LARRY A. JACKSON LIBRARY
Lander College
Greenwood, S. C. 29646

ANCIENT SOCIETY

Ancient Society

OR

RESEARCHES IN THE LINES OF HUMAN PROGRESS
FROM SAVAGERY THROUGH BARBARISM
TO CIVILIZATION

by Lewis Henry Morgan

Edited with an introduction and annotations by
ELEANOR BURKE LEACOCK

GLOUCESTER, MASS.
PETER SMITH
1974

A MERIDIAN BOOK
Published by The World Publishing Company

First published 1877
First Meridian printing September 1963

Library of Congress Catalog Card Number: 63-19730

Reprinted, 1974, by Permission of
Eleanor Burke Leacock

ISBN: 0-8446-2611

Cum prorepserunt primis animalia terris,
Mutum et turpe pecus, glandem atque cubilia propter
Unguibus et pugnis, dein fustibus, atque ita porro
Pugnabant armis, quæ post fabricaverat usus:
Donec verba, quibus voces sensusque notarent,
Nominaque invenere: dehinc absistere bello,
Oppida coeperunt munire, et ponere leges,
Ne quis fur esset, neu latro, neu quis adulter.

(As soon as animals crept forth on the first lands, a speechless and degraded crowd, they battled for the acorn and for their lairs with claws and fists, then with clubs and at length with arms, which afterwards practice had made; until they learned to use words by which to indicate vocal sounds and thoughts and to use names. After that they began to refrain from war, and fortify walled towns, and to lay down laws that no one should be a thief, nor a robber nor an adulterer.)

—Horace, Sat., I, iii, 99.

"Modern science claims to be proving, by the most careful and exhaustive study of man and his works, that our race began its existence on earth at the bottom of the scale, instead of at the top, and has been gradually working upward; that human powers have had a history of development; that all the elements of culture—as the arts of life, art, science, language, religion, philosophy—have been wrought out by slow and painful efforts, in the conflict between the soul and the mind of man on the one hand, and external nature on the other."—Whitney's "Oriental and Linguistic Studies," p. 341.

"These communities reflect the spiritual conduct of our ancestors thousands of times removed. We have passed through the same stages of development, physical and moral, and are what we are to-day because they lived, toiled, and endeavored. Our wondrous civilization is the result of the silent efforts of millions of unknown men, as the chalk cliffs of England are formed of the contributions of myriads of foraminifera."—Dr. J. Kaines, "Anthropologia," vol. i, No. 2, p. 233.

PREFACE

THE great antiquity of mankind upon the earth has been conclusively established. It seems singular that the proofs should have been discovered as recently as within the last thirty years, and that the present generation should be the first called upon to recognize so important a fact.

Mankind are now known to have existed in Europe in the glacial period, and even back of its commencement, with every probability of their origination in a prior geological age. They have survived many races of animals with whom they were contemporaneous, and passed through a process of development, in the several branches of the human family, as remarkable in its courses as in its progress.

Since the probable length of their career is connected with geological periods, a limited measure of time is excluded. One hundred or two hundred thousand years would be an unextravagant estimate of the period from the disappearance of the glaciers in the northern hemisphere to the present time. Whatever doubts may attend any estimate of a period, the actual duration of which is unknown, the existence of mankind extends backward immeasurably, and loses itself in a vast and profound antiquity.

This knowledge changes materially the views which have prevailed respecting the relations of savages to barbarians, and of barbarians to civilized men. It can now be asserted upon convincing evidence that savagery preceded barbarism in all the tribes of mankind, as barbarism is known to have preceded civilization. The history of the human race is one in source, one in experience, one in progress.

It is both a natural and a proper desire to learn, if possible, how all these ages upon ages of past time have been expended by mankind; how savages, advancing by slow, almost imperceptible steps, attained the higher condition of barbarians; how barbarians, by similar progressive advancement, finally attained to civilization; and why other tribes and nations have been left behind in the race of progress — some in civilization, some in barbarism, and others in savagery. It is not too much to expect that ultimately these several questions will be answered.

Inventions and discoveries stand in serial relations along the lines of human progress, and register its successive stages; while social and civil institutions, in virtue of their connection with perpetual human wants, have been developed from a few primary germs of thought. They exhibit a similar register of progress. These institutions, inventions and discoveries have embodied and preserved the principal facts now remaining illustrative of this experience. When collated and compared they tend to show the unity of origin of mankind, the similarity of human wants in the same stage of advancement, and the uniformity of the operations of the human mind in similar conditions of society.

Throughout the latter part of the period of savagery, and the entire period of barbarism, mankind in general were organized in gentes, phratries and tribes. These organizations prevailed throughout the entire ancient world upon all the continents, and were the instrumentalities by means of which ancient society was organized and held together. Their structure, and relations as members of an organic series, and the rights, privileges and obligations of the members of the gens, and of the members of the phratry and tribe, illustrate the growth of the idea of government in the human mind. The principal institutions of mankind originated in savagery, were developed in barbarism, and are maturing in civilization.

In like manner, the family has passed through successive forms, and created great systems of consanguinity and affinity which have remained to the present time. These systems, which record the relationships existing in the family of the period, when each system respectively was formed, contain an instructive record of the experience of mankind while the family was advancing from the consanguine, through intermediate forms, to the monogamian.

The idea of property has undergone a similar growth and development. Commencing at zero in savagery, the passion for the possession of property, as the representative of accumulated subsistence, has now become dominant over the human mind in civilized races.

The four classes of facts above indicated, and which extend themselves in parallel lines along the pathways of human progress from savagery to civilization, form the principal subjects of discussion in this volume.

There is one field of labor in which, as Americans, we have a special interest as well as a special duty. Rich as the American continent is known to be in material wealth, it is also the richest of all the continents in ethnological, philological and archæological materials, illustrative of the great period of barbarism. Since mankind were one in origin, their career has been essentially one, running in different but uniform channels upon all continents, and very similarly in all the tribes and nations of mankind down to the same status of advancement. It follows that the history and experience of the American Indian tribes represent, more or less nearly, the history and experience of our own remote ancestors when in corresponding conditions. Forming a part of the human record, their institutions, arts, inventions and practical experience possess a high and special value reaching far beyond the Indian race itself.

When discovered, the American Indian tribes represented three distinct ethnical periods, and more completely than they were elsewhere then represented upon the earth. Materials for ethnology, philology and archæology were offered in unparalleled abundance; but as these sciences scarcely existed until the present century, and are but feebly prosecuted among us at the present time, the workmen have been unequal to the work. Moreover, while fossil remains buried in the earth will keep for the future student, the remains of Indian arts, languages and institutions will not. They are perishing daily, and have been perishing for upwards of three centuries. The ethnic life of the Indian tribes is declining under the influence of American civilization, their arts and languages are disappearing, and their institutions are dissolving. After a few more years, facts that may now be gathered with ease will become impossible of discovery. These circumstances appeal strongly to Americans to enter this great field and gather its abundant harvest.

ROCHESTER, NEW YORK, MARCH, 1877.

TABLE OF CONTENTS

PART I

GROWTH OF INTELLIGENCE THROUGH INVENTIONS AND DISCOVERIES

CHAPTER III.

Ratio of Human Progress.

PART II

GROWTH OF THE IDEA OF GOVERNMENT

Editor's Introduction

CHAPTER I.

Organization of Society upon the Basis of Sex.

CHAPTER II.

The Iroquois Gens.

CHAPTER III.

The Iroquois Phratry.

CHAPTER IV.

The Iroquois Tribe.

CHAPTER V.

The Iroquois Confederacy.

CHAPTER VI.

Gentes in Other Tribes of the Ganowánian Family.

CHAPTER VII.

The Aztec Confederacy.

CHAPTER VIII.

The Grecian Gens.

CHAPTER IX.

The Grecian Phratry, Tribe and Nation.

CHAPTER X.

The Institution of Grecian Political Society.

CHAPTER XI.

The Roman Gens.

CHAPTER XII.

The Roman Curia, Tribe and Populus.

CHAPTER XIII.

The Institution of Roman Political Society.

CHAPTER XIV.

Change of Descent from the Female to the Male Line.

PART III

GROWTH OF THE IDEA OF THE FAMILY

Editor's Introduction

CHAPTER III.

The Punaluan Family.

CHAPTER IV.

The Syndyasmian and the Patriarchal Families.

CHAPTER V.

The Monogamian Family.

CHAPTER VI.

Sequence of Institutions Connected with the Family.

CONTENTS

PART IV

GROWTH OF THE IDEA OF PROPERTY

Editor's Introduction

CHAPTER I.

The Three Rules of Inheritance.

CHAPTER II.

The Three Rules of Inheritance—Continued.

PART I

GROWTH OF INTELLIGENCE THROUGH INVENTIONS AND DISCOVERIES

INTRODUCTION TO PART I

GROWTH OF INTELLIGENCE THROUGH INVENTIONS AND DISCOVERIES [1]

The reappearance in a popular edition of *Ancient Society,* in which Lewis Henry Morgan proposes his bold and all-embracing theory of the major steps in mankind's history, is an incident of greater significance to scholars in the United States than it might at first appear. Although widely acclaimed when first published, some eighty years ago, the book has since been criticized as strait-jacketing into an over-rigid scheme the myriad cultures man has developed, thus over-simplifying the complexi-

---

[1] In writing this introduction, I have attempted to point out the nature of Morgan's contribution to a science of society, as well as to summarize or refer to major lines of progress since the publication of *Ancient Society.* I have, however, dealt almost solely with anthropology in the United States; to place Morgan in the full context of world scholarship still remains to be done. In a few instances work cited or ideas developed are my own. In most cases they are derived from the entire field of American, and to some extent, British, anthropology and archaeology, and I must apologize for sparse references. On the whole, I have kept references to the minimum felt to be most useful to the reader who might wish to follow up bibliographical sources or be referred to nontechnical presentations.

I should like to acknowledge the work of the foremost scholar of Morgan, Leslie A. White, and extend to him my gratitude for his most helpful criticisms of my introductory pages. I also wish to thank Rosa Graham, Norman Klein, and Constance Sutton for reading the introduction and offering their suggestions.

In order to reissue this edition of *Ancient Society* with Morgan's original footnotes and no changes but the correction of minor typographical errors, it was felt best to break the introductory sections into four parts, one at the beginning of each section. Accordingly, pagination of the introductory sections runs separately from the original pagination of the Kerr edition of *Ancient Society,* and the introductions are set in a contemporary type face.

ties of social life. In keeping with the pragmatic social scientific climate of the early 20th century, and overwhelmed by the mounting data on the variety and richness of man's lifeways, American anthropologists felt that a cautious and empirical orientation to the study of social life was needed to counteract the elaborate "system-building" of the 19th century.

Today after mid-century, the widespread distrust of broad "systems" is in turn being replaced by a growing disillusionment with a science characterized by endless isolated studies of limited phenomena. Mankind has reached the stage of evolution where he has the power to destroy himself, and the knowledge that he can no longer afford the luxury of making serious mistakes has brought an added urgency to the desire to know the fundamental laws underlying social variability. There is a new intensity to the concern that the sciences of human behavior address themselves seriously to significant questions, lest they stand revealed as an irrelevant and esoteric playing with words, indifferent to the crucial acts of men which sweep history inexorably on.

The reawakened interest among American anthropologists in Morgan's attempt to synthesize within one broad framework the immense variety of existing human cultures, and to project an image of the future, is part of a total interest in a theory of history which can enable man's more rational control of his social life. The profundity of this interest is made dramatically evident to the anthropologist as hitherto colonial areas become forceful young nations asserting their right to independent action. Those whom the scholar has been studying are now themselves evaluating the different paths industrial societies have taken in a search for their own solutions to the basic problem before the world: how to use the technology man has developed to serve him, not only materially, but socially and intellectually, and how to prevent it from becoming an unmanageable power threatening to annihilate him.

As the author of *Ancient Society*, Morgan became the acknowledged father of "evolutionary" anthropology which is committed to the discovery of historical laws, yet he was by inclination no "system builder." Certainly, he was far from being an "arm-chair anthropologist," conjuring up grandiose ideas in the isolation of his study, as has at times been asserted. His intellectual career reveals the cautious scholar with deep respect for his material and a marked reluctance to jump at conclusions.[1] "Historical criticism demands affirmative proofs rather than deductions," he wrote in *Ancient Society* (189).

First attracted to the study of man by his contact with the Iroquois Indians in his native New York State, Morgan became interested in what appeared to him to be their unusual method of naming kinfolk. He was led to collecting material on the kinship terminologies of diverse peoples, both through personal travels and extensive correspondence. As his material piled up, it yielded the profound and exciting discovery that kinship systems existed throughout the world which were similar to each other, but at marked variance with those known to Indo-European- and Semitic-speaking peoples.

Morgan's discovery supported his belief in the unity of mankind, but it initially led him to no further historical conclusion than the Asiatic origin of the American Indians. However, when he presented his material to a publisher, as a book entitled *Systems of Consanguinity and Affinity of the Human Family*, he was informed that his findings were too diffuse and inconclusive to warrant printing the vast amount of data he had collected. Morgan reworked his text, but still unsatisfactorily. It took several years of discussing, corresponding, and thinking through the implications of his discovery before he developed the hypothesis that varying kinship systems represented different family forms, and that these had developed one from the other as the history of man unfolded.

Morgan's theory of kinship systems was, as yet, little different from other proposals for sequential stages of social and political organization which had begun to appear in Europe. Certainly the evolutionary concept of developmental stages was by no means new—indeed, it is virtually as old as written history itself, although it has waxed and waned in popularity. As a philosophy of progressive enlightenment, it had reached its zenith with Condorcet's *The Progress of the Human Mind* in the late 18th century, and Spencer had later attempted to give it a more scientific embodiment in terms of "integration," "heterogeneity,"

---

[1] Biographical material is drawn primarily from Resek, Carl, *Lewis Henry Morgan: American Scholar*, University of Chicago Press, 1960; and also from White, Leslie A., Introduction, Lewis Henry Morgan, *The Indian Journals, 1859-62*, The University of Michigan Press, Ann Arbor, 1959; White, Leslie A., editor, *Extracts from the European Travel Journal of Lewis H. Morgan*, Rochester Historical Society Publications, Vol. XVI, Rochester, New York, 1937; and Stern, Bernhard J., *Historical Sociology, Selected Papers*, The Citadel Press, New York, 1959.

"coherence," and "definiteness." Meanwhile, Boucher de Perthes had won his argument that so-called "lightning stones" were in reality the crude tools of ancient men, thus testifying to the age of man on earth; Lubbock had differentiated between an older "Stone Age," or Palaeolithic and a newer, or Neolithic; and Klemm, among others, had begun the systematic collation of data on primitive cultures to be drawn upon for building a theory of history. Maine had published *Ancient Law*, in which he elaborated on the antithesis between the "blood-tie" and the territorial tie as organizing principles; and Bachofen and McLennan had separately documented the widespread existence of matrilineality in primitive and early Mediterranean societies. Finally, Darwin's *On the Origin of Species by Means of Natural Selection*, making the statement of mankind's humble origins as a primate, had recently been published.

Morgan was to build on much of this material, but he was, as yet, reluctant to accept the full implications of Darwin's discovery for social evolution. It was not until after he had traveled in Europe and had met Darwin himself, as well as Maine, McLennan, and Lubbock, that, as he later wrote, he was "compelled" to stop "resisting" Darwin, and "to adopt the conclusion that man commenced at the bottom of the scale from which he worked himself up to his present status."[1] Morgan did not stop with this conclusion, but went on to ask the crucial question: What was the *basis* for man's progress? In giving his answer, he must be credited with the first statement of the principle underlying social evolution as it is generally understood today. "I think," he wrote in a letter, "that the real epochs of progress are connected with the arts of subsistence which includes the Darwinian idea of the 'struggle for existence.'"[2] And in *Ancient Society*, he stated:

> Without enlarging the basis of subsistence, mankind could not have propagated themselves into other areas not possessing the same kinds of food, and ultimately over the whole surface of the earth . . . without obtaining an absolute control over both its variety and amount, they could not have multiplied into populous nations. It is accordingly probable that the great epochs of human progress have been identified, more or less directly, with the enlargement of the sources of subsistence. (19)

---

[1]Resek, *op. cit.*, p. 99.
[2]*Ibid.*, pp. 136-7.

Following his discovery, Morgan turned with intensity to the writing of *Ancient Society*. In this monumental work, he outlines the manner in which man "worked himself up" from "savagery" through "barbarism" to "civilization," through the invention of successively more efficient methods of production, and he hypothesizes the forms major social, economic, and political institutions took in each period. There are inconsistencies in Morgan's work, as well as confusions and even glaring mistakes. Yet they seem insignificant in the face of his staggering accomplishment. In *Ancient Society*, he raises and clarifies all the major questions still considered basic to a science of social change. Moreover, his very presentation is something of a model. In unfolding his theory of history, Morgan does not resort to the common 19th century practice of presenting an a priori scheme and illustrating it with references to customs drawn randomly from many cultures and presented out of context. Rather he uses extensive and detailed analyses of specific cultures, either taken from his own field data or reinterpreted from ethnographic and historical materials, to give empirical embodiment to his concept of social evolution, and he interlards his empirical data with theoretical passages in a fine integration of description, analysis, and speculation.

Although Morgan served as the president of the American Association for the Advancement of Science, founded its Anthropology subsection, and was elected to the National Academy of Sciencies as its sixtieth member, he never took a university position. Like many 19th century thinkers, he remained an "amateur," and sandwiched periods of intense scholarly activity between periods of devoting himself to practical affairs as a successful lawyer and railroad investor. He also served for several terms in the New York State Legislature, first as an assemblyman and then as a senator.

Morgan had always been interested in historical research, but, curiously enough, he first became concerned with American Indians when a scholarly club of which he was an active member wished to reorganize after the pattern of the Iroquois Confederacy. Morgan's resulting acquaintanceship with the neighboring Seneca led him to be outraged at their situation, and he lent his skills as a lawyer to assisting them against an attempted land steal. Subsequently, he published numerous papers on Iroquois culture, as well as the first full ethnography of an Indian tribe, *The League of the Ho-de-no-sau-nee, or Iroquois*.

He incorporated these people into his world view as the first Americans, to be understood and respected, and allowed to take their rightful place as equals in the life of the nation. It was only when his interest in their kinship system led him to the discovery that it was shared by other non-European peoples that he was brought squarely into the field of comparative ethnology.

Morgan never deserted his direct concern for the American Indians. He first ran for state assemblyman in hopes of using his position as a step toward the office of Commissioner of Indian Affairs in the federal government. Several times during his life he came close to attaining this position, but he was always disappointed. He did become chairman of the State Committee on Indian Affairs, however, and used his office to introduce laws on behalf of the Iroquois. The year *Ancient Society* was published, toward the end of his life, Morgan defended the Sioux stand against Custer, urging that two states be set aside for the Indians, one in the East and one in the West.

A humanist, a liberal, even at times something of an iconoclast, Morgan was never a revolutionary. This has placed him in a rather curious position, for his materialistic theory of history so closely paralleled that of Marx and Engels that *Ancient Society* was used as the foundation for Engels' *The Origin of the Family, Private Property and the State,* and became a classic of socialist theory. There is much in Morgan's writing which lends itself to a socialist orientation. He deplored the "career of property" civilization had embarked upon, and his beautiful and powerful passage (561) in which he asserts that "human intelligence will rise to the mastery" over property is quoted as the closure to Engels' book. Morgan felt the antagonism between privileged and unprivileged classes, and acknowledged that his own work was "a tremendous thrust at privileged classes, who always have been a greater burden than society could afford to bear." [1] On his European travels he was appalled by the stark nature of the class differences he observed, and asked, in relation to Austria, "how long the masses will bear this . . . rather than rise in revolution and resort to force." [2] In Europe, the time was distant, he felt. He was impressed with

---

[1] Resek, *op. cit.,* p. 143.
[2] White, Leslie A., editor, *Extracts . . . ,* p. 325.

what he learned of the Paris Commune, which, he wrote, had been "unjustly condemned." [1]

On the other hand, Morgan saw class differences as fast disappearing in the United States, and the further resolution of social ills as coming about through "experience, intelligence and knowledge" as "part of the plan of the Supreme Intelligence" (562-3). Repelled as he was by extremes of rich and poor, he occasionally fell back, in good middle-class tradition, to the assumption that poverty among workers was their own fault. "I can hardly see why there should be any poor in the United States," he said in an unpublished talk, "except such as may be poor from misfortune, or owing to causes where the blame rests entirely with themselves . . ." [2]

Although Morgan's view of history was materialistic, we have seen that, strictly speaking, he was not a thoroughgoing materialist but a deist. God having set the world in motion, the business of the scientist is to discover the laws of this motion. To the regret of his wife, however, Morgan never became close to the church, although at one period in his later life he made what was apparently an unsuccessful attempt in this direction. He was suspicious of religious ritual, and, if his attitude toward primitive religion was deplorably ethnocentric—"primitive religions are grotesque and to some extent unintelligible," he wrote (5)—at least he abhorred anything he considered religious fanaticism in his own culture. Yet, he did not rule out comparative religion as a valid study. In *Ancient Society* he stated that American Indian religion was "rich in materials for the future student," and continued, "The experience of these tribes in developing their religious beliefs and mode of worship is a part of the experience of mankind; and the facts will hold an important place in the science of comparative religion" (117).

Morgan's primary commitment was to the rationality of historical law. He saw evolution as involving the development of conscious control over nature, based on principles of thought which were universal to mankind. He referred continually to the unity of mankind, which enabled him "to produce in similar conditions the same implements and utensils, the same inventions and to develop similar institutions from the same original

---

[1] White, *op. cit.,* p. 343.
[2] Stern, *op. cit.,* p. 167.

germs of thought" (562). Preeminently the natural historian, Morgan felt animals possessed similar, if less developed, mental processes. The explanation of animal behavior in terms of "instinct," he wrote in an extraordinarily profound statement, was "a system of philosophy in a definition, an instillation of the supernatural which silences at once all inquiry into the facts."[1] Among his writings appears a detailed account of *The American Beaver and His Works,* which illustrates the beaver's capacity for remembering, thinking, and learning.

Considering Morgan's assumption of basic mental processes common to men and animals, it seems surprising that he rejected evolutionary theory as long as he did. His resistance may have been due in part to the idea that only the "fittest" survive, for he saw man's progress as a unity, with the strong leading, not eliminating, the weak.[2] Or perhaps the ethnocentric inferences that lay behind much 19th century evolutionary thinking affronted both his humanism and his rationalism. Contemporary Victorian society was often seen as the epitome of man's progress, the end point, virtually, of social evolution. Although Morgan idealized the degree to which the United States had shed its European heritage of class barriers, he certainly did not see either his own country or Western culture in general as having "arrived." Society would continue to change in the future, he stated, even as it had in the past. He wrote, in *Ancient Society*, "The nature of the coming changes it may be impossible to conceive; but it seems probable that democracy, once universal in a rudimentary form and repressed in many civilized states, is destined to become again universal and supreme (351). Although he spoke of the family as having attained "its highest known perfection" in modern times, he did not see monogamy in its present form as the final perfect ending for mankind's marital career. He wrote:

> When the fact is accepted that the family has passed through four successive forms, and is now in a fifth, the question at once arises whether this form can be permanent in the future. The only answer that can be given is, that it must advance as society advances, and change as society changes, even as it has done in the past. It is the creature of the social system, and will reflect its culture. As the monogamian family has improved greatly since the commencement of civilization,

[1] Resek, *op cit.,* p. 51.
[2] *Ibid.,* pp. 102-3.

> and very sensibly in modern times, it is at least supposable that it is capable of still further improvement until the equality of the sexes is attained. Should the monogamian family in the distant future fail to answer the requirements of society, assuming the continuous progress of civilization, it is impossible to predict the nature of its successor. (499)

Morgan was clearly at odds with the view that inequalities in technological development among different peoples were due to differences in innate ability. Perhaps because of his familiarity with and respect for American Indians, Morgan was beyond crude assumptions of white supremacy. While colonial policies of the time were being buttressed with adjurations of racial inequality and the superiority of northwestern Europeans, Morgan, like Waitz before him, maintained the unity of the human race. Social diversity—or "inequality"—resulted from historical accident. In contradiction to assertions that contemporary nonliterate peoples were "abnormal" or "degraded races," Morgan portrayed them as paralleling stages of society through which "civilized" man himself had passed. "The theory of human degradation to explain the existence of savages and barbarians is no longer tenable," he wrote (7; cf. also 513-14), and he spoke of the "specific identity of the brain of all the races of mankind" (8), and the "common principle of intelligence," which "meets us in the savage, in the barbarian, and in civilized man" (562).

Morgan saw that different peoples had assumed the cultural lead at different times, with one tribe advancing, and other tribes either borrowing from the more advanced culture, or held back by geographical isolation (39). In accordance with data available at the time, he thought the Semitic-speaking and Aryan- (or Indo-European)-speaking peoples to be responsible for the rise of civilization. Their temporary cultural advantage was based on the earlier contributions of other peoples, he wrote, and was an "accident," the result of "a series of fortuitous circumstances" (563). These might be "commingling of diverse stocks, superiority of subsistence or advantage of position, and possibly . . . all together" (38). He wrote:

> When we recognize the duration of man's existence upon the earth, the wide vicissitudes through which he has passed in savagery and in barbarism, and the progress he was compelled to make, civilization might as naturally have been delayed for several thousand years in the future, as to have

> occurred when it did in the good providence of God. . . . It may well serve to remind us that we owe our present condition, with its multiplied means of safety and of happiness, to the struggles, the sufferings, the heroic exertions and the patient toil of our barbarous, and more remotely, of our savage ancestors. (563; cf. also 25, 33, 35)

Morgan's respect for early man was great. Rather than seeing him as blindly muddling through, his accomplishments outshone a thousandfold by the wonders of civilization—a not uncommon view—Morgan emphasized the fundamental importance of the first and basic inventions which were worked out slowly and painfully. Each *earlier* period showed greater relative progress than that following, as man with "an amazing amount of persistent labor with feeble means" made the major discoveries which set him on the road to civilization (41).

In the light of Morgan's views, it is surprising to find him referring occasionally to the "inferior" brain of various peoples (25, 39). This mistake arose from drawing an erroneous conclusion from two sound propositions. First, Morgan recognized that the human brain had evolved with the evolution of society itself, and second, he knew the productive techniques of society to be so basic that meaningful parallels could be drawn between the social organization of contemporary pre-literate peoples and that of "civilized" man's precursors. However, it by no means follows that any living group, no matter how simple their technology, can be equated in any respect *physically* with early man.

Fossil remains document the manner in which developing arts for living and working together intertwined with man's physical evolution from an "ape-like" to a fully human form. Only the protohuman forms which inhabited the Old World during the Palaeolithic (or Ice Age) correspond to the "primitive savage" Morgan referred to as the "earliest representative of the species," "far below the lowest savage now living upon the earth." To this "man-ape" alone can the earliest forms of social organization Morgan discussed could be inferred (507; cf. also 36, 515). By the end of the Palaeolithic one of these protohuman types had evolved into *Homo sapiens*, who, as hunting, fishing, and fruit-gathering peoples, spread over the entire earth in a few ten-thousands of years, wiping out or mixing with other hominid species, and developing ever more complex technological equipment. Almost certainly there were differences in "ability" between *Homo sapiens* as a species and his "man-ape" relatives, but there are no discernible differences in ability among different groups of *Homo sapiens* himself. Furthermore, mastering the mechanical equipment that is the heritage of "advanced" cultures involves different abilities, but not necessarily greater ability on the part of the average individual, than mastering a "simpler" technology. Anthropologists from our button-pushing culture soon learn this when they are confronted with the skill and wisdom required to live in many pre-industrial cultures. European explorers perished until they learned from the Eskimo how to survive in the Arctic. With regard to the implication that brain size is correlated with intelligence (152), Morgan was mistaken: it has since become clear that within the general human range, brain size is correlated with general body size, not with ability.

It is ironic that in spite of the disfavor into which Morgan's work fell, his general sequence of stages has been written into our understanding of prehistory and interpretation of archaeological remains, as a glance at any introductory anthropology text will indicate. However, due to the negative connotations of the words "savagery" and "barbarism," other terms for these levels are generally employed.[1] Morgan's "savagery" is "hunting and gathering" or "marginal" hunting, an economy which obtained through the Palaeolithic and persisted until recently in outlying areas such as Australia, the Kalahari Desert of South Africa, the north woods of Canada and desert and plateau areas of the American west, the tip of South America, around much of the Arctic, and in some islands and some thickly forested interior areas in Southeast Asia and Indonesia. In place of "barbarism," we speak of societies practicing horticulture, or "slash and burn agriculture," a form of agriculture using simple tools, in which the forest is burned before planting, and the gardens moved every few years when the grass and weeds get too heavy to handle. Domestication of plants was developed about ten thousand years ago, inaugurating the period called the "Neolithic" or the "New Stone Age." Simple agriculture was widespread throughout the Old and New World until the expansion of industrialization from Europe. "Civilization" is still used, although "urban culture" is increasingly being employed to denote complex societies which followed the develop-

---

[1] In the United States. In England two leading archaeologists, V. Gordon Childe and Grahame Clark, build directly upon Morgan's work and use his terminology.

ment of advanced agriculture, based on the plow and fertilization or irrigation.

Morgan wrote, "the successive arts of subsistence which arose at long intervals will ultimately, from the great influence they must have exercised upon the condition of mankind, afford the most satisfactory bases" for dividing the successive "Ethnical Periods" in man's history (9). The first of these "arts of subsistence" was "natural subsistence upon roots and fruits," in the lower stages of savagery, with fishing, and the bow and arrow for hunting, becoming important in the upper stage. The "grubbing" tool early man used before the bow and arrow transformed him into a full-fledged hunter is the archaeologically well-known "hand axe" or "fist axe." The significance of fishing has been illustrated most fully by Kroeber for North America.[1] Fishing may yield a steady source of food equal to or exceeding that made possible by horticulture, as is strikingly evident among the salmon-eating Indians in the Pacific Northwest. Morgan mentioned its importance among the Ojibwa, a reference which has only recently been taken cognizance of.[2]

Morgan placed horticulture as the third major step, achieved over a long period of time, and with immense difficulty (24). With the domestication of plants, man reached some degree of control over his source of subsistence, thus becoming less directly dependent on nature. The fourth form of subsistence was the domestication of animals, which Morgan felt predated agriculture in the eastern, though not the western, hemisphere. (The New World lacked animals like the horse, ox, and camel.) Domestication is of tremendous importance, and in large parts of pre-industrial Asia and Africa there was great dependence upon animals. However, it is generally questioned whether domestication could have been accomplished without an agricultural base. Archaeologically in the Old World the two occur together in the early village culture of the Neolithic.

There is clear consensus on Morgan's fifth type of subsistence, fully developed *agriculture*, using the plow drawn by domesticated animals, as distinguished from *horticulture*. Along with the use of iron and domesticated animals, cereal cultivation paved the way for civilization. "Dense populations in limited areas now became possible. . . . Prior to field agriculture it

---

[1] Kroeber, A. L., *Cultural and Natural Areas of Native North America*, University of California Press, Berkeley and Los Angeles, 1947.

[2] By Harold Hickerson, who has been doing extensive ethnohistorical research on these Indians.

is not probable that half a million people were developed and held together under one government in any part of the earth" (27).

Criticisms of *Ancient Society* have been myriad, but they have not dealt seriously with the major shortcoming in Morgan's exposition of his thesis, i.e., the fact that he could not take hold squarely of the basic sequence in subsistence he proposed, and make it the cornerstone of his periods. He said it was not possible at the time he wrote. Investigation had not been carried far enough, he stated, to enable him to define his periods in terms of the major subsistence types. Instead he found it necessary "at this stage of knowledge" to arrive at an approximation by "selecting such other inventions or discoveries as will afford sufficient tests of progress to characterize the commencement of successive ethnical periods" (9). Fish subsistence and fire inaugurated middle savagery; the bow and arrow, upper savagery; pottery, lower barbarism; domestication in the East and cultivation in the West, middle barbarism; and iron, upper barbarism, which led to civilization as evidenced by the use of writing.

Of Morgan's criteria for successive "ethnical" periods, the weakest is pottery. He knew it to be less significant than the others, yet he used it because it "presupposes village life, and considerable progress in the simple arts . . ." with "some degree of control over subsistence" (13). His failure was that he did not clearly pinpoint cultivation itself as enabling the more complex cultures of "barbarism." His misallocation of the Polynesians to the period of "savagery" has often been pointed out. With a few exceptions, the Polynesians did not use pottery, but much of the area lacked friable clay, and other containers were used, such as coconut shells and wooden bowls. The Polynesians were horticultural fishermen with rich and varied cultures that involved considerable differences in rank and prestige. Morgan's misclassification of their status probably arose in part from the fact that their kinship terminology was of a type he considered early. This and other problems with Morgan's theory of evolving kinship systems will be discussed below, in the introduction to Part II, "Growth of the Idea of Government."

The Indians of the Pacific Northwest also lacked pottery, and agriculture as well, and were placed by Morgan in "savagery." Yet there was a regular seasonal supply of salmon in this area, which could be dried and stored, thus affording the basis for a far more stable and complex society than is usually enabled by a hunting and fishing economy. Morgan was aware of this fact (110) but did not recognize its full significance for his theory. He knew that it would be unlikely to find criteria for each period "as will be found absolute in their application, and without exceptions upon all the continents" (9), and he spoke of the possible "adoption of equivalents" (11). However, not having been able to follow through on his theory that it was the arts of subsistence themselves which were critical, he was unable to utilize this understanding and reach the concept of parallels in productive levels and modes of production. California is a similar case. In this area the gathering of wild seeds and acorns allows an economy parallel in many respects to early agriculture, another example of "equivalence" (14).

The erroneous classifications of Polynesia and the Northwest Coast are important to note, but they have been too heavily stressed by Morgan's critics, who pick out flaws in the exposition of his thesis and bypass consideration of the theory itself. One line of attack runs: Instances like Polynesia and the Northwest Coast indicate that one cannot formulate a "unilinear" series of stages for the development of culture, since cultures take different courses under different environmental circumstances. Further, since cultures borrow freely from one another, their specific histories depart from any norm. "Diffusion plays havoc with any universal law of sequence," wrote Lowie.[1] Evolution, it has been often stated, is "multilinear," not "unilinear," and Morgan's scheme is too narrowly mechanical to take into account the complexities and richness of individual cultures. He had to force specific cultures into niches they did not fit.

Such a line of argument ignores the fact that Morgan's "law" *was not the sequence itself, but the process underlying it.* At times it seems to be forgotten that a scheme of the magnitude we are discussing should furnish a base line against which to evaluate specific situations, and does not demand that each situation duplicate it. In today's pragmatic climate, some critiques of attempts to discover social laws would lead one to assume that "laws" should describe sequences of events in all their intricacy, that they should repeat reality in all its superficial expressions, rather than stating underlying processes that might appear to be contradicted by a thousand embroideries of history. To pass the test of validity, a law must cut through superficialities, and reveal underlying but hidden causal connectives. It must explain fundamental relationships that recur so consistently that they cannot be fortuitous.

---

[1] Lowie, Robert H., *The History of Ethnological Theory,* Farrar and Rinehart, Inc., New York, 1937, p. 60.

Morgan himself was sophisticated enough to be aware that he was elaborating a hypothesis, not giving the last word on any given tribe. He saw his scheme as "provisional," though "convenient and useful" (9), as perhaps "requir[ing] modification, and perhaps essential change in some of its members," but as "afford[ing] both a rational and satisfactory explanation of the facts of human experience, so far as they are known" (515; cf. also 409). As we have seen, this qualified evaluation of his own contribution has stood the test of time.

Morgan was aware of "diffusion" and likewise aware of the differential impact varying ecological conditions have on culture. He spoke of cultures as advancing to barbarism through "original invention or adoption" (10), of the ancient Britons as affected by more advanced continental tribes (471), of the fact that geographically isolated groups retained their "arts and institutions pure and homogeneous," while others "have been adulterated through external influence" (16; cf. also 472). He was aware of so-called "multilineal" evolution, and paid considerable attention to the different endowments of the eastern and western hemispheres and the effect they had on the development of agriculture and domestication (10-11, 25). He spoke of possible "equivalents" as introducing successive stages of culture (11), and of exceptions to the general sequence of events due to "peculiar and exceptional conditions" (27; cf. also 9, 67, 190, 470-1).

It would be hard to assess the extent to which the political considerations raised by Engels' use of *Ancient Society* in *The Origin of the Family, Private Property and the State* have affected the appraisal of Morgan's work. On the one hand, the book has been uncritically accepted in its entirety by some socialist scholars. On the other, it has generally been summarily dismissed in the capitalist world, for a too favorable assessment, or even serious evaluation, may lead to crude insinuations of "disloyalty." Perhaps these considerations are less relevant to the opinions of Franz Boas, Morgan's most prominent critic and the acknowledged father of contemporary professional anthropology in the United States, than to the attitudes held by some of Boas' followers. Boas was himself something of a rebel—more so in fact than was Morgan!—and felt it his responsibility throughout his life to attack ethnocentrism and prejudice in all its forms. He emphasized the worth of each culture, the value of each group, indeed, each individual, and the importance of interpreting and recording each society's specific lifeway and history. He inaugurated a vigorous period of ethnographic research, marked by an intense emphasis on the documentation of specific cultures before they disappeared with the spread of industrialization.

Boas presents us with something of a dilemma. Although pragmatic in his approach, and cynical about the possibility of discovering useful social laws, it cannot be said that he made no contribution to a theory of history. He was primarily a methodologist, but his interests were too broad, and the problems he dealt with too profound, not to have constructive theoretical import, and he laid a solid foundation for interpreting man's language, his physical type, his art, his literature, and his culture history. When one combines his work and Morgan's, instead of placing them in opposition, one has taken a long step toward a science of society.

The nature of Boas' contribution becomes clearer when one compares his work with the writings of those among his students who seized upon his distrust of historical laws as their major emphasis. For example, in the hands of Robert H. Lowie, Morgan's *Ancient Society* became a model of what not to do, i.e., to attempt the formulation of principles underlying the history of all societies. This was virtually impossible, it was argued by Lowie and others, and violated the immense wealth and detail of specific cultures. Further and more important, it was maintained that the economic adaptation of a society in no sense serves as a foundation for other institutions. Studies supposedly demonstrated that property was individually "owned" in simple societies; that all societies had "classes"; that, in short, any type of social or political superstructure could be related to any type of economy.

In due time this trend ran its course. Further studies showed that individual property in simple societies was purely personal; that land, the basic source of subsistence, was always collectively held; that whatever the status system that obtained, it differed in simpler societies from the classes of "civilization" in that virtually all able people contributed to the food supply, and no one group controlled the main sources of subsistence. As a matter of fact, the assertion that there was no consistent causal relationship between the economic and other institutions of a society had never been totally accepted.[1] If nothing else, the

[1] In England, the so-called "functionalists" were concerned with the relationship between economic and other institutions. Cf. the classic work of Malinowski, Bronislaw, *Argonauts of the Western Pacific,*

ever widening latitude for social elaboration made possible by advancing technology was too obvious. Thus even the staunchest self-proclaimed anti-evolutionist, Lowie, wrote:

> . . . For, notwithstanding the qualifications cited, evolution is a positive fact in material culture and freely conceded by the most determined critics of its Victorian champions. To admit this, together with the possibility that material conditions may affect other phases of life, is to open the way for a fixed sequence of social and religious phenomena. . . . It [the concept of evolution] is thus very far from dead, and our duty is merely to define it with greater precision.[1]

Another order of questions about evolutionary theory is raised by the so-called "personality and culture" school of anthropology, inaugurated by Ruth Benedict and Edward Sapir in the thirties. The argument implied by most research concerned with the psychological significance of cultural differences would run: It is apparently true that certain structural forms will be found to parallel each other in societies at similar technological levels. However, it is highly questionable whether this has much relevance to people's daily lives, since the further embroidery that they build into the basic fabric of their social structure is so variable, and the things they come to value so unpredictable. For example, take the area of cooperation and competition. One would think a society based on collective production and distribution of food would value "cooperation." However, it may develop intense competition over superficial symbols of status, competition even equaling that which we experience in our competitively structured society. Thus, the argument would run, social-psychological factors are far more important than economic ones in the day-by-day impact of a culture on the individuals who live by it.

Anthropologists working in the "personality and culture"

E. P. Dutton, New York, 1922; cf. also Firth, Raymond, *Primitive Economics of the New Zealand Maori,* E. P. Dutton, New York, 1929, and *Primitive Polynesian Economy,* Routledge, London, 1939. Unlike their American contemporaries, English anthropologists in the first half of the 20th century were not explicitly anti-evolutionary, and remained committed to the notion that social laws could be discovered and should be actively sought. However, although much archaeology was built upon Morgan's work, social anthropology developed a strong non-historical orientation, and social relationships were conceived in terms of a movement toward equilibrium, with changes coming from the "outside," so to speak, rather than being inherent to social life.

[1] Lowie, *op. cit.,* p. 27.

field have documented the broad differences that exist from one culture to another in such things as socially accepted goals, definitions of desirable and undesirable behavior, and attitudes associated with various aspects of daily life. This has been important for an understanding and acceptance of varied possibilities for living. However, although such material can be meaningful, personality and culture analysis following the above line of argument has thrown little light on the basic question purportedly being studied, i.e., the nature of the relation between social processes and individual attitudes and behavior. Questions about personality are generally asked in a nonhistorical framework that fails to locate individual behavior as the means through which social processes unfold. To be significant, comparative studies of world views and life goals must be based on the objective data of philosophy and ideology, and venture cautiously from this solid grounding into the area of individual action, feeling, and understanding.

Most psychologically oriented studies in nonliterate societies make too easy an equation of "personality" among present-day peoples with that of their forebears some hundred or more years ago, virtually ignoring the profound changes—not to mention the disruption and demoralization—that have taken place among them during the period of European colonial expansion. Also, the theoretical assumptions and terminology employed in such studies are inadequate for cross-cultural comparison. They are derived from an ethnocentric Freudian framework and selectively emphasize and exaggerate limited aspects of total personality. In so doing, they employ quantitatively conceived polarities like aggression-submission, competition-cooperation, extroversion-introversion to represent the range of human response. With relation to cooperation and competition, for example, all social structures involve both, and one cannot speak purely of more or less, but of the areas in which they are practiced, their goals, and their means.

Finally, the theory of personality used is generally unclear, and lumps culturally defined directives and rationales for behavior with what are matters of individual style. This last point is beautifully documented by C. W. M. Hart when he describes the five very different sons of Turimpi, an Australian Tiwi woman. Hart writes:

> An individual in any culture will follow a "cultural course" but he will follow it cheerfully or sourly, silently or gar-

rulously, in a relaxed manner or a tense manner, like a leader or like a follower, with his eye on the gallery or regardless of the world's opinion. . . . When a man in any culture in the world is practicing a cultural pattern, he will still differ from his neighbors—or his brothers—in the way he practices it. . . . The five sons of Turimpi . . . differed not in what they did but in how they did it.[1]

Although Morgan has been criticized for ignoring the role of the individual altogether, he was most interested in formulating the relation between social processes and individual action and thought. At times he referred to the importance of conscious decision-making in history when people faced social problems; "It taxed the Greeks and Romans . . . to invent the deme or township and the city ward . . ." (7). At other times he described the way in which people are swept along by historical processes of which they are unaware. In a speech made in 1852, he said:

But there is a vast undercurrent of society moving along with irresistible power, and with an eternal flow which is destined to swallow up all things arrayed against it. This current is the unwritten thoughts of the people . . . imbibed from surrounding influences . . . they are neither books nor constitutions, nor statute laws, they are written in the bosom of humanity.[2]

In another instance, Morgan defined the limits of a solitary individual's influence on history. Speaking of Napoleon, he wrote, "Such men make some impression upon the times, but they rarely shape the course of nations." [3]

The point at which the thoroughgoing historical materialist would depart from Morgan is where he saw accumulated knowledge and experience, the *cultural* heritage of a people, as actually becoming inbred. When he entitled the sections of *Ancient Society* "Growth of the Idea of . . ." he apparently meant it quite literally. He spoke of "primary ideas which were wrought into the brains of the race in the infancy of its existence" (cf. 59-60),[4] and in discussing the French in his journals, he wrote,

---

[1] Hart, C. W. M., "The Sons of Turimpi," *American Anthropologist*, Vol. 56, No. 2, Menasha, Wisconsin, 1954.
[2] Resek, *op. cit.*, p. 53.
[3] White, *op. cit.*, p. 350.
[4] Resek, *op. cit.*, p. 85.

"There must be great inequalities of capacities in the race, otherwise they would grow into more unanimity of opinion on great questions."[1]

It was pointed out above how Morgan's notion that progressive changes in social organization became inborn capacities led him at times into a seeming support of racial inequalities. This is indeed unfortunate, since a major theme of *Ancient Society* was consistently to demonstrate otherwise. "With one principle of intelligence and one physical form," he wrote, "in virtue of a common origin, the results of human experience have been substantially the same in all times and areas in the same ethnical status" (562).

Before closing this section, we should like briefly to comment on two minor points, not wishing to add footnotes in the text itself additional to Morgan's original ones.

Morgan posited that in the evolution of language, "gesture or sign language . . . preceded articulate language," and the "monosyllabical preceded the syllabical" (5). This commonly held view may be suggested by the experience of people who speak different languages and attempt to communicate with each other, but it probably has little relation to the *genesis* of language. Considering the chattering of monkeys, who convey messages through changes in volume, pitch, and tempo, it would seem that speech developed when different combinations of pitch and sound became differentiated from a general expressive flow, and more and more clearly attached to specific meanings.

Morgan mentioned cannibalism as a source of food during the periods of savagery and early barbarism (22, 24, 537, 541). Whether or not there were ever human groups that depended upon members of their own species for food seems doubtful. Certainly this kind of dependence is not found in the animal kingdom generally, and it is unknown for any recorded culture. Such cannibalism as occurs—or is reported to have occurred, doubtless with exaggeration—is of three types: it is either a culturally reprehensible act resorted to in extremities like famine or shipwreck, or an individual aberration, or a ritual practice connected with warfare and gaining the enemy's power. In no case is human meat a regular source of food.

---

[1] White, *op. cit.*, p. 347; cf. also *Ancient Society*, pp. 6, 147-8, 468, 471, 515, 554, 562.

CHAPTER I

ETHNICAL PERIODS

The latest investigations respecting the early condition of the human race are tending to the conclusion that mankind commenced their career at the bottom of the scale and worked their way up from savagery to civilization through the slow accumulations of experimental knowledge.

As it is undeniable that portions of the human family have existed in a state of savagery, other portions in a state of barbarism, and still other portions in a state of civilization, it seems equally so that these three distinct conditions are connected with each other in a natural as well as necessary sequence of progress. Moreover, that this sequence has been historically true of the entire human family, up to the status attained by each branch respectively, is rendered probable by the conditions under which all progress occurs, and by the known advancement of several branches of the family through two or more of these conditions.

An attempt will be made in the following pages to bring forward additional evidence of the rudeness of the early condition of mankind, of the gradual evolution of their mental and moral powers through experience, and of their protracted struggle with opposing obstacles while winning their way to civilization. It will be drawn, in part, from the great sequence of inventions and discoveries which stretches along the entire pathway of human progress; but chiefly from domestic institutions, which express the growth of certain ideas and passions.

As we re-ascend along the several lines of progress toward the primitive ages of mankind, and eliminate one after the other, in the order in which they appeared, inventions and discoveries on the one hand, and institutions on the other, we are enabled to perceive that the former stand to each other in progressive, and the latter in unfolding relations. While the former class have had a connection, more or less direct, the latter have been developed from a few primary germs of thought. Modern institutions plant their roots in the period of barbarism, into which their germs were transmitted from the previous period of savagery. They have had a lineal descent through the ages, with the streams of the blood, as well as a logical development.

Two independent lines of investigations thus invite our attention. The one leads through inventions and discoveries, and the other through primary institutions. With the knowledge gained therefrom, we may hope to indicate the principal stages of human development. The proofs to be adduced will be drawn chiefly from domestic institutions; the references to achievements more strictly intellectual being general as well as subordinate.

The facts indicate the gradual formation and subsequent development of certain ideas, passions, and aspirations. Those which hold the most prominent positions may be generalized as growths of the particular ideas with which they severally stand connected. Apart from inventions and discoveries they are the following:

I. *Subsistence,*	V. *Religion,*
II. *Government,*	VI. *House Life and Architecture,*
III. *Language,*	
IV. *The Family,*	VII. *Property.*

First. Subsistence has been increased and perfected by a series of successive arts, introduced at long intervals of time, and connected more or less directly with inventions and discoveries.

Second. The germ of government must be sought in the organization into gentes in the Status of savagery; and followed down, through the advancing forms of this institution, to the establishment of political society.

Third. Human speech seems to have been developed from the rudest and simplest forms of expression. Gesture or sign language, as intimated by Lucretius, must have preceded articulate language, as thought preceded speech. The monosyllabical preceded the syllabical, as the latter did that of concrete words. Human intelligence, unconscious of design, evolved articulate language by utilizing the vocal sounds. This great subject, a department of knowledge by itself, does not fall within the scope of the present investigation.

Fourth. With respect to the family, the stages of its growth are embodied in systems of consanguinity and affinity, and in usages relating to marriage, by means of which, collectively, the family can be definitely traced through several successive forms.

Fifth. The growth of religious ideas is environed with such intrinsic difficulties that it may never receive a perfectly satisfactory exposition. Religion deals so largely with the imaginative and emotional nature, and consequently with such uncertain elements of knowledge, that all primitive religions are grotesque and to some extent unintelligible. This subject also falls without the plan of this work excepting as it may prompt incidental suggestions.

Sixth. House architecture, which connects itself with the form of the family and the plan of domestic life, affords a tolerably complete illustration of progress from savagery to civilization. Its growth can be traced from the hut of the savage, through the communal houses of the barbarians, to the house of the single family of civilized nations, with all the successive links by which one extreme is connected with the other. This subject will be noticed incidentally.

Lastly. The idea of property was slowly formed in the human mind, remaining nascent and feeble through immense periods of time. Springing into life in savagery, it required all the experience of this period and of the subsequent period of barbarism to develop the germ, and to prepare the human brain for the acceptance of its controlling influence. Its dominance as a passion over all other passions marks the commencement of civilization. It not only led mankind to overcome the obstacles which delayed civilization, but to establish political society on the basis of territory and of property. A critical knowledge of the evolution of the idea of property would embody, in some respects, the most remarkable portion of the mental history of mankind.

It will be my object to present some evidence of human progress along these several lines, and through successive ethnical periods, as it is revealed by inventions and discoveries, and by the growth of the ideas of government, of the family, and of property.

It may be here premised that all forms of government are reducible to two general plans, using the word plan in its scientific sense. In their bases the two are fundamentally distinct. The first, in the order of time, is founded upon persons, and upon relations purely personal, and may be distinguished as a society (*societas*). The gens is the unit of this organization; giving as the successive stages of integration, in the archaic period, the gens, the phratry, the tribe, and the confederacy of tribes, which constituted a people or nation (*populus*). At a later period a coalescence of tribes in the same area into a nation took the place of a confederacy of tribes occupying independent areas. Such, through prolonged ages, after the gens appeared, was the substantially universal organization of ancient society; and it remained among the Greeks and Romans after civilization supervened. The second is founded upon territory and upon property, and may be distinguished as a state (*civitas*). The township or ward, circumscribed by metes and bounds, with the property it contains, is the basis or unit of the latter, and political society is the result. Political society is organized upon territorial areas, and deals with property as well as with persons through territorial relations. The successive stages of integration are the township or ward, which is the unit of organization; the county or province, which is an aggregation of townships or wards; and the national domain or territory, which is an aggregation of counties or provinces; the people of each of which are organized into a body politic. It taxed the Greeks and Romans to the extent of their capacities, after they had gained civilization, to invent the deme or township and the city ward; and thus inaugurate the second great plan of government, which remains among civilized nations to the present hour. In ancient society this territorial plan was unknown. When it came in it fixed the boundary line between ancient and modern society, as the distinction will be recognized in these pages.

It may be further observed that the domestic institutions of the barbarous, and even of the savage ancestors of mankind, are still exemplified in portions of the human family with such completeness that, with the exception of the strictly primitive period, the several stages of this progress are tolerably well preserved. They are seen in the organization of society upon the basis of sex, then upon the basis of kin, and finally upon the basis of territory; through the successive forms of marriage and of the family, with the systems of consanguinity thereby created; through house life and architecture; and through progress in usages with respect to the ownership and inheritance of property.

The theory of human degradation to explain the existence of savages and of barbarians is no longer tenable. It came in as a corollary from the Mosaic cosmogony, and was acquiesced in from a supposed necessity which no longer exists. As a theory, it is not only incapable of explaining the existence of savages, but it is without support in the facts of human experience.

The remote ancestors of the Aryan nations presumptively passed through an experience similar to that of existing barbarous and savage tribes. Though the experience of these nations embodies all the information necessary to illustrate the periods of civilization, both ancient and modern, together with a part of that in the Later period of barbarism, their anterior experience must be deduced, in the main, from the traceable connection between the elements of their existing institutions and inventions, and similar elements still preserved in those of savage and barbarous tribes.

It may be remarked finally that the experience of mankind has run in nearly uniform channels; that human necessities in similar conditions have been substantially the same; and that the operations of the mental principle have been uniform in virtue of the specific identity of the brain of all the races of mankind. This, however, is but a part of the explanation of uniformity in results. The germs of the principal institutions and arts of life were developed while man was still a savage. To a very great extent the experience of the subsequent periods of barbarism and of civilization have been expended in the further development of these original conceptions. Wherever a connection can be traced on different continents between a present institution and a common germ, the derivation of the people themselves from a common original stock is implied.

The discussion of these several classes of facts will be facilitated by the establishment of a certain number of Ethnical Periods; each representing a distinct condition of society, and distinguishable by a mode of life peculiar to itself. The terms "Age of *Stone*," "of *Bronze*," and "of *Iron*," introduced by Danish archæologists, have been extremely useful for certain purposes, and will remain so for the classification of objects of ancient art; but the progress of knowledge has rendered other and different subdivisions necessary. Stone implements were not entirely laid aside with the introduction of tools of iron, nor of those of bronze. The invention of the process of smelting iron ore created an ethnical epoch, yet we could scarcely date another from the production of bronze. Moreover, since the period of stone implements overlaps those of bronze and of iron, and since that of bronze also overlaps that of iron, they are not capable of a circumscription that would leave each independent and distinct.

It is probable that the successive arts of subsistence which arose at long intervals will ultimately, from the great influence they must have exercised upon the condition of mankind, afford the most satisfactory bases for these divisions. But investigation has not been carried far enough in this direction to yield the necessary information. With our present knowledge the main result can be attained by selecting such other inventions or discoveries as will afford sufficient tests of progress to characterize the commencement of successive ethnical periods. Even though accepted as provisional, these periods will be found convenient and useful. Each of those about to be proposed will be found to cover a distinct culture, and to represent a particular mode of life.

The period of savagery, of the early part of which very little is known, may be divided, provisionally, into three subperiods. These may be named respectively the *Older,* the *Middle,* and the *Later* period of savagery; and the condition of society in each, respectively, may be distinguished as the *Lower,* the *Middle,* and the *Upper Status* of savagery.

In like manner, the period of barbarism divides naturally into three sub-periods, which will be called, respectively, the *Older,* the *Middle,* and the *Later* period of barbarism; and the condition of society in each, respectively, will be distinguished as the *Lower,* the *Middle,* and the *Upper Status* of barbarism.

It is difficult, if not impossible, to find such tests of progress to mark the commencement of these several periods as will be found absolute in their application, and without exceptions upon all the continents. Neither is it necessary, for the purpose in hand, that exceptions should not exist. It will be sufficient if the principal tribes of mankind can be classified, according to the degree of their relative progress, into conditions which can be recognized as distinct.

I. *Lower Status of Savagery.*

This period commenced with the infancy of the human race, and may be said to have ended with the acquisition of a fish subsistence and of a knowledge of the use of fire. Mankind were then living in their original restricted habitat, and subsisting upon fruits and nuts. The commencement of articulate speech belongs to this period. No exemplification of tribes of mankind in this condition remained to the historical period.

II. *Middle Status of Savagery.*

It commenced with the acquisition of a fish subsistence and a knowledge of the use of fire, and ended with the invention of the bow and arrow. Mankind, while in this condition, spread from their original habitat over the greater portion of the earth's surface. Among tribes still existing it will leave in the Middle Status of savagery, for example, the Australians and the greater part of the Polynesians when discovered. It will be sufficient to give one or more exemplifications of each status.

III. *Upper Status of Savagery.*

It commenced with the invention of the bow and arrow, and ended with the invention of the art of pottery. It leaves in the Upper Status of Savagery the Athapascan tribes of the Hudson's Bay Territory, the tribes of the valley of the Columbia, and certain coast tribes of North and South America; but with relation to the time of their discovery. This closes the period of Savagery.

IV. *Lower Status of Barbarism.*

The invention or practice of the art of pottery, all things considered, is probably the most effective and conclusive test that can be selected to fix a boundary line, necessarily arbitrary, between savagery and barbarism. The distinctness of the two conditions has long been recognized, but no criterion of progress out of the former into the latter has hitherto been brought forward. All such tribes, then, as never attained to the art of pottery will be classed as savages, and those possessing this art but who never attained a phonetic alphabet and the use of writing will be classed as barbarians.

The first sub-period of barbarism commenced with the manufacture of pottery, whether by original invention or adoption. In finding its termination, and the commencement of the Middle Status, a difficulty is encountered in the unequal endowments of the two hemispheres, which began to be influential upon human affairs after the period of savagery had passed. It may be met, however, by the adoption of equivalents. In the Eastern hemisphere, the domestication of animals, and the Western, the cultivation of maize and plants by irrigation, together with the use of adobe-brick and stone in house building have been selected as sufficient evidence of progress to work a transition out of the Lower and into the Middle Status of barbarism. It leaves, for example, in the Lower Status, the Indian tribes of the United States east of the Missouri River, and such tribes of Europe and Asia as practiced the art of pottery, but were without domestic animals.

V. *Middle Status of Barbarism.*

It commenced with the domestication of animals in the Eastern hemisphere, and in the Western with cultivation by irrigation and with the use of adobe-brick and stone in architecture, as shown. Its termination may be fixed with the invention of the process of smelting iron ore. This places in the Middle Status, for example, the Village Indians of New Mexico, Mexico, Central America and Peru, and such tribes in the Eastern hemisphere as possessed domestic animals, but were without a knowledge of iron. The ancient Britons, although familiar with the use of iron, fairly belong in this connection. The vicinity of more advanced continental tribes had advanced the arts of life among them far beyond the state of development of their domestic institutions.

VI. *Upper Status of Barbarism.*

It commenced with the manufacture of iron, and ended with the invention of a phonetic alphabet, and the use of writing in literary composition. Here civilization begins. This leaves in the Upper Status, for example, the Grecian tribes of the Homeric age, the Italian tribes shortly before the founding of Rome, and the Germanic tribes of the time of Cæsar.

VII. *Status of Civilization.*

It commenced, as stated, with the use of a phonetic alphabet and the production of literary records, and divides into *Ancient* and *Modern*. As an equivalent, hieroglyphical writing upon stone may be admitted.

RECAPITULATION.

Periods.	Conditions.
I. Older Period of Savagery,	I. Lower Status of Savagery,
II. Middle Period of Savagery,	II. Middle Status of Savagery,
III. Later Period of Savagery,	III. Upper Status of Savagery,
IV. Older Period of Barbarism,	IV. Lower Status of Barbarism,
V. Middle Period of Barbarism,	V. Middle Status of Barbarism,
VI. Later Period of Barbarism,	VI. Upper Status of Barbarism,
VII. Status of Civilization.	

I. Lower Status of Savagery,	From the Infancy of the Human Race to the commencement of the next Period.
II. Middle Status of Savagery,	From the acquisition of a fish subsistence and a knowledge of the use of fire, to etc.
III. Upper Status of Savagery,	From the Invention of the Bow and Arrow, to etc.
IV. Lower Status of Barbarism,	From the Invention of the Art of Pottery, to etc.
V. Middle Status of Barbarism,	From the Domestication of animals on the Eastern hemisphere, and in the Western from the cultivation of maize and plants by Irrigation, with the use of adobe-brick and stone, to etc.
VI. Upper Status of Barbarism,	From the Invention of the process of Smelting Iron Ore, with the use of iron tools, to etc.
VII. Status of Civilization,	From the Invention of a Phonetic Alphabet, with the use of writing, to the present time.

Each of these periods has a distinct culture and exhibits a mode of life more or less special and peculiar to itself. This specialization of ethnical periods renders it possible to treat a particular society according to its condition of relative advancement, and to make it a subject of independent study and discussion. It does not affect the main result that different tribes and nations on the same continent, and even of the same linguistic family, are in different conditions at the same time, since for our purpose the *condition* of each is the material fact, the *time* being immaterial.

Since the use of pottery is less significant than that of domestic animals, of iron, or of a phonetic alphabet, employed to mark the commencement of subsequent ethnical periods, the reasons for its adoption should be stated. The manufacture of pottery presupposes village life, and considerable progress in the simple arts.[1] Flint and stone implements are older than pottery, remains of the former having been found in ancient repositories in numerous instances unaccompanied by the latter. A succession of inventions of greater need and adapted to a lower condition must have occurred before the want of pottery would be felt. The commencement of village life, with some degree of control over subsistence, wooden vessels and utensils, finger weaving with filaments of bark, basket making, and the bow and arrow make their appearance before the art of pottery. The Village Indians who were in the Middle Status of barbarism, such as the Zuñians the Aztecs and the Cholulans, manufactured pottery in large quantities and in many forms of considerable excellence; the partially Village Indians of the United States, who were in the Lower Status of barbarism, such as the Iroquois, the Choctas, and the Cherokees, made it in smaller quantities and in a limited num-

[1] Mr. Edwin B. Tylor observes that Goquet "first propounded, in the last century, the notion that the way in which pottery came to be made, was that people daubed such combusible vessels as these with clay to protect them from fire, till they found that clay alone would answer the purpose, and thus the art of pottery came into the world."—"Early History of Minkind," p. 273. Goquet relates of Capt. Gonneville who visited the southeast coast of South America in 1503, that he found "their household utensils of wood, even their boiling pots, but plastered with a kind of clay, a good finger thick, which prevented the fire from burning them."—Ib. 273.

ber of forms; but the Non-horticultural Indians, who were in the Status of savagery, such as the Athapascans, the tribes of California and of the valley of the Columbia, were ignorant of its use.[1] In Lubbock's *Pre-Historic Times,* in Tylor's *Early History of Mankind,* and in Peschel's *Races of Man,* the particulars respecting this art, and the extent of its distribution, have been collected with remarkable breadth of research. It was unknown in Polynesia (with the exception of the Islands of the Tongans and Fijians), in Australia, in California, and in the Hudson's Bay Territory. Mr. Tylor remarks that "the art of weaving was unknown in most of the Islands away from Asia," and that "in most of the South Sea Islands there was no knowledge of pottery."[2] The Rev. Lorimer Fison, an English missionary residing in Australia, informed the author in answer to inquiries, that "the Australians had no woven fabrics, no pottery, and were ignorant of the bow and arrow." This last fact was also true in general of the Polynesians. The introduction of the ceramic art produced a new epoch in human progress in the direction of an improved living and increased domestic conveniences. While flint and stone implements — which came in earlier and required long periods of time to develop all their uses — gave the canoe, wooden vessels and utensils, and ultimately timber and plank in house architecture,[3] pottery gave a durable vessel for boiling food, which before that had been rudely accomplished in baskets coated with clay, and in

---

[1] Pottery has been found in aboriginal mounds in Oregon within a few years past.—Foster's "Pre-Historic Races of the United States," I, 152. The first vessels of pottery among the Aborigines of the United States seem to have been made in baskets of rushes or willows used as moulds which were burned off after the vessel hardened.—Jones's "Antiquities of the Southern Indians," p. 461. Prof. Rau's article on "Pottery." "Smithsonian Report," 1866, p. 352.

[2] "Early History of Mankind," p. 181; "Pre-Historic Times," pp. 437, 441, 462, 477, 533, 542.

[3] Lewis and Clarke (1805) found plank in use in houses among the tribes of the Columbia River.—"Travels," Longman's Ed., 1814, p. 503. Mr. John Keast Lord found "cedar plank chipped from the solid tree with chisels and hatchets made of stone," in Indian houses on Vancouver's Island.—"Naturalist in British Columbia," I, 169.

ground cavities lined with skin, the boiling being effected with heated stones.[1]

Whether the pottery of the aborigines was hardened by fire or cured by the simple process of drying, has been made a question. Prof E. T. Cox, of Indianapolis, has shown by comparing the analyses of ancient pottery and hydraulic cements, "that so far as chemical constituents are concerned it (the pottery) agrees very well with the composition of hydraulic stones." He remarks further, that "all the pottery belonging to the mound-builders' age, which I have seen, is composed of alluvial clay and sand, or a mixture of the former with pulverized fresh-water shells. A paste made of such a mixture possesses in a high degree the properties of hydraulic Puzzuolani and Portland cement, so that vessels formed of it hardened without being burned, as is customary with modern pottery. The fragments of shells served the purpose of gravel or fragments of stone as at present used in connection with hydraulic lime for the manufacture of artificial stone." The composition of Indian pottery in analogy with that of hydraulic cement suggests the difficulties in the way of inventing the art, and tends also to explain the lateness of its introduction in the course of human experience. Notwithstanding the ingenious suggestion of Prof. Cox, it is probable that pottery was hardened by artificial heat. In some cases the fact is directly attested. Thus Adair, speaking of the Gulf Tribes, remarks that "they make earthen pots of very different sizes, so as to contain from two to ten gallons, large pitchers to carry water, bowls, dishes, platters, basins, and a prodigious number of other vessels of such antiquated forms as would be tedious to describe, and impossible to name. Their method of glazing them is, they

---

[1] Tylor's "Early History of Mankind," p. 265, "et seq."

[2] "Geological Survey of Indiana," 1873, p. 119. He gives the following analysis: Ancient Pottery, "Bone Bank," Posey Co., Indiana.

Moisture at 212o F.,	1.00	Peroxide of Iron,	5.50
Silica,	36.00	Sulphuric Acid,	.20
Carbonate of Lime,	25.50	Organic Matter (alkalies and loss),	23.60
Carbonate of Magnesia,	3.02		
Alumina,	5.00		100.00

place them over a large fire of smoky pitch-pine, which makes them smooth, black and firm."[1]

Another advantage of fixing definite ethnical periods is the direction of special investigation to those tribes and nations which afford the best exemplification of each status, with the view of making each both standard and illustrative. Some tribes and families have been left in geographical isolation to work out the problems of progress by original mental effort; and have, consequently, retained their arts and institutions pure and homogeneous; while those of other tribes and nations have been adulterated through external influence. Thus, while Africa was and is an ethnical chaos of savagery and barbarism, Australia and Polynesia were in savagery, pure and simple, with the arts and institutions belonging to that condition. In like manner, the Indian family of America, unlike any other existing family, exemplified the condition of mankind in three successive ethnical periods. In the undisturbed possession of a great continent, of common descent, and with homogeneous institutions, they illustrated, when discovered, each of these conditions, and especially those of the Lower and of the Middle Status of barbarism, more elaborately and completely than any other portion of mankind. The far northern Indians and somė of the coast tribes of North and South America were in the Upper Status of savagery; the partially Village Indians east of the Mississippi were in the Lower Status of barbarism, and the Village Indians of North and South America were in the Middle Status. Such an opportunity to recover full and minute information of the course of human experience and progress in developing their arts and institutions through these successive conditions has not been offered within the historical period. It must be added that it has been indifferently improved. Our greatest deficiencies relate to the last period named.

Differences in the culture of the same period in the

---

[1] "History of the American Indians," Lond. ed., 1775, p. 424. The Iroquois affirm that in ancient times their forefathers cured their pottery before a fire.

Eastern and Western hemispheres undoubtedly existed in consequence of the unequal endowments of the continents; but the condition of society in the corresponding status must have been, in the main, substantially similar.

The ancestors of the Grecian, Roman, and German tribes passed through the stages we have indicated, in the midst of the last of which the light of history fell upon them. Their differentiation from the undistinguishable mass of barbarians did not occur, probably, earlier than the commencement of the Middle Period of barbarism. The experience of these tribes has been lost, with the exception of so much as is represented by the institutions, inventions and discoveries which they had brought with them, and possessed when they first came under historical observation. The Grecian and Latin tribes of the Homeric and Romulian periods afford the highest exemplification of the Upper Status of barbarism. Their institutions were likewise pure and homogeneous, and their experience stands directly connected with the final achievement of civilization.

Commencing, then, with the Australians and Polynesians, following with the American Indian tribes, and concluding with the Roman and Grecian, who afford the highest exemplifications respectively of the six great stages of human progress, the sum of their united experiences may be supposed fairly to represent that of the human family from the Middle Status of savagery to the end of ancient civilization. Consequently, the Aryan nations will find the type of the condition of their remote ancestors, when in savagery, in that of the Australians and Polynesians; when in the Lower Status of barbarism in that of the partially Village Indians of America; and when in the Middle Status in that of the Village Indians, with which their own experience in the Upper Status directly connects. So essentially identical are the arts, institutions and mode of life in the same status upon all the continents, that the archaic form of the principal domestic institutions of the Greeks and Romans must even now be sought in the corresponding institutions of the American aborigines, as will be shown in the course of this volume. This fact forms a part of the accumulating evidence tending to show that the principal institutions of mankind have been developed from a few primary germs of thought; and that the course and manner of their development was predetermined, as well as restricted within narrow limits of divergence, by the natural logic of the human mind and the necessary limitations of its powers. Progress has been found to be substantially the same in kind in tribes and nations inhabiting different and even disconnected continents, while in the same status, with deviations from uniformity in particular instances produced by special causes. The argument when extended tends to establish the unity of origin of mankind.

In studying the condition of tribes and nations in these several ethnical periods we are dealing, substantially, with the ancient history and condition of our own remote ancestors.

CHAPTER II

ARTS OF SUBSISTENCE

The important fact that mankind commenced at the bottom of the scale and worked up, is revealed in an expressive manner by their successive arts of subsistence. Upon their skill in this direction, the whole question of human supremacy on the earth depended. Mankind are the only beings who may be said to have gained an absolute control over the production of food; which at the outset they did not possess above other animals. Without enlarging the basis of subsistence, mankind could not have propagated themselves into other areas not possessing the same kinds of food, and ultimately over the whole surface of the earth; and lastly, without obtaining an absolute control over both its variety and amount, they could not have multiplied into populous nations. It is accordingly probable that the great epochs of human progress have been identified, more or less directly, with the enlargement of the sources of subsistence.

We are able to distinguish five of these sources of human food, created by what may be called as many successive arts, one superadded to the other, and brought out at long separated intervals of time. The first two originated in the period of savagery, and the last three, in the period of barbarism. They are the following, stated in the order of their appearance:

I. *Natural Subsistence upon Fruits and Roots on a Restricted Habitat.*

This proposition carries us back to the strictly primitive period of mankind, when few in numbers, simple in subsistence, and occupying limited areas, they were just entering upon their new career. There is neither an art, nor an institution, that can be referred to this period; and but one invention, that of language, which can be connected with an epoch so remote. The kind of subsistence indicated assumes a tropical or subtropical climate. In such a climate, by common consent, the habitat of primitive man has been placed. In fruit and nutbearing forests under a tropical sun, we are accustomed, and with reason, to regard our progenitors as having commenced their existence.

The races of animals preceded the race of mankind, in the order of time. We are warranted in supposing that they were in the plenitude of their strength and numbers when the human race first appeared. The classical poets pictured the tribes of mankind dwelling in groves, in caves and in forests, for the possession of which they disputed with wild beasts[1] — while they sustained themselves with the spontaneous fruits of the earth. If mankind commenced their career without experience, without weapons, and surrounded with ferocious animals, it is not improbable that they were at least partially, tree-livers, as a means of protection and security.

The maintenance of life, through the constant acquisition of food, is the great burden imposed upon existence in all species of animals. As we descend in the scale of structural organization, subsistence becomes more and more simple at each stage, until the mystery finally vanishes. But, in the ascending scale, it becomes increasingly difficult until the highest structural form, that of man, is reached, when it attains the maximum. Intelligence from henceforth becomes a more prominent factor. Animal food, in all probability, entered from a very early period into human consumption; but whether it was actively sought when mankind were essentially frugivorous in practice, though omnivorous in structural

[1] "Lucr. De Re. Nat.," lib. v, 951.

organization, must remain a matter of conjecture. This mode of sustenance belongs to the strictly primitive period.

II. *Fish Subsistence.*

In fish must be recognized the first kind of artificial food, because it was not fully available without cooking. Fire was first utilized, not unlikely, for this purpose. Fish were universal in distribution, unlimited in supply, and the only kind of food at all times attainable. The cereals in the primitive period were still unknown, if in fact they existed, and the hunt for game was too precarious ever to have formed an exclusive means of human support. Upon this species of food mankind became independent of climate and of locality; and by following the shores of the seas and lakes, and the courses of the rivers could, while in the savage state, spread themselves over the greater portion of the earth's surface. Of the fact of these migrations there is abundant evidence in the remains of flint and stone implements of the Status of Savagery found upon all the continents. In reliance upon fruits and spontaneous subsistence a removal from the original habitat would have been impossible.

Between the introduction of fish, followed by the wide migrations named, and the cultivation of farinaceous food, the interval of time was immense. It covers a large part of the period of savagery. But during this interval there was an important increase in the variety and amount of food. Such, for example, as the bread roots cooked in ground ovens, and in the permanent addition of game through improved weapons, and especially through the bow and arrow. This remarkable invention, which came in after the spear war club, and gave the first deadly weapon for the hunt, appeared late in savagery. It has been used to mark the commencement of

---

[1] As a combination of forces it is so abstruse that it not unlikely owed its origin to accident. The elasticity and toughness of certain kinds of wood, the tension of a cord of sinew or vegetable fibre by means of a bent bow, and finally their combination to propel an arrow by human muscle, are not very

its Upper Status. It must have given a powerful upward influence to ancient society, standing in the same relation to the period of savagery, as the iron sword to the period of barbarism, and fire-arms to the period of civilization.

From the precarious nature of all these sources of food, outside of the great fish areas, cannibalism became the dire resort of mankind. The ancient universality of this practice is being gradually demonstrated.

III. *Farinaceous Subsistence through Cultivation.*

We now leave Savagery and enter the lower Status of barbarism. The cultivation of cereals and plants was unknown in the Western hemisphere except among the tribes who had emerged from savagery; and it seems to have been unknown in the Eastern hemisphere until after the tribes of Asia and Europe had passed through the Lower, and had drawn near to the close of the Middle Status of barbarism. It gives us the singular fact that the American aborigines in the Lower Status of barbarism were in possession of horticulture one entire ethnical period earlier than the inhabitants of the Eastern hemisphere. It was a consequence of the unequal endowments of the two hemispheres; the Eastern possessing all the animals adapted to domestication, save one, and a majority of the cereals; while the Western had only one cereal fit for cultivation, but that the best. It tended to prolong the older period of barbarism in the former, to shorten it in the latter; and with the advantage of condition in this period in favor of the American aborigines. But when the most advanced tribes in the Eastern hemisphere, at the commencement of the Middle Period of barbarism, had domesticated animals which gave them meat and milk, their condition, without a knowledge of the cereals, was much superior to that of the American aborigines in the corresponding period, with maize and plants, but without domestic animals. The differentia-

---

obvious suggestions to the mind of a savage. As elsewhere noticed, the bow and arrow are unknown to the Polynesians in general, and to the Australians. From this fact alone it is shown that mankind were well advanced in the savage state when the bow and arrow made their first appearance.

tion of the Semitic and Aryan families from the mass of barbarians seems to have commenced with the domestication of animals.

That the discovery and cultivation of the cereals by the Aryan family was subsequent to the domestication of animals is shown by the fact, that there are common terms for these animals in the several dialects of the Aryan language, and no common terms for the cereals or cultivated plants. Mommsen, after showing that the domestic animals have the same names in the Sanskrit, Greek, and Latin (which Max Müller afterwards extended to the remaining Aryan dialects[1]) thus proving that they were known and presumptively domesticated before the separation of these nations from each other, proceeds as follows: "On the other hand, we have as yet no certain proofs of the existence of agriculture at this period. Language rather favors the negative view. Of the Latin-Greek names of grain none occur in the Sanskrit with the single exception of *zea,* which philologically represents the Sanskrit *yavas,* but denotes in Indian, barley; in Greek, *spelt.* It must indeed be granted that this diversity in the names of cultivated plants, which so strongly contrasts with the essential agreement in the appellations of domestic animals, does not absolutely preclude the supposition of a common original agriculture. The cultivation of rice among the Indians, that of wheat and spelt among the Greeks, and that of rye and oats among the Germans and Celts, may all be traceable to a common system of original tillage."[2] This last conclusion is forced. Horticulture preceded field culture, as the garden (*hortos*) preceded the field (*ager*); and although the latter implies boundaries, the former signifies directly an "inclosed space." Tillage, however, must have been older than the inclosed garden; the natural order being first, tillage of patches of open alluvial land, second of inclosed spaces or gardens, and third, of the field by means of the plow drawn by animal

---

[1] "Chips from a German Workshop," Comp. Table, ii, p. 42.
[2] "History of Rome," Scribner's ed., 1871, I, p. 38.

power. Whether the cultivation of such plants as the pea, bean, turnip, parsnip, beet, squash and melon, one or more of them, preceded the cultivation of the cereals, we have at present no means of knowing. Some of these have common terms in Greek and Latin; but I am assured by our eminent philologist, Prof. W. D. Whitney, that neither of them has a common term in Greek or Latin and Sanskrit.

Horticulture seems to have originated more in the necessities of the domestic animals than in those of mankind. In the Western hemisphere it commenced with maize. This new era, although not synchronous in the two hemispheres, had immense influence upon the destiny of mankind. There are reasons for believing that it requires ages to establish the art of cultivation, and render farinaceous food a principal reliance. Since in America it led to localization and to village life, it tended, especially among the Village Indians, to take the place of fish and game. From the cereals and cultivated plants, moreover, mankind obtained their first impression of the possibility of an abundance of food.

The acquisition of farinaceous food in America and of domestic animals in Asia and Europe, were the means of delivering the advanced tribes, thus provided, from the scourge of cannibalism, which as elsewhere stated, there are reasons for believing was practiced universally throughout the period of savagery upon captured enemies, and, in time of famine, upon friends and kindred. Cannibalism in war, practiced by war parties in the field, survived among the American aborigines, not only in the Lower, but also in the Middle Status of barbarism, as, for example, among the Iroquois and the Aztecs; but the general practice had disappeared. This forcibly illustrates the great importance which is exercised by a permanent increase of food in ameliorating the condition of mankind.

IV. *Meat and Milk Subsistence.*

The absence of animals adapted to domestication in

the Western hemisphere, excepting the llama, [1] and the specific differences in the cereals of the two hemispheres exercised an important influence upon the relative advancement of their inhabitants. While this inequality of endowments was immaterial to mankind in the period of savagery, and not marked in its effects in the Lower Status of barbarism, it made an essential difference with that portion who had attained to the Middle Status. The domestication of animals provided a permanent meat and milk subsistence which tended to differentiate the tribes which possessed them from the mass of other barbarians. In the Western hemisphere, meat was restricted to the precarious supplies of game. This limitation upon an essential species of food was unfavorable to the Village Indians; and doubtless sufficiently explains the inferior size of the brain among them in comparison with that of Indians in the Lower Status of barbarism. In the Eastern hemisphere, the domestication of animals enabled the thrifty and industrious to secure for themselves a permanent supply of animal food, including milk; the healthful and invigorating influence of which upon the race, and especially upon children, was undoubtedly remarkable. It is at least supposable that the Aryan and Semitic families owe their pre-eminent endowments to the great scale upon which, as far back as our knowledge extends, they have identified themselves with the maintenance in numbers of the domestic animals. In fact, they incorporated them, flesh, milk, and muscle into their plan of life. No other family of mankind have done this to an equal extent, and the Aryan have done it to a greater extent than the Semitic.

The domestication of animals gradually introduced a new mode of life, the pastoral, upon the plains of the

---

[1] The early Spanish writers speak of a "dumb dog" found domesticated in the West India Islands, and also in Mexico and Central America. (See figures of the Aztec dog in pl. iii, vol. I, of Clavigero's "History of Mexico"). I have seen no identification of the animal. They also speak of poultry as well as turkeys on the continent. The aborigines had domesticated the turkey, and the Nahuatlac tribes some species of wild fowl.

[2] We learn from the Iliad that the Greeks milked their sheep. as well as their cows and goats. See "Iliad," iv, 433.

Euphrates and of India, and upon the steppes of Asia; on the confines of one or the other of which the domestication of animals was probably first accomplished. To these areas, their oldest traditions and their histories alike refer them. They were thus drawn to regions which, so far from being the cradle lands of the human race, were areas they would not have occupied as savages, or as barbarians in the Lower Status of barbarism, to whom forest areas were natural homes. After becoming habituated to pastoral life, it must have been impossible for either of these families to re-enter the forest areas of Western Asia and of Europe with their flocks and herds, without first learning to cultivate some of the cereals with which to subsist the latter at a distance from the grass plains. It seems extremely probable, therefore, as before stated, that the cultivation of the cereals originated in the necessities of the domestic animals, and in connection with these western migrations; and that the use of farinaceous food by these tribes was a consequence of the knowledge thus acquired.

In the Western hemisphere, the aborigines were enabled to advance generally into the Lower Status of barbarism, and a portion of them into the Middle Status, without domestic animals, excepting the llama in Peru, and upon a single cereal, maize, with the adjuncts of the bean, squash, and tobacco, and in some areas, cacao, cotton and pepper. But maize, from its growth in the hill — which favored direct cultivation — from its useableness both green and ripe, and from its abundant yield and nutritive properties, was a richer endowment in aid of early human progress than all other cereals put together. It serves to explain the remarkable progress the American aborigines had made without the domestic animals; the Peruvians having produced bronze, which stands next, and quite near, in the order of time, to the process of smelting iron ore.

V. *Unlimited Subsistence through Field Agriculture.* The domestic animals supplementing human muscle with animal power, contributed a new factor of the highest value. In course of time, the production of iron gave the plow with an iron point, and a better spade and axe. Out of these, and the previous horticulture, came field agriculture; and with it, for the first time, unlimited subsistence. The plow drawn by animal power may be regarded as inaugurating a new art. Now, for the first time, came the thought of reducing the forest, and bringing wide fields under cultivation.[1] Moreover, dense populations in limited areas now became possible. Prior to field agriculture it is not probable that half a million people were developed and held together under one government in any part of the earth. If exceptions occurred, they must have resulted from pastoral life on the plains, or from horticulture improved by irrigation, under peculiar and exceptional conditions.

In the course of these pages it will become necessary to speak of the family as it existed in different ethnical periods; its form in one period being sometimes entirely different from its form in another. In Part III these several forms of the family will be treated specially. But as they will be frequently mentioned in the next ensuing Part, they should at least be defined in advance for the information of the reader. They are the following:

I. *The Consanguine Family.*

It was founded upon the intermarriage of brothers and sisters in a group. Evidence still remains in the oldest of existing systems of Consanguinity, the Malayan, tending to show that this, the first form of the family, was anciently as universal as this system of consanguinity which it created.

II. *The Punaluan Family.*

Its name is derived from the Hawaiian relationship of *Punalua.* It was founded upon the intermarriage of several brothers to each other's wives in a group; and of several sisters to each other's husbands in a group. But the term brother, as here used, included the first, second, third, and even more remote male cousins, all of whom were considered brothers to each other, as we consider own brothers; and the term sister included the first, sec-

---

[1] "Lucr. De Re. Nat.," v, 1369.

ond, third, and even more remote female cousins, all of whom were sisters to each other, the same as own sisters. This form of the family supervened upon the consanguine. It created the Turanian and Ganowanian systems of consanguinity. Both this and the previous form belong to the period of savagery.

III. *The Syndyasmian Family.*

The term is from *syndyazo,* to pair, *syndyasmos,* a joining two together. It was founded upon the pairing of a male with a female under the form of marriage, but without an exclusive cohabitation. It was the germ of the Monogamian Family. Divorce or separation was at the option of both husband and wife. This form of the family failed to create a system of consanguinity.

IV. *The Patriarchal Family.*

It was founded upon the marriage of one man to several wives. The term is here used in a restricted sense to define the special family of the Hebrew pastoral tribes, the chiefs and principal men of which practiced polygamy. It exercised but little influence upon human affairs for want of universality.

V. *The Monogamian Family.*

It was founded upon the marriage of one man with one woman, with an exclusive cohabitation; the latter constituting the essential element of the institution. It is pre-eminently the family of civilized society, and was therefore essentially modern. This form of the family also created an independent system of consanguinity.

Evidence will elsewhere be produced tending to show both the existence and the general prevalence of these several forms of the family at different stages of human progress.

CHAPTER III

RATIO OF HUMAN PROGRESS

It is well to obtain an impression of the relative amount and of the ratio of human progress in the several ethnical periods named, by grouping together the achievements of each, and comparing them with each other as distinct classes of facts. This will also enable us to form some conception of the relative duration of these periods. To render it forcible, such a survey must be general, and in the nature of a recapitulation. It should, likewise, be limited to the principal works of each period.

Before man could have attained to the civilized state it was necessary that he should gain all the elements of civilization. This implies an amazing change of condition, first from a primitive savage to a barbarian of the lowest type, and then from the latter to a Greek of the Homeric period, or to a Hebrew of the time of Abraham. The progressive development which history records in the period of civilization was not less true of man in each of the previous periods.

By re-ascending along the several lines of human progress toward the primitive ages of man's existence, and removing one by one his principal institutions, inventions, and discoveries, in the order in which they have appeared, the advance made in each period will be realized.

The principal contributions of modern civilization are the electric telegraph; coal gas; the spinning-jenny; and the power loom; the steam-engine with its numerous dependent machines, including the locomotive, the railway, and the steam-ship; the telescope; the discovery of the ponderability of the atmosphere and of the solar system; the art of printing; the canal lock; the mariner's compass; and gunpowder. The mass of other inventions, such, for example, as the Ericsson propeller, will be found to hinge upon one or another of those named as antecedents: but there are exceptions, as photography, and numerous machines not necessary to be noticed. With these also should be removed the modern sciences; religious freedom and the common schools; representative democracy; constitutional monarchy with parliaments; the feudal kingdom; modern privileged classes; international, statute and common law.

Modern civilization recovered and absorbed whatever was valuable in the ancient civilizations and although its contributions to the sum of human knowledge have been vast, brilliant and rapid, they are far from being so disproportionately large as to overshadow the ancient civilizations and sink them into comparative insignificance.

Passing over the mediæval period, which gave Gothic architecture, feudal aristocracy with hereditary titles of rank, and a hierarchy under the headship of a pope, we enter the Roman and Grecian civilizations. They will be found deficient in great inventions and discoveries, but distinguished in art, in philosophy, and in organic institutions. The principal contributions of these civilizations were imperial and kingly government; the civil law; Christianity; mixed aristocratical and democratical government, with a senate and consuls; democratical government with a council and popular assembly; the organization of armies into cavalry and infantry, with military discipline; the establishment of navies, with the practice of naval warfare; the formation of great cities, with municipal law; commerce on the seas; the coinage of money; and the state, founded upon territory and upon property; and among inventions, fire-baked brick, the crane,[1] the water-wheel for driving mills, the bridge,

[1] The Egyptians may have invented the crane (See Herodotus, ii, 125). They also had the balance scale.

acqueduct and sewer; lead pipe used as a conduit with the faucet; the arch, the balance scale; the arts and sciences of the classical period, with their results, including the orders of architecture; the Arabic numerals, and alphabetic writing.

These civilizations drew largely from, as well as rested upon, the inventions and discoveries and the institutions of the previous period of barbarism. The achievements of civilized man, although very great and remarkable, are nevertheless very far from sufficient to eclipse the works of man as a barbarian. As such he had wrought out and possessed all the elements of civilization, excepting alphabetic writing. His achievements as a barbarian should be considered in their relation to the sum of human progress; and we may be forced to admit that they transcend, in relative importance, all his subsequent works.

The use of writing, or its equivalent in hieroglyphics upon stone, affords a fair test of the commencement of civilization.[1] Without literary records neither history nor civilization can properly be said to exist. The production of the Homeric poems, whether transmitted orally or committed to writing at the time, fixes with sufficient nearness the introduction of civilization among the Greeks. These poems, ever fresh and ever marvelous, possess an ethnological value which enhances immensely their other excellences. This is especially true of the Iliad, which contains the oldest as well as the most circumstantial account now existing of the progress of mainkind up to the time of its composition. Strabo compliments Homer as the father of geographical science;[2]

[1] The phonetic alphabet came, like other great inventions, at the end of successive efforts. The slow Egyptian, advancing the hieroglyph through its several forms, had reached a syllabus composed of phonetic characters, and at this stage was resting upon his labors. He could write in permanent characters upon stone. Then came in the inquisitive Phœnician, the first navigator and trader on the sea, who, whether previously versed in hieroglyphs or otherwise, seems to have entered at a bound upon the labors of the Egyptian, and by an inspiration of genius to have mastered the problem over which the latter was dreaming. He produced that wondrous alphabet of sixteen letters which in time gave to mankind a written language and the means for literary and historical records.

[2] "Strabo," I, 2.

but the great poet has given, perhaps without design, what was infinitely more important to succeeding generations: namely, a remarkably full exposition of the arts, usages, inventions and discoveries, and mode of life of the ancient Greeks. It presents our first comprehensive picture of Aryan society while still in barbarism, showing the progress then made, and of what particulars it consisted. Through these poems we are enabled confidently to state that certain things were known among the Greeks before they entered civilization. They also cast an illuminating light far backward into the period of barbarism.

Using the Homeric poems as a guide and continuing the retrospect into the Later Period of barbarism, let us strike off from the knowledge and experience of mankind the invention of poetry; the ancient mythology in its elaborate form, with the Olympian divinities; temple architecture; the knowledge of the cereals, excepting maize and cultivated plants, with field agriculture; cities encompassed with walls of stone, with battlements, towers and gates; the use of marble in architecture; shipbuilding with plank and probably with the use of nails; the wagon and the chariot; metallic plate armor; the copper-pointed spear and embossed shield; the iron sword; the manufacture of wine, probably; the mechanical powers excepting the screw; the potter's wheel and the hand-mill for grinding grain; woven fabrics of linen and woolen from the loom; the iron axe and spade; the iron hatchet and adz; the hammer and the anvil; the bellows and the forge; and the side-hill furnace for smelting iron ore, together with a knowledge of iron. Along with the above-named acquisitions must be removed the monogamian family; military democracies of the heroic age; the later phase of the organization into gentes, phratries and tribes; the agora or popular assembly, probably; a knowledge of individual property in houses and lands; and the advanced form of municipal life in fortified cities. When this has been done, the highest class of barbarians will have surrendered the principal portion of their marvelous works, together with the mental and moral growth thereby acquired.

From this point backward through the Middle Period of barbarism the indications become less distinct, and the relative order in which institutions, inventions and discoveries appeared is less clear; but we are not without some knowledge to guide our steps even in these distant ages of the Aryan family. For reasons previously stated, other families, besides the Aryan, may now be resorted to for the desired information.

Entering next the Middle Period, let us, in like manner, strike out of human experience the process of making bronze; flocks and herds of domestic animals; communal houses with walls of adobe, and of dressed stone laid in courses with mortar of lime and sand; cyclopean walls; lake dwellings constructed on piles; the knowledge of native metals,[1] with the use of charcoal and the crucible for melting them; the copper axe and chisel; the shuttle and embryo loom; cultivation by irrigation, causeways, reservoirs and irrigating canals; paved roads; osier suspension bridges; personal gods, with a priesthood distinguished by a costume, and organized in a hierarchy; human sacrifices; military democracies of the Aztec type; woven fabrics of cotton and other vegetable fibre in the Western hemisphere, and of wool and flax in the Eastern; ornamental pottery; the sword of wood, with the edges pointed with flints; polished flint and stone implements; a knowledge of cotton and flax; and the domestic animals.

The aggregate of achievements in this period was less than in that which followed; but in its relations to the sum of human progress it was very great. It includes the domestication of animals in the Eastern hemisphere, which introduced in time a permanent meat and milk subsistence, and ultimately field agriculture; and also inaugurated those experiments with the native metals which

---

[1] Homer mentions the native metals; but they were known long before his time, and before iron. The use of charcoal and the crucible in melting them prepared the way for smelting iron ore.

resulted in producing bronze,[1] as well as prepared the way for the higher process of smelting iron ore. In the Western hemisphere it was signalized by the discovery and treatment of the native metals, which resulted in the production independently of bronze; by the introduction of irrigation in the cultivation of maize and plants, and by the use of adobe-brick and stone in the construction of great joint tenement houses in the nature of fortresses.

Resuming the retrospect and entering the Older Period of barbarism, let us next remove from human acquisitions the confederacy, based upon gentes, phratries and tribes under the government of a council of chiefs which gave a more highly organized state of society than before that had been known. Also the discovery and cultivation of maize and the bean, squash and tobacco, in the Western hemisphere, together with a knowledge of farinaceous food; finger weaving with warp and woof; the kilt, moccasin and leggin of tanned deer-skin; the blowgun for bird shooting; the village stockade for defense; tribal games; element worship, with a vague recognition of the Great Spirit; cannibalism in time of war; and lastly, the art of pottery.

As we ascend in the order of time and of development, but descend in the scale of human advancement, inventions become more simple, and more direct in their rela-

---

[1] The researches of Beckmann have left a doubt upon the existence of a true bronze earlier than a knowledge of iron among the Greeks and Latins. He thinks "electrum," mentioned in the "Iliad," was a mixture of gold and silver ("History of Inventions," Bohn's ed., ii, 212); and that the "stannum" of the Romans, which consisted of silver and lead, was the same as the "kassiteron" of Homer (Ib., ii, 217). This word has usually been interpreted as tin. In commenting upon the composition called bronze, he remarks: "In my opinion the greater part of these things were made of "stannum," properly so called, which by the admixture of the noble metals, and some difficulty of fusion, was rendered fitter for use than pure copper." (Ib., ii, 213). These observations were limited to the nations of the Mediterranean, within whose areas tin was not produced. Axes, knives, razors, swords, daggers, and personal ornaments discovered in Switzerland, Austria, Denmark, and other parts of Northern Europe, have been found, on analysis, composed of copper and tin, and therefore fall under the strict definition of bronze. They were also found in relations indicating priority to iron.

tions to primary wants; and institutions approach nearer and nearer to the elementary form of a gens composed of consanguinei, under a chief of their own election, and to the tribe composed of kindred gentes, under the government of a council of chiefs. The condition of Asiatic and European tribes in this period, (for the Aryan and Semitic families did not probably then exist), is substantially lost. It is represented by the remains of ancient art between the invention of pottery and the domestication of animals; and includes the people who formed the shell-heaps on the coast of the Baltic, who seem to have domesticated the dog, but no other animals.

In any just estimate of the magnitude of the achievements of mankind in the three sub-periods of barbarism, they must be regarded as immense, not only in number and in intrinsic value, but also in the mental and moral development by which they were necessarily accompanied.

Ascending next through the prolonged period of savagery, let us strike out of human knowledge the organization into gentes, phratries and tribes; the syndyasmian family; the worship of the elements in its lowest form; syllabical language; the bow and arrow; stone and bone implements; cane and splint baskets; skin garments; the punaluan family; the organization upon the basis of sex; the village, consisting of clustered houses; boat craft, including the bark and dug-out canoe; the spear pointed with flint, and the war club; flint implements of the ruder kinds; the consanguine family; monosyllabical language; fetichism; cannibalism; a knowledge of the use of fire; and lastly, gesture language.[1] When this

[1] The origin of language has been investigated far enough to find the grave difficulties in the way of any solution of the problem. It seems to have been abandoned, by common consent, as an unprofitable subject. It is more a question of the laws of human development and of the necessary operations of the mental principle, than of the materials of language. Lucretius remarks that with sounds and with gesture, mankind in the primitive period intimated their thoughts stammeringly to each other (—v. 1021). He assumes that thought preceded speech, and that gesture language preceded articulate language. Gesture or sign language seems to have been primitive, the elder sister of articulate speech. It is still the universal language of bar-

work of elimination has been done in the order in which these several acquisitions were made, we shall have approached quite near the infantile period of man's existence, when mankind were learning the use of fire, which rendered possible a fish subsistence and a change of habitat, and when they were attempting the formation of articulate language. In a condition so absolutely primitive, man is seen to be not only a child in the scale of humanity, but possessed of a brain into which not a thought or conception expressed by these institutions, inventions and discoveries had penetrated; — in a word, he stands at the bottom of the scale, but potentially all he has since become.

With the production of inventions and discoveries, and with the growth of institutions, the human mind necessarily grew and expanded; and we are led to recognize a gradual enlargement of the brain itself, particularly of the cerebral portion. The slowness of this mental growth was inevitable, in the period of savagery, from the extreme difficulty of compassing the simplest invention out of nothing, or with next to nothing to assist mental effort; and of discovering any substance or force

barians, if not of savages, in their mutual intercourse when their dialects are not the same. The American aborigines have developed such a language, thus showing that one may be formed adequate for general intercourse. As used by them it is both graceful and expressive, and affords pleasure in its use. It is a language of natural symbols, and therefore possesses the elements of a universal language. A sign language is easier to invent than one of sounds; and, since it is mastered with greater facility, a presumption arises that it preceded articulate speech. The sounds of the voice would first come in, on this hypothesis, in aid of gesture; and as they gradually assumed a conventional signification, they would supersede, to that extent, the language of signs, or become incorporated in it. It would also tend to develop the capacity of the vocal organs. No proposition can be plainer than that gesture has attended articulate language from its birth. It is still inseparable from it; and may embody the remains, by survival, of an ancient mental habit. If language were perfect, a gesture to lengthen out or emphasize its meaning would be a fault. As we descend through the gradations of language into its ruder forms, the gesture element increases in the quantity and variety of its forms until we find languages so dependent upon gestures that without them they would be substantially unintelligible. Growing up and flourishing side by side through savagery, and far into the period of barbarism, they remain, in modified forms, indissolubly united. Those who are curious to solve the problem of the origin of language would do well to look to the possible suggestions from gesture language.

in nature available in such a rude condition of life. It was not less difficult to organize the simplest form of society out of such savage and intractable materials. The first inventions and the first social organizations were doubtless the hardest to achieve, and were consequently separated from each other by the longest intervals of time. A striking illustration is found in the successive forms of the family. In this law of progress, which works in a geometrical ratio, a sufficient explanation is found of the prolonged duration of the period of savagery.

That the early condition of mankind was substantially as above indicated is not exclusively a recent, nor even a modern opinion. Some of the ancient poets and philosophers recognized the fact, that mankind commenced in a state of extreme rudeness from which they had risen by slow and successive steps. They also perceived that the course of their development was registered by a progressive series of inventions and discoveries, but without noticing as fully the more conclusive argument from social institutions.

The important question of the ratio of this progress, which has a direct bearing upon the relative length of the several ethnical periods, now presents itself. Human progress, from first to last, has been in a ratio not rigorously but essentially geometrical. This is plain on the face of the facts; and it could not, theoretically, have occurred in any other way. Every item of absolute knowledge gained became a factor in further acquisitions, until the present complexity of knowledge was attained. Consequently, while progress was slowest in time in the first period, and most rapid in the last, the relative amount may have been greatest in the first, when the achievements of either period are considered in their relations to the sum. It may be suggested, as not improbable of ultimate recognition, that the progress of mankind in the period of savagery, in its relations to the sum of human progress, was greater in degree than it was afterwards in the three sub-periods of barbarism; and that the progress made in the whole period of barbarism was, in like manner, greater in degree than it has been since in the entire period of civilization.

What may have been the relative length of these ethnical periods is also a fair subject of speculation. An exact measure is not attainable, but an approximation may be attempted. On the theory of geometrical progression, the period of savagery was necessarily longer in duration than the period of barbarism, as the latter was longer than the period of civilization. If we assume a hundred thousand years as the measure of man's existence upon the earth in order to find the relative length of each period,—and for this purpose, it may have been longer or shorter,—it will be seen at once that at least sixty thousand years must be assigned to the period of savagery. Three-fifths of the life of the most advanced portion of the human race, on this apportionment, were spent in savagery. Of the remaining years, twenty thousand, or one-fifth, should be assigned to the Older Period of barbarism. For the Middle and Later Periods there remain fifteen thousand years, leaving five thousand, more or less, for the period of civilization.

The relative length of the period of savagery is more likely under than over stated. Without discussing the principles on which this apportionment is made, it may be remarked that in addition to the argument from the geometrical progression under which human development of necessity has occurred, a graduated scale of progress has been universally observed in remains of ancient art, and this will be found equally true of institutions. It is a conclusion of deep importance in ethnology that the experience of mankind in savagery was longer in duration than all their subsequent experience, and that the period of civilization covers but a fragment of the life of the race.

Two families of mankind, the Aryan and Semitic, by the commingling of diverse stocks, superiority of subsistence or advantage of position, and possibly from all together, were the first to emerge from barbarism. They were substantially the founders of civilization.[1] But

[1] The Egyptians are supposed to affiliate remotely with the Semitic family.

their existence as distinct families was undoubtedly, in a comparative sense, a late event. Their progenitors are lost in the undistinguishable mass of earlier barbarians. The first ascertained appearance of the Aryan family was in connection with the domestic animals, at which time they were one people in language and nationality. It is not probable that the Aryan or Semitic families were developed into individuality earlier than the commencement of the Middle Period of barbarism, and that their differentiation from the mass of barbarians occurred through their acquisition of the domestic animals.

The most advanced portion of the human race were halted, so to express it, at certain stages of progress, until some great invention or discovery, such as the domestication of animals or the smelting of iron ore, gave a new and powerful impulse forward. While thus restrained, the ruder tribes, continually advancing, approached in different degrees of nearness to the same status; for wherever a continental connection existed, all the tribes must have shared in some measure in each other's progress. All great inventions and discoveries propagate themselves; but the inferior tribes must have appreciated their value before they could appropriate them. In the continental areas certain tribes would lead; but the leadership would be apt to shift a number of times in the course of an ethnical period. The destruction of the ethnic bond and life of particular tribes, followed by their decadence, must have arrested for a time, in many instances and in all periods, the upward flow of human progress. From the Middle Period of barbarism, however, the Aryan and Semitic families seem fairly to represent the central threads of this progress, which in the period of civilization has been gradually assumed by the Aryan family alone.

The truth of this general position may be illustrated by the condition of the American aborigines at the epoch of their discovery. They commenced their career on the American continent in savagery; and, although possessed of inferior mental endowments, the body of them had emerged from savagery and attained to the Lower

Status of barbarism; whilst a portion of them, the Village Indians of North and South America, had risen to the Middle Status. They had domesticated the llama, the only quadruped native to the continent which promised usefulness in the domesticated state, and had produced bronze by alloying copper with tin. They needed but one invention, and that the greatest, the art of smelting iron ore, to advance themselves into the Upper Status. Considering the absence of all connection with the most advanced portion of the human family in the Eastern hemisphere, their progress in unaided self-development from the savage state must be accounted remarkable. While the Asiatic and European were waiting patiently for the boon of iron tools, the American Indian was drawing near to the possession of bronze, which stands next to iron in the order of time. During this period of arrested progress in the Eastern hemisphere, the American aborigines advanced themselves, not to the status in which they were found, but sufficiently near to reach it while the former were passing through the last period of barbarism, and the first four thousand years of civilization. It gives us a measure of the length of time they had fallen behind the Aryan family in the race of progress: namely the duration of the Later Period of barbarism, to which the years of civilization must be added. The Aryan and Ganowánian families together exemplify the entire experience of man in five ethnical periods, with the exception of the first portion of the Later Period of savagery.

Savagery was the formative period of the human race. Commencing at zero in knowledge and experience, without fire, without articulate speech and without arts, our savage progenitors fought the great battle, first for existence, and then for progress, until they secured safety from the ferocious animals, and permanent subsistence. Out of these efforts there came gradually a developed speech, and the occupation of the entire surface of the earth. But society from its rudeness was still incapable of organization in numbers. When the most advanced portion of mankind had emerged from savagery, and entered the Lower Status of barbarism, the entire population of the earth must have been small in numbers. The earliest inventions were the most difficult to accomplish because of the feebleness of the power of abstract reasoning. Each substantial item of knowledge gained would form a basis for further advancement; but this must have been nearly imperceptible for ages upon ages, the obstacles to progress nearly balancing the energies arrayed against them. The achievements of savagery are not particularly remarkable in character, but they represent an amazing amount of persistent labor with feeble means continued through long periods of time before reaching a fair degree of completeness. The bow and arrow afford an illustration.

The inferiority of savage man in the mental and moral scale, undeveloped, inexperienced, and held down by his low animal appetites and passions, though reluctantly recognized, is, nevertheless, substantially demonstrated by the remains of ancient art in flint stone and bone implements, by his cave life in certain areas, and by his osteological remains. It is still further illustrated by the present condition of tribes of savages in a low state of development, left in isolated sections of the earth as monuments of the past. And yet to this great period of savagery belongs the formation of articulate language and its advancement to the syllabical stage, the establishment of two forms of the family, and possibly a third, and the organization into gentes which gave the first form of society worthy of the name. All these conclusions are involved in the proposition, stated at the outset, that mankind commenced their career at the bottom of the scale; which "modern science claims to be proving by the most careful and exhaustive study of man and his works." [1]

In like manner, the great period of barbarism was signalized by four events of pre-eminent importance: namely, the domestication of animals, the discovery of the cereals, the use of stone in architecture, and the in-

1 Whitney's "Oriental and Linguistic Studies," p. 341.

vention of the process of smelting iron ore. Commencing probably with the dog as a companion in the hunt, followed at a later period by the capture of the young of other animals and rearing them, not unlikely, from the merest freak of fancy, it required time and experience to discover the utility of each, to find means of raising them in numbers and to learn the forbearance necessary to spare them in the face of hunger. Could the special history of the domestication of each animal be known, it would exhibit a series of marvelous facts. The experiment carried, locked up in its doubtful chances, much of the subsequent destiny of mankind. Secondly, the acquisition of farinaceous food by cultivation must be regarded as one of the greatest events in human experience. It was less essential in the Eastern hemisphere, after the domestication of animals, than in the Western, where it became the instrument of advancing a large portion of the American aborigines into the Lower, and another portion into the Middle Status of barbarism. If mankind had never advanced beyond this last condition, they had the means of a comparatively easy and enjoyable life. Thirdly, with the use of adobe-brick and of stone in house building, an improved mode of life was introduced, eminently calculated to stimulate the mental capacities, and to create the habit of industry, —the fertile source of improvements. But, in its relations to the high career of mankind, the fourth invention must be held the greatest event in human experience, preparatory to civilization. When the barbarian, advancing step by step, had discovered the native metals, and learned to melt them in the crucible and to cast them in moulds; when he had alloyed native copper with tin and produced bronze; and, finally, when by a still greater effort of thought he had invented the furnace, and produced iron from the ore, nine-tenths of the battle for civilization was gained.[1] Furnished with iron tools,

1 M. Quiquerez, a Swiss engineer, discovered in the canton of Berne the remains of a number of side-hill furnaces for smelting iron ore; together with tools, fragments of iron and charcoal. To construct one, an excavation was made in the side of a hill in which a bosh was formed of clay, with a

capable of holding both an edge and a point, mankind were certain of attaining to civilization. The production of iron was the event of events in human experience, without a parallel, and without an equal, beside which all other inventions and discoveries were inconsiderable, or at least subordinate. Out of it came the metallic hammer and anvil, the axe and the chisel, the plow with an iron point, the iron sword; in fine, the basis of civilization, which may be said to rest upon this metal. The want of iron tools arrested the progress of mankind in barbarism. There they would have remained to the present hour, had they failed to bridge the chasm. It seems probable that the conception and the process of smelting iron ore came but once to man. It would be a singular satisfaction could it be known to what tribe and family we are indebted for this knowledge, and with it for civilization. The Semitic family were then in advance of the Aryan, and in the lead of the human race. They gave the phonetic alphabet to mankind and it seems not unlikely the knowledge of iron as well.

At the epoch of the Homeric poems, the Grecian tribes had made immense material progress. All the common metals were known, including the process of smelting ores, and possibly of changing iron into steel; the principal cereals had been discovered, together with the art of cultivation, and the use of the plow in field agriculture; the dog, the horse, the ass, the cow, the sow, the sheep and the goat had been domesticated and reared in flocks and herds, as has been shown. Architecture had produced a house constructed of durable materials, containing separate apartments,[1] and consisting of more than a single story;[2] ship building, weapons, textile

---

chimney in the form of a dome above it to create a draft. No evidence was found of the use of the bellows. The boshes seem to have been charged with alternate layers of pulverized ore and charcoal, combustion being sustained by fanning the flames. The result was a spongy mass of partly fused ore which was afterwards welded into a compact mass by hammering. A deposit of charcoal was found beneath a bed of peat twenty feet in thickness. It is not probable that these furnaces were coeval with the knowledge of smelting iron ore; but they were, not unlikely, close copies of the original furnace.—Vide Figuier's "Primitive Man," Putnam's ed., p. 301.

[1] Palace of Priam.—Il., vi, 242.

[2] House of Ulysses.—Od., xvi, 448.

fabrics, the manufacture of wine from the grape, the cultivation of the apple, the pear, the olive and the fig,[1] together with comfortable apparel, and useful implements and utensils, had been produced and brought into human use. But the early history of mankind was lost in the oblivion of the ages that had passed away. Tradition ascended to an anterior barbarism through which it was unable to penetrate. Language had attained such development that poetry of the highest structural form was about to embody the inspirations of genius. The closing period of barbarism brought this portion of the human family to the threshold of civilization, animated by the great attainments of the past, grown hardy and intelligent in the school of experience, and with the undisciplined imagination in the full splendor of its creative powers. Barbarism ends with the production of grand barbarians. Whilst the condition of society in this period was understood by the later Greek and Roman writers, the anterior state, with its distinctive culture and experience, was as deeply concealed from their apprehension as from our own; except as occupying a nearer stand-point in time, they saw more distinctly the relations of the present with the past. It was evident to them that a certain sequence existed in the series of inventions and discoveries, as well as a certain order of development of institutions, through which mankind had advanced themselves from the status of savagery to that of the Homeric age; but the immense interval of time between the two conditions does not appear to have been made a subject even of speculative consideration.

---

1 Od., vii, 115.

PART II

GROWTH OF THE IDEA OF GOVERNMENT

INTRODUCTION TO PART II

GROWTH OF THE IDEA OF GOVERNMENT

In developing his theory of the major steps taken by society toward full-scale political organization, Morgan built on the antithesis between personal ties and territorial ties which had been pointed out by Maine.[1] Early forms of organization were social, not political, and were based on personal relationships, not territory. Society was first organized on the basis of sex, with "classes" of intermarrying males and females. Later, through the progressive restriction of possible marriage partners, the gens developed. Subsequent steps toward formal political organization were: 1) the chief and tribal council of chiefs; 2) the confederacy of tribes; 3) the nation with a division between the council of chiefs and the assembly of the people; and, finally, 4) "out of military necessities of the united tribes came the general military commander," a third power, but subordinate to the other two (330; cf. also 61, 121-3). Full political organization could not develop, however, until the personal ties of the gens were rendered functionless, and relationships founded instead upon territory and upon property. Preliminary to the disappearance of the gens, descent shifted from matrilineal to patrilineal (63-4, 67, 315-16, 363, 366).

Morgan unfolded his theory by elaborating in detail on societies representing various stages of political growth, selecting

---

[1] Whether or not Morgan borrowed this concept directly from Maine is not clear. In his European Journal, Morgan tells of discussing the "ages of barbarism" with Maine, author of *Ancient Law* (White, Leslie A., *Extracts,* p. 375), and in *Ancient Society* Morgan wrote of Maine's "brilliant researches in the sources of ancient law, and in the early history of institutions, [which] have advanced so largely our knowledge of them" (514).

those he felt could be studied in their "normal development in areas where the institutions of the people are homogeneous," (472) meaning relatively unaffected by more complex societies. He used the Australian aborigines to represent the earliest stage, and the Iroquois, for whom he could draw on his own extensive field notes, to illustrate the gens, tribe, and confederacy. Morgan then described the Aztecs to document a stage of "military democracy" approaching that of early Greece and Rome, and presented ethnohistorical data on the latter two societies as examples of the final shift from the gentile or personal tie to the territorial or political. In closing he indicated briefly the wealth of data testifying to parallel developments in other areas.

Three major points were developed by Morgan: first, that the shift from "social" to "political" organization was a fundamental one, second, that the matrilineal gens was basic to social organization early in mankind's history, and third, that prepolitical societies generally were "democratic" in character. To appraise these points in the light of some eighty years' work since the appearance of *Ancient Society* is complicated. First, the issues have not always been clearly stated since polemics over Morgan's work have often been indirect ways of discussing Marxist theory and its implications for man's future. Second, accounts of "primitive" cultures as they existed or were remembered in the late 19th and early 20th centuries must be reinterpreted, if the aboriginal cultures are to be understood. Under the impact of Western political and economic domination, the societies from which data are drawn have all been rapidly changing, and these changes have been in the direction of male descent, formal political organization, and private property and economic classes, as individual entrepreneurs break away from the already weakened corporate body of kin.

In undertaking the present assessment of *Ancient Society*, let us say that my favorable point of view (as those in some agreement might consider it) or "bias" (as dissenters might term it) is born out of a perverse reaction to the virtually universal criticism of Morgan encountered in my student days, and reinforced both by my field experience and by the recognition that far more of Morgan's theory is already incorporated into the science of man than is generally conceded. My conviction, as I have already indicated, is that the synthesis of Morgan's theories, and the more cogent of the arguments against them, lead to refining, not rejecting, all but a few of his original propositions.

1. *The form of social organization that preceded the gens, in the earliest stage of man's history:*

Morgan's concept of the "first organized form of society" (427), the "still older and more archaic organization" than the "organization into gentes on the basis of kin" was "that into classes on the basis of sex" (47). This led to the "consanguine family . . . founded upon the intermarriage of brothers and sisters, own and collateral, in a group" (393). He inferred the existence of this form from the "Malayan" practice of naming kin found prevalently in Oceania, according to which all relations on one's own generation level are called brothers and sisters (instead of siblings and cousins), those on the parental level fathers and mothers (instead of parents, uncles, and aunts), and so forth. Morgan believed the "Malayan" terminology reflected the former custom, "fossilized" in continuing linguistic usage, of many "brothers" marrying many "sisters." Thus, any man might be one's own father, any woman one's father's wife, any boy one's brother, etc. Like other scholars of his day, Morgan used the fact that any woman could not literally be one's own mother as one reason for the gradual development of matrilineality, or descent through the mother as the certain parent.

The study of kinship systems which followed Morgan's discovery of their existence and prevalence has shown that they do not reveal actual or potential *biological* relationships, present or past, so much as *social* relationships. Kinship nomenclatures embody patterns of authority, respect, reciprocal help, sharing of food, and so forth. This can be more easily seen when one describes kin terms in a manner that does not reflect so heavily our cultural concern with the immediate nuclear family. Rather than saying, as Morgan did, "All the brothers of my father are my fathers; and all the sisters of my mother are my mothers" (420), one can say, "I call all the related men of the generation above me by the same term." The term, then, refers to a number of people with whom one relates in the same kind of way, a way that is similar, if attenuated, to the relationship with one's own father. Expectations of how one should act to other people in the tribe, band, or village in kin-organized societies can be described largely in terms of the categories defined by the kinship terminology. Morgan wrote, "to a native Indian accustomed to its daily use the apparent maze of relationships presents no difficulty" (449). The reason was that the relationship terms were daily making functional sense.

If kin terms reflect present (or but recently past) social relationships, and cannot be used as evidence for forms long past, then what evidence do we have for the type of social organization that preceded the gens? Part of Morgan's answer was to use "the condition both of savage and of barbarous tribes . . . studied in its normal development in areas where the institutions of the people are homogeneous" (472), as examples of various "stages." A number of pre-agricultural societies have persisted in outlying or otherwise unfavorable areas until recently. As we previously stated (*supra,* p. lx), these cultures cannot be equated with the earliest, or pre-*Homo sapiens,* cultures that obtained through the Ice Age. However, they do represent a wide range of adaptations that *Homo sapiens,* himself as a hunter and gatherer, made in different parts of the world.

Morgan believed the Australian tribesmen to be the best representatives of early hunting cultures. Their so-called "marriage classes" appeared to be little removed from "group marriage," which, he argued, was the form of social organization that followed "promiscuous intercourse" within the "horde" (507). However, although the Australians had a simple technology, their formal social organization is atypical among hunters, for it may have some relation to social elaborations found among the more complex societies of the nearby Melanesian Islands. Moreover, to describe the system solely according to how wives are selected gives a skewed picture of Australian marriage and family living. As Morgan himself indicated, "group marriage," if practiced literally, would be complicated and cumbersome, and in daily life, he said, individual partners paired off (424, 454). In this, aside from the special feature of "marriage classes," the Australians are fundamentally no different from other hunting cultures.[1]

Today the commonly accepted view is that the band among hunting and gathering peoples is made up of nuclear families closely approaching our own. Practices of "sexual hospitality,"

---

[1] For accounts of Australian cultures, see Service, Elman R., "The Arunta of Australia," in *Profiles in Ethnology,* Harper and Row, New York, 1963; and Hart, C. W. M., and Pilling, Arnold, *The Tiwi of North Australia,* in Case Studies in Cultural Anthropology, edited by Spindler, George, and Spindler, Louise, Holt, Rinehart & Winston, New York, 1960.

whereby a sleeping partner is available to a man away from home, or of "sexual license," particularly on festive occasions, are not seen as remnants of "group marriage," as Morgan contended, but merely as acceptable ways of handling the deviations from strictly monogamous relations which occur in all cultures, but are more strongly censured in some. Such a view has merit in placing sexual practices in proper cross-cultural perspective, but it bypasses the profound distinction between family functioning in a hunting society and in our own—*for in a hunting society the nuclear family, although seemingly a unit, is functionally merged in the band collective in a manner without parallel in Western culture.*

All evidence points to the band collective, loosely structured and disarmingly simple in appearance, flexible and adaptable in its close dependence upon the vagaries of nature, as the form preceding gentile social organization. We now have rich documentary material on band life, and since this topic is unsatisfactorily dealt with in *Ancient Society* some elaboration upon the hunting band might be worthwhile to the reader. Band size varies according to how much food a region has to offer, and movements are patterned in response to seasonal variations in food and water in different parts of an area. People living in areas where the seasonal variations of fish or root or fruit crops are relatively assured have the possibility of more regular and stable habits than hunting peoples in game areas where movements of the animal population are more unpredictable, but in either case band organization and leadership are not highly formalized. The seasonal migrations usually involve periods when bands come together for festivities and socializing, and there may be periods when bands must break up into smaller units and spread out over a wide area. Whatever the precise pattern, however, the cooperative character of the band unit is its essential characteristic. Though hunters may be scattered over wide areas, they know how to reach each other for help, and a virtually starving family will share with another in worse straits as unquestioningly as we would share a pack of chewing gum.[1]

---

[1] The cooperative character of the band has been questioned for the Eskimo and for the Northeastern Algonkian Indians. Charles Campbell Hughes counters the arguments against Eskimo collectivity ("Anomie, the Ammassalik, and the Standardization of Error," *Southwestern Journal of Anthropology*, Vol. 14, No. 4, 1958), and William Dunning has documented the persistence of cooperative patterns in a present-day

Contrary to the rather complex view of social organization among hunters presented by Morgan, the band is so simple as to be virtually anarchistic. However, the informal, the *actual*, structure of the band is highly complex—although of a different order than what we generally think of as structure—for collective decision-making involves a subtlety of communication and sensitivity to others, which are no simple matters. Decision-making in a hunting and gathering band is a topic worthy of far more attention than has been accorded it. The more so since the achievement of *real* cooperation is not at the expense of individual expression, but allows great latitude for it, a phenomenon that has been best documented for the Eskimo, and which contradicts our culture-bound psychological theories that relate self-expression and competition.

This view of the hunting band would no longer fit in its entirety any existing society, for there are today no peoples depending solely on hunting, fishing, and gathering. Those few peoples who are still not directly dependent upon agriculture are economically tied to industrial society through the trade of furs, rubber, chicle, vegetable oils, etc., which has had profound effects upon their lives. Other peoples who were first encountered as hunters may have been agriculturists in the past. Many of the American Indians of the Western Plains were former agricultural peoples who moved out onto the grasslands in search of buffalo after the introduction of the horse. In other cases, certain true hunting peoples had apparently taken on at least the superficial veneer of social practices found among neighboring agricultural tribes well before Western contact. Lastly, there are those nonagricultural tribes living in areas like California and the Pacific Northwest where the natural environment affords a regular crop in nuts, seeds, or fish that parallels the yield of an agricultural society. Clearly, if further light is to be thrown on the life of hunting peoples, ethnographic

---

Eskimo group ("An Aspect of Domestic Group Structure Among Eastern Canadian Eskimo," read at the meetings of the American Association for the Advancement of Science, December, 1962). Arguments against the collective organization of Northeastern Algonkians have been countered by myself for the Montagnais-Naskapi Indians of the Labrador Peninsula ("The Montagnais 'Hunting Territory' and the Fur Trade," *American Anthropologist,* Memoir 78, 1954), and by Harold Hickerson for the Ojibwa ("The Southwestern Chippewa, an Ethnohistorical Study," *American Anthropologist,* Memoir 92, 1962).

materials have to be assessed differently in each of these instances.[1]

2. The matrilineal gens as the basic form of organization in early agricultural societies, and the transition to patrilineality, with progressive restrictions on the inheritance of property, as steps toward the gens' disappearance (cf. esp. 63):

Whatever place different contemporary students of man cede to Morgan, no one questions how important his discovery of gens organization (or clan organization, as it is today more generally termed), and its corollary, "classificatory" kinship systems, were to the development of ethnology. The gens, clan, or sib is the basic social unit among people who are relatively settled but have not yet developed sufficiently advanced agriculture to support full "political" organization. The gens, or clan, is a unilineal-descent group, and there are several or more in a village or tribe. Every individual is born into a gens and his position within it defines his relationship to other members of his tribe. The point that has been questioned is not whether gentile organization was characteristic of a certain stage in social history, but whether or not the early gens was *matrilineally* structured, with children belonging to the clan of their mothers rather than that of their fathers.

Morgan's description of Iroquois social organization illustrates the functional fit between the matrilineal clan and simple agricultural society. Among the Iroquois, the women did most of the farming, and the working unit was the maternal lineage, consisting of the mother and her daughters, and, as they grew up, their daughters. Brothers and sons helped with the heavy work, but their primary commitment was to hunting. Thus, the

---

[1] For fuller discussions of hunting cultures, with extensive bibliographies, cf. Service, Elman, *Primitive Social Organization, An Evolutionary Perspective,* Random House, New York, 1962, Ch. 3; and Steward, Julian H., Chs. 6, 7, 8 in *Theory of Culture Change,* University of Illinois Press, Urbana, 1955. For popularized accounts of hunting cultures, cf. Washburne, Heluiz Chandler, *Land of the Good Shadows, the Life Story of Anauta, an Eskimo Woman,* John Day, New York, 1940; and Thomas, Elizabeth Marshall, *The Harmless People,* Alfred A. Knopf, New York, 1959. For a somewhat over-written and not entirely accurate novel, which, however, captures the spirit of daily life among a hunting people better than most other novels, see Mowat, Farley, *People of the Deer,* Little, Brown and Company, Boston, 1952.

matrilineal clan can be seen as the counterpart of ongoing work relations. However, Morgan's dissenters point out that, although matrilineal organization is common in simple agricultural societies, patrilineal organization is even more common, while many peoples have mixed or bilateral systems. Crucial to answering this argument is the fact that the social arrangements under discussion were not fully documented until the late 19th and early 20th centuries. It is conceded that the weight of Western cultural impact consistently favors patrilineality, that cases of a recent transition from matrilineality to patrilineality occur again and again, and that no clear case of the reverse can be cited.[1] Nonetheless, scholars are unwilling to conclude that a shift from matrilineality to patrilineality could have occurred in every simple agricultural society recorded as patrilineal or bilateral. Further ethnohistorical research is clearly necessary in order to reconstruct the history of enough cultures to clinch Morgan's argument.

Ethnohistorical reconstruction is also needed in the case of hunting bands to determine whether they were predominantly maternal or paternal in orientation. Hunting cultures, as recorded for the last century, tend to be patrilineal or bilateral, with new wives joining their husband's band, rather than vice versa. Steward argues that the case was no different prior to Western colonial expansion, and Service is in general agreement.[2] My own view is that patrilocality is a post-contact phenomenon and that, before the era of trade, hunting bands were flexible in this regard, but tended toward *matrilocality*. (Meaning that post-marital residence tended to be close to the wife's parents, or specifically, her mother. *Matrilineality* and *patrilineality* are really misnomers for band society, since their formal kinship organization is so minimal.)

Among the bilateral and patrilocal Montagnais-Naskapi of the Labrador Peninsula, the direct influence of traders, missionaries, and government personnel, plus the indirect influence of the fur trade, have all favored patrilocality. However, accounts by Jesuits and other early recorders in the 17th and 18th centuries refer to matrilocality for the area, and many continuing attitudes and practices affirm the existence of earlier

---

[1] Murdock, George Peter, *Social Structure,* The Macmillan Company, New York, 1949, p. 190.

[2] Steward, *op. cit.;* Service, *op. cit.*

matrilocality.[1] The argument that patrilineality follows from the importance of hunting, and the desirability of having a man stay in an area he knows, has no relevance. Until the present, Naskapi men moved freely from band to band and talked of joining other bands to find a wife. Knowing the general conditions of hunting, they soon learned the features of a specific territory. They liked to move around, meet old friends, make new ones, meet new women, try out a different trading post, even see, perhaps, some natural wonder in the area, like the great falls at Michikamau. One can find no functionally operating pressure toward patrilocality. On the other hand, there was a pressure toward matrilocality, equally a matter of individual feelings. A mother and newly wed daughter liked to be together so the mother could deliver the daughter's first babies. Later the daughter would become more oriented toward her own growing family, and, with constantly changing family relations and movements caused by the high death rate, the tie would weaken and the two often move apart.[2]

Unfortunately, many of the reasons for clan organization and matrilineality given by Morgan and other 19th century writers were erroneous, and this has clouded the issues. Certainty of biological parentage, one reason given for counting descent through women (67), is important to Western man, but of little importance in more egalitarian cultures. Morgan mentioned a greater natural desire on the part of women for sexual exclusiveness as instrumental in limiting the marriage group and laying the basis for clan organization (470), but there is no good cross-cultural evidence for this. He also believed the clan produced healthier people by limiting inbreeding (68, 389). However, clan exogamy does not prohibit marriage of actual relatives. Cross-cousin marriage (marrying one's mother's brother's or father's sister's son or daughter, who are not mem-

---

[1] Leacock, Eleanor, "Matrilocality in a Simple Hunting Economy (Montagnais-Naskapi)," *Southwestern Journal of Anthropology,* Vol. 11, 1955.

[2] Scattered references similar to the clues for early matrilocality among the Montagnais-Naskapi can be found for other hunting peoples. After reviewing the literature on these cultures, however, Service comes again to the conclusion that hunting peoples were more characteristically patrilineal (*op. cit.*). Nonetheless, since I do not agree with his rephrasing of my conclusions on the Montagnais-Naskapi case, which I feel shows them conclusively to have been in the main matrilocal, I feel the argument is far from closed.

bers of one's own clan) is often a preferential match, since it has the unique advantage of strengthening already close ties (one's uncle becomes one's father-in-law, or one's aunt one's mother-in-law), while at the same time building alliances across different clan groups. In fact, the occurrence of cross-cousin marriage in hunting groups, prior to the emergence of the clan, may indicate the kind of relationships that laid the basis for clan organization, when people began to produce food, rather than simply finding or capturing it, and needed more formal ways of regulating their mutual efforts.

In a recent book that brings together full and rich material on matrilineal descent systems, as well as varying points of view as to their significance, Aberle writes:

> The origins of matrilineal systems are probably to be sought in technology, division of labor, organization of work groups, control of resources, types of subsistence activities, and the ecological niches in which these activities occur. In general, matriliny is associated with horticulture, in the absence of major activities carried on and coordinated by males, of the type of cattle raising or extensive public works. It tends to disappear with plough cultivation and vanishes with industrialization. . . .[1]

The various accounts in this book illustrate variations in the functioning of matrilineal systems which arise from exigencies of history and specific environment. Gough writes:

> I have argued that in matrilineal societies, the higher the productivity of the society from subsistence cultivation, the weaker the shared interests of spouses, father and child, patrilateral kin, and affines, relative to those of matrilineal kin. . . . [This] situation ceases to exist, however, when economic changes occur which permit men to enter individual positions of access to livelihood or to accumulate personal property as a source of livelihood. The conditions which brought this about in Kerala—as in many other matrilineal societies in modern times—were those of entry into a market system in the second half of the nineteenth century, in which both land and the labor of individuals became treated as commodities. Then, even though the Nayars had probably had

---

[1] Schneider, David M., and Gough, Kathleen, *Matrilineal Kinship*, University of California Press, Berkeley and Los Angeles, 1961, p. 725.

the "strongest" matrilineal system in the world, the disintegration of matrilineal groups, and the emergence of the elementary family as the key unit in a bilateral system, proceeded apace.[1]

3. *The emergence of "political" organization as fundamentally distinct from "social" organization:*

Morgan's discussion of emerging political organization involved six propositions of major importance. Two pertained directly to the nature of political organization as such and laid the basis for what is currently an active archaeological and ethnohistorical concern with the development of economic classes and states. Two propositions involved the reinterpretation of materials on Aztec and Greek society, and, in the former case, initiated a long and fruitful debate. Two are concerned with related changes in social organization, and defined what are still important questions for the functional analysis of social systems.

i. Morgan's first proposition was that the transformation from social to political organization became necessary when agriculture and the domestication of animals grew to be sufficiently productive to enable city living and the development of private property. "It is evident," he wrote in connection with classical Greece, "that the failure of gentile institutions to meet the now complicated wants of society originated the movement to withdraw all civil powers from the gentes, phratries and tribes, and re-invest them in new constituencies" (263). In discussing "wherein the gentile organization had failed to meet the requirements of society" (263), Morgan referred to the growth of cities, which "imply the existence of a stable and developed field agriculture, the possession of domestic animals in flocks and herds, of merchandise in masses and of property in houses and lands. The city brought with it new demands in the art of government by creating a changed condition of society" (264).

Although Morgan may have originally borrowed the notion of antithesis between social and political organization from Maine, it was he who gave it concrete historical embodiment, using the instances of Greece and Rome. The origins of the first urban societies, however, lie some three thousands of years earlier in the Ancient East, and the evolution of the city was repeated at different times around the world—in the great river

[1] Schneider and Gough, *op. cit.*, pp. 595-6.

valleys of China and India, in West Africa, in the area stretching from Mexico to Bolivia in the New World. Not only are many scholars engaged in tracing the growth in each of these areas from relatively self-sufficient villages to true urban centers, dependent upon imported food and goods, but recently there has been a marked interest among them in pooling their knowledge in order to arrive at valid generalizations about the process of urban growth.[1]

ii. The solution to the new condition of society, from the viewpoint of political organization, Morgan maintained, was "to deal with persons through their territorial relations" (272). The discovery of this solution "was gradual, extending through a long period of time, and was embodied in a series of successive experiments by means of which a remedy was sought for existing evils" (263; cf. also 223-4, 281). Morgan unfolded his thesis through detailed reconstruction of Grecian and Roman history, and dealt extensively, although not always as pointedly as we might wish, with the interrelation of economic and political developments. He saw property as "the new element that had been gradually remoulding Grecian institutions to prepare the way for political society, of which it was to be the mainspring as well as the foundation" (223-4). Political organization, however, was not successful when built on property alone. In Greece, "the idea of property, as the basis of a system of government, was . . . incorporated by Solon in the new plan of property classes . . ." but fell apart, in Morgan's view, because it failed to deal with persons through their territorial relations (272). It remained for Cleisthenes to arrive at a viable solution by establishing demes or townships.

In Rome, the government that replaced the gens was based both on property classes and on city wards. Morgan stressed how important were these property classes, which became "the commanding element, as is shown by the lodgment of the controlling power of the government" in the highest of them (348). "A privileged class was . . . created at a stroke, and intrenched first in the gentile and afterwards in the political system, which ultimately overthrew the democratic principles inherited from

---

[1] For general discussions of urban growth, cf. Childe, V. Gordon, *What Happened in History,* Penguin Books, Great Britain, 1954; Steward, Julian H., *op. cit.,* Chapter 11; and Braidwood, Robert J., and Willey, Gordon R., editors, *Courses Toward Urban Life,* Aldine Publishing Company, Chicago, 1962.

the gentes. It was the Roman senate, with the patrician class it created, that changed the institutions and the destiny of the Roman people" (289). The *mélange* of property and territory he saw as the Roman solution "was the product of the superior craft of the wealthy classes who intended to seize the substance of power while they pretended to respect the rights and interests of all" (349). "Henceforth the creation and protection of property became the primary objects of the government, with a superadded career of conquest for domination over distant tribes and nations" (348). Had Rome instead, he said, been organized on the basis of territory alone, with the wards being given the power of local self-government, and the senate made elective, it would have become a democracy similar to Greece.

In this final argument of Morgan's, we recognize a shortcoming, for, in his evaluation of classical Greece, he virtually ignored the fact that it was a slave society. Morgan's emphasis on *property* as such, rather than on *classes* as groups with different relationships to property, prevented a fuller view of the structural relations lying behind its production. When he spoke of classes, he referred mainly to the distinction between commoners and an aristocracy, and not to differences in accessibility to and control over major sources of subsistence. He saw the United States of his day as having abandoned classes, although as being still too largely founded on property. In *The Origin of the Family, Private Property and the State,* when Engels summarizes Morgan's discussion of Greece and Rome, he defines more clearly the changes that occurred in economic structure as specialization and trade developed, and more precisely relates the economic structure thus created with developing political forms.[1]

iii. The third point developed by Morgan was that the democratic traditions of Greece were not something new in the world, but the heritage of a vanishing gentile society (cf. 222, 254, 282). The Greek office of "basileus" could not be translated as "king." It did not pertain to a royal line but to the tribal chiefs, or the military commander of the combined tribes, in a democratic system built on gentilism (222, 248-9, 253-4, 260,

[1] For a discussion by an interdisciplinary group of contemporary scholars on the processes and results of ancient urbanization, cf. Kraeling, Carl H., and Adams, Robert M., *City Invincible,* University of Chicago Press, Chicago, 1960.

282).[1] The democratic heritage of Greece was important to Morgan's argument that egalitarian traditions are ancient and universal in the history of man, and this theme recurs throughout *Ancient Society*. Morgan wrote, "That remarkable development of genius and intelligence, which raised the Athenians to the highest eminence among the historical nations of mankind, occurred under the inspiration of democratic institutions" (284). When comparing Greece and Rome, he said:

> The human race is gradually learning the simple lesson, that the people as a whole are wiser for the public good and the public prosperity, than any privileged class of men, however refined and cultivated, have ever been, or, by any possibility, can ever become. Governments over societies the most advanced are still in a transitional stage; and they are necessarily and logically moving, as President Grant, not without reason, intimated in his last inaugural address, in the direction of democracy; that form of self-government which represents and expresses the average intelligence and virtue of a free and educated people. (344)

iv. Morgan's fourth point was that Aztec society, despite its richness and pageantry, was not the "kingdom" described by the Spanish chroniclers, but was a "military democracy" based on gentile social organization (193, 199-200, 209-10, 219). He wrote, "Until the idea of property had advanced very far beyond the point they [North American Indians] had attained, the substitution of political for gentile society was impossible" (220). Some time prior to writing *Ancient Society*, Morgan had won the Mexican scholar Bandelier over to his point of view, and Bandelier had undertaken a thorough reinterpretation of Aztec materials.

That Aztec society could not be equated with feudal Spain of the 16th and 17th centuries is clear. However, just how far it had advanced toward classes and statehood, just what the nature of social stratification and of production and distribution of wealth were, are still questions. In his summary of early Mexican history, Wolf, drawing upon Kirchoff, writes that the "calpulli" of Aztec society were neither city wards nor egalitarian gentes,

---

[1] For an extremely full and detailed elaboration on Morgan's theoretical scheme, as it relates to ancient Greece, cf. Thompson, George, *Studies in Ancient Greek Society, Vol. I, The Prehistoric Aegean*, Camelot Press, London and Southampton, 1949, and *Vol. II, The First Philosophers*, Lawrence & Wishart, London, 1955.

but were "conical clans" which distributed "wealth, social standing and power most unequally among the members of the pseudo-family." [1] In other words, class differences, though not yet crystallized, were developing.

In stressing the "democratic" character of Aztec and early Greek society, Morgan was contrasting them with the monarchies of Europe. By "democracy," he referred to machinery for popular selection or recall of a leader, as opposed to strictly hereditary rules of succession (231-2, 254-5). This was an important distinction to make when many "rulers," surrounded with pomp and ritual, were considered "kings" after the European pattern. However, it is not only important to distinguish between what are still essentially gentile societies and what are fully developed class and state societies. It is equally important for an understanding of social evolution, and of individual cultures, not to blur the distinction between societies that are already well advanced toward a class system and political organization, and truly egalitarian hunting and gathering or horticultural societies.

As his fifth and sixth propositions, Morgan posed two social correlates of political and economic growth: the patrilineal monogamous family, and the lowered status of women.

v. The monogamous family could not become strong as long as gentile institutions were in force, for the two were mutually contradictory. ". . . every family in the archaic as well as in the later period, was partly within and partly without the gens, because husband and wife must belong to different gentes. . . . A family of the monogamian type might have become individualized and powerful in a gens, and in society at large [in ancient Greece and Rome]; but the gens nevertheless did not and could not recognize or depend upon the family as an integer of itself" (233). The development of property in cattle and land, however, led to the desire on the part of men to transmit it to their own children. First patrilineality in the gens, and second monogamy, were the consequences (67, 153-4, 238, 355-6, 363). "It is impossible to overestimate the influence of property in the civilization of mankind," wrote Morgan, and continued:

> It was the power that brought the Aryan and Semitic nations out of barbarism into civilization. The growth of the idea of

[1] Wolf, Eric R., *Sons of the Shaking Earth,* University of Chicago Press, Chicago, 1959, p. 136.

property in the human mind commenced in feebleness and ended in becoming its master passion. Governments and laws are instituted with primary reference to its creation, protection and enjoyment. It introduced human slavery as an instrument in its production; and, after the experience of several thousand years, it caused the abolition of slavery upon the discovery that a freeman was a better property-making machine. . . . With the establishment of the inheritance of property in the children of its owner, came the first possibility of a strict monogamian family. Gradually, though slowly, this form of marriage, with an exclusive cohabitation, became the rule rather than the exception; but it was not until civilization had commenced that it became permanently established. (511-12)

vi. The position of women changed adversely with the transition from gentile to political society and the emergence of the monogamous patriarchal family. Morgan was forceful on this point, although he minimized the significance of *patriarchy* as linked with monogamy. Patriarchy will be dealt with more fully in the introduction to Part III of *Ancient Society*. However, it is important to point out here that such patrilineal elements as might have existed in horticultural societies would be altogether different from patrilineality as it developed in societies with class structures, private property, and political organization. In class-structured societies, direct power of one individual over another becomes possible in a way that is foreign to collective society. The *patriarchal* family, in which an individual male could have complete control over the household of wives, children, and servants or slaves, who could be virtually isolated from the larger society, has no parallel in the pre-political world.

Morgan's view of social change has already been touched upon. In Part II of *Ancient Society* a recurrent theme was the combination of unrecognized social processes and conscious decisions that to Morgan made up history. He spoke of "the necessities of mankind for the organization of society" which produced the gens (330); and of kinship systems as "identified in their origin with organic movements of society which produced a great change of condition" (407). In another instance, we read:

It fortunately so happens that the events of human progress embody themselves, independently of particular men, in a

> material record, which is crystallized in institutions, usages and customs, and preserved in inventions and discoveries. Historians, from a sort of necessity, give to individuals great prominence in the production of events; thus placing persons, who are transient, in the place of principles, which are enduring. The work of society in its totality, by means of which all progress occurs, is ascribed far too much to individual men, and far too little to the public intelligence. It will be recognized generally that the substance of human history is bound up in the growth of ideas, which are wrought out by the people and expressed in their institutions, usages, inventions and discoveries. (311)

On the other hand, when speaking of Greece and Rome, and new social problems that had to be faced, Morgan discussed conscious attempts on the part of individuals to reach viable solutions.

Intertwined with Morgan's sociological view of history, however, there was a strong teleological thread. His rhetorical bow to the Almighty—man's labors "were a part of the plan of the Supreme Intelligence" (563)—was no more than a ritual gesture, but there is also in the pages of *Ancient Society* a Platonic inference of an ideal toward which society was striving. Morgan wrote of "a movement, still pending, in the direction of the true ideal of the gens" (56), of "unconscious reformations" (47), of "a progressive connected series, each of which represents the results of unconscious reformatory movements to extricate society from existing evils" (58), and he said, "Mankind rise in the scale and the family advances through its successive forms, as these [sexual] rights sink down before the efforts of society to improve its internal organization" (58-9).

In other instances, Morgan described the development of an institution in more utilitarian terms. "Thus, every essential institution in the government or administration of the affairs of society may generally be traced to a simple germ," he wrote, "which springs up in a rude form from human wants, and, when able to endure the test of time and experience, is developed into a permanent institution" (330). His concept was apparently one of a continuous, rather than uneven, growth from a "germ" of an idea: "[The monogamous family] was a slow growth, planting its roots far back in the period of savagery—a final result toward which the experience of ages steadily tended" (512).

At times the notion of evolution was expressed by Morgan as *cultural* growth, an accretion of social knowledge. When he spoke of the "progress of the Athenian people in knowledge and intelligence" (270), he apparently meant "intelligence" as a cultural aggregate, rather than a matter of individual ability, for in another instance he wrote:

> Mankind owe a debt of gratitude to their savage ancestors for devising an institution able to carry the advancing portion of the human race out of savagery into barbarism, and through the successive stages of the latter into civilization. *It also accumulated by experience the intelligence and knowledge necessary to devise political society while the . . . [gens] yet* remained. (350) (italics ours)

Unfortunately, however, as has previously been mentioned, Morgan's concept of cultural accretion became linked with the notion, resulting from the recent discovery of human physical evolution, of cultural knowledge as becoming embedded in the body, "interwoven with every fibre of their brains" (261; cf. also 59-60, 123, 152, 252, 471). The theory of physiological incorporation of what we might call social aptitude in mankind's ancestors, as society slowly evolved, is sound. However, it would involve a much longer time span—hundreds of thousands of years—and more generalized predispositions than Morgan assumed. The "abilities" called for would be at the level of sensitivity to others, need for self-expression, desire for gratifications beyond the directly physical, and so forth—a potential for social living which cultural traditions then supply with specific goals. The notions of private property, or the monogamous family, are culturally learned goals; our present state of knowledge shows no grounds for speaking of such social goals as incorporated into the brain, especially in the some ten thousand years between "savagery" and "civilization."

Let me now refer to several minor passages in *Ancient Society* that require specific comment. Despite his broad vision and his attempt to see beyond the limits of his own culture, Morgan was unable to escape occasional ethnocentric judgments. He dismissed Africa as a "barren ethnological field," partly because the indigenous cultures had been distorted by outside influences, and partly because it was already culturally heterogeneous—"a chaos of savagery and barbarism." True, little was known of Africa at the time, but Morgan's choice of terms was not only incorrect, but deplorably subjective. He wrote, "savagery in its lowest forms, cannibalism included, and barbarism in its lowest forms prevail over the greater part of the continent" (382). In East Africa are found centers of ancient civilization, and, while the precise nature of the great West African kingdoms is still being argued, some of them included populations well into the millions. The only people still in "savagery" were the hard-working and peaceful hunters of the Kalahari. Morgan was guilty of equally inappropriate references to the Australians, mentioning the "low level of the mental and moral life of the people," and the "dark shade of their savage state" (385).[1]

On pages 105 to 111, Morgan discussed the peopling of the New World, as successive groups of immigrants pushed south. He mentioned the long time it must have taken, as evidenced by the number of languages that had evolved from a parent stock. Carbon 14 dates have helped refine estimates of man's earliest known cultures in the New World, which are now placed at about 15,000 years ago, although there are some slight suggestions that this figure might finally be doubled or even tripled. In any case, relationships among different American Indian languages are continually being discovered, and the number of seemingly independent stocks constantly reduced. That all American Indian languages need theoretically to be reducible to one stock, however, is not necessarily true. Different waves of migrants from Asia might already have spoken divergent languages.

With regard to the movement of people south, the Valley of the Colombia probably did not play such a central role as it might have appeared when Morgan wrote. Nor would movement necessarily continue to be from north to south. By the time maize cultivation developed in Central America, the entire New World had long been peopled, and pressure would then begin to be outward, both north and south, from the new centers of population growth that agriculture produced.

On page 468, Morgan wrote, "When two advancing tribes, with strong mental and physical characters, are brought together

---

[1] References have already been given for the hunting cultures of Australia and the Kalahari. Ethnographic materials on African cultures are virtually endless, but for specific discussions of African high civilizations prior to European conquest, see DuBois, W. E. Burghardt, *The World and Africa,* Viking Press, New York, 1946; and Davidson, Basil, *The Lost Cities of Africa,* Little, Brown and Company, Boston, 1959.

and blended into one people by the accidents of barbarous life, the new skull and brain would widen and lengthen to the sum of the capabilities of both." Human skull shape is generally becoming rounder as people become more urbanized, but the process is a more obscure and complicated one than that described, although there was absolutely no evidence for this at the time Morgan wrote. To his credit, however, he recognized here and elsewhere that so-called "miscegenation" is healthy for the peoples concerned.

CHAPTER I

ORGANIZATION OF SOCIETY UPON THE BASIS OF SEX

In treating the subject of the growth of the idea of government, the organization into gentes on the basis of kin naturally suggests itself as the archaic framework of ancient society; but there is a still older and more archaic organization, that into classes on the basis of sex, which first demands attention. It will not be taken up because of its novelty in human experience, but for the higher reason that it seems to contain the germinal principle of the gens. If this inference is warranted by the facts it will give to this organization into male and female classes, now found in full vitality among the Australian aborigines, an ancient prevalence as wide spread, in the tribes of mankind, as the original organization into gentes.

It will soon be perceived that low down in savagery community of husbands and wives, within prescribed limits, was the central principle of the social system. The marital rights and privileges, (*jura conjugialia,*) [1] established in the group, grew into a stupendous scheme, which became the organic principle on which society was constituted. From the nature of the case these rights and privileges rooted themselves so firmly that emancipation from them was slowly accomplished through movements which resulted in unconscious reformations. Accordingly it will be found that the family has ad-

---

[1] The Romans made a distinction between "connubium," which related to marriage considered as a civil institution, and "conjugium," which was a mere physical union.

vanced from a lower to a higher form as the range of this conjugal system was gradually reduced. The family, commencing in the consanguine, founded upon the intermarriage of brothers and sisters in a group, passed into the second form, the punaluan, under a social system akin to the Australian classes, which broke up the first species of marriage by substituting groups of brothers who shared their wives in common, and groups of sisters who shared their husbands in common,—marriage in both cases being in the group. The organization into classes upon sex, and the subsequent higher organization into gentes upon kin, must be regarded as the results of great social movements worked out unconsciously through natural selection. For these reasons the Australian system, about to be presented, deserves attentive consideration, although it carries us into a low grade of human life. It represents a striking phase of the ancient social history of our race.

The organization into classes on the basis of sex, and the inchoate organization into gentes on the basis of kin, now prevail among that portion of the Australian aborigines who speak the Kamilaroi language. They inhabit the Darling River district north of Sydney. Both organizations are also found in other Australian tribes, and so wide spread as to render probable their ancient universal prevalence among them. It is evident from internal considerations that the male and female classes are older than the gentes: firstly, because the gentile organization is higher than that into classes; and secondly, because the former, among the Kamilaroi, are in process of overthrowing the latter. The class in its male and female branches is the unit of their social system, which place rightfully belongs to the gens when in full development. A remarkable combination of facts is thus presented; namely, a sexual and a gentile organization, both in existence at the same time, the former holding the central position, and the latter inchoate but advancing to completeness through encroachments upon the former.

This organization upon sex has not been found, as yet, in any tribes of savages out of Australia, but the slow development of these islanders in their secluded habitat, and the more archaic character of the organization upon sex than that into gentes, suggests the conjecture, that the former may have been universal in such branches of the human family as afterwards possessed the gentile organization. Although the class system, when traced out fully, involves some bewildering complications, it will reward the attention necessary for its mastery. As a curious social organization among savages it possesses but little interest; but as the most primitive form of society hitherto discovered, and more especially with the contingent probability that the remote progenitors of our own Aryan family were once similarly organized, it becomes important, and may prove instructive.

The Australians rank below the Polynesians, and far below the American aborigines. They stand below the African Negro and near the bottom of the scale. Their social institutions, therefore, must approach the primitive type as nearly as those of any existing people.[1]

Inasmuch as the gens is made the subject of the succeeding chapter, it will be introduced in this without discussion, and only for the necessary explanation of the classes.

The Kamilaroi are divided into six gentes, standing with reference to the right of marriage, in two divisions, as follows:

I. 1. Iguana, (Duli). 2. Kangaroo, (Murriira). 3. Opossum, (Mute).

II. 4. Emu, (Dinoun). 5. Bandicoot, (Bilba. 6. Blacksnake, (Nurai).

Originally the first three gentes were not allowed to

1 For the detailed facts of the Australian system I am indebted to the Rev. Lorimer Fison, an English missionary in Australia, who received a portion of them from the Rev. W. Ridley, and another portion from T. E. Lance, Esq., both of whom had spent many years among the Australian aborigines, and enjoyed excellent opportunities for observation. The facts were sent by Mr. Fison with a critical analysis and discussion of the system, which, with observations of the writer, were published in the "Proceedings of the Am. Acad. of Arts and Sciences for 1872." See vol. viii, p. 412. A brief notice of the Kamilaroi classes is given in McLennan's "Primitive Marriage," p. 118; and in Tylor's "Early History of Mankind," p. 288.

2 Padymelon: a species of kangaroo.

intermarry with each other, because they were subdivisions of an original gens; but they were permitted to marry into either of the other gentes, and *vice versâ.* This ancient rule is now modified, among the Kamilaroi, in certain definite particulars but not carried to the full extent of permitting marriage into any gens but that of the individual. Neither males nor females can marry into their own gens, the prohibition being absolute. Descent is in the female line, which assigns the children to the gens of their mother. These are among the essential characteristics of the gens, wherever this institution is found in its archaic form. In its external features, therefore, it is perfect and complete among the Kamilaroi.

But there is a further and older division of the people into eight classes, four of which are composed exclusively of males, and four exclusively of females. It is accompanied with a regulation in respect to marriage and descent which obstructs the gens, and demonstrates that the latter organization is in process of development into its true logical form. One only of the four classes of males can marry into one only of the four classes of females. In the sequel it will be found that all the males of one class are, theoretically, the husbands of all the females of the class into which they are allowed to marry. Moreover, if the male belongs to one of the first three gentes the female must belong to one of the opposite three. Marriage is thus restricted to a portion of the males of one gens, with a portion of the females of another gens, which is opposed to the true theory of the gentile institution, for all the members of each gens should be allowed to marry persons of the opposite sex in all the gentes except their own.

The classes are the following:

Male.	*Female.*
1. Ippai.	1. Ippata.
2. Kumbo.	2. Buta.
3. Murri.	3. Mata.
4. Kubbi.	4. Kapota.

All the Ippais, of whatever gens, are brothers to each

other. Theoretically, they are descended from a supposed common female ancestor. All the Kumbos are the same; and so are all the Murris and Kubbis, respectively, and for the same reason. In like manner, all the Ippatas, of whatever gens, are sisters to each other, and for the same reason; all the Butas are the same, and so are all the Matas and Kapotas, respectively. In the next place, all the Ippais and Ippatas are brothers and sisters to each other, whether children of the same mother or collateral consanguinei, and in whatever gens they are found. The Kumbos and Butas are brothers and sisters; and so are the Murris and Matas, and the Kubbis and Kapotas respectively. If an Ippai and Ippata meet, who have never seen each other before, they address each other as brother and sister. The Kamilaroi, therefore, are organized into four great primary groups of brothers and sisters, each group being composed of a male and a female branch; but intermingled over the areas of their occupation. Founded upon sex, instead of kin, it is older than the gentes, and more archaic, it may be repeated, than any form of society hitherto known.

The classes embody the germ of the gens, but fall short of its realization. In reality the Ippais and Ippatas form a single class in two branches, and since they cannot intermarry they would form the basis of a gens but for the reason that they fall under two names, each of which is integral for certain purposes, and for the further reason that their children take different names from their own. The division into classes is upon sex instead of kin, and has its primary relation to a rule of marriage as remarkable as it is original.

Since brothers and sisters are not allowed to intermarry, the classes stand to each other in a different order with respect to the right of marriage, or rather, of cohabitation, which better expresses the relation. Such was the original law, thus:

Ippai can marry Kapota, and no other.
Kumbo can marry Mata, and no other.
Murri can marry Buta, and no other.
Kubbi can marry Ippata, and no other.

This exclusive scheme has been modified in one particular, as will hereafter be shown: namely, in giving to each class of males the right of intermarriage with one additional class of females. In this fact, evidence of the encroachment of the gens upon the class is furnished, tending to the overthrow of the latter.

It is thus seen that each male in the selection of a wife, is limited to one-fourth part of all the Kamilaroi females. This, however, is not the remarkable part of the system. Theoretically every Kapota is the wife of every Ippai; every Mata is the wife of every Kumbo; every Buta is the wife of every Murri; and every Ippata of every Kubbi. Upon this material point the information is specific. Mr. Fison, before mentioned, after observing that Mr. Lance had "had much intercourse with the natives, having lived among them many years on frontier cattle-stations on the Darling River, and in the trans-Darling country," quotes from his letter as follows: "If a Kubbi meets a stranger Ippata, they address each other as *Goleer* = Spouse. . . . A Kubbi thus meeting an Ippata, even though she were of another tribe, would treat her as his wife, and his right to do so would be recognized by her tribe." Every Ippata within the immediate circle of his acquaintance would consequently be his wife as well.

Here we find, in a direct and definite form, punaluan marriage in a group of unusual extent; but broken up into lesser groups, each a miniature representation of the whole, united for habitation and subsistence. Under the conjugal system thus brought to light one-quarter of all the males are united in marriage with one-quarter of all the females of the Kamilaroi tribes. This picture of savage life need not revolt the mind, because to them it was a form of the marriage relation, and therefore devoid of impropriety. It is but an extended form of polygyny and polyandry, which, within narrower limits, have prevailed universally among savage tribes. The evidence of the fact still exists, in unmistakable form, in their systems of consanguinity and affinity, which have outlived the customs and usages in which they originated. It will be noticed that this scheme of intermarriage is but a step from promiscuity, because it is tantamount to that with the addition of a method. Still, as it is made a subject of organic regulation, it is far removed from general promiscuity. Moreover, it reveals an existing state of marriage and of the family of which no adequate conception could have been formed apart from the facts. It affords the first direct evidence of a state of society which had previously been deduced, as extremely probable, from systems of consanguinity and affinity.[1]

Whilst the children remained in the gens of their mother, they passed into another class, in the same gens, different from that of either parent. This will be made apparent by the following table:

Male.		*Female.*		*Male.*		*Female.*
Ippai	marries	Kapota.	Their children are	Murri	and	Mata.
Kumbo	marries	Mata.	Their children are	Kubbi	and	Kapota.
Murri	marries	Buta.	Their children are	Ippai	and	Ippata.
Kubbi	marries	Ippata.	Their children are	Kumbo	and	Buta.

If these descents are followed out it will be found that, in the female line, Kapota is the mother of Mata, and Mata in turn is the mother of Kapota; so Ippata is the mother of Buta, and the latter in turn is the mother of Ippata. It is the same with the male classes; but since descent is in the female line, the Kamilaroi tribes derive themselves from two supposed female ancestors, which laid the foundation for two original gentes. By tracing these descents still further it will be found that the blood of each class passes through all the classes.

Although each individual bears one of the class names above given, it will be understood that each has in addition the single personal name, which is common among savage as well as barbarous tribes. The more closely this organization upon sex is scrutinized, the more remarkable it seems as the work of savages. When once established, and after that transmitted through a few

---

"Systems of Consanguinity and Affinity of the Human Family, (Smithsonian Contributions to Knowledge)," vol. xvii, p. 420, "et seq."

generations, it would hold society with such power as to become difficult of displacement. It would require a similar and higher system, and centuries of time, to accomplish this result; particularly if the range of the conjugal system would thereby be abridged.

The gentile organization supervened naturally upon the classes as a higher organization, by simply enfolding them unchanged. That it was subsequent in point of time, is shown by the relations of the two systems, by the inchoate condition of the gentes, by the impaired condition of the classes through encroachments by the gens, and by the fact that the class is still the unit of organization. These conclusions will be made apparent in the sequel.

From the preceding statements the composition of the gentes will be understood when placed in their relations to the classes. The latter are in pairs of brothers and sisters derived from each other; and the gentes themselves, through the classes, are in pairs, as follows:

Gentes.		Male.	Female.	Male.	Female.
1. Iguana.	All are	Murri	& Mata, or	Kubbi	& Kapota.
2. Emu.	All are	Kumbo	& Buta, or	Ippai	& Ippata.
3. Kangaroo.	All are	Murri	& Mata, or	Kubbi	& Kapota.
4. Bandicoot.	All are	Kumbo	& Buta, or	Ippai	& Ippata.
5. Opossum.	All are	Murri	& Mata, or	Kubbi	& Kapota.
6. Blacksnake.	All are	Kumbo	& Buta, or	Ippai	& Ippata.

The connection of children with a particular gens is proven by the law of marriage. Thus, Iguana-Mata must marry Kumbo; her children are Kubbi and Kapota, and necessarily Iguana in gens, because descent is in the female line. Iguana-Kapota must marry Ippai; her children are Murri and Mata, and also Iguana in gens, for the same reason. In like manner Emu-Buta must marry Murri; her children are Ippai and Ippata, and of the Emu gens. So Emu-Ippata must marry Kubbi; her children are Kumbo and Buta, and also of the Emu gens. In this manner the gens is maintained by keeping in its membership the children of all its female members. The same is true in all respects of each of the remaining gentes.

It will be noticed that each gens is made up, theoretically, of the descendants of two supposed female ancestors, and contains four of the eight classes. It seems probable that originally there were but two male, and two female classes, which were set opposite to each other in respect to the right of marriage; and that the four afterward subdivided into eight. The classes as an anterior organization were evidently arranged within the gentes, and not formed by the subdivision of the latter.

Moreover, since the Iguana, Kangaroo and Opossum gentes are found to be counterparts of each other, in the classes they contain, it follows that they are subdivisions of an original gens. Precisely the same is true of Emu, Bandicoot and Blacksnake, in both particulars; thus reducing the six to two original gentes, with the right in each to marry into the other, but not into itself. It is confirmed by the fact that the members of the first three gentes could not originally intermarry; neither could the members of the last three. The reason which prevented intermarriage in the gens, when the three were one, would follow the subdivisions because they were of the same descent although under different gentile names. Exactly the same thing is found among the Seneca-Iroquois, as will hereafter be shown.

Since marriage is restricted to particular classes, when there were but two gentes, one-half of all the females of one were, theoretically, the wives of one-half of all the males of the other. After their subdivision into six the benefit of marrying out of the gens, which was the chief advantage of the institution, was arrested, if not neutralized, by the presence of the classes together with the restrictions mentioned. It resulted in continuous in-and-in marriages beyond the immediate degree of brother and sister. If the gens could have eradicated the classes this evil would, in a great measure, have been removed.

---

[1] If a diagram of descents is máde, for example, of Ippai and Kapota, and carried to the fourth generation, giving to each intermediate pair two children, a male and a female, the following results will appear. The children of Ippai and Kapota are Murri and Mata. As brothers and sisters the latter cannot marry. At the second degree, the children of Murri, married to Buta, are Ippai and Ippata, and of Mata married to Kumbo,

The organization into classes seems to have been directed to the single object of breaking up the intermarriage of brothers and sisters, which affords a probable explanation of the origin of the system. But since it did not look beyond this special abomination it retained a conjugal system nearly as objectionable, as well as cast it in a permanent form.

It remains to notice an innovation upon the original constitution of the classes, and in favor of the gens, which reveals a movement, still pending, in the direction of the true ideal of the gens. It is shown in two particulars: firstly, in allowing each triad of gentes to intermarry with each other, to a limited extent; secondly, to marry into classes not before permitted. Thus, Iguana-Murri can now marry Mata in the Kangaroo gens, his collateral sister, whereas originally he was restricted to Buta in the opposite three. So Iguana-Kubbi can now marry Kapota, his collateral sister. Emu-Kumbo can now marry Buta, and Emu-Ippai can marry Ippata in the Blacksnake gens, contrary to original limitations. Each class of males in each triad of gentes seems now to be allowed one additional class of females in the two remaining gentes of the same triad, from which they were before excluded. The memoranda sent by Mr. Fison,

---

are Kubbi and Kapota. Of these, Ippai marries his cousin Kapota, and Kubbi marries his cousin Ippata. It will be noticed that the eight classes are reproduced from two in the second and third generations, with the exception of Kumbo and Buta. At the next or third degree, there are two Murris, two Matas, two Kumbos, and two Butas; of whom the Murris marry the Butas, their second cousins, and the Kubbis the Matas, their second cousins. At the fourth generation there are four each of Ippais Kapotas Kubbis and Ippatas, who are third cousins. Of these, the Ippais marry the Kapotas, and the Kubbis the Ippatas; and thus it runs from generation to generation. A similar chart of the remaining marriageable classes will produce like results. These details are tedious, but they make the fact apparent that in this condition of ancient society they not only intermarry constantly, but are compelled to do so through this organization upon sex. Cohabitation would not follow this invariable course because an entire male and female class were married in a group; but its occurrence must have been constant under the system. One of the primary objects secured by the gens, when fully matured, was thus defeated: namely, the segregation of a moiety of the descendants of a supposed common ancestor under a prohibition of intermarriage, followed by a right of marrying into any other gens.

however, do not show a change to the full extent here indicated.[1]

This innovation would plainly have been a retrograde movement but that it tended to break down the classes. The line of progress among the Kamilaroi, so far as any is observable, was from classes into gentes, followed by a tendency to make the gens instead of the class the unit of the social organism. In this movement the overshadowing system of cohabitation was the resisting element. Social advancement was impossible without diminishing its extent, which was equally impossible so long as the classes, with the privileges they conferred, remained in full vitality. The *jura conjugialia,* which appertained to these classes, were the dead weight upon the Kamilaroi, without emancipation from which they would have remained for additional thousands of years in the same condition, substantially, in which they were found.

An organization somewhat similar is indicated by the *punalua* of the Hawaiians which will be hereafter explained. Wherever the middle or lower stratum of savagery is uncovered, marriages of entire groups under usages defining the groups, have been discovered either in absolute form, or such traces as to leave little doubt that such marriages were normal throughout this period of man's history. It is immaterial whether the group, theoretically, was large or small, the necessities of their condition would set a practical limit to the size of the group living together under this custom. If then community of husbands and wives is found to have been a law of the savage state, and, therefore, the essential condition of society in savagery, the inference would be conclusive that our own savage ancestors shared in this common experience of the human race.

In such usages and customs an explanation of the low condition of savages is found. If men in savagery had not been left behind, in isolated portions of the earth, to testify concerning the early condition of mankind in general, it would have been impossible to form any definite

---

1 "Proc. Am. Acad. Arts and Sciences," viii, 436.

conception of what it must have been. An important inference at once arises, namely, that the institutions of mankind have sprung up in a progressive connected series, each of which represents the result of unconscious reformatory movements to extricate society from existing evils. The wear of ages is upon these institutions, for the proper understanding of which they must be studied in this light. It cannot be assumed that the Australian savages are now at the bottom of the scale, for their arts and institutions, humble as they are, show the contrary; neither is there any ground for assuming their degradation from a higher condition, because the facts of human experience afford no sound basis for such an hypothesis. Cases of physical and mental deterioration in tribes and nations may be admitted, for reasons which are known, but they never interrupted the general progress of mankind. All the facts of human knowledge and experience tend to show that the human race, as a whole, have steadily progressed from a lower to a higher condition. The arts by which savages maintain their lives are remarkably persistent. They are never lost until superseded by others higher in degree. By the practice of these arts, and by the experience gained through social organizations, mankind have advanced under a necessary law of development, although their progress may have been substantially imperceptible for centuries. It was the same with races as with individuals, although tribes and nations have perished through the disruption of their ethnic life.

The Australian classes afford the first, and, so far as the writer is aware, the only case in which we are able to look down into the incipient stages of the organization into gentes, and even through it upon an interior organization so archaic as that upon sex. It seems to afford a glimpse at society when it verged upon the primitive. Among other tribes the gens seems to have advanced in proportion to the curtailment of the conjugal system. Mankind rise in the scale and the family advances through its successive forms, as these rights sink down before the efforts of society to improve its internal organization.

The Australians might not have effected the overthrow of the classes in thousands of years if they had remained undiscovered; while more favored continental tribes had long before perfected the gens, then advanced it through its successive phases, and at last laid it aside after entering upon civilization. Facts illustrating the rise of successive social organizations, such as that upon sex, and that upon kin are of the highest ethnological value. A knowledge of what they indicate is eminently desirable, if the early history of mankind is to be measurably recovered.

Among the Polynesian tribes the gens was unknown; but traces of a system analogous to the Australian classes appear in the Hawaiian custom of punalua. Original ideas, absolutely independent of previous knowledge and experience, are necessarily few in number. Were it possible to reduce the sum of human ideas to underived originals, the small numerical result would be startling. Development is the method of human progress.

In the light of these facts some of the excrescences of modern civilization, such as Mormonism, are seen to be relics of the old savagism not yet eradicated from the human brain. We have the same brain, perpetuated by reproduction, which worked in the skulls of barbarians and savages in by-gone ages; and it has come down to us ladened and saturated with the thoughts, aspirations and passions, with which it was busied through the intermediate periods. It is the same brain grown older and larger with the experience of the ages. These outcrops of barbarism are so many revelations of its ancient proclivities. They are explainable as a species of mental atavism.

Out of a few germs of thought, conceived in the early ages, have been evolved all the principal institutions of mankind. Beginning their growth in the period of savagery, fermenting through the period of barbarism, they have continued their advancement through the period of civilization. The evolution of these germs of thought has been guided by a natural logic which formed an essential attribute of the brain itself. So unerringly has this principle performed its functions in all conditions of experience, and in all periods of time, that its results are uniform, coherent and traceable in their courses. These results alone will in time yield convincing proofs of the unity of origin of mankind. The mental history of the human race, which is revealed in institutions, inventions and discoveries, is presumptively the history of a single species, perpetuated through individuals, and developed through experience. Among the original germs of thought, which have exercised the most powerful influence upon the human mind, and upon human destiny, are these which relate to government, to the family, to language, to religion, an to property. They had a definite beginning far back in savagery, and a logical progress, but can have no final consummation, because they are still progressing, and must ever continue to progress.

CHAPTER II

THE IROQUOIS GENS

The experience of mankind, as elsewhere remarked, has developed but two plans of government, using the word *plan* in its scientific sense. Both were definite and systematic organizations of society. The first and most ancient was a *social organization,* founded upon gentes, phratries and tribes. The second and latest in time was a *political organization,* founded upon territory and upon property. Under the first a gentile society was created, in which the government dealt with persons through their relations to a gens and tribe. These relations were purely personal. Under the second a political society was instituted, in which the government dealt with persons through their relations to territory, *e. g.* —the township, the county, and the state. These relations were purely territorial. The two plans were fundamentally different. One belongs to ancient society, and the other to modern.

The gentile organization opens to us one of the oldest and most widely prevalent institutions of mankind. It furnished the nearly universal plan of government of ancient society, Asiatic, European, African and Australian. It was the instrumentality by means of which society was organized and held together. Commencing in savagery, and continuing through the three sub-periods of barbarism, it remained until the establishment of political society, which did not occur until after civilization had commenced. The Grecian gens, phratry and tribe, the Roman gens, *curia* and tribe find their analogues in the gens, phratry and tribe of the American aborigines. In like manner, the Irish *sept,* the Scottish *clan,* the *phrara* of the Albanians, and the Sanskrit *ganas,* without extending the comparison further, are the same as the American Indian gens, which has usually been called a clan. As far as our knowledge extends, this organization runs through the entire ancient world upon all the continents, and it was brought down to the historical period by such tribes as attained to civilization. Nor is this all. Gentile society wherever found is the same in structural organization and in principles of action; but changing from lower to higher forms with the progressive advancement of the people. These changes give the history of development of the same original conceptions.

Gens, genos, and *ganas* in Latin, Greek and Sanskrit have alike the primary signification of *kin.* They contain the same element as *gigno, gignomai,* and *ganamai,* in the same languages, signifying *to beget*; thus implying in each an immediate common descent of the members of a gens. A gens, therefore, is a body of consanguinei descended from the same common ancestor, distinguished by a gentile name, and bound together by affinities of blood. It includes a moiety only of such descendants. Where descent is in the female line, as it was universally in the archaic period, the gens is composed of a supposed female ancestor and her children, together with the children of her female descendants, through females, in perpetuity; and where descent is in the male line—into which it was changed after the appearance of property in masses—of a supposed male ancestor and his children, together with the children of his male descendants, through males, in perpetuity. The family name among ourselves is a survival of the gentile name, with descent in the male line, and passing in the same manner. The modern family, as expressed by its name, is an unorganized gens; with the bond of kin broken, and its members as widely dispersed as the family name is found.

Among the nations named, the gens indicated a social organization of a remarkable character, which had prevailed from an antiquity so remote that its origin was lost in the obscurity of far distant ages. It was also the unit of organization of a social and governmental system, the fundamental basis of ancient society. This organization was not confined to the Latin, Grecian and Sanskrit speaking tribes, with whom it became such a conspicuous institution. It has been found in other branches of the Aryan family of nations, in the Semitic, Uralian and Turanian families, among the tribes of Africa and Australia, and of the American aborigines.

An exposition of the elementary constitution of the gens, with its functions, rights, and privileges, requires our first attention; after which it will be traced, as widely as possible, among the tribes and nations of mankind in order to prove, by comparisons, its fundamental unity. It will then be seen that it must be regarded as one of the primary institutions of mankind.

The gens has passed through successive stages of development in its transition from its archaic to its final form with the progress of mankind. These changes were limited, in the main, to two: firstly, changing descent from the female line, which was the archaic rule, as among the Grecian and Roman gentes; and, secondly, changing the inheritance of the property of a deceased member of the gens from his gentiles, who took it in the archaic period, first to his agnatic kindred, and finally to his children. These changes, slight as they may seem, indicate very great changes of condition as well as a large degree of progressive development.

The gentile organization, originating in the period of savagery, enduring through the three sub-periods of barbarism, finally gave way, among the more advanced tribes, when they attained civilization, the requirements of which it was unable to meet. Among the Greeks and Romans, political society supervened upon gentile society, but not until civilization had commenced. The township (and its equivalent, the city ward), with its fixed property, and the inhabitants it contained, organized as a body politic, became the unit and the basis of a new and radically different system of government. After political society was instituted, this ancient and time-honored organization, with the phratry and tribe development from it, gradually yielded up their existence. It will be my object, in the course of this volume, to trace the progress of this organization from its rise in savagery to its final overthrow in civilization; for it was under gentile institutions that barbarism was won by some of the tribes of mankind while in savagery, and that civilization was won by the descendants of some of the same tribes while in barbarism. Gentile institutions carried a portion of mankind from savagery to civilization.

This organization may be successfully studied both in its living and in its historical forms in a large number of tribes and races. In such an investigation it is preferable to commence with the gens in its archaic form, and then to follow it through its successive modifications among advanced nations, in order to discover both the changes and the causes which produced them. I shall commence, therefore, with the gens as it now exists among the American aborigines, where it is found in its archaic form, and among whom its theoretical constitution and practical workings can be investigated more successfully than in the historical gentes of the Greeks and Romans. In fact to understand fully the gentes of the latter nations a knowledge of the functions, and of the rights, privileges and obligations of the members of the American Indian gens is imperatively necessary.

In American Ethnography *tribe* and *clan* have been used in the place of gens as an equivalent term, from not perceiving its universality. In previous works, and folowing my predecessors, I have so used them.[1] A comparison of the Indian clan with the gens of the Greeks and Romans reveals at once their identity in structure and functions. It also extends to the phratry and tribe. If the identity of these several organizations

---

1 In "Letters on the Iroquois by Skenandoah," published in the "American Review" in 1847; in the "League of the Iroquois," published in 1851; and in "Systems of Consanguinity and Affinity of the Human Family," published in 1871. ("Smithsonian Contributions to Knowledge," vol. xvii.) I have used "tribe" as the equivalent of "gens," and in its place; but with an exact definition of the group.

can be shown, of which there can be no doubt, there is a manifest propriety in returning to the Latin and Grecian terminologies which are full and precise as well as historical. I have made herein the substitutions required, and propose to show the parallelism of these several organizations.

The plan of government of the American aborigines commenced with the gens and ended with the confederacy, the latter being the highest point to which their governmental institutions attained. It gave for the organic series: first, the gens, a body of consanguinei having a common gentile name; second, the phratry, an assemblage of related gentes united in a higher association for certain common objects; third, the tribe, an assemblage of gentes, usually organized in phratries, all the members of which spoke the same dialect; and fourth, a confederacy of tribes, the members of which respectively spoke dialects of the same stock language. It resulted in a gentile society (*societas*), as distinguised from a political society or state (*civitas*). The difference between the two is wide and fundamental. There was neither a political society, nor a citizen, nor a state, nor any civilization in America when it was discovered. One entire ethnical period intervened between the highest American Indian tribes and the beginning of civilization, as that term is properly understood.

In like manner the plan of government of the Grecian tribes, anterior to civilization, involved the same organic series, with the exception of the last member: first, the gens, a body of consanguinei bearing a common gentile name; second, the phratry, an assemblage of gentes, united for social and religious objects; third, the tribe, an assemblage of gentes of the same lineage organized in phratries; and fourth, a nation, an assemblage of tribes who had coalesced in a gentile society upon one common territory, as the four tribes of the Athenians in Attica, and the three Dorian tribes at Sparta. Coalescence was a higher process than confederating. In the latter case the tribes occupied independent territories.

The Roman plan and series were the same: First, the gens, a body of consanguinei bearing a common gentile name; second, the *curia,* an assemblage of gentes united in a higher association for the preformance of religious and governmental functions; third, the tribe, an assemblage of gentes organized in *curiae;* and fourth, a nation, an assemblage of tribes who had coalesced in a gentile society. The early Romans styled themselves, with entire propriety, the *Populus Romanus.*

Wherever gentile institutions prevailed, and prior to the establishment of political society, we find peoples or nations in gentile societies, and nothing beyond. The *state* did not exist. Their goverments were essentially democratical, because the principles on which the gens, phratry and tribe were organized were democratical. This last proposition, though contrary to received opinions, is historically important. The truth of it can be tested as the gens, phratry and tribe of the American aborigines, and the same organizations among the Greeks and Romans are successively considered. As the gens, the unit of organization, was essentially democratical, so necessarily was the phratry composed of gentes, the tribe composed of phraties, and the gentile society formed by the confederating, or coalescing of tribes.

The gens, though a very ancient social organization founded upon kin, does not include all the descendants of a common ancestor. It was for the reason that when the gens came in, marriage between single pairs was unknown, and descent through males could not be traced with certainty. Kindred were linked together chiefly through the bond of their maternity. In the ancient gens descent was limited to the female line. It embraced all such persons as traced their descent from a supposed common female ancestor, through females, the evidence of the fact being the possession of a common gentile name. It would include this ancestor and her children, the children of her daughters, and the children of her female descendants, through females, in perpetuity; whilst the children of her sons, and the children of her male descendants, through males, would belong to other gentes; namely, those of their respective mothers. Such was the gens in its archaic form, when the paternity of children was not certainly ascertainable, and when their maternity afforded the only certain criterion of descents.

This state of descents, which can be traced back to the Middle Status of savagery, as among the Australians, remained among the American aborigines through the Upper Status of savagery, and into and through the Lower Status of barbarism, with occasional exceptions. In the Middle Status barbarism, the Indian tribes began to change descent from the female line to the male, as the syndyasmian family of the period began to assume monogamian characteristics. In the Upper Status of barbarism, descent had become changed to the male line among the Grecian tribes, with the exception of the Lycians, and among the Italian tribes, with the exception of the Etruscans. The influence of property and its inheritance in producing the monogamian family which assured the paternity of children, and in causing a change of descent from the female line to the male, will be considered elsewhere. Between the two extremes, represented by the two rules of descent, three entire ethnical periods intervene, covering many thousands of years.

With descent in the male line, the gens embraced all persons who traced their descent from a supposed common male ancestor, through males only, the evidence of the fact being, as in the other case, the possession of a common gentile name. It would include this ancestor and his children, the children of his sons, and the children of his male descendants, through males, in perpetuity; whilst the children of his daughters, and the children of his female descendants, through females, would belong to other gentes; namely, those of their respective fathers. Those retained in the gens in one case were those excluded in the other, and *vice versâ.* Such was the gens in its final form, after the paternity of children became ascertainable through the rise of monogamy. The transition of a gens from one form into the other was perfectly simple, without involving its overthrow. All that was needed was an adequate motive, as will elsewhere be shown. The same gens, with descent changed to the male line, remained the unit of the social system. It could not have reached the second form without previously existing in the first.

As intermarriage in the gens was prohibited, it withdrew its members from the evils of consanguine marriages, and thus tended to increase the vigor of the stock. The gens came into being upon three principal conceptions, namely; the bond of kin, a pure lineage through descent in the female line, and non-intermarriage in the gens. When the idea of a gens was developed, it would naturally have taken the form of gentes in pairs, because the children of the males were excluded, and because it was equally necessary to organize both classes of descendants. With two gentes started into being simultaneously the whole result would have been attained; since the males and females of one gens would marry the females and males of the other; and the children, following the gentes of their respective mothers, would be divided between them. Resting on the bond of kin as its cohesive principle the gens afforded to each individual member that personal protection which no other existing power could give.

After considering the rights, privileges and obligations of its members it will be necessary to follow the gens in its organic relations to a phratry, tribe and confederacy, in order to find the uses to which it was applied, the privileges which it conferred, and the principles which it fostered. The gentes of the Iroquois will be taken as the standard exemplification of this institution in the Ganowánian family. They had carried their scheme of government from the gens to the confederacy, making it complete in each of its parts, and an excellent illustration of the capabilities of the gentile organization in its archaic form. When discovered the Iroquois were in the Lower Status of barbarism, and well advanced in the arts of life pertaining to this condition. They manufactured nets, twine and rope from filaments of bark; wove belts and burden straps, with warp and woof, from the same materials; they manufactured earthen vessels and pipes from clay mixed with siliceous materials and hardened by fire, some of which were ornamented with rude medallions; they cultivated maize, beans, squashes, and tobacco, in garden beds, and made unleavened bread from pounded maize which they boiled in earthern vessels;[1] they tanned skins into leather with which they manufactured kilts, leggins, and moccasins; they used the bow and arrow and warclub as their principal weapons; used flint stone and bone implements, wore skin garments, and were expert hunters and fishermen. They constructed long joint-tenement houses large enough to accommodate five, ten, and twenty families, and each household practiced communism in living; but they were unacquainted with the use of stone or adobe-brick in house architecture, and with the use of the native metals. In mental capacity and in general advancement they were the representative branch of the Indian family north of New Mexico. General F. A. Walker has sketched their military career in two paragraphs: "The career of the Iroquois was simply terrific. They were the scourge of God upon the aborigines of the continent."

From lapse of time the Iroquois tribes have come to differ slightly in the number, and in the names of their respective gentes. The largest number being eight, as follows:

Senecas.—1. Wolf. 2. Bear. 3. Turtle. 4. Beaver. 5. Deer. 6. Snipe. 7. Heron. 8. Hawk.

Cayugas.—1. Wolf. 2. Bear. 3. Turtle. 4. Beaver. 5. Deer. 6. Snipe. 7. Eel. 8. Hawk.

Onondagas.—1. Wolf. 2. Bear. 3. Turtle. 4. Beaver. 5. Deer. 6. Snipe. 7. Eel. 8. Ball.

Oneidas.—1. Wolf. 2. Bear. 3. Turtle.

Mohawks.—1. Wolf. 2. Bear. 3. Turtle.

Tuscaroras.—1. Gray Wolf. 2. Bear. 3. Great Turtle. 4. Beaver. 5. Yellow Wolf. 6. Snipe. 7. Eel. 8. Little Turtle.

These changes show that certain gentes in some of the

---

1 These loaves or cakes were about six inches in diameter and an inch thick.

2 "North American Review," April No., 1873, p. 370 Note.

tribes have become extinct through the vicissitudes of time; and that others have been formed by the segmentation of over-full gentes.

With a knowledge of the rights, privileges and obligations of the members of a gens, its capabilities as the unit of a social and governmental system will be more fully understood, as well as the manner in which it entered into the higher organizations of the phratry, tribe, and confederacy.

The gens is individualized by the following rights, privileges, and obligations conferred and imposed upon its members, and which made up the *jus gentilicium.*

I. *The right of electing its sachem and chiefs.*
II. *The right of deposing its sachem and chiefs.*
III. *The obligation not to marry in the gens.*
IV. *Mutual rights of inheritance of the property of deceased members.*
V. *Reciprocal obligations of help, defense, and redress of injuries.*
VI. *The right of bestowing names upon its members.*
VII. *The right of adopting strangers into the gens.*
VIII. *Common religious rites, query.*
IX. *A common burial place.*
X. *A council of the gens.*

These functions and attributes gave vitality as well as individuality to the organization, and protected the personal rights of its members.

I. *The right of electing its sachem and chiefs.*

Nearly all the American Indian tribes had two grades of chiefs, who may be distinguished as sachems and common chiefs. Of these two primary grades all other grades were varieties. They were elected in each gens from among its members. A son could not be chosen to succeed his father, where descent was in the female line, because he belonged to a different gens, and no gens would have a chief or sachem from any gens but its own. The office of sachem was hereditary in the gens, in the sense that it was filled as often as a vacancy occurred; while the office of chief was non-hereditary, because it was bestowed in reward of personal merit, and died with the individual. Moreover, the duties of a sachem were confined to the affairs of peace. He could not go out to war as a sachem. On the other hand, the chiefs who were raised to office for personal bravery, for wisdom in affairs, or for eloquence in council, were usually the superior class in ability, though not in authority over the gens. The relation of the sachem was primarily to the gens, of which he was the official head; while that of the chief was primarily to the tribe, of the council of which he, as well as the sachem, were members.

The office of sachem had a natural foundation in the gens, as an organized body of consanguinei which, as such, needed a representative head. As an office, however, it is older than the gentile organization, since it is found among tribes not thus organized, but among whom it had a similar basis in the punaluan group, and even in the anterior horde. In the gens the constituency of the sachem was clearly defined, the basis of the relation was permanent, and its duties paternal. While the office was hereditary in the gens it was elective among its male members. When the Indian system of consanguinity is considered, it will be found that all the male members of a gens were either brothers to each other, own or collateral, uncles or nephews, own or collateral, or collateral grandfathers and grandsons.[1] This will explain the succession of the office of sachem which passed from brother to brother, or from uncle to nephew, and very rarely from grandfather to grandson. The choice, which was by free suffrage of both males and females of adult age, usually fell upon a brother of the decased sachem, or upon one of the sons of a sister; an own brother, or the son of an own sister being most likely to be preferred. As between several brothers, own and collateral, on the one hand, and the sons of several sisters, own and collateral, on the other, there was no priority of right,

1 The sons of several sisters are brothers to each other, instead of cousins. The latter are here distinguished as collateral brothers. So a man's brother's son is his son instead of his nephew; while his collateral sister's son is his nephew, as well as his own sister's son. The former is distinguished as a collateral nephew.

for the reason that all the male members of the gens were equally eligible. To make a choice between them was the function of the elective principle.

Upon the death of a sachem, for example among the Seneca-Iroquois, a council of his gentiles[1] was convened to name his successor. Two candidates, according to their usages, must be voted upon, both of them members of the gens. Each person of adult age was called upon to express his or her preference, and the one who received the largest number of affirmative declarations was nominated. It still required the assent of the seven remaining gentes before the nomination was complete. If these gentes, who met for the purpose by phratries, refused to confirm the nomination it was thereby set aside, and the gens proceeded to make another choice. When the person nominated by his gens was accepted by the remaining gentes the election was complete; but it was still necessary that the new sachem should be *raised up,* to use their expression, or invested with his office by a council of the confederacy, before he could enter upon its duties. It was their method of conferring the *imperium.* In this manner the rights and interests of the several gentes were consulted and preserved; for the sachem of a gens was *ex officio* a member of the council of the tribe, and of the higher council of the confederacy. The same method of election and of confirmation existed with respect to the office of chief, and for the same reasons. But a general council was never convened to raise up chiefs below the grade of a sachem. They awaited the time when sachems were invested.

The principle of democracy, which was born of the gentes, manifested itself in the retention by the gentiles of the right to elect their sachem and chiefs, in the safeguards thrown around the office to prevent usurpation, and in the check upon the election held by the remaining gentes.

The chiefs in each gens were usually proportioned

---

1 Pronounced "gen'-ti-les," it may be remarked to those unfamiliar with Latin.

to the number of its members. Among the Seneca-Iroquois there is one chief for about every fifty persons. They now number in New York some three thousand, and have eight sachems and about sixty chiefs. There are reasons for supposing that the proportionate number is now greater than in former times. With respect to the number of gentes in a tribe, the more numerous the people the greater, usually, the number of gentes. The number varied in the different tribes, from three among the Delawares and Munsees to upwards of twenty among the Ojibwas and Creeks; six, eight, and ten being common numbers.

II. *The right of deposing its sachem and chiefs.*

This right, which was not less important than that to elect, was reserved by the members of the gens. Although the office was nominally for life, the tenure was practically during good behavior, in consequence of the power to depose. The installation of a sachem was symbolized as "putting on the horns," and his deposition as "taking off the horns." Among widely separated tribes of mankind horns have been made the emblem of office and of authority, suggested probably, as Tylor intimates, by the commanding appearance of the males among ruminant animals bearing horns. Unworthy behavior, followed by a loss of confidence, furnished a sufficient ground for deposition. When a sachem or chief had been deposed in due form by a council of his gens, he ceased thereafter to be recognized as such, and became thenceforth a private person. The council of the tribe also had power to depose both sachems and chiefs, without waiting for the action of the gens, and even against its wishes. Through the existence and occasional exercise of this power the supremacy of the gentiles over their sachem and chiefs was asserted and preserved. It also reveals the democratic constitution of the gens.

III. *The obligation not to marry in the gens.*

Although a negative proposition it was fundamental. It was evidently a primary object of the organization to isolate a moiety of the descendants of a supposed founder, and prevent their intermarriage for reasons of kin. When the gens came into existence brothers were intermarried to each other's wives in a group, and sisters to each other's husbands in a group, to which the gens interposed no obstacle. But it sought to exclude brothers and sisters from the marriage relation which was effected, as there are good reasons for stating, by the prohibition in question. Had the gens attempted to uproot the entire conjugal system of the period by its direct action, there is not the slightest probability that it would have worked its way into general establishment. The gens, originating probably in the ingenuity of a small band of savages, must soon have proved its utility in the production of superior men. Its nearly universal prevalence in the ancient world is the highest evidence of the advantages it conferred, and of its adaptability to human wants in savagery and in barbarism. The Iroquois still adhere inflexibly to the rule which forbids persons to marry in their own gens.

IV. *Mutual rights of inheritance of the property of deceased members.*

In the Status of savagery, and in the Lower Status of barbarism, the amount of property was small. It consisted in the former condition of personal effects, to which, in the latter, were added possessory rights in joint-tenement houses and in gardens. The most valuable personal articles were buried with the body of the deceased owner. Nevertheless, the question of inheritance was certain to arise, to increase in importance with the increase of property in variety and amount, and to result in some settled rule of inheritance. Accordingly we find the principle established low down in barbarism, and even back of that in savagery, that the property should remain in the gens, and be distributed among the gentiles of the deceased owner. It was customary law in the Grecian and Latin gentes in the Upper Status of barbarism, and remained as written law far into civilization, that the property of a deceased person should remain in the gens. But after the time of Solon among the Athenians it was limited to cases of intestacy.

The question, who should take the property, has given

rise to three great and successive rules of inheritance. First, that it should be distributed among the gentiles of the deceased owner. This was the rule in the Lower Status of barbarism, and so far as is known in the Status of savagery. Second, that the property should be distributed among the agnatic kindred of the deceased owner, to the exclusion of the remaining gentiles. The germ of this rule makes its appearance in the Lower Status of barbarism, and it probably became completely established in the Middle Status. Third, that the property should be inherited by the children of the deceased owner, to the exclusion of the remaining agnates. This became the rule in the Upper Status of barbarism.

Theoretically, the Iroquois were under the first rule; but, practically, the effects of a deceased person were appropriated by his nearest relations within the gens. In the case of a male his own brothers and sisters and maternal uncles divided his effects among themselves. This practical limitation of the inheritance to the nearest gentile kin discloses the germ of agnatic inheritance. In the case of a female her property was inherited by her children and her sisters, to the exclusion of her brothers. In every case the property remained in the gens. The children of the deceased males took nothing from their father because they belonged to a different gens. It was for the same reason that the husband took nothing from the wife, or the wife from her husband. These mutual right of inheritance strengthened the autonomy of the gens.

V. *Reciprocal obligations of help, defense, and redress of injuries.*

In civilized society the state assumes the protection of persons and of property. Accustomed to look to this source for the maintenance of personal rights, there has been a corresponding abatement of the strength of the bond of kin. But under gentile society the individual depended for security upon his gens. It took the place afterwards held by the state, and possessed the requisite numbers to render its guardianship effective. Within its membership the bond of kin was a powerful element for mutual support. To wrong a person was to wrong his gens; and to support a person was to stand behind him with the entire array of his gentile kindred.

In their trials and difficulties the members of the gens assisted each other. Two or three illustrations may be given from the Indian tribes at large. Speaking of the Mayas of Yucatan, Herrera remarks, that "when any satisfaction was to be made for damages, if he who was adjudged to pay was like to be reduced to poverty, the kindred contributed." [1] By the term kindred, as here used, we are justified in understanding the gens. And of the Florida Indians: "When a brother or son dies the people of the house will rather starve than seek anything to eat during three months, but the kindred and relations send it all in." [2] Persons who removed from one village to another could not transfer their possessory right to cultivated lands or to a section of a joint-tenement house to a stranger; but must leave them to his gentile kindred. Herrera refers to this usage among the Indian tribes of Nicaragua; "He that removed from one town to another could not sell what he had, but must leave it to his nearest relation." [3] So much of their property was held in joint ownership that their plan of life would not admit of its alienation to a person of another gens. Practically, the right to such property was possessory, and when abandoned it reverted to the gens. Garcilasso de la Vega remarks of the tribes of the Peruvian Andes, that "when the commonalty, or ordinary sort, married, the communities of the people were obliged to build and provide them houses." [4] For *communities,* as here used, we are justified in understanding the gens. Herrera speaking of the same tribes observes that "this variety of tongues proceed from the nations being divided into races, tribes, or clans." [5] Here the gentiles were required to assist newly married pairs in the construction of their houses.

---

1 "History of America," Lond. ed., 1725, Stevens' Trans., iv, 171.
2 Ib., iv, 34.
3 "History of America," iii, 298.
4 "Royal Commentaries," Lond. ed., 1688, Rycaut's Trans., p. 107.
5 Herrera, iv, 231.

The ancient practice of blood revenge, which has prevailed so widely in the tribes of mankind, had its birthplace in the gens. It rested with this body to avenge the murder of one of its members. Tribunals for the trial of criminals and laws prescribing their punishment, came late into existence in gentile society; but they made their appearance before the institution of political society. On the other hand, the crime of murder is as old as human society, and its punishment by the revenge of kinsmen is as old as the crime itself. Among the Iroquois and other Indian tribes generally, the obligation to avenge the murder of a kinsman was universally recognized.[1]

It was, however, the duty of the gens of the slayer, and of the slain, to attempt an adjustment of the crime before proceeding to extremities. A council of the members of each gens was held separately, and propositions were made in behalf of the murderer for a condonation of the act, usually in the nature of expressions of regret and of presents of considerable value. If there were justifying or extenuating circumstances it generally resulted in a composition; but if the gentile kindred of the slain person were implacable, one or more avengers were appointed by his gens from among its members, whose duty is was to pursue the criminal until discovered, and then to slay him wherever he might be found. If they accomplished the deed it was no ground of complaint by any member of the gens of the victim. Life having answered for life the demands of justice were appeased.

The same sentiment of fraternity manifested itself in other ways in relieving a fellow gentilis in distress, and in protecting him from injuries.

VI. *The right of bestowing names upon its members.* Among savage and barbarous tribes there is no name for the family. The personal names of individuals of the same family do not indicate any family connection

---

1 "Their hearts burn violently day and night without intermission till they have shed blood for blood. They transmit from father to son the memory of the loss of their relations, or one of their own tribe, or family, though it was an old woman."—Adair's "Hist. Amer. Indians," Lond. ed., 1775, p. 150.

between them. The family name is no older than civilization.[1] Indian personal names, however, usually indicate the gens of the individual to persons of other gentes in the same tribe. As a rule each gens had names for persons that were its special property, and, as such, could not be used by other gentes of the same tribe. A gentile name conferred of itself gentile rights. These names either proclaimed by their signification the gens to which they belonged, or were known as such by common reputation.[2]

After the birth of a child a name was selected by its mother from those not in use belonging to the gens, with the concurrence of her nearest relatives, which was then bestowed upon the infant. But the child was not fully christened until its birth and name, together with the name and gens of its mother and the name of its father, had been announced at the next ensuing council of the tribe. Upon the death of a person his name could not be used again in the life-time of the oldest surviving son without the consent of the latter.[3]

Two classes of names were in use, one adapted to childhood, and the other to adult life, which were exchanged at the proper period in the same formal manner; one being taken away, to use their expression, and the other bestowed in its place. *O-wi'-go, a canoe floating down the stream,* and *Ah-wou'-ne-ont, hanging flower;* are names for girls among the Seneca-Iroquois; and *Gä-ne-o-di'-yo, handsome lake,* and *Do-ne-ho-gä'-weh door-keeper,* are names of adult males. At the age of sixteen or eighteen, the first name was taken away, usually by a chief of the gens, and one of the second class

---

1 Mommsen's "History of Rome," Scribner's ed., Dickson's Trans., i, 49.

2 One of the twelve gentes of the Omahas is Lä'-ta-dä, the Pigeon-Hawk, which has, among others, the following names:

Boys' Names.

Ah-hise'-na-da, "Long Wing."
Gla-dan'-noh-che, "Hawk balancing itself in the air."
Nes-tase'-kä, "White-Eyed Bird."

Girls' Names.

Me-ta'-na, "Bird singing at daylight."
Lä-tä-dä'-win, "One of the Birds."
Wä-tä'-na, "Bird's Egg."

3 When particular usages are named it will be understood they are Iroquois unless the contrary is stated.

bestowed in its place. At the next council of the tribe the change of names was publicly announced, after which the person, if a male, assumed the duties of manhood. In some Indian tribes the youth was required to go out upon the war-path and earn his second name by some act of personal bravery. After a severe illness it was not uncommon for the person, from superstitious considerations, to solicit and obtain a second change of name. It was sometimes done again in extreme old age. When a person was elected a sachem or a chief his name was taken away, and a new one conferred at the time of his installation. The individual had no control over the question of a change. It is the prerogative of the female relatives and of the chiefs; but an adult person might change his name provided he could induce a chief to announce it in council. A person having the control of a particular name, as the eldest son of that of his deceased father, might lend it to a friend in another gens; but after the death of the person thus bearing it the name reverted to the gens to which it belonged.

Among the Shawnees and Delawares the mother has now the right to name her child into any gens she pleases; and the name given transfers the child to the gens to which the name belongs. But this is a wide departure from archaic usages, and exceptional in practice. It tends to corrupt and confound the gentile lineage. The names now in use among the Iroquois and among other Indian tribes are, in the main, ancient names handed down in the gentes from time immemorial.

The precautions taken with respect to the use of names belonging to the gens sufficiently prove the importance attached to them, and the gentile rights they confer.

Although this question of personal names branches out in many direction it is foreign to my purpose to do more than illustrate such general usages as reveal the relations of the members of a gens. In familiar intercourse and in formal salutation the American Indians address each other by the term of relationship the person spoken to sustains to the speaker. When related they salute by kin; when not related "my friend" is substituted. It would be esteemed an act of rudeness to address an Indian by his personal name, or to inquire his name directly from himself.

Our Saxon ancestors had single personal names down to the Norman conquest, with none to designate the family. This indicates the late appearance of the monogamian family among them; and it raises a presumption of the existence in an earlier period of a Saxon gens.

VII. *The right of adopting strangers into the gens.*

Another distinctive right of the gens was that of admitting new members by adoption. Captives taken in war were either put to death, or adopted into some gens. Women and children taken prisoners usually experienced clemency in this form. Adoption not only conferred gentile rights, but also the nationality of the tribe. The person adopting a captive placed him or her in the relation of a brother or sister; if a mother adopted, in that of a son or daughter; and ever afterwards treated the person in all respects as though born in that relation. Slavery, which in the Upper Status of barbarism became the fate of the captive, was unknown among tribes in the Lower Status in the aboriginal period. The gauntlet also had some connection with adoption, since the person who succeeded, through hardihood or favoritism, in running through the lines in safety was entitled to this reward. Captives when adopted were often assigned in the family the places of deceased persons slain in battle, in order to fill up the broken ranks of relatives. A declining gens might replenish its numbers, through adoption, although such instances are rare. At one time the Hawk gens of the Senecas were reduced to a small number of persons, and its extinction became imminent. To save the gens a number of persons from the Wolf gens by mutual consent were transferred in a body by adoption to that of the Hawk. The right to adopt seems to be left to the discretion of each gens.

Among the Iroquois the ceremony of adoption was

performed at a public council of the tribe, which turned it practically into a religious rite.[1]

VIII. *Religious rites in the gens. Query.*

Among the Grecian and Latin tribes these rites held a conspicuous position. The highest polytheistic form of religion which had then appeared seems to have sprung from the gentes in which religious rites were constantly maintained. Some of them, from the sanctity they were supposed to possess, were nationalized. In some cities the office of high priest of certain divinities was hereditary in a particular gens.[2] The gens became the natural centre of religious growth and the birthplace of religious ceremonies.

But the Indian tribes, although they had a polytheistic system, not much unlike that from which the Grecian and Roman must have sprung, had not attained that religious development which was so strongly impressed upon the gentes of the latter tribes. It can scarcely be said any Indian gens had special religious rites; and yet their religious worship had a more or less direct connection with the gentes. It was here that religious ideas would naturally germinate and that forms of worship would be instituted. But they would expand from the gens over the tribe, rather than remain special to the gens. Accordingly we find among the Iroquois six annual religious festivals, (Maple, Planting, Berry, Green-Corn, Harvest, and New Years Festivals)[3] which were common to all the gentes united in a tribe, and which were observed at stated seasons of the year.

Each gens furnished a number of "Keepers of the

---

1 After the people had assembled at the council house one of the chiefs made an address giving some account of the person, the reason for his adoption, the nåme and gens of the person adopting, and the name bestowed upon the novitiate. Two chiefs taking the person by the arms then marched with him through the council house and back, chanting the song of adoption. To this the people responded in musical chorus at the end of each verse. The march continued until the verses were ended, which required three rounds. With this the ceremony concluded. Americans are sometimes adopted as a compliment. It fell to my lot some years ago to be thus adopted into the Hawk gens of the Senecas, when this ceremony was repeated.

2 Grote's "Hist. of Greece," i, 194.

3 "League of the Iroquois," p. 182.

Faith," both male and female, who together were charged with the celebration of these festivals.[1] The number advanced to this office by each was regarded as evidence of the fidelity of the gens to religion. They designated the days for holding the festivals, made the necessary arrangements for the celebration, and conducted the ceremonies in conjunction with the sachems and chiefs of the tribe, who were, *ex officio*, "Keepers of the Faith." With no official head, and none of the marks of a priesthood, their functions were equal. The female "Keepers of the Faith" were more especially charged with the preparation of the feast, which was provided at all councils at the close of each day for all persons in attendance. It was a dinner in common. The religious rites appertaining to these festivals, which have been described in a previous work,[2] need not be considered further than to remark, that their worship was one of thanksgiving, with invocations to the Great Spirit, and to the Lesser Spirits to continue to them the blessings of life.

With the progress of mankind out of the Lower into the Middle, and more especially out of the latter into the Upper Status of barbarism, the gens became more the centre of religious influence and the source of religious development. We have only the grosser part of the Aztec religious system; but in addition to national gods, there seem to have been other gods, belonging to smaller divisions of the people than the phratries. The existence of an Aztec ritual and priesthood would lead us to expect among them a closer connection of religious rites with the gentes than is found among the Iroquois; but

1 The "Keepers of the Faith" were about as numerous as the chiefs, and were selected by the wise-men and matrons of each gens. After their selection they were raised up by a council of the tribe with ceremonies adapted to the occasion. Their names were taken away and new ones belonging to this class bestowed in their place. Men and women in about equal numbers were chosen. They were censors of the people, with power to report the evil deeds of persons to the council. It was the duty of individuals selected to accept the office; but after a reasonable service each might relinquish it, which was done by dropping his name as a Keeper of the Faith, and resuming his former name.

2 "League of the Iroquois," p. 182.

their religious beliefs and observances are under the same cloud of obscurity as their social organization.

IX. *A common burial place.*

An ancient but not exclusive mode of burial was by scaffolding the body until the flesh had wasted, after which the bones were collected and preserved in bark barrels in a house constructed for their reception. Those belonging to the same gens were usually placed in the same house. The Rev. Dr. Cyrus Byington found these practices among the Choctas in 1827; and Adair mentions usages among the Cherokees substantially the same. "I saw three of them," he remarks, "in one of their towns pretty near each other; * * Each house contained the bones of one tribe separately, with the hieroglyphical figures of each family [gens] on each of the oddshaped arks. They reckoned it irreligious to mix the bones of a relative with those of a stranger, as bone of bone and flesh of flesh should always be jointed together."[1] The Iroquois in ancient times used scaffolds and preserved the bones of deceased relatives in bark barrels, often keeping them in the house they occupied. They also buried in the ground. In the latter case those of the same gens were not always buried locally together unless they had a common cemetery for the village. The late Rev. Ashur Wright, so long a missionary among the Senecas, and a noble specimen of the American missionary, wrote to the author as follows; "I find no trace of the influence of clanship in the burial places of the dead. I believe that they buried promiscuously. However, they say that formerly the members of the different clans more frequently resided together than they do at the present time. As one family they were more under the influence of family feeling, and had less of individual interest. Hence, it might occasionally happen that a large proportion of the dead in some partiular burying place might be of the same clan." Mr. Wright is undoubtedly correct that in a particular cemetery members of all the gentes established in a village would be buried;

1 "History of the American Indians," p. 183.

but they might keep those of the same gens locally together. An illustration in point is now found at the Tuscarora reservation near Lewiston, where the tribe has one common cemetery, and where individuals of the same gens are buried in a row by themselves. One row is composed of the graves of the deceased members of the Beaver gens, two rows of the members of the Bear gens, one row of the Gray Wolf, one of the Great Turtle, and so on to the number of eight rows. Husband and wife are separated from each other and buried in different rows; fathers and their children the same; but mothers and their children and brothers and sisters are found in the same row. It shows the power of gentile feeling, and the quickness with which ancient usages are reverted to under favorable conditions; for the Tuscaroras are now christianized without surrendering the practice. An Onondaga Indian informed the writer that the same mode of burial by gentes now prevailed at the Onondaga and Oneida cemeteries. While this usage, perhaps, cannot be declared general among the Indian tribes, there was undoubtedly in ancient times a tendency to, and preference for this mode of burial.

Among the Iroquois, and what is true of them is generally true of other Indian tribes in the same status of advancement, all the members of the gens are mourners at the funeral of a deceased gentilis. The addresses at the funeral, the preparation of the grave, and the burial of the body were performed by members of other gentes.

The Village Indians of Mexico and Central America practiced a slovenly cremation, as well as scaffolding, and burying in the ground. The former was confined to chiefs and prominent men.

X. *A council of the gens.*

The council was the great feature of ancient society, Asiatic, European and American, from the institution of the gens in savagery to civilization. It was the instrument of government as well as the supreme authority over the gens, the tribe, and the confederacy. Ordinary affairs were adjusted by the chiefs; but those of general interest were submitted to the determination of a council. As the council sprang from the gentile organization the two institutions have come down together through the ages. The Council of Chiefs represents the ancient method of evolving the wisdom of mankind and applying it to human affairs. Its history, gentile, tribal, and confederate, would express the growth of the idea of government in its whole development, until political society supervened into which the council, changed into a senate, was transmitted.

The simplest and lowest form of the council was that of the gens. It was a democratic assembly because every adult male and female member had a voice upon all questions brought before it. It elected and deposed its sachem and chiefs, it elected Keepers of the Faith, it condoned or avenged the murder of a gentiles, and it adopted persons into the gens. It was the germ of the higher council of the tribe, and of that still higher of the confederacy, each of which was composed exclusively of chiefs as representatives of the gentes.

Such were the rights, privileges and obligations of the members of an Iroquois gens; and such were those of the members of the gentes of the Indian tribes generally, as far as the investigation has been carried. When the gentes of the Grecian and Latin tribes are considered, the same rights, privileges and obligations will be found to exist, with the exception of the I, II, and VI; and with respect to these their ancient existence is probable though the proof is not perhaps attainable.

All the members of an Iroquois gens were personally free, and they were bound to defend each other's freedom; they were equal in privileges and in personal rights, the sachem and chiefs claiming no superiority; and they were a brotherhood bound together by the ties of kin. Liberty, equality, and fraternity, though never formulated, were cardinal principles of the gens. These facts are material, because the gens was the unit of a social and governmental system, the foundation upon which Indian society was organized. A structure composed of such units would of necessity bear the impress of their character, for as the unit so the compound. It serves to explain that sense of independence and personal dignity universally an attribute of Indian character.

Thus substantial and important in the social system was the gens as it anciently existed among the American aborigines, and as it still exists in full vitality in many Indian tribes. It was the basis of the phratry, of the tribe, and the confederacy of tribes. Its functions might have been presented more elaborately in several particulars; but sufficient has been given to show its permanent and durable character.

At the epoch of European discovery the American Indian tribes generally were organized in gentes, with descent in the female line. In some tribes, as among the Dakotas, the gentes had fallen out; in others, as among the Ojibwas, the Omahas, and the Mayas of Yucatan, descent had been changed from the female to the male line. Throughout aboriginal America the gens took its name from some animal, or inanimate object, and never from a person. In this early condition of society, the individuality of persons was lost in the gens. It is at least presumable that the gentes of the Grecian and Latin tribes were so named at some anterior period; but when they first came under historical notice, they were named after persons. In some of the tribes, as the Moqui Village Indians of New Mexico, the members of the gens claimed their descent from the animal whose name they bore—their remote ancestors having been transformed by the Great Spirit from the animal into the human form. The Crane gens of the Ojibwas have a similar legend. In some tribes the members of a gens will not eat the animal whose name they bear, in which they are doubtless influenced by this consideration.

With respect to the number of persons in a gens it varied with the number of the gentes, and with the prosperity or decadence of the tribe. Three thousand Senecas divided equally among eight gentes would give an average of three hundred and seventy-five persons to a gens. Fifteen thousand Ojibwas divided equally among twenty-three gentes would give six hundred and fifty persons to a gens. The Cherokees would average more than a thousand to a gens. In the present condition of the principal Indian tribes the number of persons in each gens would range from one hundred to a thousand.

One of the oldest and most widely prevalent institutions of mankind, the gentes have been closely identified with human progress upon which they have exercised a powerful influence. They have been found in tribes in the Status of savagery, in the Lower, in the Middle, and in the Upper Status of barbarism on different continents, and in full vitality in the Grecian and Latin tribes after civilization had commenced. Every family of mankind, except the Polynesian, seems to have come under the gentile organization, and to have been indebted to it for preservation, and for the means of progress. It finds its only parallel in length of duration in systems of consanguinity, which, springing up at a still earlier period, have remained to the present time, although the marriage usages in which they originated have long since disappeared.

From its early institution, and from its maintenance through such immense stretches of time, the peculiar adaption of the gentile organization to mankind, while in a savage and in a barbarous state, must be regarded as abundantly demonstrated.

CHAPTER III

THE IROQUOIS PHRATRY

The phratry is a brotherhood, as the term imports, and a natural growth from the organization into gentes. It is an organic union or association of two or more gentes of the same tribe for certain common objects. These gentes were usually such as had been formed by the segmentation of an original gens.

Among the Grecian tribes, where the phratric organization was nearly as constant as the gens, it became a very conspicuous institution. Each of the four tribes of the Athenians was organized in three phratries, each composed of thirty gentes, making a total of twelve phratries and three hundred and sixty gentes. Such precise numerical uniformity in the composition of each phratry and tribe could not have resulted from the subdivision of gentes through natural processes. It must have been produced, as Mr. Grote suggests, by legislative procurement in the interests of a symmetrical organization. All the gentes of a tribe, as a rule, were of common descent and bore a common tribal name, consequently it would not require severe constraint to unite the specified number in each phratry, and to form the specified number of phratries in each tribe. But the phratric organization had a natural foundation in the immediate kinship of certain gentes as subdivisions of an original gens, which undoubtedly was the basis on which the Grecian phratry was originally formed. The incorporation of alien gentes, and transfers by consent or constraint, would explain the numerical adjustment of the gentes and phratries in the Athenian tribes.

The Roman *curia* was the analogue of the Grecian phratry. It is constantly mentioned by Dionysius as a phratry.[1] There were ten gentes in each *curia,* and ten *curiae* in each of the three Roman tribes, making thirty *curiae* and three hundred gentes of the Romans. The functions of the Roman *curia* are much better known than those of the Grecian phratry, and were higher in degree because the *curia* entered directly into the functions of government. The assembly of the gentes (*comitia curiata*) voted by *curiae,* each having one collective vote. This assembly was the sovereign power of the Roman People down to the time of Servius Tullius.

Among the functions of the Grecian phratry was the observance of special religious rites, the condonation or revenge of the murder of a phrator, and the purification of a murderer after he had escaped the penalty of his crime preparatory to his restoration to society.[2] At a later period among the Athenians—for the phratry at Athens survived the institution of political society under Cleisthenes—it looked after the registration of citizens, thus becoming the guardian of descents and of the evidence of citizenship. The wife upon her marriage was enrolled in the phratry of her husband, and the children of the mariage were enrolled in the gens and phratry of their father. It was also the duty of this organization to prosecute the murderer of a phrator in the courts of justice. These are among its known objects and functions in the earlier and later periods. Were all the particulars fully ascertained, the phratry would probably manifest itself in connection with the common tables, the public games, the funerals of distinguished men, the earliest army organization, and the proceedings of councils, as well as in the observance of religious rites and in the guardianship of social privileges.

The phratry existed in a large number of the tribes of the American aborigines, where it is seen to arise by natural growth, and to stand as the second member of

---

1 —"Dionysius," lib. II, cap. vii; and vid. lib. II, c. xiii.

2 That purification was performed by the phratry is intimated by Æschylus: "Eumenides," 656.

the organic series, as among the Grecian and Latin tribes. It did not possess original governmental functions, as the gens, tribe and confederacy possessed them; but it was endowed with certain useful powers in the social system, from the necessity for some organization larger than a gens and smaller than a tribe, and especially when the tribe was large. The same institution in essential features and in character, it presents the organization in its archaic form and with its archaic functions. A knowledge of the Indian phratry is necessary to an intelligent understanding of the Grecian and the Roman.

The eight gentes of the Seneca-Iroquois tribe were reintegrated in two phratries as follows:

First Phratry.

Gentes—1. Bear. 2. Wolf. 3. Beaver. 4. Turtle.

Second Phratry.

Gentes—5. Deer. 6. Snipe. 7. Heron. 8. Hawk.

Each phratry (De-ă-non-dă′-yoh) is a brotherhood as this term also imports. The gentes in the same phratry are brother gentes to each other, and cousin gentes to those of the other phratry. They are equal in grade, character and privileges. It is a common practice of the Senecas to call the gentes of their own phratry brother gentes, and those of the other phratry their cousin gentes, when they mention them in their relation to the phratries. Originally marriage was not allowed between the members of the same phratry; but the members of either could marry into any gens of the other. This prohibition tends to show that gentes of each phratry were subdivisions of an original gens, and therefore the prohibition against marrying into a person's own gens had followed to its subdivisions. This restriction, however, was long since removed, except with respect to the gens of the individual. A tradition of the Senecas affirms that the Bear and the Deer were the original gentes, of which the others were subdivisions. It is thus seen that the phratry had a natural foundation in the kinship of the gentes of which it was composed. After their subdivision from increase of numbers there was a natural tendency to their reunion in a higher organization for objects common to them all. The same gentes are not constant in a phratry indefinitely, as will appear when the composition of the phratries in the remaining Iroquois tribes is considered. Transfers of particular gentes from one phratry to the other must have occurred when the equilibrium in their respective numbers was disturbed. It is important to know the simple manner in which this organization springs up, and the facility with which it is managed, as a part of the social system of ancient society. With the increase of numbers in a gens, followed by local separation of its members, segmentation occurred, and the seceding portion adopted a new gentile name. But a tradition of their former unity would remain, and become the basis of their reorganization in a phratry.

In like manner the Cayuga-Iroquois have eight gentes in two phratries; but these gentes are not divided equally between them. They are the following:

First Phratry.

Gentes.—1. Bear. 2. Wolf. 3. Turtle. 4. Snipe. 5. Eel.

Second Phratry.

Gentes.—6. Deer. 7. Beaver. 8. Hawk.

Seven of these gentes are the same as those of the Senecas; but the Heron gens has disappeared, and the Eel takes its place, but transferred to the opposite phratry. The Beaver and the Turtle gentes also have exchanged phratries. The Cayugas style the gentes of the same phratry brother gentes to each other, and those of the opposite phratry their cousin gentes.

The Onondaga-Iroquois have the same number of gentes, but two of them differ in name from those of the Senecas. They are organized in two phratries as follows:

First Phratry.

Gentes.—1. Wolf. 2. Turtle. 3. Snipe. 4. Beaver. 5. Ball.

Second Phratry.

Gentes.—6. Deer. 7. Eel. 8. Bear.

Here again the composition of the phratries is different from that of the Senecas. Three of the gentes in the first phratry are the same in each; but the Bear gens has been transferred to the opposite phratry and is now found with the Deer. The division of gentes is also unequal, as among the Cayugas. The gentes in the same phratry are called brother gentes to each other, and those in the other their cousin gentes. While the Onondagas have no Hawk, the Senecas have no Eel gens; but the members of the two fraternize when they meet, claiming that there is a connection between them.

The Mohawks and Oneidas have but three gentes, the Bear, the Wolf, and the Turtle, and no phratries. When the confederacy was formed, seven of the eight Seneca gentes existed in the several tribes as is shown by the establishment of sachemships in them; but the Mohawks and Oneidas then had only the three named. It shows that they had then lost an entire phratry, and one gens of that remaining, if it is assumed that the original tribes were once composed of the same gentes. When a tribe organized in gentes and phratries subdivides, it might occur on the line of the phratric organization. Although the members of a tribe are intermingled throughout by marriage, each gens in a phratry is composed of females with their children and descendants, through females, who formed the body of the phratry. They would incline at least to remain locally together, and thus might become detached in a body. The male members of the gens married to women of other gentes and remaining with their wives would not affect the gens since the children of the males do not belong to its connection. If the minute history of the Indian tribes is ever recovered it must be sought through the gentes and phratries, which can be followed from tribe to tribe. In such an investigation it will deserve attention whether tribes ever disintegrated by phratries. It is at least improbable.

The Tuscarora-Iroquois became detached from the main stock at some unknown period in the past, and inhabited the Neuse river region in North Carolina at the time of their discovery. About A. D. 1712 they were forced out of this area, whereupon they removed to the country of the Iroquois and were admitted into the confederacy as a sixth member. They have eight gentes organized in two phratries, as follows:

First Phratry.

Gentes.—1. Bear. 2. Beaver. 3. Great Turtle. 4. Eel.

Second Phratry.

Gentes. 5. Gray Wolf. 6. Yellow Wolf. 7. Little Turtle. 8. Snipe.

They have six gentes in common with the Cayugas and Onondagas, five in common with the Senecas, and three in common with the Mohawks and Oneidas. The Deer gens, which they once possessed, became extinct in modern times. It will be noticed, also, that the Wolf gens is now divided into two, the Gray and the Yellow, and the Turtle into two, the Great and Little. Three of the gentes in the first phratry are the same with three in the first phratry of the Senecas and Cayugas, with the exception that the Wolf gens is double. As several hundred years elapsed between the separation of the Tuscaroras from their congeners and their return, it affords some evidence of permanence in the existence of a gens. The gentes in the same phratry are called brother gentes to each other, and those in the other phratry their cousin gentes, as among the other tribes.

From the differences in the composition of the phratries in the several tribes it seems probable that the phratries are modified in their gentes at intervals of time to meet changes of condition. Some gentes prosper and increase in numbers, while others through calamities decline, and others become extinct; so that transfers of gentes from one phratry to another were found necessary to preserve some degree of equality in the number of phrators in each. The phratric organization has existed among the Iroquois from time immemorial. It is probably older than the confederacy which was established more than four centuries ago. The amount of difference in their composition, as to the gentes they contain, represents the vicissitudes through which each tribe has passed in the interval. In any view of the matter it is small, tending to illustrate the permanence of the phratry as well as the gens.

The Iroquois tribes had a total of thirty-eight gentes, and in four of the tribes a total of eight phratries.

In its objects and uses the Iroquois phratry falls below the Grecian, as would be supposed, although our knowledge of the functions of the latter is limited; and below what is known of the uses of the phratry among the Roman tribes. In comparing the latter with the former we pass backward through two ethnical periods, and into a very different condition of society. The difference is in the degree of progress, and not in kind; for we have the same institution in each race, derived from the same or a similar germ, and preserved by each through immense periods of time as a part of a social system. Gentile society remained of necessity among the Grecian and Roman tribes until political society supervened; and it remained among the Iroquois tribes because they were still two ethnical periods below civilization. Every fact, therefore, in relation to the functions and uses of the Indian phratry is important, because it tends to illustrate the archaic character of an institution which became so influential in a more developed condition of society.

The phratry, among the Iroquois, was partly for social and partly for religious objects. Its functions and uses can be best shown by practical illustrations. We begin with the lowest, with games, which were of common occurrence at tribal and confederate councils. In the ball game, for example, among the Senecas, they play by phratries, one against the other; and they bet against each other upon the result of the game. Each phratry puts forward its best players, usually from six to ten on a side, and the members of each phratry assemble together but upon opposite sides of the field in which the game is played. Before it commences, articles of personal property are hazarded upon the result by members of the opposite phratries. These are deposited with keepers to abide the event. The game is played with spirit and enthusiasm, and is an exciting spectacle.

The members of each phratry, from their opposite stations, watch the game with eagerness, and cheer their respective players at every successful turn of the game.[1]

In many ways the phratric organization manifested itself. At a council of the tribe the sachems and chiefs in each phratry usually seated themselves on opposite sides of an imaginary council-fire, and the speakers addressed the two opposite bodies as the representatives of the phratries. Formalities, such as these, have a peculiar charm for the Red Man in the transaction of business.

Again; when a murder had been committed it was usual for the gens of the murdered person to meet in council; and, after ascertaining the facts, to take measures for avenging the deed. The gens of the criminal also held a council, and endeavored to effect an adjustment or condonation of the crime with the gens of the murdered person. But it often happened that the gens of the criminal called upon the other gentes of their phratry, when the slayer and the slain belonged to opposite phratries, to unite with them to obtain a condonation of the crime. In such a case the phratry held a council, and then addressed itself to the other phratry to which it sent a delegation with a belt of white wampum asking for a council of the phratry, and for an adjustment of the crime. They offered reparation to the family and gens of the murdered person in expressions of regret and in presents of value. Negotiations were continued between the two councils until an affirmative or a negative conclusion was reached. The influence of a phratry composed of several gentes would be greater than that of a single gens; and by calling into action the opposite phratry the probability of a condonation would be increased, especially if there were extenuating circumstances. We may thus see how naturally the Grecian phratry, prior to civilization, assumed the principal though not exclusive management of cases of murder, and also of the purification of the murderer if he escaped

1 "League of the Iroquois," p. 294.

punishment; and, after the institution of political society, with what proprietry the phratry assumed the duty of prosecuting the murderer in the courts of justice.

At the funerals of persons of recognized importance in the tribe, the phratric organization manifested itself in a conspicuous manner. The phrators of the decedent in a body were the mourners, and the members of the opposite phratry conducted the ceremonies. In the case of a sachem it was usual for the opposite phratry to send, immediately after the funeral, the official wampum belt of the deceased ruler to the central council fire at Onondaga, as a notification of his demise. This was retained until the installation of his successor, when it was bestowed upon him as the insignia of his office. At the funeral of Handsome Lake (Gä-ne-o-di'-yo), one of the eight Seneca sachems (which occurred some years ago), there was an assemblage of sachems and chiefs to the number of twenty-seven, and a large concourse of members of both phratries. The customary address to the dead body, and the other addressess before the removal of the body, were made by members of the opposite phratry. After the addressess were concluded, the body was borne to the grave by persons selected from the last named phratry, followed, first, by the sachems and chiefs, then by the family and gens of the decedent, next by his remaining phrators, and last by the members of the opposite phratry. After the body had been deposited in the grave the sachems and chiefs formed in a circle around it for the purpose of filling it with earth. Each in turn, commencing with the senior in years, cast in three shovelfuls, a typical number in their religious system; of which the first had relation to the Great Spirit, the second to the Sun, and the third to Mother Earth. When the grave was filled the senior sachem, by a figure of speech, deposited "the horns" of the departed sachem, emblematical of his office, upon the top of the grave over his head, there to remain until his successor was installed. In that subsequent ceremony, "the horns" were said to be taken from the grave of the deceased ruler, and placed upon the head of his successor.[1] The social and religious functions of the phratry, and its naturalness in the organic system of ancient society, are rendered apparent by this single usage.

The phratry was also directly concerned in the election of sachems and chiefs of the several gentes, upon which they had a negative as well as a confirmative vote. After the gens of a deceased sachem had elected his successor, or had elected a chief of the second grade, it was necessary, as elsewhere stated, that their choice should be accepted and confirmed by each phratry. It was expected that the gentes of the same phratry would confirm the choice almost as a matter of course; but the opposite phratry also must acquiesce, and from this source opposition sometimes appeared. A council of each phratry was held and pronounced upon the question of acceptance or rejection. If the nomination made was accepted by both it became complete; but if either refused it was thereby set aside, and a new election was made by the gens. When the choice made by the gens had been accepted by the phratries, it was still necessary, as before stated, that the new sachem, or the new chief, should be invested by the council of the confederacy, which alone had power to invest with office.

The Senecas have now lost their Medicine Lodges which fell out in modern times; but they formerly existed and formed a prominent part of their religious system. To hold a Medicine Lodge was to observe their highest religious rites, and to practice their highest religious mysteries. They had two such organizations, one in each phratry, which shows still further the natural connection of the phratry with religious observances. Very little is now known concerning these lodges or

---

1 It was a journey of ten days from earth to heaven for the departed spirit, according to Iroquois belief. For ten days after the death of a person, the mourners met nightly to lament the deceased, at which they indulged in excessive grief. The dirge or wail was performed by women. It was an ancient custom to make a fire on the grave each night for the same period. On the eleventh day they held a feast; the spirit of the departed having reached heaven, the place of rest, there was no further cause for mourning. With the feast it terminated.

their ceremonies. Each was a brotherhood, into which new members were admitted by a formal initiation.

The phratry was without governmental functions in the strict sense of the phrase, these being confined to the gens, tribe and confederacy; but it entered into their social affairs with large administrative powers, and would have concerned itself more and more with their religious affairs as the condition of the people advanced. Unlike the Grecian phratry and the Roman *curia* it had no official head. There was no chief of the phratry as such, and no religious functionaries belonging to it as distinguished from the gens and tribe. The phratric institution among the Iroquois was in its rudimentary archaic form, but it grew into life by natural and inevitable development, and remained permanent because it met necessary wants. Every institution of mankind which attained permanence will be found linked with a perpetual want. With the gens, tribe and confederacy in existence the presence of the phratry was substantially assured. It required time, however, and further experience to manifest all the uses to which it might be made subservient.

Among the Village Indians of Mexico and Central America the phratry must have existed, reasoning upon general priciples; and have been a more fully developed and influential organization than among the Iroquois. Unfortunately, mere glimpses at such an institution are all that can be found in the teeming narratives of the Spanish writers within the first century after the Spanish conquest. The four "lineages" of the Tlascalans who occupied the four quarters of the pueblo of Tlascala, were, in all probability, so many phratries. They were sufficiently numerous for four tribes; but as they occupied the same pueblo and spoke the same dialect the phratric organization was apparently a necessity. Each lineage, or phratry so to call it, had a distinct military organization, a peculiar costume and banner, and its head war-chief (*Teuctli*), who was its general military commander. They went forth to battle by phratries. The organization of a military force by phratries and by tribes was not unknown to the Homeric Greeks. Thus;

Nestor advises Agamemnon to "separate the troops by phratries and by tribes, so that phratry may support phratry and tribe tribe."[1] Under gentile institutions of the most advanced type the principle of kin became, to a considerable extent, the basis of the army organization. The Aztecs, in like manner, occupied the pueblo of Mexico in four distinct divisions, the people of each of which were more nearly related to each other than to the people of the other divisions. They were separate lineages, like the Tlascalan, and it seems highly probably were four phratries, separately organized as such. They were distinguished from each other by costumes and standards, and went out to war as separate divisions. Their geographical areas were called the four quarters of Mexico. This subject will be referred to again.

With respect to the prevalence of this organization, among the Indian tribes in the Lower Status of barbarism, the subject has been but slightly investigated. It is probable that it was general in the principal tribes, from the natural manner in which it springs up as a necessary member of the organic series, and from the uses, other than governmental, to which it was adapted.

In some of the tribes the phratries stand out prominently upon the face of their organization. Thus, the Chocta gentes are united in two phratries which must be mentioned first in order to show the relation of the gentes to each other. The first phratry is called "Divided People," and also contains four gentes. The second is called "Beloved People," and also contains four gentes. This separation of the people into two divisions by gentes created two phratries. Some knowledge of the functions of these phratries is of course desirable; but without it the fact of their existence is established by the divisions themselves. The evolution of a confederacy from a pair of gentes, for less than two are never found in any tribe, may be deduced, theoretically, from the known facts of Indian experience. Thus, the gens increases in the number of its members and divides into

1 "Iliad," ii, 362.

two; these again subdivide, and in time reunite in two or more phratries. These phratries form a tribe, and its members speak the same dialect. In course of time this tribe falls into several by the process of segmentation, which in turn reunite in a confederacy. Such a confederacy is a growth, through the tribe and phratry, from a pair of gentes.

The Chickasas are organized in two phratries, of which one contains four, and the other eight gentes, as follows:

I. *Panther Phratry.*

Gentes.—1. Wild Cat. 2. Bird. 3. Fish. 4. Deer.

II. *Spanish Phratry.*

Gentes.—5. Raccoon. 6. Spanish. 7. Royal. 8. Hush-ko'ni. 9. Squirrel. 10. Alligator. 11. Wolf. 12. Blackbird.

The particulars with respect to the Chocta and Chickasa phratries I am unable to present. Some fourteen years ago these organizations were given to me by Rev. Doctor Cyrus Byington and Rev. Charles C. Copeland, but without discussing their uses and functions.

A very complete illustration of the manner in which phratries are formed by natural growth, through the subdivision of gentes, is presented by the organization of the Mohegan tribe. It had three original gentes, the Wolf, the Turtle, and the Turkey.

Each of these subdivided, and the subdivisions became independent gentes; but they retained the names of the original gentes as their respective phratric names. In other words the subdivisions of each gens reorganized in a phratry. It proves conclusively the natural process by which, in course of time, a gens breaks up into several, and these remain united in a phratric organization, which is expressed by assuming a phratric name. They are as follows:

I. *Wolf Phratry.*

Gentes.—1. Wolf. 2. Bear. 3. Dog. 4. Opossum.

II. *Turtle Phratry.*

Gentes.—5. Little Turtle. 6. Mud Turtle. 7. Great Turtle. 8. Yellow Eel.

III. *Turkey Phratry.*

Gentes.—9. Turkey. 10. Crane. 11. Chicken.

It is thus seen that the original Wolf gens divided into four gentes, the Turtle into four, and the Turkey into three. Each new gens took a new name, the original retaining its own, which became, by seniority, that of the phratry. It is rare among the American Indian tribes to find such plain evidence of the segmentation of gentes in their external organization, followed by the formation into phratries of their respective subdivisions. It shows also that the phratry is founded upon the kinship of the gentes. As a rule the name of the original gens out of which others had formed is not known; but in each of these cases it remains as the name of the phratry. Since the latter, like the Grecian, was a social and religious rather than a governmental organization, it is externally less conspicuous than a gens or tribe which were essential to the goverment of society. The name of but one of the twelve Athenian phratries has come down to us in history. Those of the Iroquois had no name but that of a brotherhood.

The Delawares and Munsees have the same three gentes, the Wolf, the Turtle, and the Turkey. Among the Delawares there are twelve embryo gentes in each tribe, but they seem to be lineages within the gentes and had not taken gentile names. It was a movement, however, in that direction.

The phratry also appears among the Thlinkeets of the Northwest coast, upon the surface of their organization into gentes. They have two phratries, as follows:

I. *Wolf Phratry.*

Gentes.—1. Bear. 2. Eagle. 3. Dolphin. 4. Shark. 5. Elca.

II. *Raven Phratry.*

Gentes.—6. Frog. 7. Goose. 8. Sea-lion. 9. Owl. 10. Salmon.

Intermarriage in the phratry is prohibited, which shows, of itself, that the gentes of each phratry were derived from an original gens.[1] The members of any gens in the Wolf phratry could marry into any gens of the opposite phratry, and *vice versâ.*

From the foregoing facts the existence of the phratry is established in several linguistic stocks of the American aborigines. Its presence in the tribes named raises a presumption of its general prevalence in the Ganowánian family. Among the Village Indians, where the numbers in a gens and tribe were greater, it would necessarily have been more important and consequently more fully developed. As an institution it was still in its archaic form, but it possessed the essential elements of the Grecian and the Roman. It can now be asserted that the full organic series of ancient society exists in full vitality upon the American continent; namely, the gens, the phratry, the tribe, and the confederacy of tribes. With further proofs yet to be adduced, the universality of the gentile organization upon all the continents will be established.

If future investigation is directed specially to the functions of the phratric organization among the tribes of the American aborigines, the knowledge gained will explain many peculiarities of Indian life and manners not well understood, and throw additional light upon their usages and customs, and upon their plan of life and government.

---

1 Bancroft's "Native Races of the Pacific States," I, 109.

CHAPTER IV

THE IROQUOIS TRIBE

It is difficult to describe an Indian tribe by the affirmative elements of its composition. Nevertheless it is clearly marked, and the ultimate organization of the great body of the American aborigines. The large number of independent tribes into which they had fallen by the natural process of segmentation, is the striking characteristic of their condition. Each tribe was individualized by a name, by a separate dialect, by a supreme government, and by the possession of a territory which it occupied and defended as its own. The tribes were as numerous as the dialects, for separation did not become complete until dialectical variation had commenced. Indian tribes, therefore, are natural growths through the separation of the same people in the area of their occupation, followed by divergence of speech, segmentation, and independence.

We have seen that the phratry was not so much a governmental as a social organization, while the gens, tribe, and confederacy, were necessary and logical stages of progress in the growth of the idea of government. A confederacy could not exist, under gentile society, without tribes as a basis; nor could tribes exist without gentes, though they might without phratries. In this chapter I will endeavor to point out the manner in which these numerous tribes were formed, and, presumptively out of one original people; the causes which produced their perpetual segmentation; and the principal attributes which distinguished an Indian tribe as an organization.

The exclusive possession of a dialect and of a territory has led to the application of the term *nation* to many Indian tribes, notwithstanding the fewness of the people in each. *Tribe* and *nation,* however, are not strict equivalents. A nation does not arise, under gentile institutions, until the tribes united under the same government have coalesced into one people, as the four Athenian tribes coalesced in Attica, three Dorian tribes at Sparta, and three Latin and Sabine tribes at Rome. Federation requires independent tribes in separate territorial areas; but coalescence unites them by a higher process in the same area, although the tendency to local separation by gentes and by tribes would continue. The confederacy is the nearest analogue of the nation, but not strictly equivalent. Where the gentile organization exists, the organic series gives all the terms which are needed for a correct description.

An Indian tribe is composed of several gentes, developed from two or more, all the members of which are intermingled by marriage, and all of whom speak the same dialect. To a stranger the tribe is visible, and not the gens. The instances are extremely rare, among the American aborigines, in which the tribe embraced peoples speaking different dialects. When such cases are found, it resulted from the union of a weaker with a stronger tribe, speaking a closely related dialect, as the union of the Missouris with the Otoes after the overthrow of the former. The fact that the great body of the aborigines were found in independent tribes illustrates the slow and difficult growth of the idea of government under gentile institutions. A small portion only had attained to the ultimate stage known among them, that of a confederacy of tribes speaking dialects of the same stock language. A coalescence of tribes into a nation had not occurred in any case in any part of America.

A constant tendency to disintegration, which has proved such a hindrance to progress among savage and barbarous tribes, existed in the elements of the gentile organization. It was aggravated by a further tendency to divergence of speech, which was inseparable from their social state and the large areas of their occupation. A verbal language, although remarkably persistent in its vocables, and still more persistent in its grammatical forms, is incapable of permanence. Separation of the people in area was followed in time by variation in speech; and this, in turn, led to separation in interests and ultimate independence. It was not the work of a brief period, but of centuries of time, aggregating finally into thousands of years. The great number of dialects and stock languages in North and South America, which presumptively were derived, the Eskimo excepted, from one original language, require for their formation the time measured by three ethnical periods.

New tribes as well as new gentes were constantly forming by natural growth; and the process was sensibly accelerated by the great expanse of the American continent. The method was simple. In the first place there would occur a gradual outflow of people from some overstocked geographical centre, which possessed superior advantages in the means of subsistence. Continued from year to year, a considerable population would thus be developed at a distance from the original seat of the tribe. In course of time the emigrants would become distinct in interests, strangers in feeling, and last of all, divergent in speech. Separation and independence would follow, although their territories were contiguous. A new tribe was thus created. This is a concise statement of the manner in which the tribes of the American aborigines were formed, but the statement must be taken as general. Repeating itself from age to age in newly acquired as well as in old areas, it must be regarded as a natural as well as inevitable result of the gentile organization, united with the necessities of their condition. When increased numbers pressed upon the means of subsistence, the surplus removed to a new seat where they established themselves with facility, because the government was perfect in every gens, and in any number of gentes united in a band. Among the Village Indians the same repeated itself in a slightly different manner. When a village became overcrowded with numbers, a colony went up or down on the same stream and commenced a new village. Repeated at intervals of time several such villages would appear, each independent of the other and a self-governing body; but united in a league or confederacy for mutual protection. Dialectical variation would finally spring up, and thus complete their growth into tribes.

The manner in which tribes are evolved from each other can be shown directly by examples. The fact of separation is derived in part from tradition, in part from the possession by each of a number of the same gentes, and deduced in part from the relations of their dialects. Tribes formed by the subdivisions of an original tribe would possess a number of gentes in common, and speak dialects of the same language. After several centuries of separation they would still have a number of the same gentes. Thus, the Hurons, now Wyandotes, have six gentes of the same name with six of the gentes of the Seneca-Iroquois, after at least four hundred years of separation. The Potawattamies have eight gentes of the same name with eight among the Ojibwas, while the former have six, and the latter fourteen, which are different; showing that new gentes have been formed in each tribe by segmentation since their separation. A still older offshoot from the Ojibwas, or from the common parent tribe of both, the Miamis, have but three gentes in common with the former, namely, the Wolf, the Loon, and the Eagle. The minute social history of the tribes of the Ganowánian family is locked up in the life and growth of the gentes. If investigation is ever turned strongly in this direction, the gentes themselves would become reliable guides, both in respect to the order of separation from each other of the tribes of the same stock, and possibly of the great stocks of the aborigines.

The following illustrations are drawn from tribes in the Lower Status of barbarism. When discovered, the eight Missouri tribes occupied the banks of the Missouri river for more than a thousand miles; together with the banks of its tributaries, the Kansas and the Platte; and also the smaller rivers of Iowa. They also occupied the west bank of the Mississippi down to the Arkansas. Their dialects show that the people were in three tribes before the last subdivisions; namely, first, the Punkas and Omahas, second, the Iowas, Otoes and Missouris, and third, the Kaws, Osages and Quappas. These three were undoubtedly subdivisions of a single original tribe, because their several dialects are still much nearer to each other than to any other dialect of the Dakotian stock language to which they belong. There is, therefore, a linguistic necessity for their derivation from an original tribe. A gradual spread from a central point on this river along its banks, both above and below, would lead to a separation in interests with the increase of distance between their settlements, followed by divergence of speech, and finally by independence. A people thus extending themselves along a river in a prairie country might separate, first into three tribes, and afterwards into eight, and the organization of each subdivision remain complete. Division was neither a shock, nor an appreciated calamity; but a separation into parts by natural expansion over a larger area, followed by a complete segmentation. The uppermost tribe on the Missouri were the Punkas at the mouth of the Niobrara river, and the lowermost the Quappas at the mouth of the Arkansas on the Mississippi, with an interval of near fifteen hundred miles between them. The intermediate region, confined to the narrow belt of forest upon the Missouri, was held by the remaining six tribes. They were strictly River Tribes.

Another illustration may be found in the tribes of Lake Superior. The Ojibwas, Otawas[1] and Potawattamies are subdivisions of an original tribe; the Ojibwas representing the stem, because they remained at the original seat at the great fisheries upon the outlet of the lake. Moreover, they are styled "Elder Brother" by the remaining two; while the Otawas were styled "Next Older Brother," and the Potawattamies "Younger Brother." The

---

[1] O-tä'-was.

last tribe separated first, and the Otawas last, as is shown by the relative amount of dialectical variation, that of the former being greatest. At the time of their discovery, A. D. 1641, the Ojibwas were seated at the Rapids on the outlet of Lake Superior, from which point they had spread along the southern shore of the lake to the site of Ontonagon, along its northeastern shore, and down the St. Mary River well toward Lake Huron. Their position possessed remarkable advantages for a fish and game subsistence, which, as they did not cultivate maize and plants, was their main reliance.[1] It was second to none, in North America, with the single exception of the Valley of the Columbia. With such advantages they were certain to develop a large Indian population, and to send out successive bands of emigrants to become independent tribes. The Potawattamies occupied a region on the confines of Upper Michigan and Wisconsin, from which the Dakotas in 1641, were in the act of expelling them. At the same time the Otawas, whose earlier residence is supposed to have been on the Otawa river of Canada, had drawn westward and were then seated upon the Georgian Bay, the Manitouline Islands and at Mackinaw, from which points they were spreading southward over Lower Michigan. Originally one people, and possessing the same gentes, they had succeeded in appropriating a large area. Separation in place, and distance between their settlements, had long before their discovery resulted in the formation of dialects, and in tribal independence. The three tribes, whose territories were contiguous, had formed an alliance for mutual protection, known among Americans as "the Otawa Confederacy." It was a league, offensive and defensive, and not, probably, a close confederacy like that of the Iroquois.

Prior to these secessions another affiliated tribe, the Miamis, had broken off from the Ojibwa stock, or the common parent tribe, and migrated to central Illinois

---

1 The Objiwas manufactured earthen pipes, water jars, and vessels in ancient times, as they now assert. Indian pottery has been dug up at different times at the Sault St. Mary, which they recognize as the work of their forefathers.

and western Indiana. Following in the track of this migration were the Illinois, another and later offshoot from the same stem, who afterwards subdivided into the Peorias, Kaskaskias, Weaws, and Piankeshaws. Their dialects, with that of the Miamis, find their nearest affinity with the Ojibwa, and next with the Cree.[1] The outflow of all these tribes from the central seat at the great fisheries of Lake Superior is a significant fact, because it illustrates the manner in which tribes are formed in connection with natural centres of subsistence. The New England, Delaware, Maryland, Virginia and Carolina Algonkins were, in all probability, derived from the same source. Several centuries would be required for the formation of the dialects first named, and for the production of the amount of variation they now exhibit.

The foregoing examples represent the natural process by which tribes are evolved from each other, or from a parent tribe established in an advantageous position. Each emigrating band was in the nature of a military colony, if it may be so strongly characterized, seeking to acquire and hold a new area; preserving at first, and as long as possible, a connection with the mother tribe. By these successive movements they sought to expand their joint possessions, and afterward to resist the intrusion of alien people within their limits. It is a noticeable fact that Indian tribes speaking dialects of the same stock language have usually been found in territorial continuity, however extended their common area. The same has, in the main, been true of all the tribes of mankind linguistically united. It is because the people, spreading from some geographical centre, and maintaining an arduous struggle for subsistence, and for the possession of their new territories, have preserved their connection with the mother land as a means of succor in times of danger, and as a place of refuge in calamity.

---

1 The Potawattamie and the Cree have diverged about equally. It is probable that the Ojibwas. Otawas and Crees were one people in dialect after the Potawattamies became detached.

It required special advantages in the means of subsistence to render any area an initial point of migration through the gradual development of a surplus population. These natural centres were few in number in North America. There are but three. First among them is the Valley of the Columbia, the most extraordinary region on the face of the earth in the variety and amount of subsistence it afforded, prior to the cultivation of maize and plants; second, the peninsula between Lakes Superior, Huron and Michigan, the seat of the Ojibwas, and the nursery land of many Indian tribes; and third, the lake region in Minnesota, the nursery ground of the present Dakota tribes. These are the only regions in North America that can be called natural centres of subsistence, and natural sources of surplus numbers. There are reasons for believing that Minnesota was a part of the Algonkin area before it was occupied by the Dakotas. When the cultivation of maize and plants came in, it tended to localize the people and support them in smaller areas, as well as to increase their numbers; but it failed to transfer the control of the continent to the most advanced tribes of Village Indians, who subsisted almost entirely by cultivation. Horticulture spread among the principal tribes in the Lower Status of barbarism and greatly improved their condition. They held, with the nonhorticultural tribes, the great areas of North America when it was discovered, and from their ranks the continent was being replenished with inhabitants.[2]

---

1 As a mixture of forest and prairie it was an excellent game country. A species of bread-root, the kamash, grew in abundance in the prairies. In the summer there was a profusion of berries. But in these respects it was not superior to other areas. That which signalized the region was the inexhaustible supply of salmon in the Columbia, and other rivers of the coast. They crowded these streams in millions, and were taken in the season with facility, and in the greatest abundance. After being split open and dried in the sun, they were packed and removed to their villages, and formed their principal food during the greater part of the year. Beside these were the shell fisheries of the coast, which supplied a large amount of food during the winter months. Superadded to these concentrated advantages, the climate was mild and equable throughout the year—about that of Tennessee and Virginia. It was the paradise of tribes without a knowledge of the cereals.

2 It can be shown with a great degree of probability, that the Valley of the Columbia was the seed land of the Ganowánian

The multiplication of tribes and dialects nas been the fruitful source of the incessant warfare of the aborigines

ian family, from which issued, in past ages, successive streams of migrating bands, until both divisions of the continent were occupied. And further, that both divisions continued to be replenished with inhabitants from this source down to the epoch of European discovery. These conclusions may be deduced from physical causes, from the relative conditions, and from the linguistic relations of the Indian tribes. The great expanse of the central prairies, which spread continuously more than fifteen hundred miles from north to south, and more than a thousand miles from east to west, interposed a barrier to a free communication between the Pacific and Atlantic sides of the continent in North America. It seems probable, therefore, that an original family commencing its spread from the Valley of the Columbia, and migrating under the influence of physical causes, would reach Patagonia sooner than they would Florida. The known facts point so strongly to this region as the original home of the Indian family, that a moderate amount of additional evidence will render the hypothesis conclusive.

The discovery and cultivation of maize did not change materially the course of events, or suspend the operation of previous causes; though it became an important factor in the progress of improvement. It is not known where this American cereal was indigenous; but the tropical region of Central America, where vegetation is intensely active, where this plant is peculiarly fruitful, and where the oldest seats of the Village Indians were found, has been assumed by common consent, as the probable place of its nativity. If, then, cultivation commenced in Central America, it would have propagated itself first over Mexico, and from thence to New Mexico and the valley of the Mississippi, and thence again eastward to the shores of the Atlantic; the volume of cultivation diminishing from the starting-point to the extremities. It would spread, independently of the Village Indians, from the desire of more barbarous tribes to gain the new subsistence; but it never extended beyond New Mexico to the Valley of the Columbia, though cultivation was practiced by the Minnitarees and Mandans of the Upper Missouri, by the Shyans on the Red River of the North, by the Hurons of Lake Simcoe in Canada, and by the Abenakies of the Kennebec, as well as generally by the tribes between the Mississippi and the Atlantic. Migrating bands from the Valley of the Columbia, following upon the track of their predecessors would press upon the Village Indians of New Mexico and Mexico, tending to force displaced and fragmentary tribes toward and through the Isthmus into South America. Such expelled bands would carry with them the first germs of progress developed by Village Indian life. Repeated at intervals of time it would tend to bestow upon South America a class of inhabitants far superior to the wild bands previously supplied, and at the expense of the northern section thus impoverished. In the final result, South America would attain the advanced position in development, even in an inferior country, which seems to have been the fact. The Peruvian legend of Manco Capac and Mama Oello, children of the sun, brother and sister, husband and wife, shows, if it can be said to show anything, that a band of Village Indians migrating from a distance, though not necessarily from North America direct, had gathered together and taught the rude tribes of the Andes the higher arts of life, including the cultivation of maize and plants. By a simple and quite natural process the legend has dropped out the band, and retained only the leader and his wife.

upon each other. As a rule the most persistent warfare has been waged between tribes speaking different stock languages; as, for example, between the Iroquois and Algonkin tribes, and between the Dakota tribes and the same. On the contrary the Algonkin and Dakota tribes severally have, in general, lived at peace among themselves. Had it been otherwise they would not have been found in the occupation of continuous areas. The worst exception were the Iroquois, who pursued a war of extermination against their kindred tribes, the Eries, the Neutral Nation, the Hurons and the Susquehannocks. Tribes speaking dialects of the same stock language are able to communicate orally and thus compose their differences. They also learned, in virtue of their common descent, to depend upon each other as natural allies.

Numbers within a given area were limited by the amount of subsistence it afforded. When fish and game were the main reliance for food, it required an immense area to maintain a small tribe. After farinaceous food was superadded to fish and game, the area occupied by a tribe was still a large one in proportion to the number of the people. New York, with its forty-seven thousand square miles, never contained at any time more than twenty-five thousand Indians, including with the Iroquois the Algonkins on the east side of the Hudson and upon Long Island, and the Eries and Neutral Nation in the western section of the state. A personal government founded upon gentes was incapable of developing sufficient central power to follow and control the increasing numbers of the people, unless they remained within a reasonable distance from each other.

Among the Village Indians of New Mexico, Mexico, and Central America an increase of numbers in a small area did not arrest the process of disintegration. Each pueblo was usually an independent self-governing community. Where several pueblos were seated near each other on the same stream, the people were usually of common descent, and either under a tribal or confederate government. There are some seven stock languages in New Mexico alone, each spoken in several dialects.

At the time of Coronado's expedition, 1540-1542, the villages found were numerous but small. There were seven each of Cibola, Tucayan, Quivira, and Hemez, and twelve of Tiguex,[1] and other groups indicating a linguistic connection of their members. Whether or not each group was confederated we are not informed. The seven Moqui Pueblos (the Tucayan Villages of Coronado's expedition), are said to be confederated at the present time, and probably were at the time of their discovery.

The process of subdivision, illustrated by the foregoing examples, has been operating among the American aborigines for thousands of years, until upwards of forty stock languages, as near as is known, have been developed in North America alone; each spoken in a number of dialects, by an equal number of independent tribes. Their experience, probably, was but a repetition of that of the tribes of Asia, Europe and Africa, when they were in corresponding conditions.

From the preceding observations, it is apparent that an American Indian tribe is a very simple as well as humble organization. It required but a few hundreds, and, at most, a few thousand people to form a tribe, and place it in a respectable position in the Ganowánian family.

It remains to present the functions and attributes of an Indian tribe, which may be discussed under the following propositions:

I. *The possession of a territory and a name.*
II. *The exclusive possession of a dialect.*
III. *The right to invest sachems and chiefs elected by the gentes.*
IV. *The right to depose these sachems and chiefs.*
V. *The possession of a religious faith and worship.*
VI. *A supreme government consisting of a council of chiefs.*
VII. *A head-chief of the tribe in some instances.*

1 "Coll. Ternaux-Compans," IX, pp. 181-183.

It will be sufficient to make a brief reference to each of these several attributes of a tribe.

I. *The possession of a territory and a name.*

Their territory consisted of the area of their actual settlements, and so much of the surrounding region as the tribe ranged over in hunting and fishing, and were able to defend against the encroachments of other tribes. Without this area was a wide margin of neutral grounds, separating them from their nearest frontegers if they spoke a different language, and claimed by neither; but less wide, and less clearly marked, when they spoke dialects of the same language. The country thus imperfectly defined, whether large or small, was the domain of the tribe, recognized as such by other tribes, and defended as such by themselves.

In due time the tribe became individualized by a name, which, from their usual character, must have been in many cases accidental rather than deliberate. Thus, the Senecas styled themselves the "Great Hill People" (Nun-da'-wä-o-no), the Tuscaroras, "Shirt-wearing People" (Dus-ga'-o-weh-o-no'), the Sissetons, "Village of the Marsh" (Sis-se'-to-wän), the Ogalallas, "Camp Movers" (O-ga-lal'-lä), the Omahas, "Upstream People" (O-mä'-hä), the Iowas, "Dusty Noses" (Pa-ho'-cha), the Minnitarees, "People from Afar" (E-năt'-zä), the Cherokees, "Great People" (Tsä-lo'-kee), the Shawnees, "Southerners" (Sä-wan-wäkee'), the Mohegans, "Sea-side People" (Mo-he-kun-e-uk), the Slave Lake Indians, "People of the Lowlands" (A-cha'o-tin-ne). Among the Village Indians of Mexico, the Sochimilcos styled themselves "Nation of the Seeds of Flowers," the Chalcans, "People of Mouths," the Tepanecans, "People of the Bridge," the Tezcucans or Culhuas "A Crooked People," and the Tlascalans "Men of Bread." When European colonization began in the northern part of America, the names of Indian tribes were obtained, not usually from the tribe direct, but from other tribes who had bestowed

---

1 Acosta. "The Natural and Moral History of the East and West Indies," Lond. ed., 1604, Grimstone's Trans., pp. 500-503.

names upon them different from their own. As a consequence, a number of tribes are now known in history under names not recognized by themselves.

II. *The exclusive possession of a dialect.*

Tribe and dialect are substantially co-extensive, but there are exceptions growing out of special cicumstances. Thus, the twelve Dakota bands are now properly tribes, because they are distinct in interests and in organization; but they were forced into premature separation by the advance of Americans upon their original area which forced them upon the plains. They had remained in such intimate connection previously that but one new dialect had commenced forming, the *Teeton,* on the Missouri; the *Isauntie* on the Mississippi being the original speech. A few years ago the Cherokees numbered twenty-six thousand, the largest number of Indians ever found within the limits of the United States speaking the same dialect. But in the mountain districts of Georgia a slight divergence of speech had occurred, though not sufficient to be distinguished as a dialect. There are a few other similar cases, but they do not break the general rule during the aboriginal period which made tribe and dialect co-extensive. The Ojibwas, who are still in the main non-horticultural, now number about fifteen thousand, and speak the same dialect; and the Dakota tribes collectively about twenty-five thousand who speak two very closely related dialects, as stated. These several tribes are exceptionally large. The tribes within the United States and British America would yield, on an average, less than two thousand persons to a tribe.

III. *The right of investing sachems and chiefs elected by the gentes.*

Among the Iroquois the person elected could not become a chief until his investiture by a council of chiefs. As the chiefs of the gentes composed the council of the tribe, with power over common interests, there was a manifest propriety in reserving to the tribal council the function of investing persons with office. But after the confederacy was formed, the power of "raising up" sachems and chiefs was transferred from the council of the tribe to the council of the confederacy. With respect to the tribes generally, the accessible information is insufficient to explain their usages in relation to the mode of investiture. It is one of the numerous subjects requiring further investigation before the social system of the Indian tribes can be fully explained. The office of sachem and chief was universally elective among the tribes north of Mexico; with sufficient evidence, as to other parts of the continent, to leave no doubt of the universality of the rule.

Among the Delawares each gens had one sachem (Sä-ke'mä), whose office was hereditary in the gens, besides two common chiefs, and two war-chiefs—making fifteen in three gentes—who composed the council of the tribe. Among the Ojibwas, the members of some one gens usually predominated at each settlement. Each gens had a sachem, whose office was hereditary in the gens, and several common chiefs. Where a large number of persons of the same gens lived in one locality they would be found similarly organized. There was no prescribed limit to the number of chiefs. A body of usages, which have never been collected, undoubtedly existed in the several Indian tribes respecting the election and investiture of sachems and chiefs. A knowledge of them would be valuable. An explanation of the Iroquois method of "raising up" sachems and chiefs will be given in the next chapter.

IV. *The right to depose these sachems and chiefs.*

This right rested primarily with the gens to which the sachem and chief belonged. But the council of the tribe possessed the same power, and could proceed independently of the gens, and even in opposition to its wishes. In the Status of savagery, and in the Lower and also in the Middle Status of barbarism, office was bestowed for life, or during good behavior. Mankind had not learned to limit an elective office for a term of years. The right to depose, therefore, became the more essential for the maintenance of the principle of self-government. This right was a perpetual assertion of the sovereignty of the gens and also of the tribe; a sovereignty feebly understood, but nevertheless a reality.

V. *The possession of a religious faith and worship.*

After the fashion of barbarians the American Indians were a religious people. The tribes generally held religious festivals at particular seasons of the year, which were observed with forms of worship, dances and games. The Medicine Lodge, in many tribes, was the centre of these observances. It was customary to announce the holding of a Medicine Lodge weeks and months in advance to awaken a general interest in its ceremonies. The religious system of the aborigines is another of the subjects which has been but partially investigated. It is rich in materials for the future student. The experience of these tribes in developing their religious beliefs and mode of worship is a part of the experience of mankind; and the facts will hold an important place in the science of comparative religion.

Their system was more or less vague and indefinite, and loaded with crude superstitions. Element worship can be traced among the principal tribes, with a tendency to polytheism in the advanced tribes. The Iroquois, for example, recognized a Great, and an Evil Spirit, and a multitude of inferior spiritual beings, the immortality of the soul, and a future state. Their conception of the Great Spirit assigned to him a human form; which was equally true of the Evil Spirit of *He'-no,* the Spirit of Thunder, of *Gă'-oh,* the Spirit of the Winds, and of the *Three Sisters,* the Spirit of Maize, the Spirit of the Bean, and the Spirit of the Squash. The latter were styled, collectively, "Our Life," and also "Our Supporters." Beside these were the spirits of the several kinds of trees and plants, and of the running streams. The existence and attributes of these numerous spiritual beings were but feebly imagined. Among the tribes in the Lower Status of barbarism idolatry was unknown.[1] The Az-

1 Near the close of the last century the Seneca-Iroquois, at one of their villages on the Alleghany river, set up an idol of wood, and performed dances and other religious ceremonies around it. My informer, the late William Parker, saw this idol in the river into which it had been cast. Whom it personated he did not learn.

tecs had personal gods, with idols to represent them, and a temple worship. If the particulars of their religious system were accurately known, its growth out of the common beliefs of the Indian tribes would probably be made apparent.

Dancing was a form of worship among the American aborigines, and formed a part of the ceremonies at all religious festivals. In no part of the earth, among barbarians, has the dance received a more studied development. Every tribe has from ten to thirty set dances; each of which has its own name, songs, musical instruments, steps, plan and costume for persons. Some of them, as the war-dance, were common to all the tribes. Particular dances are special property, belonging either to a gens, or to a society organized for its maintenance, into which new members were from time to time initiated. The dances of the Dakotas, the Crees, the Ojibwas, the Iroquois, and of the Pueblo Indians of New Mexico, are the same in general character, in step, plan, and music; and the same is true of the dances of the Aztecs so far as they are accurately known. It is one system throughout the Indian tribes, and bears a direct relation to their svstem of faith and worship.

VI. *A supreme government through a council of chiefs.*

The council had a natural foundation in the gentes of whose chiefs it was composed. It met a necessary want, and was certain to remain as long as gentile society endured. As the gens was represented by its chiefs, so the tribe was represented by a council composed of the chiefs of the gentes. It was a permanent feature of the social system, holding the ultimate authority over the tribe. Called together under circumstances known to all, held in the midst of the people, and open to their orators, it was certain to act under popular influence. Although oligarchical in form, the government was a representative democracy; the representative being elected for life, but subject to deposition. The brotherhood of the members of each gens, and the elective principle with respect to office, were the germ and the basis of the democratic principle. Imperfectly developed, as other great principles were in this early stage of advancement, democracy can boast a very ancient pedigree in the tribes of mankind.

It devolved upon the council to guard and protect the common interests of the tribe. Upon the intelligence and courage of the people, and upon the wisdom and foresight of the council, the prosperity and the existence of the tribe depended. Questions and exigencies were arising, through their incessant warfare with other tribes, which required the exercise of all these qualities to meet and manage. It was unavoidable, therefore, that the popular element should be commanding in its influence. As a general rule the council was open to any private individual who desired to address it on a public question. Even the women were allowed to express their wishes and opinions through an orator of their own selection. But the decision was made by the council. Unanimity was a fundamental law of its action among the Iroquois; but whether this usage was general I am unable to state.

Military operations were usually left to the action of the voluntary principle. Theoretically, each tribe was at war with every other tribe with which it had not formed a treaty of peace. Any person was at liberty to organize a war-party and conduct an expedition wherever he pleased. He announced his project by giving a war-dance and inviting volunteers. This method furnished a practical test of the popularity of the undertaking. If he succeeded in forming a company, which would consist of such persons as joined him in the dance, they departed immediately, while enthusiasm was at its height. When a tribe was menaced with an attack, war-parties were formed to meet it in much the same manner. Where forces thus raised were united in one body, each was under its own war-captain, and their joint movements were determined by a council of these captains. If there was among them a war-chief of established reputation he would naturally become their leader. These statements relate to tribes in the Lower Status of barbarism. The Aztecs and Tlascalans went out by phratries, each subdivision under its own captain, and distinguished by costumes and banners.

Indian tribes, and even confederacies, were weak organizations for military operations. That of the Iroquois, and that of the Aztecs, were the most remarkable for aggressive purposes. Among the tribes in the Lower Status of barbarism, including the Iroquois, the most destructive work was performed by inconsiderable war-parties, which were constantly forming and making expeditions into distant regions. Their supply of food consisted of parched corn reduced to flour, carried in a pouch attached to the belt of each warrior, with such fish and game as the route supplied. The going out of these war-parties, and their public reception on their return, were among the prominent events in Indian life. The sanction of the council for these expeditions was not sought, neither was it necessary.

The council of the tribe had power to declare war and make peace, to send and receive embassies, and to make alliances. It exercised all the powers needful in a government so simple and limited in its affairs. Intercourse between independent tribes was conducted by delegations of wise-men and chiefs. When such a delegation was expected by any tribe, a council was convened for its reception, and for the transaction of its business.

VII. *A head-chief of the tribe in some instances.*

In some Indian tribes one of the sachems was recognized as its head-chief; and as superior in rank to his associates. A need existed, to some extent, for an official head of the tribe to represent it when the council was not in session; but the duties and powers of the office were slight. Although the council was supreme in authority it was rarely in session, and questions might arise demanding the provisional action of some one authorized to represent the tribe, subject to the ratification of his acts by the council. This was the only basis, so far as the writer is aware, for the office of head-chief. It existed in a number of tribes, but in a form of authority so feeble as to fall below the conception of an executive magistrate. In the language of some of the early writers they have been designated as kings, which is simply a caricature. The Indian tribes had not advanced far enough in a knowledge of government to develop the idea of a chief executive magistrate. The Iroquois tribe recognized no head-chief, and the confederacy no executive officer. The elective tenure of the office of chief, and the liability of the person to deposition, settled the character of the office.

A council of Indian chiefs is of little importance by itself; but as the germ of the modern parliament, congress, and legislature, it has an important bearing in the history of mankind.

The growth of the idea of government commenced with the organization into gentes in savagery. It reveals three great stages of progressive development between its commencement and the institution of political society after civilization had been attained. The first stage was the government of a tribe by a council of chiefs elected by the gentes. It may be called a government of *one power;* namely, *the council.* It prevailed generally among tribes in the Lower Status of barbarism. The second stage was a government co-ordinated between a council of chiefs, and a general military commander; one representing the civil and the other the military functions. This second form began to manifest itself in the Lower Status of barbarism, after confederacies were formed, and it became definite in the Middle Status. The office of general, or principal military commander, was the germ of that of a chief executive magistrate, the king, the emperor, and the president. It may be called a government of *two powers,* namely, *the council of chiefs,* and *the general.* The third stage was the government of a people or nation by a council of chiefs, an assembly of the people, and a general military commander. It appeared among the tribes who had attained to the Upper Status of barbarism; such, for example, as the Homeric Greeks, and the Italian tribes of the period of Romulus. A large increase in the number of people united in a nation, their establishment in walled cities, and the creation of wealth in lands and in flocks and herds, brought in the assembly of the people as an instrument of government. The council of chiefs, which still remained, found it necessary, no doubt through popular constraint, to submit the most important public measures to an assembly of the people for acceptance or rejection; whence the popular assembly. This assembly did not originate measures. It was its function to adopt or reject, and its action was final. From its first appearance it became a permanent power in the government. The council no longer passed important public measures, but became a pre-considering council, with power to originate and mature public acts, to which the assembly alone could give validity. It may be called a government of *three powers;* namely, *the pre-considering council,* the *assembly of the people,* and *the general.* This remained until the institution of political society, when, for example, among the Athenians, the council of chiefs became the senate, and the assembly of the people the ecclesia or popular assembly. The same organizations have come down to modern times in the two houses of parliament, of congress, and of legislatures. In like manner the office of general military commander, as before stated, was the germ of the office of the modern chief executive magistrate.

Recurring to the tribe, it was limited in the numbers of the people, feeble in strength, and poor in resources; but yet a completely organized society. It illustrates the condition of mankind in the Lower Status of barbarism. In the Middle Status there was a sensible increase of numbers in a tribe, and an improved condition; but with a continuance of gentile society without essential change. Political society was still impossible from want of advancement. The gentes organized into tribes remained as before; but confederacies must have been more frequent. In some areas, as in the Valley of Mexico, larger numbers were developed under a common government, with improvements in the arts of life; but no evidence exists of the overthrow among them of gentile society and the substitution of political. It is impossible to found a political society or a state upon gentes. A state must rest upon territory and not upon persons, upon the township as the unit of a political system, and not upon the gens which is the unit of a social system. It required time and a vast experience, beyond that of the American Indian tribes, as a preparation for such a fundamental change of systems. It also required men of the mental stature of the Greeks and Romans, and with the experience derived from a long chain of ancestors to devise and gradually introduce that new plan of government under which civilized nations are living at the present time.

Following the ascending organic series, we are next to consider the confederacy of tribes, in which the gentes, phratries and tribes will be seen in new relations. The remarkable adaption of the gentile organization to the condition and wants of mankind, while in a barbarous state, will thereby be further illustrated.

CHAPTER V

THE IROQUOIS CONFEDERACY

A tendency to confederate for mutual defense would very naturally exist among kindred and contiguous tribes. When the advantages of a union had been appreciated by actual experience the organization, at first a league, would gradually cement into a federal unity. The state of perpetual warfare in which they lived would quicken this natural tendency into action among such tribes as were sufficiently advanced in intelligence and in the arts of life to perceive its benefits. It would be simply a growth from a lower into a higher organization by an extension of the principle which united the gentes in a tribe.

As might have been expected, several confederacies existed in different parts of North America when discovered, some of which were quite remarkable in plan and structure. Among the number may be mentioned the Iroquois Confederacy of five independent tribes, the Creek Confederacy of six, the Otawa Confederacy of three, the Dakota League of the "Seven Council-Fires," the Moqui Confederacy in New Mexico of Seven Pueblos, and the Aztec Confederacy of three tribes in the Valley of Mexico. It is probable that the Village Indians in other parts of Mexico, in Central and in South America, were quite generally organized in confederacies consisting of two or more kindred tribes. Progress necessarily took this direction from the nature of their institutions, and from the law governing their development. Nevertheless the formation of a confederacy out of such materials, and with such unstable geographical relations, was a difficult undertaking. It was easiest of achievement by the Village Indians from the nearness to each other of their pueblos, and from the smallness of their areas; but it was accomplished in occasional instances by tribes in the Lower Status of barbarism, and notably by the Iroquois. Wherever a confederacy was formed it would of itself evince the superior intelligence of the people.

The two highest examples of Indian confederacies in North America were those of the Iroquois and of the Aztecs. From their acknowledged superiority as military powers, and from their geographical positions, these confederacies, in both cases, produced remarkable results. Our knowledge of the structure and principles of the former is definite and complete, while of the latter it is far from satisfactory. The Aztec confederacy has been handled in such a manner historically as to leave it doubtful whether it was simply a league of three kindred tribes, offensive and defensive, or a systematic confederacy like that of the Iroquois. That which is true of the latter was probably in a general sense true of the former, so that a knowledge of one will tend to elucidate the other.

The conditions under which confederacies spring into being and the principles on which they are formed are remarkably simple. They grow naturally, with time, out of pre-existing elements. Where one tribe had divided into several and these subdivisions occupied independent but contiguous territories, the confederacy re-integrated them in a higher organization, on the basis of the common gentes they possessed, and of the affiliated dialects they spoke. The sentiment of kin embodied in the gens, the common lineage of the gentes, and their dialects still mutually intelligible, yielded the material elements for a confederation. The confederacy, therefore, had the gentes for its basis and centre, and stock language for its circumference. No one has been found that reached beyond the bounds of the dialects of a common language. If this natural barrier had been crossed it would have forced heterogeneous elements into the organization. Cases have occurred where the remains of a tribe, not cognate in speech, as the Natchez,[1] have been admitted into an existing confederacy; but this exception would not invalidate the general proposition. It was impossible for an Indian power to arise upon the American continent through a confederacy of tribes organized in gentes, and advance to a general supremacy unless their numbers were developed from their own stock. The multitude of stock languages is a standing explanation of the failure. There was no possible way of becoming connected on equal terms with a confederacy excepting through membership in a gens and tribe, and a common speech.

It may here be remarked, parenthetically, that it was impossible in the Lower, in the Middle, or in the Upper Status of barbarism for a kingdom to arise by natural growth in any part of the earth under gentile institutions. I venture to make this suggestion at this early stage of the discussion in order to call attention more closely to the structure and principles of ancient society, as organized in gentes, phratries and tribes. Monarchy is incompatible with gentilism. It belongs to the later period of civilization. Despotisms appeared in some instances among the Grecian tribes in the Upper Status of barbarism; but they were founded upon usurpation, were considered illegitimate by the people, and were, in fact, alien to the ideas of gentile society. The Grecian tyrannies were despotisms founded upon usurpation, and were the germ out of which the later kingdoms arose; while the so-called kingdoms of the heroic age were military democracies, and nothing more.

The Iroquois have furnished an excellent illustration of the manner in which a confederacy is formed by natural growth assisted by skillful legislation. Originally emigrants from beyond the Mississippi, and probably a branch of the Dakota stock, they first made their way

---

1 They were admitted into the Creek Confederacy after their overthrow by the French.

to the valley of the St. Lawrence and settled themselves near Montreal. Forced to leave this region by the hostility of surrounding tribes, they sought the central region of New York. Coasting the eastern shore of Lake Ontario in canoes, for their numbers were small, they made their first settlement at the mouth of the Oswego river, where, according to their traditions, they remained for a long period of time. They were then in at least three distinct tribes, the Mohawks, the Onondagas, and the Senecas. One tribe subsequently established themselves at the head of the Canandaigua lake and became the Senecas. Another tribe occupied the Onondaga Valley and became the Onondagas. The third passed eastward and settled first at Oneida near the site of Utica, from which place the main portion removed to the Mohawk Valley and became the Mohawks. Those who remained became the Oneidas. A portion of the Onondagas or Senecas settled along the eastern shore of the Cayuga lake and became the Cayugas. New York, before its occupation by the Iroquois, seems to have been a part of the area of the Algonkin tribes. According to Iroquois traditions they displaced its anterior inhabitants as they gradually extended their settlements eastward to the Hudson, and westward to the Genesee. Their traditions further declare that a long period of time elapsed after their settlement in New York before the confederacy was formed, during which they made common cause against their enemies and thus experienced the advantages of the federal principle both for aggression and defense. They resided in villages, which were usually surrounded with stockades, and subsisted upon fish and game, and the products of a limited horticulture. In numbers they did not at any time exceed 20,000 souls, if they ever reached that number. Precarious subsistence and incessant warfare repressed numbers in all the aboriginal tribes, including the Village Indians as well. The Iroquois were enshrouded in the great forests, which then overspread New York, against which they had no power to contend. They were first discovered A. D. 1608. About 1675, they attained their culminating point when their dominion reached over an area remarkably large, covering the greater parts of New York, Pennsylvania and Ohio,[1] and portions of Canada north of Lake Ontario. At the time of their discovery, they were the highest representatives of the Red Race north of New Mexico in intelligence and advancement, though perhaps inferior to some of the Gulf tribes in the arts of life. In the extent and quality of their mental endowments they must be ranked among the highest Indians in America. Although they have declined in numbers there are still four thousand Iroquois in New York, about a thousand in Canada, and near that number in the West; thus illustrating the efficiency as well as persistency of the arts of barbarous life in sustaining existence. It is now said that they are slowly increasing.

When the confederacy was formed, about A. D. 1400-1450,[2] the conditions previously named were present. The Iroquois were in five independent tribes, occupied territories contiguous to each other, and spoke dialects of the same language which were mutually intelligible. Beside these facts certain gentes were common in the several tribes as has been shown. In their relations to each other, as separated parts of the same gens, these common gentes afforded a natural and enduring basis for a confederacy. With these elements existing, the formation of a confederacy became a question of intelligence and skill. Other tribes in large numbers were standing in precisely the same relations in different parts of the continent without confederating. The fact that the Iroquois tribes accomplished the work affords evidence of their superior capacity. Moreover, as the confederacy was the ultimate stage of organization among the American aborigines its existence would be expected in the most intelligent tribes only.

1 About 1651-5, they expelled their kindred tribes, the Eries, from the region between the Genesee river and Lake Erie, and shortly afterwards the Neutral Nations from the Niagara river, and thus came into possession of the remainder of New York, with the exception of the lower Hudson and Long Island.

2 The Iroquois claimed that it had existed from one hundred and fifty to two hundred years when they first saw Europeans. The generations of sachems in the history by David Cusik (a Tuscarora) would make it more ancient.

It is affirmed by the Iroquois that the confederacy was formed by a council of wise-men and chiefs of the five tribes which met for that purpose on the north shore of Onondaga lake, near the site of Syracuse; and that before its session was concluded the organization was perfected, and set in immediate operation. At their periodical councils for raising up sachems they still explain its origin as the result of one protracted effort of legislation. It was probably a consequence of a previous alliance for mutual defense, the advantages of which they had perceived and which they sought to render permanent.

The origin of the plan is ascribed to a mythical, or, at least, traditionary person, *Hä-yo-went'-hä,* the Hiawatha of Longfellow's celebrated poem, who was present at this council and the central person in its management. In his communications with the council he used a wise-man of the Onondagas, *Da-gä-no-we'-dä,* as an interpreter and speaker to expound the structure and principles of the proposed confederacy. The same tradition further declares that when the work was accomplished *Hä-yo-went'-hä* miraculously disappeared in a white canoe, which arose with him in the air and bore him out of their sight. Other prodigies, according to this tradition, attended and signalized the formation of the confederacy, which is still celebrated among them as a masterpiece of Indian wisdom. Such in truth it was; and it will remain in history as a monument of their genius in developing gentile institutions. It will also be remembered as an illustration of what tribes of mankind have been able to accomplish in the art of government while in the Lower Status of barbarism, and under the disadvantages this condition implies.

Which of the two persons was the founder of the confederacy it is difficult to determine. The silent *Hä-yo-went'-hä* was, not unlikely, a real person of Iroquois lineage;[1] but tradition has enveloped his character so

---

1 My friend, Horatio Hale, the eminent philologist, came, as he informed me, to this conclusion.

completely in the supernatural that he loses his place among them as one of their number. If Hiawatha were a real person, *Da-gä-no-we'-dä* must hold a subordinate place; but, if a mythical person invoked for the occasion, then to the latter belongs the credit of planning the confederacy.

The Iroquois affirm that the confederacy as formed by this council, with its powers, functions and mode of administration, has come down to them through many generations to the present time with scarcely a change in its internal organization. When the Tuscaroras were subsequently admitted, their sachems were allowed by courtesy to sit as equals in the general council, but the original number of sachems was not increased, and in strictness those of the Tuscaroras formed no part of the ruling body.

The general features of the Iroquois Confederacy may be summarized in the following propositions:

I. The confederacy was a union of Five Tribes, composed of common gentes, under one government on the basis of equality; each Tribe remaining independent in all manners pertaining to local self-government.

II. It created a General Council of Sachems, who were limited in number, equal in rank and authority, and invested with supreme powers over all matters pertaining to the Confederacy.

III. Fifty Sachemships were created and named in perpetuity in certain gentes of the several Tribes; with power in these gentes to fill vacancies, as often as they occurred, by election from among their respective members, and with the further power to depose from office for cause; but the right to invest these Sachems with office was reserved to the General Council.

IV. The Sachems of the Confederacy were also Sachems in their respective Tribes, and with the Chiefs of these Tribes formed the Council of each, which was supreme over all matters pertaining to the Tribe exclusively.

V. Unanimity in the Council of the Confederacy was made essential to every public act.

VI. In the General Council the Sachems voted by Tribes, which gave to each Tribe a negative upon the others.

VII. The Council of each Tribe had power to convene the General Council; but the latter had no power to convene itself.

VIII. The General Council was open to the orators of the people for the discussion of public questions; but the Council alone decided.

IX. The Confederacy had no chief Executive Magistrate, or official head.

X. Experiencing the necessity for a General Military Commander they created the office in a dual form, that one might neutralize the other. The two principal War-chiefs created were made equal in powers.

These several propositions will be considered and illustrated, but without following the precise form or order in which they are stated.

At the institution of the confederacy fifty permanent sachemships were created and named, and made perpetual in the gentes to which they were assigned. With the exception of two, which were filled but once, they have been held by as many different persons in succession as generations have passed away between that time and the present. The name of each sachemship is also the personal name of each sachem while he holds the office, each one in succession taking the name of his predecessor. These sachems, when in session, formed the council of the confederacy in which the legislative, executive, and judicial powers were vested, although such a discrimination of functions had not come to be made. To secure order in succession, the several gentes in which these offices were made hereditary were empowered to elect successors from among their respective members when vacancies occurred, as elsewhere explained. As a further measure of protection to their own body each sachem, after his election and its confirmation, was invested with his office by a council of the confederacy. When thus installed his name was "taken away" and that of the sachemship was bestowed upon him. By this name he was afterwards known among them. They were all upon equality in rank, authority, and privileges.

These sachemships were distributed unequally among the five tribes; but without giving to either a preponderance of power; and unequally among the gentes of the last three tribes. The Mohawks had nine sachems, the Oneidas nine, the Onondagas fourteen, the Cayugas ten, and the Senecas eight. This was the number at first, and it has remained the number to the present time. A table of these sachemships is subjoined, with their names in the Seneca dialect, and their arrangement in classes to facilitate the attainment of unanimity in council. In foot-notes will be found the signification of these names, and the gentes to which they belonged.

Table of sachemships of the Iroquois, founded at the institution of the Confederacy; with the names which have been borne by their sachems in succession, from its formation to the present time:

Mohawks.

I, 1. Da-gä-e'-o-gă.[1] 2. Hä-yo-went'-hä.[2] 3. Da-gä-no-we'-dä.[3]

II. 4. So-ä-e-wä'ah.[4] 5. Da-yo'-ho-go.[5] 6. O-ä-ä'-go-wä.[6]

III. 7. Da-an-no-gä'-e-neh.[7] 8. Sä-da'-gä-e-wä-deh.[8] 9. Häs-dä-weh'-se-ont-hä.[9]

Oneidas.

I. Ho-däs'-hä-teh.[10] 2. Ga-no-gweh'-yo-do.[11] 3. Da-yo-hä-gwen-da.[12]

II. 4. So-no-sase'.[13]. 5. To-no-ä-gă'-o.[14] 6. Hä-de-ä-dun-nent'-hä.[15]

III. 7. Da-wä-dä'-o-dä-yo.[16] 8. Gä-ne-ä-dus'-ha-yeh.[17]

---

1 These names signify as follows: 1. "Neutral," or "the Shield." 2. "Man who Combs." 3. "Inexhaustible." 4. "Small Speech." 5. "At the Forks." 6. "At the Great River." 7. "Dragging his Horns." 8. "Even-Tempered." 9. "Hanging up Rattles." The sachems in class one belonged to the Turtle gens, in class two to the Wolf gens, and in class three to the Bear gens.

10. "A Man bearing a Burden." 11. "A Man covered with Cat-tail Down." 12. "Opening through the Woods." 13. "A Long String." 14. "A Man with a Headache." 15. "Swallowing Himself." 16. "Place of the Echo." 17. "War-club on the

9. Ho-wus′-hä-da-o.[18]

Onondagas.

I. 1. To-do-dä′-ho.[19] 2. To-nes′-sa-ah. 3. Da-ät-ga-dose.[20]
II. 4. Gä-neä-dä′-je-wake[21] 5. Ah-wä′-ga-yat.[22] 6. Da-ä-yat′-gwä-e.
III. 7. Ho-no-we-nă′-to.[23]
IV. 8. Gä-wă-nă′-san-do.[1] 9. Hä-e′-ho.[2] 10. Ho-yo-ne-ä′-ne.[3] 11. Sa-dä′-kwä-seh.[4]
V. 12. Sä-go-ga-hä′.[5] 13. Ho-sa-hä′-ho.[6] 14. Skä-no′-wun-de.[7]

Cayugas.

I. 1. Da-gä′-ă-yo.[8] 2. Da-je-no′dä-weh-o.[9] 3. Gä-dä′-gwä-sa.[10] 4. So-yo-wasé.[11] 5. Hä-de-äs′-yo-no.[12]
II. 6. Da-yo-o-yo′-go.[13] 7. Jote-ho-weh′-ko.[14] 8. De-ä-wate′-ho.[15]
III. 9. To-dä-e-ho′.[16] 10. Des-gä′-heh.[17]

Senecas.

I. 1. Ga-ne-o-di′-yo.[18] 2. Sä-dä-gä′-o-yase.[19]
II. 3. Gä-no-gi′-e.[20] 4. Sä-geh′-jo-wä.[21]
III. 5. Sä-de-a-no′-wus.[22] 6. Nis-hä-ne-a′-nent.[23]
IV. 7. Gä-no-go-e-dä′-we.[24] 8. Do-ne-ho-gä′-weh.[25]

Two of these sachemships have been filled but once since their creation. *Hä-yo-went′-hä* and *Da-ga-no-we′-*

Ground." 18. "A Man Steaming Himself." The sachems in the first class belong to the Wolf gens, in the second to the Turtle gens, and in the third to the Bear gens.

19. "Tangled," Bear gens. 20. "On the Watch," Bear gens. This sachem and the one before him, were hereditary councilors of the To-do-dä′-ho, who held the most illustrious sachemship. 21. "Bitter Body," Snipe gens. 22. Turtle gens. 23. This sachem was hereditary keeper of the wampum; Wolf gens.

1. Deer gens. 2. Deer gens. 3. Turtle gens. 4. Bear gens. 5. "Having a Glimpse," Deer gens. 6. "Large Mouth," Turtle gens. 7. "Over the Creek," Turtle gens.

8. "Man Frightened," Deer gens. 9. Heron gens. 10. Bear gens. 11. Bear gens. 12. Turtle gens. 13. Not ascertained. 14. "Very Cold," Turtle gens. 15. Heron gens. 16. Snipe gens. 17. Snipe gens.

18. "Handsome Lake," Turtle gens. 19. "Level Heavens," Snipe gens. 20. Turtle gens. 21. "Great Forehead," Hawk gens. 22. "Assistant," Bear gens. 23. "Falling Day," Snipe gens. 24. "Hair Burned Off," Snipe gens. 25. "Open Door," Wolf gens.

da consented to take the office among the Mohawk sachems, and to leave their names in the list upon condition that after their demise the two should remain thereafter vacant. They were installed upon these terms, and the stipulation has been observed to the present day. At all councils for the investiture of sachems their names are still called with the others as a tribute of respect to their memory. The general council, therefore, consisted of but forty-eight members.

Each sachem had an assistant sachem, who was elected by the gens of his principal from among its members, and who was installed with the same forms and ceremonies. He was styled an "aid." It was his duty to stand behind his superior on all occasions of ceremony, to act as his messenger, and in general to be subject to his directions. It gave to the aid the office of chief, and rendered probable his election as the successor of his principal after the decease of the latter. In their figurative language these aids of the sachems were styled "Braces in the Long House," which symbolized the confederacy.

The names bestowed upon the original sachems became the names of their respective successors in perpetuity. For example, upon the demise of *Gä-ne-o-di'-yo,* one of the eight Seneca sachems, his successor would be elected by the Turtle gens in which this sachemship was hereditary, and when raised up by the general council he would receive this name, in place of his own, as a part of the ceremony. On several different occasions I have attended their councils for raising up sachems both at the Onondaga and Seneca reservations, and witnessed the ceremonies herein referred to. Although but a shadow of the old confederacy now remains, it is fully organized with its complement of sachems and aids, with the exception of the Mohawk tribe which removed to Canada about 1775. Whenever vacancies occur their places are filled, and a general council is convened to install the new sachems and their aids. The present Iroquois are also perfectly familiar with the structure and principles of the ancient confederacy.

For all purposes of tribal government the five tribes were independent of each other. Their territories were separated by fixed boundary lines, and their tribal interests were distinct. The eight Seneca sachems, in conjunction with the other Seneca chiefs, formed the council of the tribe by which its affairs were administered, leaving to each of the other tribes the same control over their separate interests. As an organization the tribe was neither weakened nor impaired by the confederate compact. Each was in vigorous life within its appropriate sphere, presenting some analogy to our own states within an embracing republic. It is worthy of remembrance that the Iroquois commended to our forefathers a union of the colonies similar to their own as early as 1755. They saw in the common interests and common speech of the several colonies the elements for a confederation, which was as far as their vision was able to penetrate.

The tribes occupied positions of entire equality in the confederacy, in rights, privileges and obligations. Such special immunities as were granted to one or another indicate no intention to establish an unequal compact, or to concede unequal privileges. There were organic provisions apparently investing particular tribes with superior power; as, for example, the Onondagas were allowed fourteen sachems and the Senecas but eight; and a larger body of sachems would naturally exercise a stronger influence in council than a smaller. But in this case it gave no additional power, because the sachems of each tribe had an equal voice in forming a decision, and a negative upon the others. When in council they agreed by tribes, and unanimity in opinion was essential to every public act. The Onondagas were made "Keepers of the Wampum," and "Keepers of the Council Brand," the Mohawks, "Receivers of Tribute" from subjugated tribes, and the Senecas "Keepers of the Door" of the Long House. These and some other similar provisions were made for the common advantage.

The cohesive principle of the confederacy did not spring exclusively from the benefits of an alliance for mutual protection, but had a deeper foundation in the bond of kin. The confederacy rested upon the tribes ostensibly, but primarily upon common gentes. All the members of the same gens, whether Mohawks, Oneidas, Onondagas, Cayugas, or Senecas, were brothers and sisters to each other in virtue of their descent from the same common ancestor; and they recognized each other as such with the fullest cordiality. When they met the first inquiry was the name of each other's gens, and next the immediate pedigree of their respective sachems; after which they were usually able to find, under their peculiar system of consanguinity, [2] the relationship in which they stood to each other. Three of the gentes, namely, the Wolf, Bear and Turtle, were common to the five tribes; these and three others were common to three tribes. In effect the Wolf gens, through the division of an original tribe into five, was now in five divisions, one of which was in each tribe. It was the same with the Bear and the Turtle gentes. The Deer, Snipe and Hawk gentes were common to the Senecas, Cayugas and Onondagas. Between the separated parts of each gens, although its members spoke different dialects of the same language, there existed a fraternal connection which linked the nations together with indissoluble bonds. When the Mohawk of the Wolf gens recognized an Oneida, Onondaga, Cayuga or Seneca of the same gens as a brother, and when the members of the other divided gentes did the same, the relationship was not ideal, but a fact founded upon consanguinity, and upon faith in an assured lineage older than their dialects and coeval with their unity as one people. In the estimation of an Iroquois every member of his gens in whatever tribe was as certainly a kinsman as an own brother. This cross-relationship between persons of the same gens in the different tribes is

1 The children of brothers are themselves brothers and sisters to each other, the children of the latter were also brothers and sisters, and so downwards indefinitely; the children and descendants of sisters are the same. The children of a brother and sister are cousins, the children of the latter are cousins, and so downwards indefinitely. A knowledge of the relationships to each other of the members of the same gens is never lost

still preserved and recognized among them in all its original force. It explains the tenacity with which the fragments of the old confederacy still cling together. If either of the five tribes had seceded from the confederacy it would have severed the bond of kin, although this would have been felt but slightly. But had they fallen into collision it would have turned the gens of the Wolf against their gentile kindred, Bear against Bear, in a word brother against brother. The history of the Iroquois demonstrates the reality as well as persistency of the bond of kin, and the fidelity with which it was respected. During the long period through which the confederacy endured, they never fell into anarchy, nor ruptured the organization.

The "Long House" (*Ho-de'-no-sote*) was made the symbol of the confederacy; and they styled themselves the "People of the Long House" (*Ho-de'-no-sau-nee*). This was the name, and the only name, with which they distinguished themselves. The confederacy produced a gentile society more complex than that of a single tribe, but it was still distinctively a gentile society. It was, however, a stage of progress in the direction of a nation, for nationality is reached under gentile institutions. Coalescence is the last stage in this process. The four Athenian tribes coalesced in Attica into a nation by the intermingling of the tribes in the same area, and by the gradual disappearance of geographical lines between them. The tribal names and organizations remained in full vitality as before, but without the basis of an independent territory. When political society was instituted on the basis of the deme or township, and all the residents of the deme became a body politic, irrespective of their gens or tribe, the coalescence became complete.

The coalescence of the Latin and Sabine gentes into the Roman people and nation was a result of the same processes. In all alike the gens, phratry and tribe were the first three stages of organization. The confederacy followed as the fourth. But it does not appear, either among the Grecian or Latin tribes in the Later Period of barbarism, that it became more than a loose league for offensive and defensive purposes. Of the nature and details of organization of the Grecian and Latin confederacies our knowledge is limited and imperfect, because the facts are buried in the obscurity of the traditionary period. The process of coalescence arises later than the confederacy in gentile society; but it was a necessary as well as vital stage of progress by means of which the nation, the state, and political society were at last attained. Among the Iroquois tribes it had not manifested itself.

The valley of Onondaga, as the seat of the central tribe, and the place where the Council Brand was supposed to be perpetually burning, was the usual though not the exclusive place for holding the councils of the confederacy. In ancient times it was summoned to convene in the autumn of each year; but public exigencies often rendered its meetings more frequent. Each tribe had power to summon the council, and to appoint the time and place of meeting at the council-house of either tribe, when circumstances rendered a change from the usual place at Onondaga desirable. But the council had no power to convene itself.

Originally the principal object of the council was to raise up sachems to fill vacancies in the ranks of the ruling body occasioned by death or deposition; but it transacted all other business which concerned the common welfare. In course of time, as they multiplied in numbers and their intercourse with foreign tribes became more extended, the council fell into three distinct kinds, which may be distinguished as Civil, Mourning and Religious. The first declared war and made peace, sent and received embassies, entered into treaties with foreign tribes, regulated the affairs of subjugated tribes, and took all needful measures to promote the general welfare. The second raised up sachems and invested them with office. It received the name of Mourning Council because the first of its ceremonies was the lament for the deceased ruler whose vacant place was to be filled. The third was held for the observance of a general religious festival. It was made an occasion for the confederated tribes to unite under the auspices of a general council in the observance of common religious rites. But as the Mourning Council was attended with many of the same ceremonies it came, in time, to answer for both. It is now the only council they hold, as the civil powers of the confederacy terminated with the supremacy over them of the state.

Invoking the patience of the reader, it is necessary to enter into some details with respect to the mode of transacting business at the Civil and Mourning Councils. In no other way can the archaic condition of society under gentile institutions be so readily illustrated.

If an overture was made to the confederacy by a foreign tribe, it might be done through either of the five tribes. It was the prerogative of the council of the tribe addressed to determine whether the affair was of sufficient importance to require a council of the confederacy. After reaching an affirmative conclusion, a herald was sent to the nearest tribes in position, on the east and on the west, with a belt of wampum, which contained a message to the effect that a civil council (*Ho-de-os'-seh*) would meet at such a place and time, and for such an object, each of which was specified. It was the duty of the tribe receiving the message to forward it to the tribe next in position, until the notification was made complete.[1] No council ever assembled unless it was summoned under the prescribed forms.

---

1 A civil council, which might be called by either nation, was usually summoned and opened in the following manner: If, for example, the Onondagas made the call, they would send heralds to the Oneidas on the east, and the Cayugas on the west of them, with belts containing an invitation to meet at the Onondaga council-grove on such a day of such a moon, for purposes which were also named. It would then become the duty of the Cayugas to send the same notification to the Senecas, and of the Oneidas to notify the Mohawks. If the council was to meet for peaceful purposes, then each sachem was to bring with him a bundle of fagots of white cedar, typical of peace; if for warlike objects then the fagots were to be of red cedar, emblematical of war.

At the day appointed the sachems of the several nations, with their followers, who usually arrived a day or two before and remained encamped at a distance, were received in a formal manner by the Onondaga sachems at the rising of the sun. They marched in separate processions from their camps to the council-grove, each bearing his skin robe and bundle

When the sachems met in council, at the time and place appointed, and the usual reception ceremony had been performed, they arranged themselves in two divisions and seated themselves upon opposite sides of the council-fire. Upon one side were the Mohawk, Onondaga and Seneca sachems. The tribes they represented

---

of fagots, where the Onondaga sachems awaited them with a concourse of people. The sachems then formed themselves into a circle, an Onondaga sachem, who by appointment acted as master of the ceremonies, occupying the side toward the rising sun. At a signal they marched round the circle moving by the north. It may be here observed that the rim of the circle toward the north is called the "cold side," (o-to'-wa-ga); that on the west "the side toward the setting sun," (ha-gă-kwäs'-gwä); that on the south "the side of the high sun," (en-de-ih'-kwä); and that on the east "the side of the rising sun," (t'-kă-gwit-käs'-gwä). After marching three times around on the circle single file, the head and foot of the columm being joined, the leader stopped on the rising sun side, and deposited before him his bundle of fagots. In this he was followed by the others, one at a time, following by the north, thus forming an inner circle of fagots. After this each sachem spread his skin robe in the same order, and sat down upon it, cross-legged, behind his bundle of fagots, with his assistant sachem standing behind him. The master of the ceremonies, after a moment's pause, arose, drew from his pouch two pieces of dry wood and a piece of punk with which he proceeded to strike fire by friction. When fire was thus obtained, he stepped within the circle and set fire to his own bundle, and then to each of the others in the order in which they were laid. When they were well ignited, and at a signal from the master of the ceremonies, the sachems arose and marched three times around the Burning Circle, going as before by the north. Each turned from time to time as he walked, so as to expose all sides of his person to the warming influence of the fires. This typified that they warmed their affections for each other in order that they might transact the business of the council in friendship and unity. They then reseated themselves each upon his own robe. After this the master of the ceremonies again rising to his feet, filled and lighted the pipe of peace from his own fire. Drawing three whiffs, one after the other, he blew the first toward the zenith, the second toward the ground, and the third toward the sun. By the first act he returned thanks to the Great Spirit for the preservation of his life during the past year, and for being permitted to be present at this council. By the second, he returned thanks to his Mother, the Earth, for her various productions which had ministered to his sustenance. And by the third, he returned thanks to the Sun for his never-failing light, ever shining upon all. These words were not repeated, but such is the purport of the acts themselves. He then passed the pipe to the first upon his right toward the north, who repeated the same ceremonies, and then passed it to the next, and so on around the burning circle. The ceremony of smoking the calumet also signified that they pledged to each other their faith, their friendship, and their honor.

These ceremonies completed the opening of the council, which was then declared to be ready for the business upon which it had been convened.

were, when in council, brother tribes to each other and father tribes to the other two. In like manner their sachems were brothers to each other and fathers to those opposite. They constituted a phratry of tribes and of sachems, by an extension of the principle which united gentes in a phratry. On the opposite side of the fire were the Oneida and Cayuga, and, at a later day, the Tuscarora sachems. The tribes they represented were brother tribes to each other, and son tribes to the opposite three. Their sachems also were brothers to each other, and sons of those in the opposite division. They formed a second tribal phratry. As the Oneidas were a subdivision of the Mohawks, and the Cayugas a subdivision of the Onondagas or Senecas, they were in reality junior tribes; whence their relation of seniors and juniors, and the application of the phratric principle. When the tribes are named in council the Mohawks by precedence are mentioned first. Their tribal epithet was "The Shield" (*Da-gä-e-o'-dä*). The Onondagas came next under the epithet of "Name-Bearer" (*Ho-de-san-no'-ge-tä*), because they had been appointed to select and name the fifty original sachems.[1] Next in the order of precedence were the Senecas, under the epithet of "Door-Keeper" (*Ho-nan-ne-ho'-onte*). They were made perpetual keepers of the western door of the Long House. The Oneidas, under the epithet of "Great Tree" (*Ne-ar'-de-on-dar'-go-war*), and the Cayugas, under that of "Great Pipe" (*Sonus'-ho-gwar-to-war*), were named fourth and fifth. The Tuscaroras, who came late into the confederacy, were named last, and had no distinguishing epithet. Forms, such as these, were more important in ancient society than we would be apt to suppose.

It was customary for the foreign tribe to be represented at the council by a delegation of wise-men and chiefs, who bore their proposition and presented it in

---

1 Tradition declares that the Onondagas deputed a wise-man to visit the territories of the tribes and select and name the new sachems as circumstances should prompt; which explains the unequal distribution of the office among the several gentes.

person. After the council was formally opened and the delegation introduced, one of the sachems made a short address, in the course of which he thanked the Great Spirit for sparing their lives and permitting them to meet together; after which he informed the delegation that the council was prepared to hear them upon the affair for which it had convened. One of the delegates then submitted their proposition in form, and sustained it by such arguments as he was able to make. Careful attention was given by the members of the council that they might clearly comprehend the matter in hand. After the address was concluded, the delegation withdrew from the council to await at a distance the result of its deliberations. It then became the duty of the sachems to agree upon an answer, which was reached through the ordinary routine of debate and consultation. When a decision had been made, a speaker was appointed to communicate the answer of the council, to receive which the delegation were recalled. The speaker was usually chosen from the tribe at whose instance the council had been convened. It was customary for him to review the whole subject in a formal speech, in the course of which the acceptance, in whole or in part, or the rejection of the proposition were announced with the reasons therefor. Where an agreement was entered upon, belts of wampum were exchanged as evidence of its terms. With these proceedings the council terminated.

"This belt preserves my words" was a common remark of an Iroquois chief in council. He then delivered the belt as the evidence of what he had said. Several such belts would be given in the course of a negotiation to the opposite party. In the reply of the latter a belt would be returned for each proposition accepted. The Iroquois experienced the necessity for an exact record of some kind of a proposition involving their faith and honor in its execution, and they devised this method to place it beyond dispute.

Unanimity among the sachems was required upon all public questions, and essential to the validity of every public act. It was a fundamental law of the confederacy.[1] They adopted a method for ascertaining the opinions of the members of the council which dispensed with the necessity of casting votes. Moreover, they were entirely unacquainted with the principle of majorities and minorities in the action of councils. They voted in council by tribes, and the sachems of each tribe were required to be of one mind to form a decision, Recognizing unanimity as a necessary principle, the founders of the confederacy divided the sachems of each tribe into classes as a means for its attainment. This will be seen by consulting the table, (*supra* p. 132.) No sachem was allowed to express an opinion in council in the nature of a vote until he had first agreed with the sachem or sachems of his class upon the opinion to be expressed, and had been appointed to act as speaker for the class. Thus the eight Seneca sachems being in four classes could have but four opinions, and the ten Cayuga sachems, being in the same number of classes, could have but four. In this manner the sachems in each class were first brought to unanimity among themselves. A cross-consultation was then held between the four sachems appointed to speak for the four classes; and when they had agreed, they designated one of their number to express their resulting opinion, which was the answer of their tribe. When the sachems of the several tribes had, by this ingenious method, become of one mind separately, it remained to compare their several opinions, and if they agreed the decision of the council was made. If they failed of agreement the measure was defeated, and the council was at an end. The five persons appointed to express the decision of the five tribes may possibly

---

1 At the beginning of the American revolution the Iroquois were unable to agree upon a declaration of war against our confederacy for want of unanimity in council. A number of the Oneida sachems resisted the proposition and finally refused their consent. As neutrality was impossible with the Mohawks and the Senecas were determined to fight, it was resolved that each tribe might engage in the war upon its own responsibility, or remain neutral. The war against the Eries, against the Neutral Nation and Susquehannocks, and the several wars against the French, were resolved upon in general council. Our colonial records are largely filled with negotiations with the Iroquois Confederacy.

explain the appointment and the functions of the six electors, so called, in the Aztec confederacy, which will be noticed elsewhere.

By this method of gaining assent the equality and independence of the several tribes were recognized and preserved. If any sachem was obdurate or unreasonable, influences were brought to bear upon him, through the preponderating sentiment, which he could not well resist; so that it seldom happened that inconvenience or detriment resulted from their adherence to the rule. Whenever all efforts to procure unanimity had failed, the whole matter was laid aside because further action had become impossible.

The induction of new sachems into office was an event of great interest to the people, and not less to the sachems who retained thereby some control over the introduction of new members into their body. To perform the ceremony of raising up sachems the general council was primarily instituted. It was named at the time, or came afterwards to be called, the Mourning Council (*Hen-nun-do-nuh'-seh*), because it embraced the twofold object of lamenting the death of the departed sachem and of installing his successor. Upon the death of a sachem, the tribe in which the loss had occurred had power to summon a general council, and to name the time and place of its meeting. A herald was sent out with a belt of wampum, usually the official belt of the deceased sachem given to him at his installation, which conveyed this laconic message,—"the name" (mentioning that of the late ruler) "calls for a council." It also announced the day and place of convocation. In some cases the official belt of the sachem was sent to the central council-fire at Onondaga immediately after his burial, as a notification of his demise, and the time for holding the council was determined afterwards.

The Mourning Council, with the festivities which followed the investiture of sachems possessed remarkable attractions for the Iroquois. They flocked to its attendance from the most distant localities with zeal and enthusiasm. It was opened and conducted with many forms and ceremonies, and usually lasted five days. The first was devoted to the prescribed ceremony of lamentations for the deceased sachem, which, as a religious act, commenced at the rising of the sun. At this time the sachems of the tribe, with whom the council was held, marched out followed by their tribesmen, to receive formally the sachems and people of the other tribes, who had arrived before and remained encamped at some distance waiting for the appointed day. After exchanging greetings, a procession was formed and the lament was chanted in verse, with responses, by the united tribes, as they marched from the place of reception to the place of council. The lament, with the responses in chorus, was a tribute of respect to the memory of the departed sachem, in which not only his gens, but his tribe, and the confederacy itself participated. It was certainly a more delicate testimonial of respect and affection than would have been expected from a barbarous people. This ceremonial, with the opening of the council, concluded the first day's proceedings. On the second day, the installation ceremony commenced, and it usually lasted into the fourth. The sachems of the several tribes seated themselves in two divisions, as at the civil council. When the sachem to be raised up belonged to either of the three senior tribes the ceremony was performed by the sachems of the junior tribes, and the new sachem was installed as a father. In like manner, if he belonged to either of the three junior tribes the ceremony was performed by the sachems of the senior tribes, and the new sachem was installed as a son. These special circumstances are mentioned to show the peculiar character of their social and governmental life. To the Iroquois these forms and figures of speech were full of significance.

Among other things, the ancient wampum belts, into which the structure and principles of the confederacy "had been talked," to use their expression, were produced and read or interpreted for the instruction of the newly inducted sachem. A wise-man, not necessarily one of the sachems, took these belts one after the other and walking to and fro between the two divisions of sachems, read from them the facts which they recorded. According to the Indian conception, these belts can tell, by means of an interpreter, the exact rule, provision or transaction talked into them at the time, and of which they were the exclusive record. A strand of wampum consisting of strings of purple and white shell beads, or a belt woven with figures formed by beads of different colors, operated on the principle of associating a particular fact with a particular string or figure; thus giving a serial arrangement to the facts as well as fidelity to the memory. These strands and belts of wampum were the only visible records of the Iroquois; but they required those trained interpreters who could draw from their strings and figures the records locked up in their remembrance. One of the Onondaga sachems (Ho-no-we-nă'-to) was made "Keeper of the Wampum," and two aids were raised up with him who were required to be versed in its interpretation as well as the sachem. The interpretation of these several belts and strings brought out, in the address of the wise-man, a connected account of the occurrences at the formation of the confederacy. The tradition was repeated in full, and fortified in its essential parts by reference to the record contained in these belts. Thus the council to raise up sachems became a teaching council, which maintained in perpetual freshness in the minds of the Iroquois the structure and principles of the confederacy, as well as the history of its formation. These proceedings occupied the council until noon each day; the afternoon being devoted to games and amusements. At twilight each day a dinner in common was served to the entire body in attendance. It consisted of soup and boiled meat cooked near the council-house, and served directly from the kettle in wooden bowls, trays and ladles. Grace was said before the feast commenced. It was a prolonged exclamation by a single person on a high shrill note, falling down in cadences into stillness, followed by a response in chorus by the people. The evenings were devoted to the dance. With these ceremonies, continued for several days, and with the festivities that followed, their sachems were inducted into office.

By investing their sachems with office through a general council, the framers of the confederacy had in view the threefold object of a perpetual succession in the gens, the benefits of a free election among its members, and a final supervision of the choice through the ceremony of investiture. To render the latter effective it should carry with it the power to reject the nominee. Whether the right to invest was purely functional, or carried with it the right to exclude, I am unable to state. No case of rejection is mentioned. The scheme adopted by the Iroquois to maintain a ruling body of sachems may claim, in several respects, the merit of originality, as well as of adaptation to their condition. In form an oligarchy, taking this term in its best sense, it was yet a representative democracy of the archaic type. A powerful popular element pervaded the whole organism and influenced its action. It is seen in the right of the gentes to elect and depose their sachems and chiefs, in the right of the people to be heard in council through orators of their own selection, and in the voluntary system in the military service. In this and the next succeeding ethnical period democratic principles were the vital element of gentile society.

The Iroquois name for a sachem (*Ho-yar-na-go'-war*), which signifies "a counselor of the people," was singularly appropriate to a ruler in a species of free democracy. It not only defines the office well, but it also suggests the analogous designation of the members of the Grecian council of chiefs. The Grecian chiefs were styled "councilors of the people." [1] From the nature and tenure of the office among the Iroquois the sachems were not masters ruling by independent right, but representatives holding from the gentes by free election. It is worthy of notice that an office which originated in savagery, and continued through the three sub-periods of bar-

---

1 Æschylus, "The Seven against Thebes," 1005.

barism, should reveal so much of its archaic character among the Greeks after the gentile organization had carried this portion of the human family to the confines of civilization. It shows further how deeply inwrought in the human mind the principle of democracy had become under gentilism.

The designation for a chief of the second grade, *Ha-sa-no-wä'-na,* "an elevated name," indicates an appreciation by barbarians of the ordinary motives for personal ambition. It also reveals the sameness of the nature of man, whether high up or low down upon the rounds of the ladder of progress. The celebrated orators, wisemen, and war-chiefs of the Iroquois were chiefs of the second grade almost without exception. One reason for this may be found in the organic provision which confined the duties of the sachem to the affairs of peace. Another may have been to exclude from the ruling body their ablest men, lest their ambitious aims should disturb its action. As the office of chief was bestowed in reward of merit, it fell necessarily upon their ablest men. Red-Jacket, Brandt, Garangula, Cornplanter, Farmer's Brother, Frost, Johnson, and other well known Iroquois, were chiefs as distinguished from sachems. None of the long lines of sachems have become distinguished in American annals, with the exception of Logan, [1] Handsome Lake,[2] and at a recent day, Ely S. Parker.[3] The remainder have left no remembrance behind them extending beyond the Iroquois.

At the time the confederacy was formed *To-do-dä'-ho* was the most prominent and influential of the Onondaga chiefs. His accession to the plan of a confederacy, in which he would experience a diminution of power, was regarded as highly meritorious. He was raised up as one of the Onondaga sachems and his name placed first in the list. Two assistant sachems were raised up with him to act as his aids and to stand behind him on public

1 One of the Cayuga sachems.

2 One of the Seneca sachems, and the founder of the New Religion of the Iroquois.

3 One of the Seneca sachems.

occasions. Thus dignified, this sachemship has since been regarded by the Iroquois as the most illustrious of the forty-eight, from the services rendered by the first *To-do-dä'-ho.* The circumstance was early seized upon by the inquisitive colonists to advance the person who held this office to the position of king of the Iroquois; but the misconception was refuted, and the institutions of the Iroquois were relieved of the burden of an impossible feature. In the general council he sat among his equals. The confederacy had no chief executive magistrate.

Under a confederacy of tribes the office of general, (*Hos-gä-ä-geh'-da-go-wä*) "Great War Soldier," makes its first appearance. Cases would now arise when the several tribes in their confederate capacity would be engaged in war; and the necessity for a general commander to direct the movements of the united bands would be felt. The introduction of this office as a permanent feature in the government was a great event in the history of human progress. It was the beginning of a differentiation of the military from the civil power, which, when completed, changed essentially the external manifestation of the government. But even in later stages of progress, when the military spirit predominated, the essential character of the government was not changed. Gentilism arrested usurpation. With the rise of the office of general, the government was gradually changed from a government of one power, into a government of two powers. The functions of government became, in course of time, co-ordinated between the two. This new office was the germ of that of a chief executive magistrate; for out of the general came the king, the emperor, and the president, as elsewhere suggested. The office sprang from the military necessities of society, and had a logical development. For this reason its first appearance and subsequent growth have an important place in this discussion. In the course of this volume I shall attempt to trace the progressive development of this office, from the *Great War Soldier* of the Iroquois through the *Teuctli* of the Aztecs, to the *Basileus* of the Grecian, and the *Rex* of the Roman tribes; among all of whom, through three successive ethnical periods, the office was the same, namely, that of a general in a military democracy. Among the Iroquois, the Aztecs, and the Romans the office was elective, or confirmative, by a constituency. Presumptively, it was the same among the Greeks of the traditionary period. It is claimed that the office of *basileus* among the Grecian tribes in the Homeric period was hereditary from father to son. This is at least doubtful. It is such a wide and total departure from the original tenure of the office as to require positive evidence to establish the fact. An election, or confirmation by a constituency, would still be necessary under gentile institutions. If in numerous instances it were known that the office had passed from father to son this might have suggested the inference of hereditary succession, now adopted as historically true, while succession in this form did not exist. Unfortunately, an intimate knowledge of the organization and usages of society in the traditionary period is altogether wanting. Great principles of human action furnish the safest guide when their operation must have been necessary. It is far more probable that hereditary succession, when it first came in, was established by force, than by the free consent of the people; and that it did not exist among the Grecian tribes in the Homeric period.

When the Iroquois confederacy was formed, or soon after that event, two permanent war-chiefships were created and named, and both were assigned to the Seneca tribe. One of them (*Ta-wan'-ne-ars,* signifying needle-breaker) was made hereditary in the Wolf, and the other (*So-no'-so-wä,* signifying great oyster shell) in the Turtle gens. The reason assigned for giving them both to the Senecas was the greater danger of attack at the west end of their territories. They were elected in the same manner as the sachems, were raised up by a general council, and were equal in rank and power. Another account states that they were created later. They discovered immediately after the confederacy was formed that the structure of the Long House was incomplete because there were no officers to execute the military commands of the confederacy. A council was convened to remedy the omission, which established the two perpetual war-chiefs named. As general commanders they had charge of the military affairs of the confederacy, and the command of its joint forces when united in a general expedition. Governor Blacksnake, recently deceased, held the office first named, thus showing that the succession has been regularly maintained. The creation of two principal war-chiefs instead of one, and with equal powers, argues a subtle and calculating policy to prevent the domination of a single man even in their military affairs. They did without experience precisely as the Romans did in creating two consuls instead of one, after they had abolished the office of *rex*. Two consuls would balance the military power between them, and prevent either from becoming supreme. Among the Iroquois this office never became influential.

In Indian Ethnography the subjects of primary importance are the gens, phratry, tribe and confederacy. They exhibit the organization of society. Next to these are the tenure and functions of the office of sachem and chief, the functions of the council of chiefs, and the tenure and functions of the office of principal war-chief. When these are ascertained, the structure and principles of their governmental system will be known. A knowledge of their usages and customs, of their arts and inventions, and of their plan of life will then fill out the picture. In the work of American investigators too little attention has been given to the former. They still afford a rich field in which much information may be gathered. Our knowledge, which is now general, should be made minute and comparative. The Indian tribes in the Lower, and in the Middle Status of barbarism, represent two of the great stages of progress from savagery to civilization. Our own remote forefathers passed through the same conditions, one after the other, and possessed, there can scarcely be a doubt, the same, or very similar institutions, with many of the same usages and customs. However little we may be interested in the American Indians personally, their experience touches us more nearly, as an exemplification of the experience of our own ancestors. Our primary institutions root themselves in a prior gentile society in which the gens, phratry and tribe were the organic series, and in which the council of chiefs was the instrument of government. The phenomena of their ancient society must have presented many points in common with that of the Iroquois and other Indian tribes. This view of the matter lends an additional interest to the comparative institutions of mankind.

The Iroquois confederacy is an excellent exemplification of a gentile society under this form of organization. It seems to realize all the capabilities of gentile institutions in the Lower Status of barbarism; leaving an opportunity for further development, but no subsequent plan of government until the institutions of political society, founded upon territory and upon property, with the establishment of which the gentile organization would be overthrown. The intermediate stages were transitional, remaining military democracies to the end, except where tyrannies founded upon usurpation were temporarily established in their places. The confederacy of the Iroquois was essentially democratical; because it was composed of gentes each of which was organized upon the common principles of democracy, not of the highest but of the primitive type, and because the tribes reserved the right of local self-government. They conquered other tribes and held them in subjection, as for example the Delawares; but the latter remained under the government of their own chiefs, and added nothing to the strength of the confederacy. It was impossible in this state of society to unite tribes under one government who spoke different languages, or to hold conquered tribes under tribute with any benefit but the tribute.

This exposition of the Iroquois confederacy is far from exhaustive of the facts, but it has been carried far enough to answer my present object. The Iroquois were a vigorous and intelligent people, with a brain approaching in volume the Aryan average. Eloquent in oratory, vindictive in war, and indomitable in perseverance, they have gained a place in history. If their military achievements are dreary with the atrocities of savage warfare, they have illustrated some of the highest virtues of mankind in their relations with each other. The confederacy which they organized must be regarded as a remarkable production of wisdom and sagacity. One of its avowed objects was peace; to remove the cause of strife by uniting their tribes under one government, and then extending it by incorporating other tribes of the same name and lineage. They urged the Eries and the Neutral Nation to become members of the confederacy, and for their refusal expelled them from their borders. Such an insight into the highest objects of government is creditable to their intelligence. Their numbers were small, but they counted in their ranks a large number of able men. This proves the high grade of the stock.

From their position and military strength they exercised a marked influence upon the course of events between the English and the French in their competition for supremacy in North America. As the two were nearly equal in power and resources during the first century of colonization, the French may ascribe to the Iroquois, in no small degree, the overthrow of their plans of empire in the New World.

With a knowledge of the gens in its archaic form and of its capabilities as the unit of a social system, we shall be better able to understand the gentes of the Greeks and Romans yet to be considered. The same scheme of government composed of gentes, phratries and tribes in a gentile society will be found among them as they stood at the threshold of civilization, with the superadded experience of two entire ethnical periods. Descent among them was in the male line, property was inherited by the children of the owner instead of the agnatic kindred, and the family was now assuming the monogamian form. The growth of property, now becoming a commanding element, and the increase of numbers gathered in walled cities were slowly demonstrating the necessity for the second great plan of government—the political. The old gentile system was becoming incapable of meeting the requirements of society as it approached civilization. Glimpses of a state, founded upon territory and property, were breaking upon the Grecian and Roman minds before which gentes and tribes were to disappear. To enter upon the second plan of government, it was necessary to supersede the gentes by townships and city wards —the gentile by a territorial system. The going down of the gentes and the uprising of organized townships mark the dividing line, pretty nearly, between the barbarian and the civilized worlds — between ancient and modern society.

CHAPTER VI

GENTES IN OTHER TRIBES OF THE GANOWA'NIAN FAMILY

When America was first discovered in its several regions, the Aborigines were found in two dissimilar conditions. First were the Village Indians, who depended almost exclusively upon horticulture for subsistence; such were the tribes in this status in New Mexico, Mexico and Central America, and upon the plateau of the Andes. Second, were the Non-horticultural Indians, who depended upon fish, bread-roots and game; such were the Indians of the Valley of the Columbia, of the Hudson's Bay Territory, of parts of Canada, and of some other sections of America. Between these tribes, and connecting the extremes by insensible gradations, were the partially Village, and partially Horticultural Indians; such were the Iroquois, the New England and Virginia Indians, the Creeks, Choctas, Cherokees, Minnitarees, Dakotas and Shawnees. The weapons, arts, usages, inventions, dances, house architecture, form of government, and plan of life of all alike bear the impress of a common mind, and reveal, through their wide range, the successive stages of development of the same original conceptions. Our first mistake consisted in overrating the comparative advancement of the Village Indians; and our second in underrating that of the Non-horticultural, and of the partially Village Indians: whence resulted a third, that of separating one from the other and regarding them as different races. There was a marked difference in the conditions in which they were severally found; for a number of the Non-horticultural tribes were in the Upper Status of savagery; the intermediate tribes were in the Lower Status of barbarism, and the Village Indians were in the Middle Status. The evidence of their unity of origin has now accumulated to such a degree as to leave no reasonable doubt upon the question, although this conclusion is not universally accepted. The Eskimos belong to a different family.

In a previous work I presented the system of consanguinity and affinity of some seventy American Indian tribes; and upon the fact of their joint possession of the same system, with evidence of its derivation from a common source, ventured to claim for them the distinctive rank of a family of mankind, under the name of the Ganowánian, the "Family of the Bow and Arrow."[1]

Having considered the attributes of the gens in its archaic form, it remains to indicate the extent of its prevalence in the tribes of the Ganowánian family. In this chapter the organization will be traced among them, confining the statements to the names of the gentes in each tribe, with their rules of descent and inheritance as to property and office. Further explanations will be added when necessary. The main point to be established is the existence or non-existence of the gentile organization among them. Wherever the institution has been found in these several tribes it is the same in all essential respects as the gens of the Iroquois, and therefore needs no further exposition in this connection. Unless the contrary is stated, it may be understood that the existence of the organization was ascertained by the author from the Indian tribe or some of its members. The classification of tribes follows that adopted in "Systems of Consanguinity."

---

1 "Systems of Consanguinity and Affinity of the Human Family." ("Smithsonian Contributions to Knowledge," vol. xvii, 1871, p. 131.)

I. *Hodenosaunian Tribes.*

1. Iroquois. The gentes of the Iroquois have been considered.[1]

2. Wyandotes. This tribe, the remains of the ancient Hurons, is composed of eight gentes, as follows:

1. Wolf. 2. Bear. 3. Beaver. 4. Turtle. 5. Deer. 6. Snake. 7. Porcupine. 8. Hawk.[2]

Descent is in the female fine, with marriage in the gens prohibited. The office of sachem, or civil chief, is hereditary in the gens, but elective among its members. They have seven sachems and seven war-chiefs, the Hawk gens being now extinct. The office of sachem passes from brother to brother, or from uncle to nephew; but that of war-chief was bestowed in reward of merit, and was not hereditary. Property was hereditary in the gens, consequently children took nothing from their father; but they inherited their mother's effects. Where the rule is stated hereafter it will be understood that unmarried as well as married persons are included. Each gens had power to depose as well as elect its chiefs. The Wyandotes have been separated from the Iroquois at least four hundred years; but they still have five gentes in common, although their names have either changed beyond identification, or new names have been substituted by one or the other.

The Eries, Neutral Nation, Nottoways, Tutelos,[3] and Susquehannocks[4] now extinct or absorbed in other tribes, belong to the same lineage. Presumptively they were organized in gentes, but the evidence of the fact is lost.

---

1 1. Wolf, Tor-yoh'-ne. 2. Bear, Ne-e-ar-guy'-ee. 3. Beaver, Non-gar-ne'-e-ar-goh. 4. Turtle, Gä-ne-e-ar-teh-go'-wä. 5. Deer, Nä-o'-geh. 6. Snipe, Doo-eese-doo-we'. 7. Heron, Jo-äs'-seh. 8. Hawk, Os-sweh-gä-dä-gä'-ah.

2 1. Ah-na-rese'-kwä, Bone Gnawers. 2. Ah-nu-yeh', Tree Liver. 3. Tso-tä'-ee, Shy Animal. 4. Ge-ah'-wish, Fine Land. 5. Os-ken'-o-toh, Roaming. 6. Sine-gain'-see, Creeping. 7. Ya-ra-hats'-see, Tall Tree. 8. Dä-soak', Flying.

3 Mr. Horatio Hale has recently proved the connection of the Tutelos with the Iroquois.

4 Mr. Francis Parkman, author of the brilliant series of works on the colonization of America, was the first to establish the affiliation of the Susquehannocks with the Iroquois.

II. *Dakotian Tribes.*

A large number of tribes are included in this great stock of the American aborigines. At the time of their discovery they had fallen into a number of groups, and their language into a number of dialects; but they inhabited, in the main, continuous areas. They occupied the head waters of the Mississippi, and both banks of the Missouri for more than a thousand miles in extent. In all probability the Iroquois, and their cognate tribes, were an offshoot from this stem.

1. Dakotas or Sioux. The Dakotas, consisting at the present time of some twelve independent tribes, have allowed the gentile organization to fall into decadence. It seems substantially certain that they once possessed it because their nearest congeners, the Missouri tribes, are now thus organized. They have societies named after animals analogous to gentes, but the latter are now wanting. Carver, who was among them in 1767, remarks that "every separate body of Indians is divided into bands or tribes; which band or tribe forms a little community within the nation to which it belongs. As the nation has some particular symbol by which it is distinguished from others, so each tribe has a badge from which it is denominated; as that of the eagle, the panther, the tiger, the buffalo, etc. One band of the Naudowissies (Sioux) is represented by a Snake, another a Tortoise, a third a Squirrel, a fourth a Wolf, and a fifth a Buffalo. Throughout every nation they particularize themselves in the same manner, and the meanest person among them will remember his lineal descent, and distinguish himself by his respective family."[1] He visited the eastern Dakotas on the Mississippi. From this specific statement I see no reason to doubt that the gentile organization was then in full vitality among them. When I visited the eastern Dakotas in 1861, and the western in 1862, I could find no satisfactory traces of gentes among them. A change in the mode of life among the Dakotas occurred between these dates when they were forced upon the

---

1 "Travels in North America," Phila. ed., 1796, p. 164.

plains, and fell into nomadic bands, which may, perhaps, explain the decadence of gentilism among them.

Carver also noticed the two grades of chiefs among the western Indians, which have been explained as they exist among the Iroquois. "Every band," he observes, "has a chief who is termed the Great Chief, or the Chief Warrior, and who is chosen in consideration of his experience in war, and of his approved valor, to direct their military operations, and to regulate all concerns belonging to that department. But this chief is not considered the head of the state; besides the great warrior who is elected for his warlike qualifications, there is another who enjoys a pre-eminence as his hereditary right, and has the more immediate management of their civil affairs. This chief might with greater propriety be denominated the sachem; whose assent is necessary to all conveyances and treaties, to which he affixes the mark of the tribe or nation." [1]

2. Missouri tribes. 1. Punkas. This tribe is composed of eight gentes, as follows:

1. Grizzly Bear. 2. Many People. 3. Elk. 4. Skunk. 5. Buffalo. 6. Snake. 7. Medicine. 8. Ice. [2]

In this tribe, contrary to the general rule, descent is in the male line, the children belonging to the gens of their father. Intermarriage in the gens is prohibited. The office of sachem is hereditary in the gens, the choice being determined by election; but the sons of a deceased sachem are eligible. It is probable that the change from the archaic form was recent, from the fact that among the Otoes and Missouris, two of the eight Missouri tribes, and also among the Mandans, descent is still in the female line. Property is hereditary in the gens.

2. Omahas. This tribe is composed of the following twelve gentes:

1. Deer. 2. Black. 3. Bird. 4. Turtle. 5. Buffalo. 6. Bear. 7. Medicine. 8. Kaw. 9. Head. 10. Red. 11. Thunder. 12. Many Seasons. [3]

---

1 "Travels in North America," p. 165.

2 1. Wä-sä'-be. 2. De-a-ghe'-ta. 3. Na-ko-poz'-na. 4. Moh-kuh'. 5. Wä-shä'-ba. 6. Wä-zhä'-zha. 7. Noh'-ga. 8. Wah'-ga.

3 1. Wä'-zhese-ta. 2. Ink-ka'-sa-ba. 3. Lä'-tä-dä. 4. Kä'-ih.

Descent, inheritance, and the law of marriage are the same as among the Punkas.

3. Iowas. In like manner the Iowas have eight gentes, as follows:

1. Wolf. 2. Bear. 3. Cow Buffalo. 4. Elk. 5. Eagle. 6. Pigeon. 7. Snake. 8. Owl.[1]

A gens of the Beaver *Pä-kuh′-thä* once existed among the Iowas and Otoes, but it is now extinct. Descent, inheritance, and the prohibition of intermarriage in the gens are the same as among the Punkas.

4. Otoes and Missouris. These tribes have coalesced into one, and have the eight following gentes:

1. Wolf. 2. Bear. 3. Cow Buffalo. 4. Elk. 5. Eagle. 6. Pigeon. 7. Snake. 8. Owl.[2]

Descent among the Otoes and Missouris is in the female line, the children belonging to the gens of their mother. The office of sachem, and property are hereditary in the gens, in which intermarriage is prohibited.

5. Kaws. The Kaws (Kaw′-ză) have the following fourteen gentes:

1. Deer. 2. Bear. 3. Buffalo. 4. Eagle (white). 5. Eagle (black). 6. Duck. 7. Elk. 8. Raccoon. 9. Prairie Wolf. 10. Turtle. 11. Earth. 12. Deer Tail. 13. Tent. 14. Thunder.[3]

The Kaws are among the wildest of the American aborigines, but are an intelligent and interesting people. Descent, inheritance and marriage regulations among them are the same as among the Punkas. It will be observed that there are two Eagle gentes, and two of the Deer, which afford a good illustration of the segmenta-

---

5. Da-thun′-da. 6. Wä-sä-ba. 7. Hun′-gä. 8. Kun′-zä. 9. Tä′-pä. 10. In-grä′-zhe-da. 11. Ish-dä′-sun-da. 12. O-non-e′-kä-gä-ha.

[1] 1. Me-je′-rä-ja. 2. Too-num′-pe. 3. Ah′-ro-whä. 4. Ho′-dash. 5. Cheh′-he-tä. 6. Lu′-chih. 7. Wä-keeh′. 8. Mä′-kotch.

H represents a deep sonant guttural. It is quite common in the dialects of the Missouri tribes, and also in the Minnitaree and Crow.

[2] 1. Me-je′-rä-ja. 2. Moon′-cha. 3. Ah′-ro-whä. 4. Hoo′-ma. 5. Kha′-ă. 6. Lute′-ja. 7. Wä′-kä. 8. Mä′-kotch.

[3] 1. Tä-we-kä-she′-gä. 2. Sin′-ja-ye-ga. 3. Mo-e′-kwe-ah-hä. 4. Hu-e′-yă. 5. Hun-go-tin′-ga. 6. Me-hä-shun′-gă. 7. O′-pä. 8. Me-kä′. 9. Sh̆o′-ma-koo-sa. 10. Do-hă-kel′-yă. 11. Mo-e′-ka-ne-kä′-she-gä. 12. Dä-sin-ja-hă-gă. 13. Ic′-hä-she. 14. Lo-ne′-kä-she-gä.

tion of a gens; the Eagle gens having probably divided into two and distinguished themselves by the names of white and black. The Turtle will be found hereafter as a further illustration of the same fact. When I visited the Missouri tribes in 1859 and 1860, I was unable to reach the Osages and Quappas. The eight tribes thus named speak closely affiliated dialects of the Dakotian stock language, and the presumption that the Osages and Quappas are organized in gentes is substantially conclusive. In 1869, the Kaws, then much reduced, numbered seven hundred, which would give an average of but fifty persons to a gens. The home country of these several tribes was along the Missouri and its tributaries from the mouth of the Big Sioux river to the Mississippi, and down the west bank of the latter river to the Arkansas.

3. Winnebagoes. When discovered this tribe resided near the lake of their name in Wisconsin. An offshoot from the Dakotian stem, they were apparently following the track of the Iroquois eastward to the valley of the St. Lawrence, when their further progress in that direction was arrested by the Algonkin tribes between Lakes Huron and Superior. Their nearest affiliation is with the Missouri tribes. They have eight gentes as follows:

1. Wolf. 2. Bear. 3. Buffalo. 4. Eagle. 5. Elk. 6. Deer. 7. Snake. 8. Thunder.[1]

Descent, inheritance, and the law of marriage are the same among them as among the Punkas. It is surprising that so many tribes of this stock should have changed descent from the female line to the male, because when first known the idea of property was substantially undeveloped, or but slightly beyond the germinating stage, and could hardly, as among the Greeks and Romans, have been the operative cause. It is probable that it occurred at a recent period under American and missionary influences. Carver found traces of descent in the female line in 1787 among the Winnebagoes. "Some nations,"

[1] 1. Shonk-chun'-ga-dä. 2. Hone-cha'-dä. 3. Cha'-rä. 4. Wahk-cha'-he-dä. 5. Hoo-wun'-nä. 6. Chä'-rä. 7. Wä-kon'-nä. 8. Wa-kon'-chä-rä.

he remarks, "when the dignity is hereditary, limit the succession to the female line. On the death of a chief his sisters' son succeeds him in preference to his own son; and if he happens to have no sister the nearest female relation assumes the dignity. This accounts for a woman being at the head of the Winnebago nation, which, before I was acquainted with their laws, appeared strange to me."[1] In 1869, the Winnebagoes numbered fourteen hundred, which would give an average of one hundred and fifty persons to the gens.

4. *Upper Missouri Tribes.*

1. Mandans. In intelligence and in the arts of life the Mandans were in advance of all their kindred tribes, for which they were probably indebted to the Minnitarees. They are divided into seven gentes as follows:

1. Wolf. 2. Bear. 3. Prairie Chicken. 4. Good Knife. 5. Eagle. 6. Flathead. 7. High Village.[2]

Descent is in the female line, with office and property hereditary in the gens. Intermarriage in the gens is not permitted. Descent in the female line among the Mandans would be singular where so many tribes of the same stock have it in the male, were it not in the archaic form from which the other tribes had but recently departed. It affords a strong presumption that it was originally in the female line in all the Dakotian tribes. This information with respect to the Mandans was obtained at the old Mandan Village in the Upper Missouri, in 1862, from Joseph Kip, whose mother was a Mandan woman. He confirmed the fact of descent by naming his mother's gens, which was also his own.

2. Minnitarees. This tribe and the Upsarokas (Upsar'-o-kas) or Crows, are subdivisions of an original people. They are doubtful members of this branch of the Ganowánian family: although from the number of words in their dialects and in those of the Missouri and Dakota tribes which are common, they have been placed with

---

1 "Travels, loc. cit.," p. 166.

2 1. Ho-ra-ta'-mŭ-make. 2. Mä-to'-no-mäke. 3. See-poosh'-kä. 4. Tä-na-tsŭ'-kä. 5. Ki-tä'-ne-mäke. 6. E-stä-pa'. 7. Me-te-ah'-ke.

them linguistically. They have had an antecedent experience of which but little is known. Minnitarees carried horticulture, the timber-framed house, and a peculiar religious system into this area which they taught to the Mandans. There is a possibility that they are descendants of the Mound-Builders. They have the seven following gentes:

1. Knife. 2. Water. 3. Lodge. 4. Prairie Chicken. 5. Hill People. 6. Unknown Animal. 7. Bonnet.[1]

Descent is in the female line, intermarriage in the gens is forbidden, and the office of sachem as well as property is hereditary in the gens. The Minnitarees and Mandans now live together in the same village. In personal appearance they are among the finest specimens of the Red Man now living in any part of North America.

3. Upsarokas or Crows. This tribe has the following gentes:

1. Prairie Dog. 2. Bad Leggins. 3. Skunk. 4. Treacherous Lodges. 5. Lost Lodges. 6. Bad Honors. 7. Butchers. 8. Moving Lodges. 9. Bear's Paw Mountain. 10. Blackfoot Lodges. 11. Fish Catchers. 12. Antelope. 13. Raven.[2]

Descent, inheritance and the prohibition of intermarriage in the gens, are the same as among the Minnitarees. Several of the names of the Crow gentes are unusual, and more suggestive of bands than of gentes. For a time I was inclined to discredit them. But the existence of the organization into gentes was clearly established by their rules of descent, and marital usages, and by their laws of inheritance with respect to property. My interpreter when among the Crows was Robert Meldrum, then one of the factors of the American Fur Company, who had lived with the Crows forty years, and was one of their chiefs. He had mastered the language so com-

---

1 1. Mit-che-ro'-ka. 2. Min-ne-pä'-ta. 3. Bä-ho-hä'-ta. 4. Seech-ka-be-ruh-pä'-ka. 5. E-tish-sho'-ka. 6. Ah-nah-ha-nä'-me-te. 7. E-ku'-pä-be-ka.

2 1. A-che-pä-be'-cha. 2. E-sach'-ka-buk. 3. Ho-ka-rut'-cha. 4. Ash-bot-chee-ah. 5. Ah-shin'-nä-de'-ah. 6. Ese-kep-kä'-buk. 7. Oo-sä-bot'-see. 8. Ah-hä-chick. 9. Ship-tet'-zä. 10. Ash-kane'-na. 11. Boo-a-dă'-sha. 12. O-hot-dŭ'-sha. 13. Pet-chale-ruh-pä'-ka.

pletely that he thought in it. The following special usages with respect to inheritance were mentioned by him. If a person to whom any article of property had been presented died with it in his possession, and the donor was dead, it reverted to the gens of the latter. Property made or acquired by a wife descended after her death to her children; while that of her husband after his decease belonged to his gentile kindred. If a person made a present to a friend and died, the latter must perform some recognized act of mourning, such as cutting off the joint of a finger at the funeral, or surrender the property to the gens of his deceased friend.[1]

The Crows have a custom with respect to marriage, which I have found in at least forty other Indian tribes, which may be mentioned here, because some use will be made of it in a subsequent chapter. If a man marries the eldest daughter in a family he is entitled to all her sisters as additional wives when they attain maturity. He may waive the right, but if he insists, his superior claim would be recognized by her gens. Polygamy is allowed by usage among the American aborigines generally; but it was never prevalent to any considerable extent from the inability of persons to support more than one family. Direct proof of the existence of the custom first mentioned was afforded by Meldrum's wife, then at the age of twenty-five. She was captured when a child in a foray upon the Blackfeet, and became Meldrum's captive. He induced his mother-in-law to adopt the child into her gens and family, which made the captive the younger sister of his then wife, and gave him the right to take her as another wife when she reached maturity. He availed himself of this usage of the tribe to make his claim paramount. This usage has a great antiquity in

1 This practice as an act of mourning is very common among the Crows, and also as a religious offering when they hold a "Medicine Lodge," a great religious ceremonial. In a basket hung up in a Medicine Lodge for their reception as offerings, fifty, and sometimes a hundred finger joints, I have been told, are sometimes thus collected. At a Crow encampment on the Upper Missouri I noticed a number of women and men with their hands mutilated by this practice.

the human family. It is a survival of the old custom of *punalua.*

III. *Gulf Tribes.*

1. Muscokees or Creeks. The Creek Confederacy consisted of six Tribes; namely, the Creeks, Hitchetes, Yoochees, Alabamas, Coosatees, and Natches, all of whom spoke dialects of the same language, with the exception of the Natches, who were admitted into the confederacy after their overthrow by the French.

The Creeks are composed of twenty-two gentes as follows:

1. Wolf. 2. Bear. 3. Skunk. 4. Alligator. 5. Deer. 6. Bird. 7. Tiger. 8. Wind. 9. Toad. 10. Mole. 11. Fox. 12. Raccoon. 13. Fish. 14. Corn. 15. Potato. 16. Hickory Nut. 17. Salt. 18. Wild Cat. 19. (Sig'n Lost). 20. (Sig'n Lost).[1] 21. (Sig'n Lost). 22. (Sig'n Lost).[2]

The remaining tribes of this confederacy are said to have had the organization into gentes, as the author was informed by the Rev. S. M. Loughridge, who was for many years a missionary among the Creeks, and who furnished the names of the gentes above given. He further stated that descent among the Creeks was in the female line; that the office of sachem and the property of deceased persons were hereditary in the gens, and that intermarriage in the gens was prohibited. At the present time the Creeks are partially civilized with a changed plan of life. They have substituted a political in place of the old social system, so that in a few years all traces of their old gentile institutions will have disappeared. In 1869 they numbered about fifteen thousand, which would give an average of five hundred and fifty persons to the gens.

---

[1] 1. Yă'-hă. 2. No-kuse'. 3. Ku'-mu. 4. Kal-pŭt'-lŭ. 5. E'-cho. 6. Tus'-wă. 7. Kat'-chŭ. 8. Ho-tor'-lee. 9. So-păk'-tŭ. 10. Tŭk'-ko. 11. Chŭ'-lă. 12. Wo'tko. 13. Hŭ'-hlo. 14. U'-che. 15. Ah'-ah. 16. O-che'. 17. Ok-chŭn'-wă. 18.. Kŭ-wă'-ku-che. 19. Tă-mul'-kee. 20. Ak-tŭ-yă-chul'-kee. 21. Is-fă-nŭl'-ke. 22. Wä-hläk-kŭl-kee.

[2] Sig'n equals signification.

2. Choctas. Among the Choctas the phratric organization appears in a conspicuous manner, because each phratry is named, and stands out plainly as a phratry. It doubtless existed in a majority of the tribes previously named, but the subject has not been specially investigated. The tribe of the Creeks consists of eight gentes arranged in two phratries, composed of four gentes each, as among the Iroquois.

I. *Divided People.* (*First Phratry*).

1. Reed. 2. Law Okla. 3. Lulak. 4. Linoklusha.

II. *Beloved People.* (*Second Phratry*).

1. Beloved People. 2. Small People. 3. Large People. 4. Cray Fish. [1]

The gentes of the same phratry could not intermarry; but the members of either of the first gentes could marry into either gens of the second, and *vice versa.* It shows that the Choctas, like the Iroquois, commenced with two gentes, each of which afterwards subdivided into four, and that the original prohibition of intermarriage in the gens had followed the subdivisions. Descent among the Choctas was in the female line. Property and the office of sachem were hereditary in the gens. In 1869 they numbered some twelve thousand, which would give an average of fifteen hundred persons to a gens. The foregoing information was communicated to the author by the late Dr. Cyrus Byington, who entered the missionary service in this tribe in 1820 while they still resided in their ancient territory east of the Mississippi, who removed with them to the Indian Territory, and died in the missionary service about the year 1868, after forty-five years of missionary labors. A man of singular excellence and purity of character, he has left behind him a name and a memory of which humanity may be proud.

A Chocta once expressed to Dr. Byington a wish that he might be made a citizen of the United States, for the reason that his children would then inherit his property

1 First. Ku-shap'. Ok'-lä.
1. Kush-ik'-sä. 2. Law-ok'-lä. 3. Lu-lak Ik'-sä. 4. Lin-ok-lŭ'-sha.

Second. Wă-tăk-i-Hŭ-lä'-tä.
1. Chú-fan-ik'-sä. 2. Is-kŭ-la-ni. 3. Chi'-to. 4. Shak-chuk'-la.

instead of his gentile kindred under the old law of the gens. Chocta usages would distribute his property after his death among his brothers and sisters and the children of his sisters. He could, however, give his property to his children in his life-time, in which case they could hold it against the members of his gens. Many Indian tribes now have considerable property in domestic animals and in houses and lands owned by individuals, among whom the practice of giving it to their children in their life-time has become common to avoid gentile inheritance. As property increased in quantity the disinheritance of children began to arouse opposition to gentile inheritance; and in some of the tribes, that of the Choctas among the number, the old usage was abolished a few years since, and the right to inherit was vested exclusively in the children of the deceased owner. It came, however, through the substitution of a political system in the place of the gentile system, an elective council and magistracy being substituted in place of the old government of chiefs. Under the previous usuages the wife inherited nothing from her husband, nor he from her; but the wife's effects were divided among her children, and in default of them, among her sisters.

3. Chickasas. In like manner the Chickasas were organized in two phratries, of which the first contains four, and the second eight gentes, as follows:

I. *Panther Phratry.*

1. Wild Cat. 2. Bird. 3. Fish. 4. Deer.

II. *Spanish Phratry.*

1. Raccoon. 2. Spanish. 3. Royal. 4. Hush-ko-ni. 5. Squirrel. 6. Alligator. 7. Wolf. 8. Black-bird.[1]

Descent was in the female line, intermarriage in the gens was prohibited, and property as well as the office of sachem were hereditary in the gens. The above particulars were obtained from the Rev. Charles C. Cope-

---

[1] I. Koi.

1. Ko-in-chush. 2. Hä-täk-fu-shi. 3. Nun-ni. 4. Is-si.

II. Ish-păn-ee.

1. Shă-u-ee. 2. Ish-păn-ee. 3. Ming-ko. 4. Hush-ko-ni. 5. Tun-ni. 6. Ho-chon-chab-ba. 7. Nă-sho-lă. 8. Chuh-hlă.

land, an American missionary residing with this tribe. In 1869 they numbered some five thousand, which would give an average of about four hundred persons to the gens. A new gens seems to have been formed after their intercourse with the Spaniards commenced, or this name, for reasons, may have been substituted in the place of an original name. One of the phratries is also called the Spanish.

4. Cherokees. This tribe was anciently composed of ten gentes, of which two, the Acorn, *Ah-ne-dsu'-la,* and the Bird, *Ah-ne-dsé-skwä,* are now extinct. They are the following:

1. Wolf. 2. Red Paint. 3. Long Prairie.
4. Deaf. (A bird.) 5. Holly. 6. Deer. 7. Blue.
8. Long Hair.[1]

Descent is in the female line, and intermarriage in the gens prohibited. In 1869 the Cherokees numbered fourteen thousand which would give an average of seventeen hundred and fifty persons to each gens. This is the largest number, so far as the fact is known, ever found in a single gens among the American aborigines. The Cherokees and Ojibwas at the present time exceed all the remaining Indian tribes within the United States in the number of persons speaking the same dialect. It may be remarked further, that it is not probable that there ever was at any time in any part of North America a hundred thousand Indians who spoke the same dialect. The Aztecs, Tezcucans and Tlascalans were the only tribes of whom so large a number could, with any propriety, be claimed; and with respect to them it is difficult to perceive how the existence of so large a number in either tribe could be established, at the epoch of the Spanish Conquest, upon trustworthy evidence. The unusual numbers of the Creeks and Cherokees is due to the possession of domestic animals and a well-developed field agriculture. They are now partially civilized, having substi-

[1] 1. Ah-ne-whi'-yä. 2. Ah-ne-who'-teh. 3. Ah-ne-ga-tä-ga'-nih.. 4. Dsŭ-ni-li'-a-nä. 5. U-ni-sdä'-sdi. 6. Ah-nee-kä'-wih. 7. Ah-nee-sä-hok'-nih. 8. Ah-nŭ-ka-lo'-high.
Ah-nee signifies the plural.

tuted an elective constitutional government in the place of the ancient gentes, under the influence of which the latter are rapidly falling into decadence.

5. Seminoles. This tribe is of Creek descent. They are said to be organized into gentes, but the particulars have not been obtained.

IV. *Pawnee Tribes.*

Whether or not the Pawnees are organized in gentes has not been ascertained. Rev. Samuel Allis, who had formerly been a missionary among them, expressed to the author his belief that they were, although he had not investigated the matter specially. He named the following gentes of which he believed they were composed:

1. Bear. 2. Beaver. 3. Eagle. 4. Buffalo. 5. Deer. 6. Owl.

I once met a band of Pawnees on the Missouri, but was unable to obtain an interpreter.

The Arickarees, whose village is near that of the Minnitarees, are the nearest congeners of the Pawnees, and the same difficulty occurred with them. These tribes, with the Huecos and some two or three other small tribes residing on the Canadian river, have always lived west of the Missouri, and speak an independent stock language. If the Pawnees are organized in gentes, presumptively the other tribes are the same.

V. *Algonkin Tribes.*

At the epoch of their discovery this great stock of the American aborigines occupied the area from the Rocky Mountains to Hudson's Bay, south of the Siskatchewun, and thence eastward to the Atlantic, including both shores of Lake Superior, except at its head, and both banks of the St. Lawrence below Lake Champlain. Their area extended southward along the Atlantic coast to North Carolina, and down the east bank of the Mississippi in Wisconsin and Illinois to Kentucky. Within the eastern section of this immense region the Iroquois and their affiliated tribes were an intrusive people, their only competitor for supremacy within its boundaries.

Gitchigamian[1] Tribes. 1. Ojibwas. The Ojibwas speak the same dialect, and are organized in gentes, of which the names of twenty-three have been obtained without being certain that they include the whole number. In the Ojibwa dialect the word *totem,* quite as often pronounced *dodaim,* signifies the symbol or device of a gens; thus the figure of a wolf was the totem of the Wolf gens. From this Mr. Schoolcraft used the words "totemic system," to express the gentile organization, which would be perfectly acceptable were it not that we have both in the Latin and the Greek a terminology for every quality and character of the system which is already historical. It may be used, however, with advantage. The Ojibwas have the following gentes:

1. Wolf. 2. Bear. 3. Beaver. 4. Turtle (Mud). 5. Turtle (Snapping). 6. Turtle (Little). 7. Reindeer. 8. Snipe. 9. Crane. 10. Pigeon Hawk. 11. Bald Eagle. 12. Loon. 13. Duck. 14. Duck. 15. Snake. 16. Muskrat. 17. Marten. 18. Heron. 19. Bull-head. 20. Carp. 21. Cat Fish. 22. Sturgeon. 23. Pike.[2]

Descent is in the male line, the children belonging to their father's gens. There are several reasons for the inference that it was originally in the female line, and that the change was comparatively recent. In the first place, the Delawares, who are recognized by all Algonkin tribes as one of the oldest of their lineage, and who are styled "Grandfathers" by all alike, still have descent in the female line. Several other Algonkin tribes have the same. Secondly, evidence still remains that within two or three generations back of the present, descent was in the female line, with respect to the office of chief.[3]

---

[1] 1. From the Ojibwa, gi-tchi', great, and gä'-me, lake, the aboriginal name of Lake Superior, and other great lakes.

[2] 1. My-een'-gun. 2. Mä-kwä'. 3. Ah-mik'. 4. Me-she'-kă. 5. Mik-o-noh'. 6. Me-skwä-da'-re. 7. Ah-dik'. 8. Chu-e-skwe'-ske-wă. 9. O-jee-jok'. 10. Ka-kake'. 11. O-me-gee-ze'. 12. Mong. 13. Ah-ah'-weh. 14. She-shebe'. 15. Ke-na'-big. 16. Wa-zhush'. 17. Wa-be-zhaze'. 18. Moosh-kä-oo-ze'. 19. Ah-wah-sis'-sa. 20. Nä-ma'-bin. 21. —— 22. Nă-ma'. 23. Ke-no'-zhe.

[3] An Ojibwa sachem, Ke-we'-kons, who died about 1840, at the age of ninety years, when asked by my informant why he did not retire from office and give place to his son, replied, that his

Thirdly, American and missionary influences have generally opposed it. A scheme of descent which disinherited the sons seemed to the early missionaries, trained under very different conceptions, without justice or reason; and it is not improbable that in a number of tribes, the Ojibwas included, the change was made under their teachings. And lastly, since several Algonkin tribes now have descent in the female line, it leads to the conclusion that it was anciently universal in the Ganowánian family, it being also the archaic form of the institution.

Intermarriage in the gens is prohibited, and both property and office are hereditary in the gens. The children, however, at the present time, take the most of it to the exclusion of their gentile kindred. The property and effects of the mother pass to her children, and in default of them, to her sisters, own and collateral. In like manner the son may succeed his father in the office of sachem; but where there are several sons the choice is determined by the elective principle. The gentiles not only elect, but they also retain the power to depose. At the present time the Ojibwas number some sixteen thousand, which would give an average of about seven hundred to each gens.

2. Potawattamies. This tribe has fifteen gentes, as follows:

1. Wolf. 2. Bear. 3. Beaver. 4. Elk. 5. Loon. 6. Eagle. 7. Sturgeon. 8. Carp. 9. Bald Eagle. 10. Thunder. 11. Rabbit. 12. Crow. 13. Fox. 14. Turkey. 15. Black Hawk.[1]

Descent, inheritance, and the law of marriage are the same as among the Ojibwas.

---

son could not succeed him; that the right of succession belonged to his nephew, E-kwä'-ka-mik, who must have the office. This nephew was a son of one of his sisters. From this statement it follows that descent, anciently, and within a recent period, was in the female line. It does not follow from the form of the statement that the nephew would take by hereditary right, but that he was in the line of succession, and his election was substantially assured.

[1] 1. Mo-ăh'. 2. M'-ko'. 3. Muk. 4. Mis-shă'-wă. 5. Maak. 6. K'-nou'. 7. N'-mă'. 8. N'-mă-pe-nă'. 9. M'-ge-ze'-wä. 10. Che'-kwa. 11. Wă-bo'-zo. 12. Kŭ-käg'-she. 13. Wake-shi'. 14. Pen'-nă. 15. M'-ke-eash'-she-kă-kah'. 16. O-tă'-wa.

3. Otawas.[1] The Ojibwas, Otawas and Potawattamies were subdivisions of an original tribe. When first known they were confederated. The Otawas were undoubtedly organized in gentes, but their names have not been obtained.

4. Crees. This tribe, when discovered, held the northwest shore of Lake Superior, and spread from thence to Hudson's Bay, and westward to the Red River of the North. At a later day they occupied the region of the Siskatchewun, and south of it. Like the Dakotas they have lost the gentile organization which presumptively once existed among them. Linguistically their nearest affiliation is with the Ojibwas, whom they closely resemble in manners and customs, and in personal appearance.

Mississippi Tribes. The western Algonkins, grouped under this name, occupied the eastern banks of the Mississippi in Wisconsin and Illinois, and extended southward into Kentucky, and eastward into Indiana.

1. Miamis. The immediate congeners of the Miamis, namely, the Weas, Piankeshaws, Peorias, and Kaskaskias, known at an early day, collectively, as the Illinois, are now few in numbers, and have abandoned their ancient usages for a settled agricultural life. Whether or not they were formerly organized in gentes has not been ascertained, but it is probable that they were. The Miamis have the following ten gentes:

1. Wolf. 2. Loon. 3. Eagle. 4. Buzzard.
5. Panther. 6. Turkey. 7. Raccoon. 8. Snow.
9. Sun. 10. Water.[2]

Under their changed condition and declining numbers the gentile organization is rapidly disappearing. When its decline commenced descent was in the male line, intermarriage in the gens was forbidden, and the office of sachem together with property were hereditary in the gens.

2. Shawnees. This remarkable and highly advanced tribe, one of the highest representatives of the Algonkin

---

1 Pronounced O-tä'-wa.

2 1. Mo-wha'-wä. 2. Mon-gwä'. 3. Ken-da-wă'. 4. Ah-pă'-kose-e-ă. 5. Ka-no-zä'-wa. 6. Pi-la-wä'. 7. Ah-se-pon'-nä. 8. Mon-nă'-to. 9. Kul-swä'. 10. (Not obtained.)

stock, still retain their gentes, although they have substituted in place of the old gentile system a civil organization with a first and second head-chief and a council, each elected annually by popular suffrage. They have thirteen gentes, which they still maintain for social and genealogical purposes, as follows:
1. Wolf. 2. Loon. 3. Bear. 4. Buzzard. 5. Panther. 6. Owl. 7. Turkey. 8. Deer. 9. Raccoon. 10. Turtle. 11. Snake. 12. Horse. 13. Rabbit.[1]

Descent, inheritance, and the rule with respect to marrying out of the gens are the same as among the Miamis. In 1869 the Shawnees numbered but seven hundred, which would give an average of about fifty persons to the gens. They once numbered three or four thousand persons, which was above the average among the American Indian tribes.

The Shawnees had a practice, common also to the Miamis and Sauks and Foxes, of naming children into the gens of the father or of the mother or any other gens, under certain restrictions, which deserves a moment's notice. It has been shown that among the Iroquois each gens had its own special names for persons which no other gens had a right to use.[2] This usage was probably general. Among the Shawnees these names carried with them the rights of the gens to which they belonged, so that the name determined the gens of the person. As the sachem must, in all cases, belong to the gens over which he is invested with authority, it is not unlikely that the change of descent from the female line to the male commenced in this practice; in the first place to enable a son to succeed his father, and in the second to enable children to inherit property from their father. If

---

1 1. M'-wa-wä'. Ma-gwä'. 3. M'-kwä'. 4. We-wä'-see. 5. M'-se'-pa-se. 6. M'-ath-wa'. 7. Pa-la-wä'. 8. Psake-the. 9. Sha-pä-tä'. 10. Na-ma-thä'. 11. Ma-na-to'. 12. Pe-sa-wä'. 13. Pä-täke-e-no-the'.

2 In every tribe the name indicated the gens. Thus, among the Sauks and Foxes Long Horn is a name belonging to the Deer gens; Black Wolf, to the wolf. In the Eagle gens the following are specimen names: Ka'-po-nä, "Eagle drawing his nest;" Ja-ka-kwä-pe, "Eagle sitting with his head up;" Pe-ä-tä-na-kä-hok, "Eagle flying over a limb."

a son when christened received a name belonging to the gens of his father it would place him in his father's gens and in the line of succession, but subject to the elective principle. The father, however, had no control over the question. It was left by the gens to certain persons, most of them matrons, who were to be consulted when children were to be named, with power to determine the name to be given. By some arrangement between the Shawnee gentes these persons had this power, and the name when conferred in the prescribed manner, carried the person into the gens to which the name belonged.

There are traces of the archaic rule of descent among the Shawnees, of which the following illustration may be given as it was mentioned to the author. *Lä-ho'-weh,* a sachem of the Wolf gens, when about to die, expressed a desire that a son of one of his sisters might succeed him in the place of his own son. But his nephew (*Kos-kwa'-the*) was of the Fish and his son of the Rabbit gens, so that neither could succeed him without first being transferred, by a change of name, to the Wolf gens, in which the office was hereditary. His wish was respected. After his death the name of his nephew was changed to *Tep-a-tä-go the',* one of the Wolf names, and he was elected to the office. Such laxity indicates a decadence of the gentile organization; but it tends to show that at no remote period descent among the Shawnees was in the female line.

3. Sauks and Foxes. These tribes are consolidated into one, and have the following gentes:

1. Wolf. 2. Bear. 3. Deer. 4. Elk. 5. Hawk. 6. Eagle. 7. Fish. 8. Buffalo. 9. Thunder. 10. Bone. 11. Fox. 12. Sea. 13. Sturgeon. 14. Big Tree. [1]

Descent, inheritance, and the rule requiring marriage out of the gens, are the same as among the Miamis. In

[1] 1. Mo-whă-wis'-so-uk. 2. Ma-kwis'-so-jik. 3. Pă-sha'-ga-sa-wis-so-uk. 4. Mă-shă-wă-uk'. 5. Kă-kă-kwis'-so-uk. 6. Pă-mis'-so-uk. 7. Nă-mă-sis'-so-uk. 8. Na-nus-sus'-so-uk. Nă-nă-ma'-kew-uk. 10. Ah-kuh'-ne-näk. 11. Wä-ko-a-wis'-so-jik. 12. Kă-che-kone-a-we'-so-uk. 13. Nă-mă-we'--so-uk. 14. Mă-she'-mă-tăk.

1869 they numbered but seven hundred, which would give an average of fifty persons to the gens. The number of gentes still preserved affords some evidence that they were several times more numerous within the previous two centuries.

4. Menominees and Kikapoos. These tribes, which are independent of each other, are organized in gentes, but their names have not been procured. With respect to the Menominees it may be inferred that, until a recent period, descent was in the female line, from the following statement made to the author, in 1859, by Antoine Gookie, a member of this tribe. In answer to a question concerning the rule of inheritance, he replied: "If I should die, my brothers and maternal uncles would rob my wife and children of my property. We now expect that our children will inherit our effects, but there is no certainty of it. The old law gives my property to my nearest kindred who are not my children, but my brothers and sisters, and maternal uncles." It shows that property was hereditary in the gens, but restricted to the agnatic kindred in the female line.

Rocky Mountain Tribes. 1. Blood Blackfeet. This tribe is composed of the five following gentes:

1. Blood. 2. Fish Eaters. 3. Skunk. 4. Extinct Animal. 5. Elk.[1]

Descent is in the male line, but intermarriage in the gens is not allowed.

2. Piegan Blackfeet. This tribe has the eight following gentes:

1. Blood. 2. Skunk. 3. Web Fat. 4. Inside Fat. 5. Conjurers. 6. Never Laugh. 7. Starving. 8. Half Dead Meat.[2]

Descent is in the male line, and intermarriage in the gens is prohibited. Several of the names above given are more appropriate to bands than to gentes; but, as the information was obtained from the Blackfeet direct,

---

[1] 1. Ki'-no. 2. Mä-me-o'-ya. 3. Ah-pe-ki'. 4. A-ne'-po. 5. Po-no-kix'.

[2] 1. Ah-ah'-pi-tä-pe. 2. Ah-pe-ki'-e. 3. Ih-po'-se-mä. 4. Ka-ka'-po-ya. 5. Mo-tă'-to-sis. 6. Kä-ti'-ya-ye-mix. 7. Kä-ta'-ge-mă-ne. 8. E-ko'-to-pis-taxe.

through competent interpreters, (Mr. and Mrs. Alexander Culbertson, the latter a Blackfoot woman) I believe it reliable. It is possible that nicknames for gentes in some cases may have superseded the original names.

Atlantic Tribes.

1. Delawares. As elsewhere stated the Delawares are, in the duration of their separate existence, one of the oldest of the Algonkin tribes. Their home country, when discovered, was the region around and north of Delaware Bay. They are comprised in three gentes, as follows:

1. Wolf. Took'-seat. Round Paw.
2. Turtle. Poke-koo-un'-go. Crawling.
3. Turkey. Pul-la'-cook. Non-chewing.

These subdivisions are in the nature of phratries, because each is composed of twelve sub-gentes, each having some of the attributes of a gens. [1] The names are personal, and mostly, if not in every case, those of females. As this feature was unusual I worked it out as minutely as possible at the Delaware reservation in Kansas, in 1860, with the aid of William Adams, an educated Delaware. It proved impossible to find the origin of these subdivisions, but they seemed to be the several eponymous ancestors from whom the members of the

---

[1] I. Wolf. Took'-seat.

1. Mă-an'-greet, Big Feet. 2. Wee-sow-het'-ko, Yellow Tree. 3. Pă-sa-kun-ă'-mon, Pulling Corn. 4. We-yar-nih'-kä-to. Care Enterer. 5. Toosh-war-ka'-ma, Across the River. 6. O-lum'-a-ne, Vermilion. 7. Pun-ar'-you, Dog standing by Fireside. 8. Kwin-eek'-cha, Long Body. 9. Moon-har-tar'-ne, Digging. 10. Non-har'-min, Pulling up Stream. 11. Long-ush-har-kar'-to, Brush Log. 12. Maw-soo-toh', Bringing Along.

II. Turtle. Poke-koo-un'-go.

1. O-ka-ho'-ki, Ruler. 2. Ta-ko-ong'-o-to, High Bank Shore. 3. See-har-ong'-o-to, Drawing down Hill. 4. Ole-har-kar-me'-kar-to, Elector. 5. Mä-har-o-luk'-ti, Brave. 6. Toosh-ki-pa-kwis-i, Green Leaves. 7. Tung-ul-ung'-si, Smallest Turtle. 8. We-lun-ŭng-si, Little Turtle. 9. Lee-kwin-ă-i', Snapping Turtle. 10. Kwis-aese-kees'-to, Deer.

The two remaining sub-gentes are extinct.

III. Turkey. Pul-la'-ook.

1. Mo-har-ă'-lă, Big Bird. 2. Le-le-wa'-you, Bird's Cry. 3. Moo-kwung-wa-ho'-ki, Eye Pain. 4. Moo-har-mo-wi-kar'-nu, Scratch the Path. 5. O-ping-ho'-ki, Opossum Ground. 6. Muh-ho-we-kă'-ken, Old Shin. 7. Tong-o-nă'-o-to, Drift Log. 8. Nool-ă-mar-lar'-mo, Living in Water. 9. Muh-krent-har'-ne, Root Digger. 10. Muh-karm-huk-se, Red Face. 11. Koo-wă-ho'-ke, Pine Region. 12. Oo-chuk'--ham, Ground Scratcher.

gentes respectively derived their descent. It shows also the natural growth of the phratries from the gentes.

Descent among the Delawares is in the female line, which renders probable its ancient universality in this form in the Algonkin tribes. The office of sachem was hereditary in the gens, but elective among its members, who had the power both to elect and depose. Property also was hereditary in the gens. Originally the members of the three original gentes could not intermarry in their own gens; but in recent years the prohibition has been confined to the sub-gentes. Those of the same name in the Wolf gens, now partially become a phratry, for example, cannot intermarry, but those of different names marry. The practice of naming children into the gens of their father also prevails among the Delawares, and has introduced the same confusion of descents found among the Shawnees and Miamis. American civilization and intercourse necessarily administered a shock to Indian institutions under which the ethnic life of the people is gradually breaking down.

Examples of succession in office afford the most satisfactory illustrations of the aboriginal law of descent. A Delaware woman, after stating to the author that she, with her children, belonged to the Wolf gens, and her husband to the Turtle, remarked that when Captain Ketchum (Tä-whe′-lä-na), late head chief or sachem of the Turtle gens, died, he was succeeded by his nephew, John Conner (Tä-tä-ne′-shă), a son of one of the sisters of the deceased sachem, who was also of the Turtle gens. The decedent left a son, but he was of another gens and consequently incapable of succeeding. With the Delawares, as with the Iroquois, the office passed from brother to brother, or from uncle to nephew, because descent was in the female line.

2. Munsees. The Munsees are an offshoot from the Delawares, and have the same gentes, the Wolf, the Turtle and the Turkey. Descent is in the female line, intermarriage in the gens is not permitted, and the office of sachem, as well as property, are hereditary in the gens.

3. Mohegans. All of the New England Indians, south

of the river Kennebeck, of whom the Mohegans formed a part, were closely affiliated in language, and could understand each other's dialects. Since the Mohegans are organized in gentes, there is a presumption that the Pequots, Narragansetts, and other minor bands were not only similarly organized, but had the same gentes. The Mohegans have the same three with the Delawares, the Wolf, the Turtle and the Turkey, each of which is composed of a number of gentes. It proves their immediate connection with the Delawares and Munsees by descent, and also reveals, as elsewhere stated, the process of subdivision by which an original gens breaks up into several, which remain united in a phratry. In this case also it may be seen how the phratry arises naturally under gentile institutions. It is rare among the American aborigines to find preserved the evidence .of the segmentation of original gentes as clearly as in the present case.

The Mohegan phratries stand out more conspicuously than those of any other tribe of the American aborigines, because they cover the gentes of each, and the phratries must be stated to explain the classification of the gentes; but we know less about them than of those of the Iroquois. They are the following:

I. *Wolf Phratry. Took-se-tuk'.*

1. Wolf. 2. Bear. 3. Dog. 4. Opossum.

II. *Turtle Phratry. Tone-bä'-o.*

1. Little Turtle. 2. Mud Turtle. 3. Great Turtle. 4. Yellow Eel.

III. *Turkey Phratry.*

1. Turkey. 2. Crane. 3. Chicken.[1]

Descent is in the female line, intermarriage in the gens is forbidden, and the office of sachem is hereditary in the gens, the office passing either from brother to brother, or from uncle to nephew. Among the Pequots and Narragansetts descent was in the female line, as I

---

[1] I. Took-se-tuk'.
1. Ne-h'-jä-o. 2. Mä'-kwä. 3. N-de-yä'-o. 4. Wä-pa-kwe'.
II. Tone-bä'-o.
1. Gak-po-mute'. 2. ——— 3. Tone-bä'-o. 4. We-saw-mä'-un.
III. Turkey.
1. Nä-ah-mä'-o. 2. Gä-h'-ko. 3. ———.

learned from a Narragansett woman whom I met in Kansas.

4. Abenakis. The name of this tribe, Wä-be-nă'-kee, signifies "Rising Sun People." [1] They affiliate more closely with the Micmacs than with the New England Indians south of the Kennebeck. They have fourteen gentes, as follows:

1. Wolf. 2. Wild Cat (Black.) 3. Bear. 4. Snake. 5. Spotted Animal. 6. Beaver. 7. Cariboo. 8. Sturgeon. 9. Muskrat. 10. Pigeon Hawk. 11. Squirrel. 12. Spotted Frog. 13. Crane. 14. Porcupine. [2]

Descent is now in the male line, intermarriage in the gens was anciently prohibited, but the prohibition has now lost most of its force. The office of sachem was hereditary in the gens. It will be noticed that several of the above gentes are the same as among the Ojibwas.

VI. *Athapasco-Apache Tribes.*

Whether or not the Athapascans of Hudson's Bay Territory and the Apaches of New Mexico, who are subdivisions of an original stock, are organized in gentes has not been definitely ascertained. When in the former territory, in 1861, I made an effort to determine the question among the Hare and Red Knife Athapascans, but was unsuccessful for want of competent interpreters; and yet it seems probable that if the system existed, traces of it would have been discovered even with imperfect means of inquiry. The late Robert Kennicott made a similar attempt for the author among the A-chä'-o-ten-ne, or Slave Lake Athapascans, with no better success. He found special regulations with respect to marriage and the descent of the office of sachem, which seemed to indicate the presence of gentes, but he could not obtain satisfactory information. The Kutchin (Louchoux)' of the Yukon river region are Athapascans.

---

1 In "Systems of Consanguinity," the aboriginal names of the principal Indian tribes, with their significations, may be found.

2 1. Mals,-sŭm. 2. Pis-suh'. 3. Ah-weh'.soos. 4. Skooke. 5. Ah-lunk'-soo. 6. Ta-mä'-kwa. 7. Mä-guh-le-loo'. 8. Kä-bäh'-seh. 9. Moos-kwă-suh'. 10. K'-che-gä-gong'-go. 11. Meh-ko-ă'. 12. Che-gwä'-lis. 13. Koos-koo'. 14. Mä-dä'-weh-soos.

In a letter to the author by the late George Gibbs, he remarks: "In a letter which I have from a gentleman at Fort Simpson, Mackenzie river, it is mentioned that among the Louchoux or Kutchin there are three grades or classes of society—undoubtedly a mistake for totem, though the totems probably differ in rank, as he goes on to say—that a man does not marry into his own class, but takes a wife from some other; and that a chief from the highest may marry with a woman of the lowest without loss of caste. The children belong to the grade of the mother; and the members of the same grade in the different tribes do not war with each other."

Among the Kolushes of the Northwest Coast, who affiliate linguistically though not closely with the Athapascans, the organization into gentes exists. Mr. Gallatin remarks that they are "like our own Indians, divided into tribes or clans; a distinction of which, according to Mr. Hale, there is no trace among the Indians of Oregon. The names of the tribes [gentes] are those of animals, namely: Bear, Eagle, Crow, Porpoise and Wolf.... The right of succession is in the female line, from uncle to nephew, the principal chief excepted, who is generally the most powerful of the family." [1]

VII. *Indian Tribes of the Northwest Coast.*

In some of these tribes, beside the Kolushes, the gentile organization prevails. "Before leaving Puget's Sound," observes Mr. Gibbs, in a letter to the author, "I was fortunate enough to meet representatives of three principal families of what we call the Northern Indians, the inhabitants of the Northwest Coast, extending from the Upper end of Vancouver's Island into the Russian Possessions, and the confines of the Esquimaux. From them I ascertained positively that the totemic system exists at least among these three. The families I speak of are, beginning at the northwest, Tlinkitt, commonly called the Stikeens, after one of their bands; the Tlaidas; and Chimsyans, called by Gallatin, Weas. There are four totems common to these, the Whale, the Wolf, the

1 Trans. Am. Eth. Soc., ii, Intro., cxlix.

Eagle, and the Crow. Neither of these can marry into the same totem, although in a different nation or family. What is remarkable is that these nations constitute entirely different families. I mean by this that their languages are essentially different, having no perceptible analogy." Mr. Dall, in his work on Alaska, written still later, remarks that "the Tlinkets are divided into four totems: the Raven (Yehl), the Wolf (Kanu'kh), the Whale, and the Eagle (Chethl)..... Opposite totems only can marry, and the child usually takes the mother's totem." [1]

Mr. Hubert H. Bancroft presents their organization still more fully, showing two phratries, and the gentes belonging to each. He remarks of the Thlinkeets that the "nation is separated into two great divisions or clans, one of which is called the Wolf and the other the Raven. The Raven trunk is again divided into sub-clans, called the Frog, the Goose, the Sea-Lion, the Owl, and the Salmon. The Wolf family comprises the Bear, Eagle, Dolphin, Shark, and Alca.... Tribes of the same clan may not war on each other, but at the same time members of the same clan may not marry with each other. Thus, the young Wolf warrior must seek his mate among the Ravens." [2]

The Eskimos do not belong to the Ganowánian family. Their occupation of the American continent in comparison with that of the latter family was recent or modern. They are also without gentes.

VIII. *Salish, Sahaptin and Kootenay Tribes.*

The tribes of the Valley of the Columbia, of whom those above named represent the principal stocks, are without the gentile organization. Our distinguished philologists, Horatio Hale and the late George Gibbs, both of whom devoted special attention to the subject, failed to discover any traces of the system among them. There are strong reasons for believing that this remarkable area was the nursery land of the Ganowánian fam-

[1] "Alaska and its Resources," p. 414.
[2] "Native Races of the Pacific States," i, 109.

ily, from which, as the initial point of their migrations, they spread abroad over both divisions of the continent. It seems probable, therefore, that their ancestors possessed the organization into gentes, and that it fell into decay and finally disappeared.

IX. *Shoshonee Tribes.*

The Comanches of Texas, together with the Ute tribes, the Bonnaks, the Shoshonees, and some other tribes, belong to this stock. Mathew Walker, a Wyandote half-blood, informed the author, in 1859, that he had lived among the Comanches, and that they had the following gentes:

1. Wolf. 2. Bear. 3. Elk. 4. Deer. 5. Gopher. 6. Antelope.

If the Comanches are organized in gentes, there is a presumption that the other tribes of this stock are the same.

This completes our review of the social system of the Indian tribes of North America, north of New Mexico. The greater portion of the tribes named were in the Lower Status of barbarism at the epoch of European discovery, and the remainder in the Upper Status of savagery. From the wide and nearly universal prevalence of the organization into gentes, its ancient universality among them with descent in the female line may with reason be assumed. Their system was purely social, having the gens as its unit, and the phratry, tribe and confederacy as the remaining members of the organic series. These four successive stages of integration and re-integration express the whole of their experience in the growth of the idea of government. Since the principal Aryan and Semitic tribes had the same organic series when they emerged from barbarism, the system was substantially universal in ancient society, and inferentially had a common origin. The punaluan group, hereafter to be described more fully in connection with the growth of the idea of the family, evidently gave birth to the gentes, so that the Aryan, Semitic, Uralian, Turanian and Ganowánian families of mankind point with a distinctiveness seemingly unmistakable to a common punaluan stock, with the organization into gentes engrafted upon it, from which each and all were derived, and finally differentiated into families. This conclusion, I believe, will ultimately enforce its own acceptance, when future investigation has developed and verified the facts on a minuter scale. Such a great organic series, able to hold mankind in society through the latter part of the period of savagery, through the entire period of barbarism, and into the early part of the period of civilization, does not arise by accident, but had a natural development from pre-existing elements. Rationally and rigorously interpreted, it seems probable that it can be made demonstrative of the unity of origin of all the families of mankind who possessed the organization into gentes.

X. *Village Indians.*

1. Moqui Pueblo Indians. The Moqui tribes are still in undisturbed possession of their ancient communal houses, seven in number, near the Little Colorado in Arizona, once a part of New Mexico. They are living under their ancient institutions, and undoubtedly at the present moment fairly represent the type of Village Indian life which prevailed from Zuñi to Cuzco at the epoch of Discovery. Zuñi, Acoma, Taos, and several other New Mexican pueblos are the same structures which were found there by Coronado in 1540-1542. Notwithstanding their apparent accessibility we know in reality but little concerning their mode of life or their domestic institutions. No systematic investigation has ever been made. What little information has found its way into print is general and accidental.

The Moquis are organized in gentes, of which they have nine, as follows:

1. Deer. 2. Sand. 3. Rain. 4. Bear. 5. Hare. 6. Prairie Wolf. 7. Rattlesnake. 8. Tobacco Plant. 9. Reed Grass.

Dr. Ten Broeck, Assistant Surgeon, U. S. A., furnished to Mr. Schoolcraft the Moqui legend of their origin which he obtained at one of their villages. They said that "many years ago their Great Mother[1] brought from her home in the West nine races of men in the following form. First, the Deer race; second, the Sand race; third, the Water [Rain] race; fourth, the Bear race; fifth, the Hare race; sixth, the Prairie Wolf race; seventh, the Rattlesnake race; eighth, the Tobacco Plant race; and ninth, the Reed Grass race. Having planted them on the spot where their villages now stand, she transformed them into men who built up the present pueblos; and the distinction of race is still kept up. One told me that he was of the Sand race, another, the Deer, etc. They are firm believers in metempsychosis, and say that when they die they will resolve into their original forms, and become bears, deer, etc., again.... The government is hereditary, but does not necessarily descend to the son of the incumbent; for if they prefer any other blood relative, he is chosen."[2] Having passed, in this case, from the Lower into the Middle Status of barbarism, and found the organization into gentes in full development, its adaptation to their changed condition is demonstrated. Its existence among the Village Indians in general is rendered probable; but from this point forward in the remainder of North, and in the whole of South America, we are left without definite information except with respect to the Lagunas. It shows how incompletely the work has been done in American Ethnology, that the unit of their social system has been but partially discovered, and its significance not understood. Still, there are traces of it in the early Spanish authors, and direct knowledge of it in a few later writers, which when brought together will leave but little doubt of the ancient universal prevalence of the gentile organization throughout the Indian family.

There are current traditions in many gentes, like that of the Moquis, of the transformation of their first progenitors from the animal, or inanimate object, which became the symbol of the gens, into men and women

1 The Shawnees formerly worshiped a Female Deity, called Go-gome-tha-mä, "Our Grand-Mother."

2 "Schoolcraft's Hist., etc., of Indian Tribes," iv, 86.

Thus, the Crane gens of the Ojibwas have a legend that a pair of cranes flew over the wide area from the Gulf to the Great Lakes and from the prairies of the Mississippi to the Atlantic in quest of a place where subsistence was most abundant, and finally selected the Rapids on the outlet of Lake Superior, since celebrated for its fisheries. Having alighted on the bank of the river and folded their wings the Great Spirit immediately changed them into a man and woman, who became the progenitors of the Crane gens of the Ojibwas. There are a number of gentes in the different tribes who abstain from eating the animal whose name they bear; but this is far from universal.

2. Lagunas. The Laguna Pueblo Indians are organized in gentes, with descent in the female line, as appears from an address of Rev. Samuel Gorman before the Historical Society of New Mexico in 1860. "Each town is classed into tribes or families, and each of these groups is named after some animal, bird, herb, timber, planet, or one of the four elements. In the pueblo of Laguna, which is one of above one thousand inhabitants, there are seventeen of these tribes; some are called bear, some deer, some rattlesnake, some corn, some wolf, some water, etc., etc. The children are of the same tribe as their mother. And, according to ancient custom, two persons of the same tribe are forbidden to marry; but, recently, this custom begins to be less rigorously observed than anciently."

"Their land is held in common, as the property of the community, but after a person cultivates a lot he has a personal claim to it, which he can sell to any one of the same community; or else when he dies it belongs to his widow or daughters; or, if he were a single man, it remains in his father's family." [1] That wife or daughter inherit from the father is doubtful.

3. Aztecs, Tezcucans and Tlacopans. The question of the organization of these, and the remaining Nahuatlac tribes of Mexico, in gentes will be considered in the next ensuing chapter.

---

1 "Address," p. 12.

4. Mayas of Yucatan. Herrera makes frequent reference to the "kindred," and in such a manner with regard to the tribes in Mexico, Central and South America as to imply the existence of a body of persons organized on the basis of consanguinity much more numerous than would be found apart from gentes. Thus: "He that killed a free man was to make satisfaction to the children and kindred." [1] It was spoken of the aborigines of Nicaragua, and had it been of the Iroquois, among whom the usage was the same, the term *kindred* would have been equivalent to *gens*. And again, speaking generally of the Maya Indians of Yucatan, he remarks that "when any satisfaction was to be made for damages, if he who was adjudged to pay was like to be reduced to poverty, the kindred contributed." [2] In this another gentile usage may be recognized. Again, speaking of the Aztecs; "if they were guilty, no favor or kindred could save them from death." [3] One more citation to the same effect may be made, applied to the Florida Indians who were organized in gentes. He observes "that they were extravagantly fond of their children, and cherished them, the parents and kindred lamenting such as died a whole year."[4] The early observers noticed, as a peculiarity of Indian society, that large numbers of persons were bound together by the bond of kin, and therefore the group came to be mentioned as "the kindred." But they did not carry the scrutiny far enough to discover, what was probably the truth, that the kindred formed a gens, and, as such, the unit of their social system.

Herrera remarks further of the Mayas, that "they were wont to observe their pedigrees very much, and therefore thought themselves all related, and were helpful to one another..... They did not marry mothers, or sisters-in-law, *nor any that bore the same name* as their father, which was looked upon as unlawful." [5] The ped-

1 "General History of America," Lond. ed., 1726. Stevens' Trans., iii, 299.
2 "Ib.," iv, 171.
3 "Ib.," iii, 203.
4 "Ib.," iv, 33.
5 "General History of America," iv, 171.

igree of an Indian under their system of consanguinity could have no significance apart from a gens; but leaving this out of view, there was no possible way, under Indian institutions, by which a father and his children could bear the same *name* except through a gens, which conferred a common gentile name upon all its members. It would also require descent in the male line to bring father and children into the same gens. The statement shows, moreover, that intermarriage in the gens among the Mayas was prohibited. Assuming the correctness of Herrera's words, it is proof conclusive of the existence of gentes among the Mayas, with descent in the male line. Tylor, in his valuable work on the "Early History of Mankind," which is a repository of widely-drawn and well-digested ethnological information, cites the same fact from another source, with the following remarks: "The analogy of the North American Indian custom is therefore with that of the Australian in making clanship on the female side a bar to marriage, but if we go down further south into Central America, the reverse custom, as in China, makes its appearance. Diego de Landa says of the people of Yucatan, that no one took a wife of his name, on the father's side, for this was a very vile thing among them; but they might marry cousins german on the mother's side."[1]

XI. *South American Indian Tribes.*

Traces of the gens have been found in all parts of South America, as well as the actual presence of the Ganowánian system of consanguinity, but the subject has not been fully investigated. Speaking of the numerous tribes of the Andes brought by the Incas under a species of confederation, Herrera observes that "this variety of tongues proceeded from the nations being divided into races, tribes, or clans."[2] Here in the clans the existence of gentes is recognized. Mr. Tylor, discussing the rules with respect to marriage and descent, remarks that "further south, below the Isthmus, both the

1 "Early History of Mankind," p. 287.
2 "Gen. Hist. of Amer.," iv, 231.

clanship and the prohibition re-appear on the female side. Bernau says that among the Arrawaks of British Guiana, 'Caste is derived from the mother, and children are allowed to marry into their father's family, but not into that of their mother.' Lastly, Father Martin Dobrizhoffer says that the Guaranis avoid, as highly criminal, marriage with the most distant relations; and speaking of the Abipones, he makes the following statement:..... 'The Abipones, instructed by nature and the example of their ancestors, abhor the very thought of marrying any one related to them by the most distant tie of relationship.'"[1] These references to the social system of the aborigines are vague; but in the light of the facts already presented the existence of gentes with descent in the female line, and with intermarriage in the gens prohibited, renders them intelligible. Brett remarks of the Indian tribes in Guiana that they "are divided into families, each of which has a distinct name, as the Siwidi, Karuafudi, Onisidi, etc. Unlike our families, these all descend in the female line, and no individual of either sex is allowed to marry another of the same family name. Thus a woman of the Siwidi family bears the same name as her mother, but neither her father nor her husband can be of that family. Her children and the children of her daughters will also be called Siwidi, but both her sons and daughters are prohibited from an alliance with any individual bearing the same name; though they may marry into the family of their father if they choose. These customs are strictly observed, and any breach of them would be considered as wicked."[2] In the *family* of this writer may at once be recognized the gens in its archaic form. All the South American tribes above named, with the exception of the Andean, were when discovered either in the Lower Status of barbarism, or in the Status of savagery. Many of the Peruvian tribes concentrated under the government established by the Inca Village Indians were in the Lower Status of bar-

1 "Early History of Mankind," p. 287.
2 "Indian Tribes of Guiana," p. 98; cited by Lubbock "Origin of Civilization," p. 98.

barism, if an opinion may be formed from the imperfect description of their domestic institutions found in Garcillasso de la Vega.

To the Village Indians of North and South America, whose indigenous culture had advanced them far into, and near the end of, the Middle Period of barbarism, our attention naturally turns for the transitional history of the gentes. The archaic constitution of the gens has been shown; its latest phases remain to be presented in the gentes of the Greeks and Romans; but the intermediate changes, both of descent and inheritance, which occurred in the Middle Period, are essential to a complete history of the gentile organization. Our information is quite ample with respect to the earlier and later condition of this great institution, but defective with respect to the transitional stage. Where the gentes are found in any tribe of mankind in their latest form, their remote ancestors must have possessed them in the archaic form; but historical criticism demands affirmative proofs rather than deductions. These proofs once existed among the Village Indians. We are now well assured that their system of government was social and not political. The upper members of the series, namely, the tribe and the confederacy, meet us at many points; with positive evidence of the gens, the unit of the system, in a number of the tribes of Village Indians. But we are not able to place our hands upon the gentes among the Village Indians in general with the same precise information afforded by the tribes in the Lower Status of barbarism. The golden opportunity was presented to the Spanish conquerers and colonists, and lost, from apparent inability to understand a condition of society from which civilized man had so far departed in his onward progress. Without a knowledge of the unit of their social system, which impressed its character upon the whole organism of society, the Spanish histories fail entirely in the portrayal of their governmental institutions.

A glance at the remains of ancient architecture in Central America and Peru sufficiently proves that the Middle Period of barbarism was one of great progress in human development, of growing knowledge, and of expanding intelligence. It was followed by a still more remarkable period in the Eastern hemisphere after the invention of the process of making iron had given that final great impulse to human progress which was to bear a portion of mankind into civilization. Our appreciation of the grandeur of man's career in the Later Period of barbarism, when inventions and discoveries multiplied with such rapidity, would be intensified by an accurate knowledge of the condition of society in the Middle Period, so remarkably exemplified by the Village Indians. By a great effort, attended with patient labor, it may yet be possible to recover a large portion at least of the treasures of knowledge which have been allowed to disappear. Upon our present information the conclusion is warrantable that the American Indian tribes were universally organized in gentes at the epoch of European discovery, the few exceptions found not being sufficient to disturb the general rule.

CHAPTER VII

THE AZTEC CONFEDERACY

The Spanish adventurers, who captured the Pueblo of Mexico, adopted the erroneous theory that the Aztec government was a monarchy, analogous in essential respects to existing monarchies in Europe. This opinion was adopted generally by the early Spanish writers, without investigating minutely the structure and principles of the Aztec social system. A terminology not in agreement with their institutions came in with this misconception which has vitiated the historical narrative nearly as completely as though it were, in the main, a studied fabrication. With the capture of the only stronghold the Aztecs possessed, their governmental fabric was destroyed, Spanish rule was substituted in its place, and the subject of their internal organization and polity was allowed substantially to pass into oblivion.[1]

The Aztecs and their confederate tribes were ignorant of iron and consequently without iron tools; they had no money, and traded by barter of commodities; but they worked the native metals, cultivated by irrigation, manufactured coarse fabrics of cotton, constructed joint-tene-

1 The histories of Spanish America may be trusted in whatever relates to the acts of the Spaniards, and to the acts and personal characteristics of the Indians; in whatever relates to their weapons, implements and utensils, fabrics, food and raiment, and things of a similar character. But in whatever relates to Indian society and government, their social relations, and plan of life, they are nearly worthless, because they learned nothing and knew nothing of either. We are at full liberty to reject them in these respects and commence anew; using any facts they may contain which harmonize with what is known of Indian society.

ment houses of adobe-bricks and of stone, and made earthenware of excellent quality. They had, therefore, attained to the Middle Status of barbarism. They still held their lands in common, lived in large households composed of a number of related families; and, as there are strong reasons for believing, practiced communism in living in the household. It is rendered reasonably certain that they had but one prepared meal each day, a dinner; at which they separated, the men eating first and by themselves, and the women and children afterwards. Having neither tables nor chairs for dinner service they had not learned to eat their single daily meal in the manner of civilized nations. These features of their social condition show sufficiently their relative status of advancement.

In connection with the Village Indians of other parts of Mexico and Central America, and of Peru, they afforded the best exemplification of this condition of ancient society then existing on the earth. They represented one of the great stages of progress toward civilization in which the institutions derived from a previous ethnical period are seen in higher advancement, and which were to be transmitted, in the course of human experience, to an ethnical condition still higher, and undergo still further development before civilization was possible. But the Village Indians were not destined to attain the Upper Status of barbarism so well represented by the Homeric Greeks.

The Indian pueblos in the valley of Mexico revealed to Europeans a lost condition of ancient society, which was so remarkable and peculiar that it aroused at the time an insatiable curiosity. More volumes have been written, in the proportion of ten to one, upon the Mexican aborigines and the Spanish Conquest, than upon any other people of the same advancement, or upon any event of the same importance. And yet, there is no people concerning whose institutions and plan of life so little is accurately known. The remarkable spectacle presented so inflamed the imagination that romance swept the field, and has held it to the present hour. The failure to ascertain the structure of Aztec society which resulted was a serious loss to the history of mankind. It should not be made a cause of reproach to any one, but rather for deep regret. Even that which has been written, with such painstaking industry, may prove useful in some future attempt to reconstruct the history of the Aztec confederacy. Certain facts remain of a positive kind from which other facts may be deduced; so that it is not improbable that a well-directed original investigation may yet recover, measurably at least, the essential features of the Aztec social system.

The "kingdom of Mexico" as it stands in the early histories, and the "empire of Mexico" as it appears in the later, is a fiction of the imagination. At the time there was a seeming foundation for describing the government as a monarchy, in the absence of a correct knowledge of their institutions; but the misconception can no longer be defended. That which the Spaniards found was simply a confederacy of three Indian tribes, of which the counterpart existed in all parts of the continent, and they had no occasion in their descriptions to advance a step beyond this single fact. The government was administered by a council of chiefs, with the co-operation of a general commander of the military bands. It was a government of two powers; the civil being represented by the council, and the military by a principal war-chief. Since the institutions of the confederate tribes were essentially democratical, the government may be called a military democracy, if a designation more special than confederacy is required.

Three tribes, the Aztecs or Mexicans, the Tezcucans and the Tlacopans, were united in the Aztec confederacy, which gives the two upper members of the organic social series. Whether or not they possessed the first and the second, namely, the gens and the phratry, does not appear in a definite form in any of the Spanish writers; but they have vaguely described certain institutions which can only be understood by supplying the lost members of the series. Whilst the phratry is not essential it is otherwise with the gens, because it is the unit upon which the social system rests. Without entering the vast and unthreadable labyrinth of Aztec affairs as they now stand historically, I shall venture to invite attention to a few particulars only of the Aztec social system, which may tend to illustrate its real character. Before doing this, the relations of the confederated to surrounding tribes should be noticed.

The Aztecs were one of seven kindred tribes who had migrated from the north and settled in and near the valley of Mexico; and who were among the historical tribes of that country at the epoch of the Spanish Conquest. They called themselves collectively the Nahuatlacs in their traditions. Acosta, who visited Mexico in 1585, and whose work was published at Seville in 1589, has given the current native tradition of their migrations, one after the other, from Aztlan, with their names and places of settlement. He states the order of their arrival as follows: 1. Sochimilcas, "Nation of the Seeds of Flowers," who settled upon Lake Xochimilco, on the south slope of the valley of Mexico; 2. Chalcas, "People of Mouths," who came long after the former and settled near them, on Lake Chalco; 3. Tepanecans, "People of the Bridge," who settled at Azcopozalco, west of Lake Tezcuco, on the western slope of the valley; 4. Culhuas, "A Crooked People," who settled on the east side of Lake Tezcuco, and were afterwards known as Tezcucans; 5. Tlatluicans, "Men of the Sierra," who, finding the valley appropriated around the lake, passed over the Sierra southward and settled upon the other side; 6. Tlascalans, "Men of Bread," who, after living for a time with the Tepanecans, finally settled beyond the valley eastward, at Tlascala; 7. The Aztecs, who came last and occupied the site of the present city of Mexico.[1] Acosta further observes that they came "from far countries which lie toward the north, where now they have found a kingdom which they call New Mexico."[2] The same

1 "The Natural and Moral History of the East and West Indies," Lond. ed., 1604. Grimstone's Trans., pp. 497-504.

2 "The Natural and Moral History of the East and West Indies," p. 499.

tradition is given by Herrera,[1] and also by Clavigero.[2] It will be noticed that the Tlacopans are not mentioned. They were, in all probability, a subdivision of the Tepanecans who remained in the original area of that tribe, while the remainder seem to have removed to a territory immediately south of the Tlascalans, where they were found under the name of the Tepeacas. The latter had the same legend of the seven caves, and spoke a dialect of the Nahuatlac language.[3]

This tradition embodies one significant fact of a kind that could not have been invented; namely, that the seven tribes were of immediate common origin, the fact being confirmed by their dialects; and a second fact of importance, that they came from the north. It shows that they were originally one people, who had fallen into seven and more tribes by the natural process of segmentation. Moreover, it was this same fact which rendered the Aztec confederacy possible as well as probable, a common language being the essential basis of such organizations.

The Aztecs found the best situations in the valley occupied, and after several changes of position they finally settled upon a small expanse of dry land in the midst of a marsh bordered with fields of pedregal and with natural ponds. Here they founded the celebrated pueblo of Mexico (Tenochtitlan), A. D. 1325, according to Clavigero, one hundred and ninety-six years prior to the Spanish Conquest.[4] They were few in number and poor in condition. But fortunately for them, the outlet of Lakes Xochimilco and Chalco and rivulets from the western hills flowed past their site into Lake Tezcuco. Having the sagacity to perceive the advantages of the location they succeeded, by means of causeways and dikes, in surrounding their pueblo with an artificial pond of large extent, the waters being furnished from the sources

1 "General History of America," Lond. ed., 1725, Stevens' Trans., iii, 188.
2 "History of Mexico," Philadelphia ed., 1817, Cullen's Trans., i, 119.
3 Herrera, "Hist. of Amer.," iii, 110.
4 "History of Mexico, loc. cit.," i. 162.

named; and the level of Lake Tezcuco being higher then than at present, it gave them, when the whole work was completed, the most secure position of any tribe in the valley. The mechanical engineering by which they accomplished this result was one of the greatest achievements of the Aztecs, and one without which they would not probably have risen above the level of the surrounding tribes. Independence and prosperity followed, and in time a controlling influence over the valley tribes. Such was the manner, and so recent the time of founding the pueblo according to Aztec traditions which may be accepted as substantially trustworthy.

At the epoch of the Spanish Conquest five of the seven tribes, namely, the Aztecs, Tezcucans, Tlacopans, Sochimilcas, and Chalcans resided in the valley, which was an area of quite limited dimensions, about equal to the state of Rhode Island. It was a mountain or upland basin having no outlet, oval in form, being longest from north to south, one hundred and twenty miles in circuit, and embracing about sixteen hundred square miles excluding the surface covered by water. The valley, as described, is surrounded by a series of hills, one range rising above another with depressions between, encompassing the valley with a mountain barrier. The tribes named resided in some thirty pueblos, more or less, of which that of Mexico was the largest. There is no evidence that any considerable portion of these tribes had colonized outside of the valley and the adjacent hill-slopes; but, on the contrary, there is abundant evidence that the remainder of modern Mexico was then occupied by numerous tribes who spoke languages different from the Nahuatlac, and the majority of whom were independent. The Tlascalans, the Cholulans, a supposed subdivision of the former, the Tepeacas, the Huexotzincos, the Meztitlans, a supposed subdivision of the Tezcucans, and the Tlatluicans were the remaining Nahuatlac tribes living without the valley of Mexico, all of whom were independent excepting the last, and the Tepeacas. A large number of other tribes, forming some seventeen territorial groups, more or less, and speaking as many stock languages, held the remainder of Mexico. They present, in their state of disintegration and independence, a nearly exact repetition of the tribes of the United States and British America, at the time of their discovery, a century or more later.

Prior to A. D. 1426, when the Aztec confederacy was formed, very little had occurred in the affairs of the valley tribes of historical importance. They were disunited and belligerent, and without influence beyond their immediate localities. About this time the superior position of the Aztecs began to manifest its results in a preponderance of numbers and of strength. Under their war-chief, Itzcoatl, the previous supremacy of the Tezcucans and Tlacopans was overthrown, and a league or confederacy was established as a consequence of their previous wars against each other. It was an alliance between the three tribes, offensive and defensive, with stipulations for the division among them, in certain proportions, of the spoils, and the after tributes of subjugated tribes.[1] These tributes, which consisted of the manufactured fabrics and horticultural products of the villages subdued, seem to have been enforced with system, and with rigor of exaction.

The plan of organization of this confederacy has been lost. From the absence of particulars it is now difficult to determine whether it was simply a league to be continued or dissolved at pleasure; or a consolidated organization, like that of the Iroquois, in which the parts were adjusted to each other in permanent and definite relations. Each tribe was independent in whatever related to local self-government; but the three were externally one people in whatever related to aggression or defense. While each tribe had its own council of chiefs, and its own head war-chief, the war-chief of the Aztecs was the commander-in-chief of the confederate bands. This may be inferred from the fact that the Tezcucans and Tlacopans had a voice either in the election or in the confirmation of the Aztec war-chief. The acquisition of the chief

1 Clavigero, "Hist. of Mex.," i. 229: Herrera, iii, 312: Prescott, "Conq. of Mex.," i, 18.

command by the Aztecs tends to show that their influence predominated in establishing the terms upon which the tribes confederated.

Nezahualcojotl had been deposed, or at least dispossessed of his office, as principal war-chief of the Tezcucans, to which he was at this time (1426) restored by Aztec procurement. The event may be taken as the date of the formation of the confederacy or league whichever it was.

Before discussing the limited number of facts which tend to illustrate the character of this organization, a brief reference should be made to what the confederacy accomplished in acquiring territorial domination during the short period of its existence.

From A. D. 1426 to 1520, a period of ninety-four years, the confederacy was engaged in frequent wars with adjacent tribes, and particularly with the feeble Village Indians southward from the valley of Mexico to the Pacific, and thence eastward well toward Guatemala. They began with those nearest in position whom they overcame, through superior numbers and concentrated action, and subjected to tribute. The villages in this area were numerous but small, consisting in many cases of a single large structure of adobe-brick or of stone, and in some cases of several such structures grouped together. These joint-tenement houses interposed serious hindrances to Aztec conquest, but they did not prove insuperable. These forays were continued from time to time for the avowed object of gathering spoil, imposing tribute, and capturing prisoners for sacrifice;[1] until the

1 The Aztecs, like the Northern Indians, neither exchanged nor released prisoners. Among the latter the stake was the doom of the captive unless saved by adoption; but among the former, under the teachings of the priesthood, the unfortunate captive was offered as a sacrifice to the principal god they worshiped. To utilize the life of the prisoner in the service of the gods, a life forfeited by the immemorial usages of savages and barbarians, was the high conception of the first hierarchy in the order of institutions. An organized priesthood first appeared among the American aborigines in the Middle Status of barbarism; and it stands connected with the invention of idols and human sacrifices, as a means of acquiring authority over mankind through the religious sentiments. It probably has a simi-

principal tribes within the area named, with some exceptions, were subdued and made tributary, including the scattered villages of the Totonacs near the present Vera Cruz.

No attempt was made to incorporate these tribes in the Aztec confederacy, which the barrier of language rendered impossible under their institutions. They were left under the government of their own chiefs, and to the practice of their own usages and customs. In some cases a collector of tribute resided among them. The barren results of these conquests reveal the actual character of their institutions. A domination of the strong over the weak for no other object than to enforce an unwilling tribute, did not even tend to the formation of a nation. If organized in gentes, there was no way for an individual to become a member of the government except through a gens, and no way for the admission of a gens except by its incorporation among the Aztec, Tezcucan, or Tlacopan gentes. The plan ascribed to Romulus of removing the gentes of conquered Latin tribes to Rome might have been resorted to by the Aztec confederacy with respect to the tribes overrun; but they were not sufficiently advanced to form such a conception, even though the barrier of language could have been obviated. Neither could colonists for the same reason, if sent among them, have so far assimilated the conquered tribes as to prepare them for incorporation in the Aztec social system. As it was the confederacy gained no strength by the terrorism it created; or by holding these tribes under burdens, inspired with enmity and ever ready to revolt. It seems, however, that they used the military bands of subjugated tribes in some cases, and shared with them the spoils. All the Aztecs could do, after

---

lar history in the principal tribes of mankind. Three successive usages with respect to captives appeared in the three subperiods of barbarism. In the first he was burned at the stake, in the second he was sacrificed to the gods, and in the third he was made a slave. All alike they proceeded upon the principle that the life of the prisoner was forfeited to his captor. This principle became so deeply seated in the human mind that civilization and Christianity combined were required for its displacement.

forming the confederacy, was to expand it over the remaining Nahuatlac tribes. This they were unable to accomplish. The Xochimilcas and Chalcans were not constituent members of the confederacy, but they enjoyed a nominal independence, though tributary.

This is about all that can now be discovered of the material basis of the so-called kingdom or empire of the Aztecs. The confederacy was confronted by hostile and independent tribes on the west, northwest, northeast, east, and southeast sides: as witness, the Mechoacans on the west, the Otomies on the northwest, (scattered bands of the Otomies near the valley had been placed under tribute), the Chichimecs or wild tribes north of the Otomies, the Meztitlans on the northeast, the Tlascalans on the east, the Cholulans and Huexotzincos on the southeast and beyond them the tribes of the Tabasco, the tribes of Chiapas, and the Zapotecs. In these several directions the dominion of the Aztec confederacy did not extend a hundred miles beyond the valley of Mexico, a portion of which surrounding area was undoubtedly neutral ground separating the confederacy from perpetual enemies. Out of such limited materials the kingdom of Mexico of the Spanish chronicles was fabricated, and afterwards magnified into the Aztec empire of current history.

A few words seem to be necessary concerning the population of the valley and of the pueblo of Mexico. No means exist for ascertaining the number of the people in the five Nahuatlac tribes who inhabited the valley. Any estimate must be conjectural. As a conjecture then, based upon what is known of their horticulture, their means of subsistence, their institutions, their limited area, and not forgetting the tribute they received, two hundred and fifty thousand persons in the aggregate would probably be an excessive estimate. It would give about a hundred and sixty persons to the square mile, equal to nearly twice the present average population of the state of New York, and about equal to the average population of Rhode Island. It is difficult to perceive what sufficient reason can be assigned for so large a number of inhabitants in all the villages within the valley, said to have been from thirty to forty. Those who claim a higher number will be bound to show how a barbarous people, without flocks and herds, and without field agriculture, could have sustained in equal areas a larger number of inhabitants than a civilized people can now maintain armed with these advantages. It cannot be shown for the simple reason that it could not have been true. Out of this population thirty thousand may, perhaps, be assigned to the pueblo of Mexico.[1]

It will be unnecessary to discuss the position and relations of the valley tribes beyond the suggestions made. The Aztec monarchy should be dismissed from American aboriginal history, not only as delusive, but as a misrepresentation of the Indians, who had neither developed nor invented monarchical institutions. The government they formed was a confederacy of tribes, and nothing more; and probably not equal in plan and symmetry with that of the Iroquois. In dealing with this organization, War-chief, Sachem, and Chief will be sufficient to distinguish their official persons.

The pueblo of Mexico was the largest in America. Romantically situated in the midst of an artificial lake, its large joint-tenement houses plastered over with gyp-

---

1 There is some difference in the estimates of the population of Mexico found in the Spanish histories; but several of them concurred in the number of houses, which, strange to say, is placed at sixty thousand. Zuazo, who visited Mexico in 1521, wrote sixty thousand inhabitants (Prescott, "Conq. of Mex.," ii, 112, note); the Anonymous Conqueror, who accompanied Cortes also wrote sixty thousand inhabitants, "soixante mille habitans" ("H. Ternaux-Compans," x, 92); but Gomora and Martyr wrote sixty thousand houses, and this estimate has been adopted by Clavigero ("Hist. of Mex.," ii, 360) by Herrera ("Hist. of Amer.," ii, 360), and by Prescott ("Conq. of Mex.," ii,112). Solis says sixty thousand families ("Hist. Conq. of Mex., l. c.," i, 393). This estimate would give a population of 300,000, although London at that time contained but 145,000 inhabitants (Black's "London." p. 5). Finally, Torquemada, cited by Clavigero (ii, 360, note), boldly writes one hundred and twenty thousand houses. There can scarcely be a doubt that the houses in this pueblo were in general large communal, or joint-tenement houses, like those in New Mexico of the same period, large enough to accommodate from ten to fifty and a hundred families in each. At either number the mistake is egregious. Zuazo and the Annonymous Conqueror came the nearest to a respectable estimate, because they did not much more than double the probable number.

sum, which made them a brilliant white, and approached by causeways, it presented to the Spaniards, in the distance, a striking and enchanting spectacle. It was a revelation of an ancient society lying two ethnical periods back of European society, and eminently calculated, from its orderly plan of life, to awaken curiosity and inspire enthusiasm. A certain amount of extravagance of opinion was unavoidable.

A few particulars have been named tending to show the extent of Aztec advancement to which some others may now be added. Ornamental gardens were found, magazines of weapons and of military costumes, improved apparel, manufactured fabrics of cotton of superior workmanship, improved implements and utensils, and an increased variety of food; picture-writing, used chiefly to indicate the tribute in kind each subjugated village was to pay; a calendar for measuring time, and open markets for the barter of commodities. Administrative offices had been created to meet the demands of a growing municipal life; a priesthood, with a temple worship and a ritual including human sacrifices, had been established. The office of head war-chief had also risen into increased importance. These, and other circumstances of their condition, not necessary to be detailed, imply a corresponding development of their institutions. Such are some of the differences between the Lower and the Middle Status of barbarism, as illustrated by the relative conditions of the Iroquois and the Aztecs, both having doubtless the same original institutions.

With these preliminary suggestions made, the three most important and most difficult questions with respect to the Aztec social system, remain to be considered. They relate first, to the existence of Gentes and Phratries; second, the existence and functions of the Council of Chiefs; and, third, the existence and functions of the office of General Military Commander, held by Montezuma.

I. *The Existence of Gentes and Phratriēs.*

It may seem singular that the early Spanish writers did not discover the Aztec gentes, if in fact they existed;

but the case was nearly the same with the Iroquois under the observation of our own people more than two hundred years. The existence among them of clans, named after animals, was pointed out at an early day, but without suspecting that it was the unit of a social system upon which both the tribe and the confederacy rested. [1] The failure of the Spanish investigators to notice the existence of the gentile organization among the tribes of Spanish America would afford no proof of its non-existence; but if it did exist, it would simply prove that their work was superficial in this respect.

There is a large amount of indirect and fragmentary evidence in the Spanish writers pointing both to the gens and the phratry, some of which will now be considered. Reference has been made to the frequent use of the term "kindred" by Herrera, showing that groups of persons were noticed who were bound together by affinities of blood. This, from the size of the group, seems to require a gens. The term "lineage" is sometimes used to indicate a still larger group, and implying a phratry.

The pueblo of Mexico was divided geographically into four quarters, each of which was occupied by a lineage, a body of people more nearly related by consanguinity among themselves than they were to the inhabitants of the other quarters. Presumptively, each lineage was a phratry. Each quarter was again subdivided, and each local subdivision was occupied by a community of persons bound together by some common tie. [2] Presumptively, this community of persons was a gens. Turning to the kindred tribe of Tlascalans, the same facts nearly re-appear. Their pueblo was divided into four quarters, each occupied by a lineage. Each had its own Teuctli or head war-chief, its distinctive military costume, and its own standard and blazon. [3] As one people they were under the government of a council of chiefs, which the Spaniards honored with the name of the Tlascalan sen-

1 "League of the Iroquois," p. 78.
2 Herrera, iii, 194, 209.
3 Herrera, ii, 279, 304: Clavigero, i, 146.

ate.[1] Cholula, in like manner, was divided into six quarters, called wards by Herrera, which leads to the same inference.[2] The Aztecs in their social subdivisions having arranged among themselves the parts of the pueblo they were severally to occupy, these geographical districts would result from their mode of settlement. If the brief account of these *quarters* at the foundation of Mexico, given by Herrera, who follows Acosta, is read in the light of this explanation, the truth of the matter will be brought quite near. After mentioning the building of a "chapel of lime and stone for the idol," Herrera proceeds as follows: "When this was done, the idol ordered a priest to bid the chief men divide themselves, with their kindred and followers, into four wards or quarters, leaving the house that had been built for him to rest in the middle, and each party to build as they liked best. These are the four quarters of Mexico now called St. John, St. Mary the Round, St. Paul and St. Sebastian. That division being acordingly made, their idol again directed them to distribute among themselves the gods he should name, and each ward to appoint peculiar places where the gods should be worshiped; and thus every quarter has several smaller wards in it according to the number of their gods this idol called them to adore . . . Thus Mexico, Tenochtitlan, was founded . . . . When the aforesaid partition was made, those who thought themselves injured, with their kindred and followers, went away to seek some other place,"[3] namely, Tlatelueco, which was adjacent. It is a reasonable interpretation of this language that they divided by kin, first into four general divisions, and these into smaller subdivisions, which is the usual formula for stating results. But the actual process was the exact reverse; namely, each body of kindred located in an area by themselves, and the several bodies in such a way as to bring those most nearly related in geographical connection with each

---

1 Clavigero, i, 147; The four war-chiefs were ex officio members of the Council. Ib., ii, 137.
2 Herrera, ii, 310.
3 Herrera, iii, 194.

other. Assuming that the lowest subdivision was a gens, and that each quarter was occupied by a phratry, composed of related gentes, the primary distribution of the Aztecs in their pueblo is perfectly intelligible. Without this assumption it is incapable of a satisfactory explanation. When a people, organized in gentes, phratries and tribes, settled in a town or city, they located by gentes and by tribes, as a necessary consequence, of their social organization. The Grecian and Roman tribes settled in their cities in this manner. For example, the three Roman tribes were organized in gentes and curiæ, the curia being the analogue of the phratry; and they settled at Rome by gentes, by curiæ and by tribes. The Ramnes occupied the Palatine Hill. The Tities were mostly on the Quirinal, and the Luceres mostly on the Esquiline. If the Aztecs were in gentes and phratries, having but one tribe, they would of necessity be found in as many quarters as they had phratries, with each gens of the same phratry in the main locally by itself. As husband and wife were of different gentes, and the children were of the gens of the father or mother as descent was in the male or the female line, the preponderating number in each locality would be of the same gens.

Their military organization was based upon these social divisions. As Nestor advised Agamemnon to arrange the troops by phratries and by tribes, the Aztecs seem to have arranged themselves by gentes and by phratries. In the *Mexican Chronicles,* by the native author Tezozomoc (for a reference to the following passage in which I am indebted to my friend Mr. Ad. F. Bandelier, of Highland, Illinois, who is now engaged upon its translation), a proposed invasion of Michoacan is referred to. Axaycatl "spoke to the Mexican captains Tlacatecatl and Tlacochcalcatl, and to all the others, and inquired whether all the Mexicans were prepared, after the usages and customs of each ward, each one with its captains; and if so that they should begin to march, and that all were to reunite at Matlatzinco Toluca."[1] It in-

1 "Cronica Mexicana," De Fernando de Alvarado Tezozomoc, ch. li, p. 83, Kingsborough, v. ix.

dicates that the military organization was by gentes and by phratries.

An inference of the existence of Aztec gentes arises also from their land tenure. Clavigero remarks that "the lands which were called *Altepetlalli* [altepetl=pueblo] that is, those of the communities of cities and villages, were divided into as many parts as there were districts in a city, and every district possessed its own part entirely distinct from, and independent of every other. These lands could not be alienated by any means whatever."[1] In each of these communities we are led to recognize a gens, whose localization was a necessary consequence of their social system. Clavigero puts the districts for the community, whereas it was the latter which made the district, and which owned the lands in common. The element of kin, which united each community, omitted by Clavigero is supplied by Herrera. "There were other lords, called major parents [sachems], whose landed property all belonged to one lineage [gens], which lived in one district, and there were many of them when the lands were distributed at the time New Spain was peopled; and each lineage received its own, and have possessed them until now; and these lands did not belong to any one in particular, but to all in common, and he who possessed them could not sell them, although he enjoyed them for life and left them to his sons and heirs; and if a house died out they were left to the nearest parent to whom they were given and to no other, who administered the same district or lineage."[2] In this remarkable statement our author was puzzled to harmonize the facts with the prevailing theory of Aztec institutions. He presents to us an Aztec lord who held the fee of the land as a feudal proprietor, and a title of rank pertaining to it, both of which he transmitted to his son and heir. But in obedience to truth he states the essential fact that the lands belonged to a body of consanguinei of whom he is styled the major

---

1 "History of Mexico," ii, 141.

2 "History of America," iii, 314. The above is a retranslation by Mr. Bandelier from the Spanish text.

parent, *i. e.,* he was the sachem, it may be supposed, of the gens, the latter owning these lands in common. The suggestion that he held the lands in trust means nothing. They found Indian chiefs connected with gentes, each gens owning a body of lands in common, and when the chief died, his place was filled by his son, according to Herrera. In so far it may have been analogous to a Spanish estate and title; and the misconception resulted from a want of knowledge of the nature and tenure of the office of chief. In some cases they found the son did not succeed his father, but the office went to some other person; hence the further statement, "if a house (*alguna casa,* another feudal feature) died out, they [the lands] were left to the nearest major parent;" *i. e.,* another person was elected sachem, as near as any conclusion can be drawn from the language. What little has been given to us by the Spanish writers concerning Indian chiefs, and the land tenure of the tribes is corrupted by the use of language adapted to feudal institutions that had no existence among them. In this *lineage* we are warranted in recognizing an Aztec gens; and in this *lord* an Aztec sachem, whose office was hereditary in the gens, in the sense elsewhere stated, and elective among its members. If descent was in the male line, the choice would fall upon one of the sons of the deceased sachem, own or collateral, upon a grandson, through one of his sons, or upon a brother, own or collateral. But if in the female line it would fall upon a brother or nephew, own or collateral, as elsewhere explained. The sachem had no title whatever to the lands, and therefore none to transmit to any one. He was thought to be the proprietor because he held an office which was perpetually maintained, and because there was a body of lands perpetually belonging to a gens over which he was a sachem. The misconception of this office and of its tenure has been the fruitful source of unnumbered errors in our aboriginal histories. The *lineage* of Herrera, and the *communities* of Clavigero were evidently organizations, and the same organization. They found in this body of kindred, without knowing the fact, the unit of their social system—a gens, as we must suppose.

Indian chiefs are described as lords by Spanish writers, and invested with rights over lands and over persons they never possessed. It is a misconception to style an Indian chief a lord in the European sense, because it implies a condition of society that did not exist. A lord holds a rank and a title by hereditary right, secured to him by special legislation in derogation of the rights of the people as a whole. To this rank and title, since the overthrow of feudalism, no duties are attached which may be claimed by the king or the kingdom as a matter of right. On the contrary, an Indian chief holds an office, not by hereditary right, but by election from a constituency, which retained the right to depose him for cause. The office carried with it the obligation to perform certain duties for the benefit of the constituency. He had no authority over the persons or property or lands of the members of the gens. It is thus seen that no analogy exists between a lord and his title, and an Indian chief and his office. One belongs to political society, and represents an aggression of the few upon the many; while the other belongs to gentile society and is founded upon the common interests of the members of the gens. Unequal privileges find no place in the gens, phratry or tribe.

Further traces of the existence of Aztec gentes will appear. A *prima facie* case of the existence of gentes among them is at least made out. There was also an antecedent probability to this effect, from the presence of the two upper members of the organic series, the tribe, and the confederacy, and from the general prevalence of the organization among other tribes. A very little close investigation by the early Spanish writers would have placed the question beyond a doubt, and, as a consequence, have given a very different complexion to Aztec history.

The usages regulating the inheritance of property among the Aztecs have come down to us in a confused and contradictory condition. They are not material in this discussion, except as they reveal the existence of bodies of consanguinei, and the inheritance by children from their fathers. If the latter were the fact it would show that descent was in the male line, and also an extraordinary advance in a knowledge of property. It is not probable that children enjoyed an exclusive inheritance, or that any Aztec owned a foot of land which he could call his own, with power to sell and convey to whomsoever he pleased.

II. *The Existence and Functions of the Council of Chiefs.*

The existence of such a council among the Aztecs might have been predicted from the necessary constitution of Indian society. Theoretically, it would have been composed of that class of chiefs, distinguished as sachems, who represented bodies of kindred through an office perpetually maintained. Here again, as elsewhere, a necessity is seen for gentes, whose principal chiefs would represent the people in their ultimate social subdivisions as among the Northern tribes. Aztec gentes are fairly necessary to explain the existence of Aztec chiefs. Of the presence of an Aztec council there is no doubt whatever; but of the number of its members and of its functions we are left in almost total ignorance. Brasseur de Bourbourg remarks generally that "nearly all the towns or tribes are divided into four clans or quarters whose chiefs constitute the great council."[1] Whether he intended to limit the number to one chief from each quarter is not clear; but elsewhere he limits the Aztec council to four chiefs. Diego Duran, who wrote his work in 1579-1581, and thus preceded both Acosta and Tezozomoc, remarks as follows: "First we must know, that in Mexico after having elected a king they elected four lords of the brothers or near relations of this king to whom they gave the titles of princes, and from whom they had to choose the king. [To the offices he gives the names of Tlacachcalcatl, Tlacatecal, Ezuauacatl, and Fillancalque] ..... These four lords and titles after being elected princes, they made them the royal council, like the presidents and judges of the supreme council, without whose opinion nothing could be

---

1 "Popol Vuh," Intro. p. 117, note 2.

done."[1] Acosta, after naming the same offices, and calling the persons who held them "electors," remarks that "all these four dignities were of the great council, without whose advice the king might not do anything of importance."[2] And Herrera, after placing these offices in four grades, proceeds: "These four sorts of noblemen were of the supreme council, without whose advice the king was to do nothing of moment, and no king could be chosen but what was of one of these four orders."[3] The use of the term king to describe a principal war-chief and of princes to describe Indian chiefs cannot create a state or a political society where none existed; but as misnomers they stilt up and disfigure our aboriginal history and for that reason ought to be discarded. When the Huexotzincos sent delegates to Mexico proposing an alliance against the Tlascalans, Montezuma addressed them, according to Tezozomoc, as follows: "Brothers and sons, you are welcome, rest yourselves awhile, for although I am king indeed I alone cannot satisfy you, but only together with all the chiefs of the sacred Mexican senate."[4] The above accounts recognize the existence of a supreme council, with authority over the action of the principal war-chief, which is the material point. It tends to show that the Aztecs guarded themselves against an irresponsible despot, by subjecting his action to a council of chiefs, and by making him elective and deposable. If the limited and incomplete statements of these authors intended to restrict this council to four members, which Duran seems to imply, the limitation is improbable. As such the council would represent, not the Aztec tribe, but the small body of kinsmen from whom the military commander was to be chosen. This is not the theory of a council of chiefs. Each chief represents a constituency, and the chiefs together represent the tribe. A selection from their num-

---

1 "History of the Indies of New Spain and Islands of the Main Land," Mexico, 1867. Ed. by Jose F. Ramirez, p. 102. Published from the original MS. Translated by Mr. Bandelier.

2 "The Natural and Moral History of the East and West Indies," Lond. ed., 1604. Grimstone's Trans., p. 485.

3 "History of America," iii, 224.

4 "Cronica Mexicana," cap. xcvii. Bandelier's Trans.

ber is sometimes made to form a general council; but it is through an organic provision which fixes the number, and provides for their perpetual maintenance. The Tezcucan council is said to have consisted of fourteen members,[1] while the council at Tlascala was a numerous body. Such a council among the Aztecs is required by the structure and principles of Indian society, and therefore would be expected to exist. In this council may be recognized the lost element in Aztec history. A knowledge of its functions is essential to a comprehension of Aztec society.

In the current histories this council is treated as an advisory board of Montezuma's, as a council of ministers of his own creation; thus Clavigero: "In the history of the conquest we shall find Montezuma in frequent deliberation with his council on the pretensions of the Spaniards. We do not know the number of each council, nor do historians furnish us with the lights necessary to illustrate such a subject."[2] It was one of the first questions requiring investigation, and the fact that the early writers failed to ascertain its composition and functions is proof conclusive of the superficial character of their work. We know, however, that the council of chiefs is an institution which came in with the gentes, which represents electing constituencies, and which from time immemorial had a vocation as well as original governing powers. We find a Tezcucan and Tlacopan council, a Tlascalan, a Cholulan and a Michoacan council, each composed of chiefs. The evidence establishes the existence of an Aztec council of chiefs; but so far as it is limited to four members, all of the same lineage, it is presented in an improbable form. Every tribe in Mexico and Central America, beyond a reasonable doubt, had its council of chiefs. It was the governing body of the tribe, and a constant phenomenon in all parts of aboriginal America. The council of chiefs is the oldest institution of government of mankind. It can show an unbroken

1 Ixtlilxochitl, "Hist. Chichimeca," Kingsborough, "Mex. Antiq.," ix, p. 243.
2 "History of Mexico," ii, 132.

succession on the several continents from the Upper Status of savagery through the three sub-periods of barbarism to the commencement of civilization, when, having been changed into a preconsidering council with the rise of the assembly of the people, it gave birth to the modern legislature in two bodies.

It does not appear that there was a general council of the Aztec confederacy, composed of the principal chiefs of the three tribes, as distinguished from the separate councils of each. A complete elucidation of this subject is required before it can be known whether the Aztec organization was simply a league, offensive and defensive, and as such under the primary control of the Aztec tribe, or a confederacy in which the parts were integrated in a symmetrical whole. This problem must await future solution.

III. *The Tenure and Functions of the Office of Principal War-chief.*

The name of the office held by Montezuma, according to the best accessible information, was simply *Teuctli,* which signifies a *war-chief.* As a member of the council of chiefs he was sometimes called *Tlatoani,* which signifies *speaker.* This office of a general military commander was the highest known to the Aztecs. It was the same office and held by the same tenure as that of principal war-chief in the Iroquois confederacy. It made the person, *ex officio,* a member of the council of chiefs, as may be inferred from the fact that in some of the tribes the principal war-chief had precedence in the council both in debate and in pronouncing his opinion.[1] None of the Spanish writers apply this title to Montezuma or his successors. It was superseded by the inappropriate title of king. *Ixtlilxochitl,* who was of mixed Tezcucan and Spanish descent, describes the head war-chiefs of

1 "The title of 'Teuctli' was added in the manner of a surname to the proper name of the person advanced to this dignity, as 'Chichimeca-Teuctli,' 'Pil-Teuctli,' and others. The 'Teuctli' took precedency of all others in the senate, both in the order of sitting and voting, and were permitted to have a servant behind them with a seat, which was esteemed a privilege of the highest honor."—Clavigero, ii, 137. This is a re-appearance of the sub-sachem of the Iroquois behind his principal.

Mexico, Tezcuco and Tlacopan, by the simple title of war-chief, with another to indicate the tribe. After speaking of the division of powers between the three chiefs when the confederacy was formed, and of the assembling of the chiefs of the three tribes on that occasion, he proceeds: "The king of Tezcuco was saluted by the title of *Aculhua Teuctli,* also by that of *Chichimecatl Teuctli* which his ancestors had worn, and which was the mark of the empire; *Itzcoatzin,* his uncle, received the title of *Culhua Teuctli,* because he reigned over the Toltecs-Culhuas; and *Totoquihuatzin* that of *Tecpanuatl Teuctli,* which had been the title of *Azcaputzalco.* Since that time their successors have received the same title." [1] *Itzcoatzin* (*Itzcoatl*), here mentioned, was war-chief of the Aztecs when the confederacy was formed. As the title was that of war-chief, then held by many other persons, the compliment consisted in connecting with it a tribal designation. In Indian speech the office held by Montezuma was equivalent to head war-chief, and in English to general.

Clavigero recognizes this office in several Nahuatlac tribes, but never applies it to the Aztec war-chief. "The highest rank of nobility in Tlascala, in Huexotzinco and in Cholula was that of *Teuctli.* To obtain this rank it was necessary to be of noble birth, to have given proofs in several battles of the utmost courage, to have arrived at a certain age, and to command great riches for the enormous expenses which were necessary to be supported by the possessor of such a dignity." [2] After Montezuma had been magnified into an absolute potentate, with civil as well as military functions, the nature and powers of the office he held were left in the background — in fact uninvestigated. As their general military commander he possessed the means of winning the popular favor, and of commanding the popular respect. It was a dangerous but necessary office to the tribe and to the confederacy. Throughout human experience, from the Lower Status of barbarism to the present time, it has

1 "Historia Chichimeca," ch. xxxii, Kingsborough: "Mex. Antiq.," ix, 219.
2 "History of Mexico," l. c., ii, 136.

ever been a dangerous office. Constitutions and laws furnish the present security of civilized nations, so far as they have any. A body of usages and customs grew up, in all probability, among the advanced Indian tribes and among the tribes of the valley of Mexico, regulating the powers and prescribing the duties of this office. There are general reasons warranting the supposition that the Aztec council of chiefs was supreme, not only in civil affairs, but over military affairs, the person and direction of the war-chief included. The Aztec polity under increased numbers and material advancement, had undoubtedly grown complex, and for that reason a knowledge of it would have been the more instructive. Could the exact particulars of their governmental organization be ascertained they would be sufficiently remarkable without embellishment.

The Spanish writers concur generally in the statement that the office held by Montezuma was elective, with the choice confined to a particular family. The office was found to pass from brother to brother, or from uncle to nephew. They were unable, however, to explain why it did not in some cases pass from father to son. Since the mode of succession was unusual to the Spaniards there was less possibility of a mistake with regard to the principal fact. Moreover, two successions occurred under the immediate notice of the conquerors. Montezuma was succeeded by Cuitlahua. In this case the office passed from brother to brother, although we cannot know whether they were own or collateral brothers without a knowledge of their system of consanguinity. Upon the death of the latter Guatemozin was elected to succeed him. Here the office passed from uncle to nephew, but we do not know whether he was an own or a collateral nephew. (See Part Third, ch. iii.) In previous cases the office had passed from brother to brother and also from uncle to nephew. [1] An elective office implies a constituency; but who were the constituents in this case? To meet this question the four chiefs mentioned by Duran (*supra*) are introduced as electors, to whom one

1 Clavigero, ii, 126.

elector from Tezcuco and one from Tlacopan are added, making six, who are then invested with power to choose from a particular family the principal war-chief. This is not the theory of an elective Indian office, and it may be dismissed as improbable. Sahagun indicates a much larger constituency. "When the king or lord died," he remarks, "all the senators called *Tecutlatoques,* and the old men of the tribe called *Achcacauhti,* and also the captains and old warriors called *Yautequioaques,* and other prominent captains in warlike matters, and also the priests called *Tlenamacaques,* or *Papasaques* — all these assembled in the royal houses. Then they deliberated upon and determined who had to be lord, and chose one of the most noble of the lineage of the past lords, who should be a valiant man, experienced in warlike matters, daring and brave.... When they agreed upon one they at once named him as lord, but this election was not made by ballot or votes, but all together conferring at last agreed upon the man. The lord once elected they also elected four others which were like senators, and had to be always with the lord, and be informed of all the business of the kingdom." [1] This scheme of election by a large assembly, while it shows the popular element in the government which undoubtedly existed, is without the method of Indian institutions. Before the tenure of this office and the mode of election can be made intelligible, it is necessary to find whether or not they were organized in gentes, whether descent was in the female line or the male, and to know something of their system of consanguinity. If they had the system found in many other tribes of the Ganowánian family, which is probable, a man would call his brother's son his son, and his sister's son his nephew; he would call his father's brother his father, and his mother's brother his uncle; the children of his father's brother his brothers and sisters, and the children of his mother's brother his cousins, and so on. If organized into gentes with descent in the female line, a man would have brothers, uncles and nephews, collateral grandfathers and grandsons within his own

1 "Historia General," ch. xviii.

gens; but neither own father, own son, nor lineal grandson. His own sons and his brother's sons would belong to other gentes. It cannot as yet be affirmed that the Aztecs were organized in gentes; but the succession to the office of principal war-chief is of itself strong proof of the fact, because it would explain this succession completely. Then with descent in the female line the office would be hereditary in a particular gens, but elective among its members. In that case the office would pass, by election within the gens, from brother to brother, or from uncle to nephew, precisely as it did among the Aztecs, and never from father to son. Among the Iroquois at that same time the offices of sachem and of principal war-chief were passing from brother to brother or from uncle to nephew, as the choice might happen to fall, and never to the son. It was the gens, with descent in the female line, which gave this mode of succession, and which could have been secured in no other conceivable way. It is difficult to resist the conclusions, from these facts alone, that the Aztecs were organized in gentes, and that in respect to this office at least, descent was still in the female line.

It may therefore be suggested, as a probable explanation, that the office held by Montezuma was hereditary in a gens (the eagle was the blazon or totem on the house occupied by Montezuma), by the members of which the choice was made from among their number; that their nomination was then submitted separately to the four lineages or divisions of the Aztecs (conjectured to be phratries), for acceptance or rejection; and also to the Tezcucans and Tlacopans, who were directly interested in the selection of the general commander. When they had severally considered and confirmed the nomination each division appointed a person to signify their concurrence; whence the six miscalled electors. It is not unlikely that the four high chiefs of the Aztecs, mentioned as electors by a number of authors, were in fact the war-chiefs of the four divisions of the Aztecs, like the four war-chiefs of the four lineages of the Tlascalans. The function of these persons was not to elect, but to ascertain by a conference with each other whether the choice made by the gens had been concurred in, and if so to announce the result. The foregoing is submitted as a conjectural explanation, upon the fragments of evidence remaining, of the mode of succession to the Aztec office of principal war-chief. It is seen to harmonize with Indian usages, and with the theory of the office of an elective Indian chief.

The right to depose from office follows as a necessary consequence of the right to elect, where the term was for life. It is thus turned into an office during good behavior. In these two principles of electing and deposing, universally established in the social system of the American aborigines, sufficient evidence is furnished that the sovereign power remained practically in the hands of the people. This power to depose, though seldom exercised, was vital in the gentile organization. Montezuma was no exception to the rule. It required time to reach this result from the peculiar circumstances of the case, for a good reason was necessary. When Montezuma allowed himself, through intimidation, to be conducted from his place of residence to the quarters of Cortes where he was placed under confinement, the Aztecs were paralyzed for a time for the want of a military commander. The Spaniards had possession both of the man and of his office. [1] They waited some weeks, hoping the Spaniards would retire; but when they found the latter intended to remain they met the necessity, as there are sufficient reasons for believing, by deposing Montezuma for want of resolution, and elected his brother to fill his place. Immediately thereafter they assaulted the Spanish quarters

1 In the West India Islands the Spaniards discovered that when they captured the cacique of a tribe and held him a prisoner, the Indians became demoralized and refused to fight. Taking advantage of this knowledge when they reached the main-land they made it a point to entrap the principal chief, by force or fraud, and hold him a prisoner until their object was gained. Cortes simply acted upon this experience when he captured Montezuma and held him a prisoner in his quarters; and Pizaarro did the same when he seized Atahuallpa. Under Indian customs the prisoner was put to death, and if a principal chief, the office reverted to the tribe and was at once filled. But in these cases the prisoner remained alive, and in possession of his office, so that it could not be filled. The action of the people was paralyzed by novel circumstances. Cortes put the Aztecs in this position.

with great fury, and finally succeeded in driving them from their pueblo. This conclusion respecting the deposition of Montezuma is fully warranted by Herrera's statement of the facts. After the assault conmmenced, Cortes, observing the Aztecs obeying a new commander, at once suspected the truth of the matter, and "sent Marina to ask Montezuma whether he thought they had put the government into his hands,"[1] *i. e.*, the hands of the new commander. Montezuma is said to have replied "that they would not presume to choose a king in Mexico whilst he was living."[2] He then went upon the roof of the house and addressed his countrymen, saying among other things, "that he had been informed they had chosen another king because he was confined and loved the Spaniards;" to which he received the following ungracious reply from an Aztec warrior: "Hold your peace, you effeminate scoundrel, born to weave and spin; these dogs keep you a prisoner, you are a coward."[3] Then they discharged arrows upon him and stoned him, from the effects of which and from deep humiliation he shortly afterwards died. The war-chief in the command of the Aztecs in this assault was Cuitlahua, the brother of Montezuma and his successor.[4]

Respecting the functions of this office very little satisfactory information can be derived from the Spanish writers. There is no reason for supposing that Montezuma possessed any power over the civil affairs of the Aztecs. Moreover, every presumption is against it. In military affairs when in the field he had the powers of a general; but military movements were probably decided upon by the council. It is an interesting fact to be noticed that the functions of a priest were attached to the office of principal war-chief, and, as it is claimed, those of a judge.[5] The early appearance of these functions in the natural growth of the military office will be referred to again in connection with that of basileus. Although the government was of two powers it is probable that

1 "History of Mexico," iii, 66.
2 Ib., iii, 67.
3 Clavigero, ii, 406.
4 Ib., ii, 404.
5 Herrera, iii, 393.

the council was supreme, in case of a conflict of authority, over civil and military affairs. It should be remembered that the council of chiefs was the oldest in time, and possessed a solid basis of power in the needs of society and in the representative character of the office of chief.

The tenure of the office of principal war-chief and the presence of a council with power to depose from office, tend to show that the institutions of the Aztecs were essentially democratical. The elective principle with respect to war-chief, and which we must suppose existed with respect to sachem and chief, and the presence of a council of chiefs, determine the material fact. A pure democracy of the Athenian type was unknown in the Lower, in the Middle, or even in the Upper Status of barbarism; but it is very important to know whether the institutions of a people are essentially democratical, or essentially monarchical, when we seek to understand them. Institutions of the former kind are separated nearly as widely from those of the latter, as democracy is from monarchy. Without ascertaining the unit of their social system, if organized in gentes as they probably were, and without gaining a knowledge of the system that did exist, the Spanish writers boldly invented for the Aztecs an absolute monarchy with high feudal characteristics, and have succeeded in placing it in history. This misconception has stood, through American indolence, quite as long as it deserves to stand. The Aztec organization presented itself plainly to the Spaniards as a league or confederacy of tribes. Nothing but the grossest perversion of obvious facts could have enabled the Spanish writers to fabricate the Aztec monarchy out of a democratic organization.

Theoretically, the Aztecs, Tezcucans and Tlacopans should severally have had a head-sachem to represent the tribe in civil affairs when the council of chiefs was not in session, and to take the initiative in preparing its work. There are traces of such an officer among the Aztecs in the *Ziahuacatl,* who is sometimes called the second chief, as the war-chief is called the first. But the accessible information respecting this office is too limited to warrant a discussion of the subject.

It has been shown among the Iroquois that the warriors could appear before the council of chiefs and express their views upon public questions; and that the women could do the same through orators of their own selection. This popular participation in the government led in time to the popular assembly, with power to adopt or reject public measures submitted to them by the council. Among the Village Indians there is no evidence, so far as the author is aware, that there was an assembly of the people to consider public questions with power to act upon them. The four lineages probably met for special objects, but this was very different from a general assembly for public objects. From the democratic character of their institutions and their advanced condition the Aztecs were drawing near the time when the assembly of the people might be expected to appear.

The growth of the idea of government among the American aborigines, as elsewhere remarked, commenced with the gens and ended with the confederacy. Their organizations were social and not political. Until the idea of property had advanced very far beyond the point they had attained, the substitution of political for gentile society was impossible. There is not a fact to show that any portion of the aborigines, at least in North America, had reached any conception of the second great plan of government founded upon territory and upon property. The spirit of the government and the condition of the people harmonize with the institutions under which they live. When the military spirit predominates, as it did among the Aztecs, a military democracy rises naturally under gentile institutions. Such a government neither supplants the free spirit of the gentes, nor weakens the principles of democracy, but accords with them harmoniously.

CHAPTER VIII

THE GRECIAN GENS

Civilization may be said to have commenced among the Asiatic Greeks with the composition of the Homeric poems about 850 B. C.; and among the European Greeks about a century later with the composition of the Hesiodic poems. Anterior to these epochs, there was a period of several thousand years during which the Hellenic tribes were advancing through the Later Period of barbarism, and preparing for their entrance upon a civilized career. Their most ancient traditions find them already established in the Grecian peninsula, upon the eastern border of the Mediterranean, and upon the intermediate and adjacent islands. An older branch of the same stock, of which the Pelasgians were the chief representatives, had preceded them in the occupation of the greater part of these areas, and were in time either Hellenized by them, or forced into emigration. The anterior condition of the Hellenic tribes and of their predecessors, must be deduced from the arts and inventions which they brought down from the previous period, from the state of development of their language, from their traditions and from their social institutions, which severally survived into the period of civilization. Our discussion will be restricted, in the main, to the last class of facts.

Pelasgians and Hellenes alike were organized in gentes, phratries [1] and tribes; and the latter united by coalescence into nations. In some cases the organic series

1 The phratries were not common to the Dorian tribes.—Müller's "Dorians," Tufnel and Law's Trans., Oxford ed., ii, 82.

was not complete. Whether in tribes or nations their government rested upon the gens as the unit of organization, and resulted in a gentile society or a people, as distinguished from a political society or a state. The instrument of government was a council of chiefs, with the co-operation of an agora or assembly of the people, and of a basileus or military commander. The people were free, and their institutions democratical. Under the influence of advancing ideas and wants the gens had passed out of its archaic into its ultimate form. Modifications had been forced upon it by the irresistible demands of an improving society; but, notwithstanding the concessions made, the failure of the gentes to meet these wants was constantly becoming more apparent. The changes were limited, in the main, to three particulars: firstly, descent was changed to the male line; secondly, intermarriage in the gens was permitted in the case of female orphans and heiresses; and thirdly, children had gained an exclusive inheritance of their father's property. An attempt will elsewhere be made to trace these changes, briefly, and the causes by which they were produced.

The Hellenes in general were in fragmentary tribes, presenting the same characteristics in their form of government as the barbarous tribes in general, when organized in gentes and in the same stage of advancement. Their condition was precisely such as might have been predicted would exist under gentile institutions, and therefore presents nothing remarkable.

When Grecian society came for the first time under historical observation, about the first Olympiad (776 B. C.) and down to the legislation of Cleisthenes (509 B. C.), it was engaged upon the solution of a great problem. It was no less than a fundamental change in the plan of government, involving a great modification of institutions. The people were seeking to transfer themselves out of gentile society, in which they had lived from time immemorial, into political society based upon territory and upon property, which had become essential to a career of civilization. In fine, they were striving to establish a state, the first in the experience of the Aryan family, and to place it upon a territorial foundation, such as the state has occupied from that time to the present. Ancient society rested upon an organization of persons, and was governed through the relations of persons to a gens and tribe; but the Grecian tribes were outgrowing this old plan of government, and began to feel the necessity of a political system. To accomplish this result it was only necessary to invent a deme or township, circumscribed with boundaries, to christen it with a name, and organize the people therein as a body politic. The township, with the fixed property it contained, and with the people who inhabited it for the time being, was to become the unit of organization in the new plan of government. Thereafter the gentilis, changed into a citizen, would be dealt with by the state through his territorial relations, and not through his personal relations to a gens. He would be enrolled in the deme of his residence, which enrollment was the evidence of his citizenship; would vote and be taxed in his deme; and from it be called into the military service. Although apparently a simple idea, it required centuries of time and a complete revolution of pre-existing conceptions of government to accomplish the result. The gens, which had so long been the unit of a social system, had proved inadequate, as before suggested, to meet the requirements of an advancing society. But to set this organization aside, together with the phratry and tribe, and substitute a number of fixed areas, each with its community of citizens, was, in the nature of the case, a measure of extreme difficulty. The relations of the individual to his gens, which were personal, had to be transferred to the township and become territorial; the demarch of the township taking, in some sense, the place of the chief of the gens. A township with its fixed property would be permanent, and the people therein sufficiently so; while the gens was a fluctuating aggregate of persons, more or less scattered, and now growing incapable of permanent establishment in a local circumscription. Anterior to experience, a township, as the unit of a political system, was abstruse enough to tax the Greeks and Romans to the depths of their capacities before the conception was formed and set in practical operation. Property was the new element that had been gradually remoulding Grecian institutions to prepare the way for political society, of which it was to be the mainspring as well as the foundation. It was no easy task to accomplish such a fundamental change, however simple and obvious it may now seem; because all the previous experience of the Grecian tribes had been identified with the gentes whose powers were to be surrendered to the new political bodies.

Several centuries elapsed, after the first attempts were made to found the new political system, before the problem was solved. After experience had demonstrated that the gentes were incapable of forming the basis of a state, several distinct schemes of legislation were tried in the various Grecian communities, who copied more or less each other's experiments, all tending to the same result. Among the Athenians from whose experience the chief illustrations will be drawn, may be mentioned the legislation of Theseus, on the authority of tradition; that of Draco (624 B. C.); that of Solon (594 B. C.); and that of Cleisthenes (509 B. C.), the last three of which were within the historical period. The development of municipal life and institutions, the aggregation of wealth in walled cities, and the great changes in the mode of life thereby produced, prepared the way for the overthrow of gentile society, and for the establishment of political society in its place.

Before attempting to trace the transition from gentile into political society, with which the closing history of the gentes is identified, the Grecian gens and its attributes will be first considered.

Athenian institutions are typical of Grecian institutions in general, in whatever relates to the constitution of the gens and tribe, down to the end of ancient society among them. At the commencement of the historical period, the Ionians of Attica were subdivided, as is well known, into four tribes (Geleontes, Hopletes, Aegicores, and Argades), speaking the same dialect, and occupying a common territory. They had coalesced into a nation as distinguished from a confederacy of tribes; but such a confederacy had probably existed in anterior times.[1] Each Attic tribe was composed of three phratries, and each phratry of thirty gentes, making an aggregate of twelve phratries, and of three hundred and sixty gentes in the four tribes. Such is the general form of the statement, the fact being constant with respect to the number of tribes, and the number of phratries in each, but liable to variation in the number of gentes in each phratry. In like manner the Dorians were generally found in three tribes (Hylleis, Pamphyli, and Dymanes), although forming a number of nationalities; as at Sparta, Argos, Sicyon, Corinth, Epidaurus and Troezen; and beyond the Peloponnesus at Megara, and elsewhere. One or more non-Dorian tribes were found in some cases united with them, as at Corinth, Sicyon and Argos.

In all cases the Grecian tribe presupposes the gentes, the bond of kin and of dialect forming the basis upon which they united in a tribe; but the tribe did not presuppose the phratry, which, as an intermediate organization, although very common among all these tribes, was liable to be intermitted. At Sparta, there were subdivisions of the tribes called obês, each tribe containing ten, which were analogous to phratries; but concerning the functions of these organizations some uncertainty prevails.[2]

The Athenian gentes will now be considered as they appeared in their ultimate form and in full vitality; but with the elements of an incipient civilization arrayed against them, before which they were yielding step by step, and by which they were to be overthrown with the social system they created. In some respects it is the

---

1 Hermann mentions the confederacies of Ægina, Athens, Prasia, Nauplia, etc.—"Political Antiquities of Greece," Oxford Trans., ch. i, s. 11.

2 "In the ancient "Rhetra" of Lycurgus, the tribes and obes are directed to be maintained unaltered: but the statement of O. Müller and Boeckh—that there were thirty obes in all, ten to each tribe,—rests upon no higher evidence than a peculiar punctuation in this "Rhetra," which various other critics reject; and seemingly with good reason. We are thus left without any information respecting the obe, though we know that it was an old peculiar and lasting division among the Spartan people." —Grote's "History of Greece," Murray's ed., ii, 362. But see Müller's "Dorians," l. c., ii, 80.

most interesting portion of the history of this remarkable organization, which had brought human society out of savagery, and carried it through barbarism into the early stages of civilization.

The social system of the Athenians exhibits the following series: first, the gens (*genos*) founded upon kin; second, the phratry (*phratra* and *phratria*), a brotherhood of gentes derived by segmentation, probably, from an original gens; third, the tribe (*phylon,* later *phyle*), composed of several phratries, the members of which spoke the same dialect; and fourth, a people or nation, composed of several tribes united by coalescence into one gentile society, and occupying the same territory. These integral and ascending organizations exhausted their social system under the gentes, excepting the confederacy of tribes occupying independent territories, which, although it occurred in some instances in the early period and sprang naturally out of gentile institutions, led to no important results. It is likely that the four Athenian tribes confederated before they coalesced, the last occurring after they had collected in one territory under pressure from other tribes. If true of them, it would be equally true of the Dorian and other tribes. When such tribes coalesced into a nation, there was no term in the language to express the result, beyond a national name. The Romans, under very similar institutions, styled themselves the *Populus Romanus,* which expressed the fact exactly. They were then simply a people, and nothing more; which was all that could result from an aggregation of gentes, *curiae* and tribes. The four Athenian tribes formed a society or people, which became completely autonomous in the legendary period under the name of the Athenians. Throughout the early Grecian communities, the gens, phratry and tribe were constant phenomena of their social systems, with the occasional absence of the phratry.

Mr. Grote has collected the principal facts with respect to the Grecian gentes with such critical ability that they cannot be presented in a more authoritative manner than in his own language, which will be quoted where he treats the subject generally. After commenting upon the tribal divisions of the Greeks, he proceeds as follows: "But the Phratries and Gentes are a distribution completely different from this. They seem aggregations of small primitive unities into larger; they are independent of, and do not presuppose, the tribe; they arise separately and spontaneously, without preconcerted uniformity, and without reference to a common political purpose; the legislator finds them pre-existing, and adapts or modifies them to answer some national scheme. We must distinguish the general fact of the classification, and the successive subordination in the scale, of the families to the gens, of the gentes to the phratry, and of the phratries to the tribe — from the precise numerical symmetry with which this subordination is invested, as we read it, — thirty families to a gens, thirty gentes to a phratry, three phratries to each tribe. If such nice equality of numbers could ever have been procured, by legislative constraint, operating upon pre-existent natural elements, the proportions could not have been permanently maintained. But we may reasonably doubt whether it did ever so exist.... That every phratry contained an equal number of gentes, and every gens an equal number of families. is a supposition hardly admissible without better evidence than we possess. But apart from this questionable precision of numerical scale, the Phratries and Gentes themselves were real, ancient, and durable associations among the Athenian people, highly important to be understood. The basis of the whole was the house, hearth, or family, — a number of which, greater or less, composed the Gens or Genos. This gens was therefore a clan, sept, or enlarged, and partly factitious, brotherhood, bound together by, — 1. Common religious ceremonies, and exclusive privilege of priesthood, in honor of the same god, supposed to be the primitive ancestor, and characterized by a special surname. 2. By a common burial place.[1] 3. By mutual rights of succession to property. 4. By reciprocal obligations of help, defense, and redress of injuries. 5. By mutual right and obligation to intermarry in certain determinate cases, especially where there was an orphan

1 —Demosthenes, "Eubulides," 1307.

daughter or heiress. 6. By possession, in some cases, at least, of common property, an archon and treasurer of their own. Such were the rights and obligations characterizing the gentile union. The phratric union, binding together several gentes, was less intimate, but still included some mutual rights and obligations of an analogous character; especially a communion of particular sacred rites, and mutual privileges of prosecution in the event of a phrator being slain. Each phratry was considered as belonging to one of the four tribes, and all the phratries of the same tribe enjoyed a certain periodical communion of sacred rites under the presidency of a magistrate called the Phylo-Basileus or tribe-king selected from the Eupatrids."[1]

The similarities between the Grecian and the Iroquois gens will at once be recognized. Differences in characteristics will also be perceived, growing out of the more advanced condition of Grecian society, and a fuller development of their religious system. It will not be necessary to verify the existence of the several attributes of the gens named by Mr. Grote, as the proof is plain in the classical authorities. There were other characteristics which doubtless pertained to the Grecian gens, although it may be difficult to establish the existence of all of them; such as: 7. The limitation of descent to the male line; 8. The prohibition of intermarriage in the gens excepting in the case of heiresses; 9. The right of adopting strangers into the gens; and 10. The right of electing and deposing its chiefs.

The rights, privileges and obligations of the members of the Grecian gens may be recapitulated, with the additions named, as follows:

I. *Common religious rites.*

II. *A common burial place.*

III. *Mutual rights of succession to property of deceased members.*

IV. *Reciprocal obligations of help, defense and redress of injuries.*

---

1 "History of Greece," III, 53, et seq.

V. *The right to intermarry in the gens in the cases of orphan daughters and heiresses.*
VI. *The possession of common property, an archon, and a treasurer.*
VII. *The limitation of descent to the male line.*
VIII. *The obligation not to marry in the gens except in specified cases.*
IX. *The right to adopt strangers into the gens.*
X. *The right to elect and depose its chiefs.*

A brief reference to the added characteristics should be made.

7. *The limitation of descent to the male line.* There is no doubt that such was the rule, because it is proved by their genealogies. I have not been able to find in any Greek author a definition of a gens or of a gentilis that would furnish a sufficient test of the right of a given person to the gentile connection. Cicero, Varro and Festus have defined the Roman gens and gentilis, which were strictly analogous to the Grecian, with sufficient fullness to show that descent was in the male line. From the nature of the gens, descent was either in the female line or the male, and included but a moiety of the descendants of the founder. It is precisely like the family among ourselves. Those who are descended from the males bear the family name, and they constitute a gens in the full sense of the term, but in a state of dispersion, and without any bond of union excepting those nearest in degree. The females lose, with their marriage, the family name, and with their children are transferred to another family. Grote remarks that Aristotle was the "son of the physician Nikomachus who belonged to the gens of the Asklepiads."[1] Whether Aristotle was of the gens of his father depends upon the further question whether they both derived their descent from Aesculapius, through males exclusively. This is shown by Laertius, who states that "Aristotle was the son of Nikomachus . . . . . and Nikomachus was descended from Nikomachus the son of Machaon, the son of Aesculapius."[2] Although the higher members of the series

1 "History of Greece," iii, 60.
2 Diogenes, Laertius, "Vit. Aristotle," v, I.

may be fabulous, the manner of tracing the descent would show the gens of the person. The statement of Hermann, on the authority of Isaeus, is also to the point. "Every infant was registered in the phratria and clan of its father."[1] Registration in the gens of the father implies that his children were of his gens.

8. *The obligation not to marry in the gens excepting in specified cases.* This obligation may be deduced from the consequences of marriage. The wife by her marriage lost the religious rites of her gens, and acquired those of her husband's gens. The rule is stated as so general as to imply that marriage was usually out of the gens. "The virgin who quits her father's house," Wachsmuth remarks, "is no longer a sharer of the paternal sacrificial hearth, but enters the religious communion of her husband, and this gave sanctity to the marriage tie."[2] The fact of her registration is stated by Hermann as follows: "Every newly married woman, herself a citizen, was on this account enrolled in the phratry of her husband."[3] Special religious rites (*sacra gentilicia*) were common in the Grecian and Latin gens. Whether the wife forfeited her agnatic rights by her marriage, as among the Romans, I am unable to state. It is not probable that marriage severed all connection with her gens, and the wife doubtless still counted herself of the gens of her father.

The prohibition of intermarriage in the gens was fundamental in the archaic period; and it undoubtedly remained after descent was changed to the male line, with the exception of heiresses and female orphans for whose case special provision was made. Although a tendency to free marriage, beyond certain degrees of consanguinity, would follow the complete establishment of the monogamian family, the rule requiring persons to marry out of their own gens would be apt to remain so long as the gens was the basis of the social system. The special provision in respect to heiresses tends to confirm this

1 "Political Antiquities of the Greeks," c. v, s. 100; and vide "Eubulides" of Demosthenes, 24.

2 "Historical Antiquities of the Greeks," Woolrych's Trans., Oxford ed., 1837, i, 451.

3 "Political Antiquities, l. c.," cap. v, s. 100.

supposition. Becker remarks upon this question, that "relationship was, with trifling limitations, no hindrance to marriage, which could take place within all degrees of *anchisteia,* or *sungeneia,* though naturally not in the gens itself."[1]

9. *The right to adopt strangers into the gens.* This right was practiced at a later day, at least in families; but it was done with public formalities, and was doubtless limited to special cases. [2] Purity of lineage became a matter of high concern in the Attic gentes, interposing no doubt serious obstacles to the use of the right except for weighty reasons.

10. *The right to elect and depose its chiefs.* This right undoubtedly existed in the Grecian gentes in the early period. Presumptively it was possessed by them while in the upper Status of barbarism. Each gens had its archon, which was the common name for a chief. Whether the office was elective, for example, in the Homeric period, or was transmitted by hereditary right to the eldest son, is a question. The latter was not the ancient theory of the office; and a change so great and radical, affecting the independence and personal rights of all the members of the gens, requires positive proof to override the presumption against it. Hereditary right to an office, carrying with it authority over, and obligations from, the members of a gens is a very different thing from an office bestowed by a free election, with the reserved power to depose for unworthy behavior. The free spirit of the Athenian gentes down to the time of Solon and Cleisthenes forbids the supposition, as to them, that they had parted with a right so vital to the independence of the members of the gens. I have not been able to find any satisfactory explanation of the tenure of this office. Hereditary succession, if it existed, would indicate a remarkable development of the aristocratical element in ancient society, in derogation of the democratical constitution of the gentes. Moreover, it would be a

---

1 "Charicles," Metcalfe's Trans., Lond. ed., 1866, p. 477; citing "Isaeus de Cir. her." 217: "Demosthenes adv. Ebul.," 1304: "Plutarch, Themist.," 32: "Pausanias," i, 7, 1: "Achill. Tat.," i, 3.

2 Hermann, "l. c.," v, s. 100 and 101.

sign of the commencement, at least, of their decadence. All the members of a gens were free and equal, the rich and the poor enjoying equal rights and privileges, and acknowledging the same in each other. We find liberty, equality and fraternity, written as plainly in the constitution of the Athenian gentes as in those of the Iroquois. Hereditary right to the principal office of the gens is totally inconsistent with the older doctrine of equal rights and privileges.

Whether the higher offices of anax, koiranos, and basileus were transmitted by hereditary right from father to son, or were elective or confirmative by a larger constituency, is also a question. It will be considered elsewhere. The former would indicate the subversion, as the latter the conservation, of gentile institutions. Without decisive evidence to the contrary every presumption is adverse to hereditary right. Some additional light will be gained on this subject when the Roman gentes are considered. A careful re-investigation of the tenure of this office would, not unlikely, modify essentially the received accounts.

It may be considered substantially assured that the Grecian gentes possessed the ten principal attributes named. All save three, namely, descent in the male line, marrying into the gens in the case of heiresses, and the possible transmission of the highest military office by hereditary right, are found with slight variations in the gentes of the Iroquois. It is thus rendered apparent that in the gentes, both the Grecian and the Iroquois tribes possessed the same original institution, the one having the gens in its later, and the other in its archaic form.

Recurring now to the quotation from Mr. Grote, it may be remarked that had he been familiar with the archaic form of the gens, and with the several forms of the family anterior to the monogamian, he would probably have modified essentially some portion of his statement. An exception must be taken to his position that the basis of the social system of the Greeks "was the house, hearth, or family." The form of the family in the mind of the distinguished historian was evidently the Roman, under the iron-clad rule of a *pater familias,* to which the Grecian family of the Homeric period approximated in the complete domination of the father over the household. It would have been equally untenable had other and anterior forms of the family been intended. The gens, in its origin, is older than the monogamian family, older than the syndyasmian, and substantially contemporaneous with the punaluan. In no sense was it founded upon either. It does not recognize the existence of the family of any form as a constituent of itself. On the contrary, every family in the archaic as well as in the later period, was partly within and partly without the gens, because husband and wife must belong to different gentes. The explanation is both simple and complete; namely, that the family springs up independently of the gens with entire freedom to advance from a lower into a higher form, while the gens is constant, as well as the unit of the social system. The gens entered entire into the phratry, the phratry entered entire into the tribe, and the tribe entered entire into the nation; but the family could not enter entire into the gens because husband and wife must belong to different gentes.

The question here raised is important, since not only Mr. Grote, but also Niebuhr, Thirlwall, Maine, Mommsen, and many other able and acute investigators have taken the same position with respect to the monogamian family of the patriarchal type as the integer around which society integrated in the Grecian and Roman systems. Nothing whatever was based upon the family in any of its forms, because it was incapable of entering a gens as a whole. The gens was homogeneous and to a great extent permanent in duration, and as such, the natural basis of a social system. A family of the monogamian type might have become individualized and powerful in a gens, and in society at large; but the gens nevertheless did not and could not recognize or depend upon the family as an integer of itself. The same remarks are equally true with respect to the modern family and political society. Although individualized by property rights and privileges, and recognized as a legal entity by statutory enactment, the family is not the unit of the political system. The state recognizes the counties of which it is composed, the county its townships, but the township takes no note of the family; so the nation recognized its tribes, the tribe its phratries, and the phratry its gentes; but the gens took no note of the family. In dealing with the structure of society, organic relations alone are to be considered. The township stands in the same relation to political society that the gens did to gentile society. Each is the unit of a system.

There are a number of valuable observations by Mr. Grote, upon the Grecian gentes, which I desire to incorporate as an exposition of them; although these observations seem to imply that they are no older than the then existing mythology, or hierarchy of the gods from the members of which some of the gentes claimed to have derived their eponymous ancestor. In the light of the facts presented, the gentes are seen to have existed long before this mythology was developed — before Jupiter or Neptune, Mars or Venus were conceived in the human mind.

Mr. Grote proceeds: "Thus stood the primitive religious and social union of the population of Attica in its gradually ascending scale — as distinguished from the political union, probably of later introduction, represented at first by the trittyes and naukraries, and in after times by the ten Kleisthenean tribes, subdivided into trittyes and demes. The religious and family bond of aggregation is the earlier of the two; but the political bond, though beginning later, will be found to acquire constantly increasing influence throughout the greater part of this history. In the former, personal relation is the essential and predominant characteristic — local relation being subordinate; in the latter, property and residence become the chief considerations, and the personal element counts only as measured along with these accompaniments. All these phratric and gentile associations, the larger as well as the smaller, were founded upon the same principles and tendencies of the Grecian mind — a coalescence of the idea of worship with that of ancestry, or of communion in certain special religious rites with communion of blood, real or supposed. The god or hero, to whom the assembled members offered their sacrifices, was conceived as the primitive ancestor to whom they owed their origin; often through a long list of intermediate names, as in the case of the Milesian Hekatæus, so often before referred to. Each family had its own sacred rites and funeral commemorations of ancestors, celebrated by the master of the house, to which none but members of the family were admissible. . . . The larger associations, called gens, phratry, tribe, were formed by an extension of the same principle — of the family considered as a religious brotherhood, worshiping some common god or hero with an appropriate surname, and recognizing him as their joint ancestor; and the festival of Theoenia, and Apaturia (the first Attic, the second common to all the Ionian race) annually brought together the members of these phratries and gentes for worship, festivity, and maintenance of special sympathies; thus strengthening the larger ties without effacing the smaller. . . . But the historian must accept as an ultimate fact the earliest state of things which his witnesses make known to him, and in the case now before us, the gentile and phratric unions are matters into the beginning of which we cannot pretend to penetrate."[1]

"The gentes both at Athens, and in other parts of Greece, bore a patronymic name, the stamp of their believed common paternity.[2] . . . But at Athens, at least after the revolution of Kleisthenês, the gentile name was not employed: a man was described by his own single name, followed first by the name of his father, and next by that of the deme to which he belonged,—as *Aeschinês son of Atromêtus, a Kothôkid*. . . . The gens constituted a close incorporation, both as to property and as to persons. Until the time of Solon, no man had any power

1 "History of Greece," iii, 55.

2 "We find the Asklepiadæ in many parts of Greece—the Aleuadæ in Thessaly—the Midylidæ, Psalychidæ, Belpsiadæ, Euxenidae, at Aegina—the Branchidæ at Miletus—the Nebridæ at Kôs—the Iamidæ and Klytiadæ at Olympia—the Akestoridæ at Argos—the Kinyradæ at Cyprus—the Penthilidæ at Mitylene—the Talthybiadæ at Sparta—not less than the Kodridæ, Eumolpidæ, Phytalidæ, Lykomêdæ, Butadæ, Euneidæ, Hesychidæ, Brytiadæ, etc., in Attica. To each of these corresponded a mythical ancestor more or less known, and passing for the first father as well as the eponymous hero of the gens—Kodrus, Eumolpus, Butes, Phytalus, Hesychus, etc."—Grote's "Hist. of Greece," iii, 62.

of testamentary disposition. If he died without children, his gennêtes succeeded to his property, and so they continued to do even after Solon, if he died intestate. An orphan girl might be claimed in marriage of right by any member of the gens, the nearest agnates being preferred; if she was poor, and he did not choose to marry her himself, the law of Solon compelled him to provide her with a dowry proportional to his enrolled scale of property, and to give her out in marriage to another. . . . If a man was murdered, first his near relations, next his gennêtes and phrators, were both allowed and required to prosecute the crime at law; while his fellow demots, or inhabitants of the same deme, did not possess the like right of prosecuting. All that we hear of the most ancient Athenian laws is based upon the gentile and phratric divisions, which are treated throughout as extensions of the family. It is to be observed that this division is completely independent of any property qualification — rich men as well as poor being comprehended in the same gens. Moreover, the different gentes were very unequal in dignity, arising chiefly from the religious ceremonies of which each possessed the hereditary and exclusive administration, and which, being in some cases considered of pre-eminent sanctity in reference to the whole city, were therefore nationalized. Thus the Eumolpidæ and Kêrykes, who supplied the hierophant and superintendent of the mysteries of the Eleusinian Dêmêtêr — and the Butadæ, who furnished the priestess of Athênê Polias, as well as the priest of Poseidôn Erechtheus in the Acropolis — seem to have been reverenced above all the other gentes."[1]

Mr. Grote speaks of the gens as an extension of the family, and as presupposing its existence; treating the family as primary and the gens as secondary. This view, for the reasons stated, is untenable. The two organizations proceed upon different principles and are independent of each other. The gens embraces a part only of the descendants of a supposed common ancestor, and excludes the remainder; it also embraces a part only of a

1 "History of Greece," iii, 62, et seq.

family, and excludes the remainder. In order to be a constituent of the gens, the family should enter entire within its folds, which was impossible in the archaic period, and constructive only in the later. In the organization of gentile society the gens is primary, forming both the basis and the unit of the system. The family also is primary, and older than the gens; the punaluan and the consanguine families having preceded it in the order of time; but it was not a member of the organic series in ancient society any more than it is in modern.

The gens existed in the Aryan family when the Latin, Grecian and Sanskrit speaking tribes were one people, as is shown by the presence in their dialects of the same term (gens, *genos,* and *ganas*) to express the organization. They derived it from their barbarous ancestors, and more remotely from their savage progenitors. If the Aryan family became differentiated as early as the Middle period of barbarism, which seems probable, the gens must have been transmitted to them in its archaic form. After that event, and during the long periods of time which elapsed between the separation of these tribes from each other and the commencement of civilization, those changes in the constitution of the gens, which have been noticed hypothetically, must have occurred. It is impossible to conceive of the gens as appearing, for the first time, in any other than its archaic form; consequently the Grecian gens must have been originally in this form. If, then, causes can be found adequate to account for so great a change of descent as that from the female line to the male, the argument will be complete, although in the end it substituted a new body of kindred in the gens in place of the old. The growth of the idea of property, and the rise of monogamy, furnished motives sufficiently powerful to demand and obtain this change in order to bring children into the gens of their father, and into a participation in the inheritance of his estate. Monogamy assured the paternity of children, which was unknown when the gens was instituted, and the exclusion of children from the inheritance was no longer possible. In the face of the new circumstances, the gens would be forced into reconstruction or dissolution. When the gens of the Iroquois, as it appeared in the Lower Status of barbarism, is placed beside the gens of the Grecian tribes as it appeared in the Upper Status, it is impossible not to perceive that they are the same organization, the one in its archaic and the other in its ultimate form. The differences between them are precisely those which would have been forced upon the gens by the exigencies of human progress.

Along with these mutations in the constitution of the gens are found the parallel mutations in the rule of inheritance. Property, always hereditary in the gens, was first hereditary among the gentiles; secondly, hereditary among the agnates, to the exclusion of the remaining gentiles; and now, thirdly, hereditary among the agnates in succession, in the order of their nearness to the decedent, which gave an exclusive inheritance to the children as the nearest agnates. The pertinacity with which the principle was maintained down to the time of Solon, that the property should remain in the gens of the deceased owner, illustrates the vitality of the organization through all these periods. It was this rule which compelled the heiress to marry in her own gens to prevent a transfer of the property by her marriage to another gens. When Solon allowed the owner of property to dispose of it by will, in case he had no children, he made the first inroad upon the property rights of the gens.

How nearly the members of a gens were related, or whether they were related at all, has been made a question. Mr. Grote remarked that "Pollux informs us distinctly that the members of the same gens at Athens were not commonly related by blood, — and even without any express testimony we might have concluded such to be the fact. To what extent the gens, at the unknown epoch of its formation was based upon actual relationship, we have no means of determining, either with regard to the Athenian or the Roman gentes, which were in the main points analogous. Gentilism is a tie by itself; distinct from the family ties, but presupposing their existence and extending them by an artificial analogy, partly founded in religious belief, and partly on positive compact, so as to comprehend strangers in blood. All the members of one gens, or even of one phratry, believed themselves to be sprung, not indeed from the same grandfather or great-grandfather, but from the same divine or heroic ancestor. . . . And this fundamental belief, into which the Greek mind passed with so much facility, was adopted and converted by positive compact into the gentile and phratric principle of union. . . . Doubtless Niebuhr, in his valuable discussion of the ancient Roman gentes, is right in supposing that they were not real families, procreated from any common historical ancestor. Still it is not the less true (although he seems to suppose otherwise) that the idea of the gens involved *the belief* in a common first father, divine or heroic — a genealogy which we may properly call fabulous, but which was consecrated and accredited among the members of the gens itself; and served as one important bond of union between them. . . . The natural families of course changed from generation to generation, some extending themselves, while others diminished or died out; but the gens received no alterations, except through the procreation, extinction, or subdivision of these component families. Accordingly the relations of the families with the gens were in perpetual course of fluctuation, and the gentile ancestorial genealogy, adapted as it doubtless was to the early condition of the gens, became in process of time partially obsolete and unsuitable. We hear of this genealogy but rarely, because it is only brought before the public in certain cases pre-eminent and venerable. But the humbler gentes had their common rites, and common superhuman ancestor and genealogy, as well as the more celebrated: the scheme and ideal basis was the same in all." [1]

The several statements of Pollux, Niebuhr and Grote are true in a certain sense, but not absolutely so. The lineage of a gens ran back of the acknowledged ancestor, and therefore the gens of ancient date could not have had a known progenitor; neither could the fact of a blood connection be proved by their system of consanguinity; nevertheless the gentiles not only *believed* in their com-

1 "Hist. of Greece," iii, 58, et seq.

mon descent, but were justified in so believing. The system of consanguinity which pertained to the gens in its archaic form, and which the Greeks probably once possessed, preserved a knowledge of the relationships of all the members of a gens to each other. This fell into desuetude with the rise of the monogamian family, as I shall endeavor elsewhere to show. The gentile name created a pedigree beside which that of a family was insignificant. It was the function of this name to preserve the fact of the common descent of those who bore it; but the lineage of the gens was so ancient that its members could not prove the actual relationship existing between them, except in a limited number of cases through recent common ancestors. The name itself was the evidence of a common descent, and conclusive, except as it was liable to interruption through the adoption of strangers in blood in the previous history of the gens. The practical denial of all relationship between its members made by Pollux and Niebuhr, which would change the gens into a purely fictitious association, has no ground to rest upon. A large proportion of the number could prove their relationship through descent from common ancestors within the gens, and as to the remainder the gentile name they bore was sufficient evidence of common descent for practical purposes. The Grecian gens was not usually a large body of persons. Thirty families to a gens, not counting the wives of the heads of families, would give, by the common rule of computation, an average of one hundred and twenty persons to the gens.

As the unit of the organic social system, the gens would naturally become the centre of social life and activity. It was organized as a social body, with its archon or chief, and treasurer; having common lands to some extent, a common burial place, and common religious rites. Beside these were the rights, privileges and obligations which the gens conferred and imposed upon all its members. It was in the gens that the religious activity of the Greeks originated, which expanded over the phratries, and culminated in periodical festivals common to all the tribes. This subject has been admirably treated by M. De Coulanges in his recent work on "The Ancient City."

In order to understand the condition of Grecian society, anterior to the formation of the state, it is necessary to know the constitution and principles of the Grecian gens; for the character of the unit determines the character of its compounds in the ascending series, and can alone furnish the means for their explanation.

CHAPTER IX

THE GRECIAN PHRATRY, TRIBE AND NATION

The phratry, as we have seen, was the second stage of organization in the Grecian social system. It consisted of several gentes united for objects, especially religious, which were common to them all. It had a natural foundation in the bond of kin, as the gentes in a phratry were probably subdivisions of an original gens, a knowledge of the fact having been preserved by tradition. "All the contemporary members of the phratry of Hekatæus," Mr. Grote remarks, "had a common god for their ancestor at the sixteenth degree,"[1] which could not have been asserted unless the several gentes comprised in the phratry of Hekatæus, were supposed to be derived by segmentation from an original gens. This genealogy, although in part fabulous, would be traced according to gentile usages. Dikæarchus supposed that the practice of certain gentes in supplying each other with wives, led to the phratric organization for the performance of common religious rites. This is a plausible explanation, because such marriages would intermingle the blood of the gentes. On the contrary, gentes formed, in the course of time, by the division of a gens and by subsequent subdivisions, would give to all a common lineage, and form a natural basis for their re-integration in a phratry. As such the phratry would be a natural growth, and as such only can it be explained as a gentile institution. The gentes thus united were brother gentes, and the association itself was a brotherhood as the term imports.

---

1 "History of Greece," iii, 58.

Stephanus of Byzantium has preserved a fragment of Dikæarchus, in which an explanation of the origin of the gens, phratry and tribe is suggested. It is not full enough, with respect to either, to amount to a definition: but it is valuable as a recognition of the three stages of organization in ancient Grecian society. He uses patry in the place of gens, as Pindar did in a number of instances, and Homer occasionally. The passage may be rendered: "Patry is one of three forms of social union among the Greeks, according to Dikæarchus, which we call respectively, patry, phratry, and tribe. The patry comes into being when relationship, originally solitary, passes over into the second stage [the relationship of parents with children and children with parents], and derives its eponym from the oldest and chief member of the patry, as Aicidas, Pelopidas."

"But it came to be called phatria and phratria when certain ones gave their daughters to be married into another patry. For the woman who was given in marriage participated no longer in her paternal sacred rites, but was enrolled in the patry of her husband; so that for the union, formerly subsisting by affection between sisters and brothers, there was established another union based on community of religious rites, which they denominated a phratry; and so that again, while the patry took its rise in the way we have previously mentioned, from the blood relation between parents and children and children and parents, the phratry took its rise from the relationship between brothers."

"But tribe and tribesmen were so called from the coalescence into communities and nations so called, for each of the coalescing bodies was called a tribe." [1]

It will be noticed that marriage out of the gens is here recognized as a custom, and that the wife was enrolled in the gens, rather than the phratry, of her husband. Dikæarchus, who was a pupil of Aristotle, lived at a time when the gens existed chiefly as a pedigree of individuals, its powers having been transferred to new political bodies.

---

1 Wachsmuth's "Historical Antiquities of the Greeks," l. c., i, 449, app. for text.

He derived the origin of the gens from primitive times; but his statement that the phratry originated in the matrimonial practices of the gentes, while true doubtless as to the practice, is but an opinion as to the origin of the organization. Intermarriages, with common religious rites, would cement the phratric union; but a more satisfactory foundation of the phratry may be found in the common lineage of the gentes of which it was composed. It must be remembered that the gentes have a history running back through the three sub-periods of barbarism into the previous period of savagery, antedating the existence even of the Aryan and Semitic families. The phratry has been shown to have appeared among the American aborigines in the Lower Status of barbarism; while the Greeks were familiar with so much only of their former history as pertained to the Upper Status of barbarism.

Mr. Grote does not attempt to define the functions of the phratry, except generally. They were doubtless of a religious character chiefly; but they probably manifested themselves, as among the Iroquois, at the burial of the dead, at public games, at religious festivals, at councils, and at the agoras of the people, where the grouping of chiefs and people would be by phratries rather than by gentes. It would also naturally show itself in the array of the military forces, of which a memorable example is given by Homer in the address of Nestor to Agamemnon.[1] "Separate the troops by tribes and by phratries, Agamemnon, so that phratry may support phratry, and tribes, tribes. If thou wilt thus act, and the Greeks obey, thou wilt then ascertain which of the commanders and which of the soldiers is a coward, and which of them may be brave, for they will fight their best." The number from the same gens in a military force would be too small to be made a basis in the organization of an army; but the larger aggregations of the phratries and tribes would be sufficient. Two things may be inferred from the advice of Nestor: first, that the organization of armies by phratries and tribes had then ceased to be common;

1 "Iliad," ii, 362.

and secondly, that in ancient times it had been the usual plan of army organization, a knowledge of which had not then disappeared. We have seen that the Tlascalans and Aztecs, who were in the Middle Status of barbarism, organized and sent out their military bands by phratries which, in their condition, was probably the only method in which a military force could be organized. The ancient German tribes organized their armies for battle on a similar principle.[1] It is interesting to notice how closely shut in the tribes of mankind have been to the theory of their social system.

The obligation of blood revenge, which was turned at a later day into a duty of prosecuting the murderer before the legal tribunals, rested primarily upon the gens of the slain person; but it was also shared in by the phratry, and became a phratric obligation.[2] In the Eumenides of Aeschylus, the Erinnys, after speaking of the slaying of his mother by Orestes, put the question: "What lustral water of his phrators shall await him?"[3] which seems to imply that if the criminal escaped punishment final purification was performed by his phratry instead of his gens. Moreover, the extension of the obligation from the gens to the phratry implies a common lineage of all the gentes in a phratry.

Since the phratry was intermediate between the gens and the tribe, and not invested with governmental functions, it was less fundamental and less important than either of the others; but it was a common, natural and perhaps necessary stage of re-integration between the two. Could an intimate knowledge of the social life of the Greeks in that early period be recovered, the phenomena would centre probably in the phratric organization far more conspicuously than our scanty records lead us to infer. It probably possessed more power and influence than is usually ascribed to it as an organization. Among the Athenians it survived the overthrow of the gentes as the basis of a system, and retained, under the

1 Tacitus, "Germania," cap. vii.
2 Grote's "History of Greece," iii, 55. The Court of Areopagus took jurisdiction over homicides.—Ib., iii, 79.
3 —"Eum.," 656.

new political system, some control over the registration of citizens, the enrollment of marriages and the prosecution of the murderer of a phrator before the courts.

It is customary to speak of the four Athenian tribes as divided each into three phratries, and of each phratry as divided into thirty gentes; but this is merely for convenience in description. A people under gentile institutions do not divide themselves into symmetrical divisions and subdivisions. The natural process of their formation was the exact reverse of this method; the gentes fell into phratries, and ultimatelv into tribes, which reunited in a society or a people. Each was a natural growth. That the number of gentes in each Athenian phratry was thirty is a remarkable fact incapable of explanation by natural causes. A motive sufficiently powerful, such as a desire for a symmetrical organization of the phratries and tribes, might lead to a subdivision of gentes by consent until the number was raised to thirty in each of these phratries; and when the number in a tribe was in excess, by the consolidation of kindred gentes until the number was reduced to thirty. A more probable way would be by the admission of alien gentes into phratries needing an increase of number. Having a certain number of tribes, phratries and gentes by natural growth, the reduction of the last two to uniformity in the four tribes could thus have been secured. Once cast in this numerical scale of thirty gentes to a phratry and three phratries to a tribe, the proportion might easily have been maintained for centuries, except perhaps as to the number of gentes in each phratry.

The religious life of the Grecian tribes had its centre and source in the gentes and phratries. It must be supposed that in and through these organizations, was perfected that marvelous polytheistic system, with its hierarchy of gods, its symbols and forms of worship, which impressed so powerfully the mind of the classical world. In no small degree this mythology inspired the great achievements of the legendary and historical periods, and created that enthusiasm which produced the temple and ornamental architecture in which the modern world has taken so much delight. Some of the religious rites, which originated in these social aggregates, were nationalized from the superior sanctity they were supposed to possess; thus showing to what extent the gentes and phratries were nurseries of religion. The events of this extraordinary period, the most eventful in many respects in the history of the Aryan family, are lost, in the main, to history. Legendary genealogies and narratives, myths and fragments of poetry, concluding with the Homeric and Hesiodic poems, make up its literary remains. But their institutions, arts, inventions, mythological system, in a word the substance of civilization which they wrought out and brought with them, were the legacy they contributed to the new society they were destined to found. The history of the period may yet be reconstructed from these various sources of knowledge, reproducing the main features of gentile society as they appeared shortly before the institution of political society.

As the gens had its archon, who officiated as its priest in the religious observances of the gens, so each phratry had its phratriarch, who presided at its meetings, and officiated in the solemnization of its religious rites. "The phratry," observes M. De Coulanges, "had its assemblies and its tribunals, and could pass decrees. In it, as well as in the family, there was a god, a priesthood, a legal tribunal and a government."[1] The religious rites of the phratries were an expansion of those of the gentes of which it was composed. It is in these directions that attention should be turned in order to understand the religious life of the Greeks.

Next in the ascending scale of organization was the tribe, consisting of a number of phratries, each composed of gentes. The persons in each phratry were of the same common lineage, and spoke the same dialect. Among the Athenians as before stated each tribe contained three phratries, which gave to each a similar organization. The tribe corresponds with the Latin tribe, and also with those of the American aborigines, an independent dialect for each tribe being necessary to render

1 "The Ancient City," Small's Trans., p. 157. Boston, Lee & Shepard.

the analogy with the latter complete. The concentration of such Grecian tribes as had coalesced into a people, in a small area, tended to repress dialectical variation, which a subsequent written language and literature tended still further to arrest. Each tribe from antecedent habits, however, was more or less localized in a fixed area, through the requirements of a social system resting on personal relations. It seems probable that each tribe had its council of chiefs, supreme in all matters relating to the tribe exclusively. But since the functions and powers of the general council of chiefs, who administered the general affairs of the united tribes, were allowed to fall into obscurity, it would not be expected that those of an inferior and subordinate council would be preserved. If such a council existed, which was doubtless the fact from its necessity under their social system, it would have consisted of the chiefs of the gentes.

When the several phratries of a tribe united in the commemoration of their religious observances it was in their higher organic constitution as a tribe. As such, they were under the presidency, as we find it expressed, of a phylo-basileus, who was the principal chief of the tribe. Whether he acted as their commander in the military service I am unable to state. He possessed priestly functions, always inherent in the office of basileus, and exercised a criminal jurisdiction in cases of murder; whether to try or to prosecute a murderer, I am unable to state. The priestly and judicial functions attached to the office of basileus tend to explain the dignity it acquired in the legendary and heroic periods. But the absence of civil functions, in the strict sense of the term, of the presence of which we have no satisfactory evidence, is sufficient to render the term king, so constantly employed in history as the equivalent of basileus, a misnomer. Among the Athenians we have the tribe-basileus, where the term is used by the Greeks themselves as legitimately as when applied to the general military commander of the four united tribes. When each is described as a king it makes the solecism of four tribes each under a king separately, and the four tribes together under another king. There is a larger amount of fictitious royalty here than the occasion requires. Moreover, when we know that the institutions of the Athenians at the time were essentially democratical it becomes a caricature of Grecian society. It shows the propriety of returning to simple and original language, using the term basileus where the Greeks used it, and rejecting king as a false equivalent. Monarchy is incompatible with gentilism, for the reason that gentile institutions are essentially democratical. Every gens, phratry and tribe was a completely organized self-governing body; and where several tribes coalesced into a nation the resulting government would be constituted in harmony with the principles animating its constituent parts.

The fourth and ultimate stage of organization was the nation united in a gentile society. Where several tribes, as those of the Athenians and the Spartans, coalesced into one people, it enlarged the society, but the aggregate was simply a more complex duplicate of a tribe. The tribes took the same place in the nation which the phratries held in the tribe, and the gentes in the phratry. There was no name for the organism[1] which was simply a society (*societas*), but in its place a name sprang up for the people or nation. In Homer's description of the forces gathered against Troy, specific names are given to these nations, where such existed, as Athenians, Ætolians, Locrians; but in other cases they are described by the name of the city or country from which they came. The ultimate fact is thus reached, that the Greeks, prior to the times of Lycurgus and Solon, had but the four stages of social organization (gens, phratry, tribe and nation), which was so nearly universal in ancient society, and which has been shown to exist, in part, in the Status of savagery, and complete in the Lower, in the Middle and in the Upper Status of barbarism, and still subsisting after civilization had commenced. This organic series expresses the extent of the growth of the idea of government among mankind down to the institution of political society. Such was the Grecian social system. It

1 Aristotle, Thucydides, and other writers, use the term basileia for the governments of the heroic period.

gave a society, made up of a series of aggregates of persons, with whom the government dealt through their personal relations to a gens, phratry or tribe. It was also a gentile society as distinguished from a political society, from which it was fundamentally different and easily distinguishable.

The Athenian nation of the heroic age presents in its government three distinct, and in some sense co-ordinate, departments or powers, namely: first, the council of chiefs, second, the agora, or assembly of the people; and third, the basileus, or general military commander. Although municipal and subordinate military offices in large numbers had been created, from the increasing necessities of their condition, the principal powers of the government were held by the three instrumentalities named. I am unable to discuss in an adequate manner the functions and powers of the council, the agora or the basileus, but will content myself with a few suggestions upon subjects grave enough to deserve re-investigation at the hands of professed Hellenists.

I. *The Council of Chiefs.* The office of basileus in the Grecian tribes has attracted far more attention than either the council or the agora. As a consequence it has been unduly magnified while the council and the agora have either been depreciated or ignored. We know, however, that the council of chiefs was a constant phenomenon in every Grecian nation from the earliest period to which our knowledge extends down to the institution of political society. Its permanence as a feature of their social system is conclusive evidence that its functions were substantial, and that its powers, at least presumptively, were ultimate and supreme. This presumption arises from what is known of the archaic character and functions of the council of chiefs under gentile institutions, and from its vocation. How it was constituted in the heroic age, and under what tenure the office of chief was held, we are not clearly informed; but it is a reasonable inference that the council was composed of the chiefs of the gentes. Since the number who formed the council was usually less than the number of gentes, a selection must have been made in some way from the body of chiefs. In what manner the selection was made we are not informed. The vocation of the council as a legislative body representing the principal gentes, and its natural growth under the gentile organization, rendered it supreme in the first instance, and makes it probable that it remained so to the end of its existence. The increasing importance of the office of basileus, and the new offices created in their military and municipal affairs with their increase in numbers and in wealth, would change somewhat the relations of the council to public affairs, and perhaps diminish its importance; but it could not be overthrown without a radical change of institutions. It seems probable, therefore, that every office of the government, from the highest to the lowest, remained accountable to the council for their official acts. The council was fundamental in their social system;[1] and the Greeks of the period were free self-governing peoples, under institutions essentially democratical. A single illustration of the existence of the council may be given from Aeschylus, simply to show that in the Greek conception it was always present and ready to act. In *The Seven against Thebes,* Eteocles is represented in command of the city, and his brother Polynices as one of the seven chiefs who had invested the place. The assault was repelled, but the brothers fell in a personal combat at one of the gates. After this occurrence a herald says: "It is necessary for me to announce the decree and good pleasure of the councilors of the people of this city of Cadmus. It is resolved,"[2] etc. A council which can make and promulgate a decree at any moment, which the people are expected to obey, possesses the supreme powers of government. Aeschylus, although dealing in this case with events in the legendary period, recognizes the council of chiefs as a necessary part of the system of government of every Grecian people. The boulê of ancient Grecian society was the prototype and pattern of the senate under the subsequent political system of the state.

---

1 Dionysius, 2, xii.
2 Aeschylus, "The Seven against Thebes," 1005.

II. *The Agora.* Although an assembly of the people became established in the legendary period, with a recognized power to adopt or reject public measures submitted by the council, it is not as ancient as the council. The latter came in at the institution of the gentes; but it is doubtful whether the agora existed, with the functions named, back of the Upper Status of barbarism. It has been shown that among the Iroquois, in the Lower Status, the people presented their wishes to the council of chiefs through orators of their own selection, and that a popular influence was felt in the affairs of the confederacy; but an assembly of the people, with the right to adopt or reject public measures, would evince an amount of progress in intelligence and knowledge beyond the Iroquois. When the agora first appears, as represented in Homer, and in the Greek Tragedies, it had the same characteristics which it afterwards maintained in the ecclesia of the Athenians, and in the *comitia curiata* of the Romans. It was the prerogative of the council of chiefs to mature public measures, and then submit them to the assembly of the people for acceptance or rejection, and their decision was final. The functions of the agora were limited to this single act. It could neither originate measures, nor interfere in the administration of affairs; but nevertheless it was a substantial power, eminently adapted to the protection of their liberties. In the heroic age certainly, and far back in the legendary period, the agora is a constant phenomenon among the Grecian tribes, and, in connection with the council, is conclusive evidence of the democratical constitution of gentile society throughout these periods. A public sentiment, as we have reason to suppose, was created among the people on all important questions, through the exercise of their intelligence, which the council of chiefs found it desirable as well as necessary to consult, both for the public good and for the maintenance of their own authority. After hearing the submitted question discussed, the assembly of the people, which was free to all who desired to speak,[1] made their decision in ancient

1 Euripides, "Orestes," 884.

times usually by a show of hands.[1] Through participation in public affairs, which affected the interests of all, the people were constantly learning the art of self-government, and a portion of them, as the Athenians, were preparing themselves for the full democracy subsequently established by the constitutions of Cleisthenes. The assembly of the people to deliberate upon public questions, not unfrequently derided as a mob by writers who were unable to understand or appreciate the principle of democracy, was the germ of the ecclesia of the Athenians, and of the lower house of modern legislative bodies.

III. *The Basileus.* This officer became a conspicuous character in the Grecian society of the heroic age, and was equally prominent in the legendary period. He has been placed by historians in the centre of the system. The name of the office was used by the best Grecian writers to characterize the government, which was styled a basileia. Modern writers, almost without exception, translate basileus by the term *king,* and basileia by the term *kingdom,* without qualification, and as exact equivalents, I wish to call attention to this office of basileus, as it existed in the Grecian tribes, and to question the correctness of this interpretation. There is no similarity whatever between the basileia of the ancient Athenians and the modern kingdom or monarchy; certainly not enough to justify the use of the same term to describe both. Our idea of a kingly government is essentially of a type in which a king, surrounded by a privileged and titled class in the ownership and possession of the lands, rules according to his own will and pleasure by edicts and decrees; claiming an hereditary right to rule, because he cannot allege the consent of the governed. Such governments have been self-imposed through the principle of hereditary right, to which the priesthood have sought to superadd a divine right. The Tudor kings of England and the Bourbon kings of France are illustrations. Constitutional monarchy is a modern development, and essentially different from the basileia of the Greeks. The basileia was neither an absolute nor a constitutional mon-

1 Aeschylus, "The Suppliants," 607.

archy; neither was it a tyranny or a despotism. The question then is, what was it.

Mr. Grote claims that "the primitive Grecian government is essentially monarchical, reposing on personal feeling and divine right;"[1] and to confirm this view he remarks further, that "the memorable dictum in the Iliad is borne out by all that we hear in actual practice: 'the rule of many is not a good thing; let us have one ruler only — one king — him to whom Zeus has given the sceptre, with the tutelary sanctions.'"[2] This opinion is not peculiar to Mr. Grote, whose eminence as a historian all delight to recognize; but it has been steadily and generally affirmed by historical writers on Grecian themes, until it has come to be accepted as historical truth. Our views upon Grecian and Roman questions have been moulded by writers accustomed to monarchical government and privileged classes, who were perhaps glad to appeal to the earliest known governments of the Grecian tribes for a sanction of this form of government, as at once natural, essential and primitive.

The true statement, as it seems to an American, is precisely the reverse of Mr. Grote's; namely, that the primitive Grecian government was essentially democratical, reposing on gentes, phratries and tribes, organized as self-governing bodies, and on the principles of liberty, equality and fraternity. This is borne out by all we know of the gentile organization, which has been shown to rest on principles essentially democratical. The question then is, whether the office of basileus passed in reality from father to son by hereditary right; which, if true, would tend to show a subversion of these principles. We have seen that in the Lower Status of barbarism the office of chief was hereditary in a gens, by which is meant that the vacancy was filled from the members of the gens as often as it occurred. Where descent was in the female line, as among the Iroquois, an own brother was usually selected to succeed the deceased chief, and where descent was in the male line, as among the Ojibwas and

1 "History of Greece," ii, 69.
2 "History of Greece," ii, 69, and "Iliad," ii, 204.

Omahas, the oldest son. In the absence of objections to the person such became the rule; but the elective principle remained, which was the essence of self-government. It cannot be claimed, on satisfactory proof, that the oldest son of the basileus took the office, upon the demise of his father, by absolute hereditary right. This is the essential fact; and it requires conclusive proof for its establishment. The fact that the oldest, or one of the sons, usually succeeded, which is admitted, does not establish the fact in question; because by usage he was in the probable line of succession by a free election from a constituency. The presumption, on the face of Grecian institutions, is against succession to the office of basileus by hereditary right; and in favor either of a free election, or of a confirmation of the office by the people through their recognized organizations, as in the case of the Roman rex.[1] With the office of basileus transmitted in the manner last named, the government would remain in the hands of the people. Because without an election or confirmation he could not assume the office; and because further, the power to elect or confirm implies the reserved right to depose.

The illustration of Mr. Grote, drawn from the Iliad, is without significance on the question made. Ulysses, from whose address the quotation is taken, was speaking of the command of an army before a besieged city. He might well say: "All the Greeks cannot by any means rule here. The rule of many is not a good thing. Let us have one koiranos, one basileus, to whom Zeus has given the sceptre, and the divine sanctions in order that he may command us." Koiranos and basileus are used as equivalents, because both alike signified a general military commander. There was no occasion for Ulysses to discuss or endorse any plan of government; but he had sufficient reasons for advocating obedience to a single commander of the army before a besieged city.

1 Mr. Gladstone, who presents to his readers the Grecian chiefs of the heroic age as kings and princes, with the superadded qualities of gentlemen, is forced to admit that "on the whole we seem to have the custom or law of primogeniture sufficiently, but not oversharply defined."—"Juventus Mundi," Little & Brown's ed., p. 428.

Basileia may be defined as a military democracy, the people being free, and the spirit of the government, which is the essential thing, being democratical. The basileus was their general, holding the highest, the most influential and the most important office known to their social system. For the want of a better term to describe the government, basileia was adopted by Grecian writers, because it carried the idea of a generalship which had then become a conspicuous feature in the government. With the council and the agora both existing with the basileus, if a more special definition of this form of government is required, military democracy expresses it with at least reasonable correctness; while the use of the term kingdom, with the meaning it necessarily conveys, would be a misnomer.

In the heroic age the Grecian tribes were living in walled cities, and were becoming numerous and wealthy through field agriculture, manufacturing industries, and flocks and herds. New offices were required, as well as some degree of separation of their functions; and a new municipal system was growing up apace with their increasing intelligence and necessities. It was also a period of incessant military strife for the possession of the most desirable areas. Along with the increase of property the aristocratic element in society undoubtedly increased, and was the chief cause of those disturbances which prevailed in Athenian society from the time of Theseus to the times of Solon and Cleisthenes. During this period, and until the final abolition of the office some time before the first Olympiad, (776 B. C.) the basileus, from the character of his office and from the state of the times, became more prominent and more powerful than any single person in their previous experience. The functions of a priest and of a judge were attached to or inherent in his office; and he seems to have been *ex officio* a member of the council of chiefs. It was a great as well as a necessary office, with the powers of a general over the army in the field, and over the garrison in the city, which gave him the means of acquiring influence in civil affairs as well. But it does not appear that he possessed civil functions. Prof. Mason remarks, that "our information respecting the Grecian kings in the more historical age is not ample or minute enough to enable us to draw out a detailed scheme of their functions."[1] The military and priestly functions of the basileus are tolerably well understood, the judicial imperfectly, and the civil functions cannot properly be said to have existed. The powers of such an office under gentile institutions would gradually become defined by the usage of experience, but with a constant tendency in the basileus to assume new ones dangerous to society. Since the council of chiefs remained as a constituent element of the government, it may be said to have represented the democratic principles of their social system, as well as the gentes, while the basileus soon came to represent the aristocratic principle. It is probable that a perpetual struggle was maintained between the council and the basileus, to hold the latter within the limits of powers the people were willing to concede to the office. Moreover, the abolition of the office by the Athenians makes it probable that they found the office unmanageable, and incompatible with gentile institutions, from the tendency to usurp additional powers.

Among the Spartan tribes the ephoralty was instituted at a very early period to limit the powers of the basileus in consequence of a similar experience. Although the functions of the council in the Homeric and the legendary periods are not accurately known, its constant presence is evidence sufficient that its powers were real, essential and permanent. With the simultaneous existence of the agora, and in the absence of proof of a change of institutions, we are led to the conclusion that the council, under established usages, was supreme over gentes, phratries, tribes and nation, and that the basileus was amenable to this council for his official acts. The freedom of the gentes, of whom the members of the council were representatives, presupposes the independence of the council, as well as its supremacy.

---

1 Smith's "Dic., Art. Rex," p. 991.

Thucydides refers incidentally to the governments of the traditionary period, as follows: "Now when the Greeks were becoming more powerful, and acquiring possession of property still more than before, many tyrannies were established in the cities, from their revenues becoming greater; whereas before there had been hereditary basileia with specified powers."[1] The office was hereditary in the sense of perpetual because it was filled as often as a vacancy occurred, but probably hereditary in a gens, the choice being by a free election by his gennetes, or by nomination possibly by the council, and confirmation by the gentes, as in the case of the rex of the Romans.

Aristotle has given the most satisfactory definition of the basileia and of the basileus of the heroic period of any of the Grecian writers. These then are the four kinds of basileia he remarks: the first is that of the heroic times, which was a government over a free people, with restricted rights in some particulars; for the basileus was their general, their judge and their chief priest. The second, that of the barbarians which is an hereditary despotic government, regulated by laws; the third is that which they call Aesymnetic, which is an elective tyranny. The fourth is the Lacedaemonian, which is nothing more than an hereditary generalship. [2] Whatever may be said of the last three forms, the first does not answer to the idea of a kingdom of the absolute type, nor to any recognizable form of monarchy. Aristotle enumerates with striking clearness the principal functions of the basileus, neither of which imply civil powers, and all of which are consistent with an office for life, held by an elective tenure. They are also consistent with his entire subordination to the council of chiefs. The "restricted rights," and the "specified powers" in the definitions of these authors, tend to show that the government had grown into this form in harmony with, as well as under, gentile institutions. The essential element in the definition of Aristotle is the freedom of the people, which in ancient

1 "Thucydides," i, 13.
2 Aristotle, "Politics," iii, c. x.

society implies that the people held the powers of the government under their control, that the office of basileus was voluntarily bestowed, and that it could be recalled for sufficient cause. Such a government as that described by Aristotle can be understood as a military democracy, which, as a form of government under free institutions, grew naturally out of the gentile organization when the military spirit was dominant, when wealth and numbers appeared, with habitual life in fortified cities, and before experience had prepared the way for a pure democracy.

Under gentile institutions, with a people composed of gentes, phratries and tribes, each organized as independent self-governing bodies, the people would necessarily be free. The rule of a king by hereditary right and without direct accountability in such a society was simply impossible. The impossibility arises from the fact that gentile institutions are incompatible with a king or with a kingly government. It would require, what I think cannot be furnished, positive proof of absolute hereditary right in the office of basileus, with the presence of civil functions, to overcome the presumption which arises from the structure and principles of ancient Grecian society. An Englishman, under his constitutional monarchy, is as free as an American under the republic, and his rights and liberties are as well protected; but he owes that freedom and protection to a body of written laws, created by legislation and enforced by courts of justice. In ancient Grecian society, usages and customs supplied the place of written laws, and the person depended for his freedom and protection upon the institutions of his social system. His safeguard was pre-eminently in such institutions as the elective tenure of office implies.

The reges of the Romans were, in like manner, military commanders, with priestly functions attached to their office; and this so-called kingly government falls into the same category of a military democracy. The rex, as before stated, was nominated by the senate, and confirmed by the *comitia curiata;* and the last of the number was deposed. With his deposition the office was abolished, as incompatible with what remained of the democratic principle, after the institution of Roman political society.

The nearest analogues of kingdoms among the Grecian tribes were the tyrannies, which sprang up here and there, in the early period, in different parts of Greece. They were governments imposed by force, and the power claimed was no greater than that of the feudal kings of mediæval times. A transmission of the office from father to son through a few generations in order to superadd hereditary right was needed to complete the analogy. But such governments were so inconsistent with Grecian ideas, and so alien to their democratic institutions, that none of them obtained a permanent footing in Greece. Mr. Grote remarks that "if any energetic man could by audacity or craft break down the constitution and render himself permanent ruler according to his own will and pleasure — even though he might rule well — he could never inspire the people with any sentiment of duty towards him. His sceptre was illegitimate from the beginning, and even the taking of his life, far from being interdicted by that moral feeling which condemned the shedder of blood in other cases, was considered meritorious." [1] It was not so much the illegitimate sceptre which aroused the hostility of the Greeks, as the antagonism of democratical with monarchical ideas, the former of which were inherited from the gentes.

When the Athenians established the new political system, founded upon territory and upon property, the government was a pure democracy. It was no new theory, or special invention of the Athenian mind, but an old and familiar system, with an antiquity as great as that of the gentes themselves. Democratic ideas had existed in the knowledge and practice of their forefathers from time immemorial, and now found expression in a more elaborate, and in many respects, in an improved government. The false element, that of aristocracy, which had penetrated the system and created much of the strife in

1 "History of Greece," ii, 61, and see 69.

the transitional period connected itself with the office of basileus, and remained after this office was abolished; but the new system accomplished its overthrow. More successfully than the remaining Grecian tribes, the Athenians were able to carry forward their ideas of government to their logical result. It is one reason why they became, for their numbers, the most distinguished, the most intellectual and the most accomplished race of men the entire human family has yet produced. In purely intellectual achievements they are still the astonishment of mankind. It was because the ideas which had been germinating through the previous ethnical period, and which had become interwoven with every fibre of their brains, had found a happy fruition in a democratically constituted state. Under its life-giving impulses their highest mental development occurred.

The plan of government instituted by Cleisthenes rejected the office of a chief executive magistrate, while it retained the council of chiefs in an elective senate, and the agora in the popular assembly. It is evident that the council, the agora and the basileus of the gentes were the germs of the senate, the popular assembly, and the chief executive magistrate (king, emperor and president) of modern political society. The latter office sprang from the military necessities of organized society, and its development with the upward progress of mankind is instructive. It can be traced from the common war-chief, first to the Great War Soldier, as in the Iroquois Confederacy; secondly, to the same military commander in a confederacy of tribes more advanced, with the functions of a priest attached to the office, as the Teuctli of the Aztec Confederacy; thirdly, to the same military commander in a nation formed by a coalescence of tribes, with the functions of a priest and of a judge attached to the office, as in the basileus of the Greeks; and finally, to the chief magistrate in modern political society. The elective archon of the Athenians, who succeeded the basileus, and the president of modern republics, from the elective tenure of the office, were the natural outcome of gentilism. We are indebted to the experience of barbarians for instituting and developing the three principal instrumentalities of government now so generally incorporated in the plan of government in civilized states. The human mind, specifically the same in all individuals in all the tribes and nations of mankind, and limited in the range of its powers, works and must work, in the same uniform channels, and within narrow limits of variation. Its results in disconnected regions of space, and in widely separated ages of time, articulate in a logically connected chain of common experiences. In the grand aggregate may still be recognized the few primary germs of thought, working upon primary human necessities, which, through the natural process of development, have produced such vast results.

CHAPTER X

THE INSTITUTION OF GRECIAN POLITICAL SOCIETY

The several Grecian communities passed through a substantially similar experience in transferring themselves from gentile into political society; but the mode of transition can be best illustrated from Athenian history, because the facts with respect to the Athenians are more fully preserved. A bare outline of the material events will answer the object in view, as it is not proposed to follow the growth of the idea of government beyond the inauguration of the new political system.

It is evident that the failure of gentile institutions to meet the now complicated wants of society originated the movement to withdraw all civil powers from the gentes, phratries and tribes, and re-invest them in new constituencies. This movement was gradual, extending through a long period of time, and was embodied in a series of successive experiments by means of which a remedy was sought for existing evils. The coming in of the new system was as gradual as the going out of the old, the two for a part of the time existing side by side. In the character and objects of the experiments tried we may discover wherein the gentile organization had failed to meet the requirements of society, the necessity for the subversion of the gentes, phratries and tribes as sources of power, and the means by which it was accomplished.

Looking backward upon the line of human progress, it may be remarked that the stockaded village was the usual home of the tribe in the Lower Status of barbarism. In the Middle Status joint-tenement houses of adobe-bricks and of stone, in the nature of fortresses, make their appearance. But in the Upper Status, cities surrounded with ring embankments, and finally with walls of dressed stone, appear for the first time in human experience. It was a great step forward when the thought found expression in action of surrounding an area ample for a considerable population with a defensive wall of dressed stone, with towers, parapets and gates, designed to protect all alike and to be defended by the common strength. Cities of this grade imply the existence of a stable and developed field agriculture, the possession of domestic animals in flocks and herds, of merchandise in masses and of property in houses and lands. The city brought with it new demands in the art of government by creating a changed condition of society. A necessity gradually arose for magistrates and judges, military and municipal officers of different grades, with a mode of raising and supporting military levies which would require public revenues. Municipal life and wants must have greatly augmented the duties and responsibilities of the council of chiefs, and perhaps have overtaxed its capacity to govern.

It has been shown that in the Lower Status of barbarism the government was of one power, the council of chiefs; that in the Middle Status it was of two powers, the council of chiefs and the military commander; and that in the Upper Status it was of three powers, the council of chiefs, the assembly of the people and the military commander. But after the commencement of civilization, the differentiation of the powers of the government had proceeded still further. The military power, first devolved upon the basileus, was now exercised by generals and captains under greater restrictions. By a further differentiation the judicial power had now appeared among the Athenians. It was exercised by the archons and dicasts. Magisterial powers were now being devolved upon municipal magistrates. Step by step, and with the progress of experience and advancement, these several powers had been taken by differentiation from the sum of the powers of the original council of chiefs, so far as they could be said to have passed from the people into this council as a representative body.

The creation of these municipal offices was a necessary consequence of the increasing magnitude and complexity of their affairs. Under the increased burden gentile institutions were breaking down. Unnumbered disorders existed, both from the conflict of authority, and from the abuse of powers not as yet well defined. The brief and masterly sketch by Thucydides of the condition of the Grecian tribes in the transitional period,[1] and the concurrent testimony of other writers to the same effect, leave no doubt that the old system of government was failing, and that a new one had become essential to further progress. A wider distribution of the powers of the government, a clearer definition of them, and a stricter accountability of official persons were needed for the welfare as well as safety of society; and more especially the substitution of written laws, enacted by competent authority, in the place of usages and customs. It was through the experimental knowledge gained in this and the previous ethnical period that the idea of political society or a state was gradually forming in the Grecian mind. It was a growth running through centuries of time, from the first appearance of a necessity for a change in the plan of government, before the entire result was realized.

The first attempt among the Athenians to subvert the gentile organization and establish a new system is ascribed to Theseus, and therefore rests upon tradition; but certain facts remained to the historical period which confirm some part at least of his supposed legislation. It will be sufficient to regard Theseus as representing a period, or a series of events. From the time of Cecrops to Theseus, according to Thucydides, the Attic people had always lived in cities, having their own prytaneums and archons, and when not in fear of danger did not consult their basileus, but governed their own affairs separately according to their own councils. But when The-

1 "Thucydides," lib. i, 2-13.

seus was made basileus, he persuaded them to break up the council-houses and magistracies of their several cities and come into relation with Athens, with one council-house (*bouleuterios*), and one prytaneum, to which all were considered as belonging.[1] This statement embodies or implies a number of important facts; namely, that the Attic population were organized in independent tribes, each having its own territory in which the people were localizéd, with its own council-house and prytaneum; and that while they were self-governing societies they were probably confederated for mutual protection, and elected their basileus or general to command their common forces. It is a picture of communities democratically organized, needing a military commander as a necessity of their condition, but not invested with civil functions which their gentile system excluded. Under Theseus they were brought to coalesce into one people, with Athens as their seat of government, which gave them a higher organization than before they had been able to form. The coalescence of tribes into a nation in one territory is later in time than confederations, where the tribes occupy independent territories. It is a higher organic process. While the gentes had always been intermingled by marriage, the tribes were now intermingled by obliterating territorial lines, and by the use of a common council-hall and prytaneum. The act ascribed to Theseus explains the advancement of their gentile society from a lower to a higher organic form, which must have occurred at some time, and probably was effected in the manner stated.

But another act is ascribed to Theseus evincing a more radical plan, as well as an appreciation of the necessity for a fundamental change in the plan of government. He

---

1 "Thucyd.," lib. ii, c. 15. Plutarch speaks nearly to the same effect: "He settled all the inhabitants of Attica in Athens, and made them one people in one city, who before were scattered up and down, and could with difficulty be assembled on any urgent occasion for the public welfare. . . . Dissolving therefore the associations, the councils, and the courts in each particular town, he built one common prytaneum and court hall, where it stands to this day. The citadel with its dependencies, and the city or the old and new town, he united under the common name of Athens."—Plutarch. "Vit. Theseus," cap. 24.

divided the people into three classes, irrespective of gentes, called respectively the *Eupatridae* or "well-born" the *Geomori* or "Husbandmen," and the *Demiurgi* or "artisans." The principal offices were assigned to the first class both in the civil administration and in the priesthood. This classification was not only a recognition of property and of the aristocratic element in the government of society, but it was a direct movement against the governing power of the gentes. It was the evident intention to unite the chiefs of the gentes with their families, and the men of wealth in the several gentes, in a class by themselves, with the right to hold the principal offices in which the powers of society were vested. The separation of the remainder into two great classes traversed the gentes again. Important results might have followed if the voting power had been taken from the gentes, phraties and tribes, and given to the classes, subject to the right of the first to hold principal offices. This does not appear to have been done although absolutely necessary to give vitality to the classes. Moreover, it did not change essentially the previous order of things with respect to holding office. Those now called Eupatrids were probably the men of the several gentes who had previously been called into office. This scheme of Theseus died out, because there was in reality no transfer of powers from the gentes, phratries and tribes to the classes, and because such classes were inferior to the gentes as the basis of a system.

The centuries that elapsed from the unknown time of Theseus to the legislation of Solon (594 B. C.) formed one of the most important periods in Athenian experience; but the succession of events is imperfectly known. The office of basileus was abolished prior to the first Olympiad (776 B. C.), and the archonship established in its place. The latter seems to have been hereditary in a gens, and it is stated to have been hereditary in a particular family within the gens, the first twelve archons being called the Medontidæ from Medon, the first archon, claimed to have been the son of Codrus, the last basileus.

In the case of these archons, who held for life, the same question exists which has elsewhere been raised with respect to the basileus; that an election or confirmation by a constituency was necessary before the office could be assumed. The presumption is against the transmission of the office by hereditary right. In 711 B. C. the office of archon was limited to ten years, and bestowed by free election upon the person esteemed most worthy of the position. We are now within the historical period, though near its threshold, where we meet the elective principle with respect to the highest office in the gift of the people clearly and completely established. It is precisely what would have been expected from the constitution and principles of the gentes, although the aristocratical principle, as we must suppose, had increased in force with the increase of property, and was the source through which hereditary right was introduced wherever found. The existence of the elective principle with respect to the later archons is not without significance in its relation to the question of the previous practice of the Athenians. In 683 B. C. the office was made elective annually, the number was increased to nine, and their duties were made ministerial and judicial.[1] We may notice, in these events, evidence of a gradual progress in knowledge with respect to the tenure of office. The Athenian tribes had inherited from their remote ancestors the office of archon as chief of the gens. It was hereditary in the gens as may fairly be supposed, and elective among its members. After descent was changed to the male line the sons of the deceased chief were within the line of succession, and one of their

---

1 "Of the nine archons, whose number continued unaltered from 683 B. C. to the end of the democracy, three bore special titles—the Archon Eponymus, from whose name the designation of the year was derived, and who was spoken of as "the Archon," the Archon Basileus (King), or more frequently, the Basileus; and the Polemarch. The remaining six passed by the general name of Thesmothetæ. . . . . The Archon Eponymus determined all disputes relative to the family, the gentile, and the phratric relations: he was the legal protector of orphans and widows. The Archon Basileus (or King Archon) enjoyed competence in complaints respecting offenses against the religious sentiment and respecting homicide. The Polemarch (speaking of times anterior to Kleisthenês) was the leader of military force, and judge in disputes between citizens and non-citizens."—Grote's "History of Greece," l. c., iii, 74.

number would be apt to be chosen in the absence of personal objections. But now they reverted to this original office for the name of their highest magistrate, made it elective irrespective of any gens, and limited its duration, first to ten years and finally to one. Prior to this, the tenure of office to which they had been accustomed was for life. In the Lower and also in the Middle Status of barbarism we have found the office of chief, elective and for life; or during good behavior, for this limitation follows from the right of the gens to depose from office. It is a reasonable inference that the office of chief in a Grecian gens was held by a free election and by the same tenure. It must be regarded as proof of a remarkable advancement in knowledge at this early period that the Athenian tribes substituted a term of years for their most important office, and allowed a competition of candidates. They thus worked out the entire theory of an elective and representative office, and placed it upon its true basis.

In the time of Solon, it may be further noticed, the Court of Areopagus, composed of ex-archons, had come into existence with power to try criminals and with a censorship over morals, together with a number of new offices in the military, naval and administrative services. But the most important event that occurred about this time was the institution of the *naucraries,* twelve in each tribe, and forty-eight in all: each of which was a local circumscription of householders from which levies were drawn into the military and naval service, and from which taxes were probably collected. The naucrary was the incipient deme or township which, when the idea of a territorial basis was fully developed, was to become the foundation of the second great plan of government. By whom the naucraries were instituted is unknown. "They must have existed even before the time of Solon," Boeckh remarks, "since the presiding officers of the naucraries are mentioned before the time of his legislation; and when Aristotle ascribes their institution to Solon, we may refer this account only to their confirmation by the political constitution of Solon."[1] Twelve naucraries formed a trittys, a larger territorial circumscription, but they were not necessarily contiguous. It was, in like manner, the germ of the county, the next territorial aggregate above the township.

Notwithstanding the great changes that had occurred in the instrumentalities by which the government was administered, the people were still in a gentile society, and living under gentile institutions. The gens, phratry and tribe were in full vitality, and the recognized sources of power. Before the time of Solon no person could become a member of this society except through connection with a gens and tribe. All other persons were beyond the pale of the government. The council of chiefs remained, the old and time-honored instrument of government; but the powers of the government were now co-ordinated between itself, the agora or assembly of the people, the Court of Areopagus, and the nine archons. It was the prerogative of the council to originate and mature public measures for submission to the people, which enabled it to shape the policy of the government. It doubtless had the general administration of the finances, and it remained to the end, as it had been from the beginning, the central feature of the government. The assembly of the people had now come into increased prominence. Its functions were still limited to the adoption or rejection of public measures submitted to its decision by the council; but it began to exercise a powerful influence upon public affairs. The rise of this assembly as a power in the government is the surest evidence of the progress of the Athenian people in knowledge and intelligence. Unfortunately the functions and powers of the council of chiefs and of the assembly of the people in this early period have been imperfectly preserved, and but partially elucidated.

In 624 B. C. Draco had framed a body of laws for the Athenians which were chiefly remarkable for their unnecessary severity; but this code demonstrated that the

---

1 "Public Economy of Athens," Lamb's Trans., Little & Brown's ed., p. 353.

time was drawing near in Grecian experience when usages and customs were to be superseded by written laws. As yet the Athenians had not learned the art of enacting laws as the necessity for them appeared, which required a higher knowledge of the functions of legislative bodies than they had attained. They were in that stage in which lawgivers appear, and legislation is in a scheme or in gross, under the sanction of a personal name. Thus slowly the great sequences of human progress unfold themselves.

When Solon came into the archonship (594 B. C.) the evils prevalent in society had reached an unbearable degree. The struggle for the possession of property, now a commanding interest, had produced singular results. A portion of the Athenians had fallen into slavery, through debt,—the person of the debtor being liable to enslavement in default of payment; others had mortgaged their lands and were unable to remove the encumbrances; and as a consequence of these and other embarrassments society was devouring itself. In addition to a body of laws, some of them novel, but corrective of the principal financial difficulties, Solon renewed the project of Theseus of organizing society into classes, not according to callings as before, but according to the amount of their property. It is instructive to follow the course of these experiments to supersede the gentes and substitute a new system, because we shall find the Roman tribes, in the time of Servius Tullius, trying the same experiment for the same purpose. Solon divided the people into four classes according to the measure of their wealth, and going beyond Theseus, he invested these classes with certain powers, and imposed upon them certain obligations. It transferred a portion of the civil powers of the gentes, phratries and tribes to the property classes. In proportion as the substance of power was drawn from the former and invested in the latter, the gentes would be weakened and their decadence would commence. But so far as classes composed of persons were substituted for gentes composed of persons, the government was still founded upon person, and upon relations purely personal. The scheme failed to reach the substance of the question. Moreover, in changing the council of chiefs into the senate of four hundred, the members were taken in equal numbers from the four tribes, and not from the classes. But it will be noticed that the idea of property, as the basis of a system of government, was now incorporated by Solon in the new plan of property classes. It failed, however, to reach the idea of political society, which must rest upon territory as well as property, and deal with persons through their territorial relations. The first class alone were eligible to the high offices, the second performed military service on horseback, the third as infantry, and the fourth as light-armed soldiers. This last class were the numerical majority. They were disqualified from holding office, and paid no taxes; but in the popular assembly of which they were members, they possessed a vote upon the election of all magistrates and officers, with power to bring them to an account. They also had power to adopt or reject all public measures submitted by the senate to their decision. Under the constitution of Solon their powers were real and durable, and their influence upon public affairs was permanent and substantial. All freemen, though not connected with a gens and tribe, were now brought into the government, to a certain extent, by becoming citizens and members of the assembly of the people with the powers named. This was one of the most important results of the legislation of Solon.

It will be further noticed that the people were now organized as an army, consisting of three divisions; the cavalry, the heavy-armed infantry, and the light-armed infantry, each with its own officers of different grades. The form of the statement limits the array to the last three classes, which leaves the first class in the unpatriotic position of appropriating to themselves the principal offices of the government, and taking no part in the military service. This undoubtedly requires modification. The same plan of organization, but including the five classes, will re-appear among the Romans under Servius Tullius, by whom the body of the people were organized as an army (*exercitus*) fully officered and equipped in each subdivision. The idea of a military democracy, different in organization but the same theoretically as that of the previous period, re-appears in a new dress both in the Solonian and in the Servian constitution.

In addition to the property element, which entered into the basis of the new system, the territorial element was partially incorporated through the naucraries before adverted to, in which it is probable there was an enrollment of citizens and of their property to form a basis for military levies and for taxation. These provisions, with the senate, the popular assembly now called the ecclesia, the nine archons, and the Court of Areopagus, gave to the Athenians a much more elaborate government than they had before known, and requiring a higher degree of intelligence for its management. It was also essentially democratical in harmony with their antecedent ideas and institutions; in fact a logical consequence of them, and explainable only as such. But it fell short of a pure system in three respects: firstly, it was not founded upon territory; secondly, all the dignities of the state were not open to every citizen; and thirdly, the principle of local self-government in primary organizations was unknown, except as it may have existed imperfectly in the naucraries. The gentes, phratries and tribes still remained in full vitality, but with diminished powers. It was a transitional condition, requiring further experience to develop the theory of a political system toward which it was a great advance. Thus slowly but steadily human institutions are evolved from lower into higher forms, through the logical operations of the human mind working in uniform but predetermined channels.

There was one weighty reason for the overthrow of the gentes and the substitution of a new plan of government. It was probably recognized by Theseus, and undoubtedly by Solon. From the disturbed condition of the Grecian tribes and the unavoidable movements of the people in the traditionary period and in the times prior to Solon, many persons transfered themselves from one nation to another, and thus lost their connection with their own gens without acquiring a connection with another. This would repeat itself from time to time, through personal adventure, the spirit of trade, and the exigencies of warfare, until a considerable number with their posterity would be developed in every tribe unconnected with any gens. All such persons, as before remarked, would be without the pale of the government with which there could be no connection excepting through a gens and tribe. The fact is noticed by Mr. Grote. "The phratries and gentes," he remarks, "probably never at any time included the whole population of the country—and the population not included in them tended to become larger and larger in the times anterior to Kleisthenes, as well as afterwards."[1] As early as the time of Lycurgus there was a considerable immigration into Greece from the islands of the Mediterranean and from the Ionian cities of its eastern coasts, which increased the number of persons unattached to any gens. When they came in families they would bring a fragment of a new gens with them; but they would remain aliens unless the new gens was admitted into a tribe. This probably occurred in a number of cases, and it may assist in explaining the unusual number of gentes in Greece. The gentes and phratries were close corporations, both of which would have been adulterated by the absorption of these aliens through adoption into a native gens. Persons of distinction might be adopted into some gens, or secure the admission of their own gens into some tribe; but the poorer class would be refused either privilege. There can be no doubt that as far back as the time of Theseus, and more especially in the time of Solon, the number of the unattached class, exclusive of the slaves, had become large. Having neither gens nor phratry they were also without direct religious privileges, which were inherent and exclusive in these organizations. It is not difficult to see in this class of persons a growing element of discontent dangerous to the security of society.

---

1 "History of Greece," iii, 65.

The schemes of Theseus and of Solon made imperfect provision for their admission to citizenship through the classes; but as the gentes and phratries remained from which they were excluded, the remedy was still incomplete. Mr. Grote further remarks, that "it is not easy to make out distinctly what was the political position of the ancient Gentes and Phratries, as Solon left them. The four tribes consisted altogether of gentes and phratries, insomuch that no one could be included in any one of the tribes who was not also a member of some gens and phratry. Now the new probouleutic or pre-considering senate consisted of 400 members,—100 from each of the tribes: persons not included in any gens and phratry could therefore have had no access to it. The conditions of eligibility were similar, according to ancient custom, for the nine archons—of course, also, for the senate of Areopagus. So that there remained only the public assembly, in which an Athenian, not a member of these tribes, could take part: yet he was a citizen, since he could give his vote for archons and senators, and could take part in the annual decision of their accountability, besides being entitled to claim redress for wrong from the archons in his own person—while the alien could ouly do so through the intervention of an avouching citizen, or Prostatês. It seems therefore that all persons not included in the four tribes, whatever their grade or fortune might be, were on the same level in respect to political privilege as the fourth and poorest class of the Solonian census. It has already been remarked, that even before the time of Solon, the number of Athenians not included in the gentes or phratries was probably considerable: it tended to become greater and greater, since these bodies were close and unexpansive, while the policy of the new lawgiver tended to invite industrious settlers from other parts of Greece to Athens."[1] The Roman Plebeians orginated from causes precisely similar. They were not members of any gens, and therefore formed no part of the *Populus Romanus.* We may find

1 "History of Greece," iii, 133.

in the facts stated one of the reasons of the failure of the gentile organization to meet the requirements of society. In the time of Solon, society had outgrown their ability to govern, its affairs had advanced so far beyond the condition in which the gentes originated. They furnished a basis too narrow for a state, up to the measure of which the people had grown.

There was also an increasing difficulty in keeping the members of a gens, phratry and tribe locally together. As parts of a governmental organic series, this fact of localization was higly necessary. In the earlier period, the gens held its lands in common, the phratries held certain lands in common for religious uses, and the tribe probably held other lands in common. When they established themselves in country or city, they settled locally together by gentes, by phratries and by tribes, as a consequence of their social organization. Each gens was in the main by itself—not all of its members, for two gentes were represented in every family, but the body who propagated the gens. Those gentes belonging to the same phratry naturally sought contiguous or at least near areas, and the same with the several phratries of the tribe. But in the time of Solon, lands and houses had come to be owned by individuals in severalty, with power of alienation as to lands, but not of houses out of the gens. It doubtless became more and more impossible to keep the members of a gens locally together, from the shifting relations of persons to land, and from the creation of new property by its members in other localities. The unit of their social system was becoming unstable in place, and also in character. Without stopping to develop this fact of their condition further, it must have proved one of the reasons of the failure of the old plan of government. The township, with its fixed property and its inhabitants for the time being, yielded that element of permanence now wanting in the gens. Society had made immense progress from its former condition of extreme simplicity. It was very different from that which the gentile organization was instituted to govern. Nothing but the unsettled condition and incessant warfare of the

Athenian tribes, from their settlement in Attica to the time of Solon, could have preserved this organization from overthrow. After their establishment in walled cities, that rapid development of wealth and numbers occurred which brought the gentes to the final test, and demonstrated their inability to govern a people now rapidly approaching civilization. But their displacement even then required a long period of time.

The seriousness of the difficulties to be overcome in creating a political society are strikingly illustrated in the experience of the Athenians. In the time of Solon, Athens had already produced able men; the useful arts had attained a very considerable development; commerce on the sea had become a national interest; agriculture and manufactures were well advanced; and written composition in verse had commenced. They were in fact a civilized people, and had been for two centuries; but their institutions of government were still gentile, and of the type prevalent throughout the Later Period of barbarism. A great impetus had been given to the Athenian commonwealth by the new system of Solon; nevertheless, nearly a century elapsed, accompanied with many disorders, before the idea of a state was fully developed in the Athenian mind. Out of the naucrary, a conception of a township as the unit of a political system was finally elaborated; but it required a man of the highest genius, as well as great personal influence, to seize the idea in its fullness, and give it an organic embodiment. That man finally appeared in Cleisthenes (509 B. C.), who must be regarded as the first of Athenian legislators —the founder of the second great plan of human government, that under which modern civilized nations are organized.

Cleisthenes went to the bottom of the question, and placed the Athenian political system upon the foundation on which it remained to the close of the independent existence of the commonwealth. He divided Attica into a hundred demes, or townships, each circumscribed by metes and bounds, and distinguished by a name. Every citizen was required to register himself, and to cause an enrollment of his property in the deme in which he resided. This enrollment was the evidence as well as the foundation of his civil privileges. The deme displaced the naucrary. Its inhabitants were an organized body politic with powers of local self-government, like the modern American township. This is the vital and the remarkable feature of the system. It reveals at once its democratic character. The government was placed in the hands of the people in the first of the series of territorial organizations. The demotæ elected a demarch, who had the custody of the public register; he had also power to convene the demotæ for the purpose of electing magistrates and judges, for revising the registry of citizens, and for the enrollment of such as became of age during the year. They elected a treasurer, and provided for the assessment and collection of taxes, and for furnishing the quota of troops required of the deme for the service of the state. They also elected thirty dicasts or judges, who tried all causes arising in the deme where the amount involved fell below a certain sum. Besides these powers of local self-government, which is the essence of a democratic system, each deme had its own temple and religious worship, and its own priest, also elected by the demotæ. Omitting minor particulars, we find the instructive and remarkable fact that the township, as first instituted, possessed all the powers of local self-government, and even upon a fuller and larger scale than an American township. Freedom in religion is also noticeable, which was placed where it rightfully belongs, under the control of the people. All registered citizens were free, and equal in their rights and privileges, with the exception of equal eligibility to the higher offices. Such was the new unit of organization in Athenian political society, at once a model for a free state, and a marvel of wisdom and knowledge. The Athenians commenced with a democratic organization at the point where every people must commence who desire to create a free state, and place the control of the government in the hands of its citizens.

The second member of the organic territorial series

consisted of ten demes, united in a larger geographical district. It was called a local tribe, to preserve some part of the terminology of the old gentile system.[1] Each district was named after an Attic hero, and it was the analogue of the modern county. The demes in each district were usually contiguous, which should have been true in every instance to render the analogy complete: but in a few cases one or more of the ten were detached, probably in consequence of the local separation of portions of the original consanguine tribe who desired to have their deme incorporated in the district of their immediate kinsmen. The inhabitants of each district or county were also a body politic, with certain powers of local self-government. They elected a phylarch, who commanded the cavalry; a taxiarch, who commanded the foot-soldiers and a general, who commanded both; and as each district was required to furnish five triremes, they probably elected as many trierarchs to command them. Cleisthenes increased the senate to five hundred, and assigned fifty to each district. They were elected by its inhabitants. Other functions of this larger body politic doubtless existed, but they have been imperfectly explained.

The third and last member of the territorial series was the Athenian commonwealth or state, consisting of ten local tribes or districts. It was an organized body politic, embracing the aggregate of Athenian citizens. It was represented by a senate, an ecclesia, the court of Areopagus, the archons, and judges, and the body of elected military and naval commanders.

Thus the Athenians founded the second great plan of government upon territory and upon property. They substituted a series of territorial aggregates in the place of an ascending series of aggregates of persons. As a plan of government it rested upon territory which was necessarily permanent, and upon property which was

1 The Latin "tribus"—tribe, signified originally "a third part," and was used to designate a third part of the people when composed of three tribes; but in course of time, after the Latin tribes were made local instead of consanguine, like the Athenian local tribes, the term tribe lost its numerical quality, and came, like the phylon of Cleisthenes to be a local designation. —See Mommsen's "Hist. of Rome", l. c., i, 71.

more or less localized; and it dealt with its citizens, now localized in demes though their territorial relations. To be a citizen of the state it was necessary to be a citizen of a deme. The person voted and was taxed in his deme, and he was called into the military service from his deme. In like manner he was called by election into the senate, and to the command of a division of the army or navy from the larger district of his local tribe. His relations to a gens or phratry ceased to govern his duties as a citizen. The contrast between the two systems is as marked as their difference was fundamental. A coalescence of the people into bodies politic in territorial areas now became complete.

The territorial series enters into the plan of government of modern civilized nations. Among ourselves, for example, we have the township, the county, the state, and the United States; the inhabitants of each of which are an organized body politic with powers of local self-government. Each organization is in full vitality and performs its functions within a definite sphere in which it is supreme. France has a similar series in the commune, the arrondissement, the department, and the empire, now the republic. In Great Britain the series is the parish, the shire, the kingdom, and the three kingdoms. In the Saxon period the hundred seems to have been the analogue of the township;[1] but already emasculated of the powers of local self-government, with the exception of the hundred court. The inhabitants of these several areas were organized as bodies politic, but those below the highest with very limited powers. The tendency to centralization under monarchical institutions has atrophied, practically, all the lower organizations.

As a consequence of the legislation of Cleisthenes, the gentes, phratries end tribes were divested of their influence, because their powers were taken from them and vested in the deme, the local tribe and the state, which became from thenceforth the sources of all political power. They were not dissolved, however, even after this

1 "Anglo Saxon Law," by Henry Adams and others, pp. 20, 23.

overthrow, but remained for centuries as a pedigree and lineage, and as fountains of religious life. In certain orations of Demosthenes, where the cases involved personal or property rights, descents or rights of sepulture, both the gens and phratry appear as living organizations in his time.[1] They were left undisturbed by the new system so far as their connection with religious rites, with certain criminal proceedings, and with certain social practices were concerned, which arrested their total dissolution. The classes, however, both those instituted by Theseus and those afterwards created by Solon, disappeared after the time of Cleisthenes.[2]

Solon is usually regarded as the founder of Athenian democracy, while some writers attribute a portion of the work to Cleisthenes and Theseus. We shall draw nearer the truth of the matter by regarding Theseus, Solon and Cleisthenes as standing connected with three great movements of the Athenian people, not to found a democracy, for Athenian democracy was older than either, but to change the plan of government from a gentile into a political organization. Neither sought to change the existing principles of democracy which had been inherited from the gentes. They contributed in their respective times to the great movement for the formation of a state, which required the substitution of a political in the place of gentile society. The invention of a township, and the organization of its inhabitants as a body politic, was the main feature in the problem. It may seem to us a simple matter; but it taxed the capacities of the Athenians to their lowest depths before the idea of a township found expression in its actual creation. It was an inspiration of the genius of Cleisthenes; and it stands as the master work of a master mind. In the new political society they realized that complete democracy which already existed in every essential principle, but which required a change in the plan of government to give it a more ample field

1 See particularly the Orations against Eubulides, and Marcatus.

2 Hermann's "Political Antiquities of Greece", l. c. p. 187, s. 96.

and a fuller expression. It is precisely here, as it seems to the writer, that we have been misled by the erroneous assumption of the great historian, Mr. Grote, whose general views of Grecian institutions are so sound and perspicuous, namely, that the early governments of the Grecian tribes were *essentially monarchical.*[1] On this assumption it requires a revolution of institutions to explain the existence of that Athenian democracy under which the great mental achievements of the Athenians were made. No such revolution occurred, and no radical change of institutions was ever effected, for the reason that they were and always had been *essentially democratical.* Usurpations not unlikely occurred, followed by controversies for the restoration of the previous order; but they never lost their liberties, or those ideas of freedom and of the right of self-government which had been their inheritance in all ages.

Recurring for a moment to the basileus, the office tended to make the man more conspicuous than any other in their affairs. He was the first person to catch the mental eye of the historian by whom he has been metamorphosed into a king, notwithstanding he was made to reign, and by divine right, over a rude democracy. As a general in a military democracy, the basileus becomes intelligible, and without violating the institutions that actually existed. The introduction of this office did not change the principles of the gentes, phratries and tribes, which in their organization were essentially democratical, and which of necessity impressed that character on their gentile system. Evidence is not wanting that the popular element was constantly active to resist encroachments on personal rights. The basileus belongs to the traditionary period, when the powers of government were more or less undefined; but the council of chiefs existed in the centre of the system, and also the gentes, phratries and

---

1 "The primitive Grecian government is essentially monarchical, reposing on personal feeling and divine right."—"History of Greece," ii, 69.

tribes in full vitality. These are sufficient to determine the character of the government.[1]

The government as reconstituted by Cleisthenes contrasted strongly with that previous to the time of Solon. But the transition was not only natural but inevitable if the people followed their ideas to their logical results. It was a change of plan, but not of principles nor even of instrumentalities. The council of chiefs remained in the senate, the agora in the ecclesia; the three highest archons were respectively ministers of state, of religion, and of justice as before, while the six inferior archons exercised judicial functions in connection with the courts, and the large body of dicasts now elected annually for judicial service. No executive officer existed under the system, which is one of its striking peculiarities. The nearest approach to it was the president of the senate, who was elected by lot for a single day, without the possibility of a re-election during the year. For a single day he presided over the popular assembly, and held the keys of the citadel and of the treasury. Under the new government the popular assembly held the substance of power, and guided the destiny of Athens. The new element which gave stability and order to the state was the deme or township, with its complete autonomy, and local self-government. A hundred demes similarly organized would determine the general movement of the commonwealth. As the unit, so the compound. It is here that the people, as before remarked, must begin if they would learn the art of self-government, and maintain equal laws and equal rights and privileges. They must retain in their hands, all the powers of society not necessary to the state to insure an efficient general administration, as well as the control of the administration itself.

---

1 Sparta retained the office of basileus in the period of civilization. It was a dual generalship, and hereditary in a particular family. The powers of government were co-ordinated between the Gerousia or council, the popular assembly, the five ephors, and two military commanders. The ephors were elected annually, with powers analogous to the Roman tribunes. Royalty at Sparta needs qualification. The basileis commanded the army, and in their capacity of chief priests offered the sacrifices to the gods.

Athens rose rapidly into influence and distinction under the new political system. That remarkable development of genius and intelligence, which raised the Athenians to the highest eminence among the historical nations of mankind, occurred under the inspiration of democratic institutions.

With the institution of political society under Cleisthenes, the gentile organization was laid aside as a portion of the rags of barbarism. Their ancestors had lived for untold centuries in gentilism, with which they had achieved all the elements of civilization, including a written language, as well as entered upon a civilized career. The history of the gentile organization will remain as a perpetual monument of the anterior ages, identified as it has been with the most remarkable and extended experience of mankind. It must ever be ranked as one of the most remarkable institutions of the human family.

In this brief and inadequate review the discussion has been confined to the main course of events in Athenian history. Whatever was true of the Athenian tribes will be found substantially true of the remaining Grecian tribes, though not exhibited on so broad or so grand a scale. The discussion tends to render still more apparent one of the main propositions advanced — that the idea of government in all the tribes of mankind has been a growth through successive stages of development.

CHAPTER XI

THE ROMAN GENS

When the Latins, and their congeners the Sabellians, the Oscans and the Umbrians, entered the Italian peninsula probably as one people, they were in possession of domestic animals, and probably cultivated cereals and plants. [1] At the least they were well advanced in the

1 "During the period when the Indo-Germanic nations which are now separated still formed one stock speaking the same language, they attained a certain stage of culture, and they had a vocabulary corresponding to it. This vocabulary the several nations carried along with them, in its conventionally established use, as a common dowry and a foundation for further structures of their own. . . . In this way we possess evidence of the development of pastoral life at that remote epoch in the unalterably fixed names of domestic animals; the Sanskrit "gâus" is the Latin "bos," the Greek "bous"; Sanskrit "avis," is the Latin "ovis." the Greek "ois;" Sanskrit "açvas," Latin "equus," Greek "hippos," Sanskrit "hañsas," Latin "anser," Greek "chen;" . . . on the other hand, we have as yet no certain proofs of the existence of agriculture at this period. Language rather favors the negative view."—Mommsen's "History of Rome," Dickson's Trans., Scribner's ed., 1871, i, 37. In a note he remarks that "barley, wheat, and spelt were found growing together in a wild state on the right bank of the Euphrates, northwest from Anah. The growth of barley and wheat in a wild state in Mesopotamia had already been mentioned by the Babylonian historian, Berosus."

Fick remarks upon the same subject as follows: "While pasturage evidently formed the foundation of primitive social life we can find in it but very slight beginnings of agriculture. They were acquainted to be sure with a few of the grains, but the cultivation of these was carried on very incidentally in order to gain a supply of milk and flesh. The material existence of the people rested in no way upon agriculture. This becomes entirely clear from the small number of primitive words which have reference to agriculture. These words are "yava," wild fruit, "varka," hoe, or plow, "rava," sickle, together with "pio, pinsere" (to bake) and "mak," Gk. "masso," which give indications of threshing out and grinding of grain." —Fick's "Primitive Unity of Indo-European Languages," Göttingen, 1873, p. 280. See also "Chips From a German Workshop," ii, 42.

With reference to the possession of agriculture by the Graeco-Italic people, see Mommsen, i, p. 47, et seq.

Middle Status of barbarism; and when they first came under historical notice they were in the Upper Status, and near the threshold of civilization.

The traditional history of the Latin tribes, prior to the time of Romulus, is much more scanty and imperfect than that of the Grecian, whose earlier relative literary culture and stronger literary proclivities enabled them to preserve a larger proportion of their traditionary accounts. Concerning their anterior experience, tradition did not reach beyond their previous life on the Alban hills, and the ranges of the Appenines eastward from the site of Rome. For tribes so far advanced in the arts of life it would have required a long occupation of Italy to efface all knowledge of the country from which they came. In the time of Romulus[1] they had already fallen by segmentation into thirty independent tribes, still united in a loose confederacy for mutual protection. They also occupied contiguous territorial areas. The Sabellians, Oscans, and Umbrians were in the same general condition; their respective tribes were in the same relations; and their territorial circumscriptions, as might have been expected, were founded upon dialect. All alike, including their northern neighbors the Etruscans, were organized in gentes, with institutions similar to those of the Grecian tribes. Such was their general condition when they first emerged from behind the dark curtain of their previous obscurity, and the light of history fell upon them.

Roman history has touched but slightly the particulars of a vast experience anterior to the founding of Rome (about 753 B. C.) The Italian tribes had then become numerous and populous; they had become strictly agricultural in their habits, possessed flocks and herds of domestic animals, and had made great progress in the arts of life. They had also attained the monogamian family. All this is shown by their condition when first made known to us; but the particulars of their progress

---

1 The use of the word Romulus, and of the names of his successors, does not involve the adoption of the ancient Roman traditions. These names personify the great movements which then took place with which we are chiefly concerned.

from a lower to a higher state had, in the main, fallen out of knowledge. They were backward in the growth of the idea of government; since the confederacy of tribes was still the full extent of their advancement. Although the thirty tribes were confederated, it was in the nature of a league for mutual defense, and neither sufficiently close or intimate to tend to a nationality.

The Etruscan tribes were confederated; and the same was probably true of the Sabellian, Oscan and Umbrian tribes. While the Latin tribes possessed numerous fortified towns and country strongholds, they were spread over the surface of the country for agricultural pursuits, and for the maintenance of their flocks and herds. Concentration and coalescence had not occurred to any marked extent until the great movement ascribed to Romulus which resulted in the foundation of Rome. These loosely united Latin tribes furnished the principal materials from which the new city was to draw its strength. The accounts of these tribes from the time of the supremacy of the chiefs of Alba down to the time of Servius Tullius, were made up to a great extent of fables and traditions; but certain facts remained in the institutions and social usages transmitted to the historical period which tend, in a remarkable manner, to illustrate their previous condition. They are even more important than an outline history of actual events.

Among the institutions of the Latin tribes existing at the commencement of the historical period were the gentes, curiæ and tribes upon which Romulus and his successors established the Roman power. The new government was not in all respects a natural growth; but modified in the upper members of the organic series by legislative procurement. The gentes, however, which formed the basis of the organization, were natural growths, and in the main either of common or cognate lineage. That is, the Latin gentes were of the same lineage while the Sabine and other gentes, with the exception of the Etruscans, were of cognate descent. In the time of Tarquinius Priscus, the fourth in succession from Romulus, the organization had been brought to a numerical scale, namely: ten gentes to a curia, ten curiæ to a tribe, and three tribes of the Romans; giving a total of three hundred gentes integrated in one gentile society.

Romulus had the sagacity to perceive that a confederacy of tribes, composed of gentes and occupying separate areas, had neither the unity of purpose nor sufficient strength to accomplish more than the maintenance of an independent existence. The tendency to disintegration counteracted the advantages of the federal principle. Concentration and coalescence were the remedy proposed by Romulus and the wise men of his time. It was a remarkable movement for the period, and still more remarkable in its progress from the epoch of Romulus to the institution of political society under Servius Tullius. Following the course of the Athenian tribes and concentrating in one city, they wrought out in five generations a similar and complete change in the plan of government, from a gentile into a political organization.

It will be sufficient to remind the reader of the general facts that Romulus united upon and around the Palatine Hill a hundred Latin gentes, organized as a tribe, the Ramnes; that by a fortunate concurrence of circumstances a large body of Sabines were added to the new community whose gentes, afterwards increased to one hundred, were organized as a second tribe, the Tities; and that in the time of Tarquinius Priscus a third tribe, the Luceres, had been formed, composed of a hundred gentes drawn from surrounding tribes, including the Etruscans. Three hundred gentes, in about the space of a hundred years, were thus gathered at Rome, and completely organized under a council of chiefs now called the Roman Senate, an assembly of the people now called the *comitia curiata,* and one military commander, the *rex;* and with one purpose, that of gaining a military ascendency in Italy.

Under the constitution of Romulus, and the subsequent legislation of Servius Tullius, the government was essentially a military democracy, because the military spirit predominated in the government. But it may be remarked in passing that a new and antagonistic element, the Roman senate, was now incorporated in the centre of the social system, which conferred patrician rank upon its members and their posterity. A privileged class was thus created at a stroke, and intrenched first in the gentile and afterwards in the political system, which ultimately overthrew the democratic principles inherited from the gentes. It was the Roman senate, with the patrician class it created, that changed the institutions and the destiny of the Roman people, and turned them from a career, analogous to that of the Athenians, to which their inherited principles naturally and logically tended.

In its main features the new organization was a masterpiece of wisdom for military purposes. It soon carried them entirely beyond the remaining Italian tribes, and ultimately into supremacy over the entire peninsula.

The organization of the Latin and other Italian tribes into gentes has been investigated by Niebuhr, Hermann, Mommsen, Long and others; but their several accounts fall short of a clear and complete exposition of the structure and principles of the Italian gens. This is due in part to the obscurity in which portions of the subject are enveloped, and to the absence of minute details in the Latin writers. It is also in part due to a misconception, by some of the first named writers, of the relations of the family to the gens. They regard the gens as composed of families, whereas it was composed of parts of families; so that the gens and not the family was the unit of the social system. It may be difficult to carry the investigation much beyond the point where they have left it; but information drawn from the archaic constitution of the gens may serve to elucidate some of its characteristics which are now obscure.

Concerning the prevalence of the organization into gentes among the Italian tribes, Niebuhr remarks as follows: "Should any one still contend that no conclusion is to be drawn from the character of the Athenian gennetes to that of the Roman gentiles, he will be bound to show how an institution which runs through the whole ancient world came to have a completely different character in Italy and in Greece.... Every body of citizens was divided in this manner; the Gephyræans and Salaminians as well as the Athenians, the Tusculans as well as the Romans." [1]

Besides the existence of the Roman gens, it is desirable to know the nature of the organization; its rights, privileges and obligations, and the relations of the gentes to each other, as members of a social system. After these have been considered, their relations to the curiæ, tribes, and resulting people of which they formed a part, will remain for consideration in the next ensuing chapter.

After collecting the accessible information from various sources upon these subjects it will be found incomplete in many respects, leaving some of the attributes and functions of the gens a matter of inference. The powers of the gentes were withdrawn, and transferred to new political bodies before historical composition among the Romans had fairly commenced. There was, therefore, no practical necessity resting upon the Romans for preserving the special features of a system substantially set aside. Gaius, who wrote his *Institutes* in the early part of the second century of our era, took occasion to remark that the whole *jus gentilicium* had fallen into desuetude, and that it was then superfluous to treat the subject. [2] But at the foundation of Rome, and for several centuries thereafter, the gentile organization was in vigorous activity.

The Roman definition of a gens and of a gentilis, and the line in which descent was traced should be presented before the characteristics of the gens are considered. In the *Topics* of Cicero a gentilis is defined as follows: Those are gentiles who are of the same name among themselves. This is insufficient. Who were born of free parents. Even that is not sufficient. No one of whose ancestors has been a slave. Something still is wanting. Who have never suffered capital diminution. This perhaps may do; for I am not aware that Scaevola, the Pontiff, added anything to this definition. [3] There is one by Festus: "A

---

1 "History of Rome," l. c., i, 241, 245.
2 —"Inst.," iii, 17.
3 —"Cicero, Topica 6."

gentilis is described as one both sprung from the same stock, and who is called by the same name." [1] Also by Varro: As from an Aemilius men are born Aemilii, and gentiles; so from the name Aemilius terms are derived pertaining to gentilism. [2]

Cicero does not attempt to define a gens, but rather to furnish certain tests by which the right to the gentile connection might be proved, or the loss of it be detected. Neither of these definitions show the composition of a gens; that is, whether all, or a part only, of the descendants of a supposed genarch were entitled to bear the gentile name; and, if a part only, what part. With descent in the male line the gens would include those only who could trace their descent through males exclusively; and if in the female line, then through females only. If limited to neither, then all the descendants would be included. These definitions must have assumed that descent in the male line was a fact known to all. From other sources it appears that those only belonged to the gens who could trace their descent through its male members. Roman genealogies supply this proof. Cicero omitted the material fact that those were gentiles who could trace their descent through males exclusively from an acknowledged ancestor within the gens. It is in part supplied by Festus and Varro. From an Aemilius, the latter remarks, men are born Aemilii, and gentiles; each must be born of a male bearing the gentile name. But Cicero's definition also shows that a gentilis must bear the gentile name.

In the address of the Roman tribune Canuleius (445 B. C.), on his proposition to repeal an existing law forbidding intermarriage between patricians and plebeians, there is a statement implying descent in the male line. For what else is there in the matter, he remarks, if a patrician man shall wed a plebeian woman, or a plebeian man a patrician woman? What right in the end is thereby changed? The children surely follow the father. [3]

A practical illustration, derived from transmitted gen-

---

1 —Quoted in Smith's "Dic. Gk. & Rom. Antiq., Article, Gens."
2 —Varro, "De Lingua Latina," lib. viii, cap. 4.
3 — Livy, lib. iv, cap. 4.

tile names, will show conclusively that descent was in the male line. Julia, the sister of Caius Julius Caesar, married Marcus Attius Balbus. Her name shows that she belonged to the Julian gens.[1] Her daughter Attia, according to custom, took the gentile name of her father and belonged to the Attian gens. Attia married Caius Octavius, and became the mother of Caius Octavius, the first Roman emperor. The son, as usual, took the gentile name of his father, and belonged to the Octavian gens.[2] After becoming emperor he added the names Caesar Augustus.

In the Roman gens descent was in the male line from Augustus back to Romulus, and for an unknown period back of the latter. None were gentiles except such as could trace their descent through males exclusively from some acknowledged ancestor within the gens. But it was unnecessary, because impossible, that all should be able to trace their descent from the same common ancestor; and much less from the eponymous ancestor.

It will be noticed that in each of the above cases, to which a large number might be added, the persons married out of the gens. Such was undoubtedly the general usage by customary law.

The Roman gens was individualized by the following rights, privileges and obligations:

I. *Mutual rights of succession to the property of deceased gentiles.*

II. *The possession of a common burial place.*

III. *Common religious rites; sacra gentilicia.*

---

1 "When there was only one daughter in a family, she used to be called from the name of the gens; thus, Tullia, the daughter of Cicero, Julia, the daughter of Caesar; Octavia, the sister of Augustus, etc.; and they retained the same name after they were married. When there were two daughters, the one was called Major and the other Minor. If there were more than two, they were distinguished by their number: thus, Prima, Secunda, Tertia, Quarta, Quinta, etc.; or more softly, Tertulla, Quartilla, Quintilla, etc. . . . During the flourishing state of the republic, the names of the gentes, and surnames of the familiæ, always remained fixed and certain. They were common to all the children of the family, and descended to their posterity. But after the subversion of liberty they were changed and confounded."—Adams's "Roman Antiquities," Glasgow ed., 1825, p. 27.

2 Suetonius, "Vit. Octavianus," c. 3 and 4.

IV. *The obligation not to marry in the gens.*
V. *The possession of lands in common.*
VI. *Reciprocal obligations of help, defense, and redress of injuries.*
VII. *The right to bear the gentile name.*
VIII. *The right to adopt strangers into the gens.*
IX. *The right to elect and depose its chiefs; query.*

These several characteristics will be considered in the order named.

1. *Mutual rights of succession to the property of deceased gentiles.*

When the law of the Twelve Tables was promulgated (451 B. C.), the ancient rule, which presumptively distributed the inheritance among the gentiles, had been superseded by more advanced regulations. The estate of an intestate now passed, first, to his *sui heredes,* that is, to his children; and, in default of children, to his lineal descendants through males. [1] The living children took equally, and the children of deceased sons took the share of their father equally. It will be noticed that the inheritance remained in the gens; the children of the female descendants of the intestate, who belonged to other gentes, being excluded. Second, if there were no *sui heredes,* by the same law, the inheritance then passed to the agnates. [2] The agnatic kindred comprised all those persons who could trace their descent through males from the same common ancestor with the intestate. In virtue of such a descent they all bore the same gentile name, females as well as males, and were nearer in degree to the decedent than the remaining gentiles. The agnates nearest in degree had the preference; first, the brothers and unmarried sisters; second, the paternal uncles and unmarried aunts of the intestate, and so on until the agnatic relatives were exhausted. Third, if there were no agnates of the intestate, the same law called the gentiles to the inheritance. [3] This seems at first sight remarkable; be-

---

1 Gaius, "Institutes," lib. iii, 1 and 2. The wife was a coheiress with the children.
2 Ib., lib. iii, 9.
3 Gaius, "Inst.," lib. iii, 17.

cause the children of the intestate's sisters were excluded from the inheritance, and the preference given to gentile kinsmen so remote that their relationship to the intestate could not be traced at all, and only existed in virtue of an ancient lineage preserved by a common gentile name. The reason, however, is apparent; the children of the sisters of the intestate belonged to another gens, and the gentile right predominated over greater nearness of consanguinity, because the principle which retained the property in the gens was fundamental. It is a plain inference from the law of the Twelve Tables that inheritance began in the inverse order, and that the three classes of heirs represent the three successive rules of inheritance; namely, first, the gentiles; second, the agnates, among whom were the children of the decedent after descent was changed to the male line; and third, the children, to the exclusion of the remaining agnates.

A female, by her marriage, suffered what was technically called a loss of franchise or capital diminution (*deminutio capitis*), by which she forfeited her agnatic rights. Here again the reason is apparent. If after her marriage she could inherit as an agnate it would transfer the property inherited from her own gens to that of her husband. An unmarried sister could inherit, but a married sister could not.

With our knowledge of the archaic principles of the gens, we are enabled to glance backward to the time when descent in the Latin gens was in the female line, when property was inconsiderable, and distributed among the gentiles; not necessarily within the life-time of the Latin gens, for its existence reached back of the period of their occupation of Italy. That the Roman gens had passed from the archaic into its historical form is partially indicated by the reversion of property in certain cases to the gentiles. [1]

---

1 A singular question arose between the Marcelli and Claudii, two families of the Claudian gens, with respect to the estate of the son of a freedman of the Marcelli; the former claiming by right of family, and the latter by right of gens. The law of the Twelve Tables gave the estate of a freedman to his former master, who by the act of manumission became his patron, provided he died intestate, and without "sui heredes;" but it

"The right of succeeding to the property of members who died without kin and intestate," Niebuhr remarks, "was that which lasted the longest; so long indeed, as to engage the attention of the jurists, and even — though assuredly not as anything more than a historical question — that of Gaius, the manuscript of whom is unfortunately illegible in this part." [1]

II. *A common burial place.*

The sentiment of gentilism seems to have been stronger in the Upper Status of barbarism than in earlier conditions, through a higher organization of society, and through mental and moral advancement. Each gens usually had a burial place for the exclusive use of its members as a place of sepulture. A few illustrations will exhibit Roman usages with respect to burial.

Appius Claudius, the chief of the Claudian gens, removed from Regili, a town of the Sabines, to Rome in the time of Romulus, where in due time he was made a senator, and thus a patrician. He brought with him the Claudian gens, and such a number of clients that his accession to Rome was regarded as an important event. Suetonius remarks that the gens received from the state lands upon the Anio for their clients, and a burial place for themselves near the capitol.[2] This statement seems to imply that a common burial place was, at that time, considered indispensable to a gens. The Claudii, having abandoned their Sabine connection and identified themselves with the Roman people, received both a grant of

---

did not reach the case of the son of a freedman. The fact that the Claudii were a patrician family, and the Marcelli were not, could not affect the question. The freedman did not acquire gentile rights in his master's gens by his manumission, although he was allowed to adopt the gentile name of his patron; as Cicero's freedman, Tyro, was called M. Tullius Tyro. It is not known how the case, which is mentioned by Cicero ("De Oratore," i, 39), and commented upon by Long (Smith's "Dic. Gk. & Rom. Antiq., Art. Gens"), and Niebuhr, was decided; but the latter suggests that it was probably against the Claudii ("Hist. of Rome," i, 245, "note"). It is difficult to discover how any claim whatever could be urged by the Claudii; or any by the Marcelli, except through an extension of the patronal right by judicial construction. It is a noteworthy case, because it shows how strongly the mutual rights with respect to the inheritance of property were intrenched in the gens.

1 "History of Rome," i, 242.

2 —Suet., "Vit. Tiberius," cap. 1.

lands and a burial place for the gens, to place them in equality of condition with the Roman gentes. The transaction reveals a custom of the times.

The family tomb had not entirely superseded that of the gens in the time of Julius Caesar, as was illustrated by the case of Quintilius Varus, who, having lost his army in Germany, destroyed himself, and his body fell into the hands of the enemy. The half-burned body of Varus, says Paterculus, was mangled by the savage enemy; his head was cut off, and brought to Maroboduus, and by him having been sent to Caesar, was at length honored with burial in the gentile sepulchre. [1]

In his treatise on the laws, Cicero refers to the usages of his own times in respect to burial in the following language: now the sacredness of burial places is so great that it is affirmed to be wrong to perform the burial independently of the sacred rites of the gens. Thus in the time of our ancestors A. Torquatus decided respecting the Popilian gens. [2] The purport of the statement is that it was a religious duty to bury the dead with sacred rites, and when possible in land belonging to the gens. It further appears that cremation and inhumation were both practiced prior to the promulgation of the Twelve Tables, which prohibited the burying or burning of dead bodies within the city. [3] The columbarium, which would usually accommodate several hundred urns, was eminently adapted to the uses of a gens. In the time of Cicero the gentile organization had fallen into decadence, but certain usages peculiar to it had remained, and that respecting a common burial place among the number. The family tomb began to take the place of that of the gens, as the families in the ancient gentes rose into complete autonomy; nevertheless, remains of ancient gentile usages with respect to burial manifested themselves in various ways, and were still fresh in the history of the past.

III. *Common sacred rites; sacra gentilicia.*

The Roman *sacra* embody our idea of divine worship,

---

1 —"Velleius Paterculus," ii, 119.
2 —"De Leg.," ii, 22.
3 Cicero, "De Leg.," ii, 23.

and were either public or private. Religious rites performed by a gens were called *sacra privata,* or *sacra gentilicia.* They were performed regularly at stated periods by the gens.[1] Cases are mentioned in which the expenses of maintaining these rites had become a burden in consequence of the reduced numbers in the gens. They were gained and lost by circumstances, e. g., adoption or marriage.[2] "That the members of the Roman gens had common sacred rites," observes Niebuhr, "is well known; there were sacrifices appointed for stated days and places."[3] The sacred rites, both public and private, were under pontifical regulation exclusively, and not subject to civil cognizance.[4]

The religious rites of the Romans seem to have had their primary connection with the gens rather than the family. A college of pontiffs, of curiones, and of augurs, with an elaborate system of worship under these priesthoods, in due time grew into form and became established; but the system was tolerant and free. The priesthood was in the main elective.[5] The head of every family also was the priest of the household. The gentes of[6] the Greeks and Romans were the fountains from which flowed the stupendous mythology of the classical world.

In the early days of Rome many gentes had each their own sacellum for the performance of their religious rites. Several gentes had each special sacrifices to perform, which had been transmitted from generation to generation, and were regarded as obligatory; as those of the Nautii to Minerva, of the Fabii to Hercules, and of the Horatii in expiation of the sororicide committed by Horatius.[7] It is sufficient for my purpose to have shown

1 "There were certain sacred rites ("sacra gentilicia") which belonged to a gens, to the observance of which all the members of a gens, as such, were bound, whether they were members by birth, adoption or adrogation. A person was freed from the observance of such "sacra," and lost the privileges connected with his gentile rights when he lost his gens."—Smith's "Dic. Antiq., Gens."

2 Cicero, "Pro Domo," c. 13.

3 "History of Rome," i, 241.

4 Cicero, "De Leg.," ii, 23.

5 "Dionysius," ii, 22.

6 Ib., ii, 21.

7 Niebuhr's "History of Rome," i, 241.

generally that each gens had its own religious rites as one of the attributes of the organization.

IV. *The obligation not to marry in the gens.*

Gentile regulations were customs having the force of law. The obligation not to marry in the gens was one of the number. It does not appear to have been turned, at a later day, into a legal enactment; but evidence that such was the rule of the gens appears in a number of ways. The Roman genealogies show that marriage was out of the gens, of which instances have been given. This, as we have seen, was the archaic rule for reasons of consanguinity. A woman by her marriage forfeited her agnatic rights, to which rule there was no exception. It was to prevent the transfer of property by marriage from one gens to another, from the gens of her birth to the gens of her husband. The exclusion of the children of a female from all rights of inheritance from a maternal uncle or maternal grandfather, which followed, was for the same reason. As the female was required to marry out of her gens her children would be of the gens of their father, and there could be no privity of inheritance between members of different gentes.

V. *The possession of lands in common.*

The ownership of lands in common was so general among barbarous tribes that the existence of the same tenure among the Latin tribes is no occasion for surprise. A portion of their lands seems to have been held in severalty by individuals from a very early period. No time can be assigned when this was not the case; but at first it was probably the possessory right to lands in actual occupation, so often before referred to, which was recognized as far back as the Lower Status of barbarism.

Among the rustic Latin tribes, lands were held in common by each tribe, other lands by the gentes, and still other by households.

Allotments of lands to individuals became common at Rome in the time of Romulus, and afterwards quite general. Varro and Dionysius both state that Romulus allotted two jugera (about two and a quarter acres) to each man. [1] Similar allotments are said to have been afterwards made by Numa and Servius Tullius. They were the beginnings of absolute ownership in severalty, and presuppose a settled life as well as a great advancement in intelligence. It was not only admeasured but granted by the government, which was very different from a possessory right in lands growing out of an individual act. The idea of absolute individual ownership of land was a growth through experience, the complete attainment of which belongs to the period of civilization. These lands, however, were taken from those held in common by the Roman people. Gentes, curiæ and tribes held certain lands in common after civilization had commenced, beyond those held by individuals in severalty.

Mommsen remarks that "the Roman territory was divided in the earliest times into a number of clan-districts, which were subsequently employed in the formation of the earliest rural wards (*tribus rusticae*)...... These names are not, like those of the districts added at a later period, derived from the localities, but are formed without exception from the names of the clans." [2] Each gens held an independent district, and of necessity was localized upon it. This was a step in advance, although it was the prevailing practice not only in the rural districts, but also in Rome, for the gentes to localize in separate areas. Mommsen further observes: "As each household had its own portion of land, so the clan-household or village, had clan-lands belonging to it, which, as will afterwards be shown, were managed up to a comparatively late period after the analogy of house-lands, that is, on the system of joint possession. .... These clanships, however, were from the beginning regarded not as independent societies, but as integral parts of a political community (*civitas populi*). This first presents itself as an aggregate of a number of clan-villages of the same stock, language and manners, bound to mutual observance of

1 —Varro, "De Re Rustica," lib. i, cap. 10.
2 "History of Rome," i, 62. He names the Camillii, Galerii, Lemonii, Pollii, Pupinii, Voltinii, Aemilii, Cornelii, Fabii, Horatii, Menenii, Papirii, Romilii, Sergii, Veturii.—Ib., p. 63.

law and mutual legal redress and to united action in aggression and defense." [1] Clan is here used by Mommsen, or his translator, in the place of gens, and elsewhere canton is used in the place of tribe, which are the more singular since the Latin language furnishes specific terms for these organizations which have become historical. Mommsen represents the Latin tribes anterior to the founding of Rome as holding lands by households, by gentes and by tribes; and he further shows the ascending series of social organizations in these tribes; a comparison of which with those of the Iroquois, discloses their close parallelism, namely, the gens, tribe and confederacy. [2] The phratry is not mentioned although it probably existed. The household referred to could scarcely have been a single family. It is not unlikely that it was composed of related families who occupied a joint-

---

1 "History of Rome," i, 63.

2 "A fixed local centre was quite as necessary in the case of such a canton as in that of a clanship; but as the members of the clan, or, in other words, the constituent elements of the canton dwelt in villages, the centre of the canton cannot have been a town or place of joint settlement in the strict sense. It must, on the contrary, have been simply a place of common assembly, containing the seat of justice and the common sanctuary of the canton, where the members of the canton met every eighth day for purposes of intercourse and amusement, and where, in case of war, they obtained a safer shelter for themselves and their cattle than in the villages; in ordinary circumstances this place of meeting was not at all or but scantily inhabited. . . These cantons accordingly, having their rendezvous in some stronghold, and including a certain number of clanships, form the primitive political unities with which Italian history begins. . . . All af these cantons were in primitive times politically sovereign, and each of them was governed by its prince with the co-operation of the council of elders and the assembly of warriors. Nevertheless the feeling of fellowship based on community of descent and of language not only pervaded the whole of them, but manifested itself in an important religious and political institution—the perpetual league of the collective Latin cantons."—"Hist. of Rome," i, 64-66. The statement that the canton or tribe was governed by its prince with the co-operation of the council, etc., is a reversal of the correct statement, and therefore misleading. We must suppose that the military commander held an elective office, and that he was deposable at the pleasure of the constituency who elected him. Further than this, there is no ground for assuming that he possessed any civil functions. It is a reasonable, if not a necessary conclusion, therefore, that the tribe was governed by a council composed of the chiefs of the gentes, and by an assembly of the warriors, with the co-operation of a general military commander, whose functions were exclusively military. It was a government of three powers, common in the Upper Status of barbarism, and identified with institutions essentially democratical.

tenement house, and practiced communism in living in the household.

VI. *Reciprocal obligations of help, defense and redress of injuries.*

During the period of barbarism the dependence of the gentiles upon each other for the protection of personal rights would be constant; but after the establishment of political society, the gentilis, now a citizen, would turn to the law and to the state for the protection before administered by his gens. This feature of the ancient system would be one of the first to disappear under the new. Accordingly but slight references to these mutual obligations are found in the early authors. It does not follow, however, that the gentiles did not practice these duties to each other in the previous period; on the contrary, the inference that they did is a necessary one from the principles of the gentile organization. Remains of these special usages appear, under special circumstances, well down in the historical period. When Appius Claudius was cast into prison (about 432 B. C.), Caius Claudius, then at enmity with him, put on mourning, as well as the whole Claudian gens.[1] A calamity or disgrace falling upon one member of the body was felt and shared by all. During the second Punic war, Niebuhr remarks, "the gentiles united to ransom their fellows who were in captivity, and were forbidden to do it by the senate. This obligation is an essential characteristic of the gens."[2] In the case of Camillus, against whom a tribune had lodged an accusation on account of the Veientian spoil, he summoned to his house before the day appointed for his trial his tribes-men and clients to ask their advice, and he received for an answer that they would collect whatever sum he was condemned to pay; but to clear him was impossible.[3] The active principle of gentilism is plainly illustrated in these cases. Niebuhr further remarks that the obligation to assist their indigent gentiles rested on the members of the Roman gens.[4]

1 —Livy, vi, 20.
2 "History of Rome," i, 242.
3—Livy, v, 32.
4 "History of Rome," i, 242: citing Dionysius, ii, 10.

VII. *The right to bear the gentile name.*

This followed necessarily from the nature of the gens. All such persons as were born sons or daughters of a male member of the gens were themselves members, and of right entitled to bear the gentile name. In the lapse of time it was found impossible for the members of a gens to trace their descent back to the founder, and, consequently, for different families within the gens to find their connection through a later common ancestor. Whilst this inability proved the antiquity of the lineage, it was no evidence that these families had not sprung from a remote common ancestor. The fact that persons were born in the gens, and that each could trace his descent through a series of acknowledged members of the gens, was sufficient evidence of gentile descent, and strong evidence of the blood connection of all the gentiles. But some investigators, Niebuhr among the number,[1] have denied the existence of any blood relationship between the families in a gens, since they could not show a connection through a common ancestor. This treats the gens as a purely fictitious organization, and is therefore untenable. Niebuhr's inference against a blood connection from Cicero's definition is not sustainable. If the right of a person to bear the gentile name were questioned, proof of the right would consist, not in tracing his descent from the genarch, but from a number of acknowledged ancestors within the gens. Without written records the number of generations through which a pedigree might be traced would be limited. Few families in the same gens might not be able to find a common ancestor, but it would not follow that they were not of common descent from some remote ancestor within the gens.[2]

After descent was changed to the male line the ancient names of the gentes, which not unlikely were taken from

---

1 "History of Rome," i, 240.

2 "Nevertheless, affinity in blood always appeared to the Romans to lie at the root of the connection between the members of the clan, and still more between those of a family; and the Roman community can only have interfered with these groups to a limited extent consistent with the retention of their fundamental character of affinity."—Mommsen's "History of Rome," i, 103.

animals,[1] or inanimate objects, gave place to personal names. Some individual, distinguished in the history of the gens, became its eponymous ancestor, and this person, as elsewhere suggested, was not unlikely superseded by another at long intervals of time. When a gens divided in consequence of separation in area, one division would be apt to take a new name, but such a change of name would not disturb the kinship upon which the gens was founded. When it is considered that the lineage of the Roman gentes, under changes of names, ascended to the time when the Latins, Greeks and Sanskrit speaking people of India were one people, without reaching its source, some conception of its antiquity may be gained. The loss of the gentile name at any time by any individual was the most improbable of all occurrences; consequently its possession was the highest evidence that he shared with his gentiles the same ancient lineage. There was one way, and but one, of adulterating gentile descent, namely: by the adoption of strangers in blood into the gens. This practice prevailed, but the extent of it was small. If Niebuhr had claimed that the blood relationship of the gentiles had become attenuated by lapse of time to an inappreciable quantity between some of them, no objection could be taken to his position; but a denial of all relationship which turns the gens into a fictitious aggregation of persons, without any bond of union, controverts the principle upon which the gens came into existence, and which perpetuated it through three entire ethnical periods.

Elswhere I have called attention to the fact that the gens came in with a system of consanguinity which reduced all consanguinei to a small number of categories, and retained their descendants indefinitely in the same. The relationships of persons were easily traced, no matter

---

1 It is a curious fact that Cleisthenes of Argos changed the names of the three Dorian tribes of Sicyon, one to Hyatæ, signifying in the singular "a boar;" another to Oneatæ, signifying "an ass," and a third to Choereatæ, signifying "a little pig." They were intended as an insult to the Sicyonians; but they remained during his lifetime, and for sixty years afterwards. Did the idea of these animal names come down through tradition?—See Grote's "History of Greece," iii, 33, 36.

how remote their actual common ancestor. In an Iroquois gens of five hundred persons, all its members are related to each other and each person knows or can find his relationship to every other; so that the fact of kin was perpetually present in the gens of the archaic period. With the rise of the monogamian family, a new and totally different system of consanguinity came in, under which the relationships between collaterals soon disappeared. Such was the system of the Latin and Grecian tribes at the commencement of the historical period. That which preceded it was, presumptively at least, Turanian, under which the relationships of the gentiles to each other would have been known.

After the decadence of the gentile organization commenced, new gentes ceased to form by the old process of segmentation; and some of those existing died out. This tended to enhance the value of gentile descent as a lineage. In the times of the empire, new families were constantly establishing themselves in Rome from foreign parts, and assuming gentile names to gain social advantages.. This practice being considered an abuse, the Emperor Claudius (A. D. 40-54) prohibited foreigners from assuming Roman names, especially those of the ancient gentes.[1] Roman families, belonging to the historical gentes, placed the highest value upon their lineages both under the republic and the empire.

All the members of a gens were free, and equal in their rights and privileges, the poorest as well as the richest, the distinguished as well as the obscure; and they shared equally in whatever dignity the gentile name conferred which they inherited as a birthright. Liberty, equality and fraternity were cardinal principles of the Roman gens, not less certainly than of the Grecian, and of the American Indian.

VIII. *The right of adopting strangers in blood into the gens.*

In the times of the republic, and also of the empire, adoption into the family, which carried the person into the

1 Sueton., "Vit. Claudius," cap. 25.

gens of the family, was practiced; but it was attended with formalities which rendered it difficult. A person who had no children, and who was past the age to expect them, might adopt a son with the consent of the pontifices, and of the *comitia curiata.* The college of pontiffs were entitled to be consulted lest the sacred rites of the family, from which the adopted person was taken, might thereby be impaired:[1] as also the assembly, because the adopted person would receive the gentile name, and might inherit the estate of his adoptive father. From the precautions which remained in the time of Cicero, the inference is reasonable that under the previous system, which was purely gentile, the restrictions must have been greater and the instances rare. It is not probable that adoption in the early period was allowed without the consent of the gens, and of the curia to which the gens belonged; and if so, the number adopted must have been limited. Few details remain of the ancient usages with respect to adoption.

IX. *The right of electing and deposing its chiefs; query.*

The incompleteness of our knowledge of the Roman gentes is shown quite plainly by the absence of direct information with respect to the tenure of the office of chief (*princeps*). Before the institution of political society each gens had its chief, and probably more than one. When the office became vacant it was necessarily filled, either by the election of one of the gentiles, as among the Iroquois, or taken by hereditary right. But the absence of any proof of hereditary right, and the presence of the elective principle with respect to nearly all offices under the republic, and before that, under the *reges,* leads to the inference that hereditary right was alien to the institutions of the Latin tribes. The highest office, that of rex, was elective, the office of senator was elective or by appointment, and that of consuls and of inferior magistrates. It varied with respect to the college of pontiffs instituted by Numa. At first the pontiffs themselves filled vacancies by election. Livy speaks of

[1] Cicero, "Pro Domo," cap. 13.

the election of a *pontifex maximus* by the *comitia* about 212 B. C.[1] By the *lex Domitia* the right to elect the members of the several colleges of pontiffs and of priests was transferred to the people, but the law was subsequently modified by Sulla.[2] The active presence of the elective principle among the Latin gentes when they first come under historical notice, and from that time through the period of the republic, furnishes strong grounds for the inference that the office of chief was elective in tenure. The democratic features of their social system, which present themselves at so many points, were inherited from the gentes. It would require positive evidence that the office of chief passed by hereditary right to overcome the presumption against it. The right to elect carries with it the right to depose from office, where the tenure is for life.

These chiefs, or a selection from them, composed the council of the several Latin tribes before the founding of Rome, which was the principal instrument of government. Traces of the three powers co-ordinated in the government appear among the Latin tribes as they did in the Grecian, namely: the council of chiefs, the assembly of the people, to which we must suppose the more important public measures were submitted for adoption or rejection, and the military commander. Mommsen remarks that "All of these cantons [tribes] were in primitive times politically sovereign, and each of them was governed by its prince, and the co-operation of the council of elders, and the assembly of the warriors."[3] The order of Mommsen's statement should be reversed, and the statement qualified. This council, from its functions and from its central position in their social system, of which it was a growth, held of necessity the supreme power in civil affairs. It was the council that governed, and not the military commander. "In all the cities belonging to civilized nations on the coasts of the Mediterranean," Niebuhr observes, "a senate was a no less es-

1 Livy, xxv, 5.
2 Smith's "Dic., Art. Pontifex."
3 "History of Rome," i, 66.

sential and indispensable part of the state, than a popular assembly; it was a select body of elder citizens; such a council, says Aristotle, there always is, whether the council be aristocratical or democratical; even in oligarchies, be the number of sharers in the sovereignty ever so small, certain councilors are appointed for preparing public measures." [1] The senate of political society succeeded the council of chiefs of gentile society. Romulus formed the first Roman senate of a hundred elders; and as there were then but a hundred gentes, the inference is substantially conclusive that they were the chiefs of these gentes. The office was for life, and non-hereditary; whence the final inference, that the office of chief was at the time elective. Had it been otherwise there is every probability that the Roman senate would have been instituted as an hereditary body. Evidence of the essentially democratic constitution of ancient society meets us at many points, which fact has failed to find its way into the modern historical expositions of Grecian and Roman gentile society.

With respect to the number of persons in a Roman gens, we are fortunately not without some information. About 474 B. C. the Fabian gens proposed to the senate to undertake the Veientian war as a gens, which they said required a constant rather than a large force. [2] Their offer was accepted, and they marched out of Rome three hundred and six soldiers, all patricians, amid the applause of their countrymen. [3] After a series of successes they were finally cut off to a man through an ambuscade. But they left behind them at Rome a single male under the age of puberty, who alone remained to perpetuate the Fabian gens. [4] It seems hardly credible that three hundred should have left in their families but a single male child, below the age of puberty, but such

1 Ib., i, 258.
2 Livy, ii, 48.
3 Ib., ii, 49.
4 Trecentos sex perisse satis convenit: unum prope pubescem aetate relictum stirpem gente Fabiae, dubiisque rebus populi Romani sepe domi bellique vel maximum futurum auxilium.—Livy, ii, 50; and see Ovid, "Fasti," ii, 193.

is the statement. This number of persons would indicate an equal number of females, who, with the children of the males, would give an aggregate of at least seven hundred members of the Fabian gens.

Although the rights, obligations and functions of the Roman gens have been inadequately presented, enough has been adduced to show that this organization was the source of their social, governmental and religious activities. As the unit of their social system it projects its character upon the higher organizations into which it entered as a constituent. A much fuller knowledge of the Roman gens than we now possess is essential to a full comprehension of Roman institutions in their origin and development.

CHAPTER XII

THE ROMAN CURIA, TRIBE AND POPULUS

Having considered the Roman gens, it remains to take up the curia composed of several gentes, the tribe composed of several curiæ, and lastly the Roman people composed of several tribes. In pursuing the subject the inquiry will be limited to the constitution of society as it appeared from the time of Romulus to that of Servius Tullius, with some notice of the changes which occurred in the early period of the republic while the gentile system was giving way, and the new political system was being established.

It will be found that two governmental organizations were in existence for a time, side by side, as among the Athenians, one going out and the other coming in. The first was a society (*societas*), founded upon the gentes; and the other a state (*civitas*), founded upon territory and upon property, which was gradually supplanting the former. A government in a transitional stage is necessarily complicated, and therefore difficult to be understood. These changes were not violent but gradual, commencing with Romulus and substantially completed, though not perfected, by Servius Tullius; thus embracing a supposed period of nearly two hundred years, crowded with events of great moment to the infant commonwealth. In order to follow the history of the gentes to the overthrow of their influence in the state it will be necessary, after considering the curia, tribe and nation, to explain briefly the new political system. The last will form the subject of the ensuing chapter.

Gentile society among the Romans exhibits four stages of organization: first, the gens, which was a body of consanguinei and the unit of the social system; second, the curia, analogous to the Grecian phratry, which consisted of ten gentes united in a higher corporate body; third, the tribe, consisting of ten curiæ, which possessed some of the attributes of a nation under gentile institutions; and fourth, the Roman people (*Populus Romanus*), consisting, in the time of Tullus Hostilius, of three such tribes united by coalescence in one gentile society, embracing three hundred gentes. There are facts warranting the conclusion that all the Italian tribes were similarly organized at the commencement of the historical period; but with this difference, perhaps, that the Roman curia was a more advanced organization than the Grecian phratry, or the corresponding phratry of the remaining Italian tribes; and that the Roman tribe, by constrained enlargement, became a more comprehensive organization than in the remaining Italian stocks. Some evidence in support of these statements will appear in the sequel.

Before the time of Romulus the Italians, in their various branches, had become a numerous people. The large number of petty tribes, into which they had become subdivided, reveals that state of unavoidable disintegration which accompanies gentile institutions. But the federal principle had asserted itself among the other Italian tribes as well as the Latin, although it did not result in any confederacy that achieved important results. Whilst this state of things existed, that great movement ascribed to Romulus occurred, namely: the concentration of a hundred Latin gentes on the banks of the Tiber, which was followed by a like gathering of Sabine, Latin and Etruscan and other gentes, to the additional number of two hundred, ending in their final coalescence into one people. The foundations of Rome were thus laid, and Roman power and civilization were to follow. It was this consolidation of gentes and tribes under one government, commenced by Romulus and completed by his successors, that prepared the way for the new political system — for the transition from a government based upon persons and upon personal relations, into one based upon territory and upon property.

It is immaterial whether either of the seven so-called kings of Rome were real or mythical persons, or whether the legislation ascribed to either of them is fabulous or true, so far as this investigation is concerned: because the facts with respect to the ancient constitution of Latin society remained incorporated in Roman institutions, and thus came down to the historical period. It fortunately so happens that the events of human progress embody themselves, independently of particular men, in a material record, which is crystallized in institutions, usages and customs, and preserved in inventions and discoveries. Historians, from a sort of necessity, give to individuals great prominence in the production of events; thus placing persons, who are transient, in the place of principles, which are enduring. The work of society in its totality, by means of which all progress occurs, is ascribed far too much to individual men, and far too little to the public intelligence. It will be recognized generally that the substance of human history is bound up in the growth of ideas, which are wrought out by the people and expressed in their institutions, usages, inventions and discoveries.

The numerical adjustment, before adverted to, of ten gentes to a curia, ten curiæ to a tribe, and three tribes of the Roman people, was a result of legislative procurement not older, in the first two tribes, than the time of Romulus. It was made possible by the accessions gained from the surrounding tribes, by solicitation or conquest; the fruits of which were chiefly incorporated in the Tities and Luceres, as they were successively formed. But such a precise numerical adjustment could not be permanently maintained through centuries, especially with respect to the number of gentes in each curia.

We have seen that the Grecian phratry was rather a religious and social than a governmental organization. Holding an intermediate position between the gens and the tribe, it would be less important than either, until governmental functions were superadded. It appears among the Iroquois in a rudimentary form, its social as distinguished from its governmental character being at that early day equally well marked. But the Roman curia, whatever it may have been in the previous period, grew into an organization more integral and governmental than the phratry of the Greeks; more is known, however, of the former than of the latter. It is probable that the gentes comprised in each curia were, in the main, related gentes; and that their reunion in a higher organization was further cemented by inter-marriages, the gentes of the same curia furnishing each other with wives.

The early writers give no account of the institution of the curia; but it does not follow that it was a new creation by Romulus. It is first mentioned as a Roman institution in connection with his legislation, the number of curiæ in two of the tribes having been established in his time. The organization, as a phratry, had probably existed among the Latin tribes from time immemorial.

Livy, speaking of the favor with which the Sabine women were regarded after the establishment of peace between the Sabines and Latins through their intervention, remarks that Romulus, for this reason, when he had divided the people into thirty curiæ bestowed upon them their names.[1] Dionysius uses the term phratry as the equivalent of curia, but gives the latter also,[2] and observes further, that Romulus divided the curiæ into decades, the ten in each being of course gentes.[3] In like manner Plutarch refers to the fact that each tribe contained ten curiæ, which some say, he remarks, were called after the Sabine women.[4] He is more accurate in the use of language than Livy or Dionysius in saying that each tribe contained ten curiæ, rather than that each was divided into ten, because the curiæ were made of gentes as original unities, and not the gentes out of a curia by subdivision. The work performed by Romulus was the

1 — Livy, i, 13.
2 —Dionys., "Antiq. of Rome," ii, 7.
3 — Dionys., ii, 7.
4 —Plutarch, "Vit. Romulus," cap. 20.

adjustment of the number of gentes in each curia, and the number of curiæ in each tribe, which he was enabled to accomplish through the accessions gained from the surrounding tribes. Theoretically each curia should have been composed of gentes derived by segmentation from one or more gentes, and the tribe by natural growth through the formation of more than one curia, each composed of gentes united by the bond of a common dialect. The hundred gentes of the Ramnes were Latin gentes. In their organization into ten curiæ, each composed of ten gentes, Romulus undoubtedly respected the bond of kin by placing related gentes in the same curia, as far as possible, and then reached numerical symmetry by arbitrarily taking the excess of gentes from one natural curia to supply the deficiency in another. The hundred gentes of the tribe Tities were, in the main, Sabine gentes. These were also arranged in ten curiæ, and most likely on the same principle. The third tribe, the Luceres, was formed later from gradual accessions and conquests. It was heterogeneous in its elements, containing, among others, a number of Etruscan gentes. They were brought into the same numerical scale of ten curiæ each composed of ten gentes. Under this re-constitution, while the gens, the unit of organization, remained pure and unchanged, the curia was raised above its logical level, and made to include, in some cases, a foreign element which did not belong to a strict natural phratry; and the tribe also was raised above its natural level, and made to embrace foreign elements that did not belong to a tribe as the tribe naturally grew. By this legislative constraint the tribes, with their curiæ and gentes, were made severally equal, while the third tribe was in good part an artificial creation under the pressure of circumstances. The linguistic affiliations of the Etruscans are still a matter of discussion. There is a presumption that their dialect was not wholly unintelligible to the Latin tribes, otherwise they would not have been admitted into the Roman social system, which at the time was purely gentile. The numerical proportions thus secured, facilitated the governmental action of the society as a whole.

Niebuhr, who was the first to gain a true conception of the institutions of the Romans in this period, who recognized the fact that the people were sovereign, that the so-called kings exercised a delegated power, and that the senate was based on the principle of representation, each gens having a senator, became at variance with the facts before him in stating in connection with this graduated scale, that "such numerical proportions are an irrefragible proof that the Roman houses [gentes] [1] were not more ancient than the constitution; but corporations formed by a legislator in harmony with the rest of his scheme." [2] That a small foreign element was forced into the curiae of the second and third tribes, and particularly into the third, is undeniable; but that a gens was changed in its composition or reconstructed or made, was simply impossible. A legislator could not make a gens; neither could he make a curia, except by combining existing gentes around a nucleus of related gentes; but he might increase or decrease by constraint the number of gentes in a curia, and increase or decrease the number of curiæ in a tribe. Niebuhr has also shown that the gens was an ancient and universal organization among the Greeks and Romans, which renders his preceding declaration the more incomprehensible. Moreover it appears that the phratry was universal, at least among the Ionian Greeks, leaving it probable that the curia, perhaps under another name, was equally ancient among the Latin tribes. The numerical proportions referred to were no doubt the result of legislative procurement in the time of Romulus, and we have abundant evidence of the sources from which the new gentes were obtained with which these proportions might have been produced.

The members of the ten gentes united in a curia were called *curiales* among themselves. They elected a priest, *curio,* who was the chief officer of the fraternity. Each curia had its sacred rites, in the observance of which the

---

1 Whether Niebuhr used the word "house" in the place of gens, or it is a conceit of the translators, I am unable to state. Thirlwall, one of the translators, applies this term frequently to the Grecian gens, which at best is objectionable.

2 "History of Rome," i, 244.

brotherhood participated; its *sacellum* as a place of worship, and its place of assembly where they met for the transaction of business. Besides the *curio,* who had the principal charge of their religious affairs, the *curiales* also elected an assistant priest, *flamen curialis,* who had the immediate charge of these observances. The curia gave its name to the assembly of the gentes, the *comitia curiata,* which was the sovereign power in Rome to a greater degree than the senate under the gentile system. Such, in general terms, was the organization of the Roman curia or phratry.[1]

Next in the ascending scale was the Roman tribe, composed of ten curiæ and a hundred gentes. When a natural growth, uninfluenced externally, a tribe would be an aggregation of such gentes as were derived by segmentation from an original gens or pair of gentes; all the members of which would speak the same dialect. Until the tribe itself divided, by processes before pointed out, it would include all the descendants of the members of these gentes. But the Roman tribe, with which alone we are now concerned, was artificially enlarged for special objects and by special means, but the basis and body of the tribe was a natural growth.

---

1 Dionysius has given a definite and circumstantial analysis of the organization ascribed to Romulus, although a portion of it seems to belong to a later period. It is interesting from the parallel he runs between the gentile institutions of the Greeks, with which he was equally familiar, and those of the Romans. In the first place, he remarks, I will speak of the order of his polity which I consider the most sufficient of all political arrangements in peace, and also in time of war. It was as follows: After dividing the whole multitude into three divisions, he appointed the most prominent man as a leader over each of the divisions; in the next place dividing each of the three again into ten, he appointed the bravest men leaders, having equal rank; and he called the greater divisions tribes, and the less curiæ, as they are also still called according to usage. And these names interpreted in the Greek tongue would be the "tribus," a third part, a phylē; the "curia," a phratry, and also a band; and those men who exercised the leadership of the tribes were both phylarchs and trittyarchs, whom the Romans call tribunes; and those who had the command of the curiæ both phratriarchs and lochagoi, whom they call curiones. And the phratries were also divided into decades, and a leader called in common parlance a decadarch had command of each. And when all had been arranged into tribes and phratries, he divided the land into thirty equal shares, and gave one full share to each phratry, selecting a sufficient portion for religious festivals and temples, and leaving a certain piece of ground for common use.—"Antiq. of Rome," ii, 7.

Prior to the time of Romulus each tribe elected a chief officer whose duties were magisterial, military and religious.[1] He performed in the city magisterial duties for the tribe, as well as administered its *sacra,* and he also commanded its military forces in the field.[2] He was probably elected by the curiæ collected in a general assembly; but here again our information is defective. It was undoubtedly an ancient office in each Latin tribe, peculiar in character and held by an elective tenure. It was also the germ of the still higher office of *rex,* or general military commander, the functions of the two offices being similar. The tribal chiefs are styled by Dionysius leaders of the tribes.[3] When the three Roman tribes had coalesced into one people, under one senate, one assembly of the people, and one military commander, the office of tribal chief was overshadowed and became less important; but the continued maintenance of the office by an elective tenure confirms the inference of its original popular character.

An assembly of the tribe must also have existed, from a remote antiquity. Before the founding of Rome each Italian tribe was practically independent, although the tribes were more or less united in confederate relations. As a self-governing body each of these ancient tribes had its council of chiefs (who were doubtless the chiefs of the gentes) its assembly of the people, and its chiefs who commanded its military bands. These three elements in the organization of the tribe; namely, the council, the tribal chief, and the tribal assembly, were the types upon which were afterwards modeled the *Roman senate,* the *Roman rex,* and the *comitia curiata.* The tribal chief was in all probability called by the name of *rex* before the founding of Rome; and the same remark is applicable to the name of senators (*senex*), and the *comitia* (*con-ire*). The inference arises, from what is known of the condition and organization of these tribes, that their institutions were essentially democratical. After the

---

1 Dionysius, ii, 7.
2 Smith's Dic., l. c., Art. Tribune.
3 Dionysius, ii, 7.

coalescence of the three Roman tribes, the national character of the tribe was lost in the higher organization; but it still remained as a necessary integer in the organic series.

The fourth and last stage of organization was the Roman nation or people, formed, as stated, by the coalescence of three tribes. Externally the ultimate organization was manifested by a senate (*senatus*), a popular assembly (*comitia curiata*), and a general military commander (*rex*). It was further manifested by a city magistracy, by an army organization, and by a common national priesthood of different orders. [1]

A powerful city organization was from the first the central idea of their governmental and military systems, to which all areas beyond Rome remained provincial. Under the military democracy of Romulus, under the mixed democratical and aristocratical organization of the republic, and under the later imperialism it was a government with a great city in its centre, a perpetual nucleus, to which all additions by conquest were added as increments, instead of being made, with the city, common constituents of the government. Nothing precisely like this Roman organization, this Roman power, and the career of the Roman race, has appeared in the experience of mankind. It will ever remain the marvel of the ages.

As organized by Romulus they styled themselves the Roman People (*Populus Romanus*), which was perfectly exact. They had formed a gentile society and nothing more. But the rapid increase of numbers in the time of Romulus, and the still greater increase between this period and that of Servius Tullius, demonstrated the necessity for a fundamental change in the plan of government. Romulus and the wise men of his time had made the most of gentile institutions. We are indebted to his

1 The thirty curiones, as a body, were organized into a college of priests, one of their number holding the office of "curio maximus." He was elected by the assembly of the gentes. Besides this was the college of augurs, consisting under the Ogulnian law (300 B. C.) of nine members, including their chief officer ("magister collegii"); and the college of pontiffs, composed under the same law of nine members, including the "pontifex maximus."

legislation for a grand attempt to establish upon the gentes a great national and military power; and thus for some knowledge of the character and structure of institutions which might otherwise have faded into obscurity, if they had not perished from remembrance. The rise of the Roman power upon gentile institutions was a remarkable event in human experience. It is not singular that the incidents that accompanied the movement should have come to us tinctured with romance, not to say enshrouded in fable. Rome came into existence through a happy conception, ascribed to Romulus, and adopted by his successors, of concentrating the largest possible number of gentes in a new city, under one government, and with their united military forces under one commander. Its objects were essentially military, to gain a supremacy in Italy, and it is not surprising that the organization took the form of a military democracy.

Selecting a magnificent situation upon the Tiber, where after leaving the mountain range it had entered the campagna, Romulus occupied the Palatine Hill, the site of an ancient fortress, with a tribe of the Latins of which he was the chief. Tradition derived his descent from the chiefs of Alba, which is a matter of secondary importance. The new settlement grew with marvelous rapidity, if the statement is reliable that at the close of his life the military forces numbered 46,000 foot and 1,000 horse, which would indicate some 200,000 people in the city and in the surrounding region under its protection. Livy remarks that it was an ancient device (*vetus consilium*) of the founders of cities to draw to themselves an obscure and humble multitude, and then set up for their progeny the autocthonic claim.[1] Romulus pursuing this ancient policy is said to have opened an asylum near the Palatine, and to have invited all persons in the surrounding tribes, without regard to character or condition, to share with his tribe the advantages and the destiny of the new city. A great crowd of people, Livy further remarks, fled to this place from the surrounding territories, slave

1 Livy, 1, 8.

as well as free, which was the first accession of foreign strength to the new undertaking.[1] Plutarch,[2] and Dionysius[3] both refer to the asylum or grove, the opening of which, for the object and with the success named, was an event of probable occurrence. It tends to show that the people of Italy had then become numerous for barbarians, and that discontent prevailed among them in consequence, doubtless, of the imperfect protection of personal rights, the existence of domestic slavery, and the apprehension of violence. Of such a state of things a wise man would naturally avail himself if he possessed sufficient military genius to handle the class of men thus brought together. The next important event in this romantic narrative, of which the reader should be reminded, was the assault of the Sabines to avenge the entrapment of the Sabine virgins, now the honored wives of their captors. It resulted in a wise accommodation under which the Latins and Sabines coalesced into one society, but each division retaining its own military leader. The Sabines occupied the Quirinal and Capitoline Hills. Thus was added the principal part of the second tribe, the Tities, under Titius Tatius their military chief. After the death of the latter they all fell under the military command of Romulus.

Passing over Numa Pompilius, the successor of Romulus, who established upon a broader scale the religious institutions of the Romans, his successor, Tullus Hostilius, captured the Latin city of Alba and removed its entire population to Rome. They occupied the Cœlian Hill, with all the privileges of Roman citizens. The number of citizens was now doubled, Livy remarks;[4] but not likely from this source exclusively. Ancus Martius, the successor of Tullus, captured the Latin city of Politorium, and following the established policy, transferred the people bodily to Rome.[5] To them was as-

---

1 Eo ex finitimis populis turba omnis sine discrimine, liber an servus esset, avida novarum rerum perfugit; idque primum ad coeptam magnitudinem roboris fuit.— Livy, i, 8.

2 "Vit. Romulus," cap. 20.

3 "Antiq. of Rome," ii, 15.

4 Livy, i, 30.

5 Ib., i, 33.

signed the Aventine Hill, with similar privileges. Not long afterwards the inhabitants of Tellini and Ficana were subdued and removed to Rome, where they also occupied the Aventine.[1] It will be noticed that in each case the gentes brought to Rome, as well as the original Latin and Sabine gentes, remained locally distinct. It was the universal usage in gentile society, both in the Middle and in the Upper Status of barbarism, when the tribes began to gather in fortresses and in walled cities, for the gentes to settle locally together by gentes and by phratries.[2] Such was the manner the gentes settled at Rome. The greater portion of these accessions were united in the third tribe, the Luceres, which gave it a broad basis of Latin gentes. It was not entirely filled until the time of Tarquinius Priscus, the fourth military leader from Romulus, some of the new gentes being Etruscan.

By these and other means three hundred gentes were gathered at Rome and there organized in curiæ and tribes, differing somewhat in tribal lineage; for the Ramnes, as before remarked, were Latins, the Tities were in the main Sabines and the Luceres were probably in the main Latins with large accessions from other sources. The Roman people and organization thus grew into being by a more or less constrained aggregation of gentes into curiæ, of curiæ into tribes, and of tribes into one gentile society. But a model for each integral organization, excepting the last, had existed among them and their ancestors from time immemorial; with a natural basis for each curia in the kindred gentes actually united in each, and a similar basis for each tribe in the common lineage of a greater part of the gentes united in each. All that was new in organization was the numerical proportions of gentes to a curia, of curiæ to a tribe, and the coalescence of the latter into one people. It may be called a

---

1 Livy, i, 38.

2 In the pueblo houses in New Mexico all the occupants of each house belonged to the same tribe, and in some cases a single joint-tenement house contained a tribe. In the pueblo of Mexico there were four principal quarters, as has been shown, each occupied by a lineage, probably a phratry; while the Tlatelulcos occupied a fifth district. At Tlascala there were also four quarters occupied by four lineages, probably phratries.

growth under legislative constraint, because the tribes thus formed were not entirely free from the admixture of foreign elements; whence arose the new name *tribus*=a third part of the people, which now came in to distinguish this organism. The Latin language must have had a term equivalent to the Greek phylon=tribe, because they had the same organization; but if so it has disappeared. The invention of this new term is some evidence that the Roman tribes contained heterogeneous elements, while the Grecian were pure, and kindred in the lineage of the gentes they contained.

Our knowledge of the previous constitution of Latin society is mainly derived from the legislation ascribed to Romulus, since it brings into view the anterior organization of the Latin tribes, with such improvements and modifications as the wisdom of the age was able to suggest. It is seen in the senate as a council of chiefs, in the *comitia curiata* as an assembly of the people by curiæ, in the office of a general military commander, and in the ascending series of organizations. It is seen more especially in the presence of the gentes, with their recognized rights, privileges and obligations. Moreover, the government instituted by Romulus and perfected by his immediate successors presents gentile society in the highest structural form it ever attained in any portion of the human family. The time referred to was immediately before the institution of political society by Servius Tullius.

The first momentous act of Romulus, as a legislator, was the institution of the Roman senate. It was composed of a hundred members, one from each gens, or ten from each curia. A council of chiefs as the primary instrument of government was not a new thing among the Latin tribes. From time immemorial they had been accustomed to its existence and to its authority. But it is probable that prior to the time of Romulus it had become changed, like the Grecian councils, into a pre-considering body, obligated to prepare and submit to an assembly of the people the most important public measures for adoption or rejection. This was in effect a resumption by the people of powers before vested in the council of chiefs. Since no public measure of essential importance could become operative until it received the sanction of the popular assembly, this fact alone shows that the people were sovereign, and not the council, nor the military commander. It reveals also the extent to which democratic principles had penetrated their social system. The senate instituted by Romulus, although its functions were doubtless substantially similar to those of the previous council of chiefs, was an advance upon it in several respects. It was made up either of the chiefs or of the wise men of the gentes. Each gens, as Niebuhr remarks, "sending its decurion who was its alderman,"[1] to represent it in the senate. It was thus a representative and an elective body in its inception, and it remained elective, or selective, down to the empire. The senators held their office for life, which was the only term of office then known among them, and therefore not singular. Livy ascribes the selection of the first senators to Romulus, which is probably an erroneous statement, for the reason that it would not have been in accordance with the theory of their institutions. Romulus chose a hundred senators, he remarks, either because that number was sufficient, or because there were but a hundred who could be created Fathers. Fathers certainly they were called on account of their official dignity, and their descendants were called patricians.[2] The character of the senate as a representative body, the title of Fathers of the People bestowed upon its members, the life tenure of the office, but, more than all these considerations, the distinction of patricians conferred upon their children and lineal descendants in perpetuity, established at a stroke an aristocracy of rank in the centre of their social system where it became firmly intrenched. The Roman senate, from its high vocation, from its composition, and from the patrician rank re-

---

1 "History of Rome," i, 258.

2 Centum creat senatores: sive quia is numerus satis erat; sive quia soli centum erant, qui creari Patres possent, Patres certe ab honore, patriciique progenies eorum appellati. Livy, i, 8. And Cicero: Principes, qui appellati sunt propter caritatem, patres.—"De Rep.," ii, 8.

ceived by its members and transmitted to their descendants, held a powerful position in the subsequent state. It was this aristocratic element, now for the first time planted in gentilism, which gave to the republic its mongrel character, and which, as might have been predicted, culminated in imperialism, and with it in the final dissolution of the race. It may perhaps have increased the military glory and extended the conquests of Rome, whose institutions, from the first, aimed at a military destiny; but it shortened the career of this great and extraordinary people, and demonstrated the proposition that imperialism of necessity will destroy any civilized race. Under the republic, half aristocratic, half democratic, the Romans achieved their fame, which one can but think would have been higher in degree, and more lasting in its fruits, had liberty and equality been nationalized, instead of unequal privileges and an atrocious slavery. The long protracted struggle of the plebeians to eradicate the aristocratic element represented by the senate, and to recover the ancient principles of democracy, must be classed among the heroic labors of mankind.

After the union of the Sabines the senate was increased to two hundred by the addition of a hundred senators [1] from the gentes of the tribe Tities; and when the Luceres had increased to a hundred gentes in the time of Tarquinius Priscus, a third hundred senators were added from the gentes of this tribe. [2] Cicero has left some doubt upon this statement of Livy, by saying that Tarquinius Priscus doubled the original number of the senators. [3] But Schmitz well suggests, as an explanation of the discrepancy, that at the time of the final increase the senate may have become reduced to a hundred and fifty members, and been filled up to two hundred from the gentes of the first two tribes, when the hundred were added from the third. The senators taken from the tribes Ramnes and Tities were thenceforth called Fathers of the Greater Gentes (*patres maiorum gentium*), and those of the Luceres Fathers of the Lesser Gentes (*patres*

1 Dionysius, ii, 47.
2 —Livy, i, 35.
3 —Cicero, "De Rep.," ii, 20.

minorum gentium).[1] From the form of the statement the inference arises that the three hundred senators represented the three hundred gentes, each senator representing a gens. Moreover, as each gens doubtless had its principal chief (*princeps*), it becomes extremely probable that this person was chosen for the position either by his gens, or the ten were chosen together by the curia, from the ten gentes of which it was composed. Such a method of representation and of choice is most in accordance with what is known of Roman and gentile institutions.[2] After the establishment of the republic, the censors filled the vacancies in the senate by their own choice, until it was devolved upon the consuls. They were generally selected from the ex-magistrates of the higher grades.

The powers of the senate were real and substantial. All public measures originated in this body—those upon which they could act independently, as well as those which must be submitted to the popular assembly and be adopted before they could become operative. It had the general guardianship of the public welfare, the management of their foreign relations, the levying of taxes and of military forces, and the general control of revenues and expenditures. Although the administration of religious affairs belonged to the several colleges of priests, the senate had the ultimate power over religion as well.

---

1 Cicero, "De Rep.," ii, 20.

2 This was substantially the opinion of Niebuhr. "We may go further and affirm without hesitation, that originally, when the number of houses (gentes) was complete, they were represented immediately by the senate, the number of which was proportionate to theirs. The three hundred senators answered to the three hundred houses, which was assumed above on good grounds to be the number of them; each gens sent its decurion, who was its alderman and the president of its meetings to represent it in the senate.... That the senate should be appointed by the kings at their discretion, can never have been the original institution. Even Dionysius supposes that there was an election: his notion of it, however, is quite untenable, and the deputies must have been chosen, at least originally, by the houses and not by the curiæ."—"Hist. of Rome," i, 258. An election by the curiæ is, in principle, most probable, if the office did not fall to the chief "ex officio," because the gentes in a curia had a direct interest in the representation of each gens. It was for the same reason that a sachem elected by the members of an Iroquois gens must be accepted by the other gentes of the same tribe before his nomination was complete.

From its functions and vocation it was the most influential body which ever existed under gentile institutions.

The assembly of the people, with the recognized right of acting upon important public measures to be discussed by them and adopted or rejected, was unknown in the Lower, and probably in the Middle Status of barbarism; but it existed in the Upper Status, in the agora of the Grecian tribes, and attained its highest form in the ecclesia of the Athenians; and it also existed in the assembly of the warriors among the Latin tribes, attaining its highest form in the *comitia curiata* of the Romans. The growth of property tended to the establishment of the popular assembly, as a third power in gentile society, for the protection of personal rights and as a shield against the encroachments of the council of chiefs, and of the military commander. From the period of savagery, after the institution of the gentes, down to the times of Solon and Romulus, the popular element had always been active in ancient gentile society. The council of chiefs was usually open in the early conditions to the orators of the people, and public sentiment influenced the course of events. But when the Grecian and Latin tribes first came under historical notice the assembly of the people to discuss and adopt or reject public measures was a phenomenon quite as constant as that of a council of chiefs. It was more perfectly systematized among the Romans under the constitution of Romulus than among the Athenians in the time of Solon. In the rise and progress of this institution may be traced the growth and development of the democratic principle.

This assembly among the Romans was called the *comitia curiata*, because the members of the gentes of adult age met in one assembly by curiæ, and voted in the same manner. Each curia had one collective vote, the majority in each was ascertained separately, and determined what that vote should be.[1] It was the assembly of the gentes, who alone were members of the government. Plebeians and clients, who already formed a numerous

---

1 Livy, i, 43. Dionys., ii, 14; iv, 20, 84.

class, were excluded, because there could be no connection with the *Populus Romanus,* except through a gens and tribe. This assembly, as before stated, could neither originate public measures, nor amend such as were submitted to them; but none of a certain grade could become operative until adopted by the *comitia.* All laws were passed or repealed by this assembly; all magistrates and high public functionaries, including the *rex,* were elected by it on the nomination of the senate.[1] The *imperium* was conferred upon these persons by a law of the assembly (*lex curiata de imperio*), which was the Roman method of investing with office. Until the *imperium* was thus conferred, the person, although the election was complete, could not enter upon his office. The *comitia curiata,* by appeal, had the ultimate decision in criminal cases involving the life of a Roman citizen. It was by a popular movement that the office of *rex* was abolished. Although the assembly of the people never acquired the power of originating measures, its powers were real and influential. At this time the people were sovereign.

The assembly had no power to convene itself; but it is said to have met on the summons of the *rex,* or, in his absence, on that of the praefect (*praefectus urbi*). In the time of the republic it was convened by the consuls, or in their absence, by the praetor; and in all cases the person who convened the assembly presided over its deliberations.

In another connection the office of *rex* has been considered. The *rex* was a general and also a priest, but without civil functions, as some writers have endeavored to imply.[2] His powers as a general, though not

---

1 Numa Pompilius (Cicero, "De Rep.," ii, 11; Liv., i, 17), Tullus Hostilius (Cicero, "De Rep.," ii, 17), and Ancus Martius (Cic., "De Rep.," ii, 18; Livy, i, 32), were elected by the "comitia curiata." In the case of Tarquinius Priscus, Livy observes that the people by a great majority elected him "rex" (i, 35). It was necessarily by the "comitia curiata." Servius Tullius assumed the office which was afterwards confirmed by the "comitia" (Cicero, "De Rep.," ii, 21). The right of election thus reserved to the people, shows that the office of "rex" was a popular one, and that his powers were delegated.

2 Mr. Leonhard Schmitz, one of the ablest defenders of the theory of kingly government among the Greeks and Romans,

defined, were necessarily absolute over the military forces in the field and in the city. If he exercised any civil powers in particular cases, it must be supposed that they were delegated for the occasion. To pronounce him a king, as that term is necessarily understood, is to vitiate and mis-describe the popular government to which he belonged, and the institutions upon which it rested. The form of government under which the *rex* and basileus appeared is identified with gentile institutions and disappeared after gentile society was overthrown. It was a peculiar organization having no parallel in modern society, and is unexplainable in terms adapted to monarchical institutions. A military democracy under a senate, an assembly of the people, and a general of their nomination and election, is a near, though it may not be a perfect, characterization of a government so peculiar, which belongs exclusively to ancient society, and rested on institutions essentially democratical. Romulus, in all probability, emboldened by his great successes, assumed powers which were regarded as dangerous to the senate and to the people, and his assassination by the Roman chiefs is a fair inference from the statements concerning his mysterious disappearance which have come down to us. This act, atrocious as it must be pronounced, evinces that spirit of independence, inherited from the gentes, which would not submit to arbitrary individual power. When the office was abolished, and the consulate was established in its place, it is not surprising that two consuls were created instead of one. While the powers of the office might raise one man to a dangerous height. it could not be the case with two. The same subtlety of reasoning led the Iroquois, without original experience, to create two war-chiefs of the confederacy instead of one, lest the office of commander-in-chief, bestowed

---

with great candor remarks: "It is very difficult to determine the extent of the king's powers, as the ancient writers naturally judged of the kingly period by their own republican constitution, and frequently assigned to the king, the senate, and the "comitia" of the "curiæ" the respective powers and functions which were only true in reference to the consuls, the senate and the "comitia" of their own time."—Smith's "Dic. Gk. & Rom. Antiq., Art. Rex."

upon a single man, should raise him to a position too influential.

In his capacity of chief priest the *rex* took the auspices on important occasions, which was one of the highest acts of the Roman religious system, and in their estimation quite as necessary in the field on the eve of a battle as in the city. He performed other religious rites as well. It is not surprising that in those times priestly functions are found among the Romans, as among the Greeks, attached to or inherent in the highest military office. When the abolition of this office occurred, it was found necessary to vest in some one the religious functions appertaining to it, which were evidently special; whence the creation of the new office of *rex sacrificulus*, or *rex sacrorum*, the incumbent of which performed the religious duties in question. Among the Athenians the same idea reappears in the second of the nine archons, who was called *archon basileus,* and had a general supervision of religious affairs. Why religious functions were attached to the office of *rex* and *basileus,* among the Romans and Greeks, and to the office of *Teuctli* among the Aztecs; and why, after the abolition of the office in the two former cases, the ordinary priesthoods could not perform them, has not been explained.

Thus stood Roman gentile society from the time of Romulus to the time of Servius Tullius, through a period of more than two hundred years, during which the foundations of Roman power were laid. The government, as before remarked, consisted of three powers, a senate, an assembly of the people, and a military commander. They had experienced the necessity for definite written laws to be enacted by themselves, as a substitute for usages and customs. In the *rex* they had the germinal idea of a chief executive magistrate, which necessity pressed upon them, and which was to advance into a more complete form after the institution of political society. But they found it a dangerous office in those times of limited experience in the higher conceptions of government, because the powers of the *rex* were, in the main, undefined, as well as difficult of definition. It is not surprising that when a serious controversy arose between the people and Tarquinius Superbus, they deposed the man and abolished the office. As soon as something like the irresponsible power of a king met them face to face it was found incompatible with liberty and the latter gained the victory. They were willing, however, to admit into the system of government a limited executive, and they created the office in a dual form in the two consuls. This occurred after the institution of political society.

No direct steps were taken, prior to the time of Servius Tullius, to establish a state founded upon territory and upon property; but the previous measures were a preparation for that event. In addition to the institutions named, they had created a city magistracy, and a complete military system, including the institution of the equestrian order. Under institutions purely gentile Rome had become, in the time of Servius Tullius, the strongest military power in Italy.

Among the new magistrates created, that of warden of the city (*custos urbis*) was the most important. This officer, who was chief of the senate (*princeps senatus*), was, in the first instance, according to Dionysius, appointed by Romulus. [1] The senate, which had no power to convene itself, was convened by him. It is also claimed that the *rex* had power to summon the senate. That it would be apt to convene upon his request, through the call of its own officer, is probable; but that he could command its convocation is improbable, from its independence in functions, from its dignity, and from its representative character. After the time of the Decemvirs the name of the office was changed to præfect of the city (*praefectus urbi*), its powers were enlarged, and it was made elective by the new *comitia centuriata.* Under the republic, the consuls, and in their absence, the praetor, had power to convene the senate, and also to hold the *comitia.* At a later day, the office of praetor (*praetor urbanus*) absorbed the functions of this ancient office and became its successor. A judicial magistrate, the Roman

---

1 Dionys., ii, 12.

praetor was the prototype of the modern judge. Thus, every essential institution in the government or administration of the affairs of society may generally be traced to a simple germ, which springs up in a rude form from human wants, and, when able to endure the test of time and experience, is developed into a permanent institution.

A knowledge of the tenure of the office of chief, and of the functions of the council of chiefs, before the time of Romulus, could they be ascertained, would reflect much light upon the condition of Roman gentile society in the time of Romulus. Moreover, the several periods should be studied separately, because the facts of their social condition were changing with their advancement in intelligence. The Italian period prior to Romulus, the period of the seven *reges,* and the subsequent periods of the republic and of the empire are marked by great differences in the spirit and character of the government. But the institutions of the first period entered into the second, and these again were transmitted into the third, and remained with modifications in the fourth. The growth, development and fall of these institutions embody the vital history of the Roman people. It is by tracing these institutions from the germ through their successive stages of growth, on the wide scale of the tribes and nations of mankind, that we can follow the great movements of the human mind in its evolution from its infancy in savagery to its present high development. Out of the necessities of mankind for the organization of society came the gens; out of the gens came the chief, and the tribe with its council of chiefs; out of the tribe came by segmentation the group of tribes, afterwards re-united in a confederacy, and finally consolidated by coalescence into a nation; out of the experience of the council came the necessity of an assembly of the people with a division of the powers of the government between them; and finally, out of the military necessities of the united tribes came the general military commander, who became in time a third power in the government, but subordinate to the two superior powers. It was the germ of the office of the subsequent chief magistrate, the king and the president. The principal institutions of civilized nations are simply continuations of those which germinated in savagery, expanded in barbarism, and which are still subsisting and advancing in civilization.

As the Roman government existed at the death of Romulus, it was social, and not political; it was personal, and not territorial. The three tribes were located, it is true, in separate and distinct areas within the limits of the city; but this was the prevailing mode of settlement under gentile institutions. Their relations to each other and to the resulting society, as gentes, curiæ and tribes, were wholly personal, the government dealing with them as groups of persons, and with the whole as the Roman people. Localized in this manner within inclosing ramparts, the idea of a township or city ward would suggest itself when the necessity for a change in the plan of government was forced upon them by the growing complexity of affairs. It was a great change that was soon to be required of them, to be wrought out through experimental legislation — precisely the same which the Athenians had entered upon shortly before the time of Servius Tullius. Rome was founded, and its first victories were won under institutions purely gentile; but the fruits of these achievements by their very magnitude demonstrated the inability of the gentes to form the basis of a state. But it required two centuries of intense activity in the growing commonwealth to prepare the way for the institution of the second great plan of government based upon territory and upon property. A withdrawal of governing powers from the gentes, curiæ and tribes, and their bestowal upon new constituencies was the sacrifice demanded. Such a change would become possible only through a conviction that the gentes could not be made to yield such a form of government as their advanced condition demanded. It was practically a question of continuance in barbarism, or progress into civilization. The inauguration of the new system will form the subject of the next chapter.

CHAPTER XIII

THE INSTITUTION OF ROMAN POLITICAL SOCIETY

Servius Tullius, the sixth chief of the Roman military democracy, came to the succession about one hundred and thirty-three years after the death of Romulus, as near as the date can be ascertained.[1] This would place his accession about 576 B. C. To this remarkable man the Romans were chiefly indebted for the establishment of their political system. It will be sufficient to indicate its main features, together with some of the reasons which led to its adoption.

From the time of Romulus to that of Servius Tullius the Romans consisted of two distinct classes, the *populus* and the *plebeians.* Both were personally free, and both entered the ranks of the army; but the former alone were organized in gentes, curiæ and tribes, and held the powers of the government. The plebeians, on the other hand, did not belong to any gens, curia or tribe, and consequently were without the government.[2] They were excluded from office, from the *comitia curiata,* and from the sacred rites of the gentes. In the time of Servius they had become nearly if not quite as numerous as the *populus.* They were in the anomalous position of being subject to the military service, and of possessing families and property, which identified them with the interests of Rome, without being in any sense connected with the gov-

---

[1] Dionysius, iv, 1.

[2] Niebuhr says: "The existence of the plebs as acknowledgedly a free and very numerous portion of the nation, may be traced back to the reign of Ancus; but before the time of Servius it was only an aggregate of unconnected parts, not a united regular whole."—"History of Rome," l. c., i, 315.

ernment. Under gentile institutions, as we have seen, there could be no connection with the government except through a recognized gens, and the plebeians had no gentes. Such a state of things, affecting so large a portion of the people, was dangerous to the commonwealth. Admitting of no remedy under gentile institutions, it must have furnished one of the prominent reasons for attempting the overthrow of gentile society, and the substitution of political. The Roman fabric would, in all probability, have fallen in pieces if a remedy had not been devised. It was commenced in the time of Romulus, renewed by Numa Pompilius, and completed by Servius Tullius.

The origin both of the plebeians and of the patricians, and their subsequent relations to each other, have been fruitful themes of discussion and of disagreement. A few suggestions may be ventured upon each of these questions.

A person was a plebeian because he was not a member of a gens, organized with other gentes in a curia and tribe. It is easy to understand how large numbers of persons would have become detached from the gentes of their birth in the unsettled times which preceded and followed the founding of Rome. The adventurers who flocked to the new city from the surrounding tribes, the captives taken in their wars and afterwards set free, and the unattached persons mingled with the gentes transplanted to Rome, would rapidly furnish such a class. It might also well happen that in filling up the hundred gentes of each tribe, fragments of gentes, and gentes having less than a prescribed number of persons, were excluded. These unattached persons, with the fragments of gentes thus excluded from recognition and organization in a curia, would soon become, with their children and descendants, a great and increasing class. Such were the Roman plebeians, who, as such, were not members of the Roman gentile society. It seems to be a fair inference from the epithet applied to the senators of the Luceres, the third Roman tribe admitted, who were styled "Fathers of the Lesser Gentes," that the old gentes were reluctant to acknowledge their entire equality. For a stronger reason they debarred the plebeians from all participation in the government. When the third tribe was filled up with the prescribed number of gentes, the last avenue of admission was closed, after which the number in the plebeian class would increase with greater rapidity. Niebuhr remarks that the existence of the plebeian class may be traced to the time of Ancus, thus implying that they made their first appearance at that time.[1] He also denies that the clients were a part of the plebeian body;[2] in both of which positions he differs from Dionysius,[3] and from Plutarch.[4] The institution of the relation of patron and client is ascribed by the authors last named to Romulus, and it is recognized by Suetonius as existing in the time of Romulus.[5] A necessity for such an institution existed in the presence of a class without a gentile status, and without religious rites, who would avail themselves of this relation for the protection of their persons and property, and for the access it gave them to religious privileges. Members of a gens would not be without this protection or these privileges; neither would it befit the dignity or accord with the obligations of a gens to allow one of its members to accept a patron in another gens. The unattached class, or, in other words, the plebeians, were the only persons who would naturally seek patrons and become their clients. The clients formed no part of the *populus* for the reasons stated. It seems plain, notwithstanding the weight of Niebuhr's authority on Roman questions, that the clients were a part of the plebeian body.

The next question is one of extreme difficulty, namely: the origin and extent of the patrician class—whether it originated with the institution of the Roman Senate, and

---

1 "History of Rome." i, 315.

2 "That the clients were total strangers to the plebeian commonalty and did not coalesce with it until late, when the bond of servitude had been loosened, partly from the houses of their patrons dying off or sinking into decay, partly from the advance of the whole nation toward freedom, will be proved in the sequel of this history."—"History of Rome," i, 315.

3 Dionysius, ii, 8.

4 Plutarch, "Vit. Rom.," xiii, 16.

5 "Vit. Tiberius," cap. 1.

was limited to the senators, and to their children and descendants; or included the entire *populus,* as distinguished from the plebeians. It is claimed by the most eminent modern authorities that the entire *populus* were patricians. Niebuhr, who is certainly the first on Roman questions, adopts this view,[1] to which Long, Schmitz, and others have given their concurrence.[2] But the reasons assigned are not conclusive. The existence of the patrician class, and of the plebeian class as well, may be traced, as stated, to the time of Romulus.[3] If the *populus,* who were the entire body of the people organized in gentes, were all patricians at this early day, the distinction would have been nominal, as the plebeian class was then unimportant. Moreover, the plain statements of Cicero and of Livy are not reconcilable with this conclusion. Dionysius, it is true, speaks of the institution of the patrician class as occurring before that of the senate, and as composed of a limited number of persons distinguished for their birth, their virtue, and their wealth; thus excluding the poor and obscure in birth, although they belonged to the historical gentes.[4] Admitting a class of patricians without senatorial connection, there was still a large class remaining in the several gentes who were not patricians. Cicero has left a plain statement that the senators and their children were patricians, and without referring to the existence of any patrician class beyond their number. When that senate of Romulus, he remarks, which was constituted of the best men, whom Romulus himself respected so highly that he wished them to be called fathers, and their children patricians, attempted,[5] etc. The meaning attached to the word fathers (*patres*) as here used was a subject of disagreement among the Romans themselves; but the word *patricii,* for the class is formed upon *patres,* thus tending to show the necessary connection of the patricians with the senatorial office. Since each senator at the outset represented, in all prob-

1 "History of Rome," i, 256,450.
2 Smith's "Dic., Articles, Gens, Patricii, and Plebs."
3 Dionysius, ii, 8; Plutarch, "Vit. Rom.," xiii.
4 Ib., ii. 8
5 "De Rep.," ii, 12.

ability, a gens, and the three hundred thus represented all the recognized gentes, this fact could not of itself make all the members of the gentes patricians, because the dignity was limited to the senators, their children, and their posterity. Livy is equally explicit. They were certainly called fathers, he remarks, on account of their official dignity, and their posterity (*progenies*) patricians.[1] Under the *reges* and also under the republic, individuals were created patricians by the government; but apart from the senatorial office, and special creation by the government, the rank could not be obtained. It is not improbable that a number of persons, not admitted into the senate when it was instituted, were placed by public act on the same level with the senators as to the new patrician rank; but this would include a small number only of the members of the three hundred gentes, all of whom were embraced in the *Populus Romanus*.

It is not improbable that the chiefs of the gentes were called fathers before the time of Romulus, to indicate the paternal character of the office; and that the office may have conferred a species of recognized rank upon their posterity. But we have no direct evidence of the fact. Assuming it to have been the case, and further, that the senate at its institution did not include all the principal chiefs, and further still, that when vacancies in the senate were subsequently filled, the selection was made on account of merit and not on account of gens, a foundation for a patrician class might have previously existed independently of the senate. These assumptions might be used to explain the peculiar language of Cicero, namely; that Romulus desired that the senators might be called Fathers, possibly because this was already the honored title of the chiefs of the gentes. In this way a limited foundation for a patrician class may be found independent of the senate; but it would not be broad enough to include all the recognized gentes. It was in connection with the senators that the suggestion was made that their children and descendants should be called

1 Livy, 1, 8.

patricians. The same statement is repeated by Paterculus.[1]

It follows that there could be no patrician gens and no plebeian gens, although particular families in one gens might be patricians, and in another plebeians. There is some confusion also upon this point. All the adult male members of the Fabian gens, to the number of three hundred and six, were patricians.[2] It must be explained by the supposition that all the families in this gens could trace their descent from senators, or to some public act by which their ancestors were raised to the patriciate. There were of course patrician families in many gentes, and at a later day patrician and plebeian families in the same gens. Thus the Claudii and Marcelli, before referred to (*supra* p. 294), were two families of the Claudian gens, but the Claudii alone were patricians. It will be borne in mind, that prior to the time of Servius Tullius the Romans were divided into two classes, the *populus* and the *plebeians;* but that after his time, and particularly after the Licinian legislation (367 B. C.), by which all the dignities of the state were opened to every citizen, the Roman people, of the degree of freemen, fell into two political classes, which may be distinguished as the aristocracy and the commonalty The former class consisted of the senators, and those descended from senators, together with those who had held either of the three curule offices, (consul, praetor, and curule ædile) and their descendants. The commonalty were now Roman citizens. The gentile organization had fallen into decadence, and the old division could no longer be maintained. Persons, who in the first period as belonging to the *populus*, could not be classed with the plebeians, would in the subsequent period belong to the aristocracy without being patricians. The Claudii could trace their descent from Appius Claudius who was made a senator in the time of Romulus; but the Marcelli could not trace their descent from him, nor from any other senator, although, as Niebuhr remarks, "equal to the Apii in the

1 Velleus Paterculus, 1, 8.
2 Livy, ii, 49.

splendor of the honors they attained to, and incomparably more useful to the commonwealth."[1] This is a sufficient explanation of the position of the Marcelli without resorting to the fanciful hypothesis of Niebuhr, that the Marcelli had lost patrician rank through a marriage of disparagement.[2]

The patrician class were necessarily numerous, because the senators, rarely less than three hundred, were chosen as often as vacancies occurred, thus constantly including new families; and because it conferred patrician rank on their posterity. Others were from time to time made patricians by act of the state.[3] This distinction, at first probably of little value, became of great importance with their increase in wealth, numbers and power; and it changed the complexion of Roman society. The full effect of introducing a privileged class in Roman gentile society was not probably appreciated at the time; and it is questionable whether this institution did not exercise a more injurious than beneficial influence upon the subsequent career of the Roman people.

When the gentes had ceased to be organizations for governmental purposes under the new political system, the *populus* no longer remained as distinguished from the plebeians;[3] but the shadow of the old organization and of the old distinction remained far into the republic.[4] The plebeians under the new system were Roman citizens, but they were now the commonalty; the question of the connection or non-connection with a gens not entering into the distinction.

From Romulus to Servius Tullius the Roman organization, as before stated, was simply a gentile society, without relation to territory or to property. All we find is a series of aggregates of persons, in gentes, curiæ and tribes, by means of which the people were dealt with by the government as groups of persons forming these several organic unities. Their condition was precisely like that of the Athenians prior to the time of Solon. But

1 "History of Rome," i, 246.
2 Ib., i, 246.
3 Livy, iv, 4.
4 Livy., iv, 51.

they had instituted a senate in the place of the old council of chiefs, a *comitia curiata* in the place of the old assembly of the people, and had chosen a military commander, with the additional functions of a priest and judge. With a government of three powers, co-ordinated with reference to their principal necessities, and with a coalescence of the three tribes, composed of an equal number of gentes and curiæ, into one people, they possessed a higher and more complete governmental organization than the Latin tribes had before attained. A numerous class had gradually developed, however, who were without the pale of the government, and without religious privileges, excepting that portion who had passed into the relation of clients. If not a dangerous class, their exclusion from citizenship, and from all participation in the government, was detrimental to the commonwealth. A municipality was growing up upon a scale of magnitude unknown in their previous experience, requiring a special organization to conduct its local affairs. A necessity for a change in the plan of government must have forced itself more and more upon the attention of thoughtful men. The increase of numbers and of wealth, and the difficulty of managing their affairs, now complex from weight of numbers and diversity of interests, began to reveal the fact, it must be supposed, that they could not hold together under gentile institutions. A conclusion of this kind is required to explain the several expedients which were tried.

Numa, the successor of Romulus, made the first significant movement, because it reveals the existence of an impression, that a great power could not rest upon gentes as the basis of a system. He attempted to traverse the gentes, as Theseus did, by dividing the people into classes, some eight in number, according to their arts and trades.[1] Plutarch, who is the chief authority for this statement, speaks of this division of the people according to their vocations as the most admired of Numa's institutions; and remarks further, that it was designed to take

1 Plutarch, "Vit. Numa," xvii, 20.

away the distinction between Latin and Sabine, both name and thing, by mixing them together in a new distribution. But as he did not invest the classes with the powers exercised by the gentes, the measure failed, like the similar attempt of Theseus, and for the same reason. Each guild, as we are assured by Plutarch, had its separate hall, court and religious observances. These records, though traditionary, of the same experiment in Attica and at Rome, made for the same object, for similar reasons, and by the same instrumentalities, render the inference reasonable that the experiment as stated was actually tried in each case.

Servius Tullius instituted the new system, and placed it upon a foundation where it remained to the close of the republic, although changes were afterwards made in the nature of improvements. His period (about 576—533 B. C.) follows closely that of Solon (596 B. C.), and precedes that of Cleisthenes (509 B. C.). The legislation ascribed to him, and which was obviously modeled upon that of Solon, may be accepted as having occured as early as the time named, because the system was in practical operation when the republic was established 509 B. C., within the historical period. Moreover, the new political system may as properly be ascribed to him as great measures have been attributed to other men, although in both cases the legislator does little more than formulate what experience had already suggested and pressed upon his attention. The three principal changes which set aside the gentes and inaugurated political society based upon territory and upon property, were: first, the substitution of classes, formed upon the measure of individual wealth, in the place of the gentes; second, the institution of the *comitia centuriata,* as the new popular assembly, in the place of the *comitia curiata,* the assembly of the gentes, with a transfer of the substantial powers of the latter to the former; and third, the creation of four city wards, in the nature of townships, circumscribed by metes and bounds and named as territorial areas, in which the residents of each ward were required to enroll their names and register their property.

Imitating Solon, with whose plan of government he was doubtless familiar, Servius divided the people into five classes, according to the value of their property, the effect of which was to concentrate in one class the wealthiest men of the several gentes.[1] Each class was then subdivided into centuries, the number in each being established arbitrarily without regard to the actual number of persons it contained, and with one vote to each century in the *comitia*. The amount of political power to be held by each class was thus determined by the number of centuries given to each. Thus, the first class consisted of eighty centuries, with eighty votes in the *comitia centuriata;* the second class of twenty centuries, to which two centuries of artisans were attached, with twenty-two votes; the third class of twenty centuries, with twenty votes; the fourth class of twenty, to which two centuries of horn-blowers and trumpeters were attached, with twenty-two votes; and the fifth class of thirty centuries, with thirty votes. In addition to these, the equites consisted of eighteen centuries, with eighteen votes. To these classes Dionysius adds a sixth class, consisting of one century, with one vote. It was composed of those who had no property, or less than the amount required for admission into the fifth class. They neither paid taxes, nor served in war.[2] The whole number of centuries in the six classes with the equites added made a total of one hundred and ninety-three, according to Dionysius.[3] Livy, agreeing with the former as to the number of regular centuries in the five classes, differs from him by excluding the sixth class, the persons being formed into one century with one vote, and included in or attached to the fifth class. He also makes three centuries of horn-blowers instead of two, and the whole number of centuries one more than Dionysius.[4] Cicero remarks that ninety-six centuries were a minority, which would be

---

1 The property qualification for the first class was 100,000 asses; for the second class, 75,000 asses; for third, 50,000; for the fourth, 25,000; and for the fifth, 11,000 asses.— Livy, i, 43.
2 Dionysius, iv, 20.
3 Ib., iv, 16, 17, 18.
4 Livy, i, 43.

equally true under either statement.[1] The centuries of each class were divided into seniors and juniors, of which the senior centuries were composed of such persons as were above the age of fifty-five years, and were charged with the duty, as soldiers, of defending the city; while the junior centuries consisted of those persons who were below this age and above seventeen, and were charged with external military enterprises.[2] The armature of each class was prescribed and made different for each.[3]

It will be noticed that the control of the government, so far as the assembly of the people could influence its action, was placed in the hands of the first class, and the equites. They held together ninety-eight votes, a majority of the whole. Each century agreed upon its vote separately when assembled in the *comitia centuriata,* precisely as each curia had been accustomed to do in the *comitia curiata.* In taking a vote upon any public question, the equites were called first, and then the first class.[4] If they agreed in their votes it decided the question, and the remaining centuries were not called upon to vote; but if they disagreed, the second class was called, and so on to the last, unless a majority sooner appeared.

The powers formerly exercised by the *comitia curiata,* now transferred to the *comitia centuriata,* were enlarged in some slight particulars in the subsequent period. It elected all officers and magistrates on the nomination of the senate; it enacted or rejected laws proposed by the senate, no measure becoming a law without its sanction; it repealed existing laws on the proposition of the same body, if they chose to do so; and it declared war on the same recommendation. But the senate concluded peace without consulting the assembly. An appeal in all cases involving life could be taken to this assembly as the highest judicial tribunal of the state. These powers were substantial, but limited—control over the finances being

1 "De Rep.," ii, 20.
2 Dionysius, iv, 16.
3 Livy, i, 43.
4 Livy, i, 43; But Dionysius places the equites in the first class, and remarks that this class was first called.— Dionysius, iv, 20.

excluded. A majority of the votes, however, were lodged with the first class, including the equites, which embraced the body of the patricians, as must be supposed, and the wealthiest citizens. Property and not numbers controlled the government. They were able, however, to create a body of laws in the course of time which afforded equal protection to all, and thus tended to redeem the worst effects of the inequalities of the system.

The meetings of the *comitia* were held in the Campus Martius annually for the election of magistrates and officers, and at other times when the public necessities required. The people assembled by centuries, and by classes under their officers, organized as an army (*exercitus*); for the centuries and classes were designed to subserve all the purposes of a military as well as a civil organization. At the first muster under Servius Tullius, eighty thousand citizen soldiers appeared in the Campus Martius under arms, each man in his proper century, each century in its class, and each class by itself.[1] Every member of a century was now a citizen of Rome, which was the most important fruit of the new political system. In the time of the republic the consuls, and in their absence, the praetor, had power to convene the *comitia*, which was presided over by the person who caused it to assemble.

Such a government appears to us, in the light of our more advanced experience, both rude and clumsy; but it was a sensible improvement upon the previous gentile government, defective and illiberal as it appears. Under it, Rome became mistress of the world. The element of property, now rising into commanding importance, determined its character. It had brought aristocracy and privilege into prominence, which seized the opportunity to withdraw the control of the government in a great measure from the hands of the people, and bestow it upon the men of property. It was a movement in the opposite direction from that to which the democratic principles inherited from the gentes naturally tended. Against the

---

1 Livy, i, 44; Dionysius states the number at 84,700.—iv, 22.

new elements of aristocracy and privilege now incorporated in their governmental institutions, the Roman plebeians contended throughout the period of the republic, and at times with some measure of success. But patrician rank and property, possessed by the higher classes, were too powerful for the wiser and grander doctrines of equal rights and equal privileges represented by the plebeians. It was even then far too heavy a tax upon Roman society to carry a privileged class.

Cicero, patriot and noble Roman as he was, approved and commended this gradation of the people into classes, with the bestowment of a controlling influence in the government upon the minority of citizens. Servius Tullius, he remarks, "having created a large number of equites from the common mass of the people, divided the remainder into five classes, distinguishing between the seniors and juniors, which he so constituted as to place the suffrages, not in the hands of the multitude, but of the men of property; taking care to make it a rule of ours, as it ought to be in every government, that the greatest number should not have the greatest weight."[1] In the light of the experience of the intervening two thousand years, it may well be observed that the inequality of privileges, and the denial of the right of self-government here commended, created and developed that mass of ignorance and corruption which ultimately destroyed both government and people. The human race is gradually learning the simple lesson, that the people as a whole are wiser for the public good and the public prosperity, than any privileged class of men, however refined and cultivated, have ever been, or, by any possibility, can ever become. Governments over societies the most advanced are still in a transitional stage; and they are necessarily and logically moving, as President Grant, not without reason, intimated in his last inaugural address, in the direction of democracy; that form of self-government which represents and expresses the average intelligence and virtue of a free and educated people.

---

1 Cicero, "De Rep.," ii, 22.

The property classes subserved the useful purpose of breaking up the gentes, as the basis of a governmental system, by transferring their powers to a different body. It was evidently the principal object of the Servian legislation to obtain a deliverance from the gentes, which were close corporations, and to give the new government a basis wide enough to include all the inhabitants of Rome, with the exception of the slaves. After the classes had accomplished this work, it might have been expected that they would have died out as they did at Athens; and that city wards and country townships, with their inhabitants organized as bodies politic, would have become the basis of the new political system, as they rightfully and logically should. But the municipal organization of Rome prevented this consummation. It gained at the outset, and maintained to the end the central position in the government, to which all areas without were made subordinate. It presents the anomaly of a great central municipal government expanded, in effect, first over Italy, and finally over the conquered provinces of three continents. The five classes, with some modifications of the manner of voting, remained to the end of the republic. The creation of a new assembly of the people to take the place of the old, discloses the radical character of the Servian constitution. These classes would never have acquired vitality without a newly constituted assembly, investing them with political powers. With the increase of wealth and population the duties and responsibilities of this assembly were much increased. It was evidently the intention of Servius Tullius that it should extinguish the *comitia curiata,* and with it the power of the gentes.

This legislator is said to have instituted the *comitia tributa,* a separate assembly of each local tribe or ward, whose chief duties related to the assessment and collection of taxes, and to furnishing contingents of troops. At a later day this assembly elected the tribunes of the people. The ward was the natural unit of their political system, and the centre where local self-government should have been established had the Roman people wished to create a democratic state. But the senate and the property classes had forestalled them from that career.

One of the first acts ascribed to Servius was the institution of the census. Livy pronounces the census a most salutary measure for an empire about to become so great, according to which the duties of peace and of war were to be performed, not individually as before, but according to the measure of personal wealth.[1] Each person was required to enroll himself in the ward of his residence, with a statement of the amount of his property. It was done in the presence of the censor; and the lists when completed furnished the basis upon which the classes were formed.[2] This was accompanied by a very remarkable act for the period, the creation of four city wards, circumscribed by boundaries, and distinguished by appropriate names. In point of time it was earlier than the institution of the Attic deme by Cleisthenes; but the two were quite different in their relations to the government. The Attic deme, as has been shown, was organized as a body politic with a similar registry of citizens and of their property, and having besides a complete local self-government, with an elective magistracy, judiciary and priesthood. On the other hand, the Roman ward was a geographical area, with a registry of citizens and of their property, with a local organization, a tribune and other elective offices, and with an assembly. For a limited number of special objects the inhabitants of the wards were dealt with by the government through their territorial relations. But the government of the ward did not possess the solid attributes of that of the Attic deme. It was a nearer copy of the previous Athenian naucrary, which not unlikely furnished the model, as the Solonian classes did of the Servian. Dionysius remarks, that after Servius Tullius had inclosed the seven hills with one wall he divided the city into four parts, and gave the names of the hills to the re-divisions: to the first, Palatina, to the second, Suburra, to the third, Collina, and to the fourth, Esquilina; and made the city consist of four parts, which

---

1 Livy, i, 42.
2 Dionysius, iv, 15.

before consisted of three; and he ordered the people who dwelt in each of the four regions, like villagers, not to take any other dwelling, nor to pay taxes elsewhere, nor give in their names as soldiers elsewhere, nor pay their assessments for military purposes and other needs, which each must furnish for the common welfare; for these things were no longer to be done according to the three consanguine tribes, but according to the four local tribes, which last had been arranged by himself; and he appointed commanders over each tribe, as phylarchs or comarchs, whom he directed to note what house each inhabited.[1] Mommsen observes that "each of these four levy-districts had to furnish the fourth part not only of the force as a whole, but of each of its military subdivisions, so that each legion and each century numbered an equal proportion of conscripts from each region; evidently for the purpose of merging all distinctions of a gentile and local nature in one common levy of the community, and especially of binding, through the powerful leveling influence of the military spirit, the *meteoci* and the burgesses into one people."[2]

In like manner, the surrounding country under the government of Rome was organized in townships (*tribus rusticae*), the number of which is stated at twenty-six by some writers, and at thirty-one by others; making, with the four city wards, a total of thirty-one in one case, and of thirty-five in the other.[3] The total number was never increased beyond thirty-five. These townships did not become integral in the sense of participating in the administration of the government.

As finally established under the Servian constitution, the government was cast in the form in which it remained during the existence of the republic; the consuls taking the place of the previous military commanders. It was not based upon territory in the exclusive sense of the

---

1 Dionysius, iv, 14.

2 "History of Rome, l. c.," Scribner's ed., i, 136.

3 Dionysius, iv, 15; Niebuhr has furnished the names of sixteen country townships, as follows: Aemilian, Camilian, Cluentian, Cornelian, Fabian, Galerian, Horatian, Lemonian, Menenian, Paperian, Romilian, Sergian, Veturian, Claudian.—"History of Rome," i, 320, note.

Athenian government, or in the modern sense; ascending from the township or ward, the unit of organization, to the county or arrondissement, and from the latter to the state, each organized and invested with governmental functions as constituents of a whole. The central government overshadowed and atrophied the parts. It rested more upon property than upon territory, this being made the commanding element, as is shown by the lodgment of the controlling power of the government in the highest property classes. It had, nevertheless, a territorial basis as well, since it recognized and used territorial subdivisions for citizenship, and for financial and military objects, in which the citizen was dealt with through his territorial relations.

The Romans were now carried fairly out of gentile society into and under the second great plan of government, founded upon territory and upon property. They had left gentilism and barbarism behind them, and entered upon a new career of civilization. Henceforth the creation and protection of property became the primary objects of the government, with a superadded career of conquest for domination over distant tribes and nations. This great change of institutions, creating political society as distinguished from gentile society, was simply the introduction of the new elements of territory and property, making the latter a power in the government, which before had been simply an influence. Had the wards and rustic townships been organized with full powers of local self-government, and the senate been made elective by these local constituencies. without distinction of classes, the resulting government would have been a democracy, like the Athenian; for these local governments would have moulded the state into their own likeness. The senate, with the hereditary rank it conferred, and the property basis qualifying the voting power in the assembly of the people, turned the scale against democratical institutions, and produced a mixed government, partly aristocratic and partly democratic; eminently calculated to engender perpetual animosity between the two classes of citizens thus deliberately and unnecessarily created by affirmative legislation. It is plain, I think, that the people were circumvented by the Servian constitution and had a government put upon them which the majority would have rejected had they fully comprehended its probable results. The evidence is conclusive of the antecedent democratical principles of the gentes, which, however exclusive as against all persons not in their communion, were carried out fully among themselves. The evidence of this free spirit and of their free institutions is so decisive that the proposition elsewhere stated, that gentilism is incompatible with monarchy, seems to be incontrovertible.

As a whole, the Roman government was anomalous. The overshadowing municipality of Rome, made the centre of the state in its plan of government, was one of the producing causes of its novel character. The primary organization of the people into an army with the military spirit it fostered created the cohesive force which held the republic together, and afterwards the empire. With a selective senate holding office for life, and possessing substantial powers; with a personal rank passing to their children and descendants; with an elective magistracy graded to the needs of a central metropolis; with an assembly of the people organized into property classes, possessing an unequal suffrage, but holding both an affirmative and a negative upon all legislation; and with an elaborate military organization, no other government strictly analogous has appeared among men. It was artificial, illogical, approaching a monstrosity; but capable of wonderful achievements, because of its military spirit, and because the Romans were endowed with remarkable powers for organizing and managing affairs. The patchwork in its composition was the product of the superior craft of the wealthy classes who intended to seize the substance of power while they pretended to respect the rights and interests of all.

When the new political system became established, the old one did not immediately disappear. The functions of the senate and of the military commander remained as before; but the property classes took the place of the gentes, and the assembly of the classes took the place of the assembly of the gentes. Radical as the changes were, they were limited, in the main, to these particulars, and came in without friction or violence. The old assembly (*comitia curiata*) was allowed to retain a portion of its powers, which kept alive for a long period of time the organizations of the gentes, curiæ and consanguine tribes. It still conferred the *imperium* upon all the higher magistrates after their election was completed, though in time it became a matter of form merely; it inaugurated certain priests, and regulated the religious observances of the curiæ. This state of things continued down to the time of the first Punic war, after which the *comitia curiata* lost its importance and soon fell into oblivion. Both the assembly and the curiæ were superseded rather than abolished, and died out from inanition; but the gentes remained far into the empire, not as an organization, for that also died out in time, but as a pedigree and a lineage. Thus the transition from gentile into political society was gradually but effectually accomplished, and the second great plan of human government was substituted by the Romans in the place of the first which had prevailed from time immemorial.

After an immensely protracted duration, running back of the separate existence of the Aryan family, and received by the Latin tribes from their remote ancestors, the gentile organization finally surrendered its existence, among the Romans, to the demands of civilization. It had held exclusive possession of society through these several ethnical periods, and until it had won by experience all the elements of civilization, which it then proved unable to manage. Mankind owe a debt of gratitude to their savage ancestors for devising an institution able to carry the advancing portion of the human race out of savagery into barbarism, and through the successive stages of the latter into civilization. It also accumulated by experience the intelligence and knowledge necessary to devise political society while the institution yet remained. It holds a position on the great chart of human progress second to none in its influence, in its achievements and in its history. As a plan of government, the gentile organization was unequal to the wants of civilized man; but it is something to be said in its remembrance that it developed from the germ the principal governmental institutions of modern civilized states. Among others, as before stated, out of the ancient council of chiefs came the modern senate; out of the ancient assembly of the people came the modern representative assembly, the two together constituting the modern legislature; out of the ancient general military commander came the modern chief magistrate, whether a feudal or constitutional king, an emperor or a president, the latter being the natural and logical results; and out of the ancient *custos urbis,* by a circuitous derivation, came the Roman praetor and the modern judge. Equal rights and privileges, personal freedom and the cardinal principles of democracy were also inherited from the gentes. When property had become created in masses, and its influence and power began to be felt in society, slavery came in; an institution violative of all these principles, but sustained by the selfish and delusive consideration that the person made a slave was a stranger in blood and a captive enemy. With property also came in gradually the principle of aristocracy, striving for the creation of privileged classes. The element of property, which has controlled society to a great extent during the comparatively short period of civilization, has given mankind despotism, imperialism, monarchy, privileged classes, and finally representative democracy. It has also made the career of the civilized nations essentially a property-making career. But when the intelligence of mankind rises to the height of the great question of the abstract rights of property,—including the relations of property to the state, as well as the rights of persons to property,—a modification of the present order of things may be expected. The nature of the coming changes it may be impossible to conceive; but it seems probable that democracy, once universal in a rudimentary form and repressed in many civilized states, is destined to become again universal and supreme.

An American, educated in the principles of democracy,

and profoundly impressed with the dignity and grandeur of those great conceptions which recognize the liberty, equality and fraternity of mankind, may give free expression to a preference for self-government and free institutions. At the same time the equal right of every other person must be recognized to accept and approve any form of government, whether imperial or monarchical, that satisfies his preferences.

CHAPTER XIV

CHANGE OF DESCENT FROM THE FEMALE TO THE MALE LINE

An important question remains to be considered, namely: whether any evidence exists that descent was anciently in the female line in the Grecian and Latin gentes. Theoretically, this must have been the fact at some anterior period among their remote ancestors; but we are not compelled to rest the question upon theory alone. Since a change to the male line involved a nearly total alteration of the membership in a gens, a method by which it might have been accomplished should be pointed out. More than this, it should be shown, if possible, that an adequate motive requiring the change was certain to arise, with the progress of society out of the condition in which this form of descent originated. And lastly, the existing evidence of ancient descent in the female line among them should be presented.

A gens in the archaic period, as we have seen, consisted of a supposed female ancestor and her children together with the children of her daughters, and of her female descendants through females in perpetuity. The children of her sons, and of her male descendants, through males, were excluded. On the other hand, with descent in the male line, a gens consisted of a supposed male ancestor and his children, together with the children of his sons and of his male descendants through males in perpetuity. The children of his daughters, and of his female descendants through females, were excluded. Those excluded in the first case would be members of the gens in the second case, and *vice versâ.* The question then arises, how could descent be changed from the female line to the male without the destruction of the gens?

The method was simple and natural, provided the motive to make the change was general, urgent and commanding. When done at a given time, and by preconcerted determination, it was only necessary to agree that all the present members of the gens should remain members, but that in future all children, whose fathers belonged to the gens, should alone remain in it and bear the gentile name, while the children of its female members should be excluded. This would not break or change the kinship or relations of the existing gentiles; but thereafter it would retain in the gens the children it before excluded and exclude those it before retained. Although it may seem a hard problem to solve, the pressure of an adequate motive would render it easy, and the lapse of a few generations would make it complete. As a practical question, it has been changed from the female line to the male among the American aborigines in a number of instances. Thus, among the Ojibwas descent is now in the male line, while among their congeners, the Delawares and Mohegans, it is still in the female line. Originally, without a doubt, descent was in the female line in the entire Algonkin stock.

Since descent in the female line is archaic, and more in accordance with the early condition of ancient society than descent in the male line, there is a presumption in favor of its ancient prevalence in the Grecian and Latin gentes. Moreover, when the archaic form of any transmitted organization has been discovered and verified, it is impossible to conceive of its origination in the later more advanced form.

Assuming a change of descent among them from the female line to the male, it must have occurred very remotely from the historical period. Their history in the Middle status of barbarism is entirely lost, except it has been in some measure preserved in their arts, institutions and inventions, and in improvements in language. The Upper Status has the superadded light of tradition and of the Homeric poems to acquaint us with its experience and the measure of progress then made. But judging from the condition in which their traditions place them, it seems probable that descent in the female line had not entirely disappeared, at least among the Pelasgian and Grecian tribes, when they entered the Upper Status of barbarism.

When descent was in the female line in the Grecian and Latin gentes, the gens possessed the following among other characteristics: 1. Marriage in the gens was prohibited; thus placing children in a different gens from that of their reputed father. 2. Property and the office of chief were hereditary in the gens; thus excluding children from inheriting the property or succeeding to the office of their reputed father. This state of things would continue until a motive arose sufficiently general and commanding to establish the injustice of this exclusion in the face of their changed condition.

The natural remedy was a change of descent from the female line to the male. All that was needed to effect the change was an adequate motive. After domestic animals began to be reared in flocks and herds, becoming thereby a source of subsistence as well as objects of individual property, and after tillage had led to the ownership of houses and lands in severalty, an antagonism would be certain to arise against the prevailing form of gentile inheritance, because it excluded the owner's children, whose paternity was becoming more assured, and gave his property to his gentile kindred. A contest for a new rule of inheritance, shared in by fathers and their children, would furnish a motive sufficiently powerful to effect the change. With property accumulating in masses and assuming permanent forms, and with an increased proportion of it held by individual ownership, descent in the female line was certain of overthrow, and the substitution of the male line equally assured. Such a change would leave the inheritance in the gens as before, but it would place children in the gens of their father, and at the head of the agnatic kindred. For a time, in all probability, they would share in the distribution of the estate with the remaining agnates; but an extension of the principle by which the agnates cut off the remaining gentiles, would in time result in the exclusion of the agnates beyond the children and an exclusive inheritance in the children. Farther than this, the son would now be brought in the line of succession to the office of his father.

Such had the law of inheritance become in the Athenian gens in the time of Solon or shortly after; when the property passed to the sons equally, subject to the obligation of maintaining the daughters, and of apportioning them in marriage; and in default of sons, to the daughters equally. If there were no children, then the inheritance passed to the agnatic kindred, and in default of the latter, to the gentiles. The Roman law of the Twelve Tables was substantially the same.

It seems probable further, that when descent was changed to the male, or still earlier, animal names for the gentes were laid aside and personal names substituted in their place. The individuality of persons would assert itself more and more with the progress of society, and with the increase and individual ownership of property, leading to the naming of the gens after some ancestral hero. Although new gentes were being formed from time to time by the process of segmentation, and others were dying out, the lineage of a gens reached back through hundreds not to say thousands of years. After the supposed substitution, the eponymous ancestor would have been a shifting person, at long intervals of time, some later person distinguished in the history of the gens being put in his place, when the knowledge of the former person became obscured, and faded from view in the misty past. That the more celebrated Grecian gentes made the change of names, and made it gracefully, is shown by the fact, that they retained the name of the mother of their gentile father, and ascribed his birth to her embracement by some particular god. Thus Eumolpus, the eponymous ancestor of the Attic Eumolpidæ, was the reputed son of Neptune and Chione; but even the Grecian gens was older than the conception of Neptune.

Recurring now to the main question, the absence of direct proof of ancient descent in the female line in the Grecian and Latin gentes would not silence the presumption in its favor; but it so happens that this form of descent remained in some tribes nearly related to the Greeks with traces of it in a number of Grecian tribes.

The inquisitive and observing Herodotus found one nation, the Lycians, Pelasgian in lineage, but Grecian in affiliation, among whom in his time (440 B. C.), descent was in the female line. After remarking that the Lycians were sprung from Crete, and stating some particulars of their migration to Lycia under Sarpedon, he proceeds as follows: "Their customs are partly Cretan and partly Carian. They have, however, one singular custom in which they differ from every other nation in the world. Ask a Lycian who he is, and he answers by giving his own name, that of his mother, and so on in the female line. Moreover, if a free woman marry a man who is a slave, their children are free citizens; but if a free man marry a foreign woman, or cohabit with a concubine even though he be the first person in the state, the children forfeit all the rights of citizenship."[1] It follows necessarily from this circumstantial statement that the Lycians were organized in gentes, with a prohibition against intermarriage in the gens, and that the children belonged to the gens of their mother. It presents a clear exemplification of a gens in the archaic form, with confirmatory tests of the consequences of a marriage of a Lycian man with a foreign woman, and of a Lycian woman with a slave.[2] The aborigines of Crete were Pelasgian, Hellenic and Semitic tribes, living locally apart. Minos, the brother of Sarpedon, is usually regarded as the head of the Pelasgians in Crete; but the Lycians were already Hellenized in the time of Herodotus and quite conspicuous among the Asiatic Greeks

1 Rawlinson's "Herodotus," i, 173.

2 If a Seneca-Iroquois man marries a foreign woman, their children are aliens; but if a Seneca-Iroquois woman marries an alien, or an Onondaga, their children are Iroquois of the Seneca tribe; and of the gens and phratry of their mother. The woman confers her nationality and her gens upon her children, whoever may be their father.

for their advancement. The insulation of their ancestors upon the island of Crete, prior to their migration in the legendary period to Lycia, may afford an explanation of their retention of descent in the female line to this late period.

Among the Etruscans also the same rule of descent prevailed. "It is singular enough," observes Cramer, "that two customs peculiar to the Etruscans, as we discover from their monuments, should have been noticed by Herodotus as characteristic of the Lycians and Caunians of Asia Minor. The first is, that the Etruscans invariably describe their parentage and family with reference to the mother, and not the father. The other, that they admitted their wives to their feasts and banquets."[1]

Curtius comments on Lycian, Etruscan and Cretan descent in the female line in the following language: "It would be an error to understand the usage in question as an homage to the female sex. It is rather rooted in primitive conditions of society, in which monogamy was not yet established with sufficient certainty to enable descent upon the father's side to be affirmed with assurance. Accordingly the usage extends far beyond the territory commanded by the Lycian nationality. It occurs, even to this day, in India; it may be demonstrated to have existed among the ancient Egyptians; it is mentioned by Sanchoniathon (p. 16, Orell), where the reasons for its existence are stated with great freedom; and beyond the confines of the East it appears among the Etruscans, among the Cretans, who were so closely connected with the Lycians, and who called their father-land mother-land; and among the Athenians, consult Bachofen, etc. Accordingly, if Herodotus regards the usage in question as thoroughly peculiar to the Lycians, it must have maintained itself longest among them of all the nations related to the Greeks, as is also proved by the Lycian inscriptions. Hence we must in general regard the employment of the maternal name for a designation of descent as the remains of an imperfect condition of social life and

---

1 "Description of Ancient Italy," i, 153; citing "Lanzi," ii, 314.

family law, which, as life becomes more regulated, was relinquished in favor of usages, afterwards universal in Greece, of naming children after the father. This diversity of usages, which is extremely important for the history of ancient civilization, has been recently discussed by Bachofen in his address above named."[1]

In a work of vast research, Bachofen has collected and discussed the evidence of female authority (mother-right) and of female rule (gyneocracy) among the Lycians, Cretans, Athenians, Lemnians, Egyptians, Orchomenians, Locrians, Lesbians, Mantineans, and among eastern Asiatic nations.[2] The condition of ancient society, thus brought under review, requires for its full explanation the existence of the gens in its archaic form as the source of the phenomena. This would bring the mother and her children into the same gens, and in the composition of the communal household, on the basis of gens, would give the gens of the mothers the ascendency in the household. The family, which had probably attained the syndyasmian form, was still environed with the remains of that conjugal system which belonged to a still earlier condition. Such a family, consisting of a married pair with their children, would naturally have sought shelter with kindred families in a communal household, in which the several mothers and their children would be of the same gens, and the reputed fathers of these children would be of other gentes. Common lands and joint tillage would lead to joint-tenement houses and communism in living; so that gyneocracy seems to require for its creation, descent in the female line. Women thus entrenched in large households, supplied from common

1 "History of Greece," Scribner & Armstrong's ed., Ward's Trans., i, 94, note. The Etiocretes, of whom Minos was the hero, were doubtless Pelasgians. They occupied the east end of the Island of Crete. Sarpedon, a brother of Minos, led the emigrants to Lycia where they displaced the Solymi, a Semitic tribe probably; but the Lycians had become Hellenized, like many other Pelasgian tribes, before the time of Herodotus, a circumstance quite material in consequence of the derivation of the Grecian and Pelasgian tribes from a common original stock. In the time of Herodotus the Lycians were as far advanced in the arts of life as the European Greeks (Curtius, i, 93; Grote, i, 224). It seems probable that descent in the female line was derived from their Pelasgian ancestors.

2 "Das Mutterrecht," Stuttgart, 1861.

stores, in which their own gens so largely predominated in numbers, would produce the phenomena of mother right and gyneocracy, which Bachofen has detected and traced with the aid of fragments of history and of tradition. Elsewhere I have referred to the unfavorable influence upon the position of women which was produced by a change of descent from the female line to the male, and by the rise of the monogamian family, which displaced the joint-tenement house, and in the midst of a society purely gentile, placed the wife and mother in a single house and separated her from her gentile kindred.[1]

Monogamy was not probably established among the Grecian tribes until after they had attained the Upper Status of barbarism; and we seem to arrive at chaos in the marriage relation within this period, especially in the Athenian tribes. Concerning the latter, Bachofen remarks: "For before the time of Cecrops the children, as we have seen, had only a mother, no father; they were of one line. Bound to no man exclusively, the woman brought only spurious children into the world. Cecrops first made an end of this condition of things; led the lawless union of the sexes back to the exclusiveness of marriage; gave to the children a father and mother, and thus from being of one line (*unilateres*) made them of two lines (*bilateres*)."[2] What is here described as the lawless union of the sexes must be received with modifications. We should expect at that comparatively late day to find the syndyasmian family, but attended by the remains of an anterior conjugal system which sprang from marriages in the group. The punaluan family, which the statement fairly implies, must have disappeared before

---

1 Bachofen, speaking of the Cretan city of Lyktos, remarks that "this city was considered a Lacedaemonian colony, and as also related to the Athenians. It was in both cases only on the mother's side, for only the mothers were Spartans; the Athenian relationship, however, goes back to those Athenian women whom the Pelasgian Tyrrhenians are said to have enticed away from the Brauron promontory." — "Das Mutterrecht," ch. 13, p. 31.

With descent in the male line the lineage of the women would have remained unnoticed; but with descent in the female line the colonists would have given their pedigrees through females only.

2 "Das Mutterrecht," ch. 38, p. 73.

they reached the ethnical period named. This subject will be considered in subsequent chapters in connection with the growth of the family.

There is an interesting reference by Polybius to the hundred families of the Locrians of Italy. "The Locrians themselves," he remarks, "have assured me that their own traditions are more conformable to the account of Aristotle than to that of Timæus. Of this they mention the following proofs. The first is, that all nobility of ancestry among them is derived from women, and not from men. That those, for example, alone are noble, who derive their origin from the hundred families. That these families were noble among the Locrians before they migrated; and were the same, indeed, from which a hundred virgins were taken by lot, as the oracle had commanded, and were sent to Troy."[1] It is at least a reasonable supposition that the rank here referred to was connected with the office of chief of the gens, which ennobled the particular family within the gens, upon one of the members of which it was conferred. If this supposition is tenable, it implies descent in the female line both as to persons and to office. The office of chief was hereditary in the gens, and elective among its male members in archaic times; and with descent in the female line, it would pass from brother to brother, and from uncle to nephew. But the office in each case passed through females, the eligibility of the person depending upon the gens of his mother, who gave him his connection with the gens, and with the deceased chief whose place was to be filled. Wherever office or rank runs through females it requires descent in the female line for its explanation.

Evidence of ancient descent in the female line among the Grecian tribes is found in particular marriages which occurred in the traditionary period. Thus Salmôneus and Krêtheus were own brothers, the sons of Æolus. The former gave his daughter Tyrô in marriage to her uncle.

---

1 "Polybius," xii, extract the second, Hampton's Trans., iii, 242.

With descent in the male line, Krêtheus and Tyrô would have been of the same gens, and could not have married for that reason; but with descent in the female line, they would have been of different gentes, and therefore not of gentile kin. Their marriage in that case would not have violated strict gentile usages. It is immaterial that the persons named are mythical, because the legend would apply gentile usages correctly. This marriage is explainable on the hypothesis of descent in the female line, which in turn raises a presumption of its existence at the time, or as justified by their ancient usages which had not wholly died out.

The same fact is revealed by marriages within the historical period, when an ancient practice seems to have survived the change of descent to the male line, even though it violated the gentile obligations of the parties. After the time of Solon a brother might marry his half-sister, provided they were born of different mothers, but not conversely. With descent in the female line, they would be of different gentes, and, therefore, not of gentile kin. Their marriage would interfere with no gentile obligation. But with descent in the male line, which was the fact when the cases about to be cited occurred, they would be of the same gens, and consequently under prohibition. Cimon married his half-sister, Elpinice, their father being the same, but their mothers different. In the *Eubulides* of Demosthenes we find a similar case. "My grandfather," says Euxithius, "married his sister, she not being his sister by the same mother."[1] Such marriages, against which a strong prejudice had arisen among the Athenians as early as the time of Solon, are explainable as a survival of an ancient custom with respect to marriage, which prevailed when descent was in the female line, and which had not been entirely eradicated in the time of Demosthenes.

Descent in the female line presupposes the gens to distinguish the lineage. With our present knowledge of the ancient and modern prevalence of the gentile organi-

---

1 "Demosthenes contra Eubulides," 20.

zation upon five continents, including the Australian, and of the archaic constitution of the gens, traces of descent in the female line might be expected to exist in traditions, if not in usages coming down to historical times. It is not supposable, therefore, that the Lycians, the Cretans, the Athenians and the Locrians, if the evidence is sufficient to include the last two, invented a usage so remarkable as descent in the female line. The hypothesis that it was the ancient law of the Latin, Grecian, and other Græco-Italian gentes affords a more rational as well as satisfactory explanation of the facts. The influence of property and the desire to transmit it to children furnished adequate motives for the change to the male line.

It may be inferred that marrying out of the gens was the rule among the Athenians, before as well as after the time of Solon, from the custom of registering the wife, upon her marriage, in the phratry of her husband, and the children, daughters as well as sons, in the gens and phratry of their father.[1] The fundamental principle on which the gens was founded was the prohibition of inter marriage among its members as consanguinei. In each gens the number of members was not large. Assuming sixty thousand as the number of registered Athenians in the time of Solon, and dividing them equally among the three hundred and sixty Attic gentes, it would give but one hundred and sixty persons to each gens. The gens was a great family of kindred persons, with common religious rites, a common burial place, and, in general, common lands. From the theory of its constitution, intermarriage would be disallowed. With the change of descent to the male line, with the rise of monogamy and an exclusive inheritance in the children, and with the appearance of heiresses, the way was being gradually prepared for free marriage regardless of gens, but with a prohibition limited to certain degrees of near consanguinity. Marriages in the human family began in the

1 Demosth., "Eubul.," 24: In his time the registration was in the Deme; but it would show who were the phrators, blood relaties, fellow demots and gennetes of the person registered; as Euxitheus says; see also Hermann's "Polit. Antiq. of Greece," par. 100.

group, all the males and females of which, excluding the children, were joint husbands and wives; but the husbands and wives were of different gentes; and it ended in marriages between single pairs, with an exclusive cohabitation. In subsequent chapters an attempt will be made to trace the several forms of marriage and of the family from the first stage to the last.

A system of consanguinity came in with the gens, distinguished as the Turanian in Asia, and as the Ganowánian in America, which extended the prohibition of intermarriage as far as the relationship of brother and sister extended among collaterals. This system still prevails among the American aborigines, in portions of Asia and Africa, and in Australia. It unquestionably prevailed among the Grecian and Latin tribes in the same anterior period, and traces of it remained down to the traditionary period. One feature of the Turanian system may be restated as follows: the children of brothers are themselves brothers and sisters, and as such could not intermarry; the children of sisters stood in the same relationship, and were under the same prohibition. It may serve to explain the celebrated legend of the Danaidæ, one version of which furnished to Aeschylus his subject for the tragedy of the *Suppliants.* The reader will remember that Danaus and Ægyptus were brothers, and descendants of Argive Io. The former by different wives had fifty daughters, and the latter by different wives had fifty sons; and in due time the sons of Ægyptus sought the daughters of Danaus in marriage. Under the system of consanguinity appertaining to the gens in its archaic form, and which remained until superseded by the system introduced by monogamy, they were brothers and sisters, and for that reason could not marry. If descent at the time was in the male line, the children of Danaus and Ægyptus would have been of the same gens, which would have interposed an additional objection to their marriage, and of equal weight. Nevertheless the sons of Ægyptus sought to overstep these barriers and enforce wedlock upon the Danaidæ; whilst the latter, crossing the sea, fled from Egypt to Argos to escape what they pronounced an unlawful and incestuous union. In the *Prometheus* of the same author, this event is foretold to Io by Prometheus, namely: that in the fifth generation from her future son Epaphus, a band of fifty virgins should come to Argos, not voluntarily, but fleeing from incestuous wedlock with the sons of Ægyptus.[1] Their flight with abhorrence from the proposed nuptials finds its explanation in the ancient system of consanguinity, independently of gentile law. Apart from this explanation the event has no significance, and their aversion to the marriages would have been mere prudery.

The tragedy of the *Suppliants* is founded upon the incident of their flight over the sea to Argos, to claim the protection of their Argive kindred against the proposed violence of the sons of Ægyptus, who pursued them. At Argos the Danaidæ declare that they did not depart from Egypt under the sentence of banishment, but fled from men of common descent with themselves, scorning unholy marriage with the sons of Ægyptus.[2] Their reluctance is placed exclusively upon the fact of kin, thus implying an existing prohibition against such marriages, which they had been trained to respect. After hearing the case of the Suppliants, the Argives in council resolved to afford them protection, which of itself implies the existence of the prohibition of the marriages and the validity of their objection. At the time this tragedy was produced, Athenian law permitted and even required marriage between the children of brothers in the case of heiresses and female orphans, although the rule seems to have been confined to these exceptional cases; such marriages, therefore, would not seem to the Athenians either incestuous or unlawful; but this tradition of the Danaidæ had come down from a remote antiquity, and its whole significance depended upon the force of the custom forbidding the nuptials. The turning-point of the tradition and its incidents was their inveterate repugnance to the proposed marriages as forbidden by law and custom. No

1 "Prometheus," 853.
2 Aeschylus, "Supp.," 9.

other reason is assigned, and no other is needed. At the same time their conduct is intelligible on the assumption that such marriages were as unpermissible then, as marriage between a brother and sister would be at the present time. The attempt of the sons of Ægyptus to break through the barrier interposed by the Turanian system of consanguinity may mark the time when this system was beginning to give way, and the present system, which came in with monogamy, was beginning to assert itself, and which was destined to set aside gentile usages and Turanian consanguinity by the substitution of fixed degrees as the limits of prohibition.

Upon the evidence adduced it seems probable that among the Pelasgian, Hellenic and Italian tribes descent was originally in the female line, from which, under the influence of property and inheritance, it was changed to the male line. Whether or not these tribes anciently possessed the Turanian system of consanguinity, the reader will be better able to judge after that system has been presented, with the evidence of its wide prevalence in ancient society.

The length of the traditionary period of these tribes is of course unknown in the years of its duration, but it must be measured by thousands of years. It probably reached back of the invention of the process of smelting iron ore, and if so, passed through the Later Period of barbarism and entered the Middle Period. Their condition of advancement in the Middle Period must have at least equaled that of the Aztecs, Mayas and Peruvians, who were found in the status of the Middle Period; and their condition in the Later Period must have surpassed immensely that of the Indian tribes named. The vast and varied experience of these European tribes in the two great ethnical periods named, during which they achieved the remaining elements of civilization, is entirely lost, excepting as it is imperfectly disclosed in their traditions, and more fully by their arts of life, their customs, language and institutions, as revealed to us by the poems of Homer. Empires and kingdoms were necessarily unknown in these periods; but tribes and inconsiderable nations, city and village life, the growth and development of the arts of life, and physical, mental and moral improvement, were among the particulars of that progress. The loss of the events of these great periods to human knowledge was much greater than can easily be imagined.

CHAPTER XV

GENTES IN OTHER TRIBES OF THE HUMAN FAMILY

Having considered the organization into gentes, phratries and tribes in their archaic as well as later form, it remains to trace the extent of its prevalence in the human family, and particularly with respect to the gens, the basis of the system.

The Celtic branch of the Aryan family retained, in the Scottish clan and Irish sept, the organization into gentes to a later period of time than any other branch of the family, unless the Aryans of India are an exception. The Scottish clan in particular was existing in remarkable vitality in the Highlands of Scotland in the middle of the last century. It was an excellent type of the gens in organization and in spirit, and an extraordinary illustration of the power of the gentile life over its members. The illustrious author of Waverley has perpetuated a number of striking characters developed under clan life, and stamped with its peculiarities. Evan Dhu, Torquil, Rob Roy and many others rise before the mind as illustrations of the influence of the gens in molding the character of individuals. If Sir Walter exaggerated these characters in some respects to suit the emergencies of a tale, they had a real foundation. The same clans, a few centuries earlier, when clan life was stronger and external influences were weaker, would probably have verified the pictures. We find in their feuds and blood revenge, in their localization by gentes, in their use of lands in common, in the fidelity of the clansman to his chief and of the members of the clan to each other, the usual and persistent features of gentile society. As portrayed by Scott, it was a more intense and chivalrous gentile life than we are able to find in the gentes of the Greeks and Romans, or, at the other extreme, in those of the American aborigines. Whether the phratric organization existed among them does not appear; but at some anterior period both the phratry and the tribe doubtless did exist. It is well known that the British government were compelled to break up the Highland clans, as organizations, in order to bring the people under the authority of law and the usages of political society. Descent was in the male line, the children of the males remaining members of the clan, while the children of its female members belonged to the clans of their respective fathers.

We shall pass over the Irish *sept,* the *phis* or *phrara* of the Albanians, which embody the remains of a prior gentile organization, and the traces of a similar organization in Dalmatia and Croatia; and also the Sanskrit *ganas,* the existence of which term in the language implies that this branch of the Aryan family formerly possessed the same institution. The communities of Villeins on French estates in former times, noticed by Sir Henry Maine in his recent work, may prove to be, as he intimates, remains of ancient Celtic gentes. "Now that the explanation has once been given," he remarks, "there can be no doubt that these associations were not really voluntary partnerships, but groups of kinsmen; not, however, so often organized on the ordinary type of the Village-Community as on that of the House-Community, which has recently been examined in Dalmatia and Croatia. Each of them was what the Hindus call a Joint-Undivided family, a collection of assumed descendants from a common ancestor, preserving a common hearth and common meals during several generations."[1]

A brief reference should be made to the question whether any traces of the gentile organization remained among the German tribes when they first came under historical notice. That they inherited this institution,

1 "Early History of Institutions," Holt's ed., p. 7.

with other Aryan tribes, from the common ancestors of the Aryan family, is probable. When first known to the Romans, they were in the Upper Status of barbarism. They could scarcely have developed the idea of government further than the Grecian and Latin tribes, who were in advance of them, when each respectively became known. While the Germans may have acquired an imperfect conception of a state, founded upon territory and upon property, it is not probable that they had any knowledge of the second great plan of government which the Athenians were first among Aryan tribes to establish. The condition and mode of life of the German tribes, as described by Cæsar and Tacitus, tend to the conclusion that their several societies were held together through personal relations, and with but slight reference to territory; and that their government was through these relations. Civil chiefs and military commanders acquired and held office through the elective principle, and constituted the council which was the chief instrument of government. On lesser affairs, Tacitus remarks, the chiefs consult, but on those of greater importance the whole community. While the final decision of all important questions belonged to the people, they were first maturely considered by the chiefs.[1] The close resemblance of these to Grecian and Latin usages will be perceived. The government consisted of three powers, the council of chiefs, the assembly of the people, and the military commander.

Cæsar remarks that the Germans were not studious of agriculture, the greater part of their food consisting of milk, cheese and meat; nor had any one a fixed quantity of land, or his own individual boundaries, but the magistrates and chiefs each year assigned to the gentes and kinsmen who had united in one body (*gentibus cognationibusque hominum qui una coerint*) as much land, and in such places as seemed best, compelling them the next year to remove to another place.[2] To give effect to the

1 "Germania," c. ii.
2 "De Bell. Gall.," vi, 22.

expression in parenthesis, it must be supposed that he found among them groups of persons, larger than a family, united on the basis of kin, to whom, as groups of persons, lands were allotted. It excludes individuals, and even the family, both of whom were merged in the group thus united for cultivation and subsistence. It seems probable, from the form of the statement, that the German family at this time was syndyasmian; and that several related families were united in households and practiced communism in living.

Tacitus refers to a usage of the German tribes in the arrangement of their forces in battle, by which kinsmen were placed side by side. It would have no significance, if kinship were limited to near consanguinei. And what is an especial incitement of their courage, he remarks, neither chance nor a fortuitous gathering of the forces make up the squadron of horse, or the infantry wedge; but they were formed according to families and kinships (*familiæ et propinquitates*).[1] This expression, and that previously quoted from Cæsar, seem to indicate the remains at least of a prior gentile organization, which at this time was giving place to the mark or local district as the basis of a still imperfect political system.

The German tribes, for the purpose of military levies, had the mark (*markgenossenschaft*), which also existed among the English Saxons, and a larger group, the *gau*, to which Cæsar and Tacitus gave the name of *pagus*.[2] It is doubtful whether the mark and the *gau* were then strictly geographical districts, standing to each other in the relations of township and county, each circumscribed by bounds, with the people in each politically organized. It seems more probable that the *gau* was a group of settlements associated with reference to military levies. As such, the mark and the *gau* were the germs of the future township and county, precisely as the Athenian

---

1 "Germania," cap. 7. The line of battle, this author remarks, is formed by wedges. "Acies per cuneos componitur."—"Ger.," c. 6. Kohlrausch observes that "the confederates of one mark or hundred, and of one race or sept, fought united."—"History of Germany," Appleton's ed., trans. by J. D. Haas, p. 28.

2 "De Bell. Gall.," iv. 1. "Germania," cap. 6.

naucrary and trittys were the rudiments of the Cleisthenean deme and local tribe. These organizations seemed transitional stages between a gentile and a political system, the grouping of the people still resting on consanguinity.[1]

We naturally turn to the Asiatic continent, where the types of mankind are the most numerous, and where, consequently, the period of human occupation has been longest, to find the earliest traces of the gentile organization. But here the transformations of society have been the most extended, and the influence of tribes and nations upon each other the most constant. The early development of Chinese and Indian civilization and the overmastering influence of modern civilization have wrought such changes in the condition of Asiatic stocks that their ancient institutions are not easily ascertainable. Nevertheless, the whole experience of mankind from savagery to civilization was worked out upon the Asiatic continent, and among its fragmentary tribes the remains of their ancient institutions must now be sought.

Descent in the female line is still very common in the

---

1 Dr. Freeman, who has studied this subject specially, remarks: "The lowest unit in the political system is that which still exists under various names, as the 'mark,' the 'gemeinde,' the 'commune,' or the 'parish.' This, as we have seen, is one of many forms of the 'gens' or clan, that in which it is no longer a wandering or a mere predatory body, but when, on the other hand, it has not joined with others to form one component element of a city commonwealth. In this stage the 'gens' takes the form of an agricultural body, holding its common lands—the germ of the 'ager publicus' of Rome, and of the 'folkland' of England. This is the 'markgenossenschaft,' the village community of the West. This lowest political unit, this gathering of real or artificial kinsmen, is made up of families, each living under the rule, the 'mund' of its own father, that 'patria potestas' which survived at Rome to form so marked and lasting a feature of Roman law. As the union of families forms the 'gens,' and as the 'gens' in its territorial aspect forms the 'markgenossenschaft,' so the union of several such village communities and their 'marks' or common lands forms the next higher political union, the hundred, a name to be found in one shape or another in most lands into which the Teutonic race has spread itself. . . . . Above the hundred comes the 'pagus,' the 'gau,' the Danish 'syssel,' the English 'shire,' that is, the tribe looked at as occupying a certain territory. And each of these divisions, greater and smaller, had its chiefs. . . . The hundred is made up of villages, marks, gemeinden, whatever we call the lowest unit; the 'shire,' the 'gau,' the 'pagus,' is made up of hundreds."—"Comparative Politics," McMillan & Co.'s ed., p. 116.

ruder Asiatic tribes; but there are numerous tribes among whom it is traced in the male line. It is the limitation of descent to one line or the other, followed by the organization of the body of consanguinei, thus separated under a common name which indicates a gens.

In the Magar tribe of Nepaul, Latham remarks, "there are twelve thums. All individuals belonging to the same thum are supposed to be descended from the same male ancestor; descent from the same mother being by no means necessary. So husband and wife must belong to different thums. Within one and the same there is no marriage. Do you wish for a wife? If so, look to the thum of your neighbor; at any rate look beyond your own. This is the first time I have found occasion to mention this practice. It will not be the last; on the contrary, the principle it suggests is so common as to be almost universal. We shall find it in Australia; we shall find it in North and South America; we shall find it in Africa; we shall find it in Europe; we shall suspect and infer it in many places where the actual evidence of its existence is incomplete."[1] In this case we have in the *thum* clear evidence of the existence of a gens, with descent in the male line.

"The Munnieporees, and the following tribes inhabiting the hills round Munniepore—the Koupooes, the Mows, the Murams, and the Murring—are each and all divided into four families—Koomul, Looang, Angom, and Ningthajà. A member of any of these families may marry a member of any other, but the intermarriage of members of the same family is strictly prohibited."[2] In these families may be recognized four gentes in each of these tribes. Bell, speaking of the *Telûsh* of the Circassians, remarks that "the tradition in regard to them is, that the members of each and all sprang from the same stock or ancestry; and thus they may be considered as so many septs or clans. . . . . These cousins german, or members of the same fraternity, are not only them-

1 "Descriptive Ethnology," i. 80.
2 McLennan's "Primitive Marriage," p. 109.

selves interdicted from intermarrying, but their serfs, too, must wed with serfs of another fraternity."[1] It is probable that the *telûsh* is a gens.

Among the Bengalese "the four castes are subdivided into many different sects or classes, and each of these is again subdivided; for instance, I am of Nundy tribe [gens?], and if I were a heathen I could not marry a woman of the same tribe, although the caste must be the same. The children are of the tribe of their father. Property descends to the sons. In case the person has no sons, to his daughters; and if he leaves neither, to his nearest relatives. Castes are subdivided, such as *Shuro*, which is one of the first divisions; but it is again subdivided, such as *Khayrl, Tilly, Tamally, Tanty, Chomor, Kari,* etc. A man belonging to one of these last-named subdivisions cannot marry a woman of the same."[2] These smallest groups number usually about a hundred persons, and still retain several of the characteristics of a gens.

Mr. Tyler remarks, that "in India it is unlawful for a Brahman to marry a wife whose clan-name or *ghotra* (literally 'cow-stall') is the same as his own, a prohibition which bars marriage among relatives in the male line indefinitely. This law appears in the code of Manu as applying to the first three castes, and connexions on the female side are also forbidden to marry within certain wide limits."[3] And again: "Among the Kols of Chota-Nagpur, we find many of the Oraon and Munda clans named after animals, as eel, hawk, crow, heron, and they must not kill or eat what they are named after."[4]

The Mongolians approach the American aborgines quite nearly in physical characteristics. They are divided into numerous tribes. "The connection," says Latham, "between the members of a tribe is that of blood, pedigree, or descent; the tribe being, in some cases, named after a real or supposed patriarch. The tribe, by which

1 Quoted in "Primitive Marriage," p. 101.
2 "Letter to the Author," by Rev. Gopenath Nundy, a Native Bengalese, India.
3 "Early History of Mankind," p. 282.
4 "Primitive Culture," Holt & Co.'s ed., ii, 235.

we translate the native name *aimauk,* or *aimâk,* is a large division falling into so many *kokhums,* or banners."[1] The statement is not full enough to show the existence of gentes. Their neighbors, the Tungusians are composed of subdivisions named after animals, as the horse, the dog, the reindeer, which imply the gentile organizations, but it cannot be asserted without further particulars.

Sir John Lubbock remarks of the Kalmucks that according to De Hell, they "are divided into hordes, and no man can marry a woman of the same horde;" and of the Ostiaks, that they "regard it as a crime to marry a woman of the same family or even of the same name;" and that "when a Jakut (Siberia) wishes to marry, he must choose a girl from another clan."[2] We have in each of these cases evidence of the existence of a gens, one of the rules of which, as has been shown, is the prohibition of intermarriage among its members. The Yurak Samoyeds are organized in gentes. Klaproth, quoted by Latham, remarks that "this division of the kinsmanship is so rigidly observed that no Samoyed takes a wife from the kinsmanship to which he himself belongs. On the contrary, he seeks her in one of the other two."[3]

A peculiar family system prevails among the Chinese which seems to embody the remains of an ancient gentile organization. Mr. Robert Hart, of Canton, in a letter to the author remarks, "that the Chinese expression for the people is *Pih-sing,* which means *the Hundred Family Names;* but whether this is mere word-painting, or had its origin at a time when the Chinese general family consisted of one hundred subfamilies or tribes [gentes?] I am unable to determine. At the present day there are about four hundred family names in this country, among which I find some that have reference to animals, fruits, metals, natural objects, etc., and which may be translated as Horse, Sheep, Ox, Fish, Bird, Phœnix, Plum, Flower, Leaf, Rice, Forest, River, Hill, Water, Cloud, Gold, Hide,

1 "Descriptive Ethnology," i, 290.
2 "Origin of Civilization," 96.
3 "Descriptive Ethnology," i, 475.

Bristles, etc., etc. In some parts of the country large villages are met with, in each of which there exists but one family name; thus in one district will be found, say, three villages, each containing two or three thousand people, the one of the Horse, the second of the Sheep, and the third of the Ox family name..... Just as among the North American Indians husbands and wives are of different tribes [gentes], so in China husband and wife are always of different families, i. e., of different surnames. Custom and law alike prohibit intermarriage on the part of people having the same family surname. The children are of the father's family, that is, they take his family surname..... Where the father dies intestate the property generally remains undivided, but under the control of the oldest son during the life of the widow. On her death he divides the property between himself and his brothers, the shares of the juniors depending entirely upon the will of the elder brother."

The family here described appears to be a gens, analogous to the Roman in the time of Romulus; but whether it was reintegrated, with other gentes of common descent, in a phratry does not appear. Moreover, the gentiles are still located as an independent consanguine body in one area, as the Roman gentes were localized in the early period, and the names of the gentes are still of the archaic type. Their increase to four hundred by segmentation might have been expected; but their maintenance to the present time, after the period of barbarism has long passed away, is the remarkable fact, and an additional proof of their immobility as a people. It may be suspected also that the monogamian family in these villages has not attained its full development, and that communism in living, and in wives as well, may not be unknown among them. Among the wild aboriginal tribes, who still inhabit the mountain regions of China and who speak dialects different from the Mandarin, the gens in its archaic form may yet be discovered. To these isolated tribes, we should naturally look for the ancient institutions of the Chinese.

In like manner the tribes of Afghanistan are said to

be subdivided into clans; but whether these clans are true gentes has not been ascertained.

Not to weary the reader with further details of a similar character, a sufficient number of cases have been adduced to create a presumption that the gentile organization prevailed very generally and widely among the remote ancestors of the present Asiatic tribes and nations.

The twelve tribes of the Hebrews, as they appear in the Book of Numbers, represent a reconstruction of Hebrew society by legislative procurement. The condition of barbarism had then passed away, and that of civilization had commenced. The principle on which the tribes were organized, as bodies of consanguinei, presupposes an anterior gentile system, which had remained in existence and was now systematized. At this time they had no knowledge of any other plan of government than a gentile society formed of consanguine groups united through personal relations. Their subsequent localization in Palestine by consanguine tribes, each district named after one of the twelve sons of Jacob, with the exception of the tribe of Levi, is a practical recognition of the fact that they were organized by lineages and not into a community of citizens. The history of the most remarkable nation of the Semitic family has been concentrated around the names of Abraham, Isaac and Jacob, and the twelve sons of the latter.

Hebrew history commences essentially with Abraham the account of whose forefathers is limited to a pedigree barren of details. A few passages will show the extent of the progress then made, and the status of advancement in which Abraham appeared. He is described as "very rich in cattle, in silver, and in gold." [1] For the cave of Machpelah "Abraham weighed to Ephron the silver, which he had named in the audience of the sons of Heth, four hundred shekels of silver, current *money* with the merchant." [2] With respect to domestic life and subsistence, the following passage may be cited: "And Abra-

---

1 "Genesis," xiii, 2.
2 "Genesis," xxiii, 16.

ham hastened into the tent unto Sarah, and said, Make ready quickly three measures of fine meal; knead *it,* and make cakes upon the hearth." [1] "And he took butter and milk, and the calf which he had dressed, and set it before them." [2] With respect to implements, raiment and ornaments: "Abraham took the fire in his hand and a knife."[3] "And the servant brought forth jewels of silver, and jewels of gold, and raiment, and gave them to Rebekah: he gave also to her brother and to her mother precious things."[4] When she met Isaac, Rebekah "took a veil and covered herself." [5] In the same connection are mentioned the camel, ass, ox, sheep and goat, together with flocks and herds; the grain mill, the water pitcher, earrings, bracelets, tents, houses and cities. The bow and arrow, the sword, corn and wine, and fields sown with grain, are mentioned. They indicate the Upper Status of barbarism for Abraham, Isaac and Jacob. Writing in this branch of the Semitic family was probably then unknown. The degree of development shown corresponds substantially with that of the Homeric Greeks.

Early Hebrew marriage customs indicate the presence of the gens, and in its archaic form. Abraham, by his servant, seemingly purchased Rebekah as a wife for Isaac; the "precious things" being given to the brother, and to the mother of the bride, but not to the father. In this case the presents went to the gentile kindred, provided a gens existed, with descent in the female line. Again, Abraham married his half-sister Sarah. "And yet indeed," he says, "she *is* my sister; she is the daughter of my father, but not the daughter of my mother; and she became my wife." [6]

With an existing gens and descent in the female line Abraham and Sarah would have belonged to different gentes, and although of *blood kin* they were not of *gentile* kin, and could have married by gentile usage. The

1 Ib., xviii, 6.
2 Ib., xviii, 8.
3 Ib., xxii, 6.
4 Ib., xxiv, 53.
5 Ib., xxiv, 65.
6 Ib., xx, 12.

case would have been reversed in both particulars with descent in the male line. Nahor married his niece, the daughter of his brother Haran;[1] and Amram, the father of Moses, married his aunt, the sister of his father, who became the mother of the Hebrew lawgiver.[2] In these cases, with descent in the female line, the persons marrying would have belonged to different gentes; but otherwise with descent in the male line. While these cases do not prove absolutely the existence of gentes, the latter would afford such an explanation of them as to raise a presumption of the existence of the gentile organization in its archaic form.

When the Mosaic legislation was completed the Hebrews were a civilized people, but not far enough advanced to institute political society. The scripture account shows that they were organized in a series of consanguine groups in an ascending scale, analogous to the gens, phratry and tribe of the Greeks. In the muster and organization of the Hebrews, both as a society and as an army, while in the Sinaitic peninsula, repeated references are made to these consanguine groups in an ascending series, the seeming equivalents of a gens, phratry and tribe. Thus, the tribe of Levi consisted of eight gentes organized in three phratries, as follows:

Tribe of Levi.

Sons of Levi.	I. *Gershon.*	7,500	Males.
	II. *Kohath.*	8,600	"
	III. *Merari.*	6,200	"

I. *Gershonite Phratry.*

Gentes.—1. *Libni.* 2. *Shimei.*

II. *Kohathite Phratry.*

Gentes.—1. *Amram.* 2. *Izhar.* 3. *Hebron.* 4. *Uzziel.*

III. *Merarite Phratry.*

Gentes.—1. *Mahli.* 2. *Mushi.*

"Number the children of Levi after the house of their

1 "Genesis," xi, 29.
2 "Exodus," vi, 20.

fathers, by their families. . . . . And these were the sons of Levi by their names; Gershon, and Kohath, and Merari. And these were the names of the sons of Gershon by their families; Libni, and Shimei. And the sons of Kohath by their families; Amram, and Izhar, Hebron, and Uzziel. And the sons of Merari by their families; Mahli, and Mushi. These are the families of the Levites by the house of their fathers." [1]

The description of these groups sometimes commences with the upper member of the series, and sometimes with the lower or the unit. Thus: "Of the children of Simeon, by their generations, after their families, by the house of their fathers." [2] Here *the children of Simeon, with their generations,* constitute the *tribe;* the *families* are the *phratries;* and *the house of the father* is the *gens.* Again: "And the chief of the house of the father of the families of the Kohathites shall be Elizaphan the son of Uzziel. [3] Here we find the gens first, and then the phratry and last the tribe. The person named was the chief of the phratry. Each house of the father also had its ensign or banner to distinguish it from others. "Every man of the children of Israel shall pitch by his own standard, with the ensign of their father's house."[4] These terms describe actual organizations; and they show that their military organization was by gentes, by phratries and by tribes.

With respect to the first and smallest of these groups, "the house of the father," it must have numbered several hundred persons from the figures given of the number in each phratry. The Hebrew term *beth' ab,* signifies *paternal house, house of the father,* and *family house.* If the Hebrews possessed the gens, it was this group of persons. The use of two terms to describe it would leave a doubt, unless individual families under monogamy had then become so numerous and so prominent that this circumlocution was necessary to cover the kindred. We have literally, the house of Amram, of Izhar, of Hebron,

1 "Numbers," iii, 15-20.
2 Ib., i. 22.
3 Ib., iii, 30.
4 Ib., ii, 2.

and of Uzziel; but as the Hebrews at that time could have had no conception of a *house* as now applied to a titled family, it probably signified, as used, kindred or lineage.[1] Since each division and subdivision is headed by a male, and since Hebrew descents are traced through males exclusively, descent among them, at this time, was undoubtedly in the male line. Next in the ascending scale is the *family,* which seems to be a phratry. The Hebrew term for this organization, *mishpacah,* signifies *union, clanship.* It was composed of two or more houses of the father, derived by segmentation from an original group, and distinguished by a phratric name. It answers very closely to the phratry. The family or phratry had an annual sacrificial feast. [2] Lastly, the *tribe,* called in Hebrew *matteh,* which signifies a *branch, stem* or *shoot,* is the analogue of the Grecian tribe.

Very few particulars are given respecting the rights, privileges and obligations of the members of these bodies of consanguinei. The idea of kin which united each organization from the *house of the father* to the *tribe,* is carried out in a form much more marked and precise than in the corresponding organizations of Grecian, Latin or American Indian tribes. While the Athenian traditions claimed that the four tribes were derived from the four sons of Ion, they did not pretend to explain the origin of the gentes and phratries. On the contrary, the Hebrew account not only derives the twelve tribes genealogically from the twelve sons of Jacob, but also the gentes and phratries from the children and descendants of each. Human experience furnishes no parallel of the growth of gentes and phratries precisely in this way. The account must be explained as a classification of existing consanguine groups, according to the knowledge preserved by tradition, in doing which minor obstacles were overcome by legislative constraint.

The Hebrews styled themselves the "People of Israel,"

---

1 Kiel and Delitzschs, in their commentaries on Exodus vi, 14, remark that "father's house was a technical term applied to a collection of families called by the name of a common ancestor." This is a fair definition of a gens.

2 "I Samuel," xx, 6, 29.

and also a "Congregation."[1] It is a direct recognition of the fact that their organization was social, and not political.

In Africa we encounter a chaos of savagery and barbarism. Original arts and inventions have largely disappeared, through fabrics and utensils introduced from external sources; but savagery in its lowest forms, cannibalism included, and barbarism in its lowest forms prevail over the greater part of the continent. Among the interior tribes, there is a nearer approach to an indigenous culture and to a normal condition; but Africa, in the main, is a barren ethnological field.

Although the home of the Negro race, it is well known that their numbers are limited and their areas small. Latham significantly remarks that "the Negro is an exceptional African."[2] The Ashiras, Aponos, Ishogos and Ashangos, between the Congo and the Niger, visited by Du Chaillu, are of the true Negro type. "Each village," he remarks, "had its chief, and further in the interior the villages seemed to be governed by elders, each elder with his people having a separate portion of the village to themselves. There was in each clan the ifoumou, fumou, or acknowledged head of the clan (ifoumou meaning the *source*, the *father*). I have never been able to obtain from the natives a knowledge concerning the splitting of their tribes into clans; they seemed not to know how it happened, but the formation of new clans does not take place now among them. . . . The house of a chief or elder is not better than those of his neighbors. The despotic form of government is unknown. . . . . A council of the elders is necessary before one is put to death. . . . . Tribes and clans intermarry with each other, and this brings about a friendly feeling among the people. People of the same clan cannot intermarry with each other. The least consanguinity is considered an abomination; nevertheless the nephew has not the slightest objection to take his uncle's wives, and, as among the

1 "Numbers," i, 2.
2 "Descript. Eth.," ii, 184.

Balakai, the son takes his father's wives, except his own mother. . . . . Polygamy and slavery exist everywhere among the tribes I have visited. . . . . . The law of inheritance among the Western tribes is, that the next brother inherits the wealth of the eldest (women, slaves, etc.), but that if the youngest dies the eldest inherits his property, and if there are no brothers that the nephew inherits it. The headship of the clan or family is hereditary, following the same law as that of the inheritance of property. In the case of all the brothers having died, the eldest son of the eldest sister inherits, and it goes on thus until the branch is extinguished, for all clans are considered as descended from the female side."[1]

All the elements of a true gens are embodied in the foregoing particulars, namely, descent is limited to one line, in this case the female, which gives the gens in its archaic form. Moreover, descent is in the female line with respect to office and to property, as well as the gentile name. The office of chief passes from brother to brother, or from uncle to nephew, that nephew being the son of a sister, as among the American aborigines; whilst the sons are excluded because not members of the gens of the deceased chief. Marriage in the gens is also forbidden. The only material omission in these precise statements is the names of some of the gentes. The hereditary feature requires further explanation.

Among the Banyai of the Zambezi river, who are a people of higher grade than the Negroes, Dr. Livingstone observed the following usages: "The government of the Banyai is rather peculiar, being a sort of feudal republicanism. The chief is elected, and they choose the son of a deceased chief's sister in preference to his own offspring. When dissatisfied with one candidate, they even go to a distant tribe for a successor, who is usually of the family of the late chief, a brother, or a sister's son, but never his own son or daughter . . . . . All the wives, goods, and children of his predecessor belong to him."[2]

---

1 "Ashango Land," Appletons' ed., p. 425, et seq.
2 "Travels in South Africa," Appletons' ed., ch. 30, p. 660.— "When a young man takes a liking for a girl of another vil-

Dr. Livingstone does not give the particulars of their social organization; but the descent of the office of chief from brother to brother, or from uncle to nephew, implies the existence of the gens with descent in the female line.

The numerous tribes occupying the country watered by the Zambezi, and from thence southward to Cape Colony, are regarded by the natives themselves, according to Dr. Livingstone, as one stock in three great divisions, the Bechuanas, the Basutos, and the Kafirs.[1] With respect to the former, he remarks that "the Bechuana tribes are named after certain animals, showing probably that in ancient times they were addicted to animal worship like the ancient Egyptians. The term Bakatla means 'they of the Monkey'; Bakuona, 'they of the Alligator'; Batlapi, 'they of the Fish'; each tribe having a superstitious dread of the animal after which it is called. . . A tribe never eats the animal which is its namesake. . . . . We find traces of many ancient tribes in individual members of those now extinct; as Bátau, 'they of the Lion'; Banoga, 'they of the Serpent,' though no such tribes now exist."[2] These animal names are suggestive of the gens rather than the tribe. Moreover, the fact that single individuals are found, each of whom was the last survivor of his tribe, would be more likely to have occurred if gens were understood in the place of tribe. Among the Bangalas of the Cassange Valley, in Argola, Livingstone remarks that "a chief's brother inherits in preference to his sons. The sons of a sister belong to her brother; and he often sells his nephews to pay his debts."[3] Here again we have evidence of descent in the female line; but his statements are too brief and general in these and other cases to show definitely whether or not they possessed the gens.

---

lage, and the parents have no objection to the match, he is obliged to come and live at their village. He has to perform certain services for the mother-in-law. . . . . If he becomes tired of living in this state of vassalage, and wishes to return to his own family, he is obliged to leave all his children behind—they belong to his wife."— Ib., p. 667.

1 "Travels in South Africa," p. 219.

2 Ib., p. 471.

3 Ib., p. 471.

Among the Australians the gentes of the Kamilaroi have already been noticed. In ethnical position the aborigines of this great island are near the bottom of the scale. When discovered they were not only savages, but in a low condition of savagery. Some of the tribes were cannibals. Upon this last question Mr. Fison, before mentioned, writes as follows to the author: "Some, at least, of the tribes are cannibals. The evidence of this is conclusive. The Wide Bay tribes eat not only their enemies slain in battle, but their friends also who have been killed, and even those who have died a natural death, provided they are in good condition. Before eating they skin them, and preserve the skins by rubbing them with mingled fat and charcoal. These skins they prize very highly, believing them to have great medicinal value."

Such pictures of human life enable us to understand the condition of savagery, the grade of its usages, the degree of material development, and the low level of the mental and moral life of the people. Australian humanity, as seen in their cannibal customs, stands on as low a plane as it has been known to touch on the earth. And yet the Australians possessed an area of continental dimensions, rich in minerals, not uncongenial in climate, and fairly supplied with the means of subsistence. But after an occupation which must be measured by thousands of years, they are still savages of the grade above indicated. Left to themselves they would probably have remained for thousands of years to come, not without any, but with such slight improvement as scarcely to lighten the dark shade of their savage state.

Among the Australians, whose institutions are normal and homogeneous, the organization into gentes is not confined to the Kamilaroi, but seems to be universal. The Narrinyeri of South Australia, near Lacepede Bay are organized in gentes named after animals and insects. Rev. George Taplin, writing to my friend Mr. Fison, after stating that the Narrinyeri do not marry into their own gens, and that the children were of the gens of their father, continues as follows: "There are no castes, nor are there any classes, similar to those of the Kamilaroi-speaking tribes of New South Wales. But each tribe or family (and a tribe is a family) has its totem, or *ngaitye;* and indeed some individuals have this *ngaitye.* It is regarded as the man's tutelary genius. It is some animal, bird, or insect. . . . . The natives are very strict in their marriage arrangements. A tribe [gens] is considered a family, and a man never marries into his own tribe."

Mr. Fison also writes, "that among the tribes of the Maranoa district, Queensland, whose dialect is called *Urghi,* according to information communicated to me by Mr. A. S. P. Cameron, the same classification exists as among the Kamilaroi-speaking tribes, both as to the class names and the totems." With respect to the Australians of the Darling River, upon information communicated by Mr. Charles G. N. Lockwood, he further remarks, that "they are subdivided into tribes (gentes), mentioning the Emu, Wild Duck, and Kangaroo, but without saying whether there are others, and that the children take both the class name and totem of the mother."[1]

From the existence of the gentile organization among the tribes named its general prevalence among the Australian aborigines is rendered probable; although the institution, as has elsewhere been pointed out, is in the incipient stages of its development.

Our information with respect to the domestic institutions of the inhabitants of Polynesia, Micronesia and the Papuan Islands is still limited and imperfect. No traces of the gentile organization have been discovered among the Hawaiians, Samoans, Marquesas Islanders or New Zealanders. Their system of consanguinity is still primitive, showing that their institutions have not advanced as far as this organization presupposes.[2] In some of the Micronesian Islands the office of chief is transmitted through females;[3] but this usage might exist independently of the gens. The Fijians are subdivided into several tribes speaking dialects of the same stock lan-

1 See also Taylor's "Early History of Mankind," p. 284.
2 "Systems of Consanguinity," etc., loc. cit., pp. 451, 482.
3 "Missionary Herald," 1853, p. 90.

guage. One of these, the Rewas, consists of four subdivisions under distinctive names, and each of these is again subdivided. It does not seem probable that the last subdivisions are gentes, for the reason, among others, that its members are allowed to intermarry. Descent is in the male line. In like manner the Tongans are composed of divisions, which are again subdivided the same as the Rewas.

Around the simple ideas relating to marriage and the family, to subsistence and to government, the earliest social organizations were formed; and with them an exposition of the structure and principle of ancient society must commence. Adopting the theory of a progressive development of mankind through the experience of the ages, the insulation of the inhabitants of Oceanica, their limited local areas, and their restricted means of subsistence predetermined a slow rate of progress. They still represent a condition of mankind on the continent of Asia in times immensely remote from the present; and while peculiarities, incident to their insulation, undoubtedly exist, these island societies represent one of the early phases of the great stream of human progress. An exposition of their institutions, inventions and discoveries, and mental and moral traits, would supply one of the great needs of anthropological science.

This concludes the discussion of the organization into gentes, and the range of its distribution. The organization has been found among the Australians and African Negroes, with traces of the system in other African tribes. It has been found generally prevalent among that portion of the American aborigines who when discovered were in the Lower Status of barbarism; and also among a portion of the Village Indians who were in the Middle Status of barbarism. In like manner it existed in full vitality among the Grecian and Latin tribes in the Upper Status of barbarism; with traces of it in several of the remaining branches of the Aryan family. The organization has been found, or traces of its existence, in the Turanian, Uralian and Mongolian families; in the Tungusian and Chinese stocks, and in the Semitic family among the Hebrews. Facts sufficiently numerous and commanding have been adduced to claim for it an ancient universality in the human family, as well as a general prevalence through the latter part of the period of savagery, and throughout the period of barbarism.

The investigation has also arrayed a sufficient body of facts to demonstrate that this remarkable institution was the origin and the basis of Ancient Society. It was the first organic principle, developed through experience, which was able to organize society upon a definite plan, and hold it in organic unity until it was sufficiently advanced for the transition into political society. Its antiquity, its substantial universality and its enduring vitality are sufficiently shown by its perpetuation upon all the continents to the present time. The wonderful adaptability of the gentile organization to the wants of mankind in these several periods and conditions is sufficiently attested by its prevalence and by its preservation. It has been identified with the most eventful portion of the experience of mankind.

Whether the gens originates spontaneously in a given condition of society, and would thus repeat itself in disconnected areas; or whether it had a single origin, and was propagated from an original center, through successive migrations, over the earth's surface, are fair questions for speculative consideration. The latter hypothesis, with a simple modification, seems to be the better one, for the following reasons: We find that two forms of marriage, and two forms of the family preceded the institution of the gens. It required a peculiar experience to attain to the second form of marriage and of the family, and to supplement this experience by the invention of the gens. This second form of the family was the final result, through natural selection, of the reduction within narrower limits of a stupendous conjugal system which enfolded savage man and held him with a powerful grasp. His final deliverance was too remarkable and too improbable, as it would seem, to be repeated many different times, and in widely separated areas. Groups of consanguinei, united for protection and subsistence, doubtless, existed from the infancy of the human family; but the gens is a very different body of kindred. It takes a part and excludes the remainder; it organized this part on the bond of kin, under a common name, and with common rights and privileges. Intermarriage in the gens was prohibited to secure the benefits of marrying out with unrelated persons. This was a vital principle of the organism as well as one most difficult of establishment. Instead of a natural and obvious conception, the gens was essentially abstruse; and, as such, a product of high intelligence for the times in which it originated. It required long periods of time, after the idea was developed into life, to bring it to maturity with its uses evolved. The Polynesians had this punaluan family, but failed of inventing the gens; the Australians had the same form of the family and possessed the gens. It originates in the punaluan family, and whatever tribes had attained to it possessed the elements out of which the gens was formed. This is the modification of the hypothesis suggested. In the prior organization, on the basis of sex, the germ of the gens existed. When the gens had become fully developed in its archaic form it would propagate itself over immense areas through the superior powers of an improved stock thus created. Its propagation is more easily explained than its institution. These considerations tend to show the improbability of its repeated reproduction in disconnected areas. On the other hand, its beneficial effects in producing a stock of savages superior to any then existing upon the earth must be admitted. When migrations were flights under the law of savage life, or movements in quest of better areas, such a stock would spread in wave after wave until it covered the larger part of the earth's surface. A consideration of the principal facts now ascertained bearing upon this question seems to favor the hypothesis of a single origin of the organization into gentes, unless we go back of this to the Australian classes, which gave the punaluan family out of which the gens originated, and regard these classes as the original basis of ancient society. In this event wherever the classes were established, the gens existed potentially.

Assuming the unity of origin of mankind, the occupation of the earth occurred through migrations from an original center. The Asiatic continent must then be regarded as the cradle-land of the species, from the greater number of original types of man it contains in comparison with Europe, Africa and America. It would also follow that the separation of the Negroes and Australians from the common stem occurred when society was organized on the basis of sex, and when the family was punaluan; that the Polynesian migration occurred later, but with society similarly constituted; and finally, that the Ganowánian migration to America occurred later still, and after the institution of the gentes. These inferences are put forward simply as suggestions.

A knowledge of the gens and its attributes, and of the range of its distribution, is absolutely necessary to a proper comprehension of Ancient Society. This is the great subject now requiring special and extended investigation. This society among the ancestors of civilized nations attained its highest development in the last days of barbarism. But there were phases of that same society far back in the anterior ages, which must now be sought among barbarians and savages in corresponding conditions. The idea of organized society has been a growth through the entire existence of the human race; its several phases are logically connected, the one giving birth to the other in succession, and that form of it we have been contemplating originated in the gens. No other institution of mankind has held such an ancient and remarkable relation to the course of human progress. The real history of mankind is contained in the history of the growth and development of institutions, of which the gens is but one. It is, however, the basis of those which have exercised the most material influence upon human affairs.

PART III

GROWTH OF THE IDEA OF THE FAMILY

INTRODUCTION TO PART III

GROWTH OF THE IDEA OF THE FAMILY

In Section III of *Ancient Society*, Morgan elaborated on the following premises: First, the family has undergone basic changes through the course of history, and in all likelihood will continue to do so. Second, the monogamous family could not become strong within the context of gentile social organization, for the married pair belonged to different gentes (477). Third, the monogamous family was based on private property (474-5, 477-8). Fourth, as a stage in the transition toward monogamy, there arose the patriarchal family with extreme male dominance and severe restrictions upon the social participation of women (474-5, 477-8, 484-5).

The stages of the family projected by Morgan were the "consanguine," as the first organized family, in which own and collateral brothers married own and collateral sisters as groups; the "punaluan," which introduced the restriction of marriage between own brothers and sisters; the "syndasmian," or "pairing marriage" of gentile society, with couples living in communal households; the patriarchal family of pastoral society, with a strong male head; and, finally, the monogamian family which insured paternity of the children and the exclusive inheritance of private property.

The consanguine and punaluan families were largely conjectural, and inferred from kin terms which group brothers with cousins, fathers with uncles, and so forth. However, as we have previously stated, kin terms cannot be used to reconstruct marriage relationships from times long past. They are not fossilized remains of ancient marriage relationships, but rather express ongoing, or recently functioning, relationships involving all manner of social and economic ties in addition to marriage.

If taken at all literally, group marriage as projected by Morgan would be complicated and cumbersome, and not in accord with the informality of relationships which obtains among hunting peoples. Among hunters and gatherers we find "loose" monogamy, with easy divorce and occasional polygamy. The sororate, the custom whereby a man who married the eldest daughter of a family "became entitled by custom to all her sisters as wives when they attained the marriageable age," was not the "remains of an ancient conjugal system" (441), as far as we understand gentile society, but an institutionalized way of repeating or strengthening existing relationships should a man's wife die, or should he take a second wife.

Morgan felt Hawaiian society gave evidence of "group marriage," since it lacked the gens, had kin categories that grouped all people of the same sex and generation level, and had not only polygyny (plural wives) and polyandry (plural husbands), but occasional brother-sister marriage (87, 418, 420-1, 423-4). However, far from being a simple society, Hawaii, like much of Polynesia, had a rich culture in which clan organization had been superseded by status groupings approaching a true class system, and where occasional brother-sister marriage was carried out to preserve the purity of the royal line, as in Ancient Egypt.[1] As for Australia, "marriage classes" did not define whom one *did* marry, but whom one *could* marry.

Morgan's proposal has difficulties even when it is interpreted loosely, not as a sequence of formal marriage systems, but as progressive steps in the limitation of in-marriage. Morgan felt the first step was the limitation of marriage across generation lines, but this does not conform to the lack of concern for relative ages of married couples which characterizes hunting-and-gathering peoples.

If the earliest stages in the history of the family hypothesized by Morgan do not follow from the evidence he presented, what are the alternatives? The prior question is: What particular conditions set certain types of active, curious, sociable, chattering primates clearly on the path toward conscious and cooperative group efforts to live and to reach out. Once this direction had been taken, there is no mystery about why loose pairing, with occasional polygamy, similar, though with less stability, to that

---

[1] For a description of Polynesian social structure, cf. Sahlins, Marshall P., *Social Stratification in Polynesia,* Publication of the American Ethnological Society, University of Washington Press, Seattle, 1958.

found among hunting peoples, would have become established. Whether the prior stage was random promiscuity like that obtaining among some monkey bands and envisaged by Morgan and others for man's subhuman primate ancestor (427, 507-9, 515) or closer to the polygamous family dominated by a strong male, and encircled with an uneasy periphery of unattached males, such as obtains among some higher primates, is not of real moment.[1] On the one hand, increasing stability of pairing, and on the other, less polygamy and a more equitable pairing off of all mature adults, would each increase the possibilities of cooperative work relations and enhance group security. Marrying "out" of the immediate group would serve the same purposes. In his review of explanations offered for incest taboos, Leslie White has elaborated on the function of marrying "out" in human society to build a wider network of cooperative relationships.[2]

Marian Slater carries the discussion of incest taboos back to the prior one of whence cooperation in the first place. Early hominids "did not mate out to form bonds of mutual aid or because of cultural prohibitions," she writes, "on the contrary, the cooperative bonds as well as the prohibitions must have been consequences of their having already mated out because of structural necessity." [3] Due to the long period of sexual immaturity among hominids, in relation to their total life expectancy, mates would not be available in the immediate family, and marrying "out" would set them on the path of inter-family cooperation. One can then take up the next question: Why the long period of sexual immaturity? In any case, the point is that

---

[1] The data on the social life of primates that have been amassed reveal great variability in mating patterns. More important, they indicate that not a mere transition, but a qualitative change, introduced some primate form to a cultural career when cooperativeness replaced competitiveness. Cf. Sahlins, Marshall D., "The Social Life of Monkeys, Apes and Primitive Man," in *The Evolution of Man's Capacity for Culture,* arranged by J. N. Spuhler, Wayne State University Press, Detroit, 1959. The essays in this recent book are valuable summaries of the latest thinking among anthropologists on the subject of early social and biological evolution, although they are somewhat technical presentations. For another recent book bringing together the work of scholars concerned with this topic, cf. Washburn, Sherwood L., editor, *Social Life of Early Man,* Aldine Publishing Company, Chicago, 1962.

[2] White, Leslie A., "The Definition and Prohibition of Incest," in *The Science of Culture,* Farrar, Straus and Company, New York, 1949.

[3] Slater, Marian Kreiselman, "Ecological Factors in the Origin of Incest," *American Anthropologist,* Vol. 61, No. 6, December, 1959.

the cultural sanction against father-daughter, mother-son, and brother-sister marriage is the result, not the cause, for limitation of inbreeding. Practices resulting from commonly repeated necessities—however they may finally be conceived—gradually become culturally reinforced. They become transformed from what one *does* to what one *ought* to do, as primate social structure evolves into the consciously recognized and sanctioned network of relationships we know as human society.

To propose loose monogamy (with occasional polygamy) as having always been found among hunting peoples could mean to accept a commonly held view that the monogamous family is universal as the basic unit of society, that variations from culture to culture are relatively superficial, that, in short, there have not been qualitatively different forms of the family in human history. This view, however, is erroneous. Unfortunately, the use of the term "monogamy" for a marrying pair obscures the fact that the relation of the pair to the rest of society may be entirely different from one type of society to another. Among hunting peoples, the married pair and their children are in no sense the basic unit of society as they are in contemporary class-structured society. The band, not the family, is the collective, whether several families share a tipi or other dwelling, or whether the camp is a series of small lean-to's, wickiups, or other such simple shelters. Care and responsibility for the young, the old, and the infirm is not an individual matter, but social, the concern of the entire group, in a direct and unquestioned fashion.[1] The cumbersome and inadequate "social service" machinery set up in contemporary societies, the use of which places one outside the pale of the "solid citizenry," is no parallel.

With the "syndasmian" or "pairing" family of gentile society, as described by Morgan for the American Indians (462-6), a new factor enters into the marriage relationship. The marriage tie unites two gentes in a patterned network of reciprocal duties and responsibilities, and, while separation is still possible at the desire of either partner, there is an attempt on the part of their kindred to hold the union together. The lineage ties of the gens,

---

1 The practice of sometimes leaving the elders to die when a hunting group is faced by famine is the tragic side of the same social responsibility where life is so closely dependent on the vagaries of nature. The recourse of being left behind by the band in its desperate search for food is usually chosen by the elders themselves as necessary for the survival of the group.

however, and not husband-wife ties, are primary. It is the gens which takes final responsibility for its members. The security of the child is not impaired by divorce; nor do the old fear becoming partial outcasts as they do in a society built around young and active married pairs. Rather they become the revered and respected elders of the gens and tribe, supported without question by the gifts and services of their kindred.

Morgan's detailed description of the inroads upon the gens by political organization on the one hand, and the individual family on the other, subsequent to the development of private property, can and has been reinforced and enriched by all manner of ethnographic and ethnohistorical data from around the world. However, his sharp differentiation between the patriarchal family and the monogamian family calls for comment. Morgan wrote that the patriarchal family required "but a brief notice" (474) since "from its limited prevalence it made but little impression upon human affairs" (409; cf. also 511). The patriarchal family, however, was, and to some extent still is, found throughout the centers of early civilization, from the Mediterranean through the Near East into India and China. Morgan himself described its existence in Greece, and in Rome where "paternal authority passed beyond the bounds of reason into an excess of domination" (475). He stated that it was "the incorporation of numbers in servile and dependent relations, before that time unknown, rather than polygamy, that stamped the patriarchal family with the attributes of an original institution" (474). In *The Origin of the Family, Private Property and the State,* Engels expanded upon this aspect of the patriarchal family, pointing out that the monogamous family was monogamous in name only, and that features of the patriarchal family persist in all manner of social and legal inequalities between the sexes. Morgan too stressed that the inequalities which arose with private property had by no means disappeared, and it was with respect to social equality of the sexes that he felt the family would continue to evolve (481-2, 487, 499). Thus, if the focus is on polygamy and outright domination of women, the patriarchal and monogamous family must be differentiated, whereas if the focus is on the family as the basic unit of society, with male dominance either direct or attenuated, the patriarchal and monogamous fall into the same category as the form that replaced the pairing family of gentile society after the advent of "civilization."

In an extended note (516-31) Morgan responded to McLennan's criticism of *Systems of Consanguinity and Affinity of the Human Family*. To McLennan, early man lived in exogamous but hostile groups, where baby girls who would weaken the group were killed. Hence, he practiced polyandry, with several men sharing a wife, often relied on bride-capture, and recognized kin through the female only. McLennan cited as evidence widespread exogamous practices, instances of polyandry, and supposed survivals of earlier practices like ritual bride-capture and the levirate (whereby a man marries his dead brother's widow). He introduced the terms endogamy and exogamy into anthropological usage, although, as Morgan pointed out, they do not characterize total societies, but different aspects of social organization. "The gens is 'exogamous,' and the tribe is essentially 'endogamous' " (520). Morgan rightly asserted that there are no grounds for considering polyandry ever to have been a widespread system (525), and that in discussing kinship systems one must differentiate between "descent in the female line," and "kinship through females only" (524). To belong to one's mother's descent group does not mean one does not recognize kin on the father's side.

To McLennan, kin terms were "modes of addressing persons." To Morgan this was too trivial a concept. ". . . a system of consanguinity is a very different thing. Its relationships spring from the family and the marriage-law, and possess even greater permanence than the family itself. . . . These relationships expressed the actual facts of the social condition when the system was formed, and have had a daily importance in the life of mankind" (527). Yet McLennan was moving toward the idea of *social* relations, and his concept, "modes of address," was in all fairness somewhat broader than the phrase implies. McLennan was arguing that kin terms expressed more than *biological* relationships, and, ironically, in his rebuttal Morgan is led to make a more complete statement on the significance of kin terms than is found elsewhere in *Ancient Society*.

Morgan constantly gave due credit to the contributions of primitive man and referred to the shortcomings of our own civilization. Nonetheless, as we have already said, he occasionally allowed an ethnocentric and moralistic note to enter his analysis. He spoke of the "abyss of primitive savagery" (499), and wrote that slavery "betrays the savage origin of mankind" for it showed the "cruelty inherent in the heart of man, which civilization and Christianity have softened without eradicating" (512). Yet, as Morgan himself pointed out, slavery could not and did not exist in savage society.

Morgan's discussion of Hawaii illustrates the positive as well as the negative aspects of his attitude toward other cultures. He quoted the missionaries who thought they had discovered "the lowest level of human degradation, not to say of depravity." But, he wrote:

> the innocent Hawaiians, who had not been able to advance themselves out of savagery, were living, no doubt respectably and modestly for savages . . . as virtuously in their faithful observance, as these excellent missionaries were in the performance of their own. The shock the latter experienced from their discoveries expresses the profoundness of the expanse which separates civilized from savage man. The high moral sense and refined sensibilities, which had been a growth of the ages, were brought face to face with the feeble moral sense and the coarse sensibilities of a savage man of all these periods ago. . . . (423)

He continued, "the existence of morality, even among savages, must be recognized, although low in type; for there never could have been a time in human experience when the principle of morality did not exist" (424).

Thus, Morgan attempted to assess the morality of a people in terms of their own culture, a long and important step away from ethnocentricity, and one that opens up the possibility of real respect for others. However, he failed to place his own culture under the same scrutiny as others in taking our "high moral sense and refined sensibilities" at face value without regard for the brutal realities of our own social life.

Morgan made the mistake which is still rife today, although far less excusable, given our immeasurably greater knowledge of other lifeways. We constantly compare the lofty moral statements our culture supposedly aspires to, not with the comparably beautiful and humanistic statements of primitive philosophers and poets, but with the daily realities of life in what are often unjust and demoralized situations. The essence of the anthropologist's argument for a "culturally relativistic" point of view is not that we cannot evaluate different social practices in relation to a pan-cultural humanistic ideal, for such an ideal can be based both on philosophy and on social necessity. It

IIviii

is that we must not use a different yardstick to measure our own culture than that we employ for others. We all too often forget that our professed ideals exist in the context of a society that is responsible for the greatest and the most massive brutalities mankind has ever perpetrated on his fellow man, and this in the context of a technology so far advanced that no one need be forgotten.

CHAPTER I

THE ANCIENT FAMILY

We have been accustomed to regard the monogamian family as the form which has always existed; but interrupted in exceptional areas by the patriarchal. Instead of this, the idea of the family has been a growth through successive stages of development, the monogamian being the last in its series of forms. It will be my object to show that it was preceded by more ancient forms which prevailed universally throughout the period of savagery, through the Older and into the Middle Period of barbarism; and that neither the monogamian nor the patriarchal can be traced back of the Later Period of barbarism. They were essentially modern. Moreover, they were impossible in ancient society, until an anterior experience under earlier forms in every race of mankind had prepared the way for their introduction.

Five different and successive forms may now be distinguished, each having an institution of marriage peculiar to itself. They are the following:

I. *The Consanguine Family.*

It was founded upon the intermarriage of brothers and sisters, own and collateral, in a group.

II. *The Punaluan Family.*

It was founded upon the intermarriage of several sisters, own and collateral, with each other's husbands, in a group; the joint husbands not being necessarily kinsmen of each other. Also, on the intermarriage of several brothers, own and collateral, with each other's wives, in a group; these wives not being necessarily of kin to each other, although often the case in both instances. In each case the group of men were conjointly married to the group of women.

III. *The Syndyasmian or Pairing Family.*

It was founded upon marriage between single pairs, but without an exclusive cohabitation. The marriage continued during the pleasure of the parties.

IV. *The Patriarchal Family.*

It was founded upon the marriage of one man with several wives; followed, in general, by the seclusion of the wives.

V. *The Monogamian Family.*

It was founded upon marriage between single pairs, with an exclusive cohabitation.

Three of these forms, namely, the first, second, and fifth, were radical; because they were sufficiently general and influential to create three distinct systems of consanguinity, all of which still exist in living forms. Conversely, these systems are sufficient of themselves to prove the antecedent existence of the forms of the family and of marriage, with which they severally stand connected. The remaining two, the syndyasmian and the patriarchal, were intermediate, and not sufficiently influential upon human affairs to create a new, or modify essentially the then existing system of consanguinity. It will not be supposed that these types of the family are separated from each other by sharply defined lines; on the contrary, the first passes into the second, the second into the third, and the third into the fifth by insensible gradations. The propositions to be elucidated and established are, that they have sprung successively one from the other, and that they represent collectively the growth of the idea of the family.

In order to explain the rise of these several forms of the family and of marriage, it will be necessary to present the substance of the system of consanguinity and affinity which pertains to each. These systems embody compendious and decisive evidence, free from all suspicion of design, bearing directly upon the question. Moreover, they speak with an authority and certainty which leave no room to doubt the inferences therefrom. But a system of consanguinity is intricate and perplexing until it is brought into familiarity. It will tax the reader's patience to look into the subject far enough to be able to test the value and weight of the evidence it contains. Having treated at length, in a previous work, the "Systems of Consanguinity and Affinity of the Human Family,"[1] I shall confine the statements herein to the material facts, reduced to the lowest number consistent with intelligibility, making reference to the other work for fuller details, and for the general Tables. The importance of the main proposition as a part of the history of man, namely, that the family has been a growth through several successive forms, is a commanding reason for the presentation and study of these systems, if they can in truth establish the fact. It will require this and the four succeeding chapters to make a brief general exhibition of the proof.

The most primitive system of consanguinity yet discovered is found among the Polynesians, of which the Hawaiian will be used as typical. I have called it the Malayan system. Under it all consanguinei, near and remote, fall within some one of the following relationships; namely, parent, child, grandparent, grandchild, brother, and sister. No other blood relationships are recognized. Beside these are the marriage relationships. This system of consanguinity came in with the first form of the family, the consanguine, and contains the principal evidence of its ancient existence. It may seem a narrow basis for so important an inference; but if we are justified in assuming that each relationship as recognized was the one which actually existed, the inference is fully sustained. This system prevailed very generally in Polynesia, although the family among them had passed out of the consanguine into the punaluan. It remained unchanged because no motive sufficiently strong, and no alteration of institutions sufficiently radical had occurred to produce its modification. Intermarriage between broth-

1 "Smithsonian Contributions to Knowledge," vol. xvii.

ers and sisters had not entirely disappeared from the Sandwich Island when the American missions, about fifty years ago, were established among them. Of the ancient general prevalence of this system of consanguinity over Asia there can be no doubt, because it is the basis of the Turanian system still prevalent in Asia. It also underlies the Chinese.

In course of time, a second great system of consanguinity, the Turanian, supervened upon the first, and spread over a large part of the earth's surface. It was universal among the North American aborigines, and has been traced sufficiently among those of South America to render probable its equally universal prevalence among them. Traces of it have been found in parts of Africa; but the system of the African tribes in general approaches nearer the Malayan. It still prevails in South India among the Hindus who speak dialects of the Dravidian language, and also, in a modified form, in North India, among the Hindus who speak dialects of the Gaura language. It also prevails in Australia in a partially developed state, where it seems to have originated either in the organization into classes, or in the incipient organization into gentes, which led to the same result. In the principal tribes of the Turanian and Ganowánian families, it owes its origin to punaluan marriage in the group and to the gentile organization, the latter of which tended to repress consanguine marriages. It has been shown how this was accomplished by the prohibition of intermarriage in the gens, which permanently excluded own brothers and sisters from the marriage relation. When the Turanian system of consanguinity came in the form of the family was punaluan. This is proven by the fact that punaluan marriage in the group explains the principal relationships under the system; showing them to be those which would actually exist in virtue of this form of marriage. Through the logic of the facts we are enabled to show that the punaluan family was once as wide-spread as the Turanian system of consanguinity. To the organization into gentes and the punaluan family, the Turanian system of consanguinity must be ascribed. It will be seen in the sequel that this system was formed out of the Malayan, by changing those relationships only which resulted from the previous intermarriage of brothers and sisters, own and collateral, and which were, in fact, changed by the gentes; thus proving the direct connection between them. The powerful influence of the gentile organization upon society, and particularly upon the punaluan group, is demonstrated by this change of systems.

The Turanian system is simply stupendous. It recognizes all the relationships known under the Aryan system, besides an additional number unnoticed by the latter. Consanguinei, near and remote, are classified into categories; and are traced, by means peculiar to the system, far beyond the ordinary range of the Aryan system. In familiar and in formal salutation, the people address each other by the term of relationship, and never by the personal name, which tends to spread abroad a knowledge of the system as well as to preserve, by constant recognition, the relationship of the most distant kindred. Where no relationship exists, the form of saluation is simply "my friend." No other system of consanguinity found among men approaches it in elaborateness of discrimination or in the extent of special characteristics.

When the American aborigines were discovered, the family among them had passed out of the punaluan into the sydyasmian form; so that the relationships recognized by the system of consanguinity were not those, in a number of cases, which actually existed in the syndyasmian family. It was an exact repetition of what had occurred under the Malayan system, where the family had passed out of the consanguine into the punaluan, the system of consanguinity remaining unchanged; so that while the relationships given in the Malayan system were those which actually existed in the consanguine family, they were untrue to a part of those in the punaluan family. In like manner, while the relationships given in the Turanian system are those which actually existed in the punaluan family, they were untrue to a part of those in the syndyasmian. The form of the family advances faster of necessity than systems of consanguinity, which follow to record the family relationships. As the establishment of the punaluan family did not furnish adequate motives to reform the Malayan system, so the growth of the syndyasmian family did not supply adequate motives to reform the Turanian. It required an institution as great as the gentile organization to change the Malayan system into the Turanian; and it required an institution as great as property in the concrete, with its rights of ownership and of inheritance, together with the monogamian family which it created, to overthrow the Turanian system of consanguinity and substitute the Aryan.

In further course of time a third great system of consanguinity came in, which may be called, at pleasure, the Aryan, Semitic, or Uralian, and probably superseded a prior Turanian system among the principal nations, who afterwards attained civilization. It is the system which defines the relationships in the monogamian family. This system was not based upon the Turanian, as the latter was upon the Malayan; but it superseded among civilized nations a previous Turanian system, as can be shown by other proofs.

The last four forms of the family have existed within the historical period; but the first, the consanguine, has disappeared. Its ancient existence, however, can be deduced from the Malayan system of consanguinity. We have then three radical forms of the family, which represent three great and essentially different conditions of life, with three different and well-marked systems of consanguinity, sufficient to prove the existence of these families, if they contained the only proofs remaining. This affirmation will serve to draw attention to the singular permanence and persistency of systems of consanguinity, and to the value of the evidence they embody with respect to the condition of ancient society.

Each of these families ran a long course in the tribes of mankind, with a period of infancy, of maturity, and of decadence. The monogamian family owes its origin to property, as the syndyasmian, which contained its germ, owed its origin to the gens. When the Grecian tribes first came under historical notice, the monogamian family existed; but it did not become completely established until positive legislation had determined its status and its rights. The growth of the idea of property in the human mind, through its creation and enjoyment, and especially through the settlement of legal rights with respect to its inheritance, are intimately connected with the establishment of this form of the family. Property became sufficiently powerful in its influence to touch the organic structure of society. Certainty with respect to the paternity of children would now have a significance unknown in previous conditions. Marriage between single pairs had existed from the Older Period of barbarism, under the form of pairing during the pleasure of the parties. It had tended to grow more stable as ancient society advanced, with the improvement of institutions, and with the progress of inventions and discoveries into higher successive conditions; but the essential element of the monogamian family, an exclusive cohabitation, was still wanting. Man far back in barbarism began to exact fidelity from the wife, under savage penalties, but he claimed exemption for himself. The obligation is necessarily reciprocal, and its performance correlative. Among the Homeric Greeks, the condition of woman in the family relation was one of isolation and marital domination, with imperfect rights and excessive inequality. A comparison of the Grecian family, at successive epochs, from the Homeric age to that of Pericles, shows a sensible improvement, with its gradual settlement into a defined institution. The modern family is an unquestionable improvement upon that of the Greeks and Romans; because woman has gained immensely in social position. From standing in the relation of a daughter to her husband, as among the Greeks and Romans, she has drawn nearer to an equality in dignity and in acknowledged personal rights. We have a record of the monogamian family, running back nearly three thousand years, during which, it may be claimed, there has been a gradual but continuous improvement in its character. It is destined to progress still further, until the equality of the sexes is acknowledged, and the equities of the marriage relation are completely recognized. We have similar evidence, though not so perfect, of the progressive improvement of the syndyasmian family, which, commencing in a low type, ended in the monogamian. These facts should be held in remembrance, because they are essential in this discussion.

In previous chapters attention has been called to the stupendous conjugal system which fastened itself upon mankind in the infancy of their existence, and followed them down to civilization; although steadily losing ground with the progressive improvement of society. The ratio of human progress may be measured to some extent by the degree of the reduction of this system through the moral elements of society arrayed against it. Each successive form of the family and of marriage is a significant registration of this reduction. After it was reduced to zero, and not until then, was the monogamian family possible. This family can be traced far back in the Later Period of barbarism, where it disappears in the syndyasmian.

Some impression is thus gained of the ages which elapsed while these two forms of the family were running their courses of growth and development. But the creation of five successive forms of the family, each differing from the other, and belonging to conditions of society entirely dissimilar, augments our conception of the length of the periods during which the idea of the family was developed from the consanguine, through intermediate forms, into the still advancing monogamian. No institution of mankind has had a more remarkable or more eventful history, or embodies the results of a more prolonged and diversified experience. It required the highest mental and moral efforts through numberless ages of time to maintain its existence and carry it through its several stages into its present form.

Marriage passed from the punaluan through the syndyasmian into the monogamian form without any material change in the Turanian system of consanguinity. This system, which records the relationships in punaluan families, remained substantially unchanged until the establishment of the monogamian family, when it became almost totally untrue to the nature of descents, and even a scandal upon monogamy. To illustrate: Under the Malayan system a man calls his brother's son his son, because his brother's wife is his wife as well as his brother's; and his sister's son is also his son because his sister is his wife. Under the Turanian system his brother's son is still his son, and for the same reason, but his sister's son is now his nephew, because under the gentile organization his sister has ceased to be his wife. Among the Iroquois, where the family is syndyasmian, a man still calls his brother's son his son, although his brother's wife has ceased to be his wife; and so with a large number of relationships equally inconsistent with the existing form of marriage. The system has survived the usages in which it originated, and still maintains itself among them, although untrue in the main, to descents as they now exist. No motive adequate to the overthrow of a great and ancient system of consanguinity had arisen. Monogamy when it appeared furnished that motive to the Aryan nations as they drew near to civilization. It assured the paternity of children and the legitimacy of heirs. A reformation of the Turanian system to accord with monogamian descents was impossible. It was false to monogamy through and through. A remedy, however, existed, at once simple and complete. The Turanian system was dropped, and the descriptive method, which the Turanian tribes always employed when they wished to make a given relationship specific, was substituted in its place. They fell back upon the bare facts of consanguinity and described the relationship of each person by a combination of the primary terms. Thus, they said brother's son, brother's grandson; father's brother, and father's brother's son. Each phrase described a person, leaving the relationship a matter of implication. Such was the system of the Aryan nations, as we find it in its most ancient form among the Grecian, Latin, Sanskritic, Germanic, and Celtic tribes; and also in the Semitic, as witness the Hebrew Scripture genealogies. Traces of the Turanian system, some of which have been referred to, remained among the Aryan and Semitic nations down to the historical period; but it was essentially uprooted, and the descriptive system substituted in its place.

To illustrate and confirm these several propositions it will be necessary to take up, in the order of their origination, these three systems and the three radical forms of the family, which appeared in connection with them respectively. They mutually interpret each other.

A system of consanguinity considered in itself is of but little importance. Limited in the number of ideas it embodies, and resting apparently upon simple suggestions, it would seem incapable of affording useful information, and much less of throwing light upon the early condition of mankind. Such, at least, would be the natural conclusion when the relationships of a group of kindred are considered in the abstract. But when the system of many tribes is compared, and it is seen to rank as a domestic institution, and to have transmitted itself through immensely protracted periods of time, it assumes a very different aspect. Three such systems, one succeeding the other, represent the entire growth of the family from the consanguine to the monogamian. Since we have a right to suppose that each one expresses the actual relationships which existed in the family at the time of its establishment, it reveals, in turn, the form of marriage and of the family which then prevailed, although both may have advanced into a higher stage while the system of consanguinity remained unchanged.

It will be noticed, further, that these systems are natural growths with the progress of society from a lower into a higher condition, the change in each case being marked by the appearance of some institution affecting deeply the constitution of society. The relationship of mother and child, of brother and sister, and of grandmother and grandchild has been ascertainable in all ages with entire certainty; but those of father and child, and of grandfather and grandchild were not ascertainable with certainty until monogamy contributed the highest assurance attainable. A number of persons would stand in each of these relations at the same time as equally probable when marriage was in the group. In the rudest conditions of ancient society these relationships would be perceived, both the actual and the probable, and terms would be invented to express them. A system of consanguinity would result in time from the continued application of these terms to persons thus formed into a group of kindred. But the form of the system, as before stated, would depend upon the form of marriage. Where marriages were between brothers and sisters, own and collateral, in the group, the family would be consanguine, and the system of consanguinity Malayan. Where marriages were between several sisters with each other's husbands in a group, and between several brothers with each other's wives in a group, the family would be punaluan, and the system of consanguinity Turanian; and where marriage was between single pairs, with an exclusive cohabitation, the family would be monogamian, and the system of consanguinity would be Aryan. Consequently the three systems are founded upon three forms of marriage; and they seek to express, as near as the fact could be known, the actual relationship which existed between persons under these forms of marriage respectively. It will be seen, therefore, that they do not rest upon nature, but upon marriage; not upon fictitious considerations, but upon fact; and that each in its turn is a logical as well as truthful system. The evidence they contain is of the highest value, as well as of the most suggestive character. It reveals the condition of ancient society in the plainest manner with unerring directness.

These systems resolve themselves into two ultimate forms, fundamentally distinct. One of these is *classificatory,* and the other *descriptive.* Under the first, consanguinei are never described, but are classified into categories, irrespective of their nearness or remoteness in degree to *Ego;* and the same term of relationship is applied to all the persons in the same category. Thus my own brothers, and the sons of my father's brothers are all alike my brothers; my own sisters, and the daughters of my mother's sisters are all alike my sisters; such is the classification under both the Malayan and Turanian systems. In the second case consanguinei are described either by the primary terms of relationship or a combination of these terms, thus making the relationship of each person specific. Thus we say brother's son, father's brother, and father's brother's son. Such was the system of the Aryan, Semitic, and Uralian families, which came in with monogamy. A small amount of classification was subsequently introduced by the invention of common terms; but the earliest form of the system, of which the Erse and Scandinavian are typical, was purely descriptive, as illustrated by the above examples. The radical difference between the two systems resulted from plural marriages in the group in one case, and from single marriages between single pairs in the other.

While the descriptive system is the same in the Aryan, Semitic, and Uralian families, the classificatory has two distinct forms. First, the Malayan, which is the oldest in point of time; and second, the Turanian and Ganowánian, which are essentially alike and were formed by the modification of a previous Malayan system.

A brief reference to our own system of consanguinity will bring into notice the principles which underlie all systems.

Relationships are of two kinds: First, by consanguinity or blood; second, by affinity or marriage. Consanguinity is also of two kinds, lineal and collateral. Lineal consanguinity is the connection which subsists among persons of whom one is descended from the other. Collateral consanguinity is the connection which exists between persons who are descended from common ancestors, but not from each other. Marriage relationships exist by custom.

Not to enter too specially into the subject, it may be stated generally that in every system of consanguinity, where marriage between single pairs exists, there must be a lineal and several collateral lines, the latter diverging from the former. Each person is the centre of a group of kindred, the *Ego* from whom the degree of relationship of each person is reckoned, and to whom the relationship returns. His position is necessarily in the lineal line, and that line is vertical. Upon it may be inscribed, above and below him, his several ancestors and descendants in a direct series from father to son, and these persons together will constitute his right lineal male line. Out of this trunk line emerge the several collateral lines, male and female, which are numbered outwardly. It will be sufficient for a perfect knowledge of the system to recognize the main lineal line, and a single male and female branch of the first five collateral lines, including those on the father's side, and on the mother's side, and proceeding in each case from the parent to one only of his or her children, although it will include but a small portion of the kindred of *Ego,* either in the ascending or descending series. An attempt to follow all the divisions and branches of the several collateral lines, which increase in number in the ascending series in a geometrical ratio, would not render the system more intelligible.

The first collateral line, male, consists of my brother and his descendants; and the first, female, of my sister and her descendants. The second collateral line, male, on the father's side, consists of my father's brother and his descendants; and the second, female, of my father's sister and her descendants: the second, male, on the mother's side, is composed of my mother's brother and his descendants; and the second, female, of my mother's sister and her descendants. The third collateral line, male, on the father's side, consists of my grandfather's brother and his descendants; and the third, female, of my grandfather's sister and her descendants; on the mother's side the same line, in its male and female branches, is composed of my grandmother's brother and sister and their descendants respectively. It will be noticed, in the last case, that we have turned out of the lineal line on the father's side into that on the mother's side. The fourth collateral line, male and female, commences with great-grandfather's brother and sister: and great-grandmother's brother and sister: and the fifth collateral line, male and female, with great-great-grandfather's brother and sister; and with great-great-grandmother's brother and sister, and each line and branch is run out in the same manner as the third. These five lines, with the lineal, embrace the great body of our kindred, who are within the range of practical recognition.

An additional explanation of these several lines is required. If I have several brothers and sisters, they, with their descendants, constitute as many lines, each independent of the other, as I have brothers and sisters; but altogether they form my first collateral line in two branches, a male and a female. In like manner, the several brothers and sisters of my father, and of my mother, with their respective descendants, make up as many lines, each independent of the other, as there are brothers and sisters; but they all unite to form the second collateral line in two divisions, that on the father's side, and that on the mother's side; and in four principal branches, two male, and two female. If the third collateral line were run out fully, in its several branches, it would give four general divisions of ancestors, and eight principal branches; and the number of each would increase in the same ratio in each successive collateral line.

With such a mass of divisions and branches, embracing such a multitude of consanguinei, it will be seen at once that a method of arrangement and of description which maintained each distinct and rendered the whole intelligible would be no ordinary achievement. This task was perfectly accomplished by the Roman civilians, whose method has been adopted by the principal European nations, and is so entirely simple as to elicit admiration.[1] The development of the nomenclature to the requisite extent must have been so extremely difficult that it would probably never have occurred except under the stimulus of an urgent necessity, namely, the need of a code of descents to regulate the inheritance of property.

To render the new form attainable, it was necessary to discriminate the relationships of uncle and aunt on the father's side and on the mother's side by concrete terms,

---

1 "Pandects," lib. xxxviii, title x. De gradibus, et ad finibus et nominibus eorum: and "Institutes of Justinian," lib. iii, title vi. De gradibus cognationem.

an achievement made in a few only of the languages of mankind. These terms finally appeared among the Romans in *patruus* and *amita,* for uncle and aunt on the father's side, and in *avunculus* and *matertera* for the same on the mother's side. After these were invented, the improved Roman method of describing consanguinei became established.[1] It has been adopted, in its essential features, by the several branches of the Aryan family, with the exception of the Erse, the Scandinavian, and the Slavonic.

The Aryan system necessarily took the descriptive form when the Turanian was abandoned, as in the Erse. Every relationship in the lineal and first five collateral lines, to the number of one hundred and more, stands independent, requiring as many descriptive phases, or the gradual invention of common terms.

It will be noticed that the two radical forms—the classificatory and descriptive—yield nearly the exact line of demarkation between the barbarous and civilized nations. Such a result might have been predicted from the law of progress revealed by these several forms of marriage and of the family.

Systems of consanguinity are neither adopted, modified, nor laid aside at pleasure. They are identified in their origin with organic movements of society which produced a great change of condition. When a particular form had come into general use, with its nomenclature invented and its methods settled, it would, from the nature of the case, be very slow to change. Every human being is the centre of a group of kindred, and therefore every person is compelled to use and to understand the prevailing system. A change in any one of these relationships would be extremely difficult. This tendency to permanence is increased by the fact that these systems exist by custom rather than legal enactment, as growths rather than artificial creations, and therefore a motive to change

1 Our term aunt is from 'amita," and uncle from "avunculus. "Avus," grandfather, gives "avunculus" by adding the diminutive. It therefore signifies a "little grandfather." "Matertera" is supposed to be derived from "mater" and "altera," equal to another mother.

must be as universal as the usage. While every person is a party to the system, the channel of its transmission is the blood. Powerful influences thus existed to perpetuate the system long after the conditions under which each originated had been modified or had altogether disappeared. This element of permanence gives certainty to conclusions drawn from the facts, and has preserved and brought forward a record of ancient society which otherwise would have been entirely lost to human knowledge.

It will not be supposed that a system so elaborate as the Turanian could be maintained in different nations and families of mankind in absolute identicalness. Divergence in minor particulars is found, but the radical features are, in the main, constant. The system of consanguinity of the Tamil people, of South India, and that of the Seneca-Iroquois, of New York, are still identical through two hundred relationships; an application of natural logic to the facts of the social condition without a parallel in the history of the human mind. There is also a modified form of the system, which stands alone and tells its own story. It is that of the Hindi, Bengali, Marâthi, and other people of North India, formed by a combination of the Aryan and Turanian systems. A civilized people, the Brahmins, coalesced with a barbarous stock, and lost their language in the new vernaculars named, which retain the grammatical structure of the aboriginal speech, to which the Sanskrit gave ninety per cent of its vocables. It brought their two systems of consanguinity into collision, one founded upon monogamy or syndyasmy, and the other upon plural marriages in the group, resulting in a mixed system. The aborigines, who preponderated in number, impressed upon it a Turanian character, while the Sanskrit element introduced such modifications as saved the monogamian family from reproach. The Slavonic stock seems to have been derived from this intermixture of races. A system of consanguinity which exhibits but two phases through the periods of savagery and of barbarism and projects a third but modified form far into the period of civilization, manifests an element of permanence calculated to arrest attention.

It will not be necessary to consider the patriarchal family founded upon polygamy. From its limited prevalence it made but little impression upon human affairs.

The house life of savages and barbarians has not been studied with the attention the subject deserves. Among the Indian tribes of North America the family was syndyasmian; but they lived generally in joint-tenement houses and practiced communism within the household. As we descend the scale in the direction of the punaluan and consanguine families, the household group becomes larger, with more persons crowded together in the same apartment. The coast tribes in Venezuela, among whom the family seems to have been punaluan, are represented by the discoverers as living in bell-shaped houses, each containing a hundred and sixty persons. [1] Husbands and wives lived together in a group in the same house, and generally in the same apartment. The inference is reasonable that this mode of house life was very general in savagery.

An explanation of the origin of these systems of consanguinity and affinity will be offered in succeeding chapters. They will be grounded upon the forms of marriage and of the family which produced them, the existence of these forms being assumed. If a satisfactory explanation of each system is thus obtained, the antecedent existence of each form of marriage and of the family may be deduced from the system it explains. In a final chapter an attempt will be made to articulate in a sequence the principal institutions which have contributed to the growth of the family through successive forms. Our knowledge of the early condition of mankind is still so limited that we must take the best indications attainable. The sequence to be presented is, in part, hypothetical; but it is sustained by a sufficient body of evidence to commend it to consideration. Its complete establishment must be left to the results of future ethnological investigations.

---

1 Herrera's "History of America," i, 216. 218, 348.

CHAPTER II

THE CONSANGUINE FAMILY

The existence of the Consanguine family must be proved by other evidence than the production of the family itself. As the first and most ancient form of the institution, it has ceased to exist even among the lowest tribes of savages. It belongs to a condition of society out of which the least advanced portion of the human race have emerged. Single instances of the marriage of a brother and sister in barbarous and even in civilized nations have occurred within the historical period; but this is very different from the inter-marriage of a number of them in a group, in a state of society in which such marriages predominated and formed the basis of a social system. There are tribes of savages in the Polynesian and Papuan Islands, and in Australia, seemingly not far removed from the primitive state; but they have advanced beyond the condition the consanguine family implies. Where, then, it may be asked, is the evidence that such a family ever existed among mankind? Whatever proof is adduced must be conclusive, otherwise the proposition is not established. It is found in a system of consanguinity and affinity which has outlived for unnumbered centuries the marriage customs in which it originated, and which remains to attest the fact that such a family existed when the system was formed.

That system is the Malayan. It defines the relationships that would exist in a consanguine family; and it demands the existence of such a family to account for its own existence. Moreover, it proves with moral certainty the existence of a consanguine family when the system was formed.

This system, which is the most archaic yet discovered, will now be taken up for the purpose of showing, from its relationships, the principal facts stated. This family, also, is the most archaic form of the institution of which any knowledge remains.

Such a remarkable record of the condition of ancient society would not have been preserved to the present time but for the singular permanence of systems of consanguinity. The Aryan system, for example, has stood near three thousand years without radical change, and would endure a hundred thousand years in the future, provided the monogamian family, whose relationships it defines, should so long remain. It describes the relationships which actually exist under monogamy, and is therefore incapable of change, so long as the family remains as at present constituted. If a new form of the family should appear among Aryan nations, it would not affect the present system of consanguinity until after it became universal; and while in that case it might modify the system in some particulars, it would not overthrow it, unless the new family were radically different from the monogamian. It was precisely the same with its immediate predecessor, the Turanian system, and before that with the Malayan, the predecessor of the Turanian in the order of derivative growth. An antiquity of unknown duration may be assigned to the Malayan system which came in with the consanguine family, remained for an indefinite period after the punaluan family appeared, and seems to have been displaced in other tribes by the Turanian, with the establishment of the organization into gentes.

The inhabitants of Polynesia are included in the Malayan family. Their system of consanguinity has been called the Malayan, although the Malays proper have modified their own in some particulars. Among the Hawaiians and other Polynesian tribes there still exists in daily use a system of consanguinity which is given in the Table, and may be pronounced the oldest known among mankind. The Hawaiian and Rotuman [1] forms are used as typical of the system. It is the simplest, and therefore the oldest form, of the classificatory system, and reveals the primitive form on which the Turanian and Ganowánian were afterwards engrafted.

It is evident that the Malayan could not have been derived from any existing system, because there is none, of which any conception can be formed, more elementary. The only blood relationships recognized are the primary, which are five in number, without distinguishing sex. All consanguinei, near and remote, are classified under these relationships into five categories. Thus, myself, my brothers and sisters, and my first, second, third, and more remote male and female cousins, are the first grade or category. All these, without distinction, are my brothers and sisters. The word *cousin* is here used in our sense, the relationship being unknown in Polynesia. My father and mother, together with their brothers and sisters, and their first, second, and more remote cousins, are the second grade. All these, without distinction. are my parents. My grandfathers and grandmothers, on the father's side and on the mother's side, with their brothers and sisters, and their several cousins, are the third grade. All these are my grandparents. Below me, my sons and daughters, with their several cousins, as before, are the fourth grade. All these, without distinction, are my children. My grandsons and granddaughters, with their several cousins, are the fifth grade. All these in like manner are my grandchildren. Moreover, all the individuals of the same grade are brothers and sisters to each other. In this manner all the possible kindred of any given person are brought into five categories; each person applying to every other person in the same category with himself or herself the same term of relationship. Particular attention is invited to the five grades of relations in the Malayan system, because the same classification appears

---

1 The Rotuman is herein for the first time published. It was worked out by the Rev. John Osborn, Wesleyan missionary at Rotuma, and procured and forwarded to the author by the Rev. Lorimer Fison, of Sydney, Australia.

in the "Nine Grades of Relations" of the Chinese, which are extended so as to include two additional ancestors and two additional descendants, as will elsewhere be shown. A fundamental connection between the two systems is thus discovered.

There are terms in Hawaiian for grandparent, *Kup-pŭnă,* for parent; *Mäkŭa;* for child, *Kaikee;* and for grandchild, *Moopŭnă.* Gender is expressed by adding the terms *Käna,* for male, and *Wäheena,* for female; thus, *Kupŭnă Käna* = grandparent male, and *Kupŭnă, Wäheena,* grandparent female. They are equivalent to grandfather and grandmother, and express these relationships in the concrete. Ancestors and descendants, above and below those named, are distinguished numerically, as first, second, third, when it is necessary to be specific; but in common usage *Kupŭnă* is applied to all persons above grandparent, and *Moopŭnă* is applied to all descendants below grandchild.

The relationships of brother and sister are conceived in the twofold form of elder and younger, and separate terms are applied to each; but it is not carried out with entire completeness. Thus, in Hawaiian, from which the illustrations will be taken, we have:

Elder Brother, Male Speaking, "Kaikŭaäna." Female Speaking, "Kaikŭnäna."
Younger Brother, Male Speaking, "Kaikaina." Female Speaking, "Kaikŭnäna."
Elder Sister, Male Speaking, "Kaikŭwäheena." Female Speaking, "Kaikŭaäna."
Younger Sister, Male Speaking, "Kaikŭwäheena." Female Speaking, "Kaikaina." [1]

It will be observed that a man calls his elder brother *Kaikŭaäna,* and that a woman calls her elder sister the same; that a man calls his younger brother *Kaikaina,* and a woman calls her younger sister the same: hence these terms are in common gender, and suggest the same idea found in the Karen system, namely, that of predecessor and successor in birth.[2] A single term is used by the males for elder and younger sister, and a single term by

---

1 a as in ale; ä as a in father; ă as a in at; ĭ as i in it; ŭ as oo in food.
2 "Systems of Consanguinity," loc. cit., p. 445.

the females for elder and younger brother. It thus appears that while a man's brothers are classified into elder and younger, his sisters are not; and, while a woman's sisters are classified into elder and younger, her brothers are not. A double set of terms are thus developed, one of which is used by the males and the other by the females, a peculiarity which reappears in the system of a number of Polynesian tribes.[1] Among savage and barbarous tribes the relationships of brother and sister are seldom conceived in the abstract.

The substance of the system is contained in the five categories of consanguinei; but there are special features to be noticed which will require the presentation in detail of the first three collateral lines. After these are shown the connection of the system with the intermarriage of brothers and sisters, own and collateral, in a group, will appear in the relationships themselves.

First collateral line. In the male branch, with myself a male, the children of my brother, speaking as a Hawaiian, are my sons and daughters, each of them calling me father; and the children of the latter are my grandchildren, each of them calling me grandfather.

In the female branch my sister's children are my sons and daughters, each of them calling me father; and their children are my grandchildren, each of them calling me grandfather. With myself a female, the relationships of the persons above named are the same in both branches, with corresponding changes for sex.

The husbands and wives of these several sons and daughters are my sons-in-law and daughters-in-law; the terms being used in common gender, and having the terms for male and female added to each respectively.

Second collateral line. In the male branch on the father's side my father's brother is my father, and calls me his son; his children are my brothers and sisters, elder or younger; their children are my sons and daughters; and the children of the latter are my grandchildren, each of them in the preceding and succeeding cases applying to

1 Ib., pp. 525, 573.

me the proper correlative. My father's sister is my mother; her children are my brothers and sisters, elder or younger; their children are my sons and daughters; and the children of the latter are my grandchildren.

In the same line on the mother's side my mother's brother is my father; his children are my brothers and sisters; their children are my sons and daughters; and the children of the latter are my grandchildren. My mother's sister is my mother; her children are my brothers and sisters; their children are my sons and daughters; and the children of the latter are my grandchildren. The relationships of the persons named in all the branches of this and the succeeding lines are the same with myself a female.

The wives of these several brothers, own and collateral, are my wives as well as theirs. When addressing either one of them, I call her my wife, employing the usual term to express that connection. The husbands of these several women, jointly such with myself, are my brothers-in-law. With myself a female the husbands of my several sisters, own and collateral, are my husbands as well as theirs. When addressing either of them, I use the common term for husband. The wives of these several husbands, who are jointly such with myself, are my sisters-in-law.

Third collateral line. In the male branch of this line on the father's side, my grandfather's brother is my grandfather; his children are my fathers and mothers; their children are my brothers and sisters, elder or younger; the children of the latter are my sons and daughters; and their children are my grandchildren. My grandfather's sister is my grandmother; and her children and descendants follow in the same relationships as in the last case.

In the same line on the mother's side, my grandmother's brother is my grandfather; his sister is my grandmother; and their respective children and descendants fall into the same categories as those in the first branch of this line.

The marriage relationships are the same in this as in

the second collateral line, thus increasing largely the number united in the bonds of marriage.

As far as consanguinei can be traced in the more remote collateral lines, the system, which is all-embracing, is the same in its classifications. Thus, my great-grandfather in the fourth collateral line is my grandfather; his son is my grandfather also; the son of the latter is my father; his son is my brother, elder or younger; and his son and grandson are my son and grandson.

It will be observed that the several collateral lines are brought into and merged in the lineal line, ascending as well as descending; so that the ancestors and descendants of my collateral brothers and sisters become mine as well as theirs. This is one of the characteristics of the classificatory system. None of the kindred are lost.

From the simplicity of the system it may be seen how readily the relationships of consanguinei are known and recognized, and how a knowledge of them is preserved from generation to generation. A single rule furnishes an illustration: the children of brothers are themselves brothers and sisters; the children of the latter are brothers and sisters; and so downward indefinitely. It is the same with the children and descendants of sisters, and of brothers and sisters.

All the members of each grade are reduced to the same level in their relationships, without regard to nearness or remoteness in numerical degrees; those in each grade standing to *Ego* in an identical relationship. It follows, also, that knowledge of the numerical degrees formed an integral part of the Hawaiian system, without which the proper grade of each person could not be known. The simple and distinctive character of the system will arrest attention, pointing with such directness as it does, to the intermarriage of brothers and sisters, own and collateral, in a group, as the source from whence it sprung.

Poverty of language or indifference to relationships exercised no influence whatever upon the formation of the system, as will appear in the sequel.

The system, as here detailed, is found in other Polynesian tribes besides the Hawaiians and Rotumans, as among the Marquesas Islanders, and the Maoris of New Zealand. It prevails, also, among the Samoans, Kusaiens, and King's Mill Islanders of Micronesia,[1] and without a doubt in every inhabited island of the Pacific, except where it verges upon the Turanian.

From this system the antecedent existence of the consanguine family, with the kind of marriage appertaining thereto, is plainly deducible. Presumptively it is a natural and real system, expressing the relationships which actually existed when the system was formed, as near as the parentage of children could be known. The usages with respect to marriage which then prevailed may not prevail at the present time. To sustain the deduction it is not necessary that they should. Systems of consanguinity, as before stated, are found to remain substantially unchanged and in full vigor long after the marriage customs in which they originated have in part or wholly passed away. The small number of independent systems of consanguinity created during the extended period of human experience is sufficient proof of their permanence. They are found not to change except in connection with great epochs of progress. For the purpose of explaining the origin of the Malayan system, from the nature of descents, we are at liberty to assume the antecedent intermarriage of own and collateral brothers and sisters in a group; and if it is then found that the principal relationships recognized are those that would actually exist under this form of marriage, then the system itself becomes evidence conclusive of the existence of such marriages. It is plainly inferable that the system originated in plural marriages of consanguinei, including own brothers and sisters; in fact commenced with the intermarriage of the latter, and gradually enfolded the collateral brothers and sisters as the range of the conjugal system widened. In course of time the evils of the first form of marriage came to be perceived, leading, if not to its direct abolition, to a preference for wives beyond this degree. Among the Australians it was permanently

1 "Systems of Consanguinity," etc., l. c., Table iii, pp. 542, 573.

abolished by the organization into classes, and more widely among the Turanian tribes by the organization into gentes. It is impossible to explain the system as a natural growth upon any other hypothesis than the one named, since this form of marriage alone can furnish a key to its interpretation. In the consanguine family, thus constituted, the husbands lived in polygyny, and the wives in polyandry, which are seen to be as ancient as human society. Such a family was neither unnatural nor remarkable. It would be difficult to show any other possible beginning of the family in the primitive period. Its long continuance in a partial form among the tribes of mankind is the greater cause for surprise; for all traces of it had not disappeared among the Hawaiians at the epoch of their discovery.

The explanation of the origin of the Malayan system given in this chapter, and of the Turanian and Ganowánian given in the next, have been questioned and denied by Mr. John F. McLennan, author of "Primitive Marriage." I see no occasion, however, to modify the views herein presented, which are the same substantially as those given in "Systems of Consanguinity," etc. But I ask the attention of the reader to the interpretation here repeated, and to a note at the end of Chapter VI, in which Mr. McLennan's objections are considered.

If the recognized relationships in the Malayan system are now tested by this form of marriage, it will be found that they rest upon the intermarriage of own and collateral brothers and sisters in a group.

It should be remembered that the relationships which grow out of the family organization are of two kinds: those of blood determined by descents, and those of affinity determined by marriage. Since in the consanguine family there are two distinct groups of persons, one of fathers and one of mothers, the affiliation of the children to both groups would be so strong that the distinction between relationships by blood and by affinity would not be recognized in the system in every case.

I. All the children of my several brothers, myself a male, are my sons and daughters.

Reason: Speaking as a Hawaiian, all the wives of my several brothers are my wives as well as theirs. As it would be impossible for me to distinguish my own children from those of my brothers, if I call any one my child, I must call them all my children. One is as likely to be mine as another.

II. All the grandchildren of my several brothers are my grandchildren.

Reason: They are the children of my sons and daughters.

III. With myself a female the foregoing relationships are the same.

This is purely a question of relationship by marriage. My several brothers being my husbands, their children by other wives would be my step-children, which relationship being unrecognized, they naturally fall into the category of my sons and daughters. Otherwise they would pass without the system. Among ourselves a step-mother is called mother, and a step-son a son.

IV. All the children of my several sisters, own and collateral, myself a male, are my sons and daughters.

Reason: All my sisters are my wives, as well as the wives of my several brothers.

V. All the grandchildren of my several sisters are my grandchildren.

Reason: They are the children of my sons and daughters.

VI. All the children of my several sisters, myself a female, are my sons and daughters.

Reason: The husbands of my sisters are my husbands as well as theirs. This difference, however, exists: I can distinguish my own children from those of my sisters, to the latter of whom I am a step-mother. But since this relationship is not discriminated, they fall into the category of my sons and daughters. Otherwise they would fall without the system.

VII. All the children of several own brothers are brothers and sisters to each other.

Reason: These brothers are the husbands of all the mothers of these children. The children can distinguish their own mothers, but not their fathers, wherefore, as to the former, a part are own brothers and sisters, and step-brothers and step-sisters to the remainder; but as to the latter, they are probable brothers and sisters. For these reasons they naturally fall into this category.

VIII. The children of these brothers and sisters are also brothers and sisters to each other; the children of the latter are brothers and sisters again, and this relationship continues downward among their descendants indefinitely. It is precisely the same with the children and descendants of several own sisters, and of several brothers and sisters. An infinite series is thus created, which is a fundamental part of the system. To account for this series it must be further assumed that the marriage relation extended wherever the relationship of brother and sister was recognized to exist; each brother having as many wives as he had sisters, own or collateral, and each sister having as many husbands as she had brothers, own or collateral. Marriage and the family seem to form in the grade or category, and to be coextensive with it. Such apparently was the beginning of that stupendous conjugal system which has before been a number of times adverted to.

IX. All the brothers of my father are my fathers; and all the sisters of my mother are my mothers.

Reasons, as in I, III, and VI.

X. All the brothers of my mother are my fathers.

Reason: They are my mother's husbands.

XI. All the sisters of my mother are my mothers.

Reasons, as in VI.

XII. All the children of my collateral brothers and sisters are, without distinction, my sons and daughters.

Reasons, as in I, III, IV, VI.

XIII. All the children of the latter are my grandchildren.

Reasons, as in II.

XIV. All the brothers and sisters of my grandfather and grandmother, on the father's side and on the mother's side, are my grandfathers and grandmothers.

Reason: They are the fathers and mothers of my father and mother.

Every relationship recognized under the system is thus explained from the nature of the consanguine family, founded upon the intermarriage of brothers and sisters, own and collateral, in a group. Relationships on the father's side are followed as near as the parentage of children could be known, probable fathers being treated as actual fathers. Relationships on the mother's side are determined by the principle of affinity, step-children being regarded as actual children.

Turning next to the marriage relationships, confirmatory results are obtained, as the following table will show:

	Tongan	Hawaiian.
	Male speaking,	
My Brother's Wife,	Unoho, My Wife.	Waheena, My Wife.
My Wife's Sister,	Unoho, My Wife.	Waheena, My Wife.
	Female speaking,	
My Husband's Brother,	Unoho, My Husband.	Kane, My Husband.
	Male speaking,	
My Father's Brother's Son's Wife,	Unoho, My Wife.	Waheena, My Wife.
My Mother's Sister's Son's Wife,	Unoho, My Wife.	Waheena, My Wife.
	Female speaking,	
My Father's Brother's Daughter's Husband,	Unoho, My Husband.	Kaikoeka, My Bro.-in-law.
My Mother's Sister's Daughter's Husband,	Unoho, My Husband.	Kaikoeka, My Bro.-in-law.

Wherever the relationship of wife is found in the collateral line, that of husband must be recognized in the lineal, and conversely.[1] When this system of consanguinity and affinity first came into use the relationships, which are still preserved, could have been none other than those which actually existed, whatever may have afterwards occurred in marriage usages.

From the evidence embodied in this system of consanguinity the deduction is made that the consanguine

1 Among the Kafirs of South Africa, the wife of my father's brother's son, of my father's sister's son, of my mother's brother's son, and of my mother's sister's son, are all alike my wives, as well as theirs, as appears by their system of consanguinity.

family, as defined, existed among the ancestors of the Polynesian tribes when the system was formed. Such a form of the family is necessary to render an interpretation of the system possible. Moreover, it furnishes an interpretation of every relationship with reasonable exactness.

The following observation of Mr. Oscar Peschel is deserving of attention: "That at any time and in any place the children of the same mother have propagated themselves sexually, for any long period, has been rendered especially incredible, since it has been established that even in the case of organisms devoid of blood, such as the plants, reciprocal fertilization of the descendants of the same parents is to a great extent impossible."[1] It must be remembered that the consanguine group united in the marriage relation was not restricted to own brothers and sisters; but it included collateral brothers and sisters as well. The larger the group recognizing the marriage relation, the less the evil of close interbreeding.

From general considerations the ancient existence of such a family was probable. The natural and necessary relations of the consanguine family to the punaluan, of the punaluan to the syndyasmian, and of the syndyasmian to the monogamian, each presupposing its predecessor, lead directly to this conclusion. They stand to each other in a logical sequence, and together stretch across several ethnical periods from savagery to civilization.

In like manner the three great systems of consanguinity, which are connected with the three radical forms of the family, stand to each other in a similarly connected series, running parallel with the former, and indicating not less plainly a similar line of human progress from savagery to civilization. There are reasons for concluding that the remote ancestors of the Aryan, Semitic, and Uralian families possessed a system identical with the Malayan when in the savage state, which was finally modified into the Turanian after the establishment of the gentile organization, and then overthrown when the

---

1 "Races of Man," Appleton's ed. 1876, p. 232.

monogamian family appeared, introducing the Aryan system of consanguinity.

Notwithstanding the high character of the evidence given, there is still other evidence of the ancient existence of the consanguine family among the Hawaiians which should not be overlooked.

Its antecedent existence is rendered probably by the condition of society in the Sandwich Islands when it first became thoroughly known. At the time the American missions were established upon these Islands (1820), a state of society was found which appalled the missionaries. The relations of the sexes and their marriage customs exited their chief astonishment. They were suddenly introduced to a phase of ancient society where the monogamian family was unknown, where the syndyasmian family was unknown; but in the place of these, and without understanding the organism, they found the punaluan family, with own brothers and sisters not entirely excluded, in which the males were living in polygyny, and the females in polyandry. It seemed to them that they had discovered the lowest level of human degradation, not to say of depravity. But the innocent Hawaiians, who had not been able to advance themselves out of savagery, were living, no doubt respectably and modestly for savages, under customs and usages which to them had the force of laws. It is probable that they were living as virtuously in their faithful observance, as these excellent missionaries were in the performance of their own. The shock the latter experienced from their discoveries expresses the profoundness of the expanse which separates civilized from savage man. The high moral sense and refined sensibilities, which had been a growth of the ages, were brought face to face with the feeble moral sense and the coarse sensibilities of a savage man of all these periods ago. As a contrast it was total and complete. The Rev. Hiram Bingham, one of these veteran missionaries, has given us an excellent history of the Sandwich Islands, founded upon original investigations, in which he pictures the people as practicing the sum of human abominations. "Polygamy, implying plurality of husbands and wives," he observes, "fornication, adultery, incest, infant murder, desertion of husband and wives, parents and children; sorcery, covetousness, and oppression extensively prevailed, and seem hardly to have been forbidden by their religion."[1] Punaluan marriage and the punaluan family dispose of the principal charges in this grave indictment, and leave the Hawaiians a chance at a moral character. The existence of morality, even among savages, must be recognized, although low in type; for there never could have been a time in human experience when the principle of morality did not exist. Wakea, the eponymous ancestor of the Hawaiians, according to Mr. Bingham, is said to have married his eldest daughter. In the time of these missionaries brothers and sisters married without reproach. "The union of brother and sister in the highest ranks," he further remarks, "became fashionable, and continued until the revealed will of God was made known to them."[2] It is not singular that the intermarriage of brothers and sisters should have survived from the consanguine family into the punaluan in some cases, in the Sandwich Islands, because the people had not attained to the gentile organization, and because the punaluan family was a growth out of the consanguine not yet entirely consummated. Although the family was substantially punaluan, the system of consanguinity remained unchanged, as it came in with the consanguine family, with the exception of certain marriage relationships.

It is not probable that the actual family, among the Hawaiians, was as large as the group united in the marriage relation. Necessity would compel its subdivision into smaller groups for the procurement of subsistence, and for mutual protection; but each smaller family would be a miniature of the group. It is not improbable that individuals passed at pleasure from one of these subdivisions into another in the punaluan as well as consanguine family, giving rise to that apparent desertion by

---

1 Bingham's "Sandwich Islands," Hartford ed., 1847, p. 21.
2 Ib., p. 23.

husbands and wives of each other, and by parents of their children, mentioned by Mr. Bingham. Communism in living must, of necessity, have prevailed both in the consanguine and in the punaluan family, because it was a requirement of their condition. It still prevails generally among savage and barbarous tribes.

A brief reference should be made to the "Nine Grades of Relations of the Chinese." An ancient Chinese author remarks as follows: "All men born into the world have nine ranks of relations. My own generation is one grade, my father's is one, that of my grandfather is one, that of my grandfather's father is one, and that of my grandfather's grandfather is one; thus, above me are four grades: My son's generation is one, and that of my grandson's is one, that of my grandson's son is one, and that of my grandson's grandson is one; thus, below me are four grades; including myself in the estimate, there are, in all nine grades. These are brethren, and although each grade belongs to a different house or family, yet they are all my relations, and these are the nine grades of relations."

"The degrees of kindred in a family are like the streamlets of a fountain, or the branches of a tree; although the streams differ in being more or less remote, and the branches in being more or less near, yet there is but one trunk and one fountain head."[1]

The Hawaiian system of consanguinity realizes the nine grades of relations (conceiving them reduced to five by striking off the two upper and the two lower members) more perfectly than that of the Chinese at the present time.[2] While the latter has changed through the introduction of Turanian elements, and still more through special addition to distinguish the several collateral lines, the former has held, pure and simple, to the primary grades which presumptively were all the Chinese possessed originally. It is evident that consanguinei, in the Chinese as in the Hawaiian, are generalized into cate-

1 "Systems of Consanguinity," etc., p. 415.
2 Ib., p. 432, where the Chinese system is presented in full.

gories by generations; all collaterals of the same grade being brothers and sisters to each other. Moreover, marriage and the family are conceived as forming within the grade, and confined, so far as husbands and wives are concerned, within its limits. As explained by the Hawaiian categories it is perfectly intelligible. At the same time it indicates an anterior condition among the remote ancestors of the Chinese, of which this fragment preserves a knowledge, precisely analogous to that reflected by the Hawaiian. In other words, it indicated the presence of the punaluan family when these grades were formed, of which the consanguine was a necessary predecessor.

In the "Timæus" of Plato there is a suggestive recognition of the same five primary grades of relations. All consanguinei in the Ideal Republic were to fall into five categories, in which the women were to be in common as wives, and the children in common as to parents. "But how about the procreation of children?" Socrates says to Timæus. "This, perhaps, you easily remember, on account of the novelty of the proposal; for we ordered that marriage unions and children should be in common to all persons whatsoever, special care being taken also that no one should be able to distinguish his own children individually, but all consider all their kindred; regarding those of an equal age, and in the prime of life, as their brothers and sisters, those prior to them, and yet further back as their parents and grandsires, and those below them, as their children and grandchildren."[1] Plato undoubtedly was familiar with Hellenic and Pelasgian traditions not known to us, which reached far back into the period of barbarism, and revealed traces of a still earlier condition of the Grecian tribes. His ideal family may have been derived from these delineations, a supposition far more probable than that it was a philosophical deduction. It will be noticed that his five grades of relations are precisely the same as the Hawaiian; that the family was to form in each grade where the relationship

1 "Timæus," c. ii, Davis's trans.

was that of brothers and sisters; and that husbands and wives were to be in common in the group.

Finally, it will be perceived that the state of society indicated by the consanguine family points with logical directness to an anterior condition of promiscuous intercourse. There seems to be no escape from this conclusion, although questioned by so eminent a writer as Mr. Darwin.[1] It is not probable that promiscuity in the primitive period was long continued even in the horde; because the latter would break up into smaller groups for subsistence, and fall into consanguine families. The most that can safely be claimed upon this difficult question is, that the consanguine family was the first organized form of society, and that it was necessarily an improvement upon the previous unorganized state, whatever that state may have been. It found mankind at the bottom of the scale, from which, as a starting point, and the lowest known, we may take up the history of human progress, and trace it through the growth of domestic institutions, inventions, and discoveries, from savagery to civilization. By no chain of events can it be shown more conspicuously than in the growth of the idea of the family through successive forms. With the existence of the consanguine family established, of which the proofs adduced seem to be sufficient, the remaining families are easily demonstrated.

---

1 "Descent of Man," ii, 360.

System of Relationship of the Hawaiians and Rotumans.

Vowel Sounds.—a, as in ale; ă, as in at; ä, as in father; ĭ, as in it; ŭ, as oo in food; kä'-na = male; wä-hee'-na = female.

	Description of Persons.		By Hon. Thomas Miller. Relationship in Hawaiian.	Translation.	By Rev. John Osborne. Relationship in Rotuman.	Translation.
1	My great-grandfather		kŭ-pŭ'-na	My grandparent	mä-pĭ-ga fä	My grandparent, male
2	" " grandfather's brother		"	" "	" "	" " "
3	" " " sister		"	" "	" hon'-ĭ	" " female
4	" " grandmother		"	" "	" "	" " "
5	" " grandmother's sister		"	" "	" "	" " "
6	" grandfather		"	" "	" fä	" " male
7	" grandmother		"	" "	" hon'-ĭ	" " female
8	" father		mä-kŭ'-ă kä'-na	" parent, male	oi-fä	" father
9	" mother		mä-kŭ-ă wä-hee'-na	" parent, female	oi-hon'-ĭ	" mother
10	" son		käi'-kee kä'-na	" child, male	le'-e fä	" child, male
11	" daughter		käi'-kee wä-hee'-na	" child, female	le'-e hon'-ĭ	" " female
12	" grandson		moo-pŭ'-nă kä'-na	" grandchild, male	mä-pĭ-ga fä	" grandchild, male
13	" granddaughter		moo-pŭ'-nă wä-hee'-na	" " female	" hon'-ĭ	" " female
14	" great-grandson		" kä'-na	" " male	" fä	" " male
15	" " granddaughter		" wä-hee'-na	" " female	" hon'-ĭ	" " female
16	" great-great-grandson		" kä'-na	" " male	" fä	" " male
17	" " " granddaughter		" wä-hee'-na	" " female	" hon'-ĭ	" " female
18	" older brother	(*male speaking*)	käi-kŭ-a-ä'-na	" brother, older	sä-sĭ-gĭ	" brother, older
19	" " "	(*female* ")	käi-kŭ-nä'-na	" " "	sag'-ve-ven'-ĭ	" " "
20	" " sister	(*male* ")	käi-kŭ-wä-hee'-na	" sister, "	sag-hon'-ĭ	" sister, "
21	" " "	(*female* ")	käi-kŭ-a-ä'-na	" " "	sa-sĭ-gĭ	" " "
22	" younger brother	(*male* ")	käi-ka-i'-na	" brother, younger	sa-sĭ-gĭ	" brother, younger
23	" " "	(*female* ")	käi-kŭ-nä'-na	" " "	sag'-ve-ven'-ĭ	" " "
24	" " sister	(*male* ")	käi-kŭ-wä-hee'-na	" sister, "	sag-hon'-ĭ	" sister "
25	" " "	(*female* ")	käi-ka-i'-na	" " "	sa-sĭ-gĭ	" " "
26	" brother's son	(*male* ")	käi'-kee kä'-na	" child, male	le'-e fä	" child, male
27	" " son's wife	" "	hŭ-no'-nă	" son-in-law	le'-e hon'-ĭ	" " female
28	" " daughter	" "	käi'-kee wä-hee'-na	" child, female	le'-e-hon'-ĭ	" " "
29	" " daughter's husband	" "	hŭ-no'-nă	" daughter-in-law	le'-e fä	" " male
30	" " grandson	" "	moo-pŭ'-nă kä'-na	" grandchild, male	mä-pĭ-ga fä	" grandchild, male
31	" " granddaughter	" "	" wä-hee'-na	" " female	" hon'-ĭ	" " female
32	" " great-grandson	" "	" kä'-na	" " male	" fä	" " male
33	" " " granddaughter	" "	" wä-hee'-na	" " female	" hon'-ĭ	" " female
34	" sister's son	" "	käi'-kee kä'-na	" child, male	le'-e fä	" child, male
35	" " son's wife	" "	hŭ-no'-nă	" daughter-in-law	le'-e hon'-ĭ	" " female
36	" " daughter	" "	käi-kee wä-hee'-na	" child, female	le'-e-hon'-ĭ	" " "
37	" " daughter's husband	" "	hŭ-no'-nă	" son-in-law	le'-e fä	" " male
38	" " grandson	" "	moo-pŭ'-nă kä'-na	" grandchild, male	mä-pĭ-ga fä	" grandchild, male

	Description of Persons	Relationship in Hawaiian.	Translation.	Relationship in Rotuman.	Translation
39	My sister's granddaughter (*male speaking*)	moo-pŭ'-nă wä-hee'-na	My grandchild, female	mä-pĭ-ga hon'-ĭ	My grandchild, female
40	" " great-grandson " "	" kä'-na	" " male	" fä	" " male
41	" " " granddaughter " "	"wä-hee'-na	" " female	" hon'-ĭ	" " female
42	" brother's son (*female speaking*)	käi'-kee kä'-na	" child, male	le'-e fä	" child, male
43	" " son's wife " "	hŭ-no'-nă	" daughter-in-law	le'-e hon'-ĭ	" " female
44	" " daughter " "	käi'-kee wä-hee'-na	" child, female	le'-e hon'-ĭ	" " "
45	" " daughter's husband " "	hŭ-no'-nă	" son-in-law	le'-e fä	" " male
46	" " grandson " "	moo-pŭ'-nă kä'-na	" grandchild, male	mä-pĭ-ga fä	" grandchild, male
47	" " granddaughter " "	" wä-hee'-na	" " female	" hon'-ĭ	" " female
48	" " great-grandson " "	" kä'-na	" " male	" fä	" " male
49	" " great-granddaughter " "	" wä-hee'-na	" " female	" hon'-ĭ	" " female
50	" sister's son " "	käi'-kee kä'-na	" child, male	le'-e fä	" child, male
51	" " son's wife " "	hŭ-no'-nă	" daughter-in-law	le'-e hon'-ĭ	" " female
52	" " daughter " "	käi'-kee wä-hee' na	" child, female	le'-e hon'-ĭ	" " "
53	" " daughter's husband " "	hŭ-no'-na	" son-in-law	le'-e fä	" " male
54	" " grandson " "	moo-pŭ'-nă kä'-na	" grandchild, male	mä-pĭ-ga fä	" grandchild, male
55	" " granddaughter " "	" wä-hee'-na	" " female	" hon'-ĭ	" " female
56	" " great-grandson " "	" kä'-na	" " male	" fä	" " male
57	" " great-granddaughter " "	" wä-hee'-na	" " female	" hon'-ĭ	" " female
58	" father's brother	mä-kŭ'-ă kä'-na	" parent, male	oi-fä	" parent, male
59	" " brother's wife	mä-kŭ'-a wä-hee'-na	" " female	oi-hon'-ĭ	" " female
60	" " " son (*older*, *male speaking*)	käi'-kŭ-a-ă'-na	" brother, older	sä-sĭ-gĭ	" brother
61	" " " " (*younger*, " ")	käi'-ka-i-na	" " younger	sä-sĭ-gĭ	" "
62	" " " son's wife	wä-hee'-na	" wife	sag-hon'-ĭ	" sister
63	" " " daughter, (*older*, *male speaking*)	käi'-ku-wä-hee'-na	" sister	sag-hon'-ĭ	" "
64	" " " " (*younger*, " ")	käi'-kŭ-wä-hee'-na	" "	"	" "
65	" " " daughter's husband	käi'-ko-ee'-kä	" brother-in-law	sä-sĭ-gĭ	" brother
66	" " " son's son	käi'-kee kä'-na	" child, male	le'-e fä	" child, male
67	" " " " daughter	käi-kee wä-hee'-na	" " female	le'-e hon'-ĭ	" " female
68	" " " daughter's son	käi'-kee kä'-na	" " male	le'-e fä	" " male
69	" " " " daughter	" wä-hee'-na	" " female	le'-e hon'-ĭ	" " female
70	" " " great-grandson	moo-pŭ'-nă kä'-na	" grandchild, male	mä-pĭ-ga fä	" grandchild, male
71	" " " " granddaughter	" wä-hee'-na	" " female	" hon'-ĭ	" " female
72	" " " great-great-grandson	" kä'na	" " male	" fä	" " male
73	" " " " " granddaughter	" wä-hee'-na	" " female	" hon'-ĭ	" " female
74	" father's sister	mä-kŭ'-ă wä-hee'-na	" parent, female	oi-hon'-ĭ	" parent, female
75	" " sister's husband	" kä'-na	" " male	oi-fä	" " male
76	" " " son (*older*, *male speaking*)	käi'-kŭ-a-ă'-na	" brother, older	sä-sĭ-gĭ	" brother
77	" " " " (*younger*, " ")	käi'-ka-i-na	" " younger	"	" "
78	" " " son's wife	wä-hee'-na	" wife	sag-hon'-ĭ	" sister
79	" " " daughter	käi'-kŭ wä-hee'-na	" sister	"	" "
80	" " " daughter's husband	kai-ko-ee'-kä	" brother-in-law	sä-sĭ-gĭ	" brother
81	" " " son's son	käi'-kee kä'-na	" child, male	le'-e fä	" child, male

	Description of Persons.	Relationship in Hawaiian.	Translation.	Relationship in Rotuman.	Translation.
82	My father's sister's son's daughter	kāī'-kee wā-hee'-na	My child, female	le'-e hon'-ī	My child, female
83	" " " daughter's son	" kā'-na	" " male	" fā	" " male
84	" " " " daughter	" wā-hee'-na	" " female	" hon'-ī	" " female
85	" " " great-grandson	moo-pū'-nā kā'-na	" grandchild, male	mā-pi-ga fā	" grandchild, male
86	" " " " granddaughter	" wā-hee'-na	" " female	" hon'-ī	" " female
87	" " " great-great-grandson	" kā'-na	" " male	" fā	" " male
88	" " " " " granddaughter	" wā-hee'-na	" " female	" hon'-ī	" " female
89	" mother's brother	mā-kū-ā kā'-na	" parent, male	oi-fā	" parent, male
90	" " brother's wife	" wā-hee'-na	" " female	oi-hon'-ī	" " female
91	" " " son (*older*, *male speaking*)	kāī'-kū-a-ā'-na	" brother, older	sā-sī-gī	" brother
92	" " " " (*younger*, " ")	kāī'-ka-i'-na	" " younger	"	" "
93	" " " son's wife	wā-hee'-na	" wife	sag-hon'-ī	" sister
94	" " " daughter	kāī'-kū-wā-hee'-na	" sister	"	" "
95	" " " daughter's husband	kāī-ko-ee'-kā	" brother-in-law	sā-sī-gī	" brother
96	" " " son's son	kāī'-kee kā'-na	" child, male	le'-e fā	" child, male
97	" " " " daughter	" wā-hee'-na	" " female	" hon'-ī	" " female
98	" " " daughter's son	" kā'-na	" " male	" fā	" " male
99	" " " " daughter	" wā-hee'-na	" " female	" hon'-ī	" " female
100	" " " great-grandson	moo-pū'-nā kā'-na	" grandchild, male	mā-pi-ga fā	" grandchild, male
101	" " " " granddaughter	" wā-hee'-na	" " female	" hon'-ī	" " female
102	" " " great-great-grandson	" kā'-na	" " male	" fā	" " male
103	" " " " " granddaughter	" wā-hee'-na	" " female	" hon'-ī	" " female
104	" mother's sister	mā-kū-ā wā-hee'-na	" parent, female	oi-hon'-ī	" parent, female
105	" " sister's husband	" kā'-na	" " male	oi-fā	" " male
106	" " " son (*older*, *male speaking*)	kāī'-kū-ā-ā'-na	" brother, older	sā-sī-gī	" brother
107	" " " " (*younger*, " ")	kāī'-ka-i-na	" " younger	"	" "
108	" " " son's wife	wā-hee'-na	" wife	sag-hon'-ī	" sister
109	" " " daughter	kāī'-kū wā-hee'-na	" sister	"	" "
110	" " " daughter's husband	kāī'-ko-ee'-kā	" brother-in-law	sā-sī-gī	" brother
111	" " " son's son	kāī'-kee kā'-na	" child, male	le'-e fā	" child, male
112	" " " " daughter	" wā-hee'-na	" " female	" hon'-ī	" " female
113	" " " daughter's son	" kā'-na	" " male	" fā	" " male
114	" " " " daughter	" wā-hee'-na	" " female	" hon'-ī	" " female
115	" " " great-grandson	moo-pū'-nā kā'-na	" grandchild, male	mā-pi-ga fā	" grandchild male
116	" " " " granddaughter	" wā-hee'-na	" " female	" hon'-ī	" " female
117	" " " great-great-grandson	" kā'-na	" " male	" fā	" " male
118	" " " " " granddaughter	" wā-hee'-na	" " female	" hon'-ī	" " female
119	" father's father's brother	kū-pū'-nā kā'-na	" grandparent, male	" fā	" grandparent, male
120	" " " brother's son	mā-kū'-ā kā'-na	" parent, male	oi-fā	" parent, male
121	" " " " daughter	" wā-hee'-na	" " female	oi-hon'-ī	" " female
122	" " " " grandson (*older*)	kāī'-kū-a-ā'-na	" brother, elder	sā-sī-gī	" brother
123	" " " " granddaughter (")	kāī'-kū wā-hee'-na	" sister, elder	sag-hon'-ī	" sister
124	" " " " great-grandson	kāī'-kee kā'-na	" child, male	le'-e fā	" child, male

	Description of Persons.	Relationship in Hawaiian.	Translation.	Relationship in Rotuman.	Translation.
125	My father's father's brother's great-granddaughter	kăi'-kee wă-hee'-na	My child, female	le'-e hon'-i	My child, female
126	" " " " great-great-grandson	moo-pŭ-nă kă'-na	" grandchild, male	mä-pi-ga fä	" grandchild, male
127	" " " " " " granddaughter	" wă-hee'-na	" " female	" hon'-i	" " female
128	" father's father's sister	kŭ-pŭ'-nă wă-hee'-na	" grandparent female	" hon'-i	" grandparent, female
129	" " " sister's son	mă-kŭ'-ă kă'-na	" parent, male	oi-fä	" parent, male
130	" " " " daughter	" wă-hee'-na	" " female	oi-hon'-i	" " female
131	" " " " grandson (older)	kăi'-kŭ-a-ă'-na	" brother, elder	sä-si-gi	" brother
132	" " " " granddaughter "	kăi'-kŭ-wă-hee'-na	" sister, "	sag-hon'-i	" sister
133	" " " " great-grandson	kăi'-kee kă'-na	" child, male	le'-e fä	" child, male
134	" " " " " granddaughter	" wă-hee'-na	" " female	le'-e hon'-i	" " female
135	" " " " great-great-grandson	moo-pŭ'-nă kă'-na	" grandchild, male	mä-pi-ga fä	" grandchild, male
136	" " " " " " granddaughter	" wă-hee'-na	" " female	" hon'-i	" " female
137	" mother's mother's brother	kŭ-pŭ'-nă kă'-na	" grandparent, male	" fä	" grandparent, male
138	" " " brother's son	mă-kŭ-ă kă'-na	" parent, male	oi-fä	" parent, male
139	" " " " daughter	" wă-hee'-na	" " female	oi-hon'-i	" " female
140	" " " " grandson (older)	kăi-kŭ-a-ă'-na	" brother, elder	sä-si-gi	" brother
141	" " " " granddaughter "	kăi'-ku-wă-hee-na	" sister, "	sag-hon'-i	" sister
142	" " " " great-grandson	kăi'-kee kă'-na	" child, male	le'-e fä	" child, male
143	" " " " " granddaughter	" wă-hee'-na	" " female	le'-e hon-i	" " female
144	" " " " great-great-grandson	moo-pŭ'-nă kă'-na	" grandchild, male	mä-pi-ga fä	" grandchild, male
145	" " " " " " granddaughter	" wă-hee'-na	" " female	" hon'-i	" " female
146	" mother's mother's sister	kŭ-pŭ-nă wă-hee-na	" grandparent, male	" hon'-i	" grandparent, male
147	" " " sister's son	mă-kŭ-ă kă'-na	" parent, male	oi-fä	" parent, male
148	" " " " daughter	" wă-hee'-na	" " female	oi-hon'-i	" " female
149	" " " " grandson (older, male speaking)	kăi'-kŭ-a-ä-na	" brother, elder	sä-si-gi	" brother
150	" " " " granddaughter	kăi'-kŭ-wă-hee'-na	" sister, "	sag-hon'-i	" sister
151	" " " " great-grandson	kăi'-kee-kă'-na	" child, male	le'-e fä	" child, male
152	" " " " " granddaughter	" wă-hee'-na	" " female	le'-e hon'-i	" " female
153	" " " " great-great-grandson	moo-pŭ'-nă kă'-na	" grandchild, male	mä-pi-ga fä	" grandchild, male
154	" " " " " " granddaughter	" wă-hee'-na	" " female	mä-pi-ga hon'-i	" " female
155	" husband	kă'-na	" husband	ve-ven'-i	" husband
156	" wife	wă-hee'-na	" wife	hoi-e-nă, and hen	" wife
157	" husband's father	mă-kŭ'-ă-hŭ-nă-ai	" father-in-law	oi-fä	" father
158	" " mother	"	" mother-in-law	oi-hon'-i	" mother
159	" wife's father	"	" father-in-law	oi-fä	" father
160	" " mother	"	" mother-in-law	oi-hon'-i	" mother
161	" son-in-law	hŭ-no'-nă kă'-na	" son-in-law	le'-e fä	" child, male
162	" daughter-in-law	" wă-hee'-na	" daughter-in-law	le'-e hon'-i	" " female
163	" brother-in-law (husband's brother)	kă'-na	" husband	hom-fu'-e	" brother-in-law
164	" " " " (sister's husband, female speaking)	"	" "	me-i	" " " "
165	" " " " (wife's sister's husband)	pŏ-na-lŭ-ă	" intimate companion		
166	" " " " (wife's brother)	kăi-ko-e'-kă	" brother-in-law	me-i	" " " "
167	" sister-in-law (wife's sister)	wă-hee'-na	" wife	hom-fu'-e	" sister-in-law

	Description of Persons.	Relationship in Hawaiian.	Translation.	Relationship in Rotuman.	Translation.
168	My sister-in-law *(husband's sister)*	käi-ko-a'-kă	My sister-in-law	mo-i	My sister-in-law
169	" " " " *(brother's wife)*	wă-hee'-na	" wife	hon-fu'-e	" " " "
170	" " " " *(" " female speaking)*	käi-ko-a'-kă	" sister-in-law	"	" " " "
171	" " " " *(husband's brother's wife)*	pŭ-na-lŭ-ă	" intimate companion		
172	" " " " *(wife's brother's wife)*	wă-hee'-na	" wife		
173	" step-father	mă-kŭ'-a kă'-na	" parent, male	oi-fă	" parent, male
174	" " mother	" wă-hee'-na	" " female	oi-hon'-ĭ	" " female
175	" " son	käi'-kee kă'-na	" child, male	le'-e fă	" child, male
176	" " daughter	" wă-hee'-na	" " female	le'-e hon'ĭ	" " female

CHAPTER III

THE PUNALUAN FAMILY

The Punaluan family has existed in Europe, Asia, and America within the historical period, and in Polynesia within the present century. With a wide prevalence in the tribes of mankind in the Status of Savagery, it remained in some instances among tribes who had advanced into the Lower Status of barbarism, and in one case, that of the Britons, among tribes who had attained the Middle Status.

In the course of human progress it followed the consanguine family, upon which it supervened, and of which it was a modification. The transition from one into the other was produced by the gradual exclusion of own brothers and sisters from the marriage relation, the evils of which could not forever escape human observation. It may be impossible to recover the events which led to deliverance; but we are not without some evidence tending to show how it occurred. Although the facts from which these conclusions are drawn are of a dreary and forbidding character, they will not surrender the knowledge they contain without a patient as well as careful examination.

Given the consanguine family, which involved own brothers and sisters and also collateral brothers and sisters in the marriage relation, and it was only necessary to exclude the former from the group, and retain the latter, to change the consanguine into the punaluan family. To effect the exclusion of the one class and the retention of the other was a difficult process, because it involved a radical change in the composition of the family, not to say in the ancient plan of domestic life. It also required the surrender of a privilege which savages would be slow to make. Commencing, it may be supposed, in isolated cases, and with a slow recognition of its advantages, it remained an experiment through immense expanses of time; introduced partially at first, then becoming general, and finally universal among the advancing tribes, still in savagery, among whom the movement originated. It affords a good illustration of the operation of the principle of natural selection.

The significance of the Anstralian class system presents itself anew in this connection. It is evident from the manner in which the classes were formed, and from the rule with respect to marriage and descents, that their primary object was to exclude own brothers and sisters from the marriage relation, while the collateral brothers and sisters were retained in that relation. The former object is impressed upon the classes by an external law; but the latter, which is not apparent on the face of the organization, is made evident by tracing their descents.[1] It is thus found that first, second, and more remote cousins, who are collateral brothers and sisters under their system of consanguinity, are brought perpetually back into the marriage relation, while own brothers and sisters are excluded. The number of persons in the Australian punaluan group is greater than in the Hawaiian, and its composition is slightly different; but the remarkable fact remains in both cases, that the brotherhood of the husbands formed the basis of the marriage relation in one group, and the sisterhood of the wives the basis in the other. This difference, however, existed with respect to the Hawaiians, that it does not appear as yet that there were any classes among them between whom marriages must occur. Since the Australian classes gave birth to

1 The Ippais and Kapotas are married in a group. Ippai begets Murri, and Murri in turn begets Ippai; in like manner Kapota begets Mata, and Mata in turn begets Kapota; so that the grandchildren of Ippai and Kapota are themselves Ippais and Kapotas, as well as collateral brothers and sisters; and as such are born husbands and wives.

the punaluan group, which contained the germ of the gens, it suggests the probability that this organization into classes upon sex once prevailed among all the tribes of mankind who afterwards fell under the gentile organization. It would not be surprising if the Hawaiians, at some anterior period, were organized in such classes.

Remarkable as it may seem, three of the most important and most wide-spread institutions of mankind, namely, the punaluan family, the organization into gentes, and the Turanian system of consanguinity, root themselves in an anterior organization analogous to the punaluan group, in which the germ of each is found. Some evidence of the truth of this proposition will appear in the discussion of this family.

As punaluan marriage gave the punaluan family, the latter would give the Turanian system of consanguinity, as soon as the existing system was reformed so as to express the relationships as they actually existed in this family. But something more than the punaluan group was needed to produce this result, namely, the organization into gentes, which permanently excluded brothers and sisters from the marriage relation by an organic law, who before that, must have been frequently involved in that relation. When this exclusion was made complete it would work a change in all these relationships which depended upon these marriages; and when the system of consanguinity was made to conform to the new state of these relationships, the Turanian system would supervene upon the Malayan. The Hawaiians had the punaluan family, but neither the organization into gentes nor the Turanian system of consanguinity. Their retention of the old system of the consanguine family leads to a suspicion, confirmed by the statements of Mr. Bingham, that own brothers and sisters were frequently involved in the punaluan group, thus rendering a reformation of the old system of consanguinity impossible. Whether the punaluan group of the Hawaiian type can claim an equal antiquity with the Australian classes is questionable, since the latter is more archaic than any other known constitution of society. But the existence of a punaluan group of one or the other type was essential to the birth of the gentes, as the latter were essential to the production of the Turanian system of consanguinity. The three institutions will be considered separately.

I. *The Punaluan Family.*

In rare instances a custom has been discovered in a concrete form usable as a key to unlock some of the mysteries of ancient society, and explain what before could only be understood imperfectly. Such a custom is the *Pŭnalŭa* of the Hawaiians. In 1860 Judge Lorin Andrews, of Honolulu, in a letter accompanying a schedule of the Hawaiian system of consanguinity, commented upon one of the Hawaiian terms of relationship as follows: "The relationship of *pŭnalŭ*a is rather amphibious. It arose from the fact that two or more brothers with their wives, or two or more sisters with their husbands, were inclined to possess each other in common; but the modern use of the word is that of *dear friend,* or *intimate companion.*" That which Judge Andrews says they were inclined to do, and which may then have been a declining practice, their system of consanguinity proves to have been once universal among them. The Rev. Artemus Bishop, lately deceased, one of the oldest missionaries in these Islands, sent to the author the same year, with a similar schedule, the following statement upon the same subject: "This confusion of relationships is the result of the ancient custom among relatives of the living together of husbands and wives in common." In a previous chapter the remark of Mr. Bingham was quoted that the polygamy of which he was writing, "implied a plurality of husbands and wives." The same fact is reiterated by Dr. Bartlett: "The natives had hardly more modesty or shame than so many animals. Husbands had many wives, and wives many husbands, and exchanged with each other at pleasure."[1] The form of marriage which they found created a punaluan group, in

---

1 "Historical Sketch of the Missions, etc., in the Sandwich Islands," etc., p. 5.

which the husbands and wives were jointly intermarried in the group. Each of these groups, including the children of the marriages, was a punaluan family; for one consisted of several brothers and their wives, and the other of several sisters with their husbands.

If we now turn to the Hawaiian system of consanguinity, in the Table, it will be found that a man calls his wife's sister his wife. All the sisters of his wife, own as well as collateral, are also his wives. But the husband of his wife's sister he calls *pŭnalŭa,* i. e., *his intimate companion;* and all the husbands of the several sisters of his wife the same. They were jointly intermarried in the group. These husbands were not, probably, brothers; if they were, the blood relationship would naturally have prevailed over the affineal; but their wives were sisters, own and collateral. In this case the sisterhood of the wives was the basis upon which the group was formed, and their husbands stood to each other in the relationship of *pŭnalŭa.* In the other group, which rests upon the brotherhood of the husbands, a woman calls her husband's brother her husband. All the brothers of her husband, own as well as collateral, were also her husbands. But the wife of her husband's brother she calls *pŭnalŭa,* and the several wives of her husband's brothers stand to her in the relationship of *pŭnalŭa.* These wives were not, probably, sisters of each other, for the reason stated in the other case, although exceptions doubtless existed under both branches of the custom. All these wives stood to each other in the relationship of *pŭnalŭa.*

It is evident that the punaluan family was formed out of the consanguine. Brothers ceased to marry their own sisters; and after the gentile organization had worked upon society its complete results, their collateral sisters as well. But in the interval they shared their remaining wives in common. In like manner, sisters ceased marrying their own brothers, and after a long period of time, their collateral brothers; but they shared their remaining husbands in common. The advancement of society out of the consanguine into the punaluan family was the inception of a great upward movement, preparing the way for the gentile organization which gradually conducted to the syndyasmian family, and ultimately to the monogamian.

Another remarkable fact with respect to the custom of punalua, is the necessity which exists for its ancient prevalence among the ancestors of the Turanian and Ganowánian families when their system of consanguinity was formed. The reason is simple and conclusive. Marriages in punaluan groups explain the relationships in the system. Presumptively they are those which actually existed when this system was formed. The existence of the system, therefore, requires the antecedent prevalence of punaluan marriage, and of the punaluan family. Advancing to the civilized nations, there seems to have been an equal necessity for the ancient existence of punaluan groups among the remote ancestors of all such as possessed the gentile organization—Greeks, Romans, Germans, Celts, Hebrews — for it is reasonably certain that all the families of mankind who rose under the gentile organization to the practice of monogamy possessed, in prior times, the Turanian system of consanguinity which sprang from the punaluan group. It will be found that the great movement, which commenced in the formation of this group, was, in the main, consummated through the organization into gentes, and that the latter was generally accompained, prior to the rise of monogamy, by the Turanian system of consanguinity.

Traces of the punaluan custom remained, here and there, down to the Middle Period of barbarism, in exceptional cases, in European, Asiatic, and American tribes. The most remarkable illustration is given by Cæsar in stating the marriage customs of the ancient Britons. He observes that, "by tens and by twelves, husbands possessed their wives in common; and especially brothers with brothers and parents with their children."[1]

This passage reveals a custom of intermarriage in the group which *pŭnalŭa* explains. Barbarian mothers would not be expected to show ten and twelve sons, as a rule,

---

1 "De Bell. Gall.," v. 14.

even in exceptional cases; but under the Turanian system of consanguinity, which we are justified in supposing the Britons to have possessed, large groups of brothers are always found, because male cousins, near and remote, fall into this category with *Ego*. Several brothers among the Britons, according to Cæsar, possessed their wives in common. Here we find one branch of the punaluan custom, pure and simple. The correlative group which this presupposes, where several sisters shared their husbands in common, is not suggested directly by Cæsar; but it probably existed as the complement of the first. Something beyond the first he noticed, namely, that parents, with their children, shared their wives in common. It is not unlikely that these wives were sisters. Whether or not Cæsar by this expression referred to the other group, it serves to mark the extent to which plural marriages in the group existed among the Britons; and which was the striking fact that arrested the attention of this distinguished observer. Where several brothers were married to each other's wives, these wives were married to each other's husbands.

Herodotus, speaking of the Massagetæ, who were in the Middle Status of barbarism, remarks that every man had one wife, yet all the wives were common.[1] It may be implied from this statement that the syndyasmian family had begun to supervene upon the punaluan. Each husband paired with one wife, who thus became his principal wife, but within the limits of the group husbands and wives continued in common. If Herodotus intended to intimate a state of promiscuity, it probably did not exist. The Massagetæ, although ignorant of iron, possessed flocks and herds, fought on horseback armed with battle-axes of copper and with copper-pointed spears, and manufactured and used the wagon (*amaxa*). It is not supposable that a people living in promiscuity could have attained such a degree of advancement. He also remarks of the Agathyrsi, who were in the same status probably, that they had their wives in common

1 Lib., i, c. 216.

that they might all be brothers, and, as members of a common family, neither envy nor hate one another.[1] Punaluan marriage in the group affords a more rational and satisfactory explanation of these, and similar usages in other tribes mentioned by Herodotus, than polygamy or general promiscuity. His accounts are too meager to illustrate the actual state of society among them.

Traces of the punaluan custom were noticed in some of the least advanced tribes of the South American aborigines; but the particulars are not fully given. Thus, the first navigators who visited the coast tribes of Venezuela found a state of society which suggests for its explanation punaluan groups. "They observe no law or rule in matrimony, but took as many wives as they would, and they as many husbands, quitting one another at pleasure, without reckoning any wrong done on either part. There was no such thing as jealousy among them, all living as best pleased them, without taking offence at one another. . . . The houses they dwelt in were common to all, and so spacious that they contained one hundred and sixty persons, strongly built, though covered with palm-tree leaves, and shaped like a bell.[2] These tribes used earthen vessels and were therefore in the Lower Status of barbarism; but from this account were but slightly removed from savagery. In this case, and in those mentioned by Herodotus, the observations upon which the statements were made were superficial. It shows, at least, a low condition of the family and of the marriage relation.

When North America was discovered in its several parts, the punaluan family seems to have entirely disappeared. No tradition remained among them, so far as I am aware, of the ancient prevalence of the punaluan

---

1 Lib., iv, c. 104.

2 Herrera's "History of America," l. c., i, 216. Speaking of the coast tribes of Brazil, Herrera further remarks that "they live in bohios, or large thatched cottages, of which there are about eight in every village, full of people, with their nests or hammocks to lie in...... . They live in a beastly manner, without any regard to justice or decency."—Ib., iv, 94. Garcilasso de la Vega gives an equally unfavorable account of the marriage relation among some of the lowest tribes of Peru.—"Royal Com. of Peru," l. c., pp. 10 and 106.

custom. The family generally had passed out of the punaluan into the syndyasmian form; but it was environed with the remains of an ancient conjugal system which points backward to punaluan groups. One custom may be cited of unmistakable punaluan origin, which is still recognized in at least forty North American Indian tribes. Where a man married the eldest daughter of a family he became entitled by custom to all her sisters as wives when they attained the marriageable age. It was a right seldom enforced, from the difficulty, on the part of the individual, of maintaining several families, although polygamy was recognized universally as a privilege of the males. We find in this the remains of the custom of punalua among their remote ancestors. Undoubtedly there was a time among them when own sisters went into the marriage relation on the basis of their sisterhood; the husband of one being the husband of all, but not the only husband, for other males were joint husbands with him in the group. After the punaluan family fell out, the right remained with the husband of the eldest sister to become the husband of all her sisters if he chose to claim it. It may with reason be regarded as a genuine survival of the ancient punaluan custom.

Other traces of this family among the tribes of mankind might be cited from historical works, tending to show not only its ancient existence, but its wide prevalence as well. It is unnecessary, however, to extend these citations, because the antecedent existence of the punaluan family among the ancestors of all the tribes who possess, or did possess, the Turanian system of consanguinity can be deduced from the system itself.

II. *Origin of the Organization into Gentes.*

It has before been suggested that the time, when this institution originated, was the period of savagery, firstly, because it is found in complete development in the Lower Status of barbarism; and secondly, because it is found in partial development in the Status of savagery. Moreover, the germ of the gens is found as plainly in the Australian classes as in the Hawaiian punaluan group. The gentes are also found among the Australians, based upon the classes, with the apparent manner of their organization out of them. Such a remarkable institution as the gens would not be expected to spring into existence complete, or to grow out of nothing, that is, without a foundation previously formed by natural growth. Its birth must be sought in pre-existing elements of society, and its maturity would be expected to occur long after its origination.

Two of the fundamental rules of the gens in its archaic form are found in the Australian classes, namely, the prohibition of intermarriage between brothers and sisters, and descent in the female line. The last fact is made entirely evident when the gens appeared, for the children are then found in the gens of their mothers. The natural adaptation of the classes to give birth to the gens is sufficiently obvious to suggest the probability that it actually so occurred. Moreover, this probability is strengthened by the fact that the gens is here found in connection with an antecedent and more archaic organization, which was still the unit of a social system, a place belonging of right to the gens.

Turning now to the Hawaiian punaluan group, the same elements are found containing the germ of the gens. It is confined, however, to the female branch of the custom, where several sisters, own and collateral, shared their husbands in common. These sisters, with their children and descendants through females, furnish the exact membership of a gens of the archaic type. Descent would necessarily be traced through females, because the paternity of children was not ascertainable with certainty. As soon as this special form of marriage in the group became an established institution, the foundation for a gens existed. It then required an exercise of intelligence to turn this natural punaluan group into an organization, restricted to these mothers, their children, and descendants in the female line. The Hawaiians, although this group existed among them, did not rise to the conception of a gens. But to precisely such a group as this, resting upon the sisterhood of the mothers, or to the similar Australian group, resting upon the same principle of union, the origin of the gens must be ascribed. It took this group as it found it, and organized certain of its members, with certain of their posterity, into a gens on the basis of kin.

To explain the exact manner in which the gens originated is, of course, impossible. The facts and circumstances belong to a remote antiquity. But the gens may be traced back to a condition of ancient society calculated to bring it into existence. This is all I have attempted to do. It belongs in its origin to a low stage of human development, and to a very ancient condition of society; though later in time than the first appearance of the punaluan family. It is quite evident that it sprang up in this family, which consisted of a group of persons coincident substantially with the membership of a gens.

The influence of the gentile organization upon ancient society was conservative and elevating. After it had become fully developed and expanded over large areas, and after time enough had elapsed to work its full influence upon society, wives became scarce in place of their former abundance, because it tended to contract the size of the punaluan group, and finally to overthrow it. The syndyasmian family was gradually produced within the punaluan, after the gentile organization became predominant over ancient society. The intermediate stages of progress are not well asertained; but, given the punaluan family in the Status of savagery, and the syndyasmian family in the Lower Status of barbarism, and the fact of progress from one into the other may be deduced with reasonable certainty. It was after the latter family began to appear, and punaluan groups to disappear, that wives came to be sought by purchase and by capture. Without discussing the evidence still accessible, it is a plain inference that the gentile organization was the efficient cause of the final overthrow of the punaluan family, and of the gradual reduction of the stupendous conjugal system of the period of savagery. While it originated in the punaluan group, as we must suppose, it nevertheless carried society beyond and above its plane.

III. *The Turanian or Ganowánian System of Consanguinity.*

This system and the gentile organization, when in its archaic form, are usually found together. They are not mutually dependent; but they probably appeared not far apart in the order of human progress. But systems of consanguinity and the several forms of the family stand in direct relations. The family represents an active principle. It is never stationary, but advances from a lower to a higher form as society advances from a lower to a higher condition, and finally passes out of one form into another of higher grade. Systems of consanguinity, on the contrary, are passive; recording the progress made by the family at long intervals apart, and only changing radically when the family has radically changed.

The Turanian system could not have been formed unless punaluan marriage and the punaluan family had existed at the time. In a society wherein by general usage several sisters were married in a group to each other's husbands, and several brothers in a group to each other's wives, the conditions were present for the creation of the Turanian system. Any system formed to express the actual relationships as they existed in such a family would, of necessity, be the Turanian; and would, of itself, demonstrate the existence of such a family when it was formed.

It is now proposed to take up this remarkable system as it still exists in the Turanian and Ganowánian families, and offer it in evidence to prove the existence of the punaluan family at the time it was established. It has come down to the present time on two continents after the marriage customs in which it originated had disappeared, and after the family had passed out of the punaluan into the syndyasmian form.

In order to appreciate the evidence it will be necessary to examine the details of the system. That of the Seneca-Iroquois will be used as typical on the part of the Ganowánian tribes of America, and that of the Tamil people of South India on the part of the Turanian tribes of Asia. These forms, which are substantially identical through upwards of two hundred relationships of the same person, will be found in a Table at the end of this chapter. In a previous work[1] I have presented in full the system of consanguinity of some seventy American Indian tribes; and among Asiatic tribes and nations that of the Tamil, Telugu, and Canarese people of South India, among all of whom the system, as given in the Table, is now in practical daily use. There are diversities in the systems of the different tribes and nations, but the radical features are constant. All alike salute by kin, but with this difference, that among the Tamil people where the person addressed is younger than the speaker, the term of relationship must be used; but when older the option is given to salute by kin or by the personal name. On the contrary, among the American aborigines, the address must always be by the term of relationship. They use the system in addresses because it is a system of consanguinity and affinity. It was also the means by which each individual in the ancient gentes was able to trace his connection with every member of his gens until monogamy broke up the Turanian system. It will be found, in many cases, that the relationship of the same person to *Ego* is different as the sex of *Ego* is changed. For this reason it was found necessary to state the question twice, once with a male speaking, and again with a female. Notwithstanding the diversities it created, the system is logical throughout. To exhibit its character, it will be necessary to pass through the several lines as was done in the Malayan system. The Seneca-Iroquois will be used.

The relationships of grandfather (*Hoc'-sote*), and grandmother (*Oc'-sote*), *and of grandson* (*Ha-yä'-da*), and granddaughter (*Ka-yä'-da*), are the most remote recognized either in the ascending or descending series. Ancestors and descendants above and below these, fall into the same categories respectively.

The relationships of brother and sister are conceived in

1 "Systems of Consanguinity and Affinity of the Human Family," Smithsonian Contributions to Knowledge, vol. xvii.

the twofold form of elder and younger, and not in the abstract; and there are special terms for each, as follow:

Elder Brother, Ha'-ge. Elder Sister, Ah'-jé.
Younger Brother, Ha'-gă. Younger Sister, Ka'-gă.

These terms are used by the males and females, and are applied to all such brothers or sisters as are older or younger than the person speaking. In Tamil there are two sets of terms for these relationships, but they are now used indiscriminately by both sexes.

First Collateral Line. With myself a male, and speaking as a Seneca, my brother's son and daughter are my son and daughter (*Ha-ah'-wuk,* and *Ka-ah'-wuk*), each of them calling me father (*Hä-nih*). This is the first indicative feature of the system. It places my brother's children in the same category with my own. They are my children as well as his. My brother's grandchildren are my grandsons and granddaughters (*Ha-yä'da,* and *Ka-yä-da,* singular), each of them calling me grandfather (*Hoc'-sote*). The relationships here given are those recognized and applied; none others are known.

Certain relationships will be distinguished as indicative. They usually control those that precede and follow. When they agree in the systems of different tribes, and even of different families of mankind, as in the Turanian and Ganowánian, they establish their fundamental identity.

In the female branch of this line, myself still a male, my sister's son and daughter are my nephew and niece (*Ha-yă'-wan-da,* and *Ka-yă'wan-da*), each of them calling me uncle (*Hoc-no'seh*). This is a second indicative feature. It restricts the relationships of nephew and niece to the children of a man's sisters, own or collateral. The children of this nephew and niece are my grandchildren as before, each of them applying to me the proper correlative.

With myself a female, a part of these relationships are reversed. My brother's son and daughter are my nephew and niece (*Ha-soh'-neh,* and *Ka-soh'-neh*), each of them calling me aunt (*Ah-ga'-huc*). It will be noticed that the terms for nephew and niece used by the males are different from those used by the females. The children of these nephews and nieces are my grandchildren. In the female branch, my sister's son and daughter are my son and daughter, each of them calling me mother (*Noh-yeh'*), and their children are my grandchildren, each of them calling me grandmother (*Oc'-sote*).

The wives of these sons and nephews are my daughters-in-law (*Ka'-sä*), and the husbands of these daughters and nieces are my sons-in-law (*Oc-na'-hose*, each term singular), and they apply to me the proper correlative.

Second Collateral Line. In the male branch of this line, on the father's side, and irrespective of the sex of *Ego,* my father's brother is my father, and calls me his son or daughter as I am a male or a female. Third indicative feature. All the brothers of a father are placed in the relation of fathers. His son and daughter are my brother and sister, elder or younger, and I apply to them the same terms I use to designate own brothers and sisters. Fourth indicative feature. It places the children of brothers in the relationship of brothers and sisters. The children of these brothers, myself a male, are my sons and daughters, and their children are my grandchildren; whilst the children of these sisters are my nephews and nieces, and the children of the latter are my grandchildren. But with myself a female the children of these brothers are my nephews and nieces, the children of these sisters are my sons and daughters, and their children, alike are my grandchildren. It is thus seen that the classification in the first collateral line is carried into the second, as it is into the third and more remote as far as consanguinei can be traced.

My father's sister is my aunt, and calls me her nephew if I am a male. Fifth indicative feature. The relationship of aunt is restricted to the sisters of my father, and to the sisters of such other persons as stand to me in the relation of a father, to the exclusion of the sisters of my mother. My father's sister's children are my cousins (*Ah-gare'-seh,* singular), each of them calling me cousin. With myself a male, the children of my male cousins are my sons and daughters, and of my female cousins are my nephews and nieces; but with myself a female these last relationships are reversed. All the children of the latter are my grandchildren.

On the mother's side, myself a male, my mother's brother is my uncle, and calls me his nephew. Sixth indicative feature. The relationship of uncle is restricted to the brothers of my mother, own and collateral, to the exclusion of my father's brothers. His children are my cousins, the children of my male cousins are my sons and daughters, of my female cousins are my nephews and nieces; but with myself a female these last relationships are reversed, the children of all alike are my grandchildren.

In the female branch of the same line my mother's sister is my mother. Seventh indicative feature. All of several sisters, own and collateral, are placed in the relation of a mother to the children of each other. My mother's sister's children are my brothers and sisters, elder or younger. Eighth indicative feature. It establishes the relationship of brother and sister among the children of sisters. The children of these brothers are my sons and daughters, of these sisters are my nephews and nieces; and the children of the latter are my grandchildren. With myself a female the same relationships are reversed as in previous cases.

Each of the wives of these several brothers, and of these several male cousins is my sister-in-law (*Ah-ge-ah'-ne-ah*), each of them calling me brother-in-law (*Ha-yă'-o*). The precise meaning of the former term is not known. Each of the husbands of these several sisters and female cousins is my brother-in-law, and they all apply to me the proper correlative. Traces of the punaluan custom remain here and there in the marriage relationship of the American aborigines, namely, between *Ego* and the wives of several brothers and the husbands of several sisters. In Mandan my brother's wife is my wife, and in Pawnee and Arickaree the same. In Crow my husband's brother's wife is "my comrade" (*Bot-ze'-no-pä-che*), in Creek my "present occupant" (*Chu-hu'-cho-wä*), and in Munsee "my friend" (*Nain-jose'*). In Winnebago and Achaotinne she is "my sister." My wife's sister's husband, in some tribes is "my brother," in others my "brother-in-law," and in Creek "my little separater" (*Un-kä-pu'-che*), whatever that may mean.

Third Collateral Line. As the relationships in the several branches of this line are the same as in the corresponding branches of the second, with the exception of one additional ancestor, it will be sufficient to present one branch out of the four. My father's father's brother is my grandfather, and calls me his grandson. This is a ninth indicative feature, and the last of the number. It places these brothers in the relation of grandfathers, and thus prevents collateral ascendants from passing beyond this relationship. The principle which merges the collateral lines in the lineal line works upward as well as downward. The son of this grandfather is my father; his children are my brothers and sisters; the children of these brothers are my sons and daughters, of these sisters are my nephews and nieces; and their children are my grandchildren. With myself a female the same relationships are reversed as in previous cases. Moreover, the correlative term is applied in every instance.

Fourth Collateral Line. It will be sufficient, for the same reason, to give but a single branch of this line. My grandfather's father's brother is my grandfather; his son is also my grandfather; the son of the latter is my father; his son and daughter are my brother and sister, elder or younger; and their children and grandchildren follow in the same relationships to *Ego* as in other cases. In the fifth collateral line the classification is the same in its several branches as in the corresponding branches of the second, with the exception of additional ancestors.

It follows, from the nature of the system, that a knowledge of the numerical degrees of consanguinity is essential to a proper classification of kindred. But to a native Indian accustomed to its daily use the apparent maze of relationships presents no difficulty.

Among the remaining marriage relationships there are terms in Seneca-Iroquois for father-in-law (*Oc-na'-hose*), for a wife's father, and (*Hä-gä'-sä*) for a husband's father. The former term is also used to designate a son-in-law, thus showing it to be reciprocal. There are also terms for step-father and step-mother (*Hoc'-no-ese*) and (*Oc'-no-ese*), and for step-son and step-daughter (*Ha'-no* and *Ka'-no*). In a number of tribes two fathers-in-law and two-mothers-in-law are related, and there are terms to express the connection. The opulence of the nomenclature, although made necessary by the elaborate discriminations of the system, is nevertheless remarkable. For full details of the Seneca-Iroquois and Tamil system reference is made to the Table. Their identity is apparent on bare inspection. It shows not only the prevalence of punaluan marriage amongst their remote ancestors when the system was formed, but also the powerful impression which this form of marriage made upon ancient society. It is, at the same time, one of the most extraordinary applications of the natural logic of the human mind to the facts of the social system preserved in the experience of mankind.

That the Turanian and Ganowánian system was engrafted upon a previous Malayan, or one like it in all essential respects, is now demonstrated. In about one-half of all the relationships named, the two are identical. If those are examined, in which the Seneca and Tamil differ from the Hawaiian, it will be found that the difference is upon those relationships which depended on the intermarriage or non-intermarriage of brothers and sisters. In the former two, for example, my sister's son is my nephew, but in the latter he is my son. The two relationships express the difference between the consanguine and punaluan families. The change of relationships which resulted from substituting punaluan in the place of consanguine marriages turns the Malayan into the Turanian system. But it may be asked why the Hawaiians, who had the punaluan family, did not reform their system of consanguinity in accordance therewith? The answer has elsewhere been given, but it may be repeated. The form of the family keeps in advance of the system. In Polynesia it was punaluan while the system remained Malayan; in America it was syndyasmian while the system remained Turanian; and in Europe and Western Asia it became monogamian while the system seems to have remained Turanian for a time, but it then fell into decadence, and was succeeded by the Aryan. Furthermore, although the family has passed through five forms, but three distinct systems of consanguinity were created, so far as is now known. It required an organic change in society attaining unusual dimensions to change essentially an established system of consanguinity. I think it will be found that the organization into gentes was sufficiently influential and sufficiently universal to change the Malayan system into the Turanian; and that monogamy, when fully established in the more advanced branches of the human family, was sufficient, with the influence of property, to overthrow the Turanian system and substitute the Aryan.

It remains to explain the origin of such Turanian relationships as differ from the Malayan. Punaluan marriages and the gentile organizations form the basis of the explanation.

I. All the children of my several brothers, own and collateral, myself a male, are my sons and daughters.

Reasons: Speaking as a Seneca, all the wives of my several brothers are mine as well as theirs. We are now speaking of the time when the system was formed. It is the same in the Malayan, where the reasons are assigned.

II. All the children of my several sisters, own and collateral, myself a male, are my nephews and nieces.

Reasons: Under the gentile organization these females, by a law of the gens, cannot be my wives. Their children, therefore, can no longer be my children, but stand to me in a more remote relationship; whence the new relationships of nephew and niece. This differs from the Malayan.

III. With myself a female, the children of my several brothers, own and collateral, are my nephews and nieces.

Reasons, as in II. This also differs from the Malayan.

IV. With myself a female, the children of my several sisters, own and collateral, and of my several female cousins, are my sons and daughters.

Reasons: All their husbands are my husbands as well. In strictness these children are my step-children, and are so described in Ojibwa and several other Algonkin tribes; but in the Seneca-Iroquois, and in Tamil, following the ancient classification, they are placed in the category of my sons and daughters, for reasons given in the Malayan.

V. All the children of these sons and daughters are my grandchildren.

Reason: They are the children of my sons and daughters.

VI. All the children of these nephews and nieces are my grandchildren.

Reason: These were the relationships of the same persons under the Malayan system, which presumptively preceded the Turanian. No new one having been invented, the old would remain.

VII. All the brothers of my father, own and collateral, are my fathers.

Reason: They are the husbands of my mother. It is the same in Malayan.

VIII. All the sisters of my father, own and collateral, are my aunts.

Reason: Under the gentile organization neither can be the wife of my father; wherefore the previous relationship of mother is inadmissible. A new relationship, therefore, was required: whence that of aunt.

IX. All the brothers of my mother, own and collateral, are my uncles.

Reasons: They are no longer the husbands of my mother, and must stand to me in a more remote relationship than that of father: whence the new relationship of uncle.

X. All the sisters of my mother, own and collateral, are my mothers.

Reasons, as in IV.

XI. All the children of my father's brothers, and all the children of my mother's sisters, own and collateral, are my brothers and sisters.

Reasons: It is the same in Malayan, and for reasons there given.

XII. All the children of my several uncles and all the children of my several aunts, own and collateral, are my male and female cousins.

Reasons: Under the gentile organization all these uncles and aunts are excluded from the marriage relation with my father and mother; wherefore their children cannot stand to me in the relation of brothers and sisters, as in the Malayan, but must be placed in one more remote: whence the new relationship of cousin.

XIII. In Tamil all the children of my male cousins, myself a male, are my nephews and nieces, and all the children of my female cousins are my sons and daughters. This is the exact reverse of the rule among the Seneca-Iroquois. It tends to show that among the Tamil people, when the Turanian system came in, all my female cousins were my wives, whilst the wives of my male cousins were not. It is a singular fact that the deviation on these relationships is the only one of any importance between the two systems in the relationships to *Ego* of some two hundred persons.

XIV. All the brothers and sisters of my grandfather and of my grandmother are my grandfathers and grandmothers.

Reason: It is the same in Malayan, and for the reasons there given.

It is now made additionally plain that both the Turanian and Ganowánian systems, which are identical, supervened upon an original Malayan system; and that the latter must have prevailed generally in Asia before the Malayan migration to the Islands of the Pacific. Moreover, there are good grounds for believing that the system was transmitted in the Malayan form to the ancestors of the three families, with the streams of the blood, from a common Asiatic source, and afterward, modified into its present form by the remote ancestors of the Turanian and Ganowánian families.

The principal relationships of the Turanian system have now been explained in their origin, and are found to be those which would actually exist in the punaluan family as near as the parentage of children could be known. The system explains itself as an organic growth, and since it could not have originated without an adequate cause, the inference becomes legitimate as well as necessary that it .was created by punaluan families. It will be noticed, however, that several of the marriage relationships have been changed.

The system treats all brothers as the husbands of each other's wives, and all sisters as the wives of each other's husbands, and as intermarried in a group. At the time the system was formed, wherever a man found a brother, own or collateral, and those in that relation were numerous, in the wife of that brother he found an additional wife. In like manner, wherever a woman found a sister, own or collateral, and those in that relation were equally numerous, in the husband of that sister she found an additional husband. The brotherhood of the husbands and the sisterhood of the wives formed the basis of the relation. It is fully expressed by the Hawaiian custom of *pŭnalŭa*. Theoretically, the family of the period was co-extensive with the group united in the marriage relation; but, practically, it must have subdivided into a number of smaller families for convenience of habitation and subsistence. The brothers, by tens and twelves, of the Britons, married to each other's wives, would indicate the size of an ordinary subdivision of a punaluan group. Communism in living seems to have originated in the necessities of the consanguine family, to have been continued in the punaluan, and to have been transmitted to the syndyasmian among the American aborigines, with whom it remained a practice down to the epoch of their discovery. Punaluan marriage is now unknown among them, but the system of consanguinity it created has survived the customs in which it originated. The plan of family life and of habitation among savage tribes has been imperfectly studied. A knowledge of their usages in these respects and of their mode of subsistence would throw a strong light upon the questions under consideration.

Two forms of the family have now been explained in their origin by two parallel systems of consanguinity. The proofs seem to be conclusive. It gives the starting point of human society after mankind had emerged from a still lower condition and entered the organism of the consanguine family. From this first form to the second the transition was natural; a development from a lower into a higher social condition through observation and experience. It was a result of the improvable mental and moral qualities which belong to the human species. The consanguine and punaluan families represent the substance of human progress through the greater part of the period of savagery. Although the second was a great improvement upon the first, it was still very distant from the monogamian. An impression may be formed by a comparison of the several forms of the family, of the slow rate of progress in savagery, where the means of advancement were slight, and the obstacles were formidable. Ages upon ages of substantially stationary life, with advance and decline, undoubtedly marked the course of events; but the general movement of society was from a lower to a higher condition, otherwise mankind would have remained in savagery. It is something to find an assured initial point from which mankind started on their great and marvelous career of progress, even though so near the bottom of the scale, and though limited to a form of the family so peculiar as the consanguine.

Comparative Table of the System of Relationship of the Seneca-Iroquois Indians of New York, and of the People of South-India speaking the Tamil Dialect of the Drâvidian Language. En = my.

	Description of Persons.	Relationship in Seneca-Iroquois.	Translation.	Relationship in Tamil.	Translation.
1	My great-grandfather's father	hoc'-sote	My grandfather	En muppáddan	My 3d grandfather
2	" " mother	oc'-sote	" grandmother	" muppáddi	" " grandmother
3	" great-grandfather	hoc'-sote	" grandfather	" pûddan	" 2d grandfather
4	" " grandmother	oc'-sote	" grandmother	" pûddi	" " grandmother
5	" grandfather	hoc'-sote	" grandfather	" päddăn	" grandfather
6	" grandmother	oc'-sote	" grandmother	" päddi	" grándmother
7	" father	hä'-nih	" father	" täkkäppăn	" father
8	" mother	no-yeh'	" mother	" táy	" mother
9	" son	hâ-ah'-wuk	" son	" măkăn	" son
10	" daughter	ka-ah'-wuk	" daughter	" măkăl	" daughter
11	" grandson	ha-yä'-da	" grandson	" pêrăn	" grandson
12	" granddaughter	ka-yä'-da	" granddaughter	" pêrtti	" granddaughter
13	" great-grandson	ha-yä'-da	" grandson	" irandám pêrăn	" 2d grandson
14	" great-granddaughter	ka-yä'-da	" granddaughter	" " pêrtti	" " granddaughter
15	" great-grandson's son	ha-yä'-da	" grandson	" mŭndam pêrăn	" 3d grandson
16	" " " daughter	ka-yä'-da	" granddaughter	" " pêrtti	" " granddaughter
17	" elder brother	hä'-je	" elder brother	" tamaiyăn, b annăn	" elder brother
18	" " sister	ah'-je	" " sister	" akkàri, b tămăkay	" " sister
19	" younger brother	ha'-gä	" younger brother	" tambi	" younger brother
20	" " sister	ka'-gä	" " sister	" tangaichchi, b tangay	" " sister
21	" brothers	da-yä-guä-dan'-no-dä	" brothers	" săkothăree	" brothers (*Sanskrit*)
22	" sisters	"	" sisters	" săkothărckăl	" sisters "
23	" brother's son (*male speaking*)	ha-ah'-wuk	" son	" măkăn	" son
24	" " son's wife " "	ka'-säh'	" daughter-in-law	" mărŭmăkăl	" dau'ter-in-law & niece
25	" " daughter " "	ka-ah'-wuk	" daughter	" măkăl	" daughter
26	" " daughter's husband " "	oc-na'-hosc	" son-in-law	" mărŭmăkăn	" son-in-law & nephew
27	" " grandson " "	ha-yä'-da	" grandson	" pêrăn	" grandson
28	" " granddaughter " "	ka-yä'-da	" granddaughter	" pêrtti	" granddaughter
29	" " great-grandson " "	ha-yä'-da	" grandson	" irandám pêrăn	" 2d grandson
30	" " great-granddaughter " "	ka-yä'-da	" granddaughter	" " pêrtti	" " granddaughter
31	" sister's son	ha-yä-'-wan-da	" nephew	" mărŭmăkăn	" nephew
32	" " son's wife " "	ka'-sä	" daughter-in-law	" măkăl	" daughter
33	" " daughter " "	ka-yä'-wan-da	" niece	" mărŭmăkăl	" niece
34	" " daughter's husband " "	oc-na'-hosc	" son-in-law	" măkăn	" son
35	" " grandson " "	ha-yä'-da	" grandson	" pêrăn	" grandson
36	" " granddaughter " "	ka-yä'-da	" granddaughter	" pêrtti	" granddaughter
37	" " great-grandson " "	ha-yä'-da	" grandson	" irandám pêrăn	" 2d grandson
38	" " great-granddaughter " "	ka-yä'-da,	" granddaughter	" irandám pêrtti	" 2d granddaughter

	Description of Persons.	Relationship in Seneca-Iroquois.	Translation.	Relationship in Tamil.	Translation.
39	My brother's son (*female speaking*)	ha-soh'-neh	My nephew	En mărŭmăkăn	My nephew
40	" " son's wife " "	ka'-sä	" daughter-in-law	" măkăl	" daughter
41	" " daughter " "	ka-soh'-neh	" niece	" mărŭmăkăl	" niece
42	" " daughter's husband " "	oc-na'-hose	" son-in-law	" măkan	" son
43	" " grandson " "	ha-yä'-da	" grandson	" pêrăn	" grandson
44	" " granddaughter " "	ka-yä'-da	" granddaughter	" pêrtti	" granddaughter
45	" " great-grandson " "	ha-yä'-da	" grandson	" irandám pêrăn	" 2d grandson
46	" " great-granddaughter " "	ka-yä'-da	" granddaughter	" " pêrtti	" " granddaughter
47	" sister's son " "	ha-ah'-wuk	" son	" măkăn	" son
48	" " son's wife " "	ka'-sä	" daughter-in-law	" mărŭmăkăl	" dau'ter-in-law & niece
49	" " daughter " "	ka-ah'-wuk	" daughter	" măkăl	" daughter
50	" " daughter's husband " "	oc-na'hose	" son-in-law	" măkăn	" son
51	" " grandson " "	ha-yä'-da	" grandson	" pêrăn	" grandson
52	" " granddaughter " "	ka-yä'-da	" granddaughter	" pêrtti	" granddaughter
53	" " great-grandson " "	ha-yä'-da	" grandson	" irandám pêrăn	" 2d grandson
54	" " great-granddaughter " "	ka-yä'-da	" granddaughter	" " pêrtti	" granddaughter
55	" father's brother	hä'-nih	" father	" periya tăkkäppăn	" great-father (*if older*
				" seriya "	" little-father (*if younger*
56	" " brother's wife	uc-no'-eso	" step-mother	" táy	" mother (*th'n my fath'r*)
57	" " " son (*older than myself*)	hä'-je	" elder brother	" tămaiyăn	" elder brother
58	" " " " (*younger than myself*)	ha'-gä	" younger brother	" tambi	" younger brother
59	" " " son's wife	ah-ge-ah'-ne-ah	" sister-in-law	" maittuni (o.) anni (y.)	" cousin & sister-in-law
60	" " " daughter (*older than myself*)	ah'-je	" elder sister	" akkarl b, tamakay	" elder sister
61	" " " " (*younger than myself*)	ka'-gä	" younger sister	" tangaichchi b, tangay	" younger sister
62	" " " daughter's husband	ha-yä'-o	" brother-in-law	" măittŭnăn	" broth'r-in-law & cousin
63	" " " son's son (*male speaking*)	ha-ah'-wuk	" son	" măkăn	" son
64	" " " " " (*female* ")	ha-soh'-neh	" nephew	" mărŭmăkăn	" nephew
65	" " " " daughter (*male* ")	ka-ah'-wuk	" daughter	" măkăl	" daughter
66	" " " " " (*female* ")	ka-soh'-neh	" niece	" mărŭmăkăl	" niece
67	" " " daughter's son (*male* ")	ha-yä'-wăn-da	" nephew	" mărŭmăkăn	" nephew
68	" " " " " (*female* ")	ha-ah'-wuk	" son	" măkăn	" son
69	" " " " daughter (*male* ")	ka-yä'-wăn-da	" niece	" mărŭmăkăl	" niece
70	" " " " " (*female* ")	ka-ah'-wuk	" daughter	" măkăl	" daughter
71	" " " great-grandson	ha-yä'-da	" grandson	" pêrăn	" grandson
72	" " " great-granddaughter	ka-yä'-da	" granddaughter	" pêrtti	" granddaughter
73	" father's sister	ah-ga'-huc	" aunt	" attai	" aunt
74	" " sister's husband	hoc-no'-ese	" step-father	" máman	" uncle
75	" " " son (*male speaking*)	ah-gäre'-seh	" cousin	" attăn b, măittŭnăn	" cousin
76	" " " " (*female* ")	ah-gäre'-seh	" cousin	" măchchăn	" "
77	" " " son's wife	ah-ge-ah'-ne-ah	" sister-in-law	" tangay	" younger sister
78	" " " daughter (*male speaking*)	ah-gäre'-seh	" cousin	" măittuni	" cousin
79	" " " " (*female* ")	ah-gäre'-seh	" cousin	" măchchi b, măchchări	" "
80	" " " daughter's husband	ha-yä-o'	" brother-in-law	" aṇṇan (o.) tambi (y.)	" elder or younger bro'r

	Description of Persons.		Relationship in Seneca-Iroquois.	Translation.	Relationship in Tamil.	Translation.
81	My father's sister's son's son	(male speaking)	ha-ah'-wuk	My son	En mărŭmăkăn	My nephew
82	" " " " "	(female ")	ha-soh'-neh	" nephew	" măkăn	" son
83	" " " " daughter	(male ")	ka-ah'-wuk	" daughter	" mărŭmăkăl	" niece
84	" " " " "	(female ")	ka-soh'-neh	" niece	" măkăl	" daughter
85	" " " daughter's son	(male ")	ha-yă'-wăn-da	" nephew	" măkăn	" son
86	" " " " "	(female ")	ha-ah'-wuk	" son	" mărŭmăkăn	" nephew
87	" " " " daughter	(male ")	ka-yă'-wăn-da	" niece	" măkăl	" daughter
88	" " " " "	(female ")	ka-ah'-wuk	" daughter	" mărŭmăkăl	" niece
89	" " " great-grandson		ha-yä'-da	" grandson	" pêrăn	" grandson
90	" " " great-granddaughter		ka-yä'-da	" granddaughter	" pêrtti	" granddaughter
91	" mother's brother		hoc-no'-seh	" uncle	" mămăn	" uncle
92	" " brother's wife		ah-gă-nē-ah	" aunt-mother	" măme	" aunt
93	" " " son	(male speaking)	äh-gäre'-seh	" cousin	" măittŭnăn	" cousin
94	" " " "	(female ")	ah-gäre'-seh	" cousin	" măchchăn	" "
95	" " " son's wife		ah-ge-ah'-ne-ah	" sister-in-law	" tăngay	" younger sister
96	" " " daughter	(male speaking)	ah-gäre'-seh	" cousin	" măittŭnl	" cousin
97	" " " "	(female ")	ah-gäre'-seh	" cousin	" măchchărl	" "
98	" " " daughter's husband		ha-yă'-o	" brother-in-law	" annan (o.) tambi (y.)	" elder or younger brother
99	" " " son's son	(male speaking)	ha-ah'-wuk	" son	" mărŭmăkăn	" nephew
100	" " " " "	(female ")	ha-soh'-neh	" nephew	" măkăn	" son
101	" " " " daughter	(male ")	ka-ah'-wuk	" daughter	" mărŭmăkăl	" niece
102	" " " " "	(female ")	ka-soh'-neh	" niece	" măkăl	" daughter
103	" " " daughter's son	(male ")	ha-yă'-wăn-da	" nephew	" măkăn	" son
104	" " " " "	(female ")	ha-ah'-wuk	" son	" mărŭmăkăn	" nephew
105	" " " " daughter	(male ")	ka-yă'-wăn-da	" niece	" măkăl	" daughter
106	" " " " "	(female ")	ka-ah'-wuk	" daughter	" mărŭmăkăl	" niece
107	" " " great-grandson		ha-yä'-da	" grandson	" pêrăn	" grandson
108	" " " great-granddaughter		ka-yä'-da	" granddaughter	" pêrtti	" granddaughter
109	" mother's sister		no-yeh'	" mother	" pêriyă táy (if older than, " sĕriyă " (if y'r myself)	" mother, great or little
110	" " sister's husband		hoc-no'-see	" step-father	" takkăppăn (P. or S.)	" father, " "
111	" " " son	(older than myself)	hä'-je	" elder brother	" tămăiyăn, b, annan	" elder brother
112	" " " "	(younger than myself)	ha'-gă	" younger brother	" tambi	" younger brother
113	" " " son's wife		ah-ge-ah'-ne-ah	" sister-in-law	" măittŭnl	" sister-in-law & cousin
114	" " " daughter	(older than myself)	ah'-je	" elder sister	" akkărl b, tămăkay	" elder sister
115	" " " "	(younger " ")	ka'-gă	" younger sister	" tăngăichchi, b, tangay	" younger sister
116	" " " daughter's husband		ha-yă'-o	" brother-in-law	" măittŭnăn	" bro'r-in-law & cousin
117	" " " son's son	(male speaking)	ha-ah'-wuk	" son	" măkăn	" son
118	" " " " "	(female ")	ha-soh'-neh	" nephew	" mărŭmăkăn	nephew
119	" " " " daughter	(male ")	ka-ah'-wuk	" daughter	" măkăl	daughter
120	" " " " "	(female ")	ka-soh'-neh	" niece	" mărŭmăkăl	" niece
121	" " " daughter's son	(male ")	ha-yă'-wăn-da	" nephew	" mărŭmăkăn	" nephew
122	" " " " "	(female ")	ha-ah'-wuk	" son	" măkăn	" son

	Description of Persons	Relationship in Seneca-Iroquois.	Translation.	Relationship in Tamil.	Translation.
123	My mother's sister's daughter's daughter (*male speaking*)	ka-yä'-wän-da	My niece	En mărŭmăkăl	My niece
124	" " " " " (*female* ")	ka-ah'-wuk	" daughter	" măkăl	" daughter
125	" " " great-grandson	ha-yä'-da	" grandson	" pêrăn	" grandson
126	" " " great-granddaughter	ka-yä'-da	" granddaughter	" pêrtti	" granddaughter
127	" father's father's brother	hoc'-sote	" grandfather	" păddăn (P. and S.)	" grandfather, g't or lit.
128	" " " brother's son	hä'-nih	" father	" takkăppăn (P. and S.)	" father, great or little
129	" " " " son's son (*older than myself*)	hä'-je	" elder brother	" annan, b, tămăiyăn	" elder brother
130	" " " " " " (*younger* " ")	ha'-gä	" younger brother	" tambi	" younger brother
131	" " " " " son's son (*male speaking*)	ha-ah'-wuk	" son	" măkăn	" son
132	" " " " " " " (*female* ")	ka-soh'-neh	" nephew	" mărŭmăkăn	" nephew
133	" " " " " " dau'ter (*male* ")	ka-ah'-wuk	" daughter	" măkăl	" daughter
134	" " " " " " " (*female* ")	ka-soh'-neh	" niece	" mărŭmăkăl	" niece
135	" " " " great-great-grandson	ha-yä'-da	" grandson	" pêrăn	" grandson
136	" " " " " " granddaughter	ka-yä'-da	" granddaughter	" pêrtti	" granddaughter
137	" father's father's sister	oc'-sote	" grandmother	" păddi (P. and S.)	" grandmother, g't or lit.
138	" " " sister's daughter	ah-ga'-huc	" aunt	" táy (P. and S.)	" mother, great or little
139	" " " " daughter's daughter (*male sp'g*)	ah-gäre'-seh	" cousin	" tămăkăy (o.) tăngăy (y.)	" elder or younger sister
140	" " " " " " (*female* ")	ah-gäre'-seh	" cousin	" tămăkăy (o.) tăngăy (y.)	" " " "
141	" " " " dau'ter's dau'ter's son (*male* ")	ha-yä'-wän-da	" nephew	" mărŭmăkăn ?	" nephew
142	" " " " " " " (*female* ")	ha-ah'wuk	" son	" măkăn ?	" son
143	" " " " " " dau'ter (*male* ")	ka-yä'-wän-da	" niece	" mărŭmăkăl ?	" niece
144	" " " " " " " (*female* ")	ka-ah'-wuk	" daughter	" măkăl ?	" daughter
145	" " " " great-great-grandson	ha-yä'-da	" grandson	" pêrăn	" grandson
146	" " " " " " granddaughter	ka-yä'-da	" granddaughter	" pêrtti	" granddaughter
147	" mother's mother's brother	hoc'-sote	" grandfather	" păddăn (P. and S.)	" grandfather, g't or lit.
148	" " " brother's son	hoc-no-seh	" uncle	" mămăn	" uncle
149	" " " " son's son (*male sp'g*)	ah-gäre'-seh	" cousin	" măittŭnăn	" cousin
150	" " " " " " (*female* ")	ah-gäre'-seh	" cousin	" măchchăn	" "
151	" " " " " son's son (*male* ")	ha-ah'-wuk	" son	" mărŭmăkăn	" nephew
152	" " " " " " " (*female* ")	ha-soh'-neh	" nephew	" măkăn	" son
153	" " " " " " dau'ter (*male* ")	ka-ah'-wuk	" daughter	" mărŭmăkăl	" niece
154	" " " " " " " (*female* ")	ka-soh'-neh	" niece	" măkăl	" daughter
155	" " " " great-great-grandson	ha-yä'-da	" grandson	" pêrăn	" grandson
156	" " " " " " granddaughter	ka-yä'-da	" granddaughter	" pêrtti	" granddaughter
157	" mother's mother's sister	oc'-sote	" grandmother	" păddi (P. and S.)	" grandmother, g't or lit.
158	" " " sister's daughter	no-yeh'	" mother	" táy (P. and S.)	" mother, great or little
159	" " " " dau'ter's dau'ter (*older than myself*)	ah'-je	" elder sister	" tămăkăy	" elder sister
160	" " " " " " (*younger* " ")	ka'-ga	" younger sister	" tăngăy	" younger sister
161	" " " " daughter's son (*male sp'g*)	ha-yä'-wän-da	" nephew	" mărŭmăkăn	" nephew
162	" " " " " " (*female* ")	ha-ah'-wuk	" son	" măkăn	" son
163	" " " " " daughter (*male* ")	ka-yä'-wän-da	" niece	" mărŭmăkăl	" niece
164	" " " " " " (*female* ")	ka-ah'-wuk	" daughter	" măkăl	" daughter
165	" " " " great-great-grandson	ha-yä'-da	" grandson	" pêrăn	" grandson

	Description of Persons.	Relationship in Seneca-Iroquois.	Translation.	Relationship in Tamil.	Translation.
166	My mother's mother's sister's great-great-granddaughter	ka-yä'-da	My granddaughter	En pêrtti	My granddaughter
167	" father's father's father's brother	hoc'-sote	" grandfather	" irandám päddän	" 2d grandfather
168	" " " " brother's son	hoc'-sote	" grandfather	" päddän (P. and S.)	" grandfather, g't or lit.
169	" " " " " son's son (*older than myself*)	hä'-nih	" father	" täkäppän (P. and S.)	" father, great or little
170	" " " " " " son's son (*male speaking*)	ha-ah'-wuk	" son	" mäkän	" son
171	" " " " " " " son's son	ha-yä'-da	" grandson	" pêrän	" grandson
172	" " " "	oc'-sote	" grandmother	" irandám päddi	" 2d grandmother
173	" father's father's father's sister's daughter	oc'-sote	" grandmother	" päddi (P. and S.)	" grandmother, g't or lit.
174	" " " " " daughter's daughter	no-yeh'	" mother	" táy (P. and S.)	" mother, great or little
175	" " " " " " dau'ter's dau'ter (*male sp'g*)	ah'-je	" elder sister	" tämäkäy b, tängäy?	" sister, elder or younger
176	" " " " " " " daughter's daughter	ha-soh'-neh	" niece	" märümäkäl	" niece
177	" " " " " " " " dau'ter's dau'ter	ha-yä'-da	" granddaughter	" pêrtti	" granddaughter
178	" mother's mother's mother's brother	hoc'-sote	" grandfather	" irandám päddän	" 2d grandfather
179	" " " " brother's son	hoc'-sote	" grandfather	" päddän (P. or S.)	" grandfather, g't or lit
180	" " " " " son's son	hoc-no'-seh	" uncle	" mämän	" uncle
181	" " " " " " son's son (*male speaking*)	ah-gäre'-seh	" cousin	" mäittünän	" cousin
182	" " " " " " " son's son (*female* ")	ha-ah'-wuk	" son	" märümäkän	" nephew
183	" " " " " " " " son's son	ha-yä'-da	" grandson	" pêrän	" grandchild
184	" mother's mother's mother's sister	oc'-sote	" grandmother	" irandám päddi	" 2d grandmother
185	" " " " sister's daughter	oc'-sote	" grandmother	" päddi (P. or S.)	" grandmother, g't or lit.
186	" " " " " daughter's daughter	no-yeh'	" mother	" táy (P. or S.)	" mother, great or little
187	" " " " " " dau'ter's dau'ter (*ol'r th'n myself*)	ah'-je	" elder sister	" akkárl	" elder sister
188	" " " " " " " dau'ter's dau'ter (*female sp'g*)	ka-yä'-wän-da	" niece	" mäkäl	" daughter
189	" " " " " " " " daughter's daughter	ka-yä'-da	" granddaughter	" pêrtti	" granddaughter
190	" husband	da-yake'-ne	" husband	" känavän, b, purushan	" husband
191	" wife	da-yake'-ne	" wife	" mäinavi, b, pernchätti	" wife
192	" husband's father	hä-ga'-sä	" father-in-law	" mámän, b, mámanär	" uncle & father-in-law
193	" " mother	ong-ga'-sä	" mother-in-law	" mámi, b, mánnai	" aunt & mother-in-law
194	" wife's father	oc-na'-hose	" father-in-law	" mämän	" uncle & father
195	" " mother	oo-na'-hose	" mother-in-law	" mámi	" aunt
196	" son-in-law	oc-na'-hose	" son-in-law	" mápillai, b, märümäkän	" son-in-law & nephew
197	" daughter-in-law	ka'-sä	" daughter-in-law	" marümäkal	" dau'ter-in-law & niece
198	" step-father	hoc-no'-ese	" step-father		(Widows cannot marry.)
199	" " mother	oc-no'-ese	" step-mother	" sëriya táy	my little mother
200	" " son	ha'-no	" step-son	" mäkän	" son
201	" " daughter	ka'-no	" step-daughter	" mäkäl	" daughter
202	" " brother			" annan (o.) tambi (y.)	" bro'r, older or younger
203	" " sister			" akkárl (o.) tängäy (y.)	" sister " "
204	" brother-in-law (*husband's brother*)	ha-yä'-o	" brother-in-law	" mäittünän	" bro'r-in-law & cousin
205	" " " (*sister's husband, male speaking*)	ah-ge-ah'-ne-o	" " "	" mäittünän	" " " "
206	" " " (" " *female* ")	ha-yä'-o	" " "	" attan (o.) maichchän	" " " "
207	" " " (*wife's brother*)	ah-ge'-ah'-ne-o	" " "	" mäittünän	" " " "
208	" " " (*wife's sister's husband*)	no relation		" sakälän	" " " "

	Description of Persons.		Relationship in Seneca-Iroquois.	Translation.	Relationship in Tamil.	Translation.
209	My brother-in-law	*(husband's sister's husband)*	no relation		En sakotaran	My bro'r-in-law & cousin
210	" sister-in-law	*(wife's sister)*	ka-yä'-o	My sister-in-law	" korlunti (o.) mäittüni	" sister-in-law & cousin
211	" " "	*(husband's sister)*	ah-ge-ah'-no-o	" " "	" nättänae	" " " "
212	" " "	*(brother's wife, male speaking)*	ka-yä'-o	" " "	" anni (o.) mäittüni (y.)	" " " "
213	" " "	*(brother's wife, female speaking)*	ah-ge-ah'-no-o	" " "	" anni (o.) mäittüni (y.)	" " " "
214	" " "	*(husband's brother's wife)*	no relation		" orakatti	" " " "
215	" " "	*(wife's brother's wife)*	no relation		" tämäkäy (o.) tängäy (y.)	" " " "
216	" widow		go-no-kw'-yes'-hä'-ah	widow	" kiempun	widow
217	" widower		ho-no-kw'-yes'-hä'-ah	widower		
218	" twins		tas-geek'-hä	twins	Dithambathie	twins (Sanskrit)

CHAPTER IV

THE SYNDYASMIAN AND THE PATRIARCHAL FAMILIES

When the American aborigines were discovered, that portion of them who were in the Lower Status of barbarism, had attained to the syndyasmian or pairing family. The large groups in the marriage relation, which must have existed in the previous period, had disappeared; and in their places were married pairs, forming clearly marked, though but partially individualized families. In this family, may be recognized the germ of the monogamian, but it was below the latter in several essential particulars.

The syndyasmian family was special and peculiar. Several of them were usually found in one house, forming a communal household, in which the principle of communism in living was practiced. The fact of the conjunction of several such families in a common household is of itself an admission that the family was too feeble an organization to face alone the hardships of life. Nevertheless it was founded upon marriage between single pairs, and possessed some of the characteristics of the monogamian family. The woman was now something more than the principal wife of her husband; she was his companion, the preparer of his food, and the mother of children whom he now began with some assurance to regard as his own. The birth of children, for whom they jointly cared, tended to cement the union and render it permanent.

But the marriage institution was as peculiar as the family. Men did not seek wives as they are sought in civilized society, from affection, for the passion of love, which required a higher development than they had attained, was unknown among them. Marriage, therefore, was not founded upon sentiment but upon convenience and necessity. It was left to the mothers, in effect, to arrange the marriages of their children, and they were negotiated generally without the knowledge of the parties to be married, and without asking their previous consent. It sometimes happened that entire strangers were thus brought into the marriage relation. At the proper time they were notified when the simple nuptial ceremony would be performed. Such were the usages of the Iroquois and many other Indian tribes. Acquiescence in these maternal contracts was a duty which the parties seldom refused. Prior to the marriage, presents to the gentile relatives of the bride, nearest in degree, partaking of the nature of purchasing gifts, became a feature in these matrimonial transactions. The relation, however, continued during the pleasure of the parties, and no longer. It is for this reason that it is properly distinguished as the pairing family. The husband could put away his wife at pleasure and take another without offence, and the woman enjoyed the equal right of leaving her husband and accepting another, in which the usages of her tribe and gens were not infringed. But a public sentiment gradually formed and grew into strength against such separations. When alienation arose between a married pair, and their separation became imminent, the gentile kindred of each attempted a reconciliation of the parties, in which they were often successful; but if they were unable to remove the difficulty their separation was approved. The wife then left the home of her husband, taking with her their children, who were regarded as exclusively her own, and her personal effects, upon which her husband had no claim; or where the wife's kindred predominated in the communal household, which was usually the case, the husband left the home of his wife.[1] Thus the continuance of the marriage relation remained at the option of the parties.

There was another feature of the relation which shows that the American aborigines in the Lower Status of barbarism had not attained the moral development implied by monogamy. Among the Iroquois, who were barbarians of high mental grade, and among the equally advanced Indian tribes generally, chastity had come to be required of the wife under severe penalties which the husband might inflict; but he did not admit the reciprocal obligation. The one cannot be permanently realized without the other. Moreover, polygamy was universally recognized as the right of the males, although the practice was limited from inability to support the indulgence. There were other usages, that need not be mentioned, tending still further to show that they were below a conception of monogamy, as that great institution is properly defined. Exceptional cases very likely existed. It will be found equally true, as I believe, of barbarous tribes in general. The principal feature which distinguished the syndyasmian from the monogamian family, although liable to numerous exceptions, was the absence of an exclusive cohabitation. The old conjugal system, a record of which is still preserved in their system of consanguin-

---

1 The late Rev. A. Wright, for many years a missionary among the Senecas, wrote the author in 1873 on this subject as follows: "As to their family system, when occupying the old long-houses, it is probable that some one clan predominated, the women taking in husbands, however, from the other clans; and sometimes, for a novelty, some of their sons bringing in their young wives until they felt brave enough to leave their mothers. Usually, the female portion ruled the house, and were doubtless clannish enough about it. The stores were in common; but woe to the luckless husband or lover who was too shiftless to do his share of the providing. No matter how many children, or whatever goods he might have in the house, he might at any time be ordered to pick up his blanket and budge; and after such orders it would not be healthful for him to attempt to disobey. The house would be too hot for him; and, unless saved by the intercession of some aunt or grandmother, he must retreat to his own clan; or, as was often done, go and start a new matrimonial alliance in some other. The women were the great power among the clans, as everywhere else. They did not hesitate, when occasion required, 'to knock off the horns,' as it was technically called, from the head of a chief, and send him back to the ranks of the warriors. The original nomination of the chiefs also always rested with them." These statements illustrate the gyneocracy discussed by Bachofen in "Das Mutterrecht."

ity, undoubtedly remained, but under reduced and restricted forms.

Among the Village Indians in the Middle Status of barbarism the facts were not essentially different, so far as they can be said to be known. A comparison of the usages of the American aborigines, with respect to marriage and divorce, shows an existing similarity sufficiently strong to imply original identity of usages. A few only can be noticed. Clavigero remarks that among the Aztecs "the parents were the persons who settled all marriages, and none were ever executed without their consent." [1] "A priest tied a point of the *huepilli,* or gown of the bride, with the *tilmatli,* or mantle of the bridegroom, and in this ceremony the matrimonial contract chiefly consisted."[2] Herrera, after speaking of the same ceremony, observes that "all that the bride brought was kept in memory, that in case they should be unmarried again, as was usual among them, the goods might be parted; the man taking the daughters, and the wife the sons, with liberty to marry again."[3]

It will be noticed that the Aztec Indian did not seek his wife personally any more than the Iroquois. Among both it was less an individual than a public or gentile affair, and therefore still remained under parental control exclusively. There was very little social intercourse between unmarried persons of the two sexes in Indian life; and as attachments were not contracted, none were traversed by these marriages, in which personal wishes were unconsidered, and in fact unimportant. It appears further, that the personal effects of the wife were kept distinct among the Aztecs as among the Iroquois, that in case of separation, which was a common occurrence as this writer states, she might retain them in accordance with general Indian usage. Finally, while among the Iroquois in the case of divorce the wife took all the children, the Aztec husband was entitled to the daughters, and the wife to the sons; a modification of the an-

---

1 "History of Mexico," Phil. ed., 1817, Cullen's trans., ii, 99.
2 Ib., ii, 101.
3 "History of America," l. c., iii, 217.

cient usage which implies a prior time when the Iroquois Indian rule existed among the ancestors of the Aztecs.

Speaking of the people of Yucatan generally Herrera further remarks that "formerly they were wont to marry at twenty years of age, and afterwards came to twelve or fourteen, and having no affection for their wives were divorced for every trifle." [1] The Mayas of Yucatan were superior to the Aztecs in culture and development; but where marriages were regulated on the principle of necessity, and not through personal choice, it is not surprising that the relation was unstable, and that separation was at the option of either party. Moreover, polygamy was a recognized right of the males among the Village Indians, and seems to have been more generally practiced than among the less advanced tribes. These glimpses at institutions purely Indian as well as barbarian reveal in a forcible manner the actual condition of the aborigines in relative advancement. In a matter so personal as the marriage relation, the wishes or preferences of the parties were not consulted. No better evidence is needed of the barbarism of the people.

We are next to notice some of the influences which developed this family from the punaluan. In the latter there was more or less of pairing from the necessities of the social state, each man having a principal wife among a number of wives, and each woman a principal husband among a number of husbands; so that the tendency in the punaluan family, from the first, was in the direction of the syndyasmian.

The organization into gentes was the principal instrumentality that accomplished this result; but through long and gradual processes. Firstly. It did not at once break up intermarriage in the group, which it found established by custom; but the prohibition of intermarriage in the gens excluded own brothers and sisters, and also the children of own sisters, since all of these were of the same gens. Own brothers could still share their wives in common, and own sisters their husbands; consequently the

---

1 "History of America," iv, 171.

gens did not interfere directly with punaluan marriage, except to narrow its range. But it withheld permanently from that relation all the descendants in the female line of each ancestor within the gens, which was a great innovation upon the previous punaluan group. When the gens subdivided, the prohibition followed its branches, for long periods of time, as has been shown was the case among the Iroquois. Secondly. The structure and principles of the organization tended to create a prejudice against the marriage of consanguinei, as the advantages of marriages between unrelated persons were gradually discovered through the practice of marrying out of the gens. This seems to have grown apace until a public sentiment was finally arrayed against it which had become very general among the American aborigines when discovered.[1] For example, among the Iroquois none of the blood relatives enumerated in the Table of consanguinity were marriageable. Since it became necessary to seek wives from other gentes they began to be acquired by negotiation and by purchase. The gentile organization must have led, step by step, as its influence became general, to a scarcity of wives in place of their previous abundance; and as a consequence, have gradually contracted the numbers in the punaluan group. This conclusion is reasonable, because there are sufficient grounds for assuming the existence of such groups when the Turanian system of consanguinity was formed. They have now disappeared although the system remains. These groups must have gradually declined, and finally disappeared with the general establishment of the syndyasmian family. Fourthly. In seeking wives, they did not confine themselves to their own, nor even to friendly tribes, but captured them by force from hostile tribes. It furnishes a reason for the Indian usage of sparing the lives of female captives, while the males were put to

---

1 A case among the Shyans was mentioned to the author, by one of their chiefs, where first cousins had married against their usages. There was no penalty for the act; but they were ridiculed so constantly by their associates that they voluntarily separated rather than face the prejudice.

death. When wives came to be acquired by purchase and by capture, and more and more by effort and sacrifice, they would not be as readily shared with others. It would tend, at least, to cut off that portion of the theoretical group not immediately associated for subsistence; and thus reduce still more the size of the family and the range of the conjugal system. Practically, the group would tend to limit itself, from the first, to own brothers who shared their wives in common and to own sisters who shared their husbands in common. Lastly. The gentes created a higher organic structure of society than had before been known, with processes of development as a social system adequate to the wants of mankind until civilization supervened. With the progress of society under the gentes, the way was prepared for the appearance of the syndyasmian family.

The influence of the new practice, which brought unrelated persons into the marriage relation, must have given a remarkable impulse to society. It tended to create a more vigorous stock physically and mentally. There is a gain by accretion in the coalescence of diverse stocks which has exercised great influence upon human development. When two advancing tribes, with strong mental and physical characters, are brought together and blended into one people by the accidents of barbarous life, the new skull and brain would widen and lengthen to the sum of the capabilities of both. Such a stock would be an improvement upon both, and this superiority would assert itself in an increase of intelligence and of numbers.

It follows that the propensity to pair, now so powerfully developed in the civilized races, had remained unformed in the human mind until the punaluan custom began to disappear. Exceptional cases undoubtedly occurred where usages would permit the privilege; but it failed to become general until the syndyasmian family appeared. This propensity, therefore, cannot be called normal to mankind, but is, rather, a growth through experience, like all the great passions and powers of the mind.

Another influence may be adverted to which tended to retard the growth of this family. Warfare among barbarians is more destructive of life than among savages, from improved weapons and stronger incentives. The males, in all periods and conditions of society, have assumed the trade of fighting, which tended to change the balance of the sexes, and leave the females in excess. This would manifestly tend to strengthen the conjugal system created by marriages in the group. It would, also, retard the advancement of the syndyasmian family by maintaining sentiments of low grade with respect to the relations of the sexes, and the character and dignity of woman.

On the other hand, improvement in subsistence, which followed the cultivation of maize and plants among the American aborigines, must have favored the general advancement of the family. It led to localization, to the use of additional arts, to an improved house architecture, and to a more intelligent life. Industry and frugality, though limited in degree, with increased protection of life, must have accompanied the formation of families consisting of single pairs. The more these advantages were realized, the more stable such a family would become, and the more its individuality would increase. Having taken refuge in a communal household, in which a group of such families succeeded the punaluan group, it now drew its support from itself, from the household, and from the gentes to which the husbands and wives respectively belonged. The great advancement of society indicated by the transition from savagery into the Lower Status of barbarism, would carry with it a corresponding improvement in the condition of the family, the course of development of which was steadily upward to the monogamian. If the existence of the syndyasmian family were unknown, given the punaluan toward one extreme, and the monogamian on the other, the occurrence of such an intermediate form might have been predicted. It has had a long duration in human experience. Springing up on the confines of savagery and barbarism, it traversed the Middle and the greater part of the Later Period of barbarism, when it was superseded by a low form of the monogamian. Overshadowed by the conjugal system of the times, it gained in recognition with the gradual progress of society. The selfishness of mankind, as distinguished from womankind, delayed the realization of strict monogamy until that great fermentation of the human mind which ushered in civilization.

Two forms of the family had appeared before the syndyasmian and created two great systems of consanguinity, or rather two distinct forms of the same system; but this third family neither produced a new system nor sensibly modified the old. Certain marriage relationships appear to have been changed to accord with those in the new family; but the essential features of the system remained unchanged. In fact, the syndyasmian family continued for an unknown period of time enveloped in a system of consanguinity, false, in the main, to existing relationships, and which it had no power to break. It was for the sufficient reason that it fell short of monogamy, the coming power able to dissolve the fabric. Although this family has no distinct system of consanguinity to prove its existence, like its predecessors, it has itself existed over large portions of the earth within the historical period, and still exists in numerous barbarous tribes.

In speaking thus positively of the several forms of the family in their relative order, there is danger of being misunderstood. I do not mean to imply that one form rises complete in a certain status of society, flourishes universally and exclusively wherever tribes of mankind are found in the same status, and then disappears in another, which is the next higher form. Exceptional cases of the punaluan family may have appeared in the consanguine, and *vice versa;* exceptional cases of the syndyasmian may have appeared in the midst of the punaluan, and *vice versa;* and exceptional cases of the monogamian in the midst of the syndyasmian, and *vice versa.* Even exceptional cases of the monogamian may have appeared as low down as the punaluan, and of the syndyasmian as low down as the consanguine. Moreover, some tribes attained to a particular form earlier than other tribes more advanced; for example, the Iroquois had the syndyasmian family while in the Lower Status of barbarism, but the Britons, who were in the Middle Status, still had the punaluan. The high civilization on the shores of the Mediterranean had propagated arts and inventions into Britain far beyond the mental development of its Celtic inhabitants, and which they had imperfectly appropriated. They seem to have been savages in their brains, while wearing the art apparel of more advanced tribes. That which I have endeavored to substantiate, and for which the proofs seem to be adequate, is, that the family began in the consanguine, low down in savagery, and grew, by progressive development, into the monogamian, through two well-marked intermediate forms. Each was partial in its introduction, then general, and finally universal over large areas; after which it shaded off into the next succeeding form, which, in turn, was at first partial, then general, and finally universal in the same areas. In the evolution of these successive forms the main direction of progress was from the consanguine to the monogamian. With deviations from uniformity in the progress of mankind through these several forms, it will generally be found that the consanguine and punaluan families belong to the status of savagery—the former to its lowest, and the latter to its highest condition—while the punaluan continued into the Lower Status of barbarism; that the syndyasmian belongs to the Lower and to the Middle Status of barbarism, and continued into the Upper; and that the monogamian belongs to the Upper Status of barbarism, and continued to the period of civilization.

It will not be necessary, even if space permitted, to trace the syndyasmian family through barbarous tribes in general upon the partial descriptions of travelers and observers. The tests given may be applied by each reader to cases within his information. Among the American aborigines in the Lower Status of barbarism it was the prevailing form of the family at the epoch of their discovery. Among the Village Indians in the Middle Status, it was undoubtedly the prevailing form, although the information given by the Spanish writers is vague and general. The communal character of their joint-tenement houses is of itself strong evidence that the family had not passed out of the syndyasmian form. It had neither the individuality nor the exclusiveness which monogamy implies.

The foreign elements intermingled with the native culture in sections of the Eastern hemisphere produced an abnormal condition of society, where the arts of civilized life were remolded to the aptitudes and wants of savages and barbarians.[1] Tribes strictly nomadic have also social peculiarities, growing out of their exceptional mode of life, which are not well understood. Through influences, derived from the higher races, the indigenous culture of many tribes has been arrested, and so far adulterated as to change the natural flow of their progress. Their institutions and social state became modified in consequence.

It is essential to systematic progress in Ethnology that the condition both of savage and of barbarous tribes should be studied in its normal development in areas where the institutions of the people are homogeneous. Polynesia and Australia, as elsewhere suggested, are the best areas for the study of savage society. Nearly the whole theory of savage life may be deduced from their institutions, usages and customs, inventions and discoveries. North and South America, when discovered, afforded the best opportunities for studying the condition of society in the Lower and in the Middle Status of barbarism. The aborigines, one stock in blood and lineage, with the exception of the Eskimos, had gained possession of a great continent, more richly endowed for human occupation than the Eastern continents save in animals capable of domestication. It afforded them an ample field for undisturbed development. They came into its possession apparently in a savage state; but the establishment of the organization into gentes put them into possession of the principal germs of progress possessed by the ancestors

1 Iron has been smelted from the ore by a number of African tribes, including the Hottentots, as far back as our knowledge of them extends. After producing the metal by rude processes acquired from foreign sources, they have succeeded in fabricating rude implements and weapons.

of the Greeks and Romans.[1] Cut off thus early, and losing all further connection with the central stream of human progress, they commenced their career upon a new continent with the humble mental and moral endowments of savages. The independent evolution of the primary ideas they brought with them commenced under conditions insuring a career undisturbed by foreign influences. It holds true alike in the growth of the idea of government, of the family, of household life, of property, and of the arts of subsistence. Their institutions, inventions and discoveries, from savagery, through the Lower and into the Middle Status of barbarism, are homogeneous, and still reveal a continuity of development of the same original conceptions.

In no part of the earth, in modern times, could a more perfect exemplification of the Lower Status of barbarism be found than was afforded by the Iroquois, and other tribes of the United States east of the Mississippi. With their arts indigenous and unmixed, and with their institutions pure and homogeneous, the culture of this period, in its range, elements and possibilities, is illustrated by them in the fullest manner. A systematic exposition of these several subjects ought to be made, before the facts are allowed to disappear.

In a still higher degree all this was true with respect to the Middle Status of barbarism, as exemplified by the Village Indians of New Mexico, Mexico, Central America, Granada, Ecuador, and Peru. In no part of the earth was there to be found such a display of society in this Status, in the sixteenth century, with its advanced arts and inventions, its improved architecture, its nascent manufactures and its incipient sciences. American scholars have a poor account to render of work done in this fruitful field. It was in reality a lost condition of ancient

1 The Asiatic origin of the American aborigines is assumed. But it follows as a consequence of the unity of origin of mankind—another assumption, but one toward which all the facts of anthropology tend. There is a mass of evidence sustaining both conclusions of the most convincing character. Their advent in America could not have resulted from a deliberate migration; but must have been due to the accidents of the sea, and to the great ocean currents from Asia to the North-west coast.

society which was suddenly unveiled to European observers with the discovery of America; but they failed to comprehend its meaning, or to ascertain its structure.

There is one other great condition of society, that of the Upper Status of barbarism, not now exemplified by existing nations; but it may be found in the history and traditions of the Grecian and Roman, and later of the German tribes. It must be deduced, in the main, from their institutions, inventions and discoveries, although there is a large amount of information illustrative of the culture of this period, especially in the Homeric poems.

When these several conditions of society have been studied in the areas of their highest exemplification, and are thoroughly understood, the course of human development from savagery, through barbarism to civilization, will become intelligible as a connected whole. The course of human experience will also be found as before suggested to have run in nearly uniform channels.

The patriarchal family of the Semitic tribes requires but a brief notice, for reasons elsewhere stated; and it will be limited to little more than a definition. It belongs to the Later Period of barbarism, and remained for a time after the commencement of civilization. The chiefs, at least, lived in polygamy; but this was not the material principle of the patriarchal institution. The organization of a number of persons, bond and free, into a family, under paternal power, for the purpose of holding lands, and for the care of flocks and herds, was the essential characteristic of this family. Those held to servitude, and those employed as servants, lived in the marriage relation, and, with the patriarch as their chief, formed a patriarchal family. Authority over its members and over its property was the material fact. It was the incorporation of numbers in servile and dependent relations, before that time unknown, rather than polygamy, that stamped the patriarchal family with the attributes of an original institution. In the great movement of Semitic society, which produced this family, paternal power over the group was the object sought; and with it a higher individuality of persons.

The same motive precisely originated the Roman family under paternal power (*patria potestas*); with the power in the father of life and death over his children and descendants, as well as over the slaves and servants who formed its nucleus and furnished its name; and with the absolute ownership of all the property they created. Without polygamy, the *pater familias* was a patriarch and the family under him was patriarchal. In a less degree the ancient family of the Grecian tribes had the same characteristics. It marks that peculiar epoch in human progress when the individuality of the person began to rise above the gens, in which it had previously been merged, craving an independent life, and a wider field of individual action. Its general influence tended powerfully to the establishment of the monogamian family, which was essential to the realization of the objects sought. These striking features of the patriarchal families, so unlike any form previously known, have given to it a commanding position; but the Hebrew and Roman forms were exceptional in human experience. In the consanguine and punaluan families, paternal authority was impossible as well as unknown; under the syndyasmian it began to appear as a feeble influence; but its growth steadily advanced as the family became more and more individualized, and became fully established under monogamy, which assured the paternity of children. In the patriarchal family of the Roman type, paternal authority passed beyond the bounds of reason into an excess of domination.

No new system of consanguinity was created by the Hebrew patriarchal family. The Turanian system would harmonize with a part of its relationships; but as this form of the family soon fell out, and the monogamian became general, it was followed by the Semitic system of consanguinity, as the Grecian and Roman were by the Aryan. Each of the three great systems—the Malayan, the Turanian, and the Aryan—indicates a completed organic movement of society, and each assured the presence, with unerring certainty, of that form of the family whose relationships it recorded.

CHAPTER V

THE MONOGAMIAN FAMILY

The origin of society has been so constantly traced to the monogamian family that the comparatively modern date now assigned to this family bears the semblance of novelty. Those writers who have investigated the origin of society philosophically, found it difficult to conceive of its existence apart from the family as its unit, or of the family itself as other than monogamian. They also found it necessary to regard the married pair as the nucleus of a group of persons, a part of whom were servile, and all of whom were under power; thus arriving at the conclusion that society began in the patriarchal family, when it first became organized. Such, in fact, was the most ancient form of the institution made known to us among the Latin, Grecian and Hebrew tribes. Thus, by relation, the patriarchal family was made the typical family of primitive society, conceived either in the Latin or Hebrew form, paternal power being the essence of the organism.

The gens, as it appeared in the later period of barbarism, was well understood, but it was erroneously supposed to be subsequent in point of time to the monogamian family. A necessity for some knowledge of the institutions of barbarous and even of savage tribes, is becoming constantly more apparent as a means for explaining our own institutions. With the assumption made that the monogamian family was the unit of organization in the social system, the gens was treated as an aggregation of families, the tribe as an aggregation of gentes and the nation as an aggregate of tribes. The error lies in the first proposition. It has been shown that the gens entered entire into the phratry, the phratry into the tribe, and the tribe into the nation; but the family could not enter entire into the gens, because husband and wife were necessarily of different gentes. The wife, down to the latest period, counted herself of the gens of her father, and bore the name of his gens among the Romans. As all the parts must enter into the whole, the family could not become the unit of the gentile organization.. That place was held by the gens. Moreover, the patriarchal family, whether of the Roman or of the Hebrew type, was entirely unknown throughout the period of savagery, through the Older, and probably through the Middle, and far into the Later Period of barbarism. After the gens had appeared, ages upon ages, and even period upon period, rolled away before the monogamian family came into existence. It was not until after civilization commenced that it became permanently established.

Its modern appearance among the Latin tribes may be inferred from the signification of the word *family,* derived from *familia,* which contains the same element as *famulus,* = servant, supposed to be derived from the Oscan *famel,* = *servus,* a slave. [1] In its primary meaning the word *family* had no relation to the married pair or their children, but to the body of slaves and servants who labored for its maintenance, and were under the power of the *pater familias. Familia* in some testamentary dispositions is used as equivalent to *patrimonium,* the inheritance which passed to the heir. [2] It was introduced in Latin society to define a new organism, the head of which held wife and children, and a body of servile persons under paternal power. Mommsen uses the phrase "body of servants" as the Latin signification

1 Famuli origo ab Oscis dependet, apud quo servus Famul nominabuntur, unde "familia" vocata.—"Festus," p. 87.

2 Amico familiam suam., id est patrimonium suum mancipio dabat.—Gaius "Inst.," ii, 102.

of *familia*.[1] This term, therefore, and the idea it represents, are no older than the iron-clad family system of the Latin tribes, which came in after field agriculture and after legalized servitude, as well as after the separation of the Greeks and Latins. If any name was given to the anterior family it is not now ascertainable.

In two forms of the family, the consanguine and punaluan, paternal power was impossible. When the gens appeared in the midst of the punaluan group it united the several sisters, with their children and descendants in the female line, in perpetuity, in a gens, which became the unit of organization in the social system it created. Out of this state of things the syndyasmian family was gradually evolved, and with it the germ of paternal power. The growth of this power, at first feeble and fluctuating, then commenced, and it steadily increased, as the new family more and more assumed monogamian characteristics, with the upward progress of society. When property began to be created in masses, and the desire for its transmission to children had changed descent from the female line to the male, a real foundation for paternal power was for the first time established. Among the Hebrew and Latin tribes, when first known, the patriarchal family of the Hebrew type existed among the former, and of the Roman type among the latter; founded in both cases upon the limited or absolute servitude of a number of persons with their families, all of whom, with the wives and children of the patriarch in one case, and of the *pater familias* in the other, were under paternal power. It was an exceptional, and, in the Roman family, an excessive development of paternal authority, which, so far from being universal, was restricted in the main to the people named. Gaius declares that the power of the Roman father over his children was peculiar to the Romans, and that in general no other people had the same power.[2]

---

1 "History of Rome," l. c., 1, 95.

2 Item in potestate nostra sunt liberi nostri, quos justis nuptiis procreauimus, quod jus proprium ciuium Romanorum est: fere enim nulli alii sunt homines, qui talem in filios suos habent potestatem, qualem nos habemus.—"Inst.," 1, 55. Among

It will be sufficient to present a few illustrations of the early monogamian family from classical writers to give an impression of its character. Monogamy appears in a definite form in the Later Period of barbarism. Long prior to this time some of its characteristics had undoubtedly attached themselves to the previous syndyasmian family; but the essential element of the former, an exclusive cohabitation, could not be asserted of the latter.

One of the earliest and most interesting illustrations was found in the family of the ancient Germans. Their institutions were homogeneous and indigenous; and the people were advancing toward civilization. Tacitus, in a few lines, states their usages with respect to marriage, without giving the composition of the family or defining its attributes. After stating that marriages were strict among them, and pronouncing it commendable, he further remarks, that almost alone among barbarians they contended themselves with a single wife—a very few excepted, who were drawn into plural marriages, not from passion, but on account of their rank. That the wife did not bring a dowry to her husband, but the husband to his wife, ... a caparisoned horse, and a shield, with a spear and sword. That by virtue of these gifts the wife was espoused.[1] The presents, in the nature of purchasing gifts, which probably in an earlier condition went to the gentile kindred of the bride, were now presented to the bride

Elsewhere he mentions the two material facts in which the substance of monogamy is found:[2] firstly, that each man was contented with a single wife (*singulis uxoribus contenti sunt*); and, secondly, that the women lived fenced around with chastity, (*septæ pudicitia agunt*). It seems probable, from what is known of the condition of the family in different ethnical periods, that this of the ancient Germans was too weak an organization to face alone the hardships of life; and, as a consequence, shelt-

---

other things they had the power of life and death—jus vitæ necisque.

1 "Germania," c. 18.

2 Ib., c. 19.

ered itself in a communal household composed of related families. When slavery became an institution, these households would gradually disappear. German society was not far enough advanced at this time for the appearance of a high type of the monogamian family.

With respect to the Homeric Greeks, the family, although monogamian, was low in type. Husbands required chastity in their wives, which they sought to enforce by some degree of seclusion; but they did not admit the reciprocal obligation by which alone it could be permanently secured. Abundant evidence appears in the Homeric poems that woman had few rights men were bound to respect. Such female captives as were swept into their vessels by the Grecian chiefs, on their way to Troy, were appropriated to their passions without compunction and without restraint. It must be taken as a faithful picture of the times, whether the incidents narrated in the poems were real or fictitious. Although the persons were captives, it reflects the low estimate placed upon woman. Her dignity was unrecognized, and her personal rights were insecure. To appease the resentment of Achilles, Agamemnon proposed, in a council of the Grecian chiefs, to give to him, among other things, seven Lesbian women excelling in personal beauty, reserved for himself from the spoil of that city, Briseis herself to go among the number; and should Troy be taken, the further right to select twenty Trojan women, the fairest of all next to Argive Helen.[1] "Beauty and Booty" were the watchwords of the Heroic Age unblushingly avowed. The treatment of their female captives reflects the culture of the period with respect to women in general. Men having no regard for the parental, marital or personal rights of their enemies, could not have attained to any high conception of their own.

In describing the tent life of the unwedded Achilles, and of his friend Patroclus, Homer deemed it befitting the character and dignity of Achilles as a chief to show, that he slept in the recess of his well-constructed tent,

1 "Iliad," ix, 128.

and by his side lay a female, fair-cheeked Diomede, whom he had brought from Lesbos. And that Patroclus on the other side reclined, and by him also lay fair-waisted Iphis, whom noble Achilles gave him, having captured her at Scyros.[1] Such usages and customs on the part of unmarried as well as married men, cited approvingly by the great poet of the period, and sustained by public sentiment, tend to show that whatever of monogamy existed, was through an enforced constraint upon wives, while their husbands were not monogamists in the preponderating number of cases. Such a family has quite as many syndyasmian as monogamian characteristics.

The condition of woman in the Heroic Age is supposed to have been more favorable, and her position in the household more honorable than it was at the commencement of civilization, and even afterwards under their highest development. It may have been true in a far anterior period before descent was changed to the male line, but there seems to be little room for the conjecture at the time named. A great change for the better occurred, so far as the means and mode of life were concerned, but it served to render more conspicuous the real estimate placed upon her through the Later Period of barbarism.

Elsewhere attention has been called to the fact, that when descent was changed from the female line to the male, it operated injuriously upon the position and rights of the wife and mother. Her children were transferred from her own gens to that of her husband, and she forfeited her agnatic rights by her marriage without obtaining an equivalent. Before the change, the members of her own gens, in all probability, predominated in the household, which gave full force to the maternal bond, and made the woman rather more than the man the center of the family. After the change she stood alone in the household of her husband, isolated from her gentile kindred. It must have weakened the influence of the maternal bond, and have operated powerfully to lower her position and arrest her progress in the social scale.

1 "Iliad". ix, 663.

Among the prosperous classes, her condition of enforced seclusion, together with the avowed primary object of marriage, to beget children in lawful wedlock, lead to the inference that her position was less favorable in the Heroic Age than in the subsequent period, concerning which we are much better informed.

From first to last among the Greeks there was a principle of egotism or studied selfishness at work among the males, tending to lessen the appreciation of woman, scarcely found among savages. It reveals itself in their plan of domestic life, which in the higher ranks secluded the wife to enforce an exclusive cohabitation, without admitting the reciprocal obligation on the part of her husband. It implies the existence of an antecedent conjugal system of the Turanian type, against which it was designed to guard. So powerfully had the usages of centuries stamped upon the minds of Grecian women a sense of their inferiority, that they did not recover from it to the latest period of Grecian ascendency. It was, perhaps, one of the sacrifices required of womankind to bring this portion of the human race out of the syndyasmian into the monogamian family. It still remains an enigma that a race, with endowments great enough to impress their mental life upon the world, should have remained essentially barbarian in their treatment of the female sex at the height of their civilization. Women were not treated with cruelty, nor with discourtesy within the range of the privileges allowed them; but their education was superficial, intercourse with the opposite sex was denied them, and their inferiority was inculcated as a principle, until it came to be accepted as a fact by the women themselves. The wife was not the companion and the equal of her husband, but stood to him in the relation of a daughter; thus denying the fundamental principle of monogamy, as the institution in its highest form must be understood. The wife is necessarily the equal of her husband in dignity, in personal rights and in social position. We may thus discover at what a price of experience and endurance this great institution of modern society has been won.

Our information is quite ample and specific with respect to the condition of Grecian women and the Grecian family during the historical period. Becker, with the marvelous research for which his works are distinguished, has collected the principal facts and presented them with clearness and force. [1] His statements, while

1 The following condensed statement, taken from Charicles ("Excursus," xii, Longman's ed., Metcalfe's trans.), contains the material facts illustrative of the subject. After expressing the opinion that the women of Homer occupied a more honorable position in the household than the women of the historical period, he makes the following statements with respect to the condition of women, particularly at Athens and Sparta, during the high period of Grecian culture. He observes that the only excellence of which a woman was thought capable differed but little from that of a faithful slave (p. 464): that her utter want of independence led to her being considered a minor all her life long; that there were neither educational institutions for girls, nor any private teachers at home, their whole instruction being left to the mothers, and to nurses, and limited to spinning and weaving and other female avocations (p. 465); that they were almost entirely deprived of that most essential promoter of female culture, the society of the other sex; strangers as well as their nearest relatives being entirely excluded; even their fathers and husbands saw them but little, the men being more abroad than at home, and when at home inhabiting their own apartments; that the gynæconitis, though not exactly a prison, nor yet a locked harem, was still the confined abode allotted for life to the female portion of the household; that it was particularly the case with the maidens, who lived in the greatest seclusion until their marriage, and, so to speak, regularly under lock and key (p. 465); that it was unbecoming for a young wife to leave the house without her husband's knowledge, and in fact she seldom quitted it; she was thus restricted to the society of her female slaves; and her husband, if he chose to exercise it, had the power of keeping her in confinement (p. 466); that at those festivals, from which men were excluded, the women had an opportunity of seeing something of each other, which they enjoyed all the more from their ordinary seclusion; that women found it difficult to go out of their houses from these special restrictions; that no respectable lady thought of going without the attendance of a female slave assigned to her for that purpose by her husband (p. 469); that this method of treatment had the effect of rendering the girls excessively bashful and even prudish, and that even a married woman shrunk back and blushed if she chanced to be seen at the window by a man (p. 471); that marriage in reference to the procreation of children was considered by the Greeks a necessity, enforced by their duty to the gods, to the state and to their ancestors; that until a very late period, at least, no higher consideration attached to matrimony, nor was strong attachment a frequent cause of marriage (p. 473); that whatever attachment existed sprang from the soil of sensuality, and none other than sensual love was acknowledged between man and wife (p. 473); that at Athens, and probably in the other Grecian states as well, the generation of children was considered the chief end of marriage, the choice of the bride seldom depending on previous, or at least intimate acquaintance; and more attention was paid to the position of the damsel's family, and the amount of her dowry, than to her personal qualities; that such marriages were unfavorable to the existence of real affection, wherefore coldness, indifference, and

they do not furnish a complete picture of the family of the historical period, are quite sufficient to indicate the great difference between the Grecian and the modern civilized family, and also to show the condition of the monogamian family in the early stages of its development.

Among the facts stated by Becker, there are two that deserve further notice: first, the declaration that the chief object of marriage was the procreation of children in lawful wedlock; and second, the seclusion of women to insure this result. The two are intimately connected, and throw some reflected light upon the previous condition from which they had emerged. In the first place, the passion of love was unknown among the barbarians. They are below the sentiment, which is the offspring of civilization and superadded refinement. The Greeks in general, as their marriage customs show, had not attained to a knowledge of this passion, although there were, of course, numerous exceptions. Physical worth, in Grecian estimation, was the measure of all the exellences of which the female sex were capable. Marriage, therefore, was not grounded upon sentiment, but upon necessity and duty. These considerations are those which governed the Iroquois and the Aztecs; in fact they originated in barbarism, and reveal the anterior barbarous condition of the ancestors of the Grecian tribes. It seems strange

---

discontent frequently prevailed (p. 477); that the husband and wife took their meals together, provided no other men were dining with the master of the house, for no woman who did not wish to be accounted a courtesan, would think even in her own house of participating in the symposia of the men, or of being present when her husband accidentally brought home a friend to dinner (p. 490); that the province of the wife was the management of the entire household, and the nurture of the children—of the boys until they were placed under a master, of the girls until their marriage; that the infidelity of the wife was judged most harshly; and while it might be supposed that the woman, from her strict seclusion, was generally precluded from transgressing, they very frequently found means of deceiving their husbands; that the law imposed the duty of continence in a very unequal manner, for while the husband required from the wife the strictest fidelity, and visited with severity any dereliction on her part, he allowed himself to have intercourse with hetæræ, which conduct though not exactly approved, did not meet with any marked censure, and much less was it considered any violation of matrimonial rights (p. 494).

hat they were sufficient to answer the Greek ideal of the family relation in the midst of Grecian civilization. The growth of property and the desire for its transmission to children was, in reality, the moving power which brought in monogamy to insure legitimate heirs, and to limit their number to the actual progeny of the married pair. A knowledge of the paternity of children had begun to be realized under the syndyasmian family, from which the Grecian form was evidently derived, but it had not attained the requisite degree of certainty because of the survival of some portion of the ancient *jura conjugialia.* It explains the new usage which made its appearance in the Upper Status of barbarism; namely, the seclusion of wives. An implication to this effect arises from the circumstance that a necessity for the seclusion of the wife must have existed at the time, and which seems to have been so formidable that the plan of domestic life among the civilized Greeks was, in reality, a system of female confinement and restraint. Although the particulars cited relate more especially to the family among the prosperous classes, the spirit it evinces was doubtless general.

Turning next to the Roman family, the condition of woman is more favorable, but her subordination the same.

She was treated with respect in Rome as in Athens, but in the Roman family her influence and authority were greater. As *mater familias* she was mistress of the family. She went into the streets freely without restraint on the part of her husband, and frequented with the men the theaters and festive banquets. In the house she was not confined to particular apartments, neither was she excluded from the table of the men. The absence of the worst restrictions placed upon Grecian females was favorable to the growth of a sense of personal dignity and of independence among Roman women. Plutarch remarks that after the peace with the Sabines, effected through the intervention of the Sabine women, many honorable privileges were conferred upon them; the men were to give them the way when they met on the street; they were not to utter a vulgar word in the presence of females, nor appear nude before them.[1] Marriage, however, placed the wife in the power of her husband (*in manum viri*); the notion that she must remain under power following, by an apparent necessity, her emancipation by her marriage from paternal power. The husband treated his wife as his daughter, and not as his equal. Moreover, he had the power of correction, and of life and death in case of adultery; but the exercise of this last power seems to have been subject to the concurrence of the council of her gens.

Unlike other people, the Romans possessed three forms of marriage. All alike placed the wife in the hand of her husband, and recognized as the chief end of marriage the procreation of children in lawful wedlock (*liberorum querendorum causa*).[2] These forms (*confarreatio, coemptio,* and *usus*) lasted through the Republic, but fell out under the Empire, when a fourth form, the free marriage, was generally adopted, because it did not place the wife in the power of her husband. Divorce, from the earliest period, was at the option of the parties, a characteristic of the syndyasmian family, and transmitted probably from that source. They rarely occurred, however, until near the close of the Republic.[3]

The licentiousness which prevailed in Grecian and Roman cities at the height of civilization has generally been regarded as a lapse from a higher and purer condition of virtue and morality. But the fact is capable of a

---

1 "Vit. Rom.," c. 20.

2 Quinctilian.

3 With respect to the conjugal fidelity of Roman women. Becker remarks "that in the earlier times excesses on either side seldom occurred," which must be set down as a mere conjecture; but "when morals began to deteriorate, we first meet with great lapses from this fidelity, and men and women outbid each other in wanton indulgence. The original modesty of the women became gradually more rare, while luxury and extravagance waxed stronger, and of many women it could be said, as Clitipho complained of his Bacchis, (Ter., "Heaut.," ii, 1, 15), "Mea est petax, procax, magnifica, sumptuosa, nobilis." Many Roman ladies, to compensate for the neglect of their husbands, had a lover of their own, who, under the pretense of being the procurator of the lady, accompanied her at all times. As a natural consequence of this, celibacy continually increased amongst the men, and there was the greatest levity respecting divorces."—Gallus, "Excursus," i. p. 155, Longman's ed., Metcalf's trans.

different, or at least of a modified explanation. They had never attained to a pure morality in the intercourse of the sexes from which to decline. Repressed or moderated in the midst of war and strife endangering the national existence, the license revived with peace and prosperity, because the moral elements of society had not risen against it for its extirpation. This licentiousness was, in all probability, the remains of an ancient conjugal system, never fully eradicated, which had followed down from barbarism as a social taint, and now expressed its excesses in the new channel of hetærism. If the Greeks and Romans had learned to respect the equities of monogamy, instead of secluding their wives in the gynæconitis in one case, and of holding them under power in the other, there is reason to believe that society among them would have presented a very different aspect. Since neither one nor the other had developed any higher morality, they had but little occasion to mourn over a decay of public morals. The substance of the explanation lies in the fact that neither recognized in its integrity the principle of monogamy, which alone was able to place their respective societies upon a moral basis. The premature destruction of the ethnic life of these remarkable races is due in no small measure to their failure to develop and utilize the mental, moral and conservative forces of the female intellect, which were not less essential than their own corresponding forces to their progress and preservation. After a long protracted experience in barbarism, during which they won the remaining elements of civilization, they perished politically, at the end of a brief career, seemingly from the exhilaration of the new life they had created.

Among the Hebrews, whilst the patriarchal family in the early period was common with the chiefs, the monogamian, into which the patriarchal soon subsided, was common among the people. But with respect to the constitution of the latter, and the relations of husband and wife in the family, the details are scanty.

Without seeking to multiply illustrations, it is plain that the monogamian family had grown into the form in which it appeared, at the commencement of the historical period, from a lower type; and that during the classical period it advanced sensibly, though without attaining its highest form. It evidently sprang from a previous syndyasmian family as its immediate germ; and while improving with human progress it fell short of its true ideal in the classical period. Its highest known perfection, at least, was not attained until modern times. The portraiture of society in the Upper Status of barbarism by the early writers implies the general practice of monogamy, but with attending circumstances indicating that it was the monogamian family of the future struggling into existence under adverse influences, feeble in vitality, rights and immunities, and still environed with the remains of an ancient conjugal system.

As the Malayan system expressed the relationships that existed in the consanguine family, and as the Turanian expressed those which existed in the punaluan, so the Aryan expressed those which existed in the monogamian; each family resting upon a different and distinct form of marriage.

It cannot be shown absolutely, in the present state of our knowledge, that the Aryan, Semitic and Uralian families of mankind formerly possessed the Turanian system of consanguinity, and that it fell into desuetude under monogamy. Such, however, would be the presumption from the body of ascertained facts. All the evidence points in this direction so decisively as to exclude any other hypothesis. Firstly. The organization into gentes had a natural origin in the punaluan family, where a group of sisters married to each other's husbands furnished, with their children and descendants in the female line, the exact circumscription as well as the body of a gens in its archaic form. The principal branches of the Aryan family were organized in gentes when first known historically, sustaining the inference that, when one undivided people, they were thus organized. From this fact the further presumption arises that they derived the organization through a remote ancestry who lived in that same punaluan condition which gave birth to this remarkable and wide-spread institution. Besides this, the Turanian system of consanguinity is still found connected with the gens in its archaic form among the American aborigines. This natural connection would remain unbroken until a change of social condition occurred, such as monogamy would produce, having power to work its overthrow. Secondly. In the Aryan system of consanguinity there is some evidence pointing to the same conclusion. It may well be supposed that a large portion of the nomenclature of the Turanian system would fall out under monogamy, if this system had previously prevailed among the Aryan nations. The application of its terms to categories of persons, whose relationships would now be discriminated from each other, would compel their abandonment. It is impossible to explain the impoverished condition of the original nomenclature of the Aryan system except on this hypothesis. All there was of it common to the several Aryan dialects are the terms for father and mother, brother and sister, and son and daughter; and a common term (San., *naptar;* Lat., *nepos;* Gr., *anepsios;*) applied indiscriminately to nephew, grandson, and cousin. They could never have attained to the advanced condition implied by monogamy with such a scanty nomenclature of blood relationships. But with a previous system, analogous to the Turanian, this impoverishment can be explained. The terms for brother and sister were now in the abstract, and new creations, because these relationships under the Turanian system were conceived universally as elder and younger; and the several terms were applied to categories of persons, including persons not own brothers and sisters. In the Aryan system this distinction is laid aside, and for the first time these relationships were conceived in the abstract. Under monogamy the old terms were inapplicable because they were applied to collaterals. Remains of a prior Turanian system, however, still appear in the system of the Uralian family, as among the Hungarians, where brothers and sisters are classified into elder and younger by special terms. In French, also, besides *frère,* and *soeur,* we find *aîné,* elder brother, *pûnè* and *cadet,* younger brother, and *aînée* and *cadette,* elder and younger sister. So also in Sanskrit we find *agrajar,* and *amujar,* and *agrajri,* and *amujri* for the same relationships; but whether the latter are from Sanskrit or aboriginal sources, I am unable to state. In the Aryan dialects the terms for brother and sister are the same words dialectically changed, the Greek having substituted *adelphos* for *phrater.* If common terms once existed in these dialects for elder and younger brother and sister, their previous application to categories of persons would render them inapplicable, as an exclusive distinction, to own brothers and sisters. The falling out from the Aryan system of this striking and beautiful feature of the Turanian requires a strong motive for its occurrence, which the previous existence and abandonment of the Turanian system would explain. It would be difficult to find any other. It is not supposable that the Aryan nations were without a term for grandfather in the original speech, a relationship recognized universally among savage and barbarous tribes; and yet there is no common term for this relationship in the Aryan dialects. In Sanskrit we have *pitameha,* in Greek *pappos,* in Latin *avus,* in Russian *djed,* in Welsh *hendad,* which last is a compound like the German *grossvader* and the English grandfather. These terms are radically different. But with a term under a previous system, which was applied not only to the grandfather proper, his brothers, and his several male cousins, but also to the brothers and several male cousins of his grandmother, it could not be made to signify a lineal grandfather and progenitor under monogamy. Its abandonment would be apt to occur in course of time. The absence of a term for this relationship in the original speech seems to find in this manner a sufficient explanation. Lastly. There is no term for uncle and aunt in the abstract, and no special terms for uncle and aunt on the father's side and on the mother's side running through the Aryan dialects. We find *pitroya, patros,* and *patruus* for paternal uncle in Sanskrit, Greek, and Latin; *stryc* in Slavonic for the same, and a common term, *eam, oom,* and *oheim* in Anglo-Saxon, Belgian, and German, and none in the Celtic. It is equally inconceivable that there was no term in the original Aryan speech for maternal uncle, a relationship made so conspicuous by the gens among barbarous tribes. If their previous system was Turanian, there was necessarily a term for this uncle, but restricted to the own brothers of the mother, and to her several male cousins. Its application to such a number of persons in a category, many of whom could not be uncles under monogamy, would, for the reasons stated, compel its abandonment. It is evident that a previous system of some kind must have given place to the Aryan.

Assuming that the nations of the Aryan, Semitic and Uralian families formerly possessed the Turanian system of consanguinity, the transition from it to a descriptive system was simple and natural, after the old system, through monogamy, had become untrue to descents as they would then exist. Every relationship under monogamy is specific. The new system, formed under such circumstances, would describe the persons by means of the primary terms or a combination of them: as brother's son for nephew, father's brother for uncle, and father's brother's son for cousin. Such was the original of the present system of the Aryan, Semitic and Uralian families. The generalizations they now contain were of later introduction. All the tribes possessing the Turanian system describe their kindred by the same formula, when asked in what manner one person was related to another. A descriptive system precisely like the Aryan always existed both with the Turanian and the Malayan, not as a system of consanguinity, for they had a permanent system, but as a means of tracing relationships. It is plain from the impoverished conditions of their nomenclatures that the Aryan, Semitic and Uralian nations must have rejected a prior system of consanguinity of some kind. The conclusion, therefore, is reasonable that when the monogamian family became generally established these nations fell back upon the old descriptive form, always in use under the Turanian system, and allowed the previous one to die out as useless and untrue to descents. This would be the natural and obvious mode of transition from the Turanian into the Aryan system; and it explains, in a satisfactory manner, the origin as well as peculiar character of the latter.

In order to complete the exposition of the monogamian family in its relations to the Aryan system of consanguinity, it will be necessary to present this system somewhat in detail, as has been done in the two previous cases.

A comparison of its forms in the several Aryan dialects shows that the original of the present system was purely descriptive.[1] The Erse, which is the typical Aryan form, and the Esthonian, which is the typical Uralian, are still descriptive. In the Erse the only terms for the blood relationships are the primary, namely, those for father and mother, brother and sister, and son and daughter. All the remaining kindred are described by means of these terms, but commencing in the reverse order: thus brother, son of brother, and son of son of brother. The Aryan system exhibits the actual relationships under monogamy, and assumes that the paternity of children is known.

In course of time a method of description, materially different from the Celtic, was engrafted upon the new system; but without changing its radical features. It was introduced by the Roman civilians to perfect the framework of a code of descents, to the necessity for which we are indebted for its existence. Their improved method has been adopted by the several Aryan nations among whom the Roman influence extended. The Slavonic system has some features entirely peculiar and evidently of Turanian origin.[2] To obtain a knowledge historically of our present system it is necessary to resort to the Roman, as perfected by the civilians.[3] The additions were slight, but they changed the method of describing kindred. They consisted chiefly, as elsewhere stated,

---

1 "Systems of Consanguinity," Table I, p. 79.
2 "Systems of Consanguinity," etc., p. 40.
3 "Pandects," lib. xxviii, tit. x. and "Institutes" of Justinian, lib. iii, tit. vi.

in distinguishing the relationships of uncle and aunt on the father's side from those on the mother's side, with the invention of terms to express these relationships in the concrete; and in creating a term for grandfather to be used as the correlative of *nepos.* With these terms and the primary, in connection with suitable augments, they were enabled to systematize the relationships in the lineal and in the first five collateral lines, which included the body of the kindred of every individual. The Roman is the most perfect and scientific system of consanguinity under monogamy which has yet appeared; and it has been made more attractive by the invention of an unusual number of terms to express the marriage relationships. From it we may learn our own system, which has adopted its improvements, better than from the Anglo-Saxon or Celtic. In a table, at the end of this chapter, the Latin and Arabic forms are placed side by side, as representatives, respectively, of the Aryan and Semitic systems. The Arabic seems to have passed through processes similar to the Roman, and with similar results. The Roman only will be explained.

From *Ego* to *tritavus,* in the lineal line, are six generations of ascendants, and from the same to *trinepos* are the same number of descendants, in the description of which but four radical terms are used. If it were desirable to ascend above the sixth ancestor, *tritavus* would become a new starting-point of description; thus, *tritavi pater,* the father of *tritavus,* and so upward to *tritavi tritavus,* who is the twelfth ancestor of *Ego* in the lineal right line, male. In our rude nomenclature the phrase grandfather's grandfather must be repeated six times to express the same relationship, or rather to describe the same person. In like manner *trinepotis trinepos* carries us to the twelfth descendant of *Ego* in the right lineal male line.

The first collateral line, male, which commences with brother, *frater,* runs as follows: *Fratris filius,* son of brother, *fratris nepos,* grandson of brother, *fratris pronepos,* greatgrandson of brother, and on to *fratris trinepos,* the great-grandson of the great-grandson of the brother of *Ego*. If it were necessary to extend the description to the twelfth descendant, *fratris trinepos* would become a second starting-point, from which we should have *fratris trinepotis trinepos,* as the end of the series. By this simple method *frater* is made the root of descent in this line, and every person belonging to it is referred to him by the force of this term in the description; and we know at once that each person thus described belongs to the first collateral line, male. It is therefore specific and complete. In like manner, the same line, female, commences with sister, *soror,* giving for the series, *sororis filia,* sister's daughter, *sororis neptis,* sister's granddaughter, *sororis proneptis,* sister's great-granddaughter, and on to *sororis trineptis,* her sixth descendant, and to *sororis trineptis trineptis,* her twelfth descendant. While the two branches of the first collateral line originate, in strictness, in the father, *pater,* the common bond of connection between them, yet, by making the brother and sister the root of descent in the description, not only the line but its two branches are maintained distinct, and the relationship of each person to *Ego* is specialized. This is one of the chief excellences of the system, for it is carried into all the lines, as a purely scientific method of distinguishing and describing kindred.

The second collateral line, male, on the father's side, commences with father's brother, *patruus,* and is composed of him and his descendants. Each person, by the terms used to describe him, is referred with entire precision to his proper position in the line, and his relationship is indicated specifically; thus, *patrui filius,* son of paternal uncle, *patrui nepos,* grandson of, and *patrui pronepos,* great-grandson of paternal uncle, and on to *patrui trinepos,* the sixth descendant of *patruus.* If it became necessary to extend this line to the twelfth generation we should have, after passing through the intermediate degrees, *patrui trinepotis trinepos,* who is the great-grandson of the great-grandson of *patrui trinepos,* the great-grandson of the great-grandson of *patruus.* It will be observed that the term for cousin is rejected in the formal method used in the Pandects. He is described as *patrui filius,* but he was also called a brother patrual, *frater patruelis,* and among the people at large by the common term *consobrinus,* from which our term cousin is derived.[1] The second collateral line, female, on the father's side, commences with father's sister, *amita,* paternal aunt; and her descendants are described according to the same general plan; thus, *amitae filia,* paternal aunt's daughter, *amitae neptis,* paternal aunt's granddaughter, and on to *amitae trineptis,* and to *amitae trineptis trineptis.* In this branch of the line the special term for this cousin, *amitina,* is also set aside for the descriptive phrase *amitae filia.*

In like manner the third collateral line, male, on the father's side commences with grandfather's brother, who is styled *patruus magnus,* or great paternal uncle. At this point in the nomenclature, special terms fail, and compounds are resorted to, although the relationship itself is in the concrete. It is evident that this relationship was not discriminated until a comparatively modern period. No existing language, so far as the inquiry has been extended, possesses an original term for this relationship, although without it this line cannot be described except by the Celtic method. If he were called simply *grandfather's brother* the phrase would describe a person, leaving the relationship to implication; but if he is styled a great-uncle, it expresses a relationship in the concrete. With the first person in this branch of the line thus made definite, all of his descendants are referred to him, by the form of the description, as the root of descent; and the line, the side, the particular branch, and the degree of the relationship of each person are at once fully expressed. This line also may be extended to the twelfth descendant, which would give for the series *patrui magni filius,* son of the paternal great-uncle, *patrui magni nepos,* and on to *patrui magni trinepos,* and ending with *patrui*

1 Item fratres patrueles, sorores patrueles, id est qui quæ-ve ex duobus fratribus progenerantur; item consobrini consobrinæ, id est qui quæ-veex duobus sororibus nascuntur (quasi consorini); item amitini amitinæ, id est qui quæ-ve ex fratre ex sorore propagantur; sed fere vulgos istos omnes communi appellatione consobrinus vocat.—"Pand,," lib. xxxviii, tit, x.

magni trinepotis trinepos. The same line, female, commences with grandfather's sister, *amita magna,* great paternal aunt; and her descendants are similarly described.

The fourth and fifth collateral lines, male, on the father's side, commence, respectively, with great-grandfather's brother, who is styled *patruus major,* greater paternal uncle, and with great-great-grandfather's brother, *patruus maximus,* greatest paternal uncle. In extending the series we have in the fourth *patrui majoris filius,* and on to *patrui majoris trinepos;* and in the fifth *patrui maximi filius,* and on to *patrui maximi trinepos.* The female branches commence, respectively, with *amita major,* greater, and *amita maxima,* greatest paternal aunt; and the description of persons in each follows in the same order.

Thus far the lines have been on the father's side only. The necessity for independent terms for uncle and aunt on the mother's side to complete the Roman method of description is now apparent; the relatives on the mother's side being equally numerous, and entirely distinct. These terms were found in *avunculus,* maternal uncle, and *matertera,* maternal aunt. In describing the relatives on the mother's side, the lineal female line is substituted for the male, but the first collateral line remains the same. In the second collateral line, male, on the mother's side, we have for the series *avunculus,* maternal uncle, *avunculi filius, avunculi nepos,* and on to *avunculi trinepos,* and ending with *avunculi trinepotis trinepos.* In the female branch, *matertera,* maternal aunt, *materteræ filia,* and on as before. The third collateral line, male and female, commence, respectively, with *avunculus magnus,* and *matertera magna,* great maternal uncle and aunt; the fourth with *avunculus major,* and *matertera major,* greater maternal uncle, and aunt; and the fifth with *avunculus maximus,* and *matertera maxima,* greatest maternal uncle, and aunt. The descriptions of persons in each line and branch are in form corresponding with those previously given.

Since the first five collateral lines embrace as wide a circle of kindred as it was necessary to include for the practical objects of a code of descents, the ordinary formula of the Roman civilians did not extend beyond this number.

In terms for the marriage relationships, the Latin language is remarkably opulent, whilst our mother English betrays its poverty by the use of such unseemly phrases as father-in-law, son-in-law, brother-in-law, step-father, and step-son, to express some twenty very common, and very near relationships, nearly all of which are provided with special terms in the Latin nomenclature.

It will not be necessary to pursue further the details of the Roman system of consanguinity. The principal and most important of its features have been presented, and in a manner sufficiently special to render the whole intelligible. For simplicity of method, felicity of description, distinctness of arrangement by lines and branches, and beauty of nomenclature, it is incomparable. It stands in its method pre-eminently at the head of all the systems of relationship ever perfected by man, and furnishes one of many illustrations that to whatever the Roman mind had occasion to give organic form, it placed once for all upon a solid foundation.

No reference has been made to the details of the Arabic system; but, as the two forms are given in the Table, the explanation made of one will suffice for the other, to which it is equally applicable.

With its additional special terms, and its perfected method, consanguinei are assumed to be connected, in virtue of their descent, through married pairs, from common ancestors. They arrange themselves in a lineal and several collateral lines; and the latter are perpetually divergent from the former. These are necessary consequences of monogamy. The relationship of each person to the central *Ego* is accurately defined and, except as to those who stand in an identical relationship, is kept distinct from every other by means of a special term or descriptive phrase. It also implies the certainty of the parentage of every individual, which monogamy alone could assure. Moreover, it describes the relationships in the monogamian family as they actually exist. Nothing can be plainer than that this form of marriage made this form of the family, and that the latter created this system of consanguinity. The three are necessary parts of a whole where the descriptive system is exclusive. What we know by direct observation to be true with respect to the monogamian family, its law of marriage and its system of consanguinity, has been shown to be equally true with respect to the punaluan family, its law of marriage and its system of consanguinity; and not less so of the consanguine family, its form of marriage and its system of consanguinity. Any of these three parts being given, the existence of the other two with it, at some one time, may be deduced with certainty. If any difference could be made in favor of the superior materiality of any one of the three, the preference would belong to systems of consanguinity. They have crystallized the evidence declaring the marriage law and the form of the family in the relationship of every individual person; thus preserving not only the highest evidence of the fact, but as many concurring declarations thereto as there are members united by the bond of consanguinity. It furnishes a test of the high rank of a domestic institution, which must be supposed incapable of design to pervert the truth, and which, therefore, may be trusted implicitly as to whatever it necessarily teaches. Finally, it is with respect to systems of consanguinity that our information is most complete.

The five successive forms of the family, mentioned at the outset, have now been presented and explained, with such evidence of their existence, and such particulars of their structure as our present knowledge furnishes. Although the treatment of each has been general, it has touched the essential facts and attributes, and established the main proposition, that the family commenced in the consanguine, and grew, through successive stages of development, into the monogamian. There is nothing in this general conclusion which might not have been anticipated from *à priori* considerations; but the difficulties and the hindrances which obstructed its growth are seen to have been far greater than would have been supposed. As a growth with the ages of time, it has shared in all the vicissitudes of human experience, and now reveals more expressively, perhaps, than any other institution, the graduated scale of human progress from the abyss of primitive savagery, through barbarism, to civilization. It brings us near to the daily life of the human family in the different epochs of its progressive development, indicating, in some measure, its hardships, its struggles and also its victories, when different periods are contrasted. We should value the great institution of the family, as it now exists, in some proportion to the expenditure of time and of intelligence in its production; and receive it as the richest legacy transmitted to us by ancient society, because it embodies and records the highest results of its varied and prolonged experience.

When the fact is accepted that the family has passed through four successive forms, and is now in a fifth, the question at once arises whether this form can be permanent in the future. The only answer that can be given is, that it must advance as society advances, and change as society changes, even as it has done in the past. It is the creature of the social system, and will reflect its culture. As the monogamian family has improved greatly since the commencement of civilization, and very sensibly in modern times, it is at least supposable that it is capable of still further improvement until the equality of the sexes is attained. Should the monogamian family in the distant future fail to answer the requirements of society, assuming the continuous progress of civilization, it is impossible to predict the nature of its successor.

Roman and Arabic System of Relationship.

	Description of Persons.	Relationship in Latin.	Translation.	Relationship in Arabic.	Translation.
1	gt-grandfather's gt-grandfather	tritavus	gt-grandfather's gt-g'dfather	jidd jidd jiddi	grandfather of g'dfather of g'dfather my
2	" " grandfather	atavus	" " grandfather	jidd jidd abi	" " " " father my
3	" " father	abavus	great-great-grandfather	jidd jiddi	" " grandfather my
4	" " mother	abavia	" " grandmother	sitt sitti	grandmother of grandmother my
5	great-grandfather	proavus	great-grandfather	jidd abi	grandfather of father my
6	" grandmother	proavia	" grandmother	sitt abi	grandmother " " "
7	grandfather	avus	grandfather	jidd	grandfather my
8	grandmother	avia	grandmother	sitti	grandmother "
9	father	pater	father	abi	father my
10	mother	mater	mother	ummi	mother "
11	son	filius	son	ibni	son "
12	daughter	filia	daughter	ibneti b, binti	daughter "
13	grandson	nepos	grandson	ibn ibni	son of son my
14	granddaughter	neptis	granddaughter	ibnet ibni	daughter of son my
15	great-grandson	pronepos	great-grandson	ibn ibn ibni	son of son of son my
16	" grandmother	proneptis	" granddaughter	bint bint binti	daughter of daughter of daughter my
17	gt-grandson's son	abnepos	" great-grandson	ibn ibn ibn ibni	son of son of son of son my
18	" " daughter	abneptis	" " granddaughter	bint bint bint binti	dau of dau of dau of dau my
19	" " grandson	atnepos	gt-grandson's grandson	ibn ibn ibn ibn ibni	son of son of son of son of son my
20	" " granddaughter	atneptis	" " granddaughter	bint bint bint bint binti	dau of dau of dau of dau of dau my
21	" " gt-grandson	trinepos	" " gt-grandson	ibn ibn ibn ibn ibn ibni	son of son of son of son of son of son my
22	" " " granddaughter	trineptis	" " " granddau'ter	bint bint bint bint bint binti	dau of dau of dau of dau of dau of dau my
23	brothers	fratres	brothers	ahwati	brothers my
24	sisters	sorores	sisters	ahwâti	sisters "
25	brother	frater	brother	akhi	brother "
	(First Collateral Line)				
26	brother's son	fratris filius	son of brother	ibn akhi	son of brother my
27	" son's wife	fratris filii uxor	wife of son of brother	amrat ibn akhi	wife of son of brother my
28	" daughter	fratris filia	daughter of brother	bint akhi	daughter of brother my
29	" daughter's husband	fratris filiae vir	husband of dau'ter of brother	zoj bint akhi	husband of daughter of brother my
30	" grandson	fratris nepos	grandson of brother	ibn ibn "	son of son of brother my
31	" granddaughter	" neptis	granddaughter " "	bint ibn "	daughter of son of brother my
32	" gt-grandson	" pronepos	gt-grandson " "	ibn ibn ibn akhi	son of son of son of brother my
33	" " granddaughter	" proneptis	gt-granddaughter " "	bint bint bint akhi	dau of dau of dau of brother my
34	sister	soror	sister	akhti	sister my
35	sister's son	sororis filius	son of sister	ibn akhti	son of sister my
36	" son's wife	sororis filii uxor	wife of son of sister	amrât ibn akhti	wife of son of sister my
37	" daughter	" filia	daughter of sister	bint akhti	daughter of sister my
38	" daughter's husband	" filiae vir	husband of daughter of sister	zoj bint akhti	husband of daughter of sister my
39	" grandson	" nepos	sister's grandson	ibn akhti	son of sister my
40	" granddaughter	" neptis	" granddaughter	bint akhti	daughter of sister my

	Description of Persons.	Relationship in Latin.	Translation.	Relationship in Arabic.	Translation.
41	sister's great-grandson	sororis pronepos	sister's great-grandson	ibn ibn akhti	son of son of sister my
42	" " granddaughter	" proneptis	" " granddaughter	bint bint akhti	daughter of daughter of sister my
	(Second Collateral Line).				
43	father's brother	patruus	paternal uncle	ammi	paternal uncle my
44	" brother's wife	patrui uxor	wife of paternal uncle	amrât ammi	wife of paternal uncle my
45	" " son	" filius,	son of " "	ibn ammi	son of " " "
46	" " son's wife	" filii uxor	wife of son of " "	amrât ibn ammi	wife of son of " " "
47	" " daughter	" filia	daughter of " "	bint ammi	daughter of " " "
48	" " dau'ter's husband	" filiae vir	husband of dau of " "	zôj bint ammi	husband of daughter of " " "
49	" " grandson	" nepos	grandson of " "	ibn ibn ammi	son of son of " " "
50	" " granddaughter	" neptis	granddaughter of " "	bint bint ammi	daughter of daughter of " " "
51	" " gt-grandson	" pronepos	gt-grandson of " "	ibn ibn ibn ammi	son of son of son of " " "
52	" " " granddaughter	" proneptis	" granddau'ter of " "	bint bint bint ammi	dau of dau of dau of " " "
53	father's sister	amita	paternal aunt	ammeti	paternal aunt my
54	" sister's husband	amitae vir	husband of paternal aunt	arât ammeti	husband of paternal aunt my
55	" " son	" filius	son of " "	ibn ammeti	son of " " "
56	" " son's wife	" filii uxor	wife of son of " "	amrât ibn ammeti	wife of son of " " "
57	" " daughter	" filia	daughter of " "	bint ammeti	daughter of " " "
58	" " dau'ter's husband	" filiae vir	husband of dau of " "	zôj bint ammeti	husband of daughter of " " "
59	" " grandson	" nepos	grandson of " "	ibn ibn ammeti	son of son of " " "
60	" " granddaughter	" neptis	granddaughter of " "	bint bint ammeti	daughter of daughter of " " "
61	" " gt-grandson	" pronepos	gt-grandson of " "	ibn ibn ibn ammeti	son of son of son of " " "
62	" " " granddaughter	" proneptis	" granddau'ter of " "	bint bint bint ammeti	dau of dau of dau of " " "
63	mother's brother	avunculus	maternal uncle	khâli	maternal uncle my
64	" brother's wife	avunculi uxor	wife of maternal uncle	amrat khâli	wife of maternal uncle my
65	" " son	" filius	son of " "	ibn khâli	son of " " "
66	" " son's wife	" filii uxor	wife of son of " "	amrat ibn khâli	wife of son of " " "
67	" " daughter	" filia	daughter of " "	bint khâli	daughter of " " "
68	" " dau'ter's husband	" filiae vir	husband of dau of " "	zôj bint khâli	husband of daughter of " " "
69	" " grandson	" nepos	grandson of " "	ibn ibn khâli	son of son of " " "
70	" " granddaughter	" neptis	granddaughter of " "	bint bint khâli	daughter of daughter of " " "
71	" " gt-grandson	" pronepos	gt-grandson of " "	ibn ibn ibn khâli	son of son of son of " " "
72	" " gt-granddaughter	" proneptis	" granddau'ter of " "	bint bint bint khâli	dau of dau of dau of " " "
73	mother's sister	matertera	maternal aunt	khâleti	maternal aunt my
74	" sister's husband	materterae vir	husband of maternal aunt	zôj khâleti	husband of maternal aunt my
75	" " son	" filius	son of " "	ibn khâleti	son of " " "
76	" " son's wife	" filii uxor	wife of son of " "	amrât ibn khâleti	wife of son of " " "
77	" " daughter	" filia	daughter of " "	bint khâleti	daughter of " " "
78	" " dau'ter's husband	" filiae vir	husband of dau of " "	zôj bint khâleti	husband of daughter of " " "
79	" " grandson	" nepos	grandson of " "	ibn ibn khâleti	son of son of " " "
80	" " granddaughter	" neptis	granddaughter of " "	bint bint khâleti	daughter of daughter of " " "
81	" " gt-grandson	" pronepos	gt-grandson of " "	ibn ibn ibn khâleti	son of son of son of " " "
82	" " " granddaughter	" proneptis	" granddau'ter of " "	bint bint bint khâleti	dau of dau of dau of " " "

	Description of Persons.	Relationship in Latin.	Translation.	Relationship in Arabic.	Translation.
	(Third Collateral Line).				
83	father's father's brother	patruus magnus	great paternal uncle	amm âbi	paternal uncle of father my
84	" " brother's son	patrui magni filius	son of gt pat uncle	ibn ammi âbi	son of paternal uncle of father my
85	" " " grandson	" " nepos	grandson of " " "	ibn ibn ammi âbi	son of son of " " " " "
86	" " " gt-grandson	" " pronepos	gt-grandson of " " "	ibn ibn ibn ammi âbi	son of son of son of " " " " "
87	" " sister	amita magna	great paternal aunt	ammet âbi	paternal aunt of father my
88	" " sister's daughter	amitae magnae filia	daughter of gt pat aunt	bint ammet âbi	daughter of paternal aunt of father my
89	" " " granddaughter	amitae magnae neptis	granddaughter of " " "	bint bint ammet âbi	dau of dau of " " " " "
90	" " " gt-granddau'ter	" " proneptis	gt-granddau'ter of " " "	bint bint bint ammet âbi	dau of dau of dau of " " " " "
91	mother's mother's brother	avunculus magnus	great maternal uncle	khâl ŭmmi	maternal uncle of mother my
92	" " brother's son	avunculi magni filius	son of gt mat uncle	ibn khâl ŭmmi	son of maternal uncle of mother my
93	" " " grandson	" " nepos	grandson of " " "	ibn ibn khâl ŭmmi	son of son of " " " " "
94	" " " gt-grandson	" " pronepos	gt-grandson of " " "	ibn ibn ibn khâl ŭmmi	son of son of son of " " " " "
95	" " sister	matertera magna	great maternal aunt	khâlet ŭmmi	maternal aunt of mother my
96	" " sister's daughter	materterae magnae filia	daughter of gt mat aunt	bint khâlet ŭmmi	daughter of maternal aunt of mother my
97	" " " granddaughter	" " neptis	granddaughter of " " "	bint bint khâlet ŭmmi	dau of dau of " " " " "
98	" " " gt-granddau'ter	" " proneptis	gt-granddau'ter of " " "	bint bint bint khâlet ŭmmi	dau of dau of dau of " " " " "
	(Fourth Collateral Line).				
99	father's father's father's brother	patruus major	paternal great-great-uncle	amm jiddi	paternal uncle of grandfather my
100	" " " brother's son	patrui majoris filius	son of pat gt-gt-uncle	ibn amm jiddi	son of paternal uncle of g f my
101	" " " " grandson	" " nepos	grandson of " " " "	ibn ibn amm jiddi	son of son of " " " " "
102	" " " " gt-g'dson	" " pronepos	gt-grandson of " " " "	ibn ibn ibn amm jiddi	son of son of son of " " " " "
103	" " " sister	amita major	paternal great-great aunt	ammet jiddi	paternal aunt of grandfather my
104	" " " sister's daughter	amitae majoris filia	daughter of pat gt-gt-aunt	bint ammet jiddi	daughter of paternal aunt of g f my
105	father's father's father's sister's granddaughter	amitae majoris neptis	granddau'ter of pat gt-gt-aunt	bint bint ammet jiddi	dau of dau of paternal aunt of g f my
106	father's father's father's sister's great-granddaughter	amitae majoris proneptis	gt-g'ddau'ter of pat gt-gt aunt	bint bint bint ammet jiddi	dau of dau of dau of paternal aunt of g f my
107	mother's mother's mother's bro'r	avunculus major	maternal great-great uncle	khâl sitti	maternal uncle of grandmother my
108	" " " bro's son	avunculi majoris filius	son of mat gt-gt-uncle	ibn khâl sitti	son of maternal uncle of g m my
109	" " " " g'dson	" " nepos	grandson of " " " "	ibn ibn khâl sitti	son of son of " " " " "
110	mother's mother's mother's brother's great-grandson	avunculi majoris pronepos	gt-grandson of mat gt-gt-uncle	ibn ibn ibn khâl sitti	son of son of son of mat uncle of g m my
111	mother's mother's mother's sister	matertera major	maternal great-great aunt	khâlet sitti	maternal aunt of grandmother my
112	mother's mother's mother's sister's daughter	materterae majoris filia	daughter of mat gt-gt-aunt	bint khâlet sitti	daughter of maternal aunt of g m my
113	mother's mother's mother's sister's granddaughter	materterae majoris neptis	granddau'ter of mat gt-gt-aunt	bint bint khâlet sitti	dau of dau of maternal aunt of g m my
114	mother's mother's mother's sister's great-granddaughter	mater. major. proneptis	gt-g'ddau'ter of mat gt-gt-aunt	bint bint bint khâlet sitti	dau of dau of dau of mat aunt of g m my
	(Fifth Collateral Line).				

	Description of Persons.	Relationship in Latin.	Translation.	Relationship in Arabic.	Translation.
115	father's father's father's father's brother	patruus maximus	paternal gt-gt-uncle	amm jidd ăbi	paternal uncle of grandfather of father my
116	father's father's father's father's brother's son	patrui maximi filius	son of paternal gt-gt-uncle	ibn amm jidd ăbi	son of paternal uncle of g f of father my
117	father's father's father's father's grandson	patrui maximi nepos	grandson of pat gt-gt-uncle	ibn ibn amm jidd ăbi	son of son of pat uncle of g f of father my
118	father's father's father's father's great-grandson	patrui maximi pronepos	gt-grandson of pat gt-gt-uncle	ibn ibn ibn amm jidd ăbi	son of son of son of pat uncle of g f of f my
119	father's father's father's father's sister	amita maxima	paternal gt-gt-gt-aunt	ammet jidd ăbi	paternal aunt of grandfather of father my
120	father's father's father's father's sister's daughter	amitae maximae filia	daughter of pat gt-gt-gt-aunt	bint ammet jidd ăbi	daughter of pat aunt of g f of father my
121	father's father's father's father's sister's granddaughter	amitae maximae neptis	g'ddau'ter of pat gt-gt-gt-aunt	bint bint ammet jidd ăbi	dau of dau of pat aunt of g f of father my
122	father's father's father's father's sister's great-granddaughter	amitae maximae proneptis	gt-g d of pat gt-gt-gt-aunt	bint bint bint ammet jidd ăbi	dau of dau of dau of pat aunt of g f of f my
123	mother's mother's mother's mother's brother	avunculus maximus	maternal gt-gt-gt-uncle	khâl sitt ŭmmi	mat uncle of grandmother of mother my
124	mother's mother's mother's mother's brother's son	avunculi maximi filius	son of maternal gt-gt-gt-uncle	ibn khâl sitt ŭmmi	son of mat uncle of g m of mother my
125	mother's mother's mother's mother's brother's grandson	avunculi maximi nepos	g'dson of mat gt-gt-gt-uncle	ibn ibn khâl sitt ŭmmi	son of son mat uncle of g m of mother my
126	mother's mother's mother's mother's brother's gt-grandson	avunculi maximi pronepos	gt-g'dson of pat gt-gt-gt-uncle	ibn ibn ibn khâl sitt ŭmmi	s of s of s of mat uncle of g m of m my
127	mother's mother's mother's mother's sister	matertera maxima	maternal gt-gt-gt-aunt	khâlet sitt ŭmmi	mat aunt of grandmother of mother my
128	mother's mother's mother's mother's sister's daughter	materterae maximae filia	daughter of mat gt-gt-gt-aunt	bint khâlet sitt ŭmmi	daughter of mat aunt of g m of mother my
129	mother's mother's mother's mother's sister's granddaughter	mater. maximae neptis	g'ddau'ter of mat gt-gt-gt-aunt	bint bint khâlet sitt ŭmmi	dau of dau of mat aunt of g m of m my
130	mother's mother's mother's mother's sister's gt-g'ddaughter	mater. maximae proneptis	gt-g d of mat gt-gt-gt-aunt	bint bint bint khâlet sitt ŭmmi	d of d of d of mat aunt of g m of m my
	(Marriage Relationships).				
131	husband	vir b, maritus	husband	zoji	husband my
132	husband's father	socer	father-in-law	ammi	uncle my
133	" mother	socrus	mother-in-law	amrât ammi	wife of uncle my
134	" grandfather	socer magnus	great father-in-law	jidd zoji	grandfather of husband my
135	" grandmother	socrus magnus	" mother-in-law	sitt zoji	grandmother " " "
136	wife	uxor b, marita	wife	amrâti	wife
137	wife's father	socer	father-in-law	ammi	uncle my
138	" mother	socrus	mother-in-law	amrât ammi	wife of uncle my
139	" grandfather	socer magnus	great father-in-law	jidd amrâti	grandfather of wife my
140	" grandmother	socrus magnus	" mother-in-law	sitt amrâti	grandmother " " "

Description of Persons.	Relationship in Latin.	Translation.	Relationship in Arabic.	Translation.
141 step-father	vitricus	step-father	ammi	uncle my
142 " mother	noverca	" mother	khâleti	aunt my
143 " son	privignus	" son	karŭti	step-son my
144 " daughter	privigna	" daughter	karŭteti	" daughter my
145 son-in-law	gener	son-in-law	khatan b, saha	son-in-law
146 daughter-in-law	nurus	daughter-in-law	kinnet	daughter-in-law
147 brother-in-law (*husband's bro'r*)	lever	brother-in-law	ibn ămmi	son of uncle my
148 " " " (*sister's husband*)	maritus sororis	" " "	zôj akhti	husband of sister my
149 " " " (*wife's brother*)	uxoris frater	brother of wife	ibn ămmi	son of uncle my
150 sister-in-law (*wife's sister*)	" soror	sister of wife	bint ămmi	daughter of uncle my
151 " " " (*husband's sist'r*)	gloss	sister-in-law	bint ămmi	" " " "
152 " " " (*brother's wife*)	fratria	" " "	amrât akhi	wife of brother my
153 widow	vidua	widow	armelet	widow
154 widower	viduus	widower	armel	widower
155 relations by father's side	agnati	agnates		
156 " " mother's side	cognati	cognates		
157 " " marriage	affines	marriage relations		

CHAPTER VI

SEQUENCE OF INSTITUTIONS CONNECTED WITH THE FAMILY

It remains to place in their relations the customs and institutions which have contributed to the growth of the family through successive forms. Their articulation in a sequence is in part hypothetical; but there is an intimate and undoubted connection between them.

This sequence embodies the principal social and domestic institutions which have influenced the growth of the family from the consanguine to the monogamian.[1] They are to be understood as originating in the several branches of the human family substantially in the order named, and as existing generally in these branches while in the corresponding status.

First Stage of Sequence.

I. *Promiscuous Intercourse.*

II. *Intermarriage of Brothers and Sisters, own and collateral, in a Group: Giving,—*

III. *The Consanguine Family. (First Stage of the Family): Giving,—*

IV. *The Malayan System of Consanguinity and Affinity.*

Second Stage of Sequence.

V. *The Organization upon the basis of Sex, and the Punaluan Custom, tending to check the intermarriage of brothers and sisters: Giving,—*

VI. *The Punaluan Family. (Second Stage of the Family): Giving,—*

---

1 It is a revision of the sequence presented in "Systems of Consanguinity," etc., p. 480.

VII. *The Organization into Gentes, which excluded brothers and sisters from the marriage relation: Giving,—*

VIII. *The Turanian and Ganowánian System of Consanguinity and Affinity.*

Third Stage of Sequence.

IX. *Increasing Influence of Gentile Organization and improvement in the arts of life, advancing a portion of mankind into the Lower Status of barbarism: Giving,—*

X. *Marriage between Single Pairs, but without an exclusive cohabitation: Giving,—*

XI. *The Syndyasmian Family. (Third Stage of the Family.)*

Fourth Stage of Sequence.

XII. *Pastoral life on the plains in limited areas: Giving,—*

XIII. *The Patriarchal Family. (Fourth, but exceptional Stage of the Family.)*

Fifth Stage of Sequence.

XIV. *Rise of Property, and settlement of lineal succession to estates: Giving,—*

XV. *The Monogamian Family. (Fifth Stage of the Family): Giving,—*

XVI. *The Aryan, Semitic and Uralian system of Consanguinity and Affinity; and causing the overthrow of the Turanian.*

A few observations upon the foregoing sequence of customs and institutions, for the purpose of tracing their connection and relations, will close this discussion of the growth of the family.

Like the successive geological formations, the tribes of mankind may be arranged, according to their relative conditions, into successive strata. When thus arranged, they reveal with some degree of certainty the entire range of human progress from savagery to civilization. A thorough study of each successive stratum will develop whatever is special in its culture and characteristics, and yield a definite conception of the whole, in their differences and in their relations. When this has been accomplished, the successive stages of human progress will be definitely understood. Time has been an important factor in the formation of these strata; and it must be measured out to each ethnical period in no stinted measure. Each period anterior to civilization necessarily represents many thousands of years.

Promiscuous Intercourse. — This expresses the lowest conceivable stage of savagery—it represents the bottom of the scale. Man in this condition could scarcely be distinguished from the mute animals by whom he was surrounded. Ignorant of marriage, and living probably in a horde, he was not only a savage, but possessed a feeble intellect and a feebler moral sense. His hope of elevation rested in the vigor of his passions, for he seems always to have been courageous; in the possession of hands physically liberated, and in the improvable character of his nascent mental and moral powers. In corroboration of this view, the lessening volume of the skull and its increasing animal characteristics, as we recede from civilized to savage man, deliver some testimony concerning the necessary inferiority of primitive man. Were it possible to reach this earliest representative of the species, we must descend very far below the lowest savage now living upon the earth. The ruder flint implements found over parts of the earth's surface, and not used by existing savages, attest the extreme rudeness of his condition after he had emerged from his primitive habitat, and commenced, as a fisherman, his spread over continental areas. It is with respect to this primitive savage, and with respect to him alone, that promiscuity may be inferred.

It will be asked whether any evidence exists of this antecedent condition. As an answer, it may be remarked that the consanguine family and the Malayan system of consanguinity presuppose antecedent promiscuity. It was limited, not unlikely, to the period when mankind were frugivorous and within their primitive habitat, since its continuance would have been improbable after they became fishermen and commenced their spread over the earth in dependence upon food artificially acquired.

Consanguine groups would then form, with intermarriage in the group as a necessity, resulting in the formation of consanguine families. At all events, the oldest form of society which meets us in the past through deduction from systems of consanguinity is this family. It would be in the nature of a compact on the part of several males for the joint subsistence of the group, and for the defense of their common wives against the violence of society. In the second place, the consanguine family is stamped with the marks of this supposed antecedent state. It recognized promiscuity within defined limits, and those not the narrowest, and it points through its organism to a worse condition against which it interposed a shield. Between the consanguine family and the horde living in promiscuity, the step, though a long one, does not require an intermediate condition. If such existed, no known trace of it remains. The solution of this question, however, is not material. It is sufficient, for the present at least, to have gained the definite starting-point far down in savagery marked out by the consanguine family, which carries back our knowledge of the early condition of mankind well toward the primitive period.

There were tribes of savages and even of barbarians known to the Greeks and Romans who are represented as living in promiscuity. Among them were the Auseans of North Africa, mentioned by Herodotus,[1] the Garamantes of Æthiopia, mentioned by Pliny,[2] and the Celts of Ireland, mentioned by Strabo.[3] The latter repeats a similar statement concerning the Arabs.[4] It is not probable that any people within the time of recorded human observation have lived in a state of promiscuous intercourse like the gregarious animals. The perpetuation of such a people from the infancy of mankind would evidently have been impossible. The cases cited, and many others that might be added, are better explained as aris-

1 Lib. iv, c. 180.
2 Garamantes matrimonium exsortes passim cum femines degunt.—"Nat. Hist.," lib. v. c. 8.
3 Lib. iv. c. 5, par. 4.
4 Lib. xvi, c. 4, par. 25.

ing under the punaluan family, which, to the foreign observer, with limited means of observation, would afford the external indications named by these authors. Promiscuity may be deduced theoretically as a necessary condition antecedent to the consanguine family; but it lies concealed in the misty antiquity of mankind beyond the reach of positive knowledge.

II. *Intermarriage of Brothers and Sisters, own and collateral, in a Group.*—In this form of marriage the family had its birth. It is the root of the institution. The Malayan system of consanguinity affords conclusive evidence of its ancient prevalence. With the ancient existence of the consanguine family established, the remaining forms can be explained as successive derivations from each other. This form of marriage gives (III.) the consanguine family and (IV.) the Malayan system of consanguinity, which disposes of the third and fourth members of the sequence. This family belongs to the Lower Status of savagery.

V. *The Punaluan Custom.*—In the Australian male and female classes united in marriage, punaluan groups are found. Among the Hawaiians, the same group is also found, with the marriage custom it expresses. It has prevailed among the remote ancestors of all the tribes of mankind who now possess or have possessed the Turanian system of consanguinity, because they must have derived it from punaluan ancestors. There is seemingly no other explanation of the origin of this system. Attention has been called to the fact that the punaluan family included the same persons found in the previous consanguine, with the exception of own brothers and sisters, who were theoretically if not in every case excluded. It is a fair inference that the punaluan custom worked its way into general adoption through a discovery of its beneficial influence. Out of punaluan marriage came (VI.) the punaluan family, which disposes of the sixth member of the sequence. This family originated, probably, in the Middle Status of savagery.

VII. *The Organization into Gentes.*—The position of this institution in the sequence is the only question here to be considered. Among the Australian classes, the punaluan group is found on a broad and systematic scale. The people are also organized in gentes. Here the punaluan family is older than the gens, because it rested upon the classes which preceded the gentes. The Australians also have the Turanian system of consanguinity, for which the classes laid the foundation by excluding own brothers and sisters from the punaluan group united in marriage. They were born members of classes who could not intermarry. Among the Hawaiians, the punaluan family was unable to create the Turanian system of consanguinity. Own brothers and sisters were frequently involved in the punaluan group, which the custom did not prevent, although it tended to do so. This system requires both the punaluan family and the gentile organization to bring it into existence. It follows that the latter came in after and upon the former. In its relative order it belongs to the Middle Status of savagery.

VIII. and IX. These have been sufficiently considered.

X. and XI. *Marriage between Single Pairs, and the Syndyasmian Family.*—After mankind had advanced out of savagery and entered the Lower Status of barbarism, their condition was immensely improved. More than half the battle for civilization was won. A tendency to reduce the groups of married persons to smaller proportions must have begun to manifest itself before the close of savagery, because the syndyasmian family became a constant phenomenon in the Lower Status of barbarism. The custom which led the more advanced savage to recognize one among a number of wives as his principal wife, ripened in time into the practice of pairing, and in making this wife a companion and associate in the maintenance of a family. With the growth of the propensity to pair came an increased certainty of the paternity of children. But the husband could put away his wife, and the wife could leave her husband, and each seek a new mate at pleasure. Moreover, the man did not recognize, on his part, the obligations of the marriage tie, and therefore had no right to expect its recognition by his wife. The old conjugal system, now reduced to narrower limits by the gradual disappearance of the punaluan groups, still environed the advancing family, which it was to follow to the verge of civilization. Its reduction to zero was a condition precedent to the introduction of monogamy. It finally disappeared in the new form of hetærism, which still follows mankind in civilization as a dark shadow upon the family. The contrast between the punaluan and syndyasmian families was greater than between the latter and the monogamian. It was subsequent in time to the gens, which was largely instrumental in its production. That it was a transitional stage of the family between the two is made evident by its inability to change materially the Turanian system of consanguinity, which monogamy alone was able to overthrow. From the Columbia River to the Paraguay, the Indian family was syndyasmian in general, punaluan in exceptional areas, and monogamian perhaps in none.

XII. and XIII. *Pastoral Life and the Patriarchal Family.*—It has been remarked elsewhere that polygamy was not the essential feature of this family, which represented a movement of society to assert the individuality of persons. Among the Semitic tribes, it was an organization of servants and slaves under a patriarch for the care of flocks and herds, for the cultivation of lands, and for mutual protection and subsistence. Polygamy was incidental. With a single male head and an exclusive cohabitation, this family was an advance upon the syndyasmian, and therefore not a retrograde movement. Its influence upon the human race was limited; but it carries with it a confession of a state of society in the previous period against which it was designed to form a barrier.

XIV. *Rise of Property and the establishment of lineal succession to Estates.* — Independently of the movement which culminated in the patriarchal family of the Hebrew and Latin types, property, as it increased in variety and amount, exercised a steady and constantly augmenting influence in the direction of monogamy. It is impossible to overestimate the influence of property in the civilization of mankind. It was the power that brought the Aryan and Semitic nations out of barbarism into civilization. The growth of the idea of property in the human mind commenced in feebleness and ended in becoming its master passion. Governments and laws are instituted with primary reference to its creation, protection and enjoyment. It introduced human slavery as an instrument in its production; and, after the experience of several thousand years, it caused the abolition of slavery upon the discovery that a freeman was a better property-making machine. The cruelty inherent in the heart of man, which civilization and Christianity have softened without eradicating, still betrays the savage origin of mankind, and in no way more pointedly than in the practice of human slavery, through all the centuries of recorded history. With the establishment of the inheritance of property in the children of its owner, came the first possibility of a strict monogamian family. Gradually, though slowly, this form of marriage, with an exclusive cohabitation, became the rule rather than the exception; but it was not until civilization had commenced that it became permanently established.

XV. *The Monogamian Family.*—As finally constituted, this family assured the paternity of children, substituted the individual ownership of real as well as personal property for joint ownership, and an exclusive inheritance by children in the place of agnatic inheritance. Modern society reposes upon the monogamian family. The whole previous experience and progress of mankind culminated and crystallized in this pre-eminent institution. It was a slow growth, planting its roots far back in the period of savagery—a final result toward which the experience of the ages steadily tended. Although essentially modern, it was the product of a vast and varied experience.

XVI. The Aryan, Semitic and Uralian systems of consanguinity, which are essentially identical, were created by the monogamian family. Its relationships are those which actually existed under this form of marriage and of the family. A system of consanguinity is not an arbitrary enactment, but a natural growth. It expresses, and must of necessity express, the actual facts of consanguinity as they appeared to the common mind when the system was formed. As the Aryan system establishes the antecedent existence of a monogamian family, so the Turanian establishes the antecedent existence of a punaluan family, and the Malayan the antecedent existence of a consanguine family. The evidence they contain must be regarded as conclusive, because of its convincing character in each case. With the existence established of three kinds of marriage, of three forms of the family, and of three systems of consanguinity, nine of the sixteen members of the sequence are sustained. The existence and relations of the remainder are warranted by sufficient proof.

The views herein presented contravene, as I am aware, an assumption which has for centuries been generally accepted. It is the hypothesis of human degradation to explain the existence of barbarians and of savages, who were found, physically and mentally, too far below the conceived standard of a supposed original man. It was never a scientific proposition supported by facts. It is refuted by the connected series of inventions and discoveries, by the progressive development of the social system, and by the successive forms of the family. The Aryan and Semitic peoples descended from barbarous ancestors. The question then meets us, how could these barbarians have attained to the Upper Status of barbarism, in which they first appear, without previously passing through the experience and acquiring the arts and development of the Middle Status; and, further than this, how could they have attained to the Middle Status without first passing through the experience of the Lower. Back of these is the further question, how a barbarian could exist without a previous savage. This hypothesis of degradation leads to another necessity, namely; that of regarding all the races of mankind without the Aryan and Semitic connections as abnormal races —races fallen away by degeneracy from their normal state. The Aryan and Semitic nations, it is true, represent the main streams of human progress, because they have carried it to the highest point yet attained; but there are good reasons for supposing that before they became differentiated into Aryan and Semitic tribes, they formed a part of the indistinguishable mass of barbarians. As these tribes themselves sprang remotely from barbarous, and still more remotely from savage ancestors, the distinction of *normal* and *abnormal* races falls to the ground.

This sequence, moreover, contravenes some of the conclusions of that body of eminent scholars who, in their speculations upon the origin of society, have adopted the patriarchal family of the Hebrew and Latin types as the oldest form of the family, and as producing the earliest organized society. The human race is thus invested from its infancy with a knowledge of the family under paternal power. Among the latest, and holding foremost rank among them, is Sir Henry Maine, whose brilliant researches in the sources of ancient law, and in the early history of institutions, have advanced so largely our knowledge of them. The patriarchal family, it is true, is the oldest made known to us by ascending along the lines of classical and Semitic authorities; but an investigation along these lines is unable to penetrate beyond the Upper Status of barbarism, leaving at least four entire ethnical periods untouched, and their connection unrecognized. It must be admitted, however, that the facts with respect to the early condition of mankind have been but recently produced, and that judicious investigators are justly careful about surrendering old doctrines for new.

Unfortunately for the hypothesis of degradation, inventions and discoveries would come one by one; the knowledge of a cord must precede the bow and arrow, as the knowledge of gunpowder preceded the musket, and that of the steam-engine preceded the railway and the steamship; so the arts of subsistence followed each other at long intervals of time, and human tools passed through forms of flint and stone before they were formed of iron. In like manner institutions of government are a growth from primitive germs of thought. Growth, development and transmission, must explain their existence among civilized nations. Not less clearly was the monogamian family derived, by experience, through the syndyasmian from the punaluan, and the still more ancient consanguine family. If, finally, we are obliged to surrender the antiquity of the monogamian family, we gain a knowledge of its derivation, which is of more importance, because it reveals the price at which it was obtained.

The antiquity of mankind upon the earth is now established by a body of evidence sufficient to convince unprejudiced minds. The existence of the race goes back definitely to the glacial period in Europe, and even back of it into the anterior period. We are now compelled to recognize the prolonged and unmeasured ages of man's existence. The human mind is naturally and justly curious to know something of the life of man during the last hundred thousand or more years, now that we are assured his days have been so long upon the earth. All this time could not have been spent in vain. His great and marvelous achievements prove the contrary, as well as imply the expenditure of long protracted ethnical periods. The fact that civilization was so recent suggests the difficulties in the way of human progress, and affords some intimation of the lowness of the level from which mankind started on their career.

The foregoing sequence may require modification, and perhaps essential change in some of its members; but it affords both a rational and a satisfactory explanation of the facts of human experience, so far as they are known, and of the course of human progress, in developing the ideas of the family and of government in the tribes of mankind.

NOTE.

Mr. J. F. McLennan's "Primitive Marriage."

As these pages are passing through the press, I have obtained an enlarged edition of the above-named work. It is a reprint of the original, with several Essays appended; and is now styled "Studies in Ancient History Comprising a Reprint of Primitive Marriage."

In one of these Essays, entitled "The Classificatory System of Relationships," Mr. McLennan devotes one section (41 pages) to an attempted refutation of my explanation of the origin of the classificatory system; and another (36 pages) to an explanation of his own of the origin of the same system. The hypothesis first referred to is contained in my work on the "Systems of Consanguinity and Affinity of the Human Family" (pp. 479-486). The facts and their explanation are the same, substantially, as those presented in preceding chapters of this volume (Chaps. II, and III, Part III). "Primitive Marriage" was first published in 1865, and "Systems of Consanguinity," etc., in 1871.

Having collected the facts which established the existence of the classificatory system of consanguinity, I ventured to submit, with the Tables, an hypothesis explanatory of its origin. That hypotheses are useful, and often indispensable to the attainment of truth, will not be questioned. The validity of the solution presented in that work, and repeated in this, will depend upon its sufficiency in explaining all the facts of the case. Until it is superseded by one better entitled to acceptance on this ground, its position in my work is legitimate, and in accordance with the method of scientific inquiry.

Mr. McLennan has criticised this hypothesis with great freedom. His conclusion is stated generally as follows (Studies, etc., p. 371): "The space I have devoted to the consideration of the solution may seem disproportioned to its importance; but issuing from the press of the Smithsonian Institution, and its preparation having been aided by the United States Government, Mr. Morgan's work has been very generally quoted as a work of authority, and it seemed worth while to take the trouble necessary to show its utterly unscientific character." Not the hypothesis alone, but the entire work is covered by the charge.

That work contains 187 pages of "Tables of Consanguinity and Affinity," exhibiting the systems of 139 tribes and nations of mankind representing four-fifths, numerically, of the entire human family. It is singular that the bare facts of consanguinity and affinity expressed by terms of relationship, even when placed in tabular form, should possess an "utterly unscientific character." The body of the work is taken up with the dry details of these several systems. There remains a final chapter, consisting of 43 out of 590 pages, devoted to a comparison of these several systems of consanguinity, in which this solution or hypothesis appears. It was the first discussion of a large mass of new material, and had Mr. McLennan's charge been limited to this chapter, there would have been little need of a discussion here. But he has directed his main attack against the Tables; denying that the systems they exhibit are systems of consanguinity and affinity, thus going to the bottom of the subject.[1]

Mr. McLennan's position finds an explanation in the fact, that as systems of consanguinity and affinity they antagonize and refute the principal opinions and the principal theories propounded in "Primitive Marriage." The author of "Primitive Marriage" would be expected to stand by his preconceived opinions.

As systems of consanguinity, for example: (1.) They show that Mr. McLennan's new terms, "Exogamy and Endogamy" are of questionable utility — that as used in "Primitive Marriage," their positions are reversed, and that "endogamy" has very little application to the facts treated in that work, while "exogamy" is simply a rule of a gens, and should be stated as such. (2.) They refute Mr. McLennan's phrase, "kinship through females only," by showing that kinship through males was recognized as constantly as kinship through females by the same people. (3.) They show that the Nair and Tibetan polyandry could never have been general in the tribes of mankind. (4.) They deny both the necessity and the extent of "wife stealing" as propounded in "Primitive Marriage."

An examination of the grounds, upon which Mr. McLennan's charge is made, will show not only the failure of his criticisms but the insufficiency of the theories on which these criticisms are based. Such an examination leads to results disastrous to his entire work, as will be made evident by the discussion of the following propositions, namely:

1 "The "Tables," however, are the "main results" of this investigation. In their importance and value they reach beyond any present use of their contents the writer may be able to indicate."—"Systems of Consanguinity," etc., Smithsonian Contributions to Knowledge, vol. xvii, p. 8.

I. That the principal terms and theories employed in "Primitive Marriage" have no value in Ethnology.

II. That Mr. McLennan's hypothesis to account for the origin of the classificatory system of relationship does not account for its origin.

III. That Mr. McLennan's objections to the hypothesis presented in "Systems of Consanguinity," etc., are of no force.

These propositions will be considered in the order named.

I. That the principal terms and theories employed in "Primitive Marriage" have no value in Ethnology.

When this work appeared it was received with favor by ethnologists, because as a speculative treatise it touched a number of questions upon which they had long been working. A careful reading, however, disclosed deficiencies in definitions, unwarranted assumptions, crude speculations and erroneous conclusions. Mr. Herbert Spencer in his "Principles of Sociology" (Advance Sheets, Popular Science Monthly, Jan., 1877, p. 272), has pointed out a number of them. At the same time he rejects the larger part of Mr. McLennan's theories respecting "Female Infanticide," "Wife Stealing," and "Exogamy and Endogamy." What he leaves of this work, beyond its collocation of certain ethnological facts, it is difficult to find.

It will be sufficient under this head to consider three points.

1. Mr. McLennan's use of the terms "Exogamy" and "Endogamy."

"Exogamy" and "endogamy" — terms of his own coinage — imply, respectively, an obligation to "marry out," and an obligation to "marry in," a particular group of persons.

These terms are applied so loosely and so imprecisely by Mr. McLennan to the organized groups made known to him by the authors he cites, that both his terms and his conclusions are of little value. It is a fundamental difficulty with "Primitive Marriage" that the gens and the tribe, or the groups they represent, are not distinguished from each other as members of an organic series, so that it might be known of which group "exogamy" or "endogamy" is asserted. One of eight gentes of a tribe, for example, may be "exogamous" with respect to itself, and "endogamous" with respect to the seven remaining gentes. Moreover, these terms, in such a case, if correctly applied, are misleading. Mr. McLennan seems to be presenting two great principles, representing distinct conditions of society which have influenced human affairs. In point of fact, while "endogamy" has very little application to conditions of society treated in "Primitive Marriage," "exogamy" has reference to a rule or law of a gens — an institution — and as such the unit of organization of a social system. It is the gens that has influenced human affairs, and which is the primary fact. We are at once concerned to know its functions and attributes, with the rights, privileges and obligations of its members. Of these material circumstances Mr. McLennan makes no account, nor does he seem to have had the slightest conception of the gens as a governing institution of ancient society. Two of its rules are the following: (1.) Intermarriage in the gens is prohibited. This is Mr. McLennan's "exogamy"— restricted as it always is to a gens, but stated by him without any reference to a gens. (2.) In the archaic form of the gens descent is limited to the female line, which is Mr. McLennan's "kinship through females only," and which is also stated by him without any reference to a gens.

Let us follow this matter further. Seven definitions of tribal system, and of tribe are given (Studies, etc., 113-115).

"Exogamy Pure.—1. Tribal (or family) system.—Tribes separate. All the members of each tribe of the same blood, or feigning themselves to be so. Marriage prohibited between the members of the tribe.

"2. Tribal system.—Tribe a congeries of family groups, falling into divisions, clans, thums, etc. No connubium between members of same division: connubium between all the divisions.

"3. Tribal system.—Tribe a congeries of family groups. * * * No connubium between persons whose family name points them out as being of the same stock.

"4. Tribal system.—Tribe in divisions. No connubium between members of the same divisions: connubium between some of the divisions; only partial connubium between others. * * *

"5. Tribal system.—Tribe in divisions. No connubium between persons of the same stock: connubium between each division and some other. No connubium between some of the divisions. Caste.

"Endogamy Pure. 6. Tribal (or family) system.—Tribes separate. All the members of each tribe of the same blood, or feigning themselves to be so. Connubium between members of the tribe: marriage without the tribe forbidden and punished.

"7. Tribal system indistinct."

Seven definitions of the tribal system ought to define the group called a tribe, with sufficient distinctness to be recognized.

The first definition, however, is a puzzle. There are several tribes in a tribal system, but no term for the aggregate of tribes. They are not supposed to form a united body. How the separate tribes fall into a tribal system or are held together does not appear. All the members of each tribe are of the same blood, or pretend to be, and therefore cannot intermarry. This might answer for a description of a gens; but the gens is never found alone, separate from other gentes. There are several gentes intermingled by marriage in every tribe composed of gentes. But Mr. McLennan could not have used tribe here as equivalent to gens, nor as a congeries of family groups. As separate bodies of consanguinei held together in a tribal system, the bodies undefined and the system unexplained, we are offered something altogether new. Definition 6 is much the same. It is not probable that a tribe answering to either of these definitions ever existed in any part of the earth; for it is neither a gens, nor a tribe composed of gentes, nor a nation formed by the coalescence of tribes.

Definitions 2d, 3d, 4th, and 5th are somewhat more intelligible. They show in each case a tribe composed of gentes, or divisions based upon kin. But it is a gentile rather than a tribal system. As marriage is allowed between the clans, thums, or divisions of the same tribe, "exogamy" cannot be asserted of the tribe in either case. The clan, thum, or division is "exogamous," with respect to itself, but "endogamous" with respect to the other clans, thums, or divisions. Particular restrictions are stated to exist in some instances.

When Mr. McLennan applies the terms "exogamy" or "endogamy" to a tribe, how is it to be known whether it is one of several separate tribes in a tribal system, whatever this may mean, or a tribe defined as a congeries of family groups? On the next page (116) he remarks: "The separate endogamous tribes are nearly as numerous, and they are in some respects as rude, as the separate exogamous tribes." If he uses tribe as a congeries of family groups, which is a tribe composed of gentes, then "exogamy" cannot be asserted of the tribe. There is not the slightest probability that "exogamy" ever existed in a tribe composed of gentes in any part of the earth. Wherever the gentile organization has been found intermarriage in the gens is forbidden. It gives what Mr. McLennan calls "exogamy." But, as an equally general rule, intermarriage between the members of a gens and the members of all the other gentes of the same tribe is permitted. The gens is "exogamous," and the tribe is essentially "endogamous." In these cases, if in no others, it was material to know the group covered by the word tribe. Take another illustration (p.42): "If it can be shown, firstly, that exogamous tribes exist, or have existed; and, secondly, that in ruder times the relations of separate tribes were uniformly, or almost uniformly, hostile, we have found a set of circumstances in which men could get wives only by capturing them." Here we find the initial point of Mr. McLennan's theory of wife stealing. To make the "set of circumstances" (namely, hostile and therefore independent tribes), tribe as used here must refer to the larger group, a tribe composed of gentes. For the members of the several gentes of a tribe are intermingled by marriage in every family throughout the area occupied by the tribe. All the gentes must be hostile or none. If the term is applied to the smaller group, the gens, then the gens is "exogamous," and the tribe, in the given case, is seven-eighths "endogamous," and what becomes of the "set of circumstances" necessitating wife-stealing?

The principal cases cited in "Primitive Marriage" to prove "exogamy" are the Khonds, Kalmucks, Circassians, Yurak Samoyeds, certain tribes of India and Australia, and certain Indian tribes of America, the Iroquois among the number (pp. 75-100). The American tribes are generally composed of gentes. A man cannot marry a woman of the same gens with himself; but he may marry a woman of any other gens of his own tribe. For example, a man of the Wolf gens of the Seneca tribe of the Iroquois is prohibited from marrying a woman of the same gens, not only in the Seneca tribe, but also in either of the five remaining Iroquois tribes. Here we have Mr. McLennan's "exogamy," but restricted, as it always is, to the gens of the individual. But a man may marry a woman in either of the seven remaining Seneca gentes. Here we have "endogamy" in the tribe, practiced by the members of each gens in the seven remaining Seneca gentes. Both practices exist side by side at the same time, in the same tribe, and have so existed from time immemorial. The same fact is true of the American Indian tribes in general. They are cited, nevertheless, by Mr. McLennan, as examples of "exogamous tribes"; and thus enter into the basis of his theories.

With respect to "endogamy," Mr. McLennan would probably refrain from using it in the above case: firstly, because "exogamy" and "endogamy" fail here to represent two opposite principles as they exist in his imagination; and, secondly, because there is, in reality, but one fact to be indicated, namely, that intermarriage in the gens is prohibited. American Indians generally can marry in their own or in a foreign tribe as they please, but not in their gens. Mr. McLennan was able to cite one fair case of "endogamy," that of the Mantchu Tartars (p. 116), "who prohibited marriage between persons whose family names are different." A few other similar cases have been found among existing tribes.

If the organizations, for example, of the Yurak Samoyeds of Siberia (82), the Magars of Nepaul (83), the Munnieporees, Koupooees, Mows, Muram and Murring tribes of India (87), were examined upon the original evidence, it is highly probable that they would be found exactly analogous to the Iroquois tribes; the "divisions" and "thums" being gentes. Latham, speaking of the Yurak or Kasovo group of the Samoyeds, quotes from Klaproth, as follows: "This division of the kinsmanship is so rigidly observed that no Samoyed takes a wife from the kinsmanship to which he himself belongs. On the contrary he seeks her in one of the other two."[1] The same author, speaking of the Magars, remarks: "There are twelve thums. All individuals belonging to the same thum are supposed to be descended from the same male ancestor; descent from the same great mother being by no means necessary. So husband and wife must belong to different thums. With one and the same there is no marriage. Do you wish for a wife? If so, look to the thum of your neighbor; at any rate look beyond your own. This is the first time I have had occasion to mention this practice. It will not be the last: on the contrary, the principle it suggests is so common as to be almost universal."[2] The Murring and other tribes of India are in divisions, with the same rule in respect to marriage. In these cases it is probable that we have tribes composed of gentes, with intermarriage in the gens prohibited. Each gens is "exogamous" with respect to itself, and "endogamous" with respect to the remaining gentes of the tribe. They are cited by Mr. McLennan, nevertheless, as examples of "exogamous" tribes. The principal Australian tribes are known to be organized in gentes, with intermarriage in the gens prohibited. Here again the gens is "exogamous" and the tribe "endogamous."

Where the gens is "exogamous" with respect to itself, and "endogamous" with respect to the remaining gentes of the same tribe, of what use is this pair of terms to mark what is but a single fact — the prohibition of intermarriage in the gens? "Exogamy" and "endogamy" are of no value as a pair of terms, pretending as they do to represent or express opposite conditions of society. They have no application in American ethnology, and probably none in Asiatic or European. "Exogamy," standing alone and applied to the small group (the gens), of which only it can be asserted, might be tolerated. There are no "exogamous" tribes in America, but a plenty of "exogamous" gentes; and when the gens is found, we are concerned with its rules, and these should always be stated as rules of a gens. Mr. McLennan found the clan, thum, division, "exogamous," and the aggregate of clans, thums, divisions, "endogamous"; but he says nothing about the "endogamy." Neither does he say the clan, division, or thum is "exogamous," but that the tribe is "exogamous." We might suppose he intended to use tribe as equivalent to clan, thum, and division; but we are met with the difficulty that he defines a "tribe [as] a congeries of family groups, falling into divisions, clans, thums, etc." (114), and immediately (116) he remarks that "the separate endogamous tribes are nearly as numerous, and they are in some respects as

1 "Descriptive Ethnology," London ed., 1859, i, 475.
2 Ib., i, 80.

rude, as the separate exogamous tribes." If we take his principal definitions, it can be said without fear of contradiction that Mr. McLennan has not produced a single case of an "exogamous" tribe in his volume.

There is another objection to this pair of terms. They are set over against each other to indicate opposite and dissimilar conditions of society. Which of the two is the ruder, and which the more advanced? Abundant cautions are here thrown out by Mr. McLennan. "They may represent a progression from exogamy to endogamy, or from endogamy to exogamy" (115); "they may be equally archaic" (116); and "they are in some respects" equally rude (116); but before the discussion ends, "endogamy" rises to the superior position, and stands over toward civilization, while "exogamy" falls back in the direction of savagery. It became convenient in Mr. McLennan's speculations for "exogamy" to introduce heterogeneity, which "endogamy" is employed to expel, and bring in homogeneity; so that "endogamy" finally gets the better of "exogamy" as an influence for progress.

One of Mr. McLennan's mistakes was his reversal of the positions of these terms. What he calls "endogamy" precedes "exogamy" in the order of human progress, and belongs to the lowest condition of mankind. Ascending to the time when the Malayan system of consanguinity was formed, and which preceded the gens, we find consanguine groups in the marriage relation. The system of consanguinity indicates both the fact and the character of the groups and exhibits "endogamy" in its pristine force. Advancing from this state of things, the first check upon "endogamy" is found in the punaluan group, which sought to exclude own brothers and sisters from the marriage relation, while it retained in that relation first, second, and more remote cousins, still under the name of brothers and sisters. The same thing precisely is found in the Australian organization upon sex. Next in the order of time the gens appeared, with descent in the female line, and with intermarriage in the gens prohibited. It brought in Mr. McLennan's "exogamy." From this time forward "endogamy" may be dismissed as an influence upon human affairs.

According to Mr. McLennan, "exogamy" fell into decay in advancing communities; and when descent was changed to the male line it disappeared in the Grecian and Roman tribes (p. 220.) So far from this being the case, what he calls "exogamy" commenced in savagery with the gens, continued through barbarism, and remained into civilization. It existed as completely in the gentes of the Greeks and Romans in the time of Solon and of Servius Tullius as it now exists in the gentes of the Iroquois. "Exogamy" and "endogamy" have been so thoroughly tainted by the manner of their use in

"Primitive Marriage," that the best disposition which can now be made of them is to lay them aside.

2. Mr. McLennan's phrase: "The system of kinship through females only."

"Primitive Marriage" is deeply colored with this phrase. It asserts that this kinship, where it prevailed, was the only kinship recognized; and thus has an error written on its face. The Turanian, Ganowánian and Malayan systems of consanguinity show plainly and conclusively that kinship through males was recognized as constantly as kinship through females. A man had brothers and sisters, grandfathers and grandmothers, grandsons and granddaughters, traced through males as well as through females. The maternity of children was ascertainable with certainty, while their paternity was not; but they did not reject kinship through males because of uncertainty, but gave the benefit of the doubt to a number of persons — probable fathers being placed in the category of real fathers, probable brothers in that of real brothers, and probable sons in that of real sons.

After the gens appeared, kinship through females had an increased importance, because it now signified gentile kin, as distinguished from non-gentile kin. This was the kinship, in a majority of cases, made known to Mr. McLennan by the authors he cites. The children of the female members of the gens remained within it, while the children of its male members were excluded. Every member of the gens traced his or her descent through females exclusively when descent was in the female line, and through males exclusively when descent was in the male line. Its members were an organized body of consanguinei bearing a common gentile name. They were bound together by affinities of blood, and by the further bond of mutual rights, privileges, and obligations. Gentile kin became, in both cases, superior to other kin; not because no other kin was recognized, but because it conferred the rights and privileges of a gens. Mr. McLennan's failure to discover this difference indicates an insufficient investigation of the subject he was treating. With descent in the female line, a man had grandfathers and grandmothers, mothers, brothers and sisters, uncles, nephews and nieces, and grandsons and granddaughters in his gens; some own and some collateral; while he had the same out of his gens with the exception of uncles; and in addition, fathers, aunts, sons and daughters, and cousins. A woman had the same relatives in the gens as a man, and sons and daughters, in addition, while she had the same relatives out of the gens as a man. Whether in or out of the gens, a brother was recognized as a brother, a father as a father, a son as a son, and the same term was applied in either case without discrimination between them. Descent in the female line, which is all that "kinship through females only" can possibly indicate, is thus seen to be a rule of a gens and nothing more. It ought to be stated as such, because the gens is the primary fact, and gentile kinship is one of its attributes.

Prior to the gentile organization, kinship through females was undoubtedly superior to kinship through males, and was doubtless the principal basis upon which the lower tribal groups were organized. But the body of facts treated in "Primitive Marriage" have little or no relation to that condition of mankind which existed prior to the gentile system.

3. There is no evidence of the general prevalence of the Nair and Tibetan polyandry.

These forms of polyandry are used in Mr. McLennan's speculations as though universal in practice. He employs them in his attempted explanation of the origin of the classificatory system of relationship. The Nair polyandry is where several unrelated persons have one wife in common (p. 146). It is called the rudest form. The Tibetan polyandry is where several brothers have one wife in common. He then makes a rapid flight through the tribes of mankind to show the general prevalence of one or the other of these forms of polyandry, and fails entirely to show their prevalence. It does not seem to have occurred to Mr. McLennan that these forms of polyandry are exceptional, and that they could not have been general even in the Neilgherry Hills or in Tibet. If an average of three men had one wife in common (twelve husbands to one wife was the Nair limit, p. 147), and this was general through a tribe, two-thirds of the marriageable females would be without husbands. It may safely be asserted that such a state of things never existed generally in the tribes of mankind, and without better evidence it cannot be credited in the Neilgherry Hills or in Tibet. The facts in respect to the Nair polyandry are not fully known. "A Nair may be one in several combinations of husbands; that is, he may have any number of wives" (p. 148). This, however, would not help the unmarried females to husbands, although it would increase the number of husbands of one wife. Female infanticide cannot be sufficiently exaggerated to raise into general prevalence these forms of polyandry. Neither can it be said with truth that they have exercised a general influence upon human affairs.

The Malayan, Turanian and Ganowánian systems of consanguinity and affinity, however, bring to light forms of polygyny and polyandry which have influenced human affairs, because they were as universal in prevalence as these systems were, when they respectively came into existence. In the Malayan system, we find evidence of consanguine groups founded upon brother and sister marriages, but including collateral brothers and sisters in the group. Here the men lived in polygyny, and the women in polyandry. In the Turanian and Ganowánian system we find evidence of a more advanced group—the punaluan in two forms. One was founded on the brotherhood of the husbands, and the other on the sisterhood of the wives; own brothers and sisters being now excluded from the marriage relation. In each group the men were polygynous, and the women polyandrous. Both practices are found in the same group, and both are essential to an explanation of their system of consanguinity. The last-named system of consanguinity and affinity presupposes punaluan marriage in the group. This and the Malayan exhibit the forms of polygyny and polyandry with which ethnography is concerned; while the Nair and Tibetan forms of polyandry are not only insufficient to explain the systems, but are of no general importance.

These systems of consanguinity and affinity, as they stand in the Tables, have committed such havoc with the theories and opinions advanced in "Primitive Marriage" that I am constrained to ascribe to this fact Mr. McLennan's assault upon my hypothesis explanatory of their origin; and his attempt to substitute another, denying them to be systems of consanguinity and affinity.

II. That Mr. McLennan's hypothesis to account for the origin of the classificatory system does not account for its origin.

Mr. McLennan sets out with the statement (p. 372) that "the phenomena presented in all the forms [of the classificatory system] are ultimately referable to the marriage law; and that accordingly its origin must be so also." This is the basis of my explanation; it is but partially that of his own.

The marriage-law, under which he attempts to explain the origin of the Malayan system, is that found in the Nair polyandry; and the marriage-law under which he attempts to explain the origin of the Turanian and Ganowánian system is that indicated by the Tibetan polyandry. But he has neither the Nair nor Tibetan system of consanguinity and affinity, with which to explain or to test his hypothesis. He starts, then, without any material from Nair or Tibetan sources, and with forms of marriage-law that never existed among the tribes and nations possessing the classificatory system of relationship. We thus find at the outset that the explanation in question is a mere random speculation.

Mr. McLennan denies that the systems in the Tables (Consanguinity, pp. 298-382; 523-567) are systems of consanguinity and affinity. On the contrary, he asserts that together they are "a system of modes of addressing persons." He is not unequivocal in his denial, but the purport of his language is to that effect. In my work of Consanguinity I pointed out the fact that the American Indians in familiar intercourse and in formal salutation addressed each other by the exact relationship in which they stood to each other, and never by the personal name; and that the same usage prevailed in South India and in China. They use the system in salutation because it is a system of consanguinity and affinity—a reason paramount. Mr. McLennan wishes us to believe that these all-embracing systems were simply conventional, and formed to enable persons to address each other in salutation, and for no other purpose. It is a happy way of disposing of these systems, and of throwing away the most remarkable record in existence respecting the early condition of mankind.

Mr. McLennan imagines there must have been a system of consanguinity somewhere entirely independent of the system of addresses; "for it seems reasonable to believe," he remarks (p. 373), "that the system of blood-ties and the system of addresses would begin to grow up together, and for some little time would have a common history." A system of blood-ties is a system of consanguinity. Where, then, is the lost system? Mr. McLennan neither produces it nor shows its existence. But I find he uses the systems in the Tables as systems of consanguinity and affinity, so far as they serve his hypothesis, without taking the trouble to modify the assertion that they are simply "modes of addressing persons."

That savage and barbarous tribes the world over, and through untold ages, should have been so solicitous concerning the proper mode of addressing relations as to have produced the Malayan, Turanian and Ganowánian systems, in their fullness and complexity, for that purpose and no other, and no other systems than these two—that in Asia, Africa, Polynesia, and America they should have agreed, for example, that a given person's grandfather's brother should be addressed as grandfather, that brothers older than one's self should be addressed as elder brothers, and those younger as younger brothers, merely to provide a conventional mode of addressing relatives—are coincidences so remarkable and for so small a reason, that it will be quite sufficient for the author of this brilliant conception to believe it.

A system of modes of addressing persons would be ephemeral, because all conventional usages are ephemeral. They would, also, of necessity, be as diverse as the races of mankind. But a system of consanguinity is a very different thing. Its relationships spring from the family and the marriage-law, and possess even greater permanence than the family itself, which advances while the system remains unchanged. These relationships expressed the actual facts of the social condition when the system was formed, and have had a daily importance in the life of mankind. Their uniformity over immense areas of the earth, and their preservation through immense periods of time, are consequences of their connection with the marriage-law.

When the Malayan system of consanguinity was formed, it may be supposed that a mother could perceive that her own son and daughter stood to her in certain relationships that could be expressed by suitable terms; that her own mother and her mother's own mother stood to her in certain other relationships; that the other children of her own mother stood to her in still other relationships; and that the children of her own daughter stood to her in still others—all of which might be expressed by suitable terms. It would give the beginning of a system of consanguinity founded upon obvious blood-ties. It would lay the foundation of the five categories of relations in the Malayan system, and without any reference to marriage-law.

When marriage in the group and the consanguine family came in, of both of which the Malayan system affords evidence, the system would spread over the group upon the basis of these primary conceptions. With the intermarriage of brothers and sisters, own and collateral, in a group, the resulting system of consanguinity and affinity would be Malayan. Any hypothesis explanatory of the origin of the Malayan system must fail if these facts are ignored. Such a form of marriage and of the family would create the Malayan system. It would be a system of consanguinity and affinity from the beginning, and explainable only as such.

If these views are correct, it will not be necessary to consider in detail the points of Mr. McLennan's hypothesis, which is too obscure for a philosophical discussion, and utterly incapable of affording an explanation of the origin of these systems.

III. That Mr. McLennan's objections to the hypothesis presented in "Systems of Consanguinity," etc., are of no force.

The same misapprehension of the facts, and the same confusion of ideas which mark his last Essay, also appear in this. He does not hold distinct the relationships by consanguinity and those by marriage, when both exist between the same persons; and he makes mistakes in the relationships of the systems also.

It will not be necessary to follow step by step Mr. McLennan's criticisms upon this hypothesis, some of which are verbal, others of which are distorted, and none of which touch the essence of the questions involved. The first proposition he attempts to refute is stated by him as follows: "The Malayan system of relationships is a system of blood-relationships. Mr. Morgan assumes this, and says nothing of the obstacles to making the assumption" (p. 342). It is in part a system of blood-relationships, and in part of marriage-relationships. The fact is patent. The relationships of father and mother, brother and sister, elder or younger, son and daughter, uncle and aunt, nephew and niece and cousin, grandfather and mother, grandson and daughter; and also of brother-in-law and sister-in-law, son-in-law and daughter-in-law, besides others, are given in the Tables and were before Mr. McLennan. These systems speak for themselves, and could say nothing else but that they are systems of consanguinity and affinity. Does Mr. McLennan suppose that the tribes named had a system other or different from that presented in the Tables? If he did, he was bound to produce it, or to establish the fact of its existence. He does neither.

Two or three of his special points may be considered. "And indeed," he remarks (p. 346), "if a man is called the son of a woman who did not bear him, his being so called clearly defies explanation on the principle of natural descents. The reputed relationship is not, in that case, the one actually existing as near as the parentage of individuals could be known; and accordingly Mr. Morgan's proposition is not made out." On the face of the statement the question involved is not one of parentage, but of marriage-relationship. A man calls his mother's sister his mother, and she calls him her son, although she did not bear him. This is the case in the Malayan, Turanian and Ganowánian systems. Whether we have consanguine or punaluan marriages, a man's mother's sister is the wife of his reputed father. She is his step-mother as near as our system furnishes an analogue; and among ourselves a step-mother is called mother, and she calls her step-son, son. It defies explanation, it is true, as a blood-relationship, which it does not pretend to be, but as a marriage-relationship, which it pretends to be, this is the explanation. The reasoning of Mr. McLennan is equally specious and equally faulty in a number of cases.

Passing from the Malayan to the Turanian system, he remarks (p. 354): "It follows from this that a man's son and his sister's daughter, while reputed brother and sister, would have been free, when the 'tribal organization' had been established, to intermarry, for they belonged to different tribes of descent." From this he branches out in an argument of two or three pages to prove that "Mr. Morgan's reason, then, is insufficient." If Mr. McLennan had studied the Turanian or the Ganowánian system of consanguinity with very moderate attention, he would have found that a "man's son and his sister's daughter" are not "reputed brother and sister." On the contrary, they are cousins. This is one of the most obvious as well as important differences between the Malayan and Turanian systems, and the one which expresses the difference between the consanguine family of the Malayan, and the punaluan family of the Turanian system.

The general reader will hardly take the trouble necessary to master the details of these systems. Unless he can follow the relationships with ease and freedom, a discussion of the system will be a source of perplexity rather than of pleasure. Mr. McLennan uses the terms of relationship freely, but without, in all cases, using them correctly.

In another place (p. 360), Mr. McLennan attributes to me a distinction between marriage and cohabitation which I have not made; and follows it with a rhetorical flourish quite equal to the best in "Primitive Marriage."

Finally, Mr. McLennan plants himself upon two alleged mistakes which vitiate, in his opinion, my explanation of the origin of the classificatory system. "In attempting to explain the origin of the classificatory system, Mr. Morgan made two radical mistakes. His first mistake was, that he did not steadily contemplate the main peculiarity of the system—its classification of the connected persons; that he did not seek the origin of the system in the origin of the classification" (p. 360). What is the difference in this case, between the system and the classification? The two mean the same thing, and cannot by any possibility be made to mean anything different. To seek the origin of one is to seek the origin of the other.

"The second mistake, or rather I should say error, was to have so lightly assumed the system to be a system of blood-ties" (p. 361). There is no error here, since the persons named in the Tables are descended from common ancestors, or connected by marriage with some one or more of them. They are the same persons who are described in the Table showing the Aryan, Semitic, and Uralian systems (Consanguinity, pp. 79-127). In each and all of these systems they are bound to each other in fact by consanguinity and affinity. In the latter each relationship is specialized; in the former they are classified in categories; but in all alike the ultimate basis is the same, namely actual consanguinity and affinity. Marriage in the group in the former, and marriage between single pairs in the latter, produced the difference between them. In the Malayan, Turanian and Ganowánian systems, there is a solid basis for the blood-relationships they exhibit in the common descent of the persons; and for the marriage-relationships we must look to the form of marriage they indicate. Examination and comparison show that two distinct forms of marriage are requisite to explain the Malayan and Turanian systems; whence the application, as tests of consanguine marriage in one case, and a punaluan marriage in the other.

While the terms of relationship are constantly used in salutation, it is because they are terms of relationship that they are so used. Mr. McLennan's attempt to turn them into conventional modes of addressing persons is futile. Although he lays great stress upon this view he makes no use of them as "modes of address" in attempting to explain their origin. So far as he makes any use of them he employs them strictly as terms of consanguinity and affinity. It was as impossible that "a system of modes of addressing persons" should have grown up independently of the system of consanguinity and affinity (p. 373), as that language should have grown up independently of the ideas it represents and expresses. What could have given to these terms their significance as used in addressing relatives, but the relationship whether of consanguinity or affiinity which they expressed? The mere want of a mode of addressing persons could never have given such stupendous systems, identical in minute details over immense sections of the earth.

Upon the essential difference between Mr. McLennan's explanation of the origin of the classificatory system, and the one presented in this volume—whether it is a system of modes of addressing persons, or a system of consanguinity and affinity—I am quite content to submit the question to the judgment of the reader.

PART IV

GROWTH OF THE IDEA OF PROPERTY

INTRODUCTION TO PART IV

GROWTH OF THE IDEA OF PROPERTY

Morgan's last section of *Ancient Society*, "Growth of the Idea of Property," needs little comment. Here the breadth and vision of his insight is revealed in a number of brilliant passages wherein he summarized the steps that transformed gentile to "civilized" society, and where he stressed the significance man's past held for his future.

He delineated three stages in the development of property. Among hunting peoples, property scarcely existed. "A passion for its possession had scarcely been formed in their minds, because the thing itself scarcely existed" (537). However, "with the institution of the gens came in the first great rule of inheritance, which distributed the effects of a deceased person among his gentiles" (538), although in actual practice they were distributed to the nearest of kin. With the development of agriculture, property in cultivated lands appeared. Although owned by the tribe, "possessory right to cultivated land was now recognized in the individual, or in the group" (540). Such usufruct to land obtained widely among horticultural peoples, and clan lands that were not being used or were not needed by one household or lineage would be redistributed among the gentiles. In simple agricultural society true ownership, with buying and selling of land, and the possibility of being alienated from it altogether, were unknown. In early frontier days in the United States many misunderstandings arose from the difference in the Indian concept of usufruct, and the settlers' concept of outright land ownership by an individual.

As society grew in complexity and organization, as clothes and personal effects became more elaborate, as weapons, tools, utensils, sacred objects, and so forth proliferated, the common practice of giving personal belongings to nearest relatives gradually crystallized in the "second great rule of inheritance, which gave the property to the agnatic kindred, to the exclusion of the remaining gentiles" (541). Morgan raised the question: When did this principle also become applied to land and homes? And this is the crucial question for understanding the development of class-structured and politically organized society. Considerable work has been done, especially in relation to the Ancient East, to West Africa, and to the high cultures of the New World, in an attempt to define stages in the transformation of land from public domain to private property.

The third rule of inheritance gave property to the children of the deceased owner (553-4, 559), a historic step, the significance of which Morgan has already described for ancient Greece and Rome, and for the Hebrew tribes, and which he now summarized. Morgan spoke of witnessing a "repugnance to gentile inheritance" among some of the village tribes of American Indians, and "devices adopted to enable fathers to give their property, now largely increased in amount, to their children" (541). Subsequent studies have documented such instances as responses to the involvement of American Indians with an industrial society, through trade and through wage labor.[1]

Several times we have alluded to Morgan's truly monumental achievement in producing, with far less data than we have today, a scheme for historical evolution which in its essential outlines has remained unchanged by new material. It seems, therefore, most presumptuous to pick at flaws in his work. However, if we measure Morgan's theoretical approach by the rigorous yardstick demanded for building a science of society, and without regard for the limits within which he had to work, there are shortcomings in his concept of social structure and social causation. Morgan defined broad relationships among the different parts of society, and he went far in detailing the

---

[1] For a detailed account of economic life and the conflict between gentile inheritance and individualized ownership among a contemporary Indian group, the Hopi Indians of the Southwest, cf. Beaglehole, Ernest, *Notes on Hopi Economic Life,* Yale University Publications in Anthropology, No. 15, 1937. For a study of the transition toward individualized rights to property among a hunting people, cf. Leacock, Eleanor, "The Montagnais 'Hunting Territory' and the Fur Trade," *American Anthropologist,* Memoir 78, 1954. For a general bibliography of works on primitive economics, cf. Herskovits, Melville J., *Economic Anthropology,* Alfred A. Knopf, New York, 1952.

constant and conflicting interaction among these parts that is the process we call social life. However, he never squarely faced the question of how social structure operates. This failure emerges most clearly in his stress on *property* as such, rather than on *economic relationships*. Morgan saw "class" as a matter of a royalty, or an aristocracy. The United States he thought to have given up classes, and he did not see that behind the regulation of property rights he felt to be necessary lay the problem of changing an economic structure.

Ironically, contrary to what has been said of Morgan, if one wanted to launch a really salient attack on him, one could better accuse him, not of building too broad a scheme, not of being too theoretical, but of not departing far enough from historical detail. One could argue that, in a period when evolutionary ideas were common, and theories of social causation were being raised, Morgan was preeminently the optimistic, pragmatic, American empiricist, liberal, humanistic, but pushed somewhat reluctantly—albeit consistently—into theoretical areas. His ultimate theory of causation is teleological. History is enacted through people with a common "principle of intelligence" seeking "ideal standards invariably the same" (562). What has happened was supposed to happen, with some moral weight, some purpose, as the active agent, as part of the grand design of the "Supreme Intelligence" (563).

Morgan's moral in *Ancient Society* has tremendous meaning today—that "the dissolution of society bids fair to become the termination of a career of which property is the end and aim; because such a career contains the elements of self-destruction" (561)—that the "next higher plane of society" must be "a revival, in a higher form, of the liberty, equality and fraternity of the ancient gentes" (562). That the causes of our difficulties lie not in the nature of man, but in our social commitment to property, is the profoundly important message. However, to say no more than "human intelligence will rise to the mastery over property" (561), since "experience, intelligence and knowledge are steadily tending" toward full democracy and brotherhood, begs the question: What are the realities of historical process that enable, or even impel, mankind to move from where he is to where he can and wants to be?

CHAPTER I

THE THREE RULES OF INHERITANCE

It remains to consider the growth of property in the several ethnical periods, the rules that sprang up with respect to its ownership and inheritance, and the influence which it exerted upon ancient society

The earliest ideas of property were intimately associated with the procurement of subsistence, which was the primary need. The objects of ownership would naturally increase in each successive ethnical period with the multiplication of those arts upon which the means of subsistence depended. The growth of property would thus keep pace with the progress of inventions and discoveries. Each ethnical period shows a marked advance upon its predecessor, not only in the number of inventions, but also in the variety and amount of property which resulted therefrom. The multiplicity of the forms of property would be accompanied by the growth of certain regulations with reference to its possession and inheritance. The customs upon which these rules of proprietary possession and inheritance depend, are determined and modified by the condition and progress of the social organization. The growth of property is thus closely connected with the increase of inventions and discoveries, and with the improvement of social institutions which mark the several ethnical periods of human progress.

I. *Property in the Status of Savagery.*

In any view of the case, it is difficult to conceive of the condition of mankind in this early period of their existence, when divested of all they had gained through inventions and discoveries, and through the growth of ideas embodied in institutions, usages and customs. Human progress from a state of absolute ignorance and inexperience was slow in time, but geometrical in ratio. Mankind may be traced by a chain of necessary inferences back to a time when, ignorant of fire, without articulate language, and without artificial weapons, they depended, like the wild animals, upon the spontaneous fruits of the earth. Slowly, almost imperceptibly, they advanced through savagery, from gesture language and imperfect sounds to articulate speech; from the club, as the first weapon, to the spear pointed with flint, and finally to the bow and arrow; from the flint-knife and chisel to the stone axe and hammer; from the ozier and cane basket to the basket coated with clay, which gave a vessel for boiling food with fire; and, finally, to the art of pottery, which gave a vessel able to withstand the fire. In the means of subsistence, they advanced from natural fruits in a restricted habitat to scale and shell fish on the coasts of the sea, and finally to bread roots and game. Rope and string-making from filaments of bark, a species of cloth made of vegetable pulp, the tanning of skins to be used as apparel and as a covering for tents, and finally the house constructed of poles and covered with bark, or made of plank split by stone wedges, belong, with those previously named, to the Status of Savagery. Among minor inventions may be mentioned the fire-drill, the moccasin and the snow-shoe.

Before the close of this period, mankind had learned to support themselves in numbers in comparison with primitive times; they had propagated themselves over the face of the earth, and come into possession of all the possibilities of the continents in favor of human advancement. In social organization, they had advanced from the consanguine horde into tribes organized in gentes, and thus became possessed of the germs of the principal governmental institutions. The human race was now successfully launched upon its great career for the attainment of civilization, which even then, with articulate language among inventions, with the art of pottery among arts, and with the gentes among institutions, was substantially assured.

The period of savagery wrought immense changes in the condition of mankind. That portion, which led the advance, had finally organized gentile society and developed small tribes with villages here and there which tended to stimulate the inventive capacities. Their rude energies and ruder arts had been chiefly devoted to subsistence. They had not attained to the village stockade for defense, nor to farinaceous food, and the scourge of cannibalism still pursued them. The arts, inventions and institutions named represent nearly the sum of the acquisitions of mankind in savagery, with the exception of the marvelous progress in language. In the aggregate it seems small, but it was immense potentially; because it embraced the rudiments of language, of government, of the family, of religion, of house architecture and of property, together with the principal germs of the arts of life. All these their descendants wrought out more fully in the period of barbarism, and their civilized descendants are still perfecting.

But the property of savages was inconsiderable. Their ideas concerning its value, its desirability and its inheritance were feeble. Rude weapons, fabrics, utensils, apparel, implements of flint, stone and bone, and personal ornaments represent the chief items of property in savage life. A passion for its possession had scarcely been formed in their minds, because the thing itself scarcely existed. It was left to the then distant period of civilization to develop into full vitality that "greed of gain" (*studium lucri*), which is now such a commanding force in the human mind. Lands, as yet hardly a subject of property, were owned by the tribes in common, while tenement houses were owned jointly by their occupants. Upon articles purely personal which were increasing with the slow progress of inventions, the great passion was nourishing its nascent powers. Those esteemed most valuable were deposited in the grave of the deceased proprietor for his continued use in the spirit-land. What remained was sufficient to raise the question of its inheritance. Of the manner of its distribution before the organization into gentes, our information is limited, or altogether wanting. With the institution of the gens came in the first great rule of inheritance, which distributed the effects of a deceased person among his gentiles. Practically they were appropriated by the nearest of kin; but the principle was general, that the property should remain in the gens of the decedent, and be distributed among its members. This principle was maintained into civilization by the Grecian and Latin gentes. Children inherited from their mother, but took nothing from their reputed father.

II. *Property in the Lower Status of Barbarism.*

From the invention of pottery to the domestication of animals, or, as an equivalent, the cultivation of maize and plants by irrigation, the duration of the period must have been shorter than that of savagery. With the exception of the art of pottery, finger weaving and the art of cultivation, in America, which gave farinaceous food, no great invention or discovery signalized this ethnical period. It was more distinguished for progress in the development of institutions. Finger weaving, with warp and woof, seems to belong to this period, and it must rank as one of the greatest of inventions; but it cannot be certainly affirmed that the art was not attained in savagery. The Iroquois and other tribes of America in the same status manufactured belts and burden-straps with warp and woof of excellent quality and finish; using fine twine made of filaments of elm and basswood bark.[1] The principles of this great invention, which has since clothed the human family, were perfectly realized; but they were unable to extend it to the production of the woven garment. Picture writing also seems to have made its first appearance in this period. If it originated earlier, it now received a very considerable development. It is interesting as one of the stages of an art which culminated in the invention of a phonetic alphabet. The

[1] "League of the Iroquois," p. 364.

series of connected inventions seem to have been the following: 1. Gesture Language, or the language of personal symbols; 2. Picture Writing, or idiographic symbols; 3. Hieroglyphs, or conventional symbols; 4. Hieroglyphs of phonetic power, or phonetic symbols used in a syllabus; and 5, a Phonetic Alphabet, or written sounds. Since a language of written sounds was a growth through successive stages of development, the rise of its antecedent processes is both important and instructive. The characters on the Copan monuments are apparently hieroglyphs of the grade of conventional symbols. They show that the American aborigines, who practiced the first three forms, were proceeding independently in the direction of a phonetic alphabet.

The invention of the stockade as a means of village defense, of a raw-hide shield as a defense against the arrow, which had now become a deadly missile, of the several varieties of the war-club, armed with an encased stone or with a point of deer horn, seem also to belong to this period. At all events they were in common use among the American Indian tribes in the Lower Status of barbarism when discovered. The spear pointed with flint or bone was not a customary weapon with the forest tribes, though sometimes used.[1] This weapon belongs to the period of savagery, before the bow and arrow were invented, and reappears as a prominent weapon in the Upper Status of barbarism, when the copper-pointed spear came into use, and close combat became the mode of warfare. The bow and arrow and the war-club were the principal weapons of the American aborigines in the Lower Status of barbarism. Some progress was made in pottery in the increased size of the vessels produced, and in their ornamentation;[2] but it remained extremely rude to the end of the period. There was a sensible advance in house architecture, in the size and mode of con-

1 For example, the Ojibwas used the lance or spear, Shemă'-gun, pointed with flint or bone.

2 The Creeks made earthen vessels holding from two to ten gallons (Adair's "History of American Indians," p. 424); and the Iroquois ornamented their jars and pipes with miniature human faces attached as buttons. This discovery was recently made by Mr. F. A. Cushing, of the Smithsonian Institution.

struction. Among minor inventions were the air-gun for bird-shooting, the wooden mortar and pounder for reducing maize to flour, and the stone mortar for preparing paints; earthen and stone pipes, with the use of tobacco; bone and stone implements of higher grades, with stone hammers and mauls, the handle and upper part of the stone being encased in raw hide; and moccasins and belts ornamented with porcupine quills. Some of these inventions were borrowed, not unlikely, from tribes in the Middle Status; for it was by this process constantly repeated that the more advanced tribes lifted up those below them, as fast as the latter were able to appreciate and to appropriate the means of progress.

The cultivation of maize and plants gave the people unleavened bread, the Indian succotash and hominy. It also tended to introduce a new species of property, namely, cultivated lands or gardens. Although lands were owned in common by the tribe, a possessory right to cultivated land was now recognized in the individual, or in the group, which became a subject of inheritance. The group united in a common household were mostly of the same gens, and the rule of inheritance would not allow it to be detached from the kinship.

The property and effects of husband and wife were kept distinct, and remained after their demise in the gens to which each respectively belonged. The wife and children took nothing from the husband and father, and the husband took nothing from the wife. Among the Iroquois, if a man died leaving a wife and children, his property was distributed among his gentiles in such a manner that his sisters and their children, and his maternal uncles, would receive the most of it. His brothers might receive a small portion. If a woman died, leaving a husband and children, her children, her sisters, and her mother and her sisters inherited her effects; but the greater portion was assigned to her children. In each case the property remained in the gens. Among the Ojibwas, the effects of a mother were distributed among her children, if old enough to use them; otherwise, or in default of children, they went to her sisters, and to her mother and her sisters, to the exclusion of her brothers. Although they had changed descent to the male line, the inheritance still followed the rule which prevailed when descent was in the female line.

The variety and amount of property were greater than in savagery, but still not sufficient to develop a strong sentiment in relation to inheritance. In the mode of distribution above given may be recognized, as elsewhere stated, the germ of the second great rule of inheritance, which gave the property to the agnatic kindred, to the exclusion of the remaining gentiles. Agnation and agnatic kindred, as now defined, assume descent in in the male line; but the persons included would be very different from those with descent in the female line. The principle is the same in both cases, and the terms seem as applicable in the one as in the other. With descent in the female line, the agnates are those persons who can trace their descent through females exclusively from the same common ancestor with the intestate; in the other case, who can trace their descent through males exclusively. It is the blood connection of persons within the gens by direct descent, in a given line, from the same common ancestor which lies at the foundation of agnatic relationship.

At the present time, among the advanced Indian tribes, repugnance to gentile inheritance has begun to manifest itself. In some it has been overthrown, and an exclusive inheritance in children substituted in its place. Evidence of this repugnance has elsewhere been given, among the Iroquois, Creeks, Cherokees, Choctas, Menominees, Crows and Ojibwas, with references to the devices adopted to enable fathers to give their property, now largely increased in amount, to their children.

The diminution of cannibalism, that brutalizing scourge of savagery, was very marked in the Older Period of barbarism. It was abandoned as a common practice; but remained as a war practice, as elsewhere explained, through this, and into the Middle Period. In this form it was found in the principal tribes of the United States, Mexico, and Central America. The acquisition of farinaceous food was the principal means of extricating mankind from this savage custom.

We have now passed over, with a mere glance, two ethnical periods, which covered four-fifths, at least, of the entire existence of mankind upon the earth. While in the Lower Status, the higher attributes of man began to manifest themselves. Personal dignity, eloquence in speech, religious sensibility, rectitude, manliness and courage were now common traits of character; but cruelty, treachery and fanaticism were equally common. Element worship in religion, with a dim conception of personal gods, and of a Great Spirit, rude verse-making, joint-tenement houses, and bread from maize, belong to this period. It also produced the syndyasmian family, and the confederacy of tribes organized in gentes and phratries. The imagination, that great faculty which has contributed so largely to the elevation of mankind, was now producing an unwritten literature of myths, legends and traditions, which had already become a powerful stimulus upon the race.

III. *Property in the Middle Status of Barbarism.*

The condition of mankind in this ethnical period has been more completely lost than that of any other. It was exhibited by the Village Indians of North and South America in barbaric splendor at the epoch of their discovery. Their governmental institutions, their religious tenets, their plan of domestic life, their arts and their rules in relation to the ownership and inheritance of property, might have been completely obtained; but the opportunity was allowed to escape. All that remains are scattered portions of the truth buried in misconceptions and romantic tales.

This period opens in the Eastern hemisphere with the domestication of animals, and in the Western with the appearance of the Village Indians, living in large joint-tenement houses of adobe brick, and, in some areas, of stone laid in courses. It was attended with the cultivation of maize and plants by irrigation, which required artificial canals, and garden beds laid out in squares, with raised ridges to contain the water until absorbed.

When discovered, they were well advanced toward the close of the Middle Period, a portion of them having made bronze, which brought them near the higher process of smelting iron ore. The joint-tenement house was in the nature of a fortress, and held an intermediate position between the stockaded village of the Lower, and the walled city of the Upper Status. There were no cities, in the proper sense of the term, in America when discovered. In the art of war they had made but little progress, except in defense, by the construction of great houses generally impregnable to Indian assault. But they had invented the quilted mantle (*escaupiles*), stuffed with cotton, as a further shield against the arrow, [1] and the two-edged sword (*macuahuitl*), [2] each edge having a row of angular flint points imbedded in the wooden blade. They still used the bow and arrow, the spear, and the war-club, flint knives and hatchets, and stone implements, [3] although they had the copper axe and chisel, which for some reason never came into general use.

To maize, beans, squashes and tobacco, were now added cotton, pepper, tomato, cacao, and the care of certain fruits. A beer was made by fermenting the juice of the maguey. The Iroquois, however, had produced a similar beverage by fermenting maple sap. Earthen vessels of capacity to hold several gallons, of fine texture and superior ornamentation were produced by improved methods in the ceramic art. Bowls, pots and water-jars were manufactured in abundance. The discovery and use of the native metals first for ornaments, and finally for implements and utensils, such as the copper axe and chisel, belong to this period. The melting of these metals in the crucible, with the probable use of the blow-pipe and charcoal, and casting them in moulds, the production of bronze, rude stone sculptures, the woven garment of cotton, [4] the house of dressed stone, ideographs

1 Herrera, l. c., iv, 16.
2 Ib., iii, 13; iv, 16, 137. Clavigero, ii, 165.
3 Clavigero, ii, 238. Herrera, ii, 145; iv, 133.
4 Hakluyt's "Coll. of Voyages," l. c., iii, 377.

or hieroglyphs cut on the grave-posts of deceased chiefs, the calendar for measuring time, and the solstitial stone for marking the seasons, cyclopean walls, the domestication of the llama, of a species of dog, of the turkey and other fowls, belong to the same period in America. A priesthood organized in a hierarchy, and distinguished by a costume, personal gods with idols to represent them, and human sacrifices, appear for the first time in this ethnical period. Two large Indian pueblos, Mexico and Cusco, now appear, containing over twenty thousand inhabitants, a number unknown in the previous period. The aristocratic element in society began to manifest itself in feeble forms among the chiefs, civil and military, through increased numbers under the same government, and the growing complexity of affairs.

Turning to the Eastern hemisphere, we find its native tribes, in the corresponding period, with domestic animals yielding them a meat and milk subsistence, but probably without horticultural and without farinaceous food. When the great discovery was made that the wild horse, cow, sheep, ass, sow and goat might be tamed, and, when produced in flocks and herds, become a source of permanent subsistence it must have given a powerful impulse to human progress. But the effect would not become general until pastoral life for the creation and maintenance of flocks and herds became established. Europe, as a forest area in the main, was unadapted to the pastoral state; but the grass plains of high Asia, and upon the Euphrates, the Tigris and other rivers of Asia, were the natural homes of the pastoral tribes. Thither they would naturally tend; and to these areas we trace our own remote ancestors, where they were found confronting like pastoral Semitic tribes. The cultivation of cereals and plants must have preceded their migration from the grass plains into the forest areas of Western Asia and of Europe. It would be forced upon them by the necessities of the domestic animals now incorporated in their plan of life. There are reasons, therefore, for supposing that the cultivation of cereals by the Aryan tribes preceded their western migration, with the exception perhaps of the

Celts. Woven fabrics of flax and wool, and bronze implements and weapons appear in this period in the Eastern hemisphere.

Such were the inventions and discoveries which signalized the Middle Period of barbarism. Society was now more highly organized, and its affairs were becoming more complex. Differences in the culture of the two hemispheres now existed in consequence of their unequal endowments; but the main current of progress was steadily upward to a knowledge of iron and its uses. To cross the barrier into the Upper Status, metallic tools able to hold an edge and point were indispensable. Iron was the only metal able to answer these requirements. The most advanced tribes were arrested at this barrier, awaiting the invention of the process of smelting iron ore.

From the foregoing considerations it is evident that a large increase of personal property had now occurred, and some changes in the relations of persons to land. The territorial domain still belonged to the tribe in common; but a portion was now set apart for the support of the government, another for religious uses, and another and more important portion, that from which the people derived their subsistence, was divided among the several gentes, or communities of persons who resided in the same pueblo (*supra*, p. 200). That any person owned lands or houses in his own right, with power to sell and convey in fee-simple to whomsoever he pleased, is not only unestablished but improbable. Their mode of owning their lands in common, by gentes, or by communities of persons, their joint-tenement houses, and their mode of occupation by related families, precluded the individual ownership of houses or of lands. A right to sell an interest in such lands or in such houses, and to transfer the same to a stranger, would break up their plan of life.[1]

---

1 The Rev. Samuel Gorman, a missionary among the Laguna Pueblo Indians, remarks in an address before the Historical Society of New Mexico (p. 12), that "the right of property belongs to the female part of the family, and descends in that line from mother to daughter. Their land is held in common, as the property of the community, but after a person cultivates a lot he has personal claim to it, "which he can sell to one of

The possessory right, which we must suppose existed in individuals or in families, was inalienable, except within the gens, and on the demise of the person would pass by inheritance to his or her gentile heirs. Joint-tenement houses, and lands in common, indicate a plan of life adverse to individual ownership.

The Moqui Village Indians, besides their seven large pueblos and their gardens, now have flocks of sheep, horses and mules, and considerable other personal property. They manufacture earthen vessels of many sizes and of excellent quality, and woolen blankets in looms, and with yarn of their own production. Major J. W. Powell noticed the following case at the pueblo of Oraybe, which shows that the husband acquires no rights over the property of the wife, or over the children of the marriage. A Zunian married an Oraybe woman, and had by her three children. He resided with them at Oraybe until his wife died, which occurred while Major Powell was at the pueblo. The relatives of the deceased wife took possession of her children and of her household property; leaving to him his horse, clothing and weapons. Certain blankets which belonged to him he was allowed to take, but those belonging to his wife remained. He left the pueblo with Major Powell, saying he would go with him to Santa Fé, and then return to his own people at Zuñi. Another case of a similar kind occurred at another of the Moqui pueblos (She-pow-e-luv-ih), which also came to the notice of my informant. A woman died, leaving children and a husband, as well as property. The children and the property were taken by the deceased wife's relatives; all the husband was allowed to take was his clothing. Whether he was a Moqui Indian or from another tribe, Major Powell, who saw the person, did not learn. It appears from these cases that the children belonged to the mother, and not to the father, and that he

---

the community." . . . Their women, generally, have control of the granary, and they are more provident than their Spanish neighbors about the future. Ordinarily they try to have a year's provisions on hand. It is only when two years of scarcity succeed each other, that Pueblos, as a community, suffer hunger."

was not allowed to take them even after the mother's death. Such also was the usage among the Iroquois and other northern tribes. Furthermore, the property of the wife was kept distinct, and belonged to her relatives after her death. It tends to show that the wife took nothing from her husband, as an implication from the fact that the husband took nothing from the wife. Elsewhere it has been shown that this was the usage among the Village Indians of Mexico.

Women, as well as men, not unlikely, had a possessory right to such rooms and sections of these pueblo houses as they occupied; and they doubtless transmitted these rights to their nearest of kin, under established regulations. We need to know how these sections of each pueblo are owned and inherited, whether the possessor has the right to sell and transfer to a stranger, and if not, the nature and limits of his possessory right. We also need to know who inherits the property of the males, and who inherits the property of the females. A small amount of well-directed labor would furnish the information now so much desired.

The Spanish writers have left the land tenure of the southern tribes in inextricable confusion. When they found a community of persons owning lands in common, which they could not alienate, and that one person among them was recognized as their chief, they at once treated these lands as a feudal estate, the chief as a feudal lord, and the people who owned the lands in common as his vassals. At best, it was a perversion of the facts. One thing is plain, namely, that these lands were owned in common by a community of persons; but one, not less essential, is not given; namely, the bond of union which held these persons together. If a gens, or a part of a gens, the whole subject would be at once understood.

Descent in the female line still remained in some of the tribes of Mexico and Central America, while in others, and probably in the larger portion, it had been changed to the male line. The influence of property must have caused the change, that children might participate as agnates in the inheritance of their father's property.

Among the Mayas, descent was in the male line, while among the Aztecs, Tezcucans, Tlacopans and Tlascalans, it is difficult to determine whether it was in the male or the female line. It is probable that descent was being changed to the male line among the Village Indians generally, with remains of the archaic rule manifesting themselves, as in the case of the office of Teuctli. The change would not overthrow gentile inheritance. It is claimed by a number of Spanish writers that the children, and in some cases the eldest son, inherited the property of a deceased father; but such statements, apart from an exposition of their system, are of little value.

Among the Village Indians, we should expect to find the second great rule of inheritance which distributed the property among the agnatic kindred. With descent in the male line, the children of a deceased person would stand at the head of the agnates, and very naturally receive the greater portion of the inheritance. It is not probable that the third great rule, which gave an exclusive inheritance to the children of the deceased owner, had become established among them. The discussion of inheritances by the earlier and later writers is unsatisfactory, and devoid of accurate information. Institutions, usages and customs still governed the question, and could alone explain the system. Without better evidence than we now possess, an exclusive inheritance by children cannot be asserted.

CHAPTER II

THE THREE RULES OF INHERITANCE—CONTINUED

The last great period of barbarism was never entered by the American aborigines. It commenced in the Eastern, according to the scheme adopted, with the production and use of iron.

The process of smelting iron ore was the invention of inventions, as elsewhere suggested, beside which all other inventions and discoveries hold a subordinate position. Mankind, notwithstanding a knowledge of bronze, were still arrested in their progress for the want of efficient metallic tools, and for the want of a metal of sufficient strength and hardness for mechanical appliances. All these qualities were found for the first time in iron. The accelerated progress of human intelligence dates from this invention. This ethnical period, which is made forever memorable, was, in many respects, the most brilliant and remarkable in the entire experience of mankind. It is so overcrowded with achievements as to lead to a suspicion that many of the works ascribed to it belong to the previous period.

IV. *Property in the Upper Status of Barbarism.*—Near the end of this period, property in masses, consisting of many kinds and held by individual ownership, began to be common, through settled agriculture, manufactures, local trade and foreign commerce; but the old tenure of lands under which they were held in common had not given place, except in part, to ownership in severalty. Systematic slavery originated in this status. It stands directly connected with the production of property. Out of it came the patriarchal family of the Hebrew type, and the similar family of the Latin tribes under paternal power, as well as a modified form of the same family among the Grecian tribes. From these causes, but more particularly from the increased abundance of subsistence through field agriculture, nations began to develop, numbering many thousands under one government, where before they would be reckoned by a few thousands. The localization of tribes in fixed areas and in fortified cities, with the increase of the numbers of the people, intensified the struggle for the possession of the most desirable territories. It tended to advance the art of war, and to increase the rewards of individual prowess. These changes of condition and of the plan of life indicate the approach of civilization, which was to overthrow gentile and establish political society.

Although the inhabitants of the Western hemisphere had no part in the experience which belongs to this status, they were following down the same lines on which the inhabitants of the Eastern had passed. They had fallen behind the advancing columm of the human race by just the distance measured by the Upper Status of barbarism and the superadded years of civilization.

We are now to trace the growth of the idea of property in this status of advancement, as shown by its recognition in kind, and by the rules that existed with respect to its ownership and inheritance.

The earliest laws of the Greeks, Romans and Hebrews. after civilization had commenced, did little more than turn into legal enactments the results which their previous experience had embodied in usages and customs. Having the final laws and the previous archaic rules, the intermediate changes, when not expressly known, may be inferred with tolerable certainty.

At the close of the Later Period of barbarism, great changes had occurred in the tenure of lands. It was gradually tending to two forms of ownership, namely, by the state and by individuals. But this result was not fully secured until after civilization had been attained. Lands among the Greeks were still held, as we have seen, some by the tribes in common, some by the phratry in common for religious uses, and some by the gens in common; but the bulk of the lands had fallen under individual ownership in severalty. In the time of Solon, while Athenian society was still gentile, lands in general were owned by individuals, who had already learned to mortgage them;[1] but individual ownership was not then a new thing. The Roman tribes, from their first establishment, had a public domain, the *Ager Romanus;* while lands were held by the *curia* for religious uses, by the gens, and by individuals in severalty. After these social corporations died out, the lands held by them in common gradually became private property. Very little is known beyond the fact that certain lands were held by these organizations for special uses, while individuals were gradually appropriating the substance of the national areas.

These several forms of ownership tend to show that the oldest tenure, by which land was held, was by the tribe in common; that after its cultivation began, a portion of the tribe lands was divided among the gentes, each of which held their portion in common; and that this was followed, in course of time, by allotments to individuals, which allotments finally ripened into individual ownership in severalty. Unoccupied and waste lands still remained as the common property of the gens, the tribe and the nation. This, substantially, seems to have been the progress of experience with respect to the ownership of land. Personal property, generally, was subject to individual ownership.

The monogamian family made its first appearance in the Upper Status of barbarism, the growth of which out of a previous syndyasmian form was intimately connected with the increase of property, and with the usages in respect to its inheritance. Descent had been changed to the male line; but all property, real as well as personal, remained, as it had been from time immemorial, hereditary in the gens.

Our principal information concerning the kinds of

1 Plutarch, in "Solon," c. xv.

property, that existed among the Grecian tribes in this period, is derived from the Homeric poems, and from the early laws of the period of civilization which reflect ancient usages. Mention is made in the Iliad of *fences* [1] around cultivated fields, of an *enclosure of fifty acres,* half of which was fit for vines and the remainder for tillage;[2] and it is said of Tydeus that he lived in a mansion rich in resources, and had corn-producing fields in abundance.[3] There is no reason to doubt that lands were then fenced and measured, and held by individual ownership. It indicates a large degree of progress in a knowledge of property and its uses. Breeds of horses were already distinguished for particular excellence.[4] Herds of cattle and flocks of sheep possessed by individuals are mentioned, as "sheep of a rich man standing countless in the fold."[5] Coined money was still unknown, consequently trade was by barter of commodities, as indicated by the following lines: "Thence the long-haired Greeks bought wine, some for brass, some for shining iron, others for hides, some for the oxen themselves, and some for slaves."[6] Gold in bars, however, is named as passing by weight and estimated by talents.[7] Manufactured articles of gold, silver, brass and iron, and textile fabrics of linen and woolen in many forms, together with houses and palaces, are mentioned. It will not be necessary to extend the illustrations. Those given are sufficient to indicate the great advance society had attained in the Upper Status of barbarism, in contrast with that in the immediately previous period.

After houses and lands, flocks and herds, and exchangeable commodities had become so great in quantity, and had come to be held by individual ownership, the question of their inheritance would press upon human attention until the right was placed upon a basis which satisfied

---

1 "Iliad," v, 90.
2 Ib., ix, 577.
3 Ib., xiv, 121.
4 Ib., v, 265.
5 Ib., iv, 433, Buckley's trans.
6 Ib., vii, 472, Buckley's trans.
7 "Iliad," xii, 274.

the growing intelligence of the Greek mind. Archaic usages would be modified in the direction of later conceptions. The domestic animals were a possession of greater value than all kinds of property previously known put together. They served for food, were exchangeable for other commodities, were usable for redeeming captives, for paying fines, and in sacrifices in the observance of their religious rites. Moreover, as they were capable of indefinite multiplication in numbers, their possession revealed to the human mind its first conception of wealth. Following upon this, in course of time, was the systematical cultivation of the earth, which tended to identify the family with the soil, and render it a property-making organization. It soon found expression, in the Latin, Grecian and Hebrew tribes, in the family under paternal power, involving slaves and servants. Since the labor of the father and his children became incorporated more and more with the land, with the production of domestic animals, and with the creation of merchandise, it would not only tend to individualize the family, now monogamian, but also to suggest the superior claims of children to the inheritance of the property they had assisted in creating. Before lands were cultivated, flocks and herds would naturally fall under the joint ownership of persons united in a group, on a basis of kin, for subsistence. Agnatic inheritance would be apt to assert itself in this condition of things. But when lands had become the subject of property, and allotments to individuals had resulted in individual ownership, the third great rule of inheritance, which gave the property to the children of the deceased owner, was certain to supervene upon agnatic inheritance. There is no direct evidence that strict agnatic inheritance ever existed among the Latin, Grecian or Hebrew tribes, excepting in the reversion, established alike in Roman, Grecian and Hebrew law; but that an exclusive agnatic inheritance existed in the early period may be inferred from the reversion.

When field agriculture had demonstrated that the whole surface of the earth could be made the subject of property owned by individuals in severalty, and it was found that the head of the family became the natural center of accumulation, the new property career of mankind was inaugurated. It was fully done before the close of the Later Period of barbarism. A little reflection must convince any one of the powerful influence property would now begin to exercise upon the human mind, and of the great awakening of new elements of character it was calculated to produce. Evidence appears, from many sources, that the feeble impulse aroused in the savage mind had now become a tremendous passion in the splendid barbarian of the heroic age. Neither archaic nor later usages could maintain themselves in such an advanced condition. The time had now arrived when monogamy, having assured the paternity of children, would assert and maintain their exclusive right to inherit the property of their deceased father.[1]

In the Hebrew tribes, of whose experience in barbarism very little is known, individual ownership of lands existed before the commencement of their civilizaton. The purchase from Ephron by Abraham of the cave of Machpelah is an illustration.[2] They had undoubtedly passed through a previous experience in all respects similar to that of the Aryan tribes; and came out of barbarism, like them, in possession of the domestic animals and of the cereals, together with a knowledge of iron and brass, of gold and silver, of fictile wares and of textile fabrics. But their knowledge of field agriculture was limited in the time of Abraham. The reconstruction of Hebrew society, after the Exodus, on the basis of consanguine tribes, to which on reaching Palestine territorial areas were assigned, shows that civilization found them under gentile

1 The German tribes when first known historically were in the Upper Status of barbarism. They used iron, but in limited quantities, possessed flocks and herds, cultivated the cereals, and manufactured coarse textile fabrics of linen and woolen; but they had not then attained to the idea of individual ownership in lands. According to the account of Caesar, elsewhere cited, the arable lands were allotted annually by the chiefs, while the pasture lands were held in common. It would seem, therefore, that the idea of individual property in lands was unknown in Asia and Europe in the Middle Period of barbarism, but came in during the Later Period.

2 "Genesis," xxiii, 13.

institutions, and below a knowledge of political society. With respect to the ownership and inheritance of property, their experience seems to have been coincident with that of the Roman and Grecian tribes, as can be made out, with some degree of clearness, from the legislation of Moses. Inheritance was strictly within the phratry, and probably within the gens, namely "the house of the father." The archaic rule of inheritance among the Hebrews is unknown, except as it is indicated by the reversion, which was substantially the same as in the Roman law of the Twelve Tables. We have this law of reversion, and also an illustrative case, showing that after children had acquired an exclusive inheritance, daughters succeeded in default of sons. Marriage would then transfer their property from their own gens to that of their husband's, unless some restraint, in the case of heiresses, was put on the right. Presumptively and naturally, marriage within the gens was prohibited. This presented the last great question which arose with respect to gentile inheritance. It came before Moses as a question of Hebrew inheritance, and before Solon as a question of Athenian inheritance, the gens claiming a paramount right to its retention within its membership; and it was adjudicated by both, in the same manner. It may be reasonably supposed that the same question had arisen in the Roman gentes, and was in part met by the rule that the marriage of a female worked a *deminutio capitis,* and with it a forfeiture of agnatic rights. Another question was involved in this issue; namely, whether marriage should be restricted by the rule forbidding it within the gens, or become free; the degree, and not the fact of kin, being the measure of the limitation. This last rule was to be the final outcome of human experience with respect to marriage. With these considerations in mind, the case to be cited sheds a strong light upon the early institutions of the Hebrews, and shows their essential similarity with those of the Greeks and Romans under gentilism.

Zelophehad died leaving daughters, but no sons, and the inheritance was given to the former. Afterwards, these daughters being about to marry out of the tribe of

Joseph, to which they belonged, the members of the tribe objecting to such a transfer of the property, brought the question before Moses, saying: "If they be married to any of the sons of the *other* tribes of the children of Israel, then shall the inheritance be taken from the inheritance of our fathers, and shall be put to the inheritance of the tribe whereunto they are received: so shall it be taken from the lot of our inheritance." [1] Although this language is but the statement of the results of a proposed act, it implies a grievance; and that grievance was the transfer of the property from the gens and tribe to which it was conceived as belonging by hereditary right. The Hebrew lawgiver admits this right in the language of his decision. "The tribe of the sons of Joseph hath spoken well. This *is* the thing which the Lord doth command, concerning the daughters of Zelophehad saying, Let them marry to whom they think best: only to the family of the tribe of their father shall they marry. So shall not the inheritance of the children of Israel remove from tribe to tribe: for every one of the children of Israel shall keep himself to the inheritance of the tribe of his fathers. And every daughter that possesseth an inheritance in any tribe of the children of Israel shall be wife unto one of the family of the tribe of her father, that the children of Israel may enjoy every man the inheritance of his fathers." [2] They were required to marry into their own phratry (*supra,* p. 368), but not necessarily into their own gens. The daughters of Zelophehad were accordingly "married to their father's brother's sons," who were not only members of their own phratry, but also of their own gens. They were also their nearest agnates.

On a previous occasion, Moses had established the rule of inheritance and of reversion in the following explicit language. "And thou shalt speak unto the children of Israel, saying, If a man die and have no son, then you shall cause his inheritance to pass unto his daughters.

---

1 "Numbers," xxxvi, 4.
2 "Numbers," xxxvi, 5-9.
3 Ib., xxxvi, 11.

And if he have no daughter, then you shall give his inheritance unto his brothers. And if he have no brethren, then ye shall give his inheritance unto his father's brethren. And if his father have no brethren, then ye shall give his inheritance unto his kinsman, that is next to him of his family, and he shall possess it." [1]

Three classes of heirs are here named; first, the children of the deceased owner; second, the agnates, in the order of their nearness; and third, the gentiles, restricted to the members of the phratry of the decedent. The first class of the heirs were the children; but the inference would be that the sons took the property, subject to the obligation of maintaining the daughters. We find elsewhere that the eldest son had a double portion. In default of sons, the daughters received the inheritance. The second class were the agnates, divided into two grades; first, the brethren of the decedent, in default of children, received the inheritance; and second, in default of them, the brethren of the father of the decedent. The third were the gentiles, also in the order of their nearness, namely, "his kinsman that is next to him of his family." As the "family of the tribe" is the analogue of the phratry (*supra,* p. 369), the property, in default of children and of agnates, went to the nearest phrator of the deceased owner. It excluded cognates from the inheritance, so that a phrator, more distant than a father's brother, would inherit in preference to the children of a sister of the decedent. Descent is shown to have been in the male line, and the property must remain hereditary in the gens. It will be noticed that the father did not inherit from his son, nor the grandfather from his grandson. In this respect and in nearly all respects, the Mosaic law agrees with the law of the Twelve Tables. It affords a striking illustration of the uniformity of human experience, and of the growth of the same ideas in parallel lines in different races.

At a later day, the Levitical law established marriage upon a new basis independent of gentile law. It prohibited

1 "Numbers" xxvii, 8-11.

its occurrence within certain prescribed degrees of consanguinity and affinity, and declared it free beyond those degrees. This uprooted gentile usages in respect to marriage among the Hebrews; and it has now become the rule of Christian nations.

Turning to the laws of Solon concerning inheritances, we find them substantially the same as those of Moses. From this coincidence, an inference arises that the antecedent usages, customs and institutions of the Athenians and Hebrews were much the same in relation to property. In the time of Solon, the third great rule of inheritance was fully established among the Athenians. The sons took the estate of their deceased father equally; but charged with the obligation of maintaining the daughters, and of apportioning them suitably on their marriage. If there were no sons, the daughters inherited equally. This created heiresses by investing woman with estates, who like the daughters of Zelophehad, would transfer the property, by their marriage, from their own gens to that of their husband. The same question came before Solon that had been brought before Moses, and was decided in the same way. To prevent the transfer of property from gens to gens by marriage, Solon enacted that the heiress should marry her nearest male agnate, although they belonged to the same gens, and marriage between them had previously been prohibited by usage. This became such a fixed rule of Athenian law, that M. De Coulanges, in his original and suggestive work, expresses the opinion that the inheritance passed to the agnate, subject to the obligation of marrying the heiress.[1] Instances occurred where the nearest agnate, already married, put away his wife in order to marry the heiress, and thus gain the estate. Protomachus, in the Eubulides of Demosthenes, is an example.[2] But it is hardly supposable that the law compelled the agnate to divorce his wife and marry the heiress, or that he could obtain the estate without becoming her husband. If there were no children, the estate

1 "The Ancient City," Lee & Shepard's ed., Small's trans., p. 99.
2 "Demosthenes against Eubul.," 41.

passed to the agnates, and in default of agnates, to the gentiles of the deceased owner. Property was retained within the gens as inflexibly among the Athenians as among the Hebrews and the Romans. Solon turned into a law what, probably, had before become an established usage.

The progressive growth of the idea of property is illustrated by the appearance of testamentary dispositions established by Solon. This right was certain of ultimate adoption; but it required time and experience for its development. Plutarch remarks that Solon acquired celebrity by his law in relation to testaments, which before that were not allowed; but the property and homestead must remain in the gens of the decedent. When he permitted a person to devise his own property to any one he pleased, in case he had no children, he honored friendship more than kinship, and made property the rightful possession of the owner.[1] This law recognized the absolute individual ownership of property by the person while living, to which was now superadded the power of disposing of it by will to whomsoever he pleased, in case he had no children; but the gentile right to the property remained paramount so long as children existed to represent him in the gens. Thus at every point we meet the evidence that the great principles, which now govern society, were elaborated step by step proceeding in sequences, and tending invariably in the same upward direction. Although several of these illustrations are drawn from the period of civilization, there is no reason for supposing that the laws of Solon were new creations independent of antecedents. They rather embodied in positive form those conceptions, in relation to property, which had gradually developed through experience, to the full measure of the laws themselves. Positive law was now substituted for customary law.

The Roman law of the Twelve Tables (first promulgated 449 B. C.)[2] contain the rules of inheritance as then

---

1 Plutarch, "Vita Solon," c. 21.
2 Livy, iii, 54, 57.

established. The property passed first to the children, equally with whom the wife of the decedent was a co-heiress; in default of children and descendants in the male line, it passed to the agnates in the order of their nearness; and in default of agnates it passed to the gentiles.[1] Here we find again, as the fundamental basis of the law, that the property must remain in the gens. Whether the remote ancestors of the Latin, Grecian and Hebrew tribes possessed, one after the other, the three great rules of inheritance under consideration, we have no means of knowing, excepting through the reversion. It seems a reasonable inference that inheritance was acquired in the inverse order of the law as it stands in the Twelve Tables; that inheritance by the gentiles preceded inheritance by the agnates, and that inheritance by the agnates preceded an exclusive inheritance by the children.

During the Later Period of barbarism a new element, that of aristocracy, had a marked development. The individuality of persons, and the increase of wealth now possessed by individuals in masses, were laying the foundation of personal influence. Slavery, also, by permanently degrading a portion of the people, tended to establish contrasts of condition unknown in the previous ethnical periods. This, with property and official position, gradually developed the sentiment of aristocracy, which has so deeply penetrated modern society, and antagonized the democratical principles created and fostered by the gentes. It soon disturbed the balance of society by introducing unequal privileges, and degrees of respect for individuals among people of the same nationality, and thus became the source of discord and strife.

In the Upper Status of barbarism, the office of chief in its different grades, originally hereditary in the gens and elective among its members, passed, very likely, among the Grecian and Latin tribes, from father to son, as a rule. That it passed by hereditary right cannot be admitted upon existing evidence; but the possession of either of the offices of *archon, phylo-basileus,* or *basileus*

---

1 Gaius, "Inst.," iii, 1, 9, 17.

among the Greeks, and of *princeps* and *rex* among the Romans, tended to strengthen in their families the sentiment of aristocracy. It did not, however, become strong enough to change essentially the democratic constitution of the early governments of these tribes, although it attained a permanent existence. Property and office were the foundations upon which aristocracy planted itself.

Whether this principle shall live or die has been one of the great problems with which modern society has been engaged through the intervening periods. As a question between equal rights and unequal rights, between equal laws and unequal laws, between the rights of wealth, of rank and of official position, and the power of justice and intelligence, there can be little doubt of the ultimate result. Although several thousand years have passed away without the overthrow of privileged classes, excepting in the United States, their burdensome character upon society has been demonstrated.

Since the advent of civilization, the outgrowth of property has been so immense, its forms so diversified, its uses so expanding and its management so intelligent in the interests of its owners, that it has become, on the part of the people, an unmanageable power. The human mind stands bewildered in the presence of its own creation. The time will come, nevertheless, when human intelligence will rise to the mastery over property, and define the relations of the state to the property it protects, as well as the obligations and the limits of the rights of its owners. The interests of society are paramount to individual interests, and the two must be brought into just and harmonious relations. A mere property career is not the final destiny of mankind, if progress is to be the law of the future as it has been of the past. The time which has passed away since civilization began is but a fragment of the past duration of man's existence; and but a fragment of the ages yet to come. The dissolution of society bids fair to become the termination of a career of which property is the end and aim; because such a career contains the elements of self-destruction. Democracy in government, brotherhood in society, equality in rights and privileges, and universal education, foreshadow the next higher plane of society to which experience, intelligence and knowledge are steadily tending. It will be a revival, in a higher form, of the liberty, equality and fraternity of the ancient gentes.

Some of the principles, and some of the results of the growth of the idea of property in the human mind have now been presented. Although the subject has been inadequately treated, its importance at least has been shown.

With one principle of intelligence and one physical form, in virtue of a common origin, the results of human experience have been substantially the same in all times and areas in the same ethnical status.

The principle of intelligence, although conditioned in its powers within narrow limits of variation, seeks ideal standards invariably the same. Its operations, consequently, have been uniform through all the stages of human progress. No argument for the unity of origin of mankind can be made, which, in its nature, is more satisfactory. A common principle of intelligence meets us in the savage, in the barbarian, and in civilized man. It was in virtue of this that mankind were able to produce in similar conditions the same implements and utensils, the same inventions, and to develop similar institutions from the same original germs of thought. There is something grandly impressive in a principle which has wrought out civilization by assiduous application from small beginnnings; from the arrow head, which expresses the thought in the brain of a savage, to the smelting of iron ore, which represents the higher intelligence of the barbarian, and, finally, to the railway train in motion, which may be called the triumph of civilization.

It must be regarded as a marvelous fact that a portion of mankind five thousand years ago, less or more, attained to civilization. In strictness but two families, the Semitic and the Aryan, accomplished the work through unassisted self-development. The Aryan family represents the central stream of human progress, because it produced the highest type of mankind, and because it has proved its intrinsic superiority by gradually assuming the control of the earth. And yet civilization must be regarded as an accident of circumstances. Its attainment at some time was certain; but that it should have been accomplished when it was, is still an extraordinary fact. The hindrances that held mankind in savagery were great, and surmounted with difficulty. After reaching the Middle Status of barbarism, civilization hung in the balance while barbarians were feeling their way, by experiments with the native metals, toward the process of smelting iron ore. Until iron and its uses were known, civilization was impossible. If mankind had failed to the present hour to cross this barrier, it would have afforded no just cause for surprise. When we recognize the duration of man's existence upon the earth, the wide vicissitudes through which he has passed in savagery and in barbarism, and the progress he was compelled to make, civilization might as naturally have been delayed for several thousand years in the future, as to have occurred when it did in the good providence of God. We are forced to the conclusion that it was the result, as to the time of its achievement, of a series of fortuitous circumstances. It may well serve to remind us that we owe our present condition, with its multiplied means of safety and of happiness, to the struggles, the sufferings, the heroic exertions and the patient toil of our barbarous, and more remotely, of our savage ancestors. Their labors, their trials and their successes were a part of the plan of the Supreme Intelligence to develop a barbarian out of a savage, and a civilized man out of this barbarian.

INDEX

LEWIS HENRY MORGAN

Lewis Henry Morgan, considered the father of modern anthropology, was born in 1818 and died in 1881. He is noted for his pioneering studies of the American Indian culture. Among his published works are *Systems of Consanguinity and Affinity of the Human Family, The League of the Ho-de-no-sau-nee, or Iroquois, The American Beaver and His Works*, and *Houses and House-Life of the American Aborigines.*

ELEANOR BURKE LEACOCK

Eleanor Burke Leacock does research at the Bank Street College of Education and teaches at the Polytechnic Institute of Brooklyn. She has done field work in Switzerland and Italy and among American Indian tribes in Labrador. A specialist in social anthropology and the American Indian, she has also taught at Queens College, been a staff member of the Yorkville mental health project, and is the author of a large number of scholarly papers (including one on Morgan) and a monograph, "The Montagnais 'Hunting Territory' and the Fur Trade."